second edition

CASES IN BUSINESS AND SOCIETY

Scott H. Partridge

California State University, Hayward

PRENTICE HALL
Englewood Cliffs, N.J. 07632

Library of Congress Cataloging-in-Publication Data

Partridge, Scott H.
Cases in business and society / Scott H. Partridge. -- 2nd ed.
p. cm.
ISBN 0-13-115536-9 :
1. Industry--Social aspects--United States--Case studies.
2. Industry and state--United States--Case studies. I. Title.
II. Title: Business and society.
HD60.5.U5P36 1989
658.4'08--dc20 89-8740
CIP

Editorial/production supervision and interior design: Maureen Wilson
Cover design: Lundgren Graphics, Ltd.
Manufacturing buyer: Ed O'Dougherty

The following cases are hypothetical and are not intended to describe actual persons or events: *Fanny's Famous Foods, The Lomax Baby Furniture Co.*, the Lazy D Ranch in *The Case of the OSHA Cowboy*, the U.S. Copper Co. in *A Case of Lead Poisoning, The Kidd Co., The Pacific Corp.*, the ElectroVac Vacuum Cleaner Co. in *Confidential Memorandum, The Allen Cookie Co.*, and *The Boston Banana Co.*

Printed in the United States of America

10 9 8 7 6 5 4 3 2 1

ISBN 0-13-115536-9 05

Prentice-Hall International (UK) Limited, *London*
Prentice-Hall of Australia Pty. Limited, *Sydney*
Prentice-Hall Canada Inc., *Toronto*
Prentice-Hall Hispanoamericana, S.A., *Mexico*
Prentice-Hall of India Private Limited, *New Delhi*
Prentice-Hall of Japan, Inc., *Tokyo*
Simon & Schuster Asia Pte. Ltd., *Singapore*
Editora Prentice-Hall do Brasil, Ltda., *Rio de Janeiro*

TO
NADINE

ALPHABETICAL LIST OF CASES

CONTENTS

PART TWO

CORPORATE RELATIONSHIPS

PART THREE

CORPORATE INTERFACE WITH SOCIETY

PART FOUR

THE PROBLEM OF ECONOMIC CONCENTRATION

PREFACE

This second edition is very much like the first, partly because the author's original convictions have remained about the same and partly because much of the original material continues to be interesting and pertinent. Thirteen of the cases from the original edition have been replaced by fifteen new cases, and numerous revisions have been made in those cases that have been retained.

The purpose of the book is to provide an opportunity for students and general readers to come to grips with the major social issues facing business managers today. At a time when government at all levels is increasingly interested and directly involved in the activities of business firms, it is crucial that managers, of both small and large companies, understand the business-government interface and know the part they are required to play in it.

Special effort has been made to present both sides of particularly controversial issues so that the reader can develop personal conclusions based on supporting and opposing arguments. For the senior or graduate-level college student, the book can be used in conjunction with one of the many descriptive texts in business and society, or it can stand alone as the basis for a case discussion course. The material, it is hoped, will hold the interest of the general reader while informing and educating on the issues crucial to American business.

The material is organized in forty-one case studies arranged into nine divisions. Part I is concerned with the historical and literary background of American business. In addition, I have woven historical material into many of the case presentations, the purpose being to locate both the material and the student in time and events so that a broad view of the various issues might be obtained. The material on economic concentration and on government's role in maintaining competition has been put in Parts IV and V, and the remainder of the cases—most of which are concerned with the relations between business and other groups in society—are logically organized in the other sections.

I am grateful for many people who have stirred my interest and otherwise helped in this book. The late Dr. Ralph W. Hidy, Strauss Professor of Business History at the Harvard Business School, was the first to encourage my interest in government-business relations. Thanks should also go to my wife and family for their steadfast support over the years in which I worked on this project.

PART ONE
A BUSINESS SOCIETY

For much of our history it is true that the business of America has been business. Our economic development has been accomplished through the agency of free-enterprise capitalism instead of through some authoritarian alternative. In this section, consideration is given to some of the historical, philosophical, and literary underpinnings connected to the rise of big business in the United States. In particular, attention is given to some of the paradoxes that have resulted from our love-hate relationship with American corporations; our attitude toward the Founding Fathers—who are revered as idealists by some but maligned by others as rich men interested only in the more effective exploitation of the poor; upper-middle-class American liberals, many of whom preach socialism but much prefer to live under capitalism; and an early tradition of ministers and public speakers who became rich sermonizing on the spiritual significance of economic accomplishments.

In Case 1, our ambivalence toward the Rockefellers, Vanderbilts, Carnegies, and other early business leaders is shown as stemming from two sets of historical facts. On the one hand, they did many good things, they were most anxious to provide goods and services that the public wanted, and they built railroads and production facilities where none had existed before. In the process of enriching themselves, they developed a highly productive economic system that is very responsive to human wants, created economic development within the context of a democratic society (no Kulaks were sent off to Siberia), and ultimately brought about a high standard of living in this country. On the other hand, they engaged in activities such as commercial espionage, bribery, and destructive price competition—resulting in the wasting of human and material resources, the corruption of our political processes, and a marring of the moral fabric of our society.

Whether we accept these early business leaders as robber barons or as industrial statesmen is important, because much of the American public's attitude toward the role of government in the regulation of business derives from traditional ideas of business and the people who run it. Even though the average history book on the subject has a narrow audience, it helps shape the attitudes of professors in a wide variety of disciplines. They, in turn, shape the attitudes of students in class situations and through their textbooks, and this general frame of reference ultimately emerges to influence elections.

In *The Case of the Closet Capitalist,* Michael Novak and Bruce Douglass engage in the capitalist-socialist dialogue that has been going on for the past two hundred years. Joined at issue are questions regarding practicability, justice, human freedom, relative records of accomplishment, and economic equality.

The third case, *A Message to Garcia and Acres of Diamonds,* relates the impact of the nineteenth-century businessman on popular sermons and writings of the period. Before the advent of radio, newspapers, and national magazines, the fame and influence of such preachers and authors was great. For example, it is estimated that Russell H. Conwell gave his "Acres of Diamonds" oration to over six thousand audiences during the fifty years ending in 1910 and earned more than $8 million in royalties on the printed version.

The material on J. Pierpont Morgan is designed to illustrate not just the economic, political, and social power of the great banker, but also to consider his attempts to fine-tune an economy that, for all its growth and dynamism, was having some problems. In his confrontation with the Pujo Committee, Morgan laid bare the values underlying his operations as the major power on Wall Street. But in the final analysis it seemed as though Morgan and the government were after the same thing—bringing order and fairness to corporate life—but were simply approaching the problem from different perspectives.

In the case, *Debate on the Economic Significance of the Constitution,* it is suggested that our attitude regarding the genesis of that document can have serious and far-reaching implications for the manner in which we measure its provisions against new laws and administrative practices. Those who view the Constitution as a gift from the angels will certainly apply it in a different manner from those who look on it as just one among many such documents. Although this is not a burning issue at present, it is one toward which students of business-government relations should develop a point of view.

1
THE ROBBER BARONS AND THE MUCKRAKERS

The Muckrakers

The term "muckraker" was applied to an unorganized group of American reformist-writers who developed a "literature of exposure" in the early 1900s. Their work grew out of the yellow journalism of the 1890s, which was largely the result of competition between the two major American newspaper publishers of the day, William Randolph Hearst and Joseph Pulitzer. It was called "yellow journalism" because the rivals both published versions of a popular comic strip featuring a character named The Yellow Kid—which they both printed in bright yellow. To increase their respective circulations, the two publishers used lurid headlines and placed heavy emphasis on sensationalism. Their key stories were usually about crimes of passion or alleged atrocities committed by the Spanish during the Spanish-American War.

The muckrakers, who generally wrote for the popular magazines rather than for newspapers, concentrated on social evils and the need for reform. Although they were sometimes as sensational as their more flamboyant rivals on the daily papers, generally they made serious attempts to express themselves through realism and a kind of natural reporting. They were named by President Theodore Roosevelt, who, in a speech on April 14, 1906, borrowing a passage from John Bunyan's *Pilgrim's Progress,* denounced them by comparing them to "the man with the muck-rake...who could look no way but downward."

The first muckraker was probably Joseph F. Willard, whose series "The World of Graft" appeared in McClure's magazine in 1901. By January 1903 public interest had grown to such a point that an entire issue of that very popular publication was devoted to articles by muckrakers Lincoln Steffens, Ray Stannard Baker, and Ida Tarbell. Editor Samuel Sidney McClure, in summarizing what he felt was the significance of that particular issue, leaves us some clues as to the significance of the whole muckraker era.

THE CHALLENGE OF THE MUCKRAKERS

S. S. McClure, "The Challenge of the Muckrakers," *McClure's*, January 1903.

How many of those who have read through this number of the magazine noticed that it contains three articles on one subject? We did not plan it so; it is a coincidence that the January *McClure's* is such an arraignment of American character as should make every one of us stop and think. How many noticed that?

The leading article, "The Shame of Minneapolis," might have been called "The American Contempt of Law." That title could well have served for the current chapter of Miss Tarbell's History of Standard Oil. And it would have fitted perfectly Mr. Baker's "The Right to Work." All together, these articles come pretty near showing how universal is this dangerous trait of ours. Miss Tarbell has our capitalists conspiring among themselves, deliberately, shrewdly, upon legal advice, to break the law so far as it restrained them and to misuse it to restrain others who were in their way. Mr. Baker shows labor, the ancient enemy of capital and the chief complainant of the trusts' unlawful acts, itself committing and excusing crimes. And in "The Shame of Minneapolis" we see the administration of a city employing criminals to commit crimes for the profit of the elected officials, while the citizens—Americans of good stock and more than average culture, and honest, healthy Scandinavians—stood by complacent and not alarmed.

Capitalists, workingmen, politicians, citizens—all breaking the law, or letting it be broken. Who is left to uphold it? The lawyers? Some of the best lawyers in this country are hired, not to go into court to defend cases but to advise corporations and business firms how they can get around the law without too great a risk of punishment. The judges? Too many of them so respect the laws that for some "error" or quibble they restore to office and liberty men convicted on evidence overwhelmingly convincing to common sense. The churches? We know of one, an ancient and wealthy establishment, which had to be compelled by a Tammany holdover health officer to put its tenements in sanitary condition. The colleges? They do not understand.

There is no one left; none but all of us. Capital is learning (with indignation at labor's unlawful acts) that its rival's contempt of law is a menace to property. Labor has shrieked the belief that the illegal power of capital is a menace to the worker. These two are drawing together. Last November, when a strike was threatened by the yardmen on all the railroads centering in Chicago, the men got together and settled by raising wages, and raising freight rates too. They made the public pay. We all are doing our worst and making the public pay. The public is the people.

We forget that we all are the people; that while each of us in his group can shove off on the rest the bill of today, the debt is only postponed; the rest are passing it on back to us. We have to pay in the end, every one of us. And in the end the sum total of the debt will be our liberty.

Evaluation of the Muckrakers

From the original negative connotation given them by President Roosevelt, the appellation "muckraker" eventually became somewhat of a badge of honor. In addition to Ida Tarbell's popular serial about the sins of Standard Oil, Thomas W. Lawson, a Boston financier, wrote "Frenzied Finance,"[1] which also put the light of publicity on corporate irresponsibility. Additional well-received works included *The Jungle*, by Upton Sinclair, which, in describing the unsanitary conditions in the Chicago meat-packing industry, helped bring about the federal pure-food laws; *Children in Bondage*, by Edwin Markham, which attacked the evils of child labor; and David Graham Phillips' series

"The Treason of the Senate,"[2] which inspired Roosevelt's comments about "the man with the rake."

Of course, the muckrakers also had their critics. With some justification, it was pointed out that they tended to disregard the real achievements of American businessmen in their quest for ever-more-sensational stories. In addition, and most telling of all, it was argued that by offering only criticism, the muckrakers were really not helping society very much, that what was needed were solutions to the problems and conditions they had uncovered. Even the muckrakers' most ardent defenders admitted that they did not present practical programs to solve the problems they were so eager to expose.

On balance, admitting that the muckrakers did not solve problems, they did perform a valuable public service by pointing out areas where individuals and organizations were corrupting and perverting the economic and political system. They were largely responsible for the excitement in the public mind over corruption in government and business that existed during the Progressive Era, and maybe, in doing that, they were partly responsible for many of the reforms that were made.

The influence of the muckrakers, in fact the entire yellow journalism era, ended with the beginning of World War I. In addition to a tradition of investigative reporting, some of the long-lasting effects were attention-grabbing headlines, photographic illustrations, and color comics. After the war, many aspects of American life came under fire from a new breed of literary critics, such as H. L. Mencken and Sherwood Anderson. This kind of journalism has continued until today.

HISTORY OF THE STANDARD OIL COMPANY: CUTTING TO KILL

Ida Tarbell, *The History of the Standard Oil Company* (New York: The Macmillan Company, 1904), Chap. 10.

To know every detail of the oil trade, to be able to reach at any moment its remotest point, to control even its weakest factor—this was John D. Rockefeller's ideal of doing business. It seemed to be an intellectual necessity for him to be able to direct the course of any particular gallon of oil from the moment it gushed from the earth until it went into the lamp of a housewife. There must be nothing—*nothing* in his great machine he did not know to be working right. It was to complete this ideal, to satisfy this necessity, that he undertook, late in the seventies, to organize the oil markets of the world, as he had already organized oil refining and oil transportation. Mr. Rockefeller was driven to his new task of organization not only by his own curious intellect; he was driven to it by that thing so abhorrent to his mind—competition. If, as he claimed, the oil business belonged to him, and if, as he had announced, he was prepared to refine all the oil that men would consume, it followed as a corollary that the markets of the world belonged to him....

When Mr. Rockefeller began to gather the oil markets into his own hands he had a task whose field was literally the world, for already, in 1871, the year before he first appeared as an important factor in the oil trade, refined oil was going into every civilized country of the globe. Of the five and a half million barrels of crude oil produced that year, the world used five millions, over three and a half of which went to foreign lands. This was the market which had been built up in the first ten years of business by the men who had developed the oil territory and invented the processes of refining and transporting, and this was the market, still further developed, of course, that Mr. Rockefeller inherited when he succeeded in corralling the refining and transporting of oil. It was this market he proceeded to organize.

The purpose of organization seems to have been natural and highly intelligent. The entire country was buying refined oil for illumination. Many refiners had their own agents out looking for markets; others sold to wholesale dealers, or jobbers, who placed trade with local dealers, usually grocers. Mr. Rockefeller's business was to replace independent agents and jobbers by his own employees. The United States was mapped out and agents appointed over these great divisions. Thus, a certain portion of the Southwest—including Kansas, Missouri, Arkansas, and Texas—the Waters-Pierce Oil Company, of St. Louis, Missouri, had charge of; a portion of the South—including Kentucky, Tennessee, and Mississippi—Chess, Carley and Company, of Louisville, Kentucky, had charge of. These companies in turn divided their territory into sections, and put the subdivisions in the charge of local agents. These local agents had stations where oil was received and stored, and from which they and their salesmen carried on their campaigns. This system, inaugurated in the seventies, has been developed until now the Standard Oil Company of each state has its own marketing department, whose territory is divided and watched over in the above fashion. The entire oil-buying territory of the country is thus covered by local agents reporting to division headquarters. These report in turn to the head of the state marketing department, and his reports go to the general marketing headquarters in New York.

To those who know anything of the way in which Mr. Rockefeller did business, it will go without saying that this marketing department was conducted from the start with the greatest efficiency and economy. Its aim was to make every local station as nearly perfect in its service as it could be. The buyer must receive his oil promptly, in good condition, and of the grade he desired. If a customer complained, the case received prompt attention, and the cause was found and corrected. He did not only receive oil; he could have proper lamps and wicks and burners, and directions about using them.

The local stations from which the dealer is served today are always models of their kind, and one can easily believe they have always been so. Oil, even refined, is a difficult thing to handle without much disagreeable odour and stain, but the local stations of the Standard Oil Company, like its refineries, are kept orderly and clean by a rigid system of inspection. Every two or three months an inspector goes through each station and reports to headquarters on a multitude of details—whether barrels are properly bunged, filled, stenciled, painted, glued; whether tank wagons, buckets, faucets, pipes, are leaking; whether the glue is clean, the ground around the tanks dry, the locks in good condition; the horses properly cared for; the weeds cut in the yard. The time the agent gets around in the morning and the time he takes for lunch are reported. The prices he pays for feed for his horses, for coal, for repairs, are noted. In fact, the condition of every local station, at any given period, can be accurately known at marketing headquarters if desired. All of this tends, of course, to the greatest economy and efficiency in the local agents.

But the Standard Oil agents were not sent into a territory back in the seventies simply to sell all the oil they could by efficient service and aggressive pushing; they were sent there to sell all the oil that was bought. "The coal-oil business belongs to us," was Mr. Rockefeller's motto, and from the beginning of his campaign in the markets his agents accepted and acted on that principle. If a dealer bought but a barrel of oil a year, it must be from Mr. Rockefeller. This ambition made it necessary that the agents have accurate knowledge of all outside transactions in oil, however small, made in their field....

For many years independent refiners have declared that the details of their shipments were leaking regularly from their own employees or from clerks in freight offices. At every investigation made, these declarations have been repeated and occasional proof has been offered; for instance, a Cleveland refiner, John Teagle, testified in 1888 to the Congressional Committee that one day in 1883 his bookkeeper came to him and told him that he had been approached by a brother of the secretary of the Standard Oil Company at Cleveland, who had asked him if he did not wish to make some money. The bookkeeper asked how, and after some talk was informed that it would be by his giving information concerning the business of his firm to the Standard. The bookkeeper seems to have been a wary fellow, for he dismissed his interlocutor without arousing suspicion and then took the case to Mr. Teagle, who asked him to make some kind of an arrangement in order to find out just what information the Standard wanted. The man did this. For twenty-five dollars down and a small sum per year he was to make a transcript of Mr. Teagle's daily shipments with net price received for the same; he was to tell what the cost of manufacture in the refinery was; the amount of gasoline and naphtha made and the net price received for them; what was done with the tar; and what percentage of different grades of oil was made; also how much was exported. This information was to be mailed regularly to Box 164 of the Cleveland post office. Mr. Teagle, who at that moment was hot on the tracks of the Standard in the courts, got an affidavit from the bookkeeper. This he took with the money which the clerk had received to the secretary of the Standard Oil Company and charged him with bribery. At first the gentleman denied having any knowledge of the matter, but he finally confessed and even took back the money. Mr. Teagle then gave the whole story to the newspapers, where it of course made much noise.

Several gentlemen testified before the recent Industrial Commission to the belief that their business was under the constant espionage of the Standard Oil Company. Theodore Westgate, an oil refiner of Titusville, told the Commission that all of his shipments were watched. The inference from his testimony was that the Standard Oil Company received reports direct from the freight houses. Lewis Emery, Jr., of Bradford, a lifelong contestant of the Standard, declared that he knew his business was followed now in the same way as it was in 1872 under the South Improvement Company contract. He gave one or two instances from his own business experience to justify his statements, and he added that he could give many others if necessary. Mr. Gall, of Montreal, Canada, declared that these same methods were in operation in Canada.…Mrs. G. C. Butts, a daughter of George Rice, an independent refiner of Marietta, Ohio, told the Ohio Senate Committee which investigated trusts in 1898 that a railroad agent of their town had notified them that he had been approached by a Standard representative who asked him for a full report of all shipments, to whom and where going.…

But while the proofs the independents have offered of their charges show that such leaks have occurred at intervals all over the country, they do not show anything like a regular system of collecting information through this channel. From the evidence one would be able to conclude and perfectly justified in believing that the cases were rare, occurring only when a not over-nice Standard manager got into hot competition with a rival and prevailed upon a freight agent to give him information to help in his fight. In 1903, however, the writer came into possession of a large mass of documents of unquestionable authenticity, bearing out all and more than the independents charge. They show that the Standard Oil Company receives regularly today, at least from the railroads and steamship lines represented in these papers, information of all oil shipped. A study of these papers shows beyond question that somebody having access to the books of the freight offices records regularly each oil shipment passing the office—the names of consignor and consignee, the addresses of each, and the quantity and kind of oil are given in each case. This record is made out usually on a sheet of blank paper, though occasionally the recorder has been indiscreet enough to use the railroad company's stationery. The reports are evidently intended not to be signed, though there are cases in the documents where the name of the sender has been signed and erased; in one case a printed head bearing the name of the freight agent had been used. The name had been cut out, but so carelessly that it was easy to identify him. These reports have evidently been sent to the office of the Standard Oil Company, where they have received a careful examination, and the information they contained has been classified. Wherever the shipment entered was from one of the distributing stations of the Standard Oil Company, a line was drawn through it, or it was checked off in some way. In every other case in the mass of reports there was written opposite the name of the consignee, the name of a person *known* to be a Standard agent or salesman in the territory where the shipment had gone.

Now what is this for? Copies of letters and telegrams accompanying the reports show that as soon as a particular report had reached Standard headquarters and it was known that a carload, or even a barrel, of independent oil was on its way to a dealer, the Standard agent whose name was written after the shipment on the record had been notified. "If you can stop car going to X, authorize rebate to Z (name of dealer) of three-quarters cent per gallon," one of the telegrams reads. There is plenty of evidence to show how an agent receiving such information "stops" the oil. He *persuades* the dealer to countermand the order. George Rice, when before the House Committee on Manufacturers in 1888, presented a number of telegrams as samples of his experience in having orders countermanded in Texas. Four of these were sent on the same day from different dealers in the same town, San Angelo. Mr. Rice investigated the cause, and, by letters from various firms, learned that the Standard agent had been around "threatening the trade that if they bought off me they would not sell them any more," as he had put it.

Mrs. Butts in her testimony in 1898 said that the firm had a customer in New Orleans to whom they had been selling from 500 to 1,000 barrels a month, and that the Standard representative made a contract with him to pay him $10,000 a year for five years to stop handling the independent oil and take Standard Oil!...

In the Ohio investigation of 1898 John Teagle, of Cleveland, being upon his oath, said that his firm had had great difficulty in getting goods accepted because the Standard agents would persuade the dealers to cancel the orders. "They would have their local man, or some other man, call upon the trade and use their influence and talk lower prices, or make a lower retail price, or something to convince them that they'd better not take our oil, and, I suppose, to buy theirs." Mr. Teagle presented the following letter (see Exhibit 1-1), signed by a Standard representative, explaining such a countermand.

Peter Shull, of the Independent Oil Company of Mansfield, Ohio, testified before the same committee to experiences similar to those of Mr. Teagle.

"If I put a man on the road to sell goods for me," said Mr. Shull, "and he takes orders to the amount of 200 to 300 barrels a week, before I am able to ship these goods possibly, the Standard Oil Company has gone there and compelled those people to countermand those orders under a threat that, if they don't countermand them, they will put the price of oil down to such a price that they cannot afford to handle the goods."

In support of his assertion, Mr. Shull offered letters from firms he has been dealing with. The following citation shows the character of them (see Exhibit 1-2).

In case the agent cannot persuade the dealer to countermand his order, more strenuous measures are applied. The letters quoted above hint at what they will be. Many letters have been presented by witnesses under oath in various investigations showing that Standard Oil agents in all parts of the country have found it necessary for the last twenty-five years to act as these letters threaten. One of the most aggressive of these campaigns waged at the beginning of this war of exterminating independent dealers was by the Standard marketing agent at Louisville, Kentucky —Chess, Carley and Company. This concern claimed a large section of

Des Moines, Iowa
January 14, 1891

John Fowler
Hampton, Iowa

Dear Sir:

Our Marshall town manager, Mr. Ruth, has explained the circumstances regarding the purchase and subsequent countermand of a car of oil from our competitors. He desires to have us express to you our promise that we will stand all expense provided there should be any trouble growing out of the countermand of this car. We cheerfully promise to do this; we have the best legal advice which can be obtained in Iowa, bearing on the points in this case. An order can be countermanded either before or after the goods have been shipped, and, in fact, can be countermanded even if the goods have already arrived and are at the depot. A firm is absolutely obliged to accept a countermand. The fact that the order has been signed does not make any difference. We want you to absolutely refuse, under any circumstances, to accept the car of oil. We are standing back of you in this matter, and will protect you in every way, and would kindly ask you to keep this letter confidential....

Yours truly,

E. P. Pratt

EXHIBIT 1-1 Letter from a Standard Oil Representative

the South as its territory. George Rice of Marietta, Ohio, had been in this field for eight or ten years, having many regular customers. It became Chess, Carley and Company's business to secure these customers and to prevent his getting others. Mr. Rice was handicapped to begin with by railroad discrimination. He was never able to secure the rates of his big rival on any of the Southern roads. In 1888 the Interstate Commerce Commission examined his complaints against eight different Southern and Western roads and found that no one of them treated him with "relative justice." Railroad discriminations were not sufficient to drive him out of the Southwest, however, and a war of prices was begun.

Rice carried on his fight for a market in the most aggressive way, and everywhere he met disastrous competition. In 1892 he published a large pamphlet of documents illustrating Standard methods, in which he included citations from seventy letters from dealers in Texas, received by him between 1881 and 1889, showing the kind of competition his oil met there from the Waters-Pierce Oil Company, the Standard's agents:

I have had wonderful competition on this car. As soon as my car arrived the Waters-Pierce Oil Com-

EXHIBIT 1-2 Letter from an Oil Dealer

Tiffin, Ohio
February 1, 1898

Independent Oil Company
Mansfield, Ohio

Dear Sirs:

The Standard Oil Company, after your man was here, had the cheek to come in and ask how many barrels of oil we bought and so forth, then asked us to countermand the order, saying it would be for our best; we understand they have put their oil in our next door and offer it at six cents per gallon, at retail. Shall we turn tail or show them fight? If so, will you help us out any?

Yours truly,

Talbott and Son

pany, who has an agent here, slapped the price down to $1.80 per case.

...Oil was selling at this point for $2.50 per case, and as soon as your car arrived it was put down to $1.50, which it is selling at today.

The Waters-Pierce Oil Company reduced their prices on Brilliant Oil from $2.60 to $1.50 per case and is waging a fierce war.

I would like to handle your oil if I could be protected against the Waters-Pierce Oil Company. I am afraid if I would buy a car of oil from you this company would put the oil way below what I pay and make me lose big money. I can handle your oil in large quantities if you would protect me against them.

Jobbers say when they take hold of another oil they are at once boycotted by Waters-Pierce Oil Company, who not only refuse to sell to them, but put oil below what they pay for it, and thus knock them out of the oil trade, unless they sell at a loss.

Mr. Rice claims, in his preface to the collection of letters here quoted from, that he has hundreds of similar ones from different states in the union, and the writer asked to examine them. The package of documents submitted in reply to this request was made up of literally hundreds of letters. They came from twelve different states, and show everywhere the same competitive method—cutting to kill. One thing very noticeable in these letters is the indignation of the dealers at the Standard's methods of securing trade. They resent threats. They complain that the Standard agents "nose" about their business premises, that they ask impudent questions, and that they generally make the trade disgusting and humiliating. In Mississippi, in the eighties, the indignation of the small dealers against Chess, Carley and Company was so strong that they formed associations binding themselves not to deal with them....

Independent oil dealers of the present day complain bitterly of a rather novel way employed by the Standard for bringing into line dealers whose prejudices against buying from them are too strong to be overcome by the above methods. This is through what are called "bogus" oil companies. The obdurate dealer is approached by the agent of a new independent concern, call it ABC Oil Company, for illustration. The agent seeks trade on the ground that he represents an independent concern and that he can sell at lower prices than the firm from which the dealer is buying. Gradually he works into the independent's trade. As a matter of fact, the new company is merely a Standard jobbing house which makes no oil, and which conceals its real identity under a misleading name. The mass of reports from railroad freight offices quoted from in this article corroborate this claim of the independents. The ABC Oil Company is mentioned again and again as shipping oil, and in the audited reports it is always checked off in the same fashion as the known Standard companies, and none of its shipments is referred to Standard agents. Independents all over the country tell of loss of markets through underselling by these "bogus" companies. The lower price which a supposedly independent concern gives to a dealer who will not, under any condition, buy from the Standard, need not demoralize the Standard trade in the vicinity if the concession is made with caution. After the trade is secure, that is, after the genuine independent is ousted, the masquerading concern always finds itself obliged to advance prices. When the true identity of such a company becomes known, its usefulness naturally is impaired, and it withdraws from the field and a new one takes its place.

The general explanation of these competitive methods which the Standard officials have offered, is that they originate with "overzealous" employees and are disapproved of promptly if brought to the attention of the heads of the house. The cases seem rather too universal for such an explanation to be entirely satisfactory. Certainly the system of collecting information concerning competitive business is not practiced by the exceptional "overzealous" employee, but is a recognized department of the Standard Oil Company's business.

The moral effect of this system on employees is even a more serious feature of the case than the injustice it works to competition. For a consideration railway clerks give confidential information concerning freight going through their hands. It would certainly be quite as legitimate for post office clerks to allow Mr. Rockefeller to read the private letters of his competitors, as it is that the clerks of a railroad give him data concerning their shipments. Everybody through whose hands such information passes is contaminated by the knowledge. To be a factor, though even so small a one, in such a transaction, blunts one's sense of right and fairness. The effect on the local Standard agent cannot but be demoralizing.

The system results every now and then, naturally enough, in flagrant cases of bribing employees of the independents themselves. Where the freight office does not yield the information, the rival's own office may, and certainly if it is legitimate to get it from one place it is from the other. It is not an unusual thing for independent refiners to discharge a man whom they have reason to believe gives confidential information to the Standard....

For the general public, absorbed chiefly in the question, "How does all this affect what we are paying for oil?" the chief point of interest in the marketing contests is that, after they were over, the price of oil has always gone back with a jerk to the point where it was when the cutting began, and not infrequently it has gone higher—the public pays....A table was prepared in 1892 to show the effect of competition on the price of oil in various states of the union. The results were startling. In California, oil which sold at noncompetitive points at 26 ½ cents a gallon, at competitive points brought 17 ½ cents. In Denver, Colorado, there was an "oil war" on in the spring of 1892, and the same oil which was selling at Montrose and Garrison at 25 cents a gallon, in Denver sold at 7 cents. This competition finally killed all opposition and Denver thereafter paid 25 cents. The profits on this price were certainly great enough to call for competition. The same oil which was sold in Colorado in the spring of 1892 at 25 cents, sold in New York for exportation at 6.10 cents. Of course the freight rates to Colorado were high, the open rate was said to be 9 cents a gallon, but that it cost the Standard 9 cents a gallon to get its oil there, one would have to have documentary proof to believe, and, even if it did, there was still some 10 cents profit on a gallon—$5.00 on a barrel. In Kansas, this time, the difference between the price at competitive and noncompetitive points was 7 cents; in South Carolina 4 ½ cents.

Briefly put, then, the conclusion, from a careful examination of the testimony on Standard competitive methods, is this:

The marketing department of the Standard Oil Company is organized to cover the entire country, and aims to sell all the oil sold in each of its divisions. To forestall or meet competition it has organized an elaborate secret service for locating the quantity, quality, and selling price of independent shipments. Having located an order for independent oil with a dealer, it persuades him, if possible, to countermand the order. If this is impossible, it threatens "predatory competition," that is, to sell at cost or less, until the rival is worn out. If the dealer is still obstinate, it institutes an "oil war." In late years the cutting and the "oil wars" are often entrusted to so-called "bogus" companies, who retire when the real independent is put out of the way. In later years the Standard has been more cautious about beginning underselling than formerly, though if a rival offered oil at a lower price than it had been getting—and generally even small refineries can contrive to sell below the noncompetitive prices of the Standard—it does not hesitate to consider the lower price a declaration of war and to drop its prices and keep them down until the rival is out of the way. The price then goes back to the former figure or higher....At the period we have reached in this history—that is, the completion of the monopoly of the pipelines in 1884, and the end of competition in transporting oil—there seemed to the independents to be no escape from Mr. Rockefeller in the market.

The sureness and the promptness with which he located their shipments seemed uncanny to them. The ruthlessness and persistency with which he cut and continued to cut their prices drove them to despair. The character of the competition Mr. Rockefeller carried on in the markets, particularly of the South and Middle West of this country, at this time, aggravated daily the feeble refining element, and bred contempt far and wide among people who saw the cutting, and perhaps profited temporarily by it, but who had neither the power nor the courage to interfere. The knowledge of it fed greatly the bitterness in the oil regions. Part of the stock in conversation of every dissatisfied oil producer or ruined refiner became tales of disastrous conflicts in markets. They told of crippled men selling independent oil from a hand cart, whose trade had been wiped out by a Standard cart which followed him day by day, practically giving away oil. They told of grocers driven out of business by an attempt to stand by a refiner. They told endless tales, probably all exaggerated, perhaps some of them false, yet all of them believed, because of such facts as have been rehearsed above.

THE JUNGLE

Upton Sinclair, *The Jungle* (New York: Doubleday, Page and Company, 1905), pp. 113–17, 160–62.

"Bubbly Creek" is an arm of the Chicago River, and forms the southern boundary of the yards; all the drainage of the square mile of packing houses empties into it, so that it is really a great open sewer a hundred or two feet wide. One long arm of it is blind, and the filth stays there forever and a day. The grease and chemicals that are poured into it undergo all sorts of strange transformations, which are the cause of its name; it is constantly in motion, as if huge fish were feeding in it, or great leviathans disporting themselves in its depths. Bubbles of carbonic gas will rise to the surface and burst, and make rings two or three feet wide. Here and there the grease and filth have caked solid, and the creek looks like a bed of lava; chickens walk about on it feeding, and many times an unwary stranger has started to stroll across, and vanished temporarily. The packers used to leave the creek that way, till every now and then the surface would catch on fire and burn furiously, and the fire department would have to come and put it out. Once, however, an ingenious stranger came and started to gather this filth in scows, to make lard out of it; then the packers took the cue, and got out an injunction to stop him, and afterward gathered it themselves. The banks of "Bubbly Creek" are plastered thick with hairs, and this also the packers gather and clean.

And there were things even stranger than this, according to the gossip of the men. The packers had secret mains, through which they stole billions of gallons of the city's water. The newspapers had been full of this scandal—once there had been an investigation, and an actual uncovering of the pipes; but nobody had been punished, and the thing went right on. And then there was the condemned meat industry, with its endless horrors. The people of Chicago saw the government inspectors in Packingtown, and they all took that to mean that they were protected from diseased meat; then did not understand that these hundred and sixty-three inspectors had been appointed at the request of the packers, and that they were paid by the United States government to certify that all the diseased meat was kept in the state. They had no authority beyond that; for the inspection of meat to be sold in the city and state, the whole force in Packingtown consisted of three henchmen of the local political machine! And shortly afterward one of these, a physician, made the discovery that the carcasses of steers which had been condemned as tubercular by the government inspectors, and which therefore contained ptomaines, which are deadly poisons, were left upon an open platform and carted away to be sold in the city; and so he insisted that these carcasses be treated with an injection of kerosene—and was ordered to resign the same week! So indignant were the packers that they went further, and compelled the mayor to abolish the whole bureau of inspection; so that since then there has not been even a pretense of any interference with the graft. There was said to be two thousand dollars a week hush money from the tubercular steers alone; and as much again from the hogs which had died of cholera on the trains, and which you might see any day being loaded into boxcars and hauled away to a place called Globe, in Indiana, where they made a fancy grade of lard.

Jurgis heard of these things little by little, in the gossip of those who were obliged to perpetuate them. It seemed as if every time you met a person from a new department, you heard of new swindles and new crimes. There was, for instance, a Lithuanian who was a cattle butcher for the plant where Marija had worked, which killed meat for canning only; and to hear the man describe the animals which came to his place would have been worth while for a Dante or a Zola.

It seemed that they must have agencies all over the country, to hunt out old and crippled and diseased cattle to be canned. There were cattle which had been fed on "whisky-malt," the refuse of the breweries, and had become what the men called "steerly"—which means covered with boils. It was a nasty job killing these, for when you plunged your knife into them they would burst and splash foul-smelling stuff into your face; and when a man's sleeves were smeared with blood, and his hands steeped in it, how was he ever to wipe his face, or to clear his eyes so that he could see? It was stuff such as this that made the "embalmed beef" that had killed several times as many United States soldiers as all the bullets of the Spaniards, only the army beef, besides, was not fresh canned, it was old stuff that had been lying around.

Then one Sunday evening, Jurgis sat puffing his pipe by the kitchen stove, and talking with an old fellow whom Jonas had introduced, and who worked in the canning rooms at Durham's; and so Jurgis learned a few things about the great and only Durham canned goods, which had become a national institution. They were regular alchemists at Durham's; they advertised a mushroom-catsup, and the men who made it did not know what a mushroom looked liked. They advertised "potted chicken"—and it was like the boardinghouse soup of the comic papers, through which a chicken had walked with rubbers on. Perhaps they had a secret process for making chickens chemically—who knows? said Jurgis' friend; the things that went into the mixture were tripe, and the fat of pork, and beef suet, and hearts of beef, and finally the waste ends of veal, when they had any. They put these up in several grades, and sold them at several prices; but the contents of the cans all came out of the same hopper. And then there was "potted game" and "potted grouse," "potted ham, and "deviled ham"—de-vyled, as the men called it. "De-vyled" ham was made out of the waste ends of smoked beef that were too small to be sliced by the machines; and also tripe, dyed with chemicals so that it would not show white; and trimmings of hams and corned beef; and potatoes, skins and all; and finally the hard cartilagenous gullets of beef, after the tongue had been cut out. All this ingenious mixture was ground up and flavored with spices to make it taste like something. Anybody who could invent a new imitation had been sure of a fortune from old Durham, said Jurgis' friend; but it was hard to think of anything new in a place where so many sharp wits had been at work for so long; where men welcomed tuberculosis in the cattle they were feeding, because it made them fatten more quickly; and where they bought up all the old rancid butter left over in the grocery stores of a continent, and "oxydized" it by forced-air process, to take away the odor, rechurned it with skim milk, and sold it in bricks in the cities! Up to a year or two ago it had been the custom to kill horses in the yards—ostensibly for fertilizer; but after long agitation the newspapers had been able to make the public realize that the horses were being canned. Now it was against the law to kill horses in Packingtown, and the law was really complied with—for the present at any rate. Any day, however, one might see sharp-horned and shaggy-haired creatures running with the sheep—and yet what a job you would have to get the public to believe that a good part of what it buys for lamb and mutton is really goat's flesh!

There was another interesting set of statistics that a person might have gathered in Packingtown—those of the various afflictions of the workers. When Jurgis had first inspected the packing plants with Szedvilas, he had marveled while he listened to the tale of all the things that were made out of the carcasses of animals, and of all the lesser industries that were maintained there; now he found that each of these lesser industries was a separate little inferno, in its way as horrible as the killing beds, the source and fountain of them all. The workers in each of them had their own peculiar diseases. And the wandering visitor might be skeptical about all the swindles, but he could not be skeptical about these, for the worker bore the evidence of them about his own person—generally he had only to hold out his hand.

There were men in the pickle rooms for instance, where old Antanas had gotten his death; scarce a one of these that had not some spot of horror on his person. Let a man so much as scrape his finger pushing a truck in the pickle rooms, and he might have a sore that would put him out of the world; all the joints of his fingers might be eaten by the acid, one by one. Of the butchers and floorsmen, the beef-boners and trimmers, and all those who used knives, you could scarcely find a person who had the use of his thumb; time and time again the base of it had been slashed, til it was a mere lump of flesh against which the man pressed the knife to hold it. The hands of these men would be criss-crossed with cuts, until you could no longer pretend to count them or to trace them. They would have no nails—they had worn them off pulling hides; their knuckles were so swollen that their fingers spread out like a fan. There were men who worked in the cooking rooms, in the midst of steam and sickening odors, by artificial light; in these rooms the germs of tuberculosis might live for two years, but the supply was renewed every hour. There were the beef-luggers, who carried two-hundred pound quarters into the refrigerator cars; a fearful kind of work, that began at four o'clock in the morning, and that wore out the most powerful men in a few years. There were those who worked in the chilling rooms, and whose special disease was rheumatism; the time limit that a man could work in the chilling rooms was said to be five years. There were the wool-pluckers, whose hands went to pieces even sooner than the hands of the pickle men; for the pelts of the sheep had to be painted with acid to loosen the wool, and then the pluckers had to pull this wool with their bare hands, til the acid had eaten their fingers off. There were those who made the tins for the canned meat; and their hands, too, were a maze of cuts, and each cut represented a chance for blood poisoning. Some worked at the stamping machines, and it was very seldom that one could work there at the pace that was set and not give out and forget himself, and have a part of his hand chopped off. There were the "hoisters" as they were called, whose task it was to press the level which lifted the dead cattle off the floor. They ran along a rafter, peering down through the damp and the steam; and as old Durham's architects had not built the killing room for the convenience of the hoisters, at every few feet they would have to stoop under a beam, say four feet above the one they ran on; which got them into the habit of stooping, so that in a few years they would be walking like chimpanzees. Worst of any, however, were the fertilizer men, and those who served in the cooking rooms. These people could not be shown to the visitor—for the odor of a fertilizer man would scare any ordinary visitor at a hundred yards, and as for the other men, who worked in tank rooms full of steam, and in some of which there were open vats near the level of the floor, their peculiar trouble was that they fell into the vats; and when they were fished out, there was never enough of them left to be worth exhibiting—sometimes they would be overlooked for days, till all but the bones of them had gone out to the world as Durham's Pure Leaf Lard!

In the pickling of hams they had an ingenious apparatus, by which they saved time and increased the capacity of the plant—a machine consisting of a hollow needle attached to a pump; by plunging this needle into the meat and working with his foot, a man could fill a ham with pickle in a few seconds. And yet, in spite of this, there would be hams found spoiled, some of them with an odor so bad that a man could hardly bear to be in the room with them. To pump into these the packers had a second and a much stronger pickle which destroyed the odor—a process known to the workers as "giving them thirty percent."

Also, after the hams had been smoked, there would be found some that had gone to the bad. Formerly these had been sold as "Number Three Grade," but later on some ingenious person had hit upon a new device, and now they would extract the bone about which the bad part lay, and insert in the hole a white-hot iron. After this invention there was no longer Number One, Two, and Three Grade—there was only Number One Grade. The packers were always originating such schemes—they had what they called "boneless hams," which were all the odds and ends of pork stuffed into casings; and "California hams," which were the shoulders, with big knuckle joints, and nearly all the meat cut out; and fancy "skinned hams," which were made of the oldest hogs, whose skins were so heavy and coarse that no one would buy them—that is, until they had been cooked and chopped fine and labeled "headcheese!"

It was only when the whole ham was spoiled that it came into the department of Elibieta. Cut up by the two-thousand-revolutions-a-minute flyers, and mixed with half a ton of other meat, no odor that ever was in a ham could make any difference. There was never the least attention paid to what was cut up for sausage; there would come all the way back from Europe old sausage that had been rejected, and that was moldy and white—it would be dosed with borax and glycerine, and dumped into the hoppers, and made over again for home consumption. There would be meat that had tumbled out on the floor, in the dirt and sawdust, where the workers had tramped and spit uncounted billions of consumption germs. There would be meat stored in great piles in rooms; and the water from leaky roofs would drip over it, and thousands of rats would race about on it.

It was too dark in these storage places to see well, but a man could run his hand over these piles of meat and sweep off handfuls of the dried dung of rats. These rats were nuisances, and the packers would put poisoned bread out for them; they would die, and then rats, bread, and meat would go into the hoppers together. This is no fairy story and no joke; the meat would be shoveled into carts, and the man who did the shoveling would not trouble to lift out a rat even when he saw one—there were things that went into the sausage in comparison with which a poisoned rat was a tidbit.

There was no place for the men to wash their hands before they ate their dinner, and so they made a practice of washing them in the water that was to be ladled into the sausage. There were the butt ends of smoked meat, and the scraps of corned beef, and all the odds and ends of the waste of the plants that would be dumped into old barrels in the cellar and left there.

Under the system of rigid economy which the packers enforced, there were some jobs that it only paid to do once in a long time, and among these was the cleaning out of the waste barrels. Every spring they did it; and in the barrels would be dirt and rust and old nails and stale water—and cartload after cartload of it would be taken up and dumped into the hoppers with fresh meat and sent out to the public's breakfast. Some of it they would make into "smoked" sausage—but as the smoking took time, and was therefore expensive, they would call upon their chemistry department and preserve it with borax and color it with gelatine to make it brown. All of their sausage came out of the same bowl, but when they came to wrap it, they would stamp some of it "special," and for this they would charge two cents more a pound.

ASSIGNMENT QUESTIONS

1. Did the Standard Oil Company provide good-quality products and a high level of service to its customers?
2. What activities of Standard Oil were criticized by Ida Tarbell?
3. How do you account for such an unfavorable picture of early businessmen?
4. How would *you* rate the contributions of early business leaders such as Rockefeller, Armour, and Morgan? On balance, good or bad? Why?
5. Assuming that economic development is something desirable, what alternative methods could you suggest for promoting early economic development in the United States?
6. How do you rate the muckrakers? What were their major contributions? Could they have done better?

NOTES

1. Thomas W. Lawson, "Frenzied Finance," *Everybody's,* 1904–1905.
2. David Graham Phillips, "The Treason of the Senate," *Cosmopolitan,* 1906.

2
THE CASE OF THE CLOSET CAPITALIST

A CLOSET CAPITALIST CONFESSES

Michael Novak, "A Closet Capitalist Confesses," *Washington Post,* March 14, 1976, p. C1.

The day I heard Michael Harrington say that most liberals are "closet socialists," I knew by my revulsion that I had to face an ugly truth about myself. For years, I had tried to hide, even from myself, my unconscious convictions. In the intellectual circles I frequent, persons with inclinations like my own are mocked, considered to be compromised, held at arm's length as security risks. We are easily intimidated.

The truth is there are probably millions of us. Who knows? Your brother or sister may be one of us. The fellow teaching in the class next to yours; the columnist for the rival paper; even the famous liberated poetess—our kind, hiding their convictions out of fear of retribution, lurk everywhere. Even now we may be corrupting your children.

We are the closet capitalists. Now, at last, our time has come. The whole world is going socialist. Nearly 118 out of 142 nations of the world are socialist tyrannies. A bare 24 are free-economy democracies. We are the world's newest, least understood and little loved minority. It is time for us to begin, everywhere, organizing cells of the Capitalist Liberation Front.

I first realized I was a capitalist when all my friends began publicly declaring that they were socialists, Harrington and John Kenneth Galbraith having called the signal. How I wished I could be as left as they; night after night I tried to persuade myself of the coherence of their logic. I did my best to go straight. I held up in the privacy of my room pictures of every socialist land known to me: North Korea, Albania, Czechoslovakia (land of my grandparents) and even Sweden. Nothing worked.

When I quizzed my socialist intellectual

friends, I found they didn't like socialist countries, either. They all said to me, "We want socialism, but not like Eastern Europe." I said: "Cuba?" No suggestion won their assent. They didn't want to be identified with China (except that the streets seemed clean). Nor with Tanzania. They loved the *idea* of socialism.

"But what is it about this particular idea you like?" I asked. Government control? Will we have a Pentagon of heavy industry?" Not exactly. Nor did they think my suggestion witty, that under socialism everything would function like the post office. When they began to speak of "planning," I asked, who would police the planners? They had enormous faith in politicians, bureaucrats and experts. Especially in experts.

"Will Mayor Daley have 'clout' over the planners?" I asked, seeking a little comfort. "Or congressmen from Mississippi?" My friends thought liberal-minded persons would make the key decisions. Knowing the nation, I can't feel so sure. Knowing the liberal-minded, I'm not so comforted.

Since they have argued that oil companies are now too large, I couldn't see how an HEW that included oil would be smaller. My modest proposal was that they encourage monopoly in every industry and then make each surviving corporation head a cabinet office.

Practical discussions seemed beside the point. Finally I realized that socialism is not a *political* proposal, not an *economic* plan. Socialism is the residue of Judaeo-Christian faith, without religion. It is a belief in community, the goodness of the human race and paradise on earth.

That's when I discovered I was an incurable and inveterate, as well as secret, sinner. I believe in sin. I'm for capitalism, modified and made intelligent and public spirited, because it makes the world free for sinners. It allows human beings to do pretty much what they will. Socialism is a system built on belief in human goodness, so it never works. Capitalism is a system built on belief in human selfishness, given checks and balances. Check Taiwan, Japan, West Germany, Hong Kong and (one of the newest nations in one of the recently most underdeveloped sectors of the world) these United States. Two hundred years ago, there was a China, and also a Russia. The United States was only a gleam in Patrick Henry's eye.

Wherever you go in the world, sin thrives better under capitalism. It's presumptuous to believe that God is on any human's side (actually, if capitalism were godless and socialism were deeply religious, the roles of many spokesmen in America would be reversed in fascinating ways), but God did make human beings free. Free to sin. God's heart may have been socialist; his design was capitalist as hell. There is an innate tendency in socialism toward authoritarianism. Left to themselves, all human beings won't be good; most must be concerned. Capitalism, accepting human sinfulness, rubs sinner against sinner, making even dry wood yield a spark of grace.

Capitalism has given the planet its present impetus for liberation. Everywhere else they are hawking capitalist ideas: growth, liberation, democracy, investments, banking, industry, technology. Millions are alive, and living longer, because of medicine developed under capitalism. Without our enormous psychic energy, productivity and inventions, oil would still be lying under Saudi Arabia, undiscovered, unpumped and useless. Coffee, bananas, tin, sugar and other items of trade would have no markets. Capitalism has made the world rich, inventing riches other populations didn't know they had. And yielding sinful pleasures for the millions.

Six percent of the world's population consumes, they say, 40 percent of the world's goods. The same 6 percent produces more than 50 percent; far more than it can consume. No other system can make such a statement, even in lands more populous, older and richer than our own. As everybody knows, hedonism requires excess.

Look out world! The closet capitalists are coming out. You don't have to love us. We don't need your love. If we can help you out, we'll be glad to. A system built on sin is built on very solid ground indeed. The saintliness of socialism will not feed the poor. The United States may be, as many of you say, the worthless and despicable prodigal son among the nations. Just wait and see who gets the fatted calf.

SOCIALISM AND SIN

Much of the political comment coming from the theologians these days has a socialist flavor. I was surprised, therefore, to find a theologian arguing the case for capitalism in the editorial pages of the *Washington Post* ("A Closet Capitalist Confesses," March 14, 1976). Especially was it surprising to find Michael Novak in this role, for in a previous incarnation he was one of the early proponents of a theology for radical politics. Not only does Novak admit to being a "closet capitalist" (acknowledging the truth of Michael Harrington's charge about liberals in the United States), but he also sets forth elements of a theological argument for the superiority of capitalism over socialism.

Making the World Free for Sinners

Actually, Novak makes two cases—one political, the other theological. The former calls into service two time-tested claims of capitalism's defenders: (1) that free market yields greater efficiency and productivity than socialist economies, and (2) that it results in greater freedom. Novak raises the specter of a whole economy run with the well-known efficiency of the U.S. Postal Service, and then attributes to capitalism most of the world's productivity:

> Millions are alive, and living longer, because of medicine developed under capitalism. Without our enormous psychic energy, productivity and inventions, oil would still be lying under Saudi Arabia, undiscovered, unpumped and useless. Coffee, bananas, tin, sugar and other items of trade would have no markets. Capitalism has made the world rich, inventing riches other populations didn't know they had. And yielding sinful pleasures for the millions.

The only way socialism can possibly work at all, we are told, is by being authoritarian. Lacking the incentive of greed, people have to be coerced into producing. At the same time great power is concentrated in the hands of politicians, bureaucrats and experts. *They* make the momentous decisions that determine the fate of millions. The result is a command society—a result which, Novak suggests, no self-respecting liberal would want. Democratic socialists are hard put to cite an example, he notes, of a model socialist society. Everywhere we look—China, Cuba, Tanzania, eastern Europe—socialism means the same thing: the domination of society by huge, ponderous government bureaucracies.

Why is this the case? The technological part of Novak's analysis provides the answer: capitalism is more congruent with human nature—i.e., with humanity's sinful nature. It accepts selfishness as a fact of life; it doesn't require any illusions about the innate goodness of people. "God's heart may have been socialist; his design was capitalist as hell." Given the freedom to sin, human beings have of course taken abundant advantage of the opportunity, and the only way to create a productive and free society is to cater to selfishness. Socialism, presuming goodness, "never works," whereas capitalism, building upon greed, "is nearly always a smashing success."

Sin thus accounts for the greater productivity of capitalism; it also accounts for the greater freedom it allows. Capitalism "makes the world free for sinners;" it tolerates people's doing what they will. Socialism, dedicated to the cultivation of benevolence, can't leave people alone. Human beings have to be made over; sin has to be eliminated. All the while, of course, socialists place great faith in the goodness and wisdom of the politicians and social planners.

In short, capitalism is realistic while socialism is naive. For this reason, the future belongs to capitalism. A social system built on illusion simply cannot succeed—not in the long run.

But such arguments make little headway with socialists, says Novak, because contrary to appearances, socialism is not really a practical political proposal at all. It is a faith, a secular religion, "the residue of Judaeo-Christian faith," minus the theistic component and minus the idea of sin. It is a belief that paradise can be brought to earth here and now by human action. In the face of such a belief, practical considerations are "beside the point."

A Fixation with Profits

When I first read this "confession," I suspected that Novak was putting us on—that it was all tongue-in-cheek. The mid-1970s were not, after all, the most auspicious time for a spirited defense of capitalism. Devaluations, unemployment, inflation, problems with OPEC—the catalog of serious economic problems suffered by capitalist societies in the past few years does not inspire confidence. The more I thought about it, however, the more I concluded that he *was* serious and the more I felt that his argument called for a reply.

At the risk of being dismissed as a naive visionary who can't face up to reality, I want to suggest that the choice between capitalism and socialism is considerably more complex than Novak would have *Washington Post* readers believe. I have come to take his argument seriously, both because there is some truth in what he says and because he articulates sentiments widely held in this country. The problem is that his view expresses only half the truth. He conveniently overlooks certain other considerations favorable to socialism; when these considerations are given their due, even some practical people unafflicted by the need for a secular religion will find the alleged superiority of capitalism something less than obvious.

The socialist case against capitalism has never, to my knowledge, challenged the productivity of the free market. That has not been the issue. There is no better hymn of praise, after all, to the achievements of capitalism than the Communist Manifesto. The social critique has been based on other grounds—specifically, the *use* of the productive resources which capitalism generates. Because of the fixation with profits, capitalist use of this productivity necessarily is far less rational and humane than it could be.

Examples abound, but to my mind the most graphic case in point is the American automobile industry. Year after year, decade after decade, we witness the spectacle of Detroit's efforts to sell ever-increasing numbers of cars designed for quick obsolescence, though it has been clear for some time now that considerations of both space and air quality dictate that we move toward some alternative transportation system. Both transportation and ecology experts tell us that we cannot go on indefinitely multiplying the number of cars on our streets and highways without serious costs to our physical and psychological well-being. Yet this is precisely what the health of the economy is said to require.

Food production offers other illustrations. Chemical additives in our food, possibly harmful, are justified as a convenience to the producer and seller. Short of unequivocal prohibition by the government (which the industry strongly resists), these additives continue to be used because they enhance the appeal and durability of food products. The meat looks pinker; the baked goods last longer on the shelves—even if they actually may be less healthful! Then there is the irony of underproduction. For many years now the federal government has been paying farmers *not* to produce foodstuffs, while millions, in this country and abroad, go hungry. The rationale, once again, is economic necessity: prices and profits must be maintained at a level sufficient to stimulate production.

The energy crisis is another case in point. Now that there are no lines at the gas pumps and the scare has faded, consumers are once again being encouraged to use energy in all kinds of ways, many of them patently frivolous. The crisis is hardly over, of course, but the imperatives of the market require that we stop worrying about energy conservation.

Underlying the whole system is, of course, a consumption ethic, which John Kenneth Galbraith and others have analyzed. Vast sums of money and resources are invested in the creation, mainly through the mass media, of "needs" which otherwise would not exist. To make the system go, to keep sales and profits moving, people must be encouraged not to acquire only what they sensibly need but, in the words of the beer commercial, to "grab for all they can get." Whether these acquisitions will really benefit them and whether this style of consumption represents the best use of available resources are questions not seriously considered.

Public Penury

The other side of the story is what David Broder aptly characterizes as "public penury." Vital public services, which do not easily lend themselves to profit-making, are underfunded and inadequately developed: public transportation, health care, education, criminal justice. Alongside Novak's picture of the abundance which capitalism produces there needs to be placed another equally significant image—that of decaying, broken-down bus and railway systems; underpaid teachers, policemen, firemen and social workers; overcrowded and understaffed public hospitals; jails and rehabilitation facilities extended far beyond their capacities. In America at least, capitalism has resulted in a situation in which, as Broder has written (in *The Party's Over*), "every single essential service we depend on some public agency to provide is seriously underfinanced."

The case for socialism derives from the irrationality of this state of affairs. Would it not be a more intelligent use of resources, asks the socialist, to focus our productive capabilities on those things that are conducive to human well-being? Would it not be more rational (and humane) to invest more of our resources in such things as health care and education and less in providing 17 brands of breakfast cereal or dream cars with Moroccan leather upholstery? Would it not be more intelligent to seek to liberate ourselves from the tyranny of profits? Would it not be preferable to develop and utilize our productive capacities on the basis of a rational plan rather than the whims of investors? Would it not be more intelligent, in short, to try to transcend the *anarchy* of capitalism?

To speak of planning, of course, raises the other issue on which Novak makes his case for capitalism. For many people, any mention of social planning suggests dictatorship, and socialism becomes therefore almost by definition a recipe for tyranny. I have no intention of making light of this problem. It is the central problem of socialism today. But the notion that socialism need be tyrannical can be dismissed as an exaggeration. Democratic socialism as it has been practiced in Western Europe and elsewhere demonstrates clearly that this is not the case. Democratic socialist regimes have tended, however, either to be coalition governments or to be short-lived, and they have had considerable difficulty with the problem of reconciling parliamentary, bureaucratic and managerial authority. Democratic socialism still remains, therefore, much more a vision than a demonstrated possibility.

The Problem of Freedom

But to admit that freedom is a problem for socialists is one thing, and to say that capitalism solves the problem of freedom is quite another. It all depends, of course, on how you define the term. Novak defines it in negative terms—freedom means being left alone, being uncoerced by other people. This is an important part of freedom, no doubt; in this respect it must be admitted that the liberties of bourgeois capitalist society are no small achievement, and that they are not to be casually forsaken.

There remains, however, another side to the story, which people who take Novak's line characteristically neglect. Freedom has a positive aspect as well. The free person is not only free of external coercion but also has the ability to control the direction of his or her life and to develop his or her potential. In this respect I would argue that the difference which capitalism makes has been greatly exaggerated by its proponents. Perhaps in the 18th or early 19th century the simplicities of the free market made it possible for anybody with gumption to become a "rugged individualist" and shape his or her own destiny. But we are far removed from that era today. We are now confronted with a form of capitalism which concentrates economic power in vast, impersonal institutions, with the result that decisions vitally affecting the livelihood of average citizens are made in places far removed from their capacity to have any influence at all. What kinds of jobs will be available, where they will be available, how much salary they will provide, what products will be sold, how much they will sell for—these matters are settled for most of us by people who remain faceless.

It is therefore a misleading half-truth to say, as Novak does, that capitalism "allows human beings to do pretty much what they will." It all depends on what you choose. If you opt for selling insurance or making automobiles or fixing plumbing, the system will probably find a place for you. It will also tolerate your whim if you choose to "drop out" in a commune somewhere. But if you choose to do something which does not lead to profits and which requires substantial financial support, your chances of being frustrated are fairly high. If you choose, for example, to be an educator or a social worker or an artist, realism demands that you prepare for the possibility that a shrunken job market or the impossibility of making a decent living will force you to abandon your career aspirations in favor of something more "practical."

Restricted Choices

The same holds true for consumption. Strictly speaking, we are not forced to buy anything. And if we happen to like what is offered in the marketplace, then indeed capitalism does allow us to do what we wish. But what if we do not like what is being offered? What if, for example, an individual does not want to pay the price being asked for automobiles? What if he thinks the price unnecessarily high and the product undesirable in important respects? He needs transportation, and public transportation in his particular area is either inadequate or nonexistent. Such a person, I would submit, has his freedom of choice restricted *precisely because of the way the free market operates.* He will probably end up buying one of Detroit's latest models not because he really wants to but rather because it represents the only available practical answer to his needs.

The same argument applies to the life and medical insurance premiums people pay because there is no cheaper, more efficient public program for dealing with the costs of medical care and old-age security. It also applies to our food, much of which comes to us in the supermarkets overpriced and laced with chemicals of dubious value. Theoretically it is possible to grow one's own crops and bake one's own bread. But as a *practical* matter that is not a serious possibility for most people. So they end up "choosing" products about which they have serious reservations. Short of transforming their whole way of life, they are stuck with what A&P and Safeway make available—and at prices A&P and Safeway charge.

I do not mean to imply that things will be radically different under socialism. Only anarchism makes sense as a formula for the full restoration of positive freedom, and anarchism is incompatible with industrial society. If we are going to live in an industrialized world, with its economic complexity and population density, a substantial diminution of the freedom of the individual (as compared with simpler times) is probably inevitable. Concentrated economic and political power is going to be a fact of life, regardless of the economic arrangements under which we live.

Socialists have argued that it makes a considerable difference where this concentration occurs. They contend that freedom is enhanced when economic power is vested in public rather than private hands because the people who wield that power are made publicly accountable. As R. H. Tawney, a British socialist of an earlier generation, wrote: "It is the condition of economic freedom that men should not be ruled by an authority which they cannot control" (*The Acquisitive Society*). The virtue of socialism, it is argued, is that it does away with such irresponsible authority and forces those who make economic policy to appeal to the electorate and to justify their decisions in terms of the public good. Through political action, in turn, there is something average citizens can do about their fate. No longer need they be the victims of faceless, powerful people over whom they have no control.

I subscribe to this argument, but it can be confidently asserted only insofar as socialism is democratic. And by "democratic" I mean liberal democracy—i.e., a multiparty system, regular competitive elections, and civil liberties. Without these, there is no reliable check on the policies laid down by government officials, and there is a strong likelihood that the ruling elite will become just as exploitative as any capitalist (perhaps even more so).

Sinfulness and Justice

The other element in the case for socialism is, of course, justice. Down through the socialist tradition, the argument repeatedly has been made that capitalism results in gross inequities, and that socialism can do away with such foolishness. Under socialism no one goes hungry; everyone who is able works; those who work receive benefits commensurate with their social contribution; and there are not the radical disparities in wealth and opportunities characteristic of capitalism.

Curiously, Novak makes no mention of the issue of justice. But it is of critical importance to the choice between capitalism and socialism, and it is directly relevant to what he has to say about sin.

I have no quarrel with an emphasis on sin per se. The inevitability of selfishness in political and economic affairs is something which I have taken for granted ever since reading Reinhold Niebuhr. Niebuhr's arguments are thoroughly persuasive that sin is simply a fact of the human condition which no amount of education, preaching or social engineering will eliminate. I take this to be one of the principal contributions which Christian thought has to offer in the realm of social and political theory.

For Niebuhr, however, an emphasis on sin was not the whole story of human nature. It was equally important to recognize humanity's capacity for justice. If I read Niebuhr correctly, the two are roughly equal in their strength and influence in human affairs. It is for this reason that Niebuhr could be moderately optimistic about the course of history and make comparatively high demands on social institutions.

The neglect of the issue of justice is what makes Novak's case as plausible as it is. There is no question that capitalism builds upon and in fact encourages selfishness; a capitalist environment naturally inclines us to believe that people *must* be addicted to a greedy, competitive individualism. But the socialist argument is that a different environment will elicit a significantly different kind of behavior.

Socialism's Moral Appeal

"Different," I emphasize, but not sinless. There are socialists, of course, who harbor fantasies about completely rooting out selfishness. But they hardly represent the whole of the socialist tradition, and there is no reason to believe that the socialist idea requires such a belief. Many socialists have been and continue to be more modest and pragmatic. They identify socialism not with heaven on earth but simply with a better, morally superior way of life. They have no intention of remaking the soul of humanity—only of harnessing human egoism and cultivating a better human nature. They know that selfishness is a given, but they also know that its force and consequences vary enormously with the context. They believe that there is a fundamental moral distinction to be drawn between a system that encourages people to be greedy and one that instead encourages them to acquire only what they truly need.

For much the same reasons, it is simply fallacious, I think, to say that socialism *must* take the form of a secular religion. Socialism no more than capitalism need be a substitute for theistic religion, and it is worth noting that capitalist ideology, for all its alleged "realism," just as easily succumbs to this danger. (For every socialist who believes that socialism is The Answer to the problems of the human condition, there are at least as many capitalist "true believers," the preponderance located in the business world.) Admittedly, socialism does make a strong moral appeal, and in the past this appeal has often been associated with a heavy dose of secularism. But to suggest that this is a necessary connection is to mistake history for logic. Socialism no more requires a secularist foundation than does modern science.

Logic is probably beside the point, however, in dealing with this charge, because it is mainly a polemical device. Its main purpose, as Novak shows, is to dismiss socialists as impractical visionaries and thereby to protect capitalism against moral criticism. It enables the defenders of capitalism to deflect the socialist critique without having directly to address it. The argument of socialism's impracticality is nonsense which can be sustained only so long as one is ignorant of the variety and complexity of the socialist tradition.

Capitalism Naivete

A standard reply to this kind of critique is to praise capitalism's flexibility. According to capitalism's revisionist defenders, collaboration between government and private industry can curtail the anarchy of the market, and the various devices of the welfare state can be used to resolve inequities. Socialism is therefore unnecessary because welfare capitalism answers the principal objections of socialists. Such an approach is apparently what Novak has in mind when he speaks of a capitalism "made intelligent and public spirited."

Capitalism is indeed flexible. Capitalist economies have shown a remarkable resilience that has defeated the pessimistic prophecies of socialists again and again. So one would be foolish to speak dogmatically about what is possible. Still, there is ample reason for skepticism that any version of capitalism can adequately resolve the problems that agitate socialists. Where the genuinely mixed economy becomes a reality (as, for example, in Sweden), capitalism clearly becomes much more like socialism, and is therefore more palatable. But "capitalism with a human face" still is not socialism. As Michael Harrington keeps insisting, as long as the means of production remain in private ownership, there is a fundamental structural obstacle to the realization of socialist objectives.

It is here that the realism of socialists and the naivete of democratic capitalists become apparent. The democratic capitalist wants to believe that we can have most of the dividends of socialism without actually moving to public ownership of the major industries. The socialist says in reply that we cannot have it both ways. Capitalism is designed primarily to prevent the objectives which socialists seek, and its adherents will strongly resist the measures necessary to adapt private enterprise to anything seriously approaching a socialist program. They may allow "national planning" of a sort (as in France); they may allow welfare programs; they may allow some progressive taxation; but what they will not allow is an invasion of the autonomy of the private corporation so that economic decisions can be coordinated and made on a basis other than profits. That is where the line must be drawn if capitalism is to remain capitalist. And this in turn means that *real* national planning, oriented primarily toward social needs, will be impossible.

THE CLOSET SOCIALISTS

Seldom have 1,200 words of mine generated so much attention as "A Closet Capitalist Confesses" (*Washington Post*, March 14, 1976). Bruce Douglass's temperate and reasoned reply in the *Century*'s pages ("Socialism and Sin," December 1, 1976) provides a rare opportunity for discussion. On grand themes like "capitalism" and "socialism," much passion is generated. Arguments are theological rather than empirical, for the reality of any economic system is larger than the universes of empirical fact. When systems are in conflict, there is pitifully little room outside them where one can find a vantage point of neutral observation.

Douglass was wise to suspect at first that I was "putting us on—that it was all tongue-in-cheek," but upon mature reflection he was also perceptive enough to see that I "*was* serious." I have difficulty believing in socialism; I cried out in the dark for help. Douglass thinks the 1970s an inauspicious time for capitalism; my weak faith found these years inauspicious for socialism. The spectacle of Great Britain's becoming less than Great, the terrors of the Gulag Archipelago, Ingmar Bergman's problems with the Swedish tax bureaucracy, the disastrous socialism of the Third World, the flight of economic resources from socialist-leaning Quebec, the perfidy of political planners in New York City, efficient tyrannies from Cambodia to Czechoslovakia—these do not inspire me with confidence in the practice of socialism. As a religious vision, socialism has my respect. As a practical way of arranging human political and economic affairs, it evokes my skepticism. I find that even candles burned to St. Michael Harrington (my socialist patron saint) fail to quicken sluggish faith.

I

On reflection, I realized that I had never read an intelligent description, let alone a defense, of democratic capitalism. Persons trained in the humanities, history and sociology—my usual contacts in the literary and intellectual worlds—tend to speak disdainfully of capitalism, profits, business and Detroit. They tend also to be as economically illiterate as I am, who long could not read a balance sheet, do not understand "the dismal science," find business a foreign world. The only *theoretical* materials I ever encounter are socialist.

So it hit me: Socialism—to play on the Volvo slogan—is the thinking man's economics. They go together, socialism and intellectual life. Capitalism is abandoned to practical men and women of affairs. Democratic capitalism as we experience it in the U.S. has no "manifesto," and pitifully scant theoretical interests. There are many fundamentalist preachers of the creed—in Rotary clubs, at the AMA—but there is no serious theology accessible to the ordinary reader. All the fashionable theoreticians—John Kenneth Galbraith, Robert Lekachman, Michael Harrington and a scattering of others—are socialists and review each other's books.

According to the prophetic tradition, one ought to warn oneself to think against prevailing winds. It is one thing to be a nonprofit thinker; nonprophet thinking is worse indeed. It is not really very radical for a theologian to promote socialism; it is the expected niche. In *A Theology for Radical Politics,* I did not urge forms of socialism, but only those forms that strengthen rights and liberties and extend our own tradition. No doubt our own form of democratic capitalism has accepted many socialist elements over the generations; Peter Drucker's work on the effects of "pension-plan socialism" is only one such evidence. It is an advantage of our system that it is subject to continual modification—"creeping socialism," as some call it.

Intellectually speaking, a theologian should be critical of both capitalist and socialist tendencies. It is by no means plain from the historical record that all virtue and truth reside on one side. Among businesspeople one would perhaps want to raise one set of reflections; among socialist-inclined intellectuals, another. In recent years the balance of highly respected public rhetoric has plainly tipped toward the socialist side. Wisely? Critically? Or in "bad faith?"

The wisest course for a theologian today, I believe, is to be suspicious of the two ideologies—of, as Peter Berger puts it, those twin *Pyramids of Sacrifice*—and to start thinking carefully about one's own economic experience. It is necessary to begin reading economics. As I argued in *Ascent of the Mountain, Flight of the Dove,* economic systems are the most profound institutional enforcers of the prevailing "sense of reality." Economic institutions are more basic than political institutions. Sophistication in "political consciousness" must give place to sophistication in "economic consciousness." But economic consciousness is not to be gleaned solely from books of propaganda. Experience is a more reliable criterion by far. We must move from "political theology" to "economic theology." We might even speak of the "economy of salvation," if liberation theology had not already made that particular connection. But in launching out in these directions, the greatest weakness of us theologians is how little we know about economics.

II

Douglass's defense of socialism is unusual for its modesty and pragmatism. His essay is one of the best I have read on the subject. One can sense his care to submit to the evidence, not to be stampeded by desire. Still, one need not look at the evidence from within his horizon. Looked at from another standpoint, his evidence does not help a doubter.

Douglass really has only two points to make, and one of them confirms the central point of my essay. He says it best: "Democratic socialism still remains, therefore, much more a vision than a demonstrated possibility." It *is* a vision. One must approach it as one approaches a religion. Even its claims—as Douglass correctly reports them—are religious: it will generate a new type of human being, more rational, people who "acquire only what they truly need." At stake in the choice between democratic capitalism and democratic socialism "is a fundamental *moral* distinction." Dr. Douglass resists my phrase "secular religion" in order to rebut the "secular" part; it was the "religious" part that caught my attention.

"Under socialism," he writes, "no one goes hungry; everyone who is able works; those who work receive benefits commensurate with their social contribution; and there are not the radical disparities in wealth and opportunities characteristic of capitalism." My own minimal travels abroad teach me no such facts about the practice of socialism. Do most persons in, say, Czechoslovakia meet U.S. minimal standards of nutrition? By our definition, are they above the poverty line? As for unemployment, forced labor can end that anywhere. I believe I have seen evidence of "radical disparities in wealth and opportunities" in every socialist nation I have visited, even independently of reading Yugoslav social critic Milovan Djilas. As for social cooperation, here is how Soviet MIG-25 flyer Viktor Belenko, who defected to Japan, described American crewmen at work on a carrier: "I've never seen men work with such proficiency and coordination." They moved so casually, he marveled, "without anyone shouting at them."

The problem is that socialism is now several generations old; it is no longer merely a vision or a dream; it has a historical record and is embodied in actual systems—scores of them around the world. Characteristically, intellectuals deal with *ideas* and *visions* when writing of socialism—and then suddenly become ruthlessly concrete when describing the capitalism they know. This hardly seems fair, until one recognizes that democratic capitalism lacks the texts, theories and visions that might be compared point for point with those of socialism. As a body of ideas, socialism has a coherent beauty and the elaborate casuistry theologians love. That alone makes me believe that it is too good for this frail, sinful world—that it is lacking in practice and is too beautiful by half to supply a useful guide to actual human behavior.

III

Still, one tries to believe. Wouldn't it be wonderful if an economic-political system delivered *everything;* not only productivity sufficient to alleviate poverty, disease and ignorance, not only freedom for science and intellectual pursuits, but also citizens tutored to "acquire only what they truly need?" My experience with socialists suggests that they are anybody's equal as consumers, connoisseurs of good foods and expensive foreign cars (built by multi-national corporations), and not detectably less greedy than the capitalists I have known. My hunch—ingrained cynicism, perhaps—is that the coveting of goods antedates capitalism and outlives socialism. In addition, my limited international experience (both travel and reading) does not indicate that socialist systems are more "rational" or even more "humane" in the allocation of resources than capitalist systems.

As a vision, socialism encourages my longing to believe. As a system well advanced in historical experience, it prompts me to ask myself: Would I want to live under such a system? Would I like for the U.S. to become one? Until a better apologist gets to me, I will have to confess, shamefaced (since this confession proves me less humane, less just and less visionary than those with faith), that my flesh and my experience will not let my spirit soar so high.

Temporarily, therefore, I confess as a matter of considered judgment that democratic capitalism is not only a more humane and rational economic-political system than socialism has yet produced but also the most advanced human form of liberty, justice and equality of opportunity yet fashioned by the human race. When a better system comes along, or when genuine internal improvements are imagined for it, I will most happily support such. For ours is obviously a deficient human system. Nonetheless, actual socialisms are, without exception, worse.

IV

I have even formulated some reasons for this dreadful conclusion, to which my head, despite the heart's yearnings, forces me.

First, *Liberty.* Democratic capitalism "is indeed flexible," to cite Douglass once again. It is endlessly reformable. Freedom of ideas prevails, private initiatives are encouraged, and practicality has great weight. "As Michael Harrington keeps insisting," Douglass warns us, "as long as the means of production remain in private ownership, there is a fundamental structural obstacle to the realization of socialist objectives"—and also, it might be added, to total state tyranny.

I seem to lack the necessary confidence in bureaucrats, political leaders and state ownership. On reflection, I prefer a world in which private ownership is both possible and effective. I prefer the liberation of private spheres of economic activity, so that economic and political orders are kept in tension. It's ideologically impure of me, I know, but it does seem that "socialist objectives" may not be worth destroying that tension for, and that they could not survive its disappearance. In a word, the socialist dream seems not only unworkable in practice but also deficient in theory. Countervailing forces in the economic order are indispensable.

Second, *Equality*. Recently I heard civil rights spokesman Bayard Rustin ask an audience (predominantly black) which nation of the world a black would rather be living in now. Is there more opportunity for self-realization for a young black—or Hungarian, or Indian, or Dominican—in any other existing system? The American ideal is not, of course, equality of results, but equality of opportunity; but even in the (humanly unrealizable) sphere of equality of results, what system in existence draws as many immigrants year by year, or counts as "poverty" annual incomes unparalled elsewhere? (The *average* grant to a welfare family in Harlem last year was $6,100.)

Last summer I watched a bicentennial parade in Cresco, Iowa, a town just over 100 years old. The earliest farm implements were resurrected. Three generations ago, one saw vividly, America was an underdeveloped nation. No tractors, no power machines. Then, in this same midwest, industrial invention flowered as nowhere else. (My wife's grandfather himself invented the extension ladder, the grubbing machine—for pulling up stumps—and a special lightning rod.) A great historical miracle occurred. Democratic capitalism nourished it. The whole world now has new horizons.

Disparities of wealth and power, within the United States and outside it, cannot by any means be understood simply as evidence of "oppression" or sins against "equality." The subject is a complicated one. Some use inequality of results as prima facie evidence of inequality of opportunity on the one hand, or of "oppression" on the other. Would that life were so simple. Equality of results is neither a natural, nor a virtuous, nor a creative, nor a free condition. Egalitarianism is, in practice egalityranny; it must be enforced. Its social costs—in inventiveness, initiative and creativity—are exceedingly high.

Third, *Justice*. I fail to see any practicing socialist state whose schemes of justice exceed those of democratic capitalism. Justice is never fully achieved by human institutions, but in no land known to me—or to former militant Eldridge Cleaver—does the steady advance of justice have as creditable a track record as in ours. The demands we Americans characteristically make on our social institutions are both extraordinary and exorbitant. We even expect them to make us happy. Justice in Czechoslovakia—forget it.

V

And so on. Perhaps it is best, by way of conclusion, to show how Dr. Douglass's second point—the irrationality and inhumaneness of capitalism so disappointing to our academic socialists—fails to help my lack of faith.

1. *Detroit's automobiles*. Dr. Douglass can buy a car of virtually any size from Detroit, or from any other auto-producing nation. Has any socialist a wider range of choice than he? I do not share his enthusiasm for mass transportation; neither the Long Island Railroad, nor the Bay Area Rapid Transit, nor New York City's subways, nor the Paris Metro, nor Eurail, nor any other system can quite match the liberty of action and distribution of costs of the personal automobile. Social costs of various sorts will force us to live differently in the future. You and I will pay for them.
2. *Food production*. The problem is not one of underproduction, for no economic system in the world is so productive, but one of inter-

national distribution. One need not buy foods containing additives; the fastest-growing group of food stores is the "independents" catering to the advanced and purified tastes of (among others) intellectuals. Our artificial foods do not seem to lead to shorter life-spans than those of our ancestors.

3. *The energy crisis.* Having discovered oil and its uses, we will now have to find other cheap sources of energy, and live differently. Socialist nations will no doubt suffer even more than we from higher oil prices.
4. *The consumption ethic.* The most highly educated Americans—who happen to be the most affluent—provide the best markets by far for consumer goods. Who else has so much discretionary income? My socialist friends drive expensive foreign cars and have habits in consumption that are not quite so "conspicuous" as to be vulgar, but are actually even more expensive. In a society like ours, there is also freedom *not* to consume. One can teach such restraint to one's children and one's students, if one practices it. One need not care too much about the sinfulness of one's neighbors. Some like consumption, some pornography. Let them.
5. *Public penury.* Douglass's comment about "underpaid teachers, policemen, firemen and social workers" is probably intended ironically, so far as New York is concerned; but even in Washington federal salaries are notoriously high. In any case, the public pays. Government is not an efficient provider of many services. Where there is government, there is corruption—and also high motivation, well, to shrug.

Douglass wants a "rational plan" rather than "the whims of investors." Look at this meaning of "rational." Would you be satisfied with someone else's "rational plan" if you had a better idea? Investors are rather more careful about their own money than the word "whim" suggests. It seems to me more intelligent—and vastly more creative—to develop and utilize our productive capacities on the basis of the intelligent self-interest of investors than on the whims of planners (to invert a Douglass sentence). Socialist planning has not become the laughingstock of socialist citizens for nothing.

Douglass would like a world without economic accountability: "If you choose to do something which does not lead to profits and which requires substantial financial support, your chances of being frustrated are rather high." Such chances are high in any case in this imperfect world. But the amount of money available for nonprofit work, with substantial financial support, in this nation of all nations in history is astronomical. Dr. Douglass and I draw remarkable salaries from nonprofit universities, for example. Has any civilization ever paid so many so well for being unproductive?

VI

There is scarcely a sentence of Douglass's modest defense of socialism and calm attack upon capitalism which—much as I admire it—does justice to the complex facts of my own experience of democratic capitalism. Capitalism "builds upon and in fact encourages selfishness"—but also extraordinary generosity, a sense of service, voluntarism, giving. "A capitalist environment naturally inclines us to believe that people must be addicted to a greedy, competitive individualism." But how, then, explain the extraordinary innocence and moralism of Americans, so many of whom seem to believe in the essential goodness of humanity and are so deliciously outraged by each example of "greedy, competitive individualism" they encounter in the news? Dr. Douglass argues from what the socialist books say Americans must be like—not, I think, from the way his friends and associates regularly behave.

A very large proportion of Americans do *not* seek upward mobility; are content to stay at the salary level they have attained; do not work in order to consume; are not greedy, or even competitive; nourish their families and like their neighbors. The top 10 percent, the ambitious, of course, do otherwise—and pay the high personal costs. The democratic capitalist conviction is that such individualists will—subject to the checks and balances of our society—do more good than harm. The record seems to support this rather optimistic assessment of human liberty, this method of "harnessing human egoism." As to cultivating a better human nature, those of us who are Christian leave this slim possibility to the miracle of divine grace and meanwhile do not set too much store by the chance of its happening in history.

Dr. Douglass makes the best case against capitalism and for socialism that I have encountered. His vision sounds noble, moral, heroic even. At night, faith wavering, I still thumb through pictures of Sweden, Albania, China, Yugoslavia, Nigeria and other socialist experiments, trying to awaken a dying light. How fortunate are those who still believe.

ASSIGNMENT QUESTIONS

1. Summarize the basic points of Michael Novak's article, "A Closet Capitalist Confesses."
2. Compare and relate Bruce Douglass's response to Novak's arguments in the article, "Socialism and Sin."
3. Outline Novak's final response to Douglass in "The Closet Socialists." Tie in his arguments to what Douglass said and to what he, himself, stated earlier.
4. Did Novak, in your opinion, fully answer the criticisms of capitalism enumerated by Douglass? What would you add?
5. What is your personal conclusion on the subject of capitalism versus socialism? Be specific.

3
A MESSAGE TO GARCIA AND ACRES OF DIAMONDS

A MESSAGE TO GARCIA

Elbert H. Hubbaard, "A Message to Garcia," n.p., 1899.

In all this Cuban business there is one man who stands out on the horizon of my memory like Mars at perihelion. When war broke out between Spain and the United States, it was very necessary to communicate quickly with the leader of the insurgents. Garcia was somewhere in the mountain fastness of Cuba—no one knew where. No mail nor telegraph message could reach him. The President must secure his cooperation, and quickly.

What to do!

Someone said to the President, "There's a fellow by the name of Rowan will find Garcia for you, if anybody can."

Rowan was sent for and given a letter to be delivered to Garcia. How "the fellow by the name of Rowan" took the letter, sealed it up in an oilskin pouch, strapped it over his heart, in four days landed by night off the coast of Cuba from an open boat, disappeared into the jungle, and in three weeks came out on the other side of the island, having traversed a hostile country on foot and delivered his letter to Garcia, are things I have no special desire now to tell in detail.

The point I wish to make is this: McKinley gave Rowan a letter to be delivered to Garcia; Rowan took the letter and did not ask, "Where is he at?" By the Eternal! there is a man whose form should be cast in deathless bronze and the statue placed in every college of the land. It is not book learning young men need, nor instruction about this and that, but a stiffening of the vertebrae which will cause them to be loyal to a trust, to act promptly, concentrate their energies; do the thing—"Carry a message to Garcia!"

General Garcia is dead now, but there are other Garcias.

No man who has endeavored to carry out an enterprise where many hands were needed, is surprised at times by the imbecility of the average man—the inability or unwillingness to concentrate on a thing and do it. Slipshop assistance, foolish inattention, dowdy indifference, and half-hearted work seem the rule; and no man succeeds, unless by hook or crook, or threat, he forces or bribes other men to assist him; or, mayhap, God in His goodness performs a miracle and sends him an Angel of Light for an assistant.

You, reader, put this matter to a test: You are sitting now in your office—six clerks are within call. Summon any one and make this request: "Please look in the encyclopedia and make a brief memorandum for me concerning the life of Correggio."

Will the clerk quietly say, "Yes, sir," and go do the task?

On your life, he will not. He will look at you out of a fishy eye and ask one or more of the following questions:

Who was he?
Which encyclopedia?
Where is the encyclopedia?
Was I hired for that?
Don't you mean Bismarck?
What's the matter with Charlie doing it?
Is he dead?
Is there any hurry?
Shan't I bring you the book and let you look it up for yourself?
What do you want to know for?

And I will lay you ten to one that after you have answered the questions, and explained how to find the information, and why you want it, the clerk will go off and get one of the other clerks to help him try to find Correggio—and then come back and tell you there is no such man. Of course I may lose my bet, but according to the law of average, I will not.

Now if you are wise you will not bother to explain to your "assistant" that Correggio is indexed under the C's, not the K's, but you will smile sweetly and say, "Never mind," and go look it up yourself.

And this incapacity for independent action, this moral stupidity, this infirmity of the will, this unwillingness to cheerfully catch hold and lift are the things that put pure socialism so far into the future. If men will not act for themselves, what will they do when the benefit of their effort is for all? A first mate with knotted club seems necessary; and the dread of getting "the bounce" Saturday night holds many a worker to his place.

Advertise for a stenographer, and nine out of ten who apply can neither spell nor punctuate—and do not think it necessary to.

Can such a one write a letter to Garcia?

"You see that bookkeeper," said the foreman in a large factory.

"Yes, what about him?"

"Well, he's a fine accountant, but if I'd send him uptown on an errand, he might accomplish the errand all right, and, on the other hand, might stop at four saloons on the way, and when he got to Main Street would forget what he had been sent for."

Can such a man be entrusted to carry a message to Garcia?

We have recently been hearing much maudlin sympathy expressed for the "downtrodden denizen of the sweatshop" and the "homeless wanderer searching for honest employment," and with it all too often go many hard words for the men in power.

Nothing is said about the employer who grows old before his time in a vain attempt to get frowsy ne'er-do-wells to do intelligent work; and his long, patient striving with "help" that does nothing but loaf when his back is turned. In every store and factory there is a constant weeding-out process going on. The employer is constantly sending away "help" that have shown their incapacity to further the interests of the business, and others are being taken on. No matter how good times are, this sorting continues, only if times are hard and work is scarce, the sorting is done finer—but out and forever out, the incompetent and unworthy go. It is the survival of the fittest. Self-interest prompts every employer to keep the best—those who can carry a message to Garcia.

I know one man of really brilliant parts who has not the ability to manage a business of his own, and yet who is absolutely worthless to anyone else because he carries with him constantly the insane suspicion that his employer is oppressing or intending to oppress him. He cannot give orders, and he will not receive them. Should a message be given him to take to Garcia, his answer would probably be, "Take it yourself, and be damned!"

Tonight this man walks the streets looking for work, the wind whistling through his threadbare coat. No one who knows him dare employ him, for he is a regular firebrand of discontent. He is impervious to reason, and the only thing that can impress him is the toe of a thick-soled No. 9 boot.

Of course, I know that one so morally deformed is no less to be pitied than a physical cripple; but in our pitying, let us drop a tear, too, for the men who are striving to carry on a great enterprise, whose working hours are not limited by the whistle, and whose hair is fast turning white through the struggle to hold in line dowdy indifference, slipshod imbecility, and the heartless ingratitude which, but for their enterprise, would be both hungry and homeless.

Have I put the matter too strongly? Possibly I have; but when all the world has gone a-slumming I wish to speak a word of sympathy for the man who succeeds—the man who, against great odds, has directed the efforts of others, and, having succeeded, finds there's nothing in it; nothing but bare board and clothes.

I have carried a dinner pail and worked for day's wages, and I have also been an employer of labor, and I know there is something to be said on both sides. There is no excellence, per se, in poverty; rags are no recommendation; and all employers are not rapacious and high-handed, any more than all poor men are virtuous.

My heart goes out to the man who does his work when the "boss" is away as well as when he is at home. And the man who, when given a letter for Garcia, quietly takes the missive, without asking any idiotic questions, and with no lurking intention of chucking it into the nearest sewer, or of doing aught else but deliver it, never gets "laid off," nor has to go on a strike for higher wages. Civilization is one long, anxious search for just such individuals. Anything such a man asks shall be granted; his kind is so rare that no employer can afford to let him go. He is wanted in every city, town, and village—in every office, shop, store, and factory. The world cries out for such; he is needed, and needed badly—the man who can carry a message to Garcia.

ACRES OF DIAMONDS

Russell H. Conwell, "Acres of Diamonds" (Cleveland, n.p., 1905).

The acres of diamonds of which I propose to speak today are to be found in your homes, or near to them, and not in some distant land. I cannot better introduce my thought than by the relation of a little incident that occurred to a party of American travelers beyond the Euphrates River. We passed across the great Arabian Desert, coming out at Baghdad, passed down the river to the Arabian Gulf, and on our way down we hired an Arabian guide to show us all the wonderful things connected with the ancient history and scenery. And that guide was very much like the barbers...in this country today; that is, he thought it was not only his duty to guide us but also to entertain us with stories both curious and weird, and ancient and modern, many of which I have forgotten; and I am glad I have, but there is one I remember today. The old guide led the camel along by his halter, telling various stories, and once he took his Turkish cap from his head and swung it high in the air to give me to understand that he had something especially important to communicate, and then he told me this beautiful story.

"There once lived on the banks of the Indus River an ancient Persian by the name of Al Hafed. He owned a lovely cottage on a magnificent hill, from which he could look down upon the glittering river and the glorious sea; he had wealth in abundance, fields, grain, orchards, money at interest, a beautiful wife and lovely children, and he was contented. Contented because he was wealthy, and wealthy because he was contented. And one day there visited this Al Hafed an ancient priest, and that priest sat down before the fire and told him how diamonds were made, and said the old priest, 'If you had a diamond the size of your thumb you could purchase a dozen farms like this, and if you had a handful you could purchase the whole county.'

"Al Hafed was at once a poor man; he had not lost anything, he was poor because he was discontented, and he was discontented because he thought he was poor. He said: 'I want a mine of diamonds; what is the use of farming a little place like this? I want a mine and I will have it.' He could hardly sleep that night, and early in the morning he went and wakened the priest, and said: 'I want you to tell me where you can find diamonds.' Said the old priest: 'If you want diamonds, go and get them.'

'Won't you please tell me where I can find them?'

'Well, if you go and find high mountains, with a deep river running between them, over white sand, in this white sand you will find diamonds.'

'Well,' said he, 'I will go.'

"So he sold his farm, collected his money, and went to hunt for diamonds. He began, very properly, with the Mountains of the Moon, and came down through Egypt and Palestine. Years passed. He came over through Europe, and, at last, in rags and hunger, he stood a pauper on the shores of the great Bay of Barcelona; and when that great tidal wave came rolling through the Pillars of Hercules, he threw himself into the incoming tide and sank beneath its foaming crest, never again to rise in this life."

Here the guide stopped to fix some dislocated baggage, and I said to myself, "What does he mean by telling me this story! It was the first story I ever read in which the hero was killed in the first chapter." But he went on:

"The man who purchased Al Hafed's farm led his camel one day out to the stream in the garden to drink. As the camel buried his nose in the water, the man noticed a flash of light from the white sand and reached down and picked up a black stone with a strange eye of light in it which seemed to reflect all the hues of the rainbow. He said, 'It's a wonderful thing,' and took it in his house, where he put it on his mantel and forgot all about it. A few days afterward the same old priest came to visit Al Hafed's successor. He noticed a flash of light from the mantel, and taking up the stone, exclaimed:

'Here is a diamond! Has Al Hafed returned?'

'Oh, no, that is not a diamond, that is nothing but a stone that we found out in the garden.'

'But,' said the priest, 'that is a diamond!' And together they rushed out into the garden and stirred up the white sands with their fingers, and there came up other more beautiful gems, and more valuable than the first."

And that was the guide's story. And it is, in the main, historically true. Thus were discovered the wonderful mines of Golconda. Again the guide swung his cap, and said: "Had Al Hafed remained at home and dug in his own cellar or garden, or under his own wheat fields, he would have found Acres of Diamonds." And this discovery was the founding of the line of the Great Moguls, whose magnificent palaces are still the astonishment of all travelers. He did not need to add the moral.

But that I may teach by illustration, I want to tell you the story that I then told him. We were sort of exchanging works; he would tell me a story and I would tell him one, and so I told him about the man in California, living on his ranch there, who read of the discovery of gold in the southern part of the state. He became dissatisfied and sold his ranch and started for new fields in search of gold. His successor, Colonel Sutter, put a mill on the little stream below the house, and one day, when the water was shut off, his little girl went down to gather some of the white sand in the raceway; and she brought some of it into the house to dry it. And while she was sifting it through her fingers, a gentleman, a visitor there, noticed the first shining sands of gold ever discovered in Upper California. That farm that the owner sold to go somewhere else to find gold has added $18 million to the circulating medium of the world; and they told me there sixteen years ago that the owner of one-third of the farm received a $20 gold piece for every fifteen minutes of his life.

That reminds me of what Professor Agassiz told his summer class in mineralogy in reference to Pennsylvania. I live in Pennsylvania, but, being a Yankee, I enjoy telling this story. This man owned a farm, and he did just what I would do if I owned a farm in that state—sold it. Before he sold it, he concluded that he would go to Canada to collect coal oil. The professors will tell you that this stuff was first found in connection with living springs, floating on the water. This man wrote to his cousin in Canada asking for employment collecting this oil. The cousin wrote back that he did not understand the work. The farmer then studied all the books on coal oil, and when he knew all about it, and the theories of the geologists concerning it from the formation of primitive coal beds to the present day, he removed to Canada to work for his cousin, first selling his Pennsylvania farm for $1,833.

The old farmer who purchased his estate went back to the barn one day to fix a place for the horses to drink and found that the previous owner had already arranged that matter. He had fixed some plank edgewise, running from one bank toward the other and resting edgewise a few inches into the water, the purpose being to throw over to one side a dreadful scum that the cattle would not put their noses in, although they would drink the water below it. That man had been damming back for twenty-one years that substance, the discovery of which the official geologist pronounced to be worth to the state the sum of $100 million. Yet that man had sold his farm for $1,833. He sold one of the best oil-producing farms and went somewhere else to find—nothing.

That story brought to my mind the incident of the young man in Massachusetts. There was a young man in college studying mining and mineralogy, and while he was a student they employed him for a time as a tutor and paid him $15 a week for the special work. When he graduated they offered him a professorship and $45 a week. When this offer came, he went home and said to his mother:

"Mother, I know too much to work for $45 a week; let us go out to California, and I will stake out gold mines and copper and silver mines, and we will be rich."

His mother said it was better to stay there. But as he was an only son he had his way, and they sold out and started. But they only went to Wisconsin, where he went into the employ of the Superior Copper Mining Company, at a salary of $15 a week. He had scarcely left the old estate before the farmer who bought it was digging potatoes and bringing them through the yard in a large basket. The farms there are almost all stone wall, and the gate was narrow, and as he was working his basket through, pulling first one side then the other, he noticed in that stone wall a block of native silver about eight inches square. This professor of mining and mineralogy was born on that place, and when he sold out he sat on that very stone while he was making the bargain. He had passed it again and again. He had rubbed it with his sleeve until it had reflected his countenance and said: "Come, now, here is $100,000 for digging—dig me."

I should enjoy exceedingly telling these stories, but I am not here to relate incidents so much as to bring lessons that may be helpful to you. I love to laugh at the mistakes of these men until the thought comes to me, "How do you know what that man in Wisconsin is doing—and that man in Canada?" It may be that he sits by his hearth today and shakes his sides and laughs at us for making the same mistakes and feels that after all he is in comparatively good company. We have all made the same mistakes. Is there anyone here that has not? If there is one that says you have never made such a blunder, I can argue with you that you have. You may not have had the acres of diamonds and sold them. You may not have had wells of oil and sold them, and yet you may have done so. A teacher in the Wilkes-Barre schools came to me after one of my lectures and told me that he owned a farm of fifty acres that he sold for $5 an acre, and a few weeks before my lecture it was sold for $38,000 because they had found a silver mine on it.

You say you never have made any such mistakes. Are you rich today? Are you worth $5 million? Of course not!

Why not? "I never had opportunity to get it."

Now you and I can talk. Let us see!

Were you ever in the mercantile business? Why didn't you get rich? "Because I couldn't, there was so much competition and all that." Now, my friend, didn't you carry on your store just as I carried on my father's store? I don't like to tell how I conducted my father's store. But when he went away to purchase goods, he would sometimes leave me in charge; and a man would come in and say: "Do you keep jackknives?" "No, we don't keep jackknives." Then another would come in and ask: "Do you keep jackknives?" "No, we don't!" and still another. "No, we don't keep jackknives; why are you all bothering me about jackknives!!!"

Did you keep store in that way? Do you ask me what was the fault? The difficulty was that I never had learned by bitter experience the foundation of business success; and that it is the same foundation that underlies all true success, the foundation that underlies Christianity and morality. That it is the whole of man's life to live for others; and he that can do the most to elevate, enrich, and inspire others shall reap the greatest reward himself. Not only so says the Holy Book but so says business common sense.

I will go into your store and ask: "Do you know neighbor A that lives over a couple of squares from your store?" Yes, he deals here." "Where did he come from?" "I don't know." "Has he any children?" "I don't know." "Is he a married man?" "I don't know." "What ticket does he vote?" "I don't know, and I don't care!"

Is that the way you do business? If it is, then you have been conducting your business as I carried on my father's store! And you do not succeed and are poor? I understand it. You can't succeed and I am glad of it, and I will give $5 to see your failure announced in the newspaper tomorrow morning. The only way to succeed is to take an interest in the people around you and honestly work for their welfare.

"But," you say, "I have no capital." I am glad you haven't. I am sorry for the rich men's sons. Young man, if you have no capital, there is hope for you. According to the statistics collected in the city of Boston twenty years ago, ninety-six of every one hundred successful merchants were born poor; and trustworthy statistics also show that of the rich men's sons not one in a thousand dies rich. I am sorry for the rich men's sons unless their fathers be wise enough to bring them up like poor children. If you haven't any capital, life is full of hope to you.

A. T. Stewart started out with a dollar and a half to begin on and he lost all but sixty-two and a half cents the first afternoon. That was before he was a school teacher. He purchased things the people did not want. He said, "I will never do that again," and he went around to the doors and found what the people wanted and invested his sixty-two and a half cents safely, for he knew what people wanted, and went on until he was worth $42 million. And what man has done, men can do again. You may say: "I can't be acquainted with every man in the county and know his wife and children in order to succeed." If you know a few fairly well, you may judge the world by them.

John Jacob Astor is said by one of his latest biographers to have had a mortgage on a millinery establishment. I always think when I reach this point that the ladies will say: "Fools rush in where angels fear to tread." They could not pay the interest on the mortgage and he foreclosed and took possession. He went into partnership with the same man who failed and kept the old clerks and retained the old stock. He went out and set down on a bench in Union Park. What was he doing there? He was watching the women as they passed by, and when he saw a lady with her shoulders thrown back and her head up as if she didn't care if all the world was looking at her, he studied that bonnet; and before it was out of sight he knew every feather and ribbon and all about the frame; and—and—some men may be able to describe a bonnet, but I cannot. I don't believe there are words in the English language to do it. Then he went to the store and said: "put such and such a bonnet in the window, for I know that there is one woman that likes it." And then he would go and watch for another style and return and have that put in the window with the other. And success came.

Some years ago I went into that store to find out about it for myself, and there I found the descendants of that man doing business, and it is the largest millinery firm in the world, with branch houses in all the large cities on the globe. That success was made because Astor studied into the matter and knew what the women wanted before he had the articles made.

But you say, "I cannot do it." You can do it. You say you have no capital—but you have a jackknife. I could not sleep if I did not have a jackknife in my pocket—a Yankee cannot. In Massachusetts, there lived a man who was a carpenter and who was out of work. He sat around the stove until his wife told him to go outdoors, and he did—every man in Massachusetts is compelled by law to obey his wife! He sat down on the shore of the bay and whittled a soaked oak shingle, until he made a chain that his children quarreled over. Then he whittled another.

Then a neighbor, coming in, advised him to whittle toys, for sale. "I can't make toys," said he. "Yes, you can." "But I wouldn't know what to make." There is the whole thing; not in having the machinery or the capital but in knowing what the people want; and so his friend said to the carpenter: "Why don't you ask your own children? See what they like, and perhaps other children will like the same thing." He concluded to do so; and, when his little girl came down, he said: "Mary, what kind of a toy would you like to have me make?" "Oh, a little doll cradle, and carriage, and horse," and a dozen other things.

He began with his jackknife and made up these rough, unpainted toys. A friend of his sold them in a Boston shoe store at first, and brought back 25 and 50 cents at a time, and then his wife began to be better natured. The wife always does get better natured when there is a prospect of money to divide. She came out and split up the wood while he made up the toys. The last case I had as a lawyer before I entered the ministry that man was on the stand, and I said to him: "When did you commence to whittle those toys?" "In 1870." "How much are the patents on those toys worth?" His answer was, their actual value, to him, was $78,000; and it was a little less than seven years after the time when he began with his jackknife; and today I know that he is worth $100,000, and he has received it all from having consulted his own children and judging from them what other people's children wanted and trying to supply the demand. If a man takes an interest in people, and knows what they need, and endeavors to supply it, he must succeed.

Some of you who sit before me, thinking you are poor, are actually in possession of wealth; like the Baltimore lady, who, fourteen years after her father's failure, found a costly diamond bracelet he had lost seventeen years before.

Many of you smile at the thought that you are in the actual possession of wealth. A shoemaker in Massachusetts sat around in the house until his wife drove him out with a broom, and then he went out into the backyard and sat down on an ash barrel. Nearby was a beautiful mountain stream but I don't suppose that he thought of Tennyson's beautiful poem—

I chatter, chatter, as I flow,
  To join the brimming river;
Men may come, and men may go,
  But I go on forever.

It was not a poetical situation, sitting on an ash barrel and his wife in the kitchen with a mop.

Then he saw a trout flash in the stream and hide under the bank, and he reached down and got the fish and took it into the house; and his wife took it and sent it to a friend in Worcester. The friend wrote back that he would give $5 for another such trout, and our shoemaker and his wife immediately started out to find it—man and wife now perfectly united. A $5 bill in prospect! They went up the stream to its source and followed it down to the brimming river, but there was not another trout to be found. Then he went to the minister. That minister didn't know how trout grew, but he told them to go to the public library and, under a pile of dime novels, he would find Seth Green's book, and that would give them the information they wanted. They did so, and found out all about the culture of trout, and began operations.

They afterwards moved to the banks of the Connecticut River and then to the Hudson, and now that man sends trout, fresh and packed in ice, all over the country, and is a rich man. His wealth was in that backyard just as much twenty years before. But he did not discover it until his repeated failures had made his wife imperious.

I remember meeting, in western Pennsylvania, a distinguished professor who began as a country school teacher. He was determined to know his district, and he learned that the father of one of the boys was a maker of wagon wheels. He studied up all about making wagon wheels, and when that man's boy came to school he told him all about it; and the boy went home and told his father: "I know more about wagon wheels than you do!" "That teacher is teaching that boy wonderfully," said the father. He told a farmer's boy all about the value of fertilizer for the soil, and he went home and told his father, and the old gentleman said: "How that boy is learning!" That teacher is now the president of a college, and is a D.D., an LL.D., and a Ph.D. He taught what the people wanted to know, and that made him successful.

Once I went up into the mountain region of New Hampshire to lecture, and I suffered a great deal from the cold. When I came back to Harvard, I said to a friend, who was a scientific man of great culture: "Professor, I am never going into New Hampshire to lecture again, never!" "Why?" "Because I nearly shivered the teeth out of my head." "And why did you shiver?" "Because the weather was cold." "Oh, no, no!" said my friend. "Then it was because I did not have bedclothes enough?" "No, no, it wasn't that." "Well," I said, "you are a scientific man, and I wish you would tell me, then, just why I shivered?" "Well, sir," he replied, "it was because you didn't know any better." Said he: "Didn't you have in your pocket a newspaper?" "Oh, yes." "Well, why didn't you spread that over your bed? If you had you would have been as warm as the richest man in America under all his silk coverlids; and you shivered because you did not know enough to put the two-cent paper over your bed."

How many women want divorces—and ought to have them, too! How many divorces originate something like this: A workingman comes in haste to his supper and sits down to eat potatoes that are about as hard as the rocks beside which they grew. He will chop them up and eat them in a hurry, and they won't digest well. They make him cross. He frets and scolds, and perhaps he swears, he scarcely knows why, and then there is trouble. If the good woman had only enough of science to put in a pinch of salt, they would have come out mealy and luscious and eatable and ready to laugh themselves to pieces in edible joy; and he would have eaten them down in peace and satisfaction and with good digestion; and he would have arisen from the table with a smile on his face; and there would have been joy in that family—and all because of a pinch of salt. The lack in appreciating the value of little things often keeps us in poverty.

I want to ask the audience—Who are the great inventors in the world? Many will answer that it is a peculiar race of men, with intellects like lightning flashes and heads like bushel measures. But, in fact, inventors are usually ordinary practical thinkers. You may invent as much as they if you study on the question—What does the world need? It is not so difficult to prepare a machine, after all, as it is to find out just what people want. The Jacquard loom was invented by a workingwoman. So was the printing roller. So was the second-best cotton gin. So was the mowing machine. I am out of all patience with myself because I did not invent the telephone. I had the same opportunity that the other boy had; I put my ear down to the rail and heard the rumbling of the engine through the miles of track, and arose and threw snowballs—the other boy arose and asked—Why? He discovered that it was caused by the generation of electricity by the wheels, and, when he saw Edison's speaking machine, he had the whole matter at a glance.

There was the congressman once who resolved to talk sense; of course, he was an exception to the general rule. He was one day walking through the Treasury Department, when a clerk said to him that it was a fine day. As he met the other clerks, they remarked the same thing, and at last our congressman said: "Why do you tell me that it is a fine day? I know that already. Now, if you could tell me what the weather will be tomorrow, it would be of some importance." A clerk caught the idea and began to think it over, and entered into correspondence with the professor at Cincinnati. That was the origin of our signal service. Soon we will know what the weather will be a week ahead. Yes, not many years hence, we will decide what weather we will have by a popular vote. How simple all these mighty improvements and inventions seem when we study the simple steps of their evolution!

Yet civilized men and women are greater today than ever before. We often think all great men are dead, and the longer they are dead the greater they appear to have been. But, in fact, men are greater and women are nobler than ever before. We are building on the foundations of the past, and we must be exceeding small if we are not greater than they who laid them. The world knows nothing of its greatest men. Some young man may say: "I am going to be great." "How?" "How? By being elected to an office." Shall the man be greater than the men who elect him? Shall the servant be greater than his master? That a man is in public office is no evidence of greatness. Even if you are great when you are in office, they will not call you great till after you die. Another young man says: "I am going to be great when there comes a war." But success in war is not always an evidence of greatness.

Historians are apt to credit a successful man with more than he really does and with deeds that were performed by subordinates. General Thomas was one of the greatest generals of the war, yet an incident in his life illustrates this thought. After the Battle of Nashville, the soldiers, seeing him, cheered the hero and shouted, "Hurrah for the hero of Lookout Mountain." This was distasteful to the General, and he ordered it to be stopped. Said he: "Talk about the hero of Lookout Mountain! Why, I was ordered by General Grant to keep my troops at the foot of the mountain, and the enemy began to drop their shells among us, and I ordered my men to retreat, but they would not do it; and they charged and captured the works against my positive orders. Now they talk about the hero of Lookout Mountain!" Yet as he was in command of that corps he would naturally be credited with the victory of that charge, while the daring private or subordinate may never be mentioned in history.

You can be as great at home and in private life as you can on fields of awful carnage. Greatness, in its noblest sense, knows no social or official rank.

I can see again a company of soldiers in the last war going home to be received by their native town officers. Did you ever think you would like to be a king or queen? Go and be received by your town officers, and you will know what it means. I shall never see again so proud a moment as that when, at the head of a company of troops, we were marching home to be received. I was but a boy in my teens. I can hear now distinctly the band playing and see the people that were waiting. We marched into their town hall and were seated in the center. Then I was called to take a position on the platform with the town officers. Then came the address of welcome. The old gentleman had never made a speech before, but he had written this, and walked up and down the pasture until he had committed it to memory. But he had brought it with him and spread it out on the desk. The delivery of the speech by that good but nervous town official went something like this:

"Fellow Citizens—fellow citizens. We are—we are—we are very happy—we are—we are very happy to welcome back to our native town—these soldiers. Fellow citizens, we are very happy to welcome back to our native town these soldiers who have—who have—who have fought—who have fought and bled—and come back to their native town again. We are—we are—we are especially—especially pleased to see with us today this young hero. This young hero—to see this young hero—in imagination we have seen—(remember that he said 'in imagination') we have seen him leading his troops on to battle. We have seen his—his—his shining sword, flashing in the sunshine, as he shouted to his troops, 'Come on!' "

Oh, dear, dear, dear! What did he know about war? That captain, with his shining sword flashing in air, shouting to his troops, "Come on?" He never did it, never. If there had not often been a double line of flesh and blood between him and the enemy, he would not have been there that day to be received. If he had known anything about war he would have known what any soldier in this audience can tell you—that it was next to a crime for an officer of infantry in time of danger to go ahead of his men! Do you suppose he is going out there to be shot in front by the enemy and in the back by his own men? That is no place for him. And yet the hero of the reception hour was that boy. There stood in that house, unnoticed, men who had carried that boy on their backs through deep rivers, men who had given him their last draft of coffee; men who had run miles to get him food. And some were not there; some were sleeping their last sleep in their unknown graves. They had given their lives for the nation, but were scarcely noticed in the good man's speech. And the boy was the hero of the reception hour. Why? For no other reason under heaven but because he was an officer and these men were only private soldiers. Human nature often estimates men's greatness by the office they hold; yet office cannot make men great, nor noble, nor brave.

Any man may be great, but the best place to be great is at home. All men can make their kind better; they can labor to help their neighbors and instruct and improve the minds of the men, women, and children around them; they can make holier their own locality; they can build up the schools and churches around them; and they can make their own homes bright and sweet. These are the elements of greatness; it is here greatness begins; and if a man is not great in his own home or in his own school district, he will never be great anywhere.

THE ERRAND BOY

Horatio Alger, Jr., "The Errand Boy" (New York: A. L. Burt, 1888), pp. 52–68.

After a frugal breakfast at the Bowery Restaurant, Phil invested a few pennies in...two newspapers...and began to go the rounds. The first place was in Pearl Street. He entered, and was directed to a desk in the front part of the store.

"You advertised for a boy," he said.

"We've got one," was the brusque reply.

Of course no more was to be said, and Phil walked out, a little dashed at his first rebuff.

At the next place he found some half dozen boys waiting and joined the line, but the vacancy was filled before his turn came. At the next place his appearance seemed to make a good impression, and he was asked several questions.

"What is your name?"

"Philip Brent."

"How old are you?"

"Just sixteen."

"How is your education?"

"I have been to school since I was six."

"Then you ought to know something. Have you ever been in a place?"

"No sir."

"Do you live with your parents?"

"No sir; I have just come to the city, and am lodging in Fifth Street."

"Then you won't do. We wish our boys to live with their parents."

Poor Phil! He had allowed himself to hope that at length he was likely to get a place. The abrupt termination of the conversation dispirited him.

He made three more applications. In one of them he again came near succeeding, but once more the fact that he did not live with his parents defeated his application.

"It seems to be very hard getting a place," thought Phil, and it must be confessed he felt a little homesick.

"I won't make any more applications today," he decided, and being on Broadway, walked up the busy thoroughfare, wondering what the morrow would bring.

It was winter, and there was ice on the sidewalk. Directly in front of Phil walked an elderly gentleman, whose suit of fine broadcloth and gold spectacles seemed to indicate a person of some prominence and social importance. Suddenly he set foot on a treacherous piece of ice. Vainly he strove to keep his equilibrium, his arms waving wildly, and his gold-headed cane falling to the sidewalk. He would have fallen backward, had not Phil, observing his danger in time, rushed to his assistance. With some difficulty the gentleman righted himself, and then Phil picked up his cane.

"I hope you are not hurt, sir?" he said.

"I should have been but for you my good boy," said the gentleman. "I am a little shaken by the suddenness of my slipping."

"Would you wish me to go with you, sir?"

"Yes, if you please. I do not perhaps require you, but I shall be glad of your company."

"Thank you, sir."

"Do you live in the city?"

"Yes, sir; that is, I propose to do so. I have come here in search of employment."

Phil said this, thinking it possible that the old gentleman might exert his influence in his favor.

"Are you dependent on what you may earn?" asked the gentleman, regarding him attentively.

"I have a little money, sir, but when that is gone I shall need to earn something."

"That is no misfortune. It is a good thing for a boy to be employed. Otherwise he is liable to get into mischief."

"At any rate, I shall be glad to find work, sir."

"Have you applied anywhere yet?"

Phil gave a little account of his unsuccessful applications, and the objections that had been made to him.

"Yes, yes," said the old gentleman thoughtfully, "more confidence is placed in a boy who lives with his parents."

The two walked on together until they reached Twelfth Street. It was a considerable walk, and Phil was surprised that his companion should walk, when he could easily have taken a Broadway stage, but the old gentleman explained this himself.

"I find it does me good," he said, "to spend some time in the open air, and even if walking tires me it does me good."

At Twelfth Street they turned off.

"I am living with a married niece," he said, "just on the other side of Fifth Avenue."

At the door of a handsome four-story house, with a brownstone front, the old gentleman paused, and told Phil that this was his residence.

"Then, sir, I will bid you good morning," said Phil.

"No, no; come in and lunch with me," said Carter hospitably.

He had, by the way, mentioned that his name was Oliver Carter, and said that he was no longer actively engaged in business, but was a silent partner in the firm of which his nephew by marriage was the nominal head.

"Thank you, sir," answered Phil.

He was sure that the invitation was intended to be accepted, and he saw no reason why he should not accept it.

"Hannah," said the old gentleman to the servant who opened the door, "tell your mistress that I have brought a boy home to dinner with me."

"Yes, sir," answered Hannah, surveying Phil with some surprise.

"Come up to my room, my young friend," said Mr. Carter, "You may want to prepare for lunch."

Mr. Carter had two connecting rooms on the second floor, one of which he used as a bedchamber. The furniture was handsome and costly, and Phil, who was not used to city houses, thought it luxurious. Phil washed his face and hands, and brushed his hair. Then a bell rang, and following his new friend, he went down to lunch.

Lunch was set out in the front basement. When Phil and Mr. Carter entered the room a lady was standing by the fire, and beside her was a boy of about Phil's age. The lady was tall and slender, with light brown hair and cold grey eyes.

"Lavinia," said Mr. Carter, "I have brought a young friend with me to lunch."

"So I see," answered the lady. "Has he been here before?"

"No; he is a new acquaintance."

"I would speak to him if I knew his name."

"His name is—" Here the old gentleman hesitated, for in truth he had forgotten.

"Philip Brent."

"You may sit down here, Mr. Brent," said Mrs. Pitkin, for this was the lady's name.

"Thank you, ma'am."

"And so you made my uncle's acquaintance this morning?" she continued, herself taking a seat at the head of the table.

"Yes; he was of service to me," answered Mr. Carter for him. "I had lost my balance, and should have had a heavy fall if Philip had not come to my assistance."

"He is very kind, I am sure," said Mrs. Pitkin, but her tone was very cold.

"Philip," said Mr. Carter, "this is my grandnephew, Alonzo Pitkin."

He indicated the boy already referred to.

"How do you do?" said Alonzo, staring at Philip not very cordially.

"Very well, thank you," answered Philip politely.

"Where do you live?" asked Alonzo, after a moment's hesitation.

"In Fifth Street."

"That's near the Bowery, isn't it?"

"Yes."

The boy shrugged his shoulders and exchanged a significant look with his mother. Fifth Street was not a fashionable street—indeed quite the reverse, and Phil's answer showed that he was a nobody. Phil himself had begun to suspect that he was unfashionably located, but he felt that under his circumstances he might as well remain where he was.

But, though he lived in an unfashionable

street, it could not be said that Phil, in his table manners, showed any lack of good breeding. He seemed quite at home at Mrs. Pitkin's table, and in fact acted with greater propriety than Alonzo, who was addicted to fast eating and greediness.

"Couldn't you walk home alone, Uncle Oliver?" asked Mrs. Pitkin presently.

"Yes."

"Then it was a pity to trouble Mr. Brent to come with you."

"It was no trouble," responded Philip promptly, though he suspected that it was not consideration for him that prompted the remark.

"Yes, I admit that I was a little selfish in taking up my young friend's time," said the old gentleman cheerfully; "but I infer, from what he tells me that it is not particularly valuable just now."

"Are you in a business position, Mr. Brent?" asked Mrs. Pitkin.

"No, madam, I was looking for a place this morning."

"Have you lived for some time in the city?"

"No; I came here only yesterday from the country."

"I think country boys are very foolish to leave good homes in the country to seek places in the city," said Mrs. Pitkin sharply.

"There may be circumstances, Lavinia, that make it advisable," suggested Mr. Carter, who, however, did not know Phil's reason for coming.

"No doubt; I understand that," answered Mrs. Pitkin, in a tone so significant that Phil wondered whether she thought he had got into any trouble at home.

"And besides, we can't judge for everyone, so I hope Master Philip may find some good and satisfactory opening, now that he has reached the city."

After a short time, lunch, which in New York is generally a plain meal, was over, and Mr. Carter invited Philip to come upstairs again.

"I want to talk over your prospects, Philip," he said.

There was silence till after the two had left the room. Then Mrs. Pitkin said:

"Alonzo, I don't like this."

"What don't you like, Ma?"

"Uncle bringing this boy home. It is very extraordinary, this sudden interest in a perfect stranger."

"Do you think he'll leave him any money?" asked Alonzo, betraying interest.

"I don't know what it may lead to, Lonny, but it don't look right. Such things have been known."

"I'd like to punch the boy's head," remarked Alonzo, with sudden hostility. "All uncle's money ought to come to us."

"So it ought, by rights," observed his mother.

"We must see that this boy doesn't get any ascendancy over him."

Phil would have been very much amazed if he had overheard this conversation.

The old gentleman sat down in an armchair and waved his hand toward a small rocking chair, in which Phil seated himself.

"I concluded that you had a good reason for leaving home, Philip," said Mr. Carter, eyeing our hero with a keen but friendly look.

"Yes, sir; since my father's death it has not been a home to me."

"Is there a stepmother in the case?" asked the old gentleman shrewdly.

"Yes, sir."

"Anyone else?"

"She has a son."

"And you two don't agree?"

"You seem to know all about it, sir," said Phil surprised.

"I know something of the world—that is all."

Phil began to think that Mr. Carter's knowledge of the world was very remarkable. He began to wonder whether he could know anything more—could suspect the secret which Mrs. Brent had communicated to him. Should he speak of it? He decided at any rate to wait, for Mr. Carter, though kind, was a comparative stranger.

"Well," continued the old gentleman, "I

won't inquire too minutely in the circumstances. You don't look like a boy that would take such an important step as leaving home without a satisfactory reason. The next thing is to help you."

Phil's courage rose as he heard these words. Mr. Carter was evidently a rich man, and he could help him if he was willing. So he kept silence, and let his new friend do the talking.

"You want a place," continued Mr. Carter. "Now, what are you fit for?"

"That is a hard question for me to answer, sir. I don't know."

"Have you a good education?"

"Yes, sir; and I know something of Latin and French besides."

"You can write a good hand?"

"Shall I show you, sir?"

"Yes; write a few lines at my private desk."

Phil did so, and handed the paper to Mr. Carter.

"Very good," said the old gentleman approvingly. "That is in your favor. Are you good at accounts?"

"Yes, sir."

"Better still."

"Sit down there again," he continued. "I will give you a sum in interest."

Phil resumed his seat.

"What is the interest of eight hundred and forty-five dollars and sixty cents for four years, three months and twelve days, at eight and one-half per cent?"

Phil's pen moved fast in perfect silence for five minutes. Then he announced the result.

"Let me look at the paper. I will soon tell you whether it is correct."

After a brief examination, for the old gentleman was himself adept at figures, he said with a beaming smile:

"It is entirely correct. You are a smart boy."

"Thank you, sir," said Phil, gratified.

"And you deserve a good place—better than you will probably get."

Phil listened attentively. The last clause was not quite so satisfactory.

"Yes," said Mr. Carter, evidently talking to himself, "I must get Pitkin to take him."

Phil knew that the lady whom he had already met was named Pitkin, and he rightly concluded that it was her husband who was meant.

"I hope that he is more agreeable than his wife," thought Philip.

"Yes, Philip," said Mr. Carter, who had evidently made up his mind, "I will try to find you a place this afternoon."

"I shall be very much obliged, sir," said Philip gladly.

"I have already told you that my nephew and I are in business together, he being the active and I the silent partner. We do a general shipping business. Our store is on Franklin Street. I will give you a letter to my nephew and he will give you a place."

"Thank you, sir."

"Wait a minute and I will write you a note."

Five minutes later Phil was on his way downtown with his credentials in his pocket.

Phil paused before an imposing business structure, and looked up to see if he could see the sign that would show him he had reached his destination. He had not far to look. On the front of the building he saw in large letters the sign:

ENOCH PITKIN & CO.

In the doorway there was another sign, from which he learned that the firm occupied the second floor. He went upstairs, and opening a door, entered a spacious apartment which looked like a hive of industry. There were numerous clerks, counters piled with goods, and every indication that a prosperous business was being carried on.

The nearest person was a young man of eighteen, or perhaps more, with an incipient, straw-colored moustache, and a shock of hair of tow color. This young man wore a variegated necktie, a stiff standing collar, and a suit of clothes in the extreme of fashion.

Phil looked at him hesitatingly. The

young man observed the look, and asked condescendingly:

"What can I do for you, my son?"

Such an address from a person less than three years older than himself came near to upsetting the gravity of Phil.

"Is Mr. Pitkin in?" he asked.

"Yes, I believe so."

"Can I see him?"

"I have no objection," remarked the young man facetiously.

"Where shall I find him?"

The youth indicated a small room partitioned off as a private office in the extreme end of the store.

"Thank you," said Phil, and proceeded to find his way to the office in question.

When he arrived at the door, which was partly open, he looked in. In an armchair, sat a small man, with an erect figure and an air of consequence. He was not over forty-five, but looked older, for his cheeks were already seamed and his look was querulous. Cheerful natures do not so soon show signs of age as their opposites.

"Mr. Pitkin?" said Phil interrogatively.

"Well?" said the small man, frowning instinctively.

"I have a note for you, sir."

Phil stepped forward and handed the missive to Mr. Pitkin. The latter opened it quickly and read as follows:

The boy who will present this to you did me a service this morning. He is in want of employment. He seems well educated but if you can't offer him anything better than the post of errand boy, do so. I will guarantee that he will give satisfaction. You can send him to the post-office, and to other offices on such errands as you may have. Pay him five dollars a week and charge that sum to me.

Yours truly,

OLIVER CARTER

Mr. Pitkin's frown deepened as he read this note.

"Pish!" he ejaculated, in a tone which, though low, was audible to Phil. "Uncle Oliver must be crazy. What is your name?" he demanded fiercely, turning suddenly to Phil.

"Philip Brent."

"When did you meet the gentleman who gave you this letter?"

Phil told him.

"Do you know what is in this letter?"

"I suppose, sir, it is a request that you give me a place."

"Did you read it?"

"No," answered Phil indignantly.

"Humph! He wants me to give you the place of errand boy."

"I will try to suit you, sir."

"When do you want to begin?"

"As soon as possible, sir."

"Come tomorrow morning, and report to me first."

"Another freak of Uncle Oliver's!" he muttered, as he turned his back upon Phil, and so signified the interview was ended.

THE MAN WHO COULD NOT BE CORNERED

George Horace Lorimer, "The Man Who Could Not Be Cornered," *The Saturday Evening Post,* August 27, 1898, pp. 137–38.

I

For weeks, the wheat pit had been a storm center. Day after day a dull rumble and roar, rising and falling monotonously, as when the surf booms in on a distant beach, had come down to passers-by in the street below. Men hurrying along about their business had stopped as their ears caught the sound, looked up curiously at the great plate-glass windows, and joined the jostling crowd that was pushing in through the wide doors beneath the gray stone tower.

It was April when the storm began to gather, December when it burst. At first a little thing of gusts and flurries, it scarce flawed the surface of the market; but week by week it gathered strength until it broke a cyclone that swept men from their feet and shook the foundations of trade.

It began in April, when a young man placed a careless order for 100,000 bushels of May wheat; and now it was December, and the young man's little holding had swelled to millions. For that first wheat he had paid some 70 cents a bushel. Then the price had dropped and dropped until he could have bought September wheat at 64. And buy he did, 500,000 bushels of it, and kept on buying. And as his holdings grew, his horizon widened, until he was dazzled by the prospect that he saw before him.

Wheat mounted higher, slowly at first, and then by leaps and bounds; for Europe was hungry and must have bread. The young man transferred his holdings to the December delivery, and bought and bought. Already he owned more wheat than was in all the elevators in Chicago. And now, unless the men who had sold it to him discovered their plight in time to bring grain from the West before January 1, he could run the price up to a dollar, two dollars, whatever he wished. These "shorts" must fill their contracts then or pay him the difference between that final price and the one at which they had sold. To keep them ignorant of their danger until it was too late to get wheat to Chicago was the game.

Well the young man played it. The price kept rising, but there were little breaks between to lull suspicion. On December 5 it was 95 ½ cents, and all the blame was laid on hungry Europe. For the young man kept himself modestly in the background, and there was nothing but a number on a broker's books to tell who owned millions of wheat.

Old hands, who had weathered many a hard storm, began to suspect something besides Europe. They sniffed and smelt Armour, Pillsbury, Pierpont Morgan, or a New York syndicate in the market, quietly pocketed their losses, and made all snug and tight against dirty weather.

The wheat pit of the Chicago Board of Trade, that hub whose spokes radiate to the markets of the world, and which regulates the movement of prices for grain, is a circular arena of steps on which a few hundred brokers can find standing space and face each other. Around it, scattered over the floor of the great trading chamber, are smaller pits where other grains and provisions are dealt in. Even on calm days, when the pulse of the market is slow, this is not a quiet place. In the pits there is the constant clamor of buying and selling for future delivery; about the long rows of sample tables on the floor are quieter groups, offering and bidding on cash grain. In and out, among the men in the pits and on the floor, dart messengers, bawling the names of brokers for whom they have telegrams, and sharp above all the tumult comes the clatter of a hundred instruments, ticking out orders and carrying away quotations. From a spacious gallery, a dozen country visitors look down at the shouting, gesticulating men and wonder what it all means.

But on the ninth of last December, long before the hour for trading to begin, the crowd filled the wheat pit to the brim, and, overflowing down the circular steps, spread out dense on the surrounding floor. The other pits were half deserted, the floor bare, except for the messengers hurrying back and forth. Above, in the gallery, the seats were filled, the aisles were choked with curious men and women. They kept rising to their feet, like people at a circus, and peering down at the waiting crowd.

As the hands of the clock crept toward the trading hour, the laughing chat of the sightseers died down and the men in the pits, who had been conversing in low tones, gravely, earnestly, became silent. Every face reflected a fierce eagerness to grasp more in the great struggle which was coming, or a half-terror lest the rest of a dwindling fortune should be swallowed up. For in that range of 30 cents, from 65 to 95, men had made millions, had lost millions, and now a new force, an unknown quantity, loomed up large enough before them. For overnight that vague uneasiness which, through all the early winter, had been growing, had crystallized into panic.

Only a minute more! Every eye was on the clock, every ear alert for the clash of the gong. Only the clacking of the tireless instruments and the shrill cries of the messengers echoed from the lofty ceiling.

It came with a clang and a mighty roar. The crowd crushed together until the men in the pit were lifted from their feet. The wriggling, writhing, swaying mass bristled with wildly waving arms until it looked a monster with a thousand tentacles. Men, with faces reddened and distorted, howled and raved, now shaking clenched fists across the pit, now signaling frantically with crooked fingers.

To the people in the gallery, craning their necks in breathless eagerness to see, the meaning of this madness was not clear. But they knew that men were being made and ruined in those few minutes, and that was enough. They saw the hands on the indicator, which some days moved by eighths and some days scarce at all, flying around wildly, like the arrow on a wheel of fortune stopping not for eighths and quarters, but leaping halves and cents at a whirl. From 101 ½ to 109 it moved, and the highest mark that wheat had made in six years had been reached. Farther and higher the panic-stricken shorts might have driven it had not the echo of the tumult come to the young man in his office half a mile away. As yet it was not time for these big figures. Settling day was three weeks off, and there were big fish in the net who might break its meshes were they too soon lifted above water.

Into the frantic crowd, where 50 sought to buy what one would sell, his brokers came and doled out wheat until the panic was appeased and the clamor quieted.

II

While the excitement was wildest, a sharp-eyed lad, clutching tight in one hand a slip of white paper, detached himself from the outer fringe of traders and dodged across the floor to the door. Down the stairs he went, taking them three at a time, and out into La Salle Street. A short block he ran, turned into the Home Insurance building, and, breathless, burst into an office on the first floor.

To a door in the front of this office, which gave admission to a small private apartment, the lad hurried and handed his slip of paper to an older youth, who was hovering about with the anxious air of one momentarily expecting a summons from some unexpected quarter. Armed with this slip, the youth opened the door.

Within, seated before a wide oak writing desk, sat a man of medium height, snugly stout. His large head, set deep down into a strong neck, was perfectly bald except for a thin thatch of light-colored hair, which covered the base of his brain and climbed up over his ears and down his face on either side in closely-cropped whiskers. A high and well-shaped forehead, square, determined jaws, and keen, gray eyes, restless, darting and incisive, stamped his as an unusual and powerful personality. The eyes were his most distinguishing feature. They compelled a certain docile respect at all times, submission and fear when their owner wished it. Yet, withal, they were kindly eyes—eyes that could twinkle with fun or express depths of sympathy.

This man was Philip D. Armour, on whom perhaps some 50,000 people are dependent for a living. Philip D. Armour is Armour & Company, who are the largest packers of meats in the world. And Armour & Company is the Armour Elevator Company, whose warehouses dot the West and line the Chicago river; and the Armour Refrigerator Line, whose rolling stock is on all lines, east and west, north and south; and half a dozen other vast enterprises. Last of all, Philip D. Armour is "the old man." Not disrespectfully, but as the badge of his authority, is the term used.

This man began life with a country-school education. But he made up in Scotch pluck and persistence, and Yankee ingenuity and shrewdness, his natural and only inheritance, what he lacked in special equipment for life. From gold-hunting in the West, he drifted into the grain business, and thence, in a modest way, into packing provisions in Milwaukee. From Milwaukee to Chicago is but a step, and he took it.

Year by year the scope of his operations broadened. Tumble-down sheds and ramshackle shanties gave way to big brick buildings whose clustering stacks vomited forth smoke day and night. Armour & Company had become the foremost concern of its kind in the world.

Meanwhile, as the Armour Elevator Company, the head of the house had been broadening out in another direction. First of all, Mr. Armour is a merchant and warehouseman, but he has been known to speculate occasionally—in fact, all the unexplained vagaries of the market are laid at his door.

Mr. Armour is simple in his habits. At six o'clock every morning he is up, and an hour later in his office, listening to telegrams and skimming over important correspondence before passing it along to his department heads, glancing at market reports, asking quick questions and receiving careful answers. He seldom leaves his desk before five, and then it is to drive back to his unpretentious house on Prairie Avenue and pass the evening until nine in his library, when he goes to bed.

His men are notoriously well paid. Half of them tell the time by watches that the "old man" has given them, and the other half wear suits for which the bills have been sent to him. And besides his daily charities, a million and more of his money has gone into the twin institutions which bear his name. But while his left hand may give, his right attends strictly to business.

III

Mr. Armour unfolded the little white slip, and peered over the top of his glasses at the column of penciled figures and the comment scrawled beneath. His face expressed nothing.

He had been expecting something of this sort and quietly preparing for it. For the "old man" had a little business secret, too—a secret which the sharper traders had already guessed, and which he was soon to share with the rest of the world.

For once, the shrewd old speculator had been caught on the wrong side of the market. All through the fall he had been feeling pessimistic about wheat, and all through the fall he had been selling, until the aggregate which he stood committed to deliver before the first day of January had mounted into millions of bushels. And the bins in that long string of elevators along the foul river were well-nigh bare of contract-grade wheat.

But Mr. Armour possesses the saving virtue of the speculator. He can smell out an error in judgment, or a change in conditions, and take the other side with the rapidity of a flash of lightning jumping from cloud to cloud. It was late in the deal when there had come to him a suspicion that he was fairly cornered—too late unless he could accomplish the seemingly impossible. Another man must have thrown up his hands and submitted to being held up. Mr. Armour turned to fight.

It was not the money only, though no man, no matter how great his wealth, can be careless of a loss of a million dollars and more, according as the fancy of an opponent dictates. But the fierce pride of the merchant was involved—the pride of the man who had made the name of the house the synonym for success; the pride of the veteran who had stood a victor at the forks while his opponents passed under the yoke.

When he had been younger, and even in these later years of unshakable strength, there had been men of boldness and wealth who had boasted that they would break "old Armour"; that they would paint their trademarks on his yellow wagons. But after these storms had blown off to sea the rock had still been there. Armour bore no malice toward them. More than once, when some great structure of speculation had collapsed, wrecking the work of months in an hour, the head of the corner had hurried breathless to his office, and it was Armour who had saved the market from utter collapse and the man from utter ruin.

And then there were the little fellows, who, in venturing beyond their strength, had been sucked down and under. How this crowd would yelp with delight at the spectacle of the "old man" beaten at his game by a boy—and a Harvard graduate at that. For now the fight was in the open; the old man and the young man were face to face.

It was at one of the downtown clubs that the latter's secret had been discovered. Day after day there had been hasty calls for Joseph Leiter at the telephone, and the young man had talked a dozen times a morning to a mysterious someone. Even club men have that pardonable human failing—curiosity. It was discovered that the mysterious someone was the broker who was making those heavy purchases for a number on his books. Club men can put two and two together. The number became a name.

IV

It is a source of strength to Mr. Armour that he is as little deceived by flattery as he is moved by abuse. He appraises men and events at their exact value.

"No man," he is fond of saying, "is stronger than his weakest point." So he probes for that weakest point, and, once he has found it, he knows his man.

Nature and chance had combined to make Leiter's position well-nigh unassailable. Drought and wet and blight had wasted the wheat fields of Europe; except for America, the great grain-producing countries had nothing to sell; the hungry had been calling across the Atlantic for bread until the grain bins in Chicago were half empty. Leiter himself had been hurrying grain away to any port far enough removed to have it out of reach on delivery day.

But there was still wheat, plenty of it, in the West and Northwest. And if Armour could get enough of it to Chicago in time, the corner would be broken.

Here again nature sided with Leiter. Even if the grain could be scraped together, it would be impossible for the railroads alone to transport it to Chicago in the brief space. Part of it must come down by boat from Duluth.

Winter comes early on those Northern lakes. In December the last blur of trailing smoke fades from the horizon, and the vast space becomes a solitude—a stretch of white, darkened with patches of steel-blue water, silent, save for the sharp snap and crack of grinding and shifting ice. Already the harbors were ice-bound, and the narrow straits of Sault Ste. Marie, through which a steamer must steer its course to Lake Michigan, becoming locked fast against attack.

In the rear of the office at 205 La Salle Street, center wires over which every way-station in the United States, every capital in Europe, every corner of the world can be reached. Within an hour after Mr. Armour had decided where he stood, ordinary business had been sidetracked, and the operators were busy sending a constantly increasing pile of telegrams marked "rush."

Armour was calling for wheat. To every "impossible," he returned a "must." Day and night he was in the saddle, directing, watching every detail of the fierce struggle against time and the elements.

When Mr. Armour is in a hurry, there is a note in his voice which makes men hurry. When he says a thing can be done, there is a persuasiveness in his blunt logic that moves others to his way of thinking. As his telegrams were delivered, they woke up men all over the West—agents and brokers in the large cities; buyers and warehousemen at the lonely prairie stations; and farmers in Minnesota, Montana, Kansas, Nebraska, the Dakotas, and even far-off Manitoba. They started long trains of empty cars rattling across the endless prairie stretches to the stations where the loaded wagons, creaking and groaning tire-deep through the black mud, were converging and dumping the clean, sound grain. They routed out steamboat men from snug little groceries and saloons, where they had started to doze away the long winter beside squat, red-hot baseburners, and sent them aboard deserted steamers that were tied up to the warves.

They moved a fleet of tugboats down Lake Superior, and kept them stirring back and forth in endless procession through the straits during the long, still nights, when the sharp cold bound together the cakes of ice washing about in their wake. In the harbor at Duluth there were other tugboats puffing back and forth until the fleet should be loaded to the water-line. And what steam could not do, dynamite accomplished. For while the old man in Chicago might believe in his destiny, he knew that dynamite would help it through the zero weather.

Now began the race. Long trains of loaded cars bumped in quick succession across the western lines. Some were headed for Chicago; the rest poured their freight into the holds of the mighty fleet that had been gathering. From Duluth to Sault Ste. Marie, and thence down Lake Michigan, the steamers were strung out, booming along under every pound of steam. And in the midst of it all sat Armour, coaxing, planning, ordering and keeping the whole deal, from farmers to fleet, within the scope of his all-comprehending eye. Until the danger was past, nothing was too big, nothing too small, for his personal attention.

V

On December 10 the reporters found out the young man and made him talk. Something of what was going on in the West he knew, but he was flushed with the glory of what he had done, proud of the big game he had played and had not yet lost, even if his victory were to be incomplete.

"Am I in this wheat deal?" he asked, leaning back in his chair and looking about with the assurance of the young man for whom life has been a round of ready-made successes. "Well, I should remark. Without any desire to boast, I might say we are controlling the biggest individual line of wheat in the country."

On December 13 the price dropped from 105 to 97 ½, but there were other forces at work now. For the next day it was reported that stocks of wheat in storage had increased 1,356,000 bushels in two days, and the last cargoes of 3,654,000 bushels were arriving from Duluth.

All the tracks in the acres of railroad yards were stuffed and choked with cars; the enormous elevators could make room for no such extra tonnage. In the end, a fleet of 134 vessels had to be pressed into service to store the surplus wheat through the winter.

It really looked as if Mr. Leiter had not counted on having all this wheat delivered to him, when, 24 hours later, his father came hurrying on from the East. He, too, seemed rather impressed with the bigness of it all.

"I am much pleased that my son has broadened out into a first-class merchant," he said; and then he started out to borrow money to pay for the wheat which Armour was delivering to him. And there was need, for that day saw 500,000 bushels added to the stocks, 2,500,000 bushels tendered on the son's contracts, and 3,000,000 bushels more reported on the way to Chicago.

On December 30 Leiter had 8,000,000 bushels of cash wheat; Armour had filled all his contracts, and was selling out a surplus that he had on hand.

On the last day of the year a crowd gathered on 'Change to see the end of the December deal; but it had already ended—ended when, a few days before, Armour had delivered the last bushel which was due on his contracts, and left Leiter alone, with his glory and his wheat.

A DEAL IN WHEAT

Frank Norris, *A Deal in Wheat and Other Stories of the New and Old West* (New York: n.p., 1903).

I The Bear—Wheat at Sixty-two

As Sam Lewiston backed the horse into the shafts of his buckboard and began hitching the tugs to the whiffletree, his wife came out from the kitchen door of the house and drew near, and stood for some time at the horse's head, her arms folded and her apron rolled around them. For a long moment neither spoke. They had talked over the situation so long and so comprehensively the night before that there seemed to be nothing more to say.

The time was late in the summer, the place, a ranch in southwestern Kansas, and Lewiston and his wife were two of a vast population of farmers, wheat growers, who at that moment were passing through a crisis—a crisis that at any moment might culminate in tragedy. Wheat was down to sixty-two.

At length Emma Lewiston spoke.

"Well," she hazarded, looking vaguely out across the ranch toward the horizon, leagues distant; "Well, Sam, there's always that offer of brother Joe's. We can quit—and go to Chicago—if the worst comes."

"And give up!" exclaimed Lewiston, running the lines through the torets. "Leave the ranch! Give up! After all these years!"

His wife made no reply for the moment. Lewiston climbed into the buckboard and gathered up the lines. "Well, here goes for the last try, Emmie," he said. "Good-by, girl. Maybe things will look better in town today."

"Maybe," she said gravely. She kissed her husband good-by and stood for some time looking after the buckboard travelling toward the town in a moving pillar of dust.

"I don't know," she murmured at length; "I don't know just how we're going to make out."

When he reached town, Lewiston tied the horse to the iron railing in front of the Odd Fellows' Hall, the ground floor of which was occupied by the post office, and went across the street and up the stairway of a building of brick and granite—quite the most pretentious structure of the town—and knocked at a door upon the first landing. The door was furnished with a pane of frosted glass, on which, in gold letters, was inscribed, "Bridges & Co., Grain Dealers."

Bridges himself, a middle-aged man who wore a velvet skullcap and who was smoking a Pittsburgh stogie, met the farmer at the counter and the two exchanged perfunctory greetings.

"Well," said Lewiston, tentatively, after awhile.

"Well, Lewiston," said the other, "I can't take that wheat of yours at any better than sixty-two."

"Sixty-*two*."

"It's the Chicago price that does it, Lewiston, Truslow is bearing the stuff for all he's worth. It's Truslow and the bear clique that stick the knife into us. The price broke again this morning. We've just got a wire."

"Good heavens," murmured Lewiston, looking vaguely from side to side. "That—that ruins me. I *can't* carry my grain any longer—what with storage charges and—and—Bridges, I don't see just how I'm going to make out. Sixty-two cents a bushel! Why, man, what with this and with that it's cost me nearly a dollar a bushel to raise that wheat, and now Truslow—"

He turned away abruptly with a quick gesture of infinite discouragement.

He went down the stairs, and making his way to where his buckboard was hitched, got in, and, with eyes vacant, the reins slipping and sliding in his limp, half-open hands, drove slowly back to the ranch. His wife had seen him coming and met him as he drew up before the barn.

"Well?" she demanded.

"Emmie," he said as he got out of the buckboard, laying his arm across her shoulder, "Emmie, I guess we'll take up with Joe's offer. We'll go to Chicago. We're cleaned out!"

II The Bull—Wheat at a Dollar-ten

...and said Party of the Second Part further covenants and agrees to merchandise such wheat in foreign ports, it being understood and agreed between the Party of the First Part and the Party of the Second Part that the wheat hereinbefore mentioned is released and sold to the Party of the Second Part for export purposes only, and not for consumption or distribution within the boundaries of the United States of America or of Canada.

"Now, Mr. Gates, if you will sign for Mr. Truslow I guess that'll be all," remarked Hornung when he had finished reading.

Hornung affixed his signature to the two documents and passed them over to Gates, who signed for his principal and client, Truslow—or, as he had been called ever since he had gone into the fight against Hornung's corner—the Great Bear. Hornung's secretary was called in and witnessed the signatures, and Gates thrust the contract into his Gladstone bag and stood up, smoothing his hat.

"You will deliver the warehouse receipts for the grain," began Gates.

"I'll send a messenger to Truslow's office before noon," interrupted Hornung. "You can pay by certified check through the Illinois Trust people."

When the other had taken himself off, Hornung sat for some moments gazing abstractedly toward his office windows, thinking over the whole matter. He had just agreed to release to Truslow, at the rate of $1.10 per bushel, 100,000 out of the 2 million and odd bushels of wheat that he, Hornung, controlled, or actually owned. And for the moment he was wondering if, after all, he had done wisely in not goring the Great Bear to actual financial death. He had made him pay $100,000. Truslow was good for this amount. Would it not have been better to have put a prohibitive figure on the grain and forced the Bear into bankruptcy? True Hornung would then be without his enemy's money, but Truslow would have been eliminated from the situation, and that—so Hornung told himself—was always a consummation most devoutly, strenuously, and diligently to be striven for. Truslow once dead was dead, but the Bear was never more dangerous than when desperate.

"But so long as he can't get wheat," muttered Hornung at the end of his reflections, "he can't hurt me. And he can't get it. That I *know*."

For Hornung controlled the situation. So far back as the February of that year an "unknown bull" had been making his presence felt on the floor of the Board of Trade. By the middle of March the commercial reports of the daily press had begun to speak of "the powerful bull clique"; a few weeks later that legendary condition of affairs implied and epitomized in the magic words "Dollar Wheat" had been attained, and by the first of April, when the price had been boosted to $1.10 a bushel, Hornung had disclosed his hand, and in place of mere rumors, the definite and authoritative news that May wheat had been cornered in the Chicago pit went flashing around the world from Liverpool to Odessa and from Duluth to Buenos Aires.

It was—so the veteran operators were persuaded—Truslow himself who had made Hornung's corner possible. The Great Bear had for once over-reached himself, and, believing himself all-powerful, had hammered the price just the fatal fraction too far down. Wheat had gone to sixty-two—for the time, and under the circumstances, an abnormal price. When the reaction came it was tremendous. Hornung saw his chance, seized it, and in a few months had turned the tables, had cornered the product, and virtually driven the bear clique out of the pit.

On the same day that the delivery of the 100,000 bushels was made to Truslow, Hornung met his broker at his lunch club.

"Well," said the latter, "I see you let go that line of stuff to Truslow."

Hornung nodded; but the broker added:

"Remember, I was against it from the very beginning. I know we've cleaned up over a hundred thou'. I would have fifty times preferred to have lost twice that and *smashed Truslow dead*. Bet you what you like he makes us pay for it somehow."

"Huh!" grunted his principal. "How about insurance, and warehouse charges, and carrying expenses on that lot? Guess we'd have had to pay those, too, if we'd held on."

But the other put up his chin, unwilling to be persuaded. "I won't sleep easy," he declared, "till Truslow is busted."

III The Pit

Just as Going mounted the steps on the edge of the pit the great gong struck; a roar of a hundred voices developed with the swiftness of successive explosions, the rush of a hundred men surging downward to the center of the pit filled the air with the stamp and grind of feet, a hundred hands in eager strenuous gestures tossed upward from out the brown of the crowd, the official reporter in his cage on the margin of the pit leaned far forward with straining ear to catch the opening bid, and another day of battle was begun.

Since the sale of the 100,000 bushels of wheat to Truslow, the "Hornung crowd" had steadily shouldered the price higher, until on this particular morning it stood at $1.50. That was Hornung's price. No one else had any grain to sell.

But not ten minutes after the opening, Going was surprised out of all countenance to hear shouted from the other side of the pit these words:

"Sell May at one-fifty."

Going was for the moment touching elbows with Kimbark on one side and with Merriam on the other, all three belonging to the "Hornung crowd." Their answering challenge of "*Sold*" was as the voice of one man. They did not pause to reflect upon the strangeness of the circumstance. (That was for afterward.) Their response to the offer was as unconscious as reflex action and almost as rapid, and before the pit was well aware of what had happened the transaction of 1,000 bushels was down upon Going's trading card and $1,500 had changed hands. But here was a marvel—the whole available supply of wheat cornered, Hornung master of the situation, invincible, unassailable; yet behold a man willing to sell, a Bear bold enough to raise his head.

"That was Kennedy, wasn't it, who made that offer?" asked Kimbark, as Going noted down the trade—"Kennedy, that new man?"

"Yes; who do you suppose he's selling for; who's willing to go short at this stage of the game?"

"Maybe he ain't short."

"Short! Great heavens, man; where'd he get the stuff?"

"Blamed if I know. We can account for every handful of May. Steady! Oh, there he goes again."

"Sell 1,000 May at $1.50," vociferated the bear-broker, throwing out his hand, one finger raised to indicate the number of "contracts" offered. This time it was evident that he was attacking the Hornung crowd deliberately, for, ignoring the jam of traders that swept toward him, he looked across the pit to where Going and Kimbark were shouting "*Sold! Sold!*" and nodded his head.

A second time Going made memoranda of the trade, and either the Hornung holdings were increased by 2,000 bushels of May wheat or the Hornung bank account swelled by at least $3,000 of some unknown short's money.

Of late—so sure was the bull crowd of its position—no one had even thought of glancing at the inspection sheet on the bulletin board. But now one of Going's messengers hurried up to him with the announcement that this sheet showed receipts at Chicago for that morning of 25,000 bushels, and not credited to Hornung. Someone had got hold of a line of wheat overlooked by the "clique" and was dumping it upon them.

"Wire the Chief," said Going over his shoulder to Merriam. This one struggled out of the crowd, and on a telegraph blank scribbled:

Strong bear movement—New man—Kennedy—Selling in lots of five contracts—Chicago receipts twenty-five thousand.

The message was dispatched, and in a few moments the answer came back, laconic, of military terseness:

Support the market.

And Going obeyed, Merriam and Kimbark following, the new broker fairly throwing the wheat at them in thousand-bushel lots.

"Sell May at 'fifty; sell May; sell May."

A moment's indecision, an instant's hesitation, the first faint suggestion of weakness, and the market would have broken under them. But for the better part of four hours they stood their ground, taking all that was offered, in constant communication with the Chief, and from time to time stimulated and steadied by his brief, unvarying command: "Support the market."

At the close of the session they had bought in the 25,000 bushels of May. Hornung's position was as stable as a rock, and the price closed even with the opening figure—$1.50.

But the morning's work was the talk of all La Salle Street. Who was back of the raid? What was the meaning of this unexpected selling? For weeks the pit trading had been merely nominal. Truslow, the Great Bear, from whom the most serious attack might have been expected, had gone to his country seat at Geneva Lake, in Wisconsin, declaring himself to be out of the market entirely. He went bass fishing every day.

IV The Belt Line

On a certain day toward the middle of the month, at a time when the mysterious Bear had unloaded some 80,000 bushels upon Hornung, a conference was held in the library of Hornung's home. His broker attended it, and also a clean-faced, bright-eyed individual whose name of Cyrus Ryder might have been found upon the payroll of a rather well-known detective agency. For upward of half an hour after the conference began the detective spoke, the other two listening attentively, gravely.

"Then, last of all," concluded Ryder, "I made out I was a hobo, and began stealing rides on the Belt Line Railroad. Know the road? It just circles Chicago. Truslow owns it. Yes? Well, then I began to catch on. I noticed that cars of certain numbers—thirty-one nought thirty-four, thirty-two one ninety—well, the numbers don't matter, but anyhow, these cars were always switched onto the sidings by Mr. Truslow's main elevator D soon as they came in. The wheat was shunted in, and they were pulled out again. Well, I spotted one car and stole a ride on her. Say, look here, *that car went right around the city on the Belt, and came back to D again, and the same wheat in her all the time.* The grain was reinspected—it was raw, I tell you—and the warehouse receipts made out just as though the stuff had come in from Kansas or Iowa."

"The same wheat all the time!" interrupted Hornung.

"The same wheat—your wheat, that you sold to Truslow."

"Great snakes!" ejaculated Hornung's broker. "Truslow never took it abroad at all."

"Took it abroad! Say, he's just been running it around Chicago, like the supers in 'Shenandoah,' round an' round, so you'd think it was a new lot, an' selling it back to you again."

"No wonder we couldn't account for so much wheat."

"Bought it from us at $1.10, and made us buy it back—our own wheat—at $1.50."

Hornung and his broker looked at each other in silence for a moment. Then all at once Hornung struck the arm of his chair with his fist and exploded in a roar of laughter. The broker stared for one bewildered moment, then followed his example.

"Sold! Sold!" shouted Hornung almost gleefully. "Upon my soul it's as good as a Gilbert and Sullivan show. And we—Oh, Lord! Billy, shake on it, and hats off to my distinguished friend Truslow. He'll be President some day. Hey! What? Prosecute him? Not I."

"He's done us out of a neat hatful of dollars for all that," observed the broker, suddenly grave.

"Billy, it's worth the price."

"We've got to make it up somehow."

"Well, tell you what. We were going to boost the price to $1.75 next week, and make that our settlement figure."

"Can't do it now. Can't afford it."

"No. Here; we'll let out a big link; we'll put wheat at $2.00, and let it go at that."

"Two it is, then," said the broker.

V The Bread Line

The street was very dark and absolutely deserted. It was a district on the "South Side," not far from the Chicago River, given up largely to wholesale stores, and after nightfall was empty of all life. The echoes slept but lightly hereabouts, and the slightest footfall, the faintest noise, woke them upon the instant and sent them clamoring up and down the length of the pavement between the iron shuttered fronts. The only light visible came from the side door of a certain "Vienna" bakery, where at 1 o'clock in the morning loaves of bread were given away to any who should ask. Every evening about 9 o'clock the outcasts began to gather about the side door. The stragglers came in rapidly, and the line—the "bread line," as it was called—began to form. By midnight it was usually some hundred yards in length, stretching almost the entire length of the block.

Toward ten in the evening, his coat collar turned up against the fine drizzle that pervaded the air, his hands in his pockets, his elbows gripping his sides, Sam Lewiston came up and silently took his place at the end of the line.

Unable to conduct his farm upon a paying basis at the time when Truslow, the "Great Bear," had sent the price of grain down to 62 cents a bushel, Lewiston had turned over his entire property to his creditors, and, leaving Kansas for good, had abandoned farming, and had left his wife at her sister's boarding house in Topeka with the understanding that she was to join him in Chicago as soon as he had found a steady job. Then he had come to Chicago and had turned workman. His brother Joe conducted a small hat factory on Archer Avenue, and for a time he found there a meager employment. But difficulties had occurred, times were bad, the hat factory was involved in debts, the repealing of a certain import duty on manufactured felt overcrowded the home market with cheap Belgian and French products, and in the end his brother had assigned and gone to Milwaukee.

Thrown out of work, Lewiston drifted aimlessly about Chicago, from pillar to post, working a little, earning here a dollar, there a dime, but always sinking, sinking, till at last the ooze of the lowest bottom dragged at his feet and the rush of the great ebb went over him and engulfed him and shut him out from the light, and a park bench became his home and the "bread line" his chief makeshift of subsistence.

He stood now in the enfolding drizzle, sodden, stupefied with fatigue. Before and behind stretched the line. There was no talking. There was no sound. The street was empty. It was so still that the passing of a cablecar in the adjoining thoroughfare grated like prolonged rolling explosions, beginning and ending at immeasurable distances. The drizzle descended incessantly. After a long time midnight struck.

There was something ominous and gravely impressive in this interminable line of dark figures, close-pressed, soundless; a crowd, yet absolutely still; a close-packed, silent file, waiting, waiting in the vast deserted night-ridden street; waiting without a word, without a movement, there under the night and under the slow-moving mists of rain.

Few in the crowd were professional beggars. Most of them were workmen, long since out of work, forced into idleness by long-continued "hard times," by ill luck, by sickness. To them the "bread line" was a godsend. At least they could not starve. Between jobs here in the end was something to hold them up—a small platform, as it were, above the sweep of black water, where for a moment they might pause and take breath before the plunge.

The period of waiting on this night of rain seemed endless to those silent, hungry men; but at length there was a stir. The line moved. The side door opened. Ah, at last! They were going to hand out the bread.

But instead of the usual white-aproned undercook with his crowded hampers there now appeared in the doorway a new man—a young fellow who looked like a bookkeeper's assistant. He bore in his hand a placard, which he tacked to the outside of the door. Then he disappeared within the bakery, locking the door after him.

A shudder of poignant despair, an unformed, inarticulate sense of calamity, seemed to run from end to end of the line. What had happened? Those in the rear, unable to read the placard, surged forward, a sense of bitter disappointment clutching at their hearts.

The line broke up, disintegrated into a shapeless throng—a throng that crowded forward and collected in front of the shut door whereon the placard was affixed. Lewiston, with the others, pushed forward. On the placard he read these words:

Owing to the fact that the price of grain has been increased to two dollars a bushel, there will be no distribution of bread from this bakery until further notice.

Lewiston turned away, dumb, bewildered. Till morning he walked the streets, going on without purpose, without direction. But now at last his luck had turned. Overnight the wheel of his fortunes had creaked and swung upon its axis, and before noon he had found a job in the street-cleaning brigade. In the course of time he rose to be first shift boss, then deputy inspector, then inspector, promoted to the dignity of driving in a red wagon with rubber tires and drawing a salary instead of mere wages. The wife was sent for and a new start made.

But Lewiston never forgot. Dimly he began to see the significance of things. Caught once in the cogs and wheels of a great and terrible engine, he had seen—none better—its workings. Of all the men who had vainly stood in the "bread line" on that rainy night in early summer, he, perhaps, had been the only one who had struggled up to the surface again. How many others had gone down in the great ebb? Grim question; he dared not think how many.

He had seen the two ends of a great wheat operation—a battle between Bear and Bull. The stories (subsequently published in the city's press) of Truslow's countermove in selling Hornung his own wheat, supplied the unseen section. The farmer—he who raised the wheat—was ruined upon one hand; the workingman—he who consumed it—was ruined upon the other. But between the two, the great operators, who never saw the wheat they traded in, bought and sold the world's food, gambled in the nourishment of entire nations, practised their tricks, their chicanery and oblique shifty "deals," were reconciled in their differences, and went on through their appointed way, jovial, contented, enthroned, and unassailable.

ASSIGNMENT QUESTIONS

1. Summarize the meaning of "A Message to Garcia."
2. What is the message Russell H. Conwell was giving to his audiences in his exhortation, "Acres of Diamonds"?
3. "A Message to Garcia" and "Acres of Diamonds" were immensely popular in their day. What does this tell us about the environment within which businessmen operated around the turn of the century?
4. What lessons might a young boy learn from reading "The Errand Boy" by Horatio Alger?
5. "The Man Who Could Not Be Cornered" and "A Deal in Wheat" are both centered around the Chicago grain market. Contrast the view that each writing gives us of the American businessman at that time.

4
J. PIERPONT MORGAN

Among the men who ushered in the American Industrial Revolution following the Civil War, none was more powerful or more famous than the great J. Pierpont Morgan. Like many of the business leaders who were later to direct the great corporations and banks that harnessed the nation's resources, Morgan was born in the late 1830s. Yet, in contrast to most of the others, who would have made useful subjects for Horatio Alger novels, he was born to wealth, social position, and privilege. His father was the wealthy banker Junius P. Morgan, and young Morgan was given all the opportunity that money and position could give him.

"Pip," as young Pierpont was called, attended in succession, a small, expensive, private school in Hartford, Connecticut; a public grammar school; a boarding school in Cheshire, Connecticut; and English High School in Boston—a public school known for its exceptionally high standards. When his family moved to London, he attended a private school in Vevey, Switzerland; and finally, for over a year, he studied at the University of Gottingen in Germany. At the university he had an undistinguished academic record, although he had what the Germans called *rechenhaftigkeit*—the enjoyment of numbers. By the time he was twenty, he had enjoyed opportunities for travel, university education, and international acquaintance that were to serve him well in his business and banking life.

Early Business Experience

In 1857 Morgan returned to the United States and took a job with the firm of Duncan, Sherman & Company. Since he was already independently wealthy and after experience more than income, he served with no salary and spent much of his time in the unproductive study of the cotton market. In 1861 he opened his own office in New York, acting as the agent of George Peabody & Company, at the time, the leading investment bankers in London. It was obvious that he was using the connections he had made in Europe to aid him bringing success to his own firm.

In 1865, acting on the advice of his father, young Morgan took in as his partner one Charles Dabney, a seasoned and experienced older man. Six years later, Dabney, Morgan and Company combined with the firm of Anthony Drexel to form the most prestigious banking firm in America—Drexel, Morgan & Company. The company was involved in a combination of commercial and investment banking, buying and selling securities and acceptances drawn against imports; dealing in foreign exchange and gold; and passing back information on banking activities in America to its associate companies in Europe.

During these early years, Morgan honed his skills in the arts of buying and selling gold, securities, and bills of exchange. His income, which even during this early period was considerable, was based entirely on commissions. Following the Civil War, J. P. Morgan and Drexel, Morgan and Company made great progress. Dabney was a first-class accountant and manager, and Morgan was an innovative, dynamic, self-confident entrepreneur. Even in these years he believed in cooperation rather than competitiveness in his relations with others in the industry.

Morgan spent the 1870s participating in the massive refinancing of the federal government's debt. In this endeavor, his close and long relationship with the European financial sources helped him to dominate the government refunding operation. By the late 1870s, however, the government was paying off its debt and struggling to deal with the terrible problem of the federal surplus. With this avenue of enterprise closed to him, Morgan turned, in 1879, to the financing, refinancing, and reorganization of the nation's railroads. His first major sale was the disposition of 250,000 shares of the New York Central Railroad without causing more than a minor stir in the market. In 1880, his company underwrote $40 million of Northern Pacific bonds, a tremendous sum for the time.

Morgan the Man

During the years when he was rising to the top of his profession, Morgan's financial and business success was marred by personal problems. In particular, his health was never good, and he was frequently afflicted by colds and blinding headaches. Even more troublesome was the humiliation he suffered from a persistent inflammation of the skin of his face which, during the 1870s, had begun to settle in his nose. This affliction, *acne rosacea,* increasingly disfigured him as the years went by.

Some people believed that Morgan's nose was a product of his excessive style of living. In actuality, he drank moderately, usually having something during his evening meals, but not much else during the day. He usually held a cigar between his teeth, but often it was not lit. However, like many of his compatriots, he was accustomed to eating well. He had a huge breakfast—such as, fruit, porridge, eggs, hash, fried fish, and sliced tomatoes—but a modest lunch. His dinners tended to be large and expensive. Those were the days of eight- and ten-course dinners, and Morgan was known to enjoy such repasts.

He belonged to an exclusive dinner group named the Zodiac Club which met periodically to partake of a sumptuous meal. The menu of one Zodiac dinner given at the University Club was as follows:[1]

Amontillado Sherry
Cotuit oysters
Bisque of crabs à la Norfolk
Consumme de volaille sevigne
Hors d'oeuvres variés

Rhine Wine, 1893
Soft clams à Pancienne

Chateau-Latour, 1878
Saddle and rack of spring lamb
Mint sauce
Peas à la Francaise
Bermuda potatoes rissolees

Moet & Chandon, 1893
Terrapin, Maryland Club
Grapefruit au Kirsch

Clos-Vougeot, 1893
Canvasback ducks
Fried hominy
Celery à l'université

Parfait noisettes
Cheese
Fruit
Coffee
Cognac, 1805

J. Pierpont probably lived life in a more regal fashion than any American has led—or likely ever will lead. It wasn't that he made the most money—others were actually richer—it was that he had a love of grand things, worldwide travel, and restrained taste.

His home during his years as a public figure was number 219 Madison Avenue in New York City. By no means a palace, the house was large and comfortable and provided quarters for twelve servants in addition to the Morgan family. Along with this home, he owned various building sites in the neighborhood which served as homes for his children; a white marble library building in which to store his art collections; a country house, "Cragston," on the Hudson River; a thousand-acre place in the Adirondacks, "Camp Uncas"; a furnished apartment at the Jekyll Island Club on a piny island on the Georgia coast; and for a place to stop while he was yachting, a "fishing box" on Narragansett Bay with a full-time cook ready to satisfy the palates of Morgan's guests.

In London he stayed at a large double house in Prince's Gate, which, although not too pretentious, was hung with paintings by Rubens, Rembrandt, Gainsborough, Constable, Turner, and other famous artists. Outside London there was "Dover House," a comfortable country estate equipped with gardens, orchards, and a dairy farm. When traveling on the continent Morgan needed no homes of his own for he always had his choice of accommodations. In Paris and Rome, for example, the best hotels set aside suites for his use whenever he came.

When he was away from his residences he was often traveling or simply living on his yacht, *Corsair*. There were three versions of this most luxurious of all yachts, the largest of which was *Corsair III*, completed in 1898, which was 302 feet long. He used the *Corsair* as a kind of floating home and place of entertainment, but never attempted to make the Atlantic crossing on her, although he did require that the yacht be available for him in the Mediterranean after he had completed the Atlantic crossing on a White Star liner. One odd disappointment was that the *Corsair III* was too large to ascend the Nile—so Morgan had a private all-steel paddle-wheel steamer built in case he should wish to vacation in Egypt.

In his travels across America, Morgan always went in his private car—sometimes in his private train—and was known to tip the porter with a hundred-dollar bill (about two months' salary) at the end of a trip.

When he traveled, as he did about three or four months out of each year, Morgan steadily and regularly purchased art objects—paintings, statues, rugs, manuscripts, ceramics, books, and so on and so on. These he had sent home, and many were used to decorate his home, which had almost every available surface covered by some rare and expensive purchase. Like most things he did, Morgan bought art by issuing instructions and not wasting much time in bargaining. One story is as follows:[2]

George S. Hellman once brought Morgan a Vermeer to look at, and found to his surprise that the great dutchman's name was strange to the Morgan ear. Thereupon Hellman delivered a brief lecture on Vermeer, his place in the history of art, and the value set upon his work in recent sales.

Morgan gazed at the picture; then he abruptly asked the price.

"One hundred thousand dollars," said the dealer.

"I'll take it," snapped Morgan, and the deal was concluded.

In person, J. P. Morgan had such an overwhelming presence that people were frequently frightened into silence. When meeting him for the first time, the first thing they saw was his nose. In looking away from his nose they met his blazing eyes. Edward Steichen, the famous photographer, said that meeting his gaze was somewhat like confronting the headlights of an express train bearing down on one. Yet, in spite of his appearance, Morgan was a kindly man, devoted to his family and friends, who was not only generally courteous, but who often made special efforts to help those less fortunate than himself with special acts of goodwill.

Morganization

As a consequence of his successful sales of New York Central securities, Morgan was appointed as a director of the railroad. Thus, he changed from being an outside financial advisor to participating actively in the management of a firm served by his company. As additional companies, and especially railroads, turned to J. P. Morgan and Company for financial services, Morgan or one of his associates increasingly accepted memberships on the boards of directors.

Morgan was, of course, interested in making money for his clients, but he was also interested in promulgating and applying his personal antipathy toward competition and overexpansion. The Morgan representative on a board would be firmly behind the establishment of an orderly and responsible administration within a cooperative system and would work to tone down the rough edges of competition. The railroad industry with its periodic price wars and irresponsible owners particularly violated his sense of what was appropriate, and he spent much of his time during the later part of his life in restoring peace to the industry.

Prior to Morgan, railroad promoters had grown careless in loading up their companies with heavy interest burden—sometimes giving away bonds in order to sell shares of common stock. When bad times hit, a railroad would be unable to meet its interest obligations, and J. P. Morgan and Company would be called upon to reorganize it to protect the interest of its creditors. This process became known in the banking and business world as "Morganization," that is, acquiring a strong influence in the management of railroads that were in financial difficulty.

When Morgan reorganized a railroad—and he reorganized most of the railroads in the United States—he pursued the following pattern:

1. He set up a voting trust to control management.
2. He reorganized the management.
3. He did not cut the capitalization.
4. He raised the stock-bond (equity-to-debt) ratio, thus lowering fixed charges.
5. He restricted production and created reserves.

The purpose of these steps was to establish a set of rates that would make the railroad profitable—which did not go down well with all the industrialists since they enjoyed playing off the railroads against each other and getting what they felt were the cheapest of all possible rates. Morgan, through his representatives on corporate boards, was able to dominate effectively many of these firms, even though he actually was likely to be a minority shareholder. It really was true that during this period, the head of the board was wherever the Morgan man sat.

Industrial Mergers

In time, as the Morgan firm continued to grow, it branched out into and became intimately involved in the industrial merger movement in this country. It started out managing the formation of the General Electric Company in 1892 and proceeded to assist in the formation of the Federal Steel Company, the American Telephone & Telegraph Company, the Westinghouse Corporation, and finally, in 1901, directed the formation of the trust to end all trusts, the United States Steel Corporation.

The House of Morgan could not have accomplished all it did without maintaining control over a very large supply of ready funds, but even these resources were inadequate to support the numerous financial reorganizations in which it was involved. What Morgan did was to take under his leadership two other large New York financial institutions to assist him—George F. Baker's First National Bank and James Stillman's National City Bank. In addition, a Morgan partner was instrumental in organizing the Bankers' Trust Company, the Guarantee Trust Company was commonly considered to be a Morgan bank as was the National Bank of Commerce, and Morgan controlled the Equitable Life Assurance Society and served as chairman of the Mutual Life Insurance Company's Finance Committee. This interlocking group of banks and corporations became known by critics, by 1912, as "The Money Trust."

In the beginning, when investment bankers, such as Morgan, arranged for financing on behalf of industrial entrepreneurs, they remained relatively detached from the actual operations of the firms they assisted. Unfortunately, it sometimes happened that investment bankers were embarrassed by the inept performance (or dishonesty) of corporate managers for whom they had provided funds. The funds raised were misused; and sometimes the organization set up with great effort by the banker simply failed. A consequence was that Morgan and his associates in the financial world concluded that it would be wise to maintain some kind of control over their principals. As part of a refinancing effort, Morgan would regularly insist that one of his representatives be put on a company's board of directors.

Once on a board, Morgan or his representative could then exert their influence to bring the thinking of the other board members in line with that of the investment bankers. Their basic philosophy was that order, harmony, persuasion, agreement, and combination were good and that competition and instability were bad. Thus, in 1885, Morgan brought peace between the New York Central and Pennsylvania railroads, when each threatened the other with the construction of parallel railroad lines. In the next year, he settled a potentially difficult conflict in the coal industry. In both cases, he invited industry leaders to his yacht and more or less kept them there until an agreement was reached.

The Pujo Committee

As the power of Morgan and his associates—The Money Trust—grew and spread, critics of big business began a steady drumbeat of articles and books outlining what they believed were the excesses of those who controlled the country's economic activities. Morgan was criticized because of the alleged ruthlessness of the methods he used to bring order to industries which came under his influence; he was accused, with others, of "stock watering" (i.e., of creating common share interests with stated values greatly in excess of the property values underlying them); and he was charged with fraud when nearly forty of the corporations he had helped organized failed in the Panic of 1903. Finally, the concern over the concentration of power in the hands of the investment bankers reached to the U.S. Congress.

The House Committee on Banking and Currency formed a subcommittee known as the Pujo Committee after its chairman Arsene Pujo of Louisiana. The committee's purpose was to show to the American public that a small group of New York bankers, under the direction of J. Pierpont Morgan, held such an iron grip on the money and credit resources of the country through an intricate system of interlocking directorates that they, in effect, controlled the whole American economy.

For weeks the committee displayed the testimony of witnesses, as well as voluminous charts, graphs, and exhibits, for the public record. The committee's plan was for the hearings to build up to the climactic testimony of Morgan himself, and shortly before Christmas 1912, he was called to take the stand. The Pujo Committee made elaborate preparations for his testimony, apparently concerned that he would be a hostile and reluctant witness and that any useful information would have to be forced from him. Careful arrangements were also made for reporters and press photographers to cover the details of Morgan's appearance.

Morgan was not enthusiastic about having to testify and found the preparation insisted upon by his advisors boring and exhausting. He anticipated that the committee would attempt to put him in an unfavorable light and discussed with his lawyers all the possible traps and plots that confronted him. Morgan at first suggested that he just go on down to Washington more or less by himself, but his lawyers advised strongly against it, and he ended up taking with him a party of supporters and attorneys which numbered sixteen.

The trip down to Washington was not particularly a pleasant one. Morgan was an old man now. In his seventy-sixth year, his hair was white and thin, his big mustache was gray, and his nose was more swollen and flaming red than ever. Even his fierce eyes now looked tired, and reporters noted that he moved slowly as he stepped off the train.

The next morning, on December 18, he rode to the capital in a limousine and walked slowly to the committee room accompanied by his son Jack and his daughter Louisa. He seemed like a figure out of the past, a large man dressed in a heavy velvet-collared overcoat, wearing a high silk hat and carrying a walking stick. Although no one in the room could have known it, this was to be his last public appearance, and he was within four months of his death.

Testimony Before the Committee

When the morning of J. P. Morgan's appearance before the Pujo Committee arrived, it was like some major sporting event. Crowds of eager would-be spectators lined up along the hallway, out into the street, and around the corner of the building; policemen kept them in their places in line. The room itself was jammed, packed with spectators who had waited in line since early that morning. Cameramen and reporters were well situated with the light from the windows at their backs.

After some time exhibiting charts and other exhibits prepared by the committee's experts demonstrating the affiliations J. P. Morgan & Company had, through directorships, with corporations, banks, trust companies, and insurance firms, the examination of Mr. Morgan was conducted by the counsel for the committee, Samuel Untermyer—a shrewd and experienced government lawyer.[3]

Q. Where do you reside, Mr. Morgan?
A. New York City.

Q. Are you the senior member of the partnership or firm of J. P. Morgan & Co., Bankers, of New York City?

A. I am, sir....

Q. Does your New York house do a general banking business?

A. We try to, sir.

[The committee was eager to establish that Morgan, through his directorships, actually exercised control of the organizations with which he had representation.]

Q. As a member of the voting trust which year after year chooses the directors of the Southern Railway are you not, in effect, dealing with yourself when the firm of J. P. Morgan agrees with the officials of the Southern Railway on the prices at which its securities should be issued to the public?

A. I do not think so. We do not deal with ourselves.

Q. Let us see if you do not. The voting trustees name the board, do they not?

A. But when you have elected the board, then the board is independent of the voting trustees.

Q. That is only until the next election?

A. It is during that time they act independently.

Q. You think, therefore, that where you name a board of directors who remain in existence only a year and you have the power to name another board next year, that this board so named is an independent position to deal with your banking house, as would a board named by the stockholders themselves?

A. I think it would be better.

Q. You think it is a great deal better?

A. Yes, sir.

Q. More independent?

A. Better.

Q. Will you tell us why?

A. Simply because we select the best people we can find for the positions.

[When Untermyer questioned Morgan as to whether he had control over the country's banks, he responded that the presence of Morgan partners on the boards of other banks did not necessarily mean that he controlled them.]

A. There is no question of control, unless you have got a majority of the directors...in all banks.

[Untermyer further questioned him about the significance of corporate deposits with his bank.]

Q. Mr. Morgan, according to the record, some seventy-eight interstate corporations carry bank accounts with J. P. Morgan & Company, and their deposits total over $81 million. Do you think it is a wise thing to permit publicly owned corporations to make deposits with a private banker.

A. I do, sir.

[Untermyer further established that many railroads had made J. P. Morgan & Company their fiscal agent, so that Morgan became the only channel through which the railroads could sell their securities to the public. He went on to ask:]

Q. Don't you think it would be better for these great interstate railroad corporations if they were entirely free to sell their securities in open competition than that they should be tied to any banking house, however just might its methods in the issue of such securities?

A. I should not think so.

Q. Doesn't the fact that there are so few men, such as yourself and your partners, who serve on the board of directors of many banks tend to prevent those banks from competing for deposits?

A. I should doubt it. I have been in business for a great many years in New York, and I do not compete for any deposits, I do not care whether they ever come. They come.

[Exercising all his ingenuity, Untermyer attempted to get Morgan to affirm that he exercised great power. Morgan would not agree. According to him, he exercised no power whatsoever. He simply ignored all the elaborate charts and graphs that had been so carefully prepared for the committee. The high point of Morgan's testimony was with regard to credit.]

Q. Isn't it true that a man's credit depends on the money he has or the stock exchange collateral that he can furnish?
A. No. I know lots of men—businessmen, too—who can borrow any amount, whose credit is unquestionable.
Q. Is that not because it is believed that they have the money back of them?
A. No sir; it is because people believe in the man.
Q. And it is regardless of whether he had any financial backing at all, is it?
A. It is, very often.
Q. And he might not be worth anything?
A. He might not have anything. I have known a man to come into my office, and I have given him a check for a million dollars when I knew he had not a cent in the world.
Q. Mr. Morgan, is not commercial credit based upon the possession of money or property?
A. Money or property or character.
Q. Is not commercial credit based primarily upon money or property?
A. No, sir; the first thing is character.
Q. Before money or property?
A. Before money or anything else. Money cannot buy it. It is the fundamental basis of business.
Q. That is not the way money is loaned on the stock exchange?
A. That is the way *I* loan it.

After Morgan was excused from the witness stand, he walked with Jack and Louisa back to the limousine, made his way back to rest in his private railway car and soon was on his way back to New York. After his death a few months later, some said that the strain of testifying had brought on his death prematurely. They said it was not just the ordeal of testifying that had killed him but the hostile attitudes on the part of the committee members and counsel. Like many other early entrepreneurs in America, Morgan felt that he had accomplished great things for his country and was disturbed by implications that he had somehow done something wrong.

The Committee Report

The testimony and exhibits published by the Pujo Committee made up three thick volumes. In response to the question "Is there a money trust?" the committee stated[4]

> If by a money trust is meant an established and well-defined identity and community of interest between a few leaders of finance which has been created and is held together through stock holdings, interlocking directorates, and other forms of domination over banks, trust companies, railroads, public-service and industrial corporations, and which has resulted in a vast and growing concentration of control of money and credit in the hands of a comparatively few men, the committee has no hesitation in asserting as the result of its investigation up to this time that the condition thus described exists in this country today.

The Pujo Committee plainly pointed to Morgan as the leader of the "money trust." It found that if one combined together the Morgan partners and the directors of the First National and National City Banks, the Bankers Trust Company, and the Guarantee Trust Company, they controlled

118 directorships in 34 banks and trust companies,
30 directorships in 10 insurance companies,

105 directorships in 32 transportation companies,
63 directorships in 24 producing and trading corporations,
25 dictatorships in 12 public utility corporations,

making in all, 341 directorships in 112 corporations with aggregate resources or capitalization of over $22 billion in assets at a time when the national wealth was estimated at $186 billion.[5] (See Exhibit 4-1.)

EXHIBIT 4-1 Affiliations of J. P. Morgan & Co., National City Bank, First National Bank, Guarantee Trust Co., and Bankers Trust Co. of New York City with Large Corporations of the United States.

(TAKEN FROM EXHIBIT NO. 243, SHOWN TO THE PUJO COMMITTEE ON FEBRUARY 25, 1913.)

Corporation	*Capital*
Metals	
American Can Company	$ 80,000,000
U.S. Motor Company	10,000,000
W. E. Gramp & Sons	6,000,000
Edison Typewriter Company	19,000,000
International Harvester Company	178,000,000
J. I. Case Threshing Machine Company	20,000,000
Safety Car Heating and Lighting	11,000,000
Baldwin Locomotive Works	45,000,000
Allis Chalmers Corporation	10,500,000
Westinghouse Electrical Manufacturing	65,000,000
Pullman Company	194,000,000
General Electric Company	208,000,000
United States Steel Corporation	1,390,000,000
Cambria Steel Company	61,000,000
Lackawana Steel Company	59,000,000
Pennsylvania Steel Company	45,500,000
Phelps Dodge & Company	96,800,000
Old Dominion	14,600,000
International Consolidated Copper	19,000,000
American Brass	21,000,000
International Nickel Company	62,900,000
	$ 2,616,300,000
Express	
American Express Company	59,000,000
	$ 59,000,000
Railroads	
Chicago, Rock Island & Pacific	365,000,000
El Paso & Southwestern	45,000,000
Chicago, Milwaukee & St. Paul	659,000,000
Toledo, St. Louis & Western	88,000,000
Union Pacific	603,000,000
Chicago & Northwestern	455,000,000
Northern Pacific	490,000,000
Chicago, Burlington & Quincy	495,000,000
Great Northern	430,000,000
Chicago Great Western	60,000,000
Atchison, Topeka & Santa Fe	640,000,000
Southern Pacific	867,000,000
New York, New Haven & Hartford	849,000,000
Hocking Vy	42,000,000
Chesapeake & Ohio	199,000,000
Erie R. R.	342,000,000
Delaware, Lackawanna & Western	289,000,000
Delaware & Hudson	17,500,000
Pere Marq.	62,500,000
Chicago, Indianapolis & Louisville	25,000,000
Lehigh Valley	23,300,000
Norfolk & Western	265,000,000
Pennsylvania System	1,193,000,000
Baltimore & Ohio	515,000,000
Cincinnati, Hamilton & Dayton	64,000,000
Reading Company	529,600,000
Central Railroad of New Jersey	181,600,000
New York Central Lines	1,446,000,000
Kansas City & Southern	58,000,000
Missouri, Kansas & Texas	165,000,000
Illinois Central	373,000,000
Seaboard Air Line	161,000,000
Atlantic Coast Line	182,000,000
Louisville & Nashville	248,000,000
Southern Railway	402,000,000
	$12,829,500,000
Steamship	
International Mercantile Marine	74,000,000
	$ 74,000,000
Insurance Companies	
American Surety Company	8,400,000
Insurance Company of North America	17,000,000
Continental Insurance	16,700,000
Equitable Life Assurance Society	504,500,000
Mutual Life Insurance Company	587,000,000
	$ 1,133,000,000
Banks and Trust Companies	
First Trust and Savings	56,000,000
Illinois Trust and Savings	91,500,000
First National Bank	102,000,000
Continental & Commercial National	169,500,000
Title Guarantee & Trust	25,300,000
Second National Bank	18,100,000
Astor Trust	20,800,000
New York Trust	34,800,000
United States Mortgage & Trust Company	44,800,000

EXHIBIT 4-1 (Con't.)

(TAKEN FROM EXHIBIT NO. 243, SHOWN TO THE PUJO COMMITTEE ON FEBRUARY 25, 1913.)

Corporation	*Capital*
Union Trust Company	55,900,000
Mechanic & Metals National Bank	55,200,000
Chase National	113,400,000
National Bank of Commerce	117,600,000
Lincoln National	15,100,000
Liberty National	25,500,000
New York Life Insurance & Trust	32,000,000
Bank of Manhattan Company	33,400,000
United States Trust Company	49,800,000
Chemical National	25,200,000
Hanover National	84,800,000
Farmers Loan and Trust	105,100,000
	$ 1,275,800,000
Traction, Lighting, and Power	
Kansas City & Light Company	34,100,000
International Traction Company of Buffalo	40,000,000
Hudson and Manhattan Railway	73,800,000
Chicago City & Connecting Railways	70,500,000
Public Service Corporation of New Jersey	265,300,000
United Gas Improvement Co.	143,000,000
New York Edison	36,000,000
Consolidated Gas Company of New York	257,000,000
Chicago Railways	94,000,000
Chicago Elevated Railways	80,000,000
Niagara Falls Power	31,000,000
Butte Electric & Power Company	35,000,000
Pacific Gas & Electric	106,000,000
Commonwealth Edison Company of Chicago	86,000,000
New York Railways	63,000,000
Interborough Metropolitan System	359,000,000
Philadelphia Rapid Transit Company	194,000,000
	$ 1,967,700,000
Telegraph and Telephone	
Central and South America Telephone Company	10,500,000
Western Union Telegraph Co.	156,000,000
American Telephone & Telegraph	739,000,000
	$ 905,000,000
Animal and Vegetable Producers	
American Cotton Oil Company	31,000,000
Tide Water Company	24,000,000
International Agriculture Corporation	23,000,000
American Agriculture Chemical	49,700,000
Intercontinental Rubber Company	5,000,000
United States Rubber Company	113,000,000
American Bank Note	10,000,000
International Paper Company	31,000,000
American Sugar Refining	106,600,000
Armour & Company	50,000,000
National Biscuit Company	68,000,000
General Asphalt	18,000,000
United States Rubber Company	113,000,000
	$ 642,300,000
Miscellaneous	
United States Realty & Improvement	23,000,000
	$ 23,000,000
Grand Total	$ 21,525,300,000

ASSIGNMENT QUESTIONS

1. Write a paragraph or two appropriate for delivery at the funeral of J. P. Morgan, praising his accomplishments and summarizing the positive things he did for the United States.
2. Write a paragraph or two critical of the money trust and of Morgan in particular.
3. How vast was Morgan's influence on our economy in 1912? What sort of influence would he have to have today to match the $22 million of corporate assets which he affected in 1912?
4. Have the Wall Street bankers kept their position of influence in the American economy? If not, who replaced them?

NOTES

1. Herbert L. Satterlee, *J. Pierpont Morgan, An Intimate Portrait* (New York: Macmillan, 1939), p. 406.
2. Frederick Lewis Allen, *The Great Pierpont Morgan* (New York: Harper & Brothers, 1949), p. 199.
3. Report of the Committee Appointed Pursuant to House Resolution 429 and 504 to Investigate the Concentration of Control and Credit (Washington: U.S. Government Printing Office, 1913).
4. Ibid., p. 130.
5. Allen, *Morgan,* p. 274.

5
DEBATE ON THE ECONOMIC SIGNIFICANCE OF THE CONSTITUTION

Moderator

Good evening, ladies and gentlemen. We are honored, tonight, to present two gentlemen, as our speakers, who have earned national reputations as scholars in the area of American economic development. Dr. Charles Beard, as one of the most creative interpreters of America in its first hundred years, is a major figure in bringing the significance of historical events to bear on current issues. Mr. Forrest McDonald is also well known as a scholar and major interpreter of American history.

Tonight, our guests will debate the economic significance of the U.S. Constitution. Dr. Beard has written widely on the subject, in particular his influential *An Economic Interpretation of the Constitution of the United States.*[1] We are fortunate in having Mr. McDonald to present a position in opposition to that of Professor Beard, because his book, *We the People: The Economic Origins of the Constitution,*[2] is generally considered to be the best argument against Beard's thesis.

We shall begin by hearing from Professor Beard.

Comments by Professor Charles Beard

I should like to begin by sketching, as background, the three central ideas that have traditionally dominated American historical research. The first, the Teutonic School, attributes the achievements of English-speaking peoples to the peculiar genius of the Germanic race. The second, sometimes called the Bancroft School, is based on the supposition that American achievements are the consequence of the special virtues of a nation under divine protection. The final school is a kind of noninterpretative analysis based on an examination of historical documents.

The principal flaw in all of these schools

is that they neglect consideration of the economic factor in American historical development. We should keep in mind that, at their most basic, the laws that govern our society are simply the rules which determine our property relations. The Constitution, as the law of the land, is just one among many legal systems established to bring order to the economic relationships of those, who at the time of its creation, had the most property.

A Survey of Economic Interests in 1787

Careful analysis of the economic groups at the time of the Constitutional Convention shows that our population, at that time, could be divided into three main groups: the disfranchised, the real property holders, and the personal property holders. The disfranchised were slaves, indentured servants, nonproperty holders, and women. The real property holders, who had been the traditional powers in the colonies prior to the revolution, were mostly small farmers, but also included wealthy southern slaveholders and the lords of the Hudson River Valley. Personal property holders consisted of those engaged in manufacturing and shipping, as well as holders of paper money and public securities.

In looking at these three groups, it is obvious that the disfranchised had little, if any, power to influence events and can be disregarded. The holders of real property, although still possessing political, economic, and social power, were fundamentally conservative, and not strongly in favor of a new constitution. It was the last group, those holding speculative assets, who were the strongest supporters of change because the economic system under the Articles of Confederation was unfavorable to their interests. The main problem had to do with the varied and conflicting laws in the several states. In some cases, state legislatures had even considered the imposition of tariff barriers against goods imported from other states. To resolve these problems, those holding securities, paper money, or western lands, or those involved in manufacturing and trade, advocated the establishment of a new and stronger central government.

At this point, let me suggest the following conclusions. First, individuals with great economic power had been adversely affected by the government that existed under the Articles of Confederation—these groups had special interests in money, speculative securities, western lands, shipping, and manufacturing. In other words, their interest was in capital rather than land. Second, these people met with the authority to amend the Articles, but surpassed that authority by developing an entirely new and revolutionary constitutional document.

The Election of Delegates to the Constitutional Convention

With the possible exception of the states of New York and Delaware, each state had at least one prominent member of its delegation who held a significant interest in speculative wealth, and who, therefore, could speak with feeling and authority on questions of protecting personal property rights. Further, eleven representatives to the convention were engaged in manufacturing or shipping, twenty-four had money at interest, and fourteen were speculating in western lands.

In most of the states, the ownership of property was a qualification for potential delegates, and in other states, the payment of taxes was a requirement. Although, under these requirements, farmers and small property owners were able to vote for delegates, the representatives of private property interests tended to be better educated and more competent in the political process. As a consequence, they were able to secure delegates friendly to their cause.

In conclusion, it is obvious that those delegates elected to represent the states at the Constitutional Convention had a strong economic interest in the new government they were establishing.

The Constitution as a Defender of Property Rights

The document created by the convention does not treat the question of economic interests directly, but does suggest two underlying arrangements that serve to protect the rights of property. First, the government established by the proposed constitution was designed to set up a series of buffers between the opinion of the masses and rapid reaction to that opinion on the part of governing bodies. These buffers, which have the effect of modifying the force of majority rule and invasions of minority property rights are, for example: the separation of powers, the direct election of U.S. senators by state legislatures, and the indirect election of the president by the Electoral College. Second, state legislatures, which had traditionally been hostile to speculators and capital, were very much limited in their power to affect property rights.

Ratification

Careful examination of the ratification process establishes that the Constitution was supported by only a small minority of our citizens. Probably only about 5 percent of the general population was allowed to express any political opinion on the document—about 20 percent of the adult, male, white population. Even within this select group, the Constitution had a difficult time.

In four states, the ratification elections were held in such haste that it is doubtful that the general public had time to either develop or express its opinion. In three states, the popular vote was against ratification, and it was only through political tricks and heavy pressure on individual representatives—sometimes leading to repudiation of specific instructions—that approval was obtained. In two states, ratification was won only after much delay and deliberation. And, finally, in two other states, approval was, at first, refused, only to be reversed when the federal government had been established, and had set strong economic forces into motion against the majority.

Summary

It seems obvious that the Constitution of the United States, in spite of a general opinion otherwise, is basically an economic document. Further, it is based upon a fundamental presupposition that the rights of property holders come before, and exist independent of, the powers of government, and are morally beyond the power of a popular majority. The Constitution was not created by the people but was the product of a monolithic economic group which had interests transcending state boundaries and which, therefore, promoted the idea of a strong federal government.

Moderator

Thank you, Professor Beard. I know that the audience has some questions to ask you, but I think it might be better if we wait until we have had a chance to hear Mr. McDonald's reaction to what we have enjoyed so far. I am pleased to present Mr. Forrest McDonald.

Comments by Mr. Forrest McDonald

It should be obvious to all that Professor Beard sees not complexity when he examines the making of the Constitution, but simplicity—a series of clear-cut events that follow one another in logical fashion. He believes that when all those who supported the new constitution are lumped together, and when all those who opposed the constitution are lumped together, that the conflict between them will turn out to be a fundamentally simple economic one. From this, he proceeds to develop a number of proposals:

The Constitutional Convention

Professor Beard concludes that the Constitution was the product of a single, unified economic group which had national interests transcending state boundaries. Unfortunately for this viewpoint, the following facts emerge from a careful study of the convention:

1. Over a fourth of the delegates had supported debtor-relief laws in state legislatures. These were the kind of laws which, according to Professor Beard, the delegates had gathered to prevent.
2. Another fourth of the delegates had interests which were adversely affected by the constitution which they helped to write. It is obvious that the most common holding of the delegates was farm land and not personal property.
3. Finally, the delegates, during the day-to-day business of the convention, behaved in anything but a consolidated, unified manner. When Caleb Strong, in his black hat and string tie—probably traveling third class—met a delegate from South Carolina looking like one of the Three Musketeers, with a retinue of slaves, and probably on a white horse, it was a wonder that they could talk together at all. Certainly, to say that they approached the tasks of the convention with duplicate motivations is far-fetched.

In conclusion, it is impossible to support Professor Beard's analysis of the Constitution as, first, an economic document, and secondly, as drawn up by a consolidated interest group acting to protect their property rights.

The Ratification Process

Professor Beard claims that the final test of the validity of his economic interpretation of the Constitution is based on a comparison of the economic interests of those supporting and those opposing ratification. His conclusion is that those who voted for the Constitution were basically holders of personal property and that those who voted against the Constitution were basically small farmers and debtors. Again, however, as in the case of the Constitutional Convention, analysis of the actual facts surrounding the successful ratification process fails to provide support for Professor Beard's argument. For example,

1. In four states (Massachusetts, Pennsylvania, New York, and Rhode Island), although the holders of personal property were a majority, the minority agrarian interests supported the new Constitution by sizable margins.
2. In three states (Connecticut, South Carolina, and New Hampshire) farmers were dominant, but a substantial minority held speculative wealth. In *all* these states there was very little difference in the two groups between the percentage favoring and the percentage in opposition. In fact, a large majority of those supporting ratification were farmers.
3. In two states where the Constitution was approved only after a closely contested contest (Virginia and North Carolina), a high percentage of the delegates on both sides of the issue were farmers.
4. In three states (Delaware, New Jersey, and Georgia), the vote for ratification was unanimous. Yet, the conventions were made up respectively of 77 percent, 64 percent, and 50 percent agricultural interests.

Professor Beard's basic error is that he is attempting to apply a grand generalization to thirteen economically, socially, and politically diverse states. Such an attempt is bound to fail since the external political impact of any state was bound to reflect differing internal conditions.

In the United States, at the time of the struggle over the Constitution, there were at least twenty basic occupational groups with varying economic characteristics, and at least six basic kinds of capital investment. Given this diversity, it is not possible to develop a single set of political alignments that will completely explain the issue of ratification as one in which economic self-interest was the main motivator. I will admit that Professor Beard's analysis provides some interesting insights into the development of the Constitution, but like all generalizations it is, unfortunately, at best only a partial truth.

ASSIGNMENT QUESTIONS

1. Summarize the central points in the thesis advanced by Professor Beard.
2. Summarize the counter argument of Professor McDonald.
3. Decide for yourself which position is most nearly correct. What is your rationale for the choice you have made?
4. What significance does Beard's thesis have for business-government relations? Does it have any significance for us today?

NOTES

1. Charles Austin Beard, *An Economic Interpretation of the Constitution of the United States* (New York: Macmillan, 1968).
2. Forrest McDonald, *We the People: The Economic Origins of the Constitution* (Chicago: University of Chicago Press, 1958).

PART TWO
CORPORATE RELATIONSHIPS

Under the law, a corporation is a person—a person with a body you cannot kick and a soul you cannot damn, but still a person. As such, a corporation can interact with government officials, customers, owners, with other corporate persons, and with many others. In this part, attention is focused on some representative corporate relationships: within a debt relationship, within an industry association, and within the internal framework of relations between shareholders and corporate managers.

In Case 6, *The Minnesota Mortgage Moratorium Law of 1933,* the principal question is whether economic conditions can get bad enough to allow government to step in and alter otherwise perfectly legal contracts made between business firms. Other issues include the meaning of the contract clause of the Constitution, the proper roles of creditors and debtors in hard times, and the correct use of police power by the states to promote the wealth and prosperity, comfort, convenience, and happiness of the public. Peripheral issues include the causes for depressions and the proper action a business manager should take during depressed periods.

One of the few major governmental innovations made during the early 1920s—a period of general inactivity on the part of the national administration—was the development of the "association movement." Probably as a response to some of the unbridled competition brought out by the muckrakers, both business and government leaders came to believe, by this time, that businessmen should cooperate to bring some kind of order and rationality to the economy. Harding's secretary of commerce, Herbert Hoover—possibly for want of something to do in an incompetent administration—was very active in bringing businessmen together in industry groups to work up codes of conduct and to organize into formal associations. However, the proper bounds of this "cooperation" had not at this time been determined by the courts. The *Linseed Oil* case is one of a series of cases in which the courts attempted to determine when the interchange of information within an industry association becomes conspiracy in restraint of trade.

6

THE MINNESOTA MORTGAGE MORATORIUM LAW OF 1933

GENTLEMEN, THE CORN BELT!

Remley J. Glass, "Gentlemen, the Corn Belt!" *Harper's*, CIXVI (July 1933), pp. 200–206.

My home county may well be considered a fair example of Iowa and the Corn Belt. It is one of the ninety-nine counties of Iowa and similar to those throughout the Middle West. Its condition and problems are typical of the entire Corn Belt. Organized before the Civil War, its early citizenry was purely pioneer stock which successfully withstood the attacks of Indians and the vicissitudes of border existence. To this nucleus have been added a considerable group of Irish immigrants who are centered in two or three southern townships, and a larger proportion of Scandinavians who constitute the majority in five or six northern townships. The manufacturing industries in our county seat have brought groups of laborers from the south of Europe, while Mexico likewise has furnished its full quota.

The wheat and corn of pioneer farming gave place in part to hogs, beef cattle, and dairy herds, and the development of sugar beets added to its prosperity. The county seat, with the establishment of large manufacturing industries, assumed an almost metropolitan air with comfortable homes and a contented people. Railroads radiated from the town and made it the trading center of a considerable area. A conservative prosperity was ours.

In the early days of the century, Iowa, along with the rest of the Middle West, enjoyed a gradual, conservative increase in the values of farm products and farm real estate. Men who had homesteaded their farms from the government, paying $2.50 or $3.00 per acre, saw the price of land gradually increase to around $100 per acre, and thereby built up comfortable fortunes. Early investors at $7 to $15 per acre profited by the same increase. Even though sales of farm lands were rare in those days, the new values seemed definitely established.

This increase in values...did not come like the Biblical manna in the Wilderness; it was the result of pioneer effort in the building up and improvement of those farms and of the states in which the efforts were put forth.

The boom period of the last years of the World War and the extreme inflationary period of 1919 and 1920 were like the Mississippi Bubble and the Tulip Craze in Holland in their effect upon the general public. Farm prices shot high almost overnight. The town barber and the small-town merchant bought and sold options until every town square was a real estate exchange. Bankers and lawyers, doctors and ministers left their offices and clients and drove pell mell over the county to procure options and contracts upon this farm and that, paying a few hundred dollars down and expecting to sell the rights before the following March brought settlement day. Not to be in the game marked one as an old fogey, while paper profits were pyramided and Cadillac cars and pleasure trips to the cities took the place of Fords and Sunday afternoon picnics. Everyone then maintained that there was only a little land as fertile as the fields of Iowa, Illinois, and Minnesota, and everyone sought to get his part before it was gone. Like gold, it was limited in extent and of great potential value. Prices skyrocketed from $100 to $250 and $400 per acre without regard to the producing power of the land.

During this period insurance companies were bidding against one another for the privilege of making loans on Iowa farms at $90 to $100 or $150 per acre. Prices of products were soaring. Everyone was on the high road, not only to comfort, but to wealth and luxury. Second, third, and fourth mortgages were considered just as good as government bonds. Money was easy, and every bank was ready and anxious to loan money to any Tom, Dick, or Harry on the possibility that he would make enough in these trades to repay the loans almost before the day was over. Every country bank, and every county-seat town was a replica in miniature of a brisk day on the board of trade.

Settlements were made on March 1, 1920, but, alas, from then on the painful awakening from this financial carousel brought long continuing headaches to the investors, the holders of second mortgages, and the bankers who had financed these endeavors.

The next decade was marked by a gradual decrease in the price of farm commodities, a shrinkage in farm values, and increasing attempts by the holders to collect second and third mortgages given during boom times. However, the foreclosure of a first or primary mortgage on Iowa real estate was as rare during this period as it had been in prior years. The basic value of Corn Belt land was still beyond question, and what few first-mortgage foreclosure actions were brought disturbed this confidence but little. During this same decade large drainage projects were inaugurated in the Corn Belt in order to bring large areas of "border" land under cultivation. Consolidated schools were erected to bring the highest type of educational facilities to the rural children. The proverbial little red schoolhouse became a modern brick building with enlarged facilities and more faculty. Paved roads were built.

All these features had been demanded and are desirable; but the ability to pay for them has not continued. The general tax demands of school district, county, and state have equaled the interest on a thirty-dollar-per-acre mortgage over the entire State of Iowa; while special highway, drainage, and consolidated school assessments have increased the tax burden in areas affected by those improvements beyond bearing. For some years affected by these special levies, and in nearly every county the first of the flood of foreclosures was in such heavily taxed areas.

During the year after the great debacle of 1929, the flood of foreclosures did not reach any peak, but in the years 1931 and 1932 the tidal wave was upon us. Insurance companies and large investors had not as yet realized (and in some instances do not yet realize) that, with the low price of farm commodities and the gradual exhaustion of savings and reserves, the formerly safe and sane investments in farm mortgages could not be worked out, taxes and interest could not be paid, and liquidation could not be made. With an utter disregard of the possibilities of payment or refinancing, the large loan companies plunged ahead to make the Iowa farmer pay his loans in full or turn over the real estate to the mortgage holder. Deficiency judgments and the resultant receiverships were the clubs they used to make the honest but indigent farm owners yield immediate possession of the farms.

Men who had sunk every dollar they possessed in the purchase, upkeep, and improvement of their home places were turned out with small amounts of personal property as their only assets. Landowners who had regarded farm land as the ultimate in safety, after using their outside resources in vain attempts to hold their lands, saw these assets go under the sheriff's hammer on the courthouse steps.

During the two-year period of 1931–32, in this formerly prosperous Iowa county, 12 ½ percent of the farms went under the hammer, and almost 25 percent of the mortgaged farm real estate was foreclosed. And the conditions in my home county have been substantially duplicated in every one of the ninety-nine counties of Iowa and in those of the surrounding states.

From a lawyer's point of view, one of the most serious effects of the economic crisis lies in the rapid and permanent disintegration of established estates throughout the Corn Belt. Families of moderate means as well as those of considerable fortunes who have been clients of my particular office for three or four generations in many instances have lost their savings, their investments, and their homes, while their business, which for many years has been a continuous source of income, has become merely an additional responsibility as we strive to protect them from foreclosures, judicial receivership, deficiency judgments, and probable bankruptcy.

As I sit here my mind turns to one after another of the prominent land-owning families of this county who have lost their fortunes, not as a result of extravagance or carelessness, but because of conditions beyond their control which were not envisaged by the most farsighted.

Take, if you please, what seems to me to have been a typical case, one Johannes Schmidt. Johannes was descended from farming stock in Germany, came to this country as a boy, became a citizen, went overseas in the 88th Division, and on his return married the daughter of a retired farmer. He rented 120 acres from his father-in-law and 160 acres from the town banker. His livestock and equipment, purchased in the early 1920s, were well bought, for his judgment was good, and the next eight years marked a gradual increase in his livestock and reductions in his bank indebtedness. During these years two youngsters came to the young couple and all seemed rosy.

In the year 1931 a drought in this part of the Corn Belt practically eliminated his crops, while what little he did raise was insufficient to pay his rent, and he went into 1932 with increased indebtedness for feed, back taxes, and back rent. While the crops in 1932 were wonderful and justified the statement that the Middle West is the market basket of the world, prices were so low as not to pay the cost of seed and labor in production without regard to taxes and rent.

Times were hard and the reverberations of October 1929 had definitely reached the Corn Belt. The county seat which held Johannes's paper was in hard shape. Much of its reserve had been invested in bonds recommended by Eastern bankers upon which default of interest and principal had occurred. When the bottom dropped out of the bond market the banking departments and examiners insisted upon immediate collection of slow farm loans, as liquidity was the watchword of bank examiners in the years 1929 to 1932. When Johannes sought to renew his bank loan, payment or else security on all his personal property was demanded without regard to the needs of wife and family. Prices of farm products had fallen to almost nothing, oats were 10 cents a bushel, corn 12 cents per bushel, while hogs, the chief cash crop in the Corn Belt, were selling at less than 2 ½ cents a pound. In the fall of 1932, a wagon load of oats would not pay for a pair of shoes; a truckload of hogs, which in other days would have paid all a tenant's cash rent, did not pay the interest on a thousand dollars.

This man Schmidt had struggled and contrived as long as possible under the prodding of landlord and banker, and as a last resort came to see me about bankruptcy. We talked it over and with regret reached the conclusion it was the only road for him to take. He did not have even enough cash on hand to pay the $30 filing fee which I had to send to the Federal Court but finally borrowed it from his brother-in-law. The time of hearing came, and he and his wife and children sat before the Referee in Bankruptcy, while the banker and the landlord struggled over priorities of liens and rights to crops and cattle. When the day was over, this family went out from the office the owner of an old team of horses, a wagon, a couple of cows and five hogs, together with their few sticks of furniture and no place to go.

George Warner, aged seventy-four, who had for years operated one hundred and sixty acres in the northeast corner of the county and in the early boom days had purchased an additional quarter section, is typical of hundreds in the Corn Belt. He had retired and with his wife was living comfortably in his square white house in town a few blocks from my home. Sober, industrious, pillars of the church and active in good works, he and his wife may well be considered typical retired farmers. Their three boys wanted to get started in business after they were graduated from high school, and George, to finance their endeavors, put a mortgage, reasonable in amount, on his two places. Last fall a son out of a job brought his family and came home to live with the old couple. The tenants on the farm could not pay their rents, and George could not pay his interest and taxes. George's land was sold at tax sale and a foreclosure action was brought against the farms by the insurance company which held the mortgage. I did the best I could for him in the settlement, but to escape a deficiency judgment he surrendered the places beginning on March 1 of this year, and a few days ago I saw a mortgage recorded on his home in town. As he told me of it, the next day, tears came to his eyes and his lips trembled, and he and I both thought of the years he had spent building up that estate and making those acres bear fruit abundantly. Like another Job, he murmured, "The Lord gave and the Lord hath taken away"; but I wondered if it was proper to place the responsibility for the breakdown of a faulty human economic system on the shoulders of the Lord.

I have represented bankrupt farmers and holders of claims for rent, notes, and mortgages against such farmers in dozens of bankruptcy hearings and court actions, and the most discouraging, disheartening experiences of my legal life have occurred when men of middle age, with families, go out of the bankruptcy court with furniture, a team of horses and a wagon, and a little stock as all that is left from twenty-five years of work, to try once more—not to build up an estate—for that is usually impossible—but to provide clothing and food and shelter for the wife and children. And the powers that be seem to demand that these not only accept this situation but shall like it.

HOME BUILDING AND LOAN ASSOCIATION v. *BLAISDELL ET AL.*

290 U.S. 398 (1934).

A Minnesota statute, passed on April 18, 1933, declared the existence of an emergency demanding the exercise of the police power for the protection of the public, and temporarily extended the time allowed by existing law for redeeming real property from foreclosure and sale under existing mortgages.

The act provided that the mortgagor or owner in possession, by applying to a state court, could obtain an extension for such time as the court might decide was just and fair—but in no case beyond May 1, 1935. The court was to determine the reasonable income or rental value of the property, and to order the applicant to pay all, or a reasonable part, of that value toward the payment of taxes, insurance, interest, and mortgage.

Mr. and Mrs. Blaisdell owned a lot in a closely built section of Minneapolis on which a house and garage were located. They lived in part of the house and offered the other part for rental. The reasonable present market value of the entire property was around $6,000, and the reasonable rental value of the available portion of the house was $40 per month. On May 2, 1932, under a power of sale in a mortgage held by the Home Building and Loan Association, the property was sold to satisfy the debt owned by the Blaisdells. The bid price was $3,700, which would have satisfied the entire amount due, but would have left nothing to the prior owners.

A state court extended the period of redemption to May 1, 1935, upon condition that the mortgagor pay $40 per month through the extended period. The mortgage holder challenged the constitutionality of the law under which the extension was made, and the case eventually found its way to the United States Supreme Court.

Argument on Behalf of Home Building and Loan Association

Alfred W. Bowen and Karl H. Covell presented the argument for the Home Building and Loan Association:

If this extension be valid, succeeding legislatures may prolong it indefinitely, and convert the relation of mortgagee and mortgagor into that of landlord and tenant—the tenant owning the title.

The Act clearly shows its intention to protect the ownership of real property in Minnesota at all hazards. By no stretch can it be imagined that the mere recital of the economic depression indicates an intention to cure the depression. Neither the conditions recited nor those actually prevailing approach in severity the conditions that prevailed throughout this nation prior to the adoption of the contract clause in the U.S. Constitution. Rather, this recital in the Act is made solely to identify the cause of the landowner's present condition. And it is this condition only that the legislature seeks to remedy.

Practically, the Act defeats this purpose, because it aggravates the depression from which the landowners' condition is said to result. It tends naturally and inevitably to restrict the extension of credit on real estate security in Minnesota, and thus (a) to increase foreclosures by discouraging loans or renewals; (b) to decrease employment of labor and the purchase and use of building materials, because prospective builders cannot borrow to improve real estate; and (c) to freeze assets and deposits in banks and other institutions which would otherwise become liquid by payment of old loans from new loans.

The Supreme Court of Minnesota agrees that the Act tends to restrict credit. In the majority opinion, the court said: "It tends to withdraw from the borrower the funds which otherwise he might procure. Lenders will not loan their money in a state where the contract for its repayment may be impaired at the uncontrolled whim of its legislature."

The results so predicted by the court have followed swiftly and irresistibly. During the short time since the passage of the Act, new construction in Minneapolis and throughout the state has fallen off enormously.

Such a law is repugnant to the contract clause, and to the due process clause of the Fourteenth Amendment. The statute impairs the obligation of the contract and takes property without due process of law, because it arbitrarily changes the agreed remedy of foreclosure by advertisement into foreclosure by action in the courts, and subjects the mortgagee to future action by the court. It extends the redemption period from one year to three years. This arbitrary cutting down of the appellant's estate and enlargement of the mortgagors' estate is contrary to the express terms of the contract.

There is nothing before this Court to show that the existence of the State is threatened. The claim that the police power is beyond limitations in the Federal Constitution is so extravagant as hardly to merit consideration. It flies directly in the face of innumerable decisions of this court. Moreover, the contrary is twice admitted—first, in admitting that in normal times the Act would be void because violating the Federal Constitution; and second, in arguing that the emergency justifies the Act and frees the police power of the restraints otherwise imposed by the Constitution.

The appellant does not admit that the economic depression constitutes an emergency; nor that the emergency, if any is of the character recognized by this court as one which would suspend the limitations of the Federal Constitution.

The statute denies equal protection of the laws to creditors like the appellant, and also to debtors. It discriminates against debtors who have not given such security or who have no real property out of which satisfaction of the debt can be extracted.

It was the intention of the framers of the Constitution that, under depression conditions like those now prevailing, laws of this type should be forever prohibited, whether enacted under the police power or any other power. It cannot be denied that many provisions of the Federal Constitution limit the police power. The contract clause, the due process clause, and the equal protection clause all are such limitations.

The court below and the appellees concede that the police power is so limited. But they assert that the "emergency" suspends the limitations. This Court has stated positively and squarely, in a case involving an actual emergency arising during the Civil War, that even the war power of the Federal Government is not without limitations, and such an emergency does not suspend constitutional limitations and guarantees.

Limitations on the police power, as on all other powers of the state governments, are imposed both by the Federal Constitution, as shown above, and by the state constitutions. Determination by the legislature of what constitutes proper exercise of police power is not final or conclusive, but is subject to supervision by the courts.

The relationship of mortgagor and mortgagee arising out of the business of lending money on the credit of real estate, and the enforcement of the agreed remedies, are clearly private matters and are not "affected with a public interest."

Aside from the legislative declaration, there is nothing before the Court in this case to show the existence of any emergency, nor any rational basis for the period of two years prescribed in the act. Moreover, there is no reasonable compensation, for mortgagees and other creditors under the act. There are no reasonable and definite standards for applying it. It is not merely for the protection of residences, that is, homesteads as such, but applies indiscriminately to all real property, whether vacant, unimproved, agricultural or urban, and whether used for purposes of residence, investment, or speculation.

Argument for the State of Minnesota

The argument for the state of Minnesota was presented by Harry H. Peterson, attorney general of Minnesota:

Every contract is entered into subject to the implied limitation that in an emergency its terms may be varied in a reasonable manner under the exercise of the police power of the state. This limitation upon contract rights is as much a part of any contract as if it were incorporated therein in writing.

This law does not impair the contract obligation nor deprive of property without due process. It provides for an orderly proceeding to determine what extension, if any, should be made, the amount which must be paid and the other conditions which must be performed as a condition precedent in the making and continuance of the extension.

We concede that in normal times and under normal conditions the Minnesota Mortgage Moratorium Law would be unconstitutional. But these are not normal times nor normal conditions. A great economic emergency has arisen in which the State has been compelled to invoke the police power to protect its people in the possession and ownership of their homes and farms and other real estate from the disastrous effects of the wholesale foreclosure of real estate mortgages which inevitably resulted from the present state-wide, nation-wide, and world-wide economic depression.

One of the major problems arising out of the depression is the proper handling of mortgage debts. This problem has been particularly acute in Minnesota because of the fact that it is an agricultural state and the income of the majority of our people comes from land. Most of the real estate mortgages existing were contracted when the general price level was about twice, and the farm values about four times, as high as they are today. At the time of the passage of this law, real estate had practically ceased to have a market value and could scarcely be sold at any price, and the income from real estate was not sufficient in many instances to pay the interest on the mortgage and the taxes on the land. Our people, with their savings tied up in closed banks, with their earning power greatly reduced or entirely wiped out, were unable to make payments on their mortgages as they became due. And they could not refinance their loans or sell their properties so as to realize something out of their equities. Consequently, mortgage foreclosures multiplied until, in the Spring of 1933, they reached an all-time high level. The throwing upon the market of these mortgaged premises had the inevitable effect of further depreciating real estate values throughout the state. It is obvious that if these foreclosures had been allowed to continue and to increase in number, unrestricted and unabated, a large portion of the homes and farms of the people of this state would inevitably have become the property of trust companies, banks, insurance companies and other mortgagees.

For several months prior to the passage of the act, many serious breaches of the peace occurred from time to time throughout the state, especially in the rural districts, in connection with mortgage foreclosure sales, and in many instances these sales were interrupted and prevented by mobs of people, otherwise peaceful and law abiding, who had been driven to desperation by the fear of losing their homes. In some instances mobs comprising more than a thousand people gathered together and forcibly prevented the holding of foreclosure sales. These disturbances increased in violence and in number until the Governor of the state, in the interest of preserving the public safety, was compelled to issue an executive order directing sheriffs to refrain from foreclosing mortgages on homes until the legislature had an opportunity to pass a relief measure to cope with the emergency.

Unfortunately, there are many home and farm owners in Minnesota who cannot get any relief from this law because the burden of mortgage indebtedness on their land is too great. However, there are many mortgagors in this State, who if allowed to retain possession and ownership, will be able to save them, if economic conditions improve within a reasonable period of time. In the past history of this country depressions have come, run their course of one year, or a few years, and then normally prosperous times have returned. May we not expect this depression, although more intense and wider in scope, to run a similar course? This law will enable many owners of mortgaged real estate to retain the ownership and possession of their real estate until such time as economic conditions improve and real estate again has a market value, so that loans can be refinanced or real estate sold at normal prices. Moreover, the national government has passed laws providing for the making of loans to owners of farms and homes, and when these laws are put into full operation many mortgagors will be able to refinance their loans through the Government.

The early decisions of the federal courts quite generally limited the exercise by the State of its police power to matters affecting the public health, public morals and public safety; but in the last half century this limitation has been abandoned and these courts, as well as many of the state courts, have enlarged by judicial interpretation the scope of this power to meet the requirements of changing economic and industrial conditions and the growth of the States and the Nation. It is now, we think, the consensus of the judicial opinion that the State may exercise its police power not only for the promotion and protection of the public health, public morals and public safety, but also to promote the wealth and prosperity, the comfort, convenience and happiness—in short, the general welfare—of the State.

An Opinion of the Supreme Court

After arguments were presented, and following due deliberation by the Court, the following opinion was issued by Justice Sutherland:

Few questions of greater moment than that just decided have been submitted for judicial inquiry during this generation. He simply closes his eyes to the necessary implications of the decision who fails to see in it the potentiality of future gradual but ever advancing encroachments upon the sanctity of private and public contracts. The effect of the Minnesota legislation, though serious enough in itself, is of trivial consequence compared with the far more serious and dangerous inroads upon the limitations of the Constitution which are almost certain to ensue as a consequence naturally following any step beyond the boundaries fixed by that instrument.

The Constitution of the United States is a law for rulers and people, equally in war and in peace, and covers with the shield of its protection all classes of men, at all times, and under all circumstances. No doctrine, involving more pernicious consequences, was ever invented by the wit of man than that any of its provisions can be suspended during any of the great exigencies of government. Such a doctrine leads directly to anarchy or despotism.

A candid consideration of the history and circumstances which led up to and accompanied the framing and adoption of this clause will demonstrate conclusively that it was framed and adopted with the specific and studied purpose of preventing legislation designed to relieve debtors *especially* in time of financial distress.

Following the revolution, and prior to the adoption of the Constitution, the American people found themselves in a greatly impoverished condition. Their commerce had been well-nigh annihilated. They were not only without luxuries, but in great degree were destitute of the ordinary comforts and necessities of life. In these circumstances they incurred indebtedness in the purchase of imported goods and otherwise, far beyond their capacity to pay. From this situation there arose a divided sentiment. On the one hand, an exact observance of public and private engagements was insistently urged. A violation of the faith of the nation or the pledges of the private individual, it was insisted, was equally forbidden by the principles of moral justice and of sound policy. Individual distress, it was urged, should be alleviated only by industry and frugality, not by relaxation of law or by a sacrifice of the rights of others.

On the other hand, it was insisted that the case of the debtor should be viewed with tenderness, and efforts were constantly directed toward relieving him from an exact compliance with his contract. As a result of the latter view, state laws were passed suspending the collection of taxes, providing for the emission of paper money, delaying legal proceedings, etc. There followed, as there must always follow from such a course, a long trail of ills, one of the direct consequences being a loss of confidence in the government and in the good faith of the people. Bonds of men whose ability to pay their debts was unquestionable could not be negotiated except at a discount of thirty, forty, or fifty percent. Real property could be sold only at a ruinous loss. Debtors, instead of seeking to meet their obligations by painful effort, by industry and economy, began to rest their hopes entirely upon legislation. The impossibility of payment of public or private debts was widely asserted, and in some instances threats were made of suspending the administration of justice by violence. The circulation of depreciated currency became common. Resentment against lawyers and courts was freely manifested, and in many instances the course of the law was arrested and judges restrained from proceeding in the execution of their duty by popular and tumultuous assemblages.

In the midst of this confused, gloomy, and seriously exigent condition of affairs, the Constitutional Convention of 1787 met in Philadelphia. Shortly prior to the meeting, Madison had assailed a bill pending in the Virginia Assembly, proposing the payment of private debts in three annual installments, on the ground that "no legislative principle could vindicate such an interposition of the law in private contracts." The bill lost by a single vote.

In the plan of government especially urged by Sherman and Ellsworth there was an article proposing that the legislatures of the individual states ought not to possess a right to emit bills of credit, etc., "or any manner to obstruct or impede the recovery of debts, whereby the interests of foreigners of the citizens of any other state may be affected." And on July 13, 1787, Congress in New York, acutely conscious of the evils engendered by state laws interfering with existing contracts, passed the Northwest Territory Ordinance, which contained the clause: "And, in the just preservation of rights and property, it is understood and declared, that no law ought ever to be made or have force in the said territory, that shall, in any manner whatever, interfere with or affect private contracts, or engagements, bonafide, and without fraud previously formed."

It is not surprising, therefore, that, after the Convention had adopted the clauses, no state shall "emit bills of credit," or "make any thing but gold or silver coin a tender in payment of debts," Mr. King moved to add a "prohibition on the states to interfere in private contracts." This was opposed by Gouverneur Morris and Colonel Mason. Colonel Mason thought that this would be carrying the restraint too far; that some cases would happen that could not be foreseen where some kind of interference would be essential. This was on August 28. But Mason's view did not prevail, for, on September 14, following, the first clause of Article I, Para. 10, was altered so as to include the provision, "No state shall...pass...law impairing the obligation of contracts," and in that form it was adopted.

Unquestionably, the country owes much of its prosperity to the unflinching courage with which, in the face of attack, the Court has maintained its firm stand in behalf of high standards of business morale, requiring honest payment of debts and strict performance of contracts; and its rigid construction of the Constitution to this end has been one of the glories of the Judiciary. That its decisions should, at times, have met with disfavor among the debtor class was, however, entirely natural; and while, ultimately, these debtor-relief laws have always proved to be injurious to the very class they were designed to relieve and to increase the financial distress, fraud, and extortion, temporarily, debtors have always believed such laws to be their salvation and have resented judicial decisions holding them invalid.

The present exigency is nothing new. From the beginning of our existence as a nation, periods of depression, of industrial failure, of financial distress, of unpaid and unpayable indebtedness, have alternated with years of plenty.

The Minnesota statute either impairs the obligation of contracts or it does not. If it does not, the occasion to which it relates becomes immaterial, since then the passage of the statute is the exercise of a normal, unrestricted state power and requires no special occasion to render it effective. If it does, the emergency no more furnishes a proper occasion for its exercise than if the emergency were non-existent.

Whether the legislation under review is wise or unwise is a matter with which we have nothing to do. Whether it is likely to work well or work ill presents a question entirely irrelevant to the issue. The only legitimate inquiry we can make is whether it is constitutional. If it is not, its virtues, if it have any, cannot save it; if it is, its faults cannot be invoked to accomplish its destruction. If the provisions of the Constitution be not upheld when they punch as well as when they comfort, they may as well be abandoned. Being unable to reach any other conclusion than that the Minnesota statute infringes the Constitutional restriction under review, I have no choice but to say so.

ASSIGNMENT QUESTIONS

1. Explain the reasons for the plight of American farmers during the 1930s.
2. What was the purpose and provisions of the Minnesota Mortgage Moratorium Law of 1933?
3. What was the situation with the Blaisdell family? In the face of this situation, what did they do?
4. Summarize the argument presented before the Supreme Court on behalf of the Home Building and Loan Association.

5. What was the argument for the state of Minnesota?
6. What does the opinion say?
7. If you had been a member of the Court, how would you have voted in this case?

7
UNITED STATES v. AMERICAN LINSEED OIL COMPANY ET AL.

262 U.S. 371 (1923).

The defendants are twelve corporations, commonly referred to as "crushers," with principal places of business in six different states, which manufacture, sell, and distribute linseed oil, cake, and meal, and Julian Armstrong, who operates at Chicago under the name Armstrong Bureau of Related Industries. The bureau conducts an exchange through which one subscribing manufacturer may obtain detailed information concerning the affairs of others doing like business. The defendant "crushers" constitute one of the groups who contract for this service. They manufacture and distribute throughout the United States a large part of the linseed products consumed.

Prior to entering into the challenged combination, the twelve defendant firms were active, unrestrained competitors. Some time in September 1918, each of them entered into an identical "subscription agreement" with the Armstrong Bureau. This agreement is summarized as follows:

The Agreement

General Provisions

After stating that "the matter contained herein is for the exclusive and confidential use of the subscriber," the agreement recites that it and other "crushers" of flaxseed desire promptly and economically to secure from and through the bureau the following things, "which will promote better and more safe, sane, and stable conditions in the linseed oil, cake, and meal industry and increase its service to the commonwealth":

Comprehensive data as to market, trade, and manufacturing conditions in the linseed oil industry;

Economies in manufacture and sale by frank exchange of accurate information;

The latest authentic information concerning the credit of buyers;

A broader market for cake and meal;

Establishment of uniform cost accounting systems;

Fair and just freight tariffs and classifications;

Definite standardization of the products of the industry;

Stabilization of the flaxseed market so far as lawful;

Shipment of cake and meal to the consumer from the nearest point of production.

The Contracting "Crusher" Agrees:

1. To subscribe to the bureau's service for twelve months and thereafter from year to year, subject to cancellation by either party upon thirty-day notice, and pay therefore a sum reckoned upon the amount of flaxseed milled by it, but not less than $1,100 annually.
2. That all information reported or received shall be purely statistical and relevant to past operations and no part of the bureau's machinery will be used to fix prices, divide territory, limit sales, production or manufacture, or control competition.
3. That it will promptly forward to the bureau full, accurate, complete, signed, and certified reports of all sales, quotations, and offerings or other information required by the bureau and full, correct replies or answers to any and all inquiries concerning the same or seeking any information in regard thereto.
4. That upon request it will "at once turn and have turned over to the bureau's auditor for examination all vouchers, books of account, correspondence, and such other evidence or documents as he may request."
5. That "if any subscriber considers that it has good cause to question the report made by any other subscriber that it may request an investigation or audit to be made by the bureau and, if considered proper by the bureau, it will be so made," the incident expense to be paid by the party found in error.
6. That it will deposit with the bureau not less than $1,000 nor more than $10,000 of Liberty bonds, according to its milling capacity.
7. That "should the undersigned subscriber fail, in any manner whatsoever, to comply with any of the terms of this agreement or with any and all reasonable requirements of said bureau, then it shall forfeit to said bureau, at its election, all money paid for services and all further right, title, or interest in and to said bonds (so on deposit) in whole or in part," subject to the right of appeal to a council, of three subscribers, which shall have power to review the entire matter.
8. That it will (a) "immediately, and when as hereafter issued, deposit with the bureau all published price lists; (b) also report to the bureau by prepaid telegraph duplicates of all quotations made at variance with the above price lists, giving better terms to the contemplated purchaser than those quoted."
9. That directly at the close of each day's business each subscriber shall mail by special delivery to the bureau a complete report of all its carload sales for that day of oil, cake, or meal, which report shall disclose the quantity and kind, price and terms.
10. That for the purpose of compiling a weekly sales report "a map of the United States shall be divided into zones as agreed upon by all of the subscribers to this service, and each subscriber at the conclusion of the week shall send to the bureau by special delivery, not later than the following Monday night, a compiled report of all of its sales of oil, cake, or meal into each zone made during the period covered by such report."
11. That before the tenth day of each calendar month it will report to the bureau the number of gallons of oil and the total tons of meal or cake on hand not covered by sale or contract.
12. That all information received from the bureau or any meeting of subscribers will be treated as confidential.

The Bureau Undertakes, "With the Help of Each and Every Subscriber":

1. That it will use its best efforts to organize the linseed oil, cake, and meal industry of the United States.
2. That it will afford its full statistical service for the exchange of information concerning quotations, sales, shipments, production, and terms.
3. That the market information received by the bureau will be cleared and relayed promptly to subscribers in good standing.
4. That it will send to subscribers, in the form of

market letters, "news clippings" of interest to the industry and in accordance with the object and terms of the agreement.

It Is Agreed By All:

1. That monthly meetings will be held of all subscribers hereto at some convenient center with a representative of the bureau, as secretary, who shall present the matters pertaining to the industry to be therein openly discussed. All subscribers shall report at these meetings on all matters and conditions within their knowledge that they may be there discussed for mutual benefit.
2. That any subscriber who has made offerings of quotations to a prospective buyer and is advised by such buyer that it is not to be awarded such business shall have the right to immediately advise the bureau of such unsuccessful offering or quotation giving all details of such bid or offering, and may then request the bureau to bulletin all of its subscribers asking specific information regarding any quotation or sale to such prospective buyer by any of the other subscribers and the bureau, on receipt of such request, will immediately bulletin all subscribers asking therefore and on receipt of replies will send out a compilation report thereof to all subscribers, together with the details of sale, if such a sale has been reported, so that all subscribers, including the original inquirer, will have a complete report of this transaction.

Court Tests

Operation of the System

The bureau displayed great industry in making inquiries, collecting information, investigating derelictions and giving immediate advice to subscribers. Hundreds of "market letters" relating to diverse transactions were sent to subscribers. A sale of as little as two barrels of oil below schedule was deemed worthy of special attention. Also from time to time it gave counsel concerning "unfair merchandising" and the necessity for establishing sound policy by constructive cooperation. The following letters, dated February 5 and 12, 1919, are characteristic.

Will all council members please reply promptly and fully through the bureau whether or not they made the sale in question to the following?

New York, N.Y., Feb. 3, 1919

Armstrong Bureau of Related Industries, Chicago

Gentlemen:

Our Chicago manager advises us that under date of February 1st the Enterprise Paint Mfg. Co. informed him that they had bought 10 barrels linseed oil at less than $1.46 from another crusher in the Chicago territory. Will you kindly bulletin the subscribers with a view of finding out if any of the crushers sold this lot at under their published price?

Yours truly, American Linseed Company

In the file of replies today completed, 11 subscribers state, in effect, that they have neither quoted nor sold the Enterprise Paint Mfg. Co.; the sale was apparently made by subscriber No. 6 whose letter follows:

Minneapolis, Minn., Feb. 6, 1919

Armstrong Bureau of Related Industries, Chicago

Gentlemen:

Replying to your market letter No. 224, we sold Enterprise Paint Manufacturing Company on February 3rd five barrels of bleached linseed oil at $1.50 delivered to their plant. This is our price in the Chicago market at the present time.

Yours truly, Midland Linseed Products Co.

Government Action

In 1921, the Antitrust Division of the Justice Department proceeded against the American Linseed Oil Company and others, under the Sherman Act. The government challenged as a combination or conspiracy a contract between the defendants, linseed oil crushers and the Armstrong Bureau. In the District Court, Judge Carpenter dismissed the suit on the grounds (1) that the government had not proven that an illegal combination working to restrain trade actually existed and (2) that associations under open price plans were not necessarily obnoxious to antitrust laws. An appeal was made, and the case eventually made its way to the United States Supreme Court, where it was argued on April 25 and 26, 1923. The brief for the United States was presented by James A. Fowler, special assistant to the attorney general.

Argument for the Government

The competition which it was intended by the Sherman Act to preserve was that existing in the economic world at the time of its enactment; and which had always existed and continued to exist, except as now and then interfered with by unlawful agreements down to the organization of latter day associations and bureaus. Economists then supposed that prices were regulated by the law of supply and demand. Of course the price of an article was necessarily based on the cost of producing and selling it. It could not for any substantial length of time be sold at a price under cost of production and marketing, but the producer's profit depended upon the amount he could realize in excess of costs, and that was controlled by the demand and the supply in the market.

The producer then sought to manufacture his article at the lowest cost possible. He would figure a reasonable profit upon that cost, and would be satisfied if he could receive the amount thus determined. If he had an advantage in location; or for any reason he could obtain his raw material more cheaply than a competitor; or had his factory so organized that he could produce the article more economically, the public received the benefit of those advantages, unless the demand was substantially greater than the supply, in which event naturally he increased his price, thus temporarily realizing a larger profit. If this condition continued for a time others entered the field, and the production soon equaled or probably exceeded the demand; and then it became a question of the survival of the fittest.

Under these conditions but little attention was given to the prices of competitors. When the market was active because the demand was great, prices naturally advanced; when business was depressed and demand lax, prices were reduced. Then producers were endeavoring to conceal every detail of their business from their competitors, and they were in ignorance of the details of each other's business except as they were accidentally revealed to them through agents, or possibly were obtained through some devious method. All effort, therefore, was concentrated upon producing the goods as cheaply as possible, so that they could sell them upon the market against competition and yet realize a reasonable profit; and no dependence was had upon the prices of competitors.

Under the present system of so-called "constructive" competition a precisely contrary course is pursued. Each producer of an article reveals every detail of his entire business to every competitor. He reports to him every sale, and the price at which it is made, and the locality to which it is shipped. They all agree upon terms of sale, and the amount that shall be charged to every locality in lieu of the freight from the mill to such locality. They adopt uniform practices with reference to storage, and conditions under which allowances shall be made. They then meet together and personally discuss every question relating to the production and distribution of the goods made by them. In other words, every producer is as familiar with the details of the business of his competitors as he is with those of his own business, or as they are with their business. Can anyone possessing intelligence sincerely contend that this revolution does not profoundly affect the economic laws governing prices which previously existed, and does not necessarily affect prices themselves? The result is that the producer now devotes his time to studying the business of his competitors instead of his own business. He interests himself in ascertaining whether his competitors have deviated at some point from an agreed uniform practice and in calling him upon the carpet to stop such deviation, rather than in figuring upon some means of reducing the cost of production. In determining upon prices he studies the price lists of his several competitors, ascertains what they are receiving for their goods in certain markets, and fixes his price therefrom instead of studying his cost sheet and determining what is a reasonable profit upon his investment.

If it be conceded that there are plausible arguments in support of this so-called "stabilization," which is nothing less than fixing prices, and of the effects of this so-called "constructive" competition, the debate over that question is purely an economic and not a legal one. The undoubted fact is that economic laws are profoundly affected by this new system; and the Sherman Act was passed to maintain the system governing competition then existing; and any fundamental change in practice by agreement between competitors whereby prices of articles moving in interstate commerce are substantially affected is a violation of that act.

The combination between the defendants is unlawful, because when carried into effect it inevitably restrains interstate commerce.

It has been repeatedly held that any combination which necessarily results in a restraint of interstate commerce is violative of the Anti-trust Act regardless of how innocent the intention of the parties thereto may have been.

It is just as unlawful to agree upon practices as upon prices, as conveniences and favors to the trade suffer because of the elimination thereby of all competition in practices.

The relief that should be granted in this case is an adjudication that the combination described in the bill and proven in the evidence is unlawful in toto, and an injunction inhibiting any further operation under the plan as a whole or under any part thereof.

Argument for the Linseed Oil Companies

The brief for the linseed oil companies was presented by John Walsh.

The charge of the Government in this case is that the inevitable result of the exchange of true and accurate market information as to past transactions must inevitably result in a curtailment of production and the advancement of prices, and therefore is in violation of the Sherman Anti-trust Act. That act being a penal statute, proof of its violation must be clear, positive and convincing.

We contend therefore that it is incumbent upon the Government to show that the operations of the Bureau necessarily had the effect of curtailing production or enhancing prices. Further, if the Government relies on circumstantial evidence to prove a combination or conspiracy to restrain trade, as it asserts it does, it must show that the circumstances upon which reliance is placed are inconsistent with supposition of innocence.

The burden is on the government in this case to prove by a clear and satisfying preponderance of evidence that a combination or conspiracy existed among the defendants to bring about an unlawful result. The rule as to presumptions and burden of proof in a suit in equity for injunction to prohibit violations of the Sherman Act is substantially the same as in a criminal case for violation of the act.

While this a civil suit, it is based upon an alleged violation of the Sherman Act, which is a highly penal statute. Thus a judgment under the pleadings in such a civil action must necessarily rest upon the conclusion from the facts that this highly penal statute has been violated.

It is quite useless to review the decisions of the courts which condemn combinations and conspiracies in restraint of trade in violation of the Sherman Act. Each case stands upon its own facts. Each of the reported cases where acts are condemned as combinations and conspiracies in violation of the law are well supported by courses of conduct from which any discerning mind can at once come to the conclusion that the conduct complained of constitute a direct restraint upon competition, and artificially interfered with the natural course of trade. We submit that no such degree of proof is present in this case.

We do not feel that it is necessary to discuss the legal difference between reasonable and unreasonable restraint of trade. We contend that there is no proof submitted to show that any restraint was brought about through the dissemination by the Bureau of true, accurate market information as to past transactions. We feel, however, that what is the test of reasonable or unreasonable restraint of trade is not out of place in this case.

There is no proof in the record that the interests of the public were injuriously affected, or that buyers ever complained that they were being penalized by prices quoted by the members of the Council. Further, there is no proof in the record that the crushers outside of the council were injuriously affected in their efforts to compete for the business of the crusher defendants. Those who are injured are the first to complain, and the Government submitted no testimony that any one had complained against the operations of the Bureau.

It is a matter of record, however, that buyers called by the government and the defendants testified that they never considered the prices quoted by the defendant crushers while members of the Linseed Oil Council were out of line with the price of flaxseed. This fact we assert ought to be proof sufficient that no one was burdened by reason of the exchange of accurate market information set forth in this case.

It is true that the crushers did have the benefit of accurate information which assisted each in individually forming his own judgment as to the prices he should charge for his product. Everyone who has anything to sell always seeks to ascertain what others are selling the same products for. There can be no violation of law in that. Can it be said to be unlawful if persons having like products for sale agree among themselves to inform each other as to the prices that have prevailed? Nothing further was done by the linseed oil crushers. They had freedom to contract, to do a lawful thing, and they did nothing more. Not a scintilla of evidence has been presented in this case that indicates, by inference or otherwise, that the exchange of information by the linseed oil crushers brought about an artificial influence on the linseed oil market.

The Court cannot, and will not, decide this case on guess or presumptions not supported by evidence, but can, of course, only find the existence of a purpose to artificially influence prices, and the affecting thereof, by a clear and satisfying preponderance of the evidence.

We assert that before the Court can find an unlawful use by the defendants of such information, it is necessary to find that there was an agreement, express or implied, to unlawfully use the information.

So far as we can ascertain no court, state or federal, has ever held that the collection and dissemination of true, accurate market information, although obtained from and exchanged by competitors, constituted a violation of law as part of a combination or conspiracy in restraint of competition or trade.

The matter of uniformity of price of itself means nothing so far as proof of combinations or conspiracies is concerned if there is no proof of effort to bring it about by concerted action.

The operation of the Linseed Crushers Council did not affect the market price of linseed oil. The price of linseed oil was determined by the market price of flaxseed. The record shows, without any evidence to the contrary, that prices, spot and future, of linseed oil are directly based upon prices, spot and future, of flaxseed; that flaxseed, like wheat and other commodities of like nature, is bought and sold on open exchanges; and that fluctuations in flaxseed prices cannot be artificially controlled.

The members of the Linseed Crushers Council during its existence were actively competing against each other, and although there were periods during the operation of the Council, just as there had been before the Council was formed, when the prices of linseed oil were uniform, these periods of uniformity obtained at times when the market was inactive and did not obtain when the market was active and sales large.

The correspondence between the Armstrong Bureau and the members of the Linseed Crushers Council indicates clearly that the individual council members were actively competing with each other, and the very insistence by the individual members that the reports of price changes should be prompt and accurate negates the existence of any understanding or agreement to maintain arbitrary prices.

The Government's argument based upon the uniformity of prices at various periods during the operation of the Council is palpably misleading.

ASSIGNMENT QUESTIONS

1. Summarize the provisions of the agreement between the crushers and the bureau.
2. What was the argument for the government?
3. What was the argument for the linseed oil companies?
4. If you were a justice of the Supreme Court, what decision would you make in this case? Why?

PART THREE
CORPORATE INTERFACE WITH SOCIETY

Environmental problems, discrimination, affirmative action, business ethics, and competitive arrangements are all areas where the social impact of the American corporation is great. Because the largest two hundred of these corporations control about 50 percent of our economy, it is obvious that their relations with other groups will not only be important but crucial. In considering the interface between corporate leaders and the rest of society, we usually summarize the problem by suggesting that managers should be "socially responsible." In Part III we attempt to come to grips with a definition of the term and, particularly, with its application to specific problems.

In Case 8, *A Case of Lead Poisoning*, we consider the responsibilities and problems of a major American corporation as it is faced with the lead poisoning of a group of children living near one of its plants. Not only must the company decide what specific actions it must take in the face of a very complex situation, it must somehow reconcile its past behavior and must develop policies for the future that will prevent the reoccurrence of similar difficulties. At the same time, there are larger issues: Who is really responsible for pollution? How much environmental purity do we want, and are we willing to pay for? Does a corporate polluter have any obligations greater than those required by law? If so, what are these obligations? What is a proper role for government?

Case 9, *Discrimination in Employment,* consists of seven short case reviews used to illustrate what discrimination is and what it is not. Subjects considered include employment tests and educational requirements, sex discrimination, experience requirements, male and female stereotypes, affirmative action, and reverse discrimination. The final two subject areas are dealt with in much greater detail in Case 10, *Kaiser Aluminum & Chemical Corporation.* In this case, suit was brought against the company and a cooperating union for advancing a black worker to training ahead of a white worker with greater seniority. Case 11, *The Kidd Company,* completes our study of employment rights issues with a consideration of the arguments for and against "comparable worth" as the basis for compensation of women employees.

The Pacific Corporation, Case 12, uses the occasion of a worker suffering with AIDS to stimulate discussion not just on an appropriate corporate policy for dealing with this difficult problem, but for a more general consideration of how society as a whole should handle the costs, dangers, and discriminatory impact of what promises to become an epidemic. Case 13, *Welfare Facts,* continues our consideration of the less fortunate in society by suggesting that business executives should review their obligation toward those living in poverty, and Case 14, *Motorola, Inc.,* presents the challenge to a large corporation, when many of its production workers do not, apparently, have sufficient basic education to allow them to compete with similarly employed workers in foreign companies.

In Case 15, *Confidential Memorandum,* a bulletin from a sales manager to his door-to-door vacuum cleaner sales personnel raises the question of whether or not customers are people to be manipulated and cheated or people to be served. Much is said in our society about "business ethics," but few people are able to give a clear definition as a guideline for actual corporate behavior. In this case the reader is left with the obligation of deciding whether the sales manager's conduct is appropriate, and also with the responsibility for suggesting a solution to the problems presented by such behavior. This question of business ethics also arises with regard to Case 16. Although the initial issue under consideration is the validity or nonvalidity of a patent, the argument quickly moves to the question of unfair or unethical competition that might arise if Sears deliberately copied an unpatentable article. Not only was Sears much larger than the Stiffle Company, but it was selling an article that it had deliberately copied, at a much lower price, and some consumers were confused as to the source of the competing lamps in question.

The final case in this section, *The Allen Cookie Company,* presents the case of a relatively new businessman who wants to know what he should do to be socially responsible. He ends up supporting the local symphony orchestra after some pressure from his wife, but has second thoughts. The reader is asked to advise him what he should do.

8
A CASE OF LEAD POISONING

Facts on Lead

Lead is a metallic element with an atomic number of 82, an atomic weight of 207.20, a boiling point of 1,743° Centigrade, and a melting point of 327.4° Centigrade. It was one of the first metals known to us and was mentioned in the Old Testament, wherein Pharaoh's chariots "sank as lead in the mighty waters."[1] Lead was used extensively by many early civilizations. In particular, it was in especially widespread use by the Romans for everything from water pipes to kitchen receptacles. In character, lead is very heavy, soft, malleable, and ductile. When gently heated, it can be easily poured into dies.

Lead Poisoning

Lead, in the form of metal or of its soluble compounds, when taken internally, is highly toxic. Lead poisoning, technically known as "plumbism," is almost exclusively an occupational disease which is usually chronic in nature. Because of the frequency with which painters acquired it from lead-based paints, it was known in times past as "painter's colic."

Because lead can be taken into the body in a wide variety of ways—including the ingestion of fumes, dust, vapor, or mist from lead—occupations involving the use of lead almost always result in some degree of lead poisoning. Jobs involving possible lead poisoning include: the ceramic industry (where lead glaze is used), house painting, glassmaking, copper working, plumbing, gas fitting, printing, and storage-battery manufacture. Of course, the more an occupational situation calls for contact with automobile exhaust, the greater the probability for lead poisoning. Thus, automobile mechanics, traffic police officers, parking attendants, and people who live next to busy highways show particularly high lead concentrations in their blood. Of course, as the relative percentage of lead-free gasolines continues to rise with the retirement of older cars, auto-related lead poisoning will probably decline.

The Effects of Lead Poisoning

The consequences of taking lead into the body are not felt until it has accumulated over a period of time. But when that accumulation has reached the danger point, the entire body can become affected. In particular, damage can be done to the nervous system, the gastrointestinal tract, and the blood-forming tissues. Changes may occur in the red blood cells, the kidneys may become fibrotic (called granular kidney), and there may be atrophy in the optic nerve.

The symptoms of lead poisoning vary with the sensitivity of the individual and the level of lead ingested. Basically, though, the effects will begin with a deterioration in the victim's appearance, and can ultimately lead to death. In sequence, from least serious to most serious, the effects of lead poisoning can be as follows:

1. The skin becomes pale.
2. A bluish line or spots may appear on the gums.
3. Anemia—a condition in which the blood is deficient in red blood cells, in hemoglobin, or in total volume.
4. General tiredness and weakness.
5. Indigestion.
6. Constipation.
7. Colic—acute abdominal pain caused by spasm, obstruction, or twisting.
8. Palsy—a condition marked by an uncontrolled tremor of part of the body.
9. Weakness or paralysis of the wrist, ankles, or hands.
10. "Wrist drop"—in which the victim is unable to hold up or use his hands, making any kind of work impossible.
11. An extension of paralysis to the shoulders and eventually to the legs.
12. Because of optic atrophy, the sight is weakened or even lost.
13. Convulsions.
14. Death.

Because of the seriousness of its effects, lead poisoning can have large consequences when populations or subpopulations are affected by it. For example, some historians seriously believe that a main cause of the fall of the Roman Empire may have been lead poisoning. The Romans used lead pots for boiling grape juice to make a syrup used by the upper classes as a sweetener and preservative. This, it is claimed, brought on brain damage, deformities, and stillbirths among those who were the leaders of the society, and eventually lead to the collapse of government and society. In our own country, lead poisoning occurs frequently among disadvantaged children living in slum areas. They ingest peelings from old lead-based paints on toys, furniture, and especially woodwork. The consequence is often severe cerebral involvement leading to a condition known as "lead encephalopathy."

The treatment of lead poisoning includes the administration of BAL, or British anti-Lewisite, a chemical developed during World War II as an antidote for heavy-metal poisoning. In most cases, though, the seriousness of the disease calls for careful regulation of working conditions and periodic physical examination of workers exposed to lead and its compounds.

Coppertown, New Mexico

In 1894, the U.S. Copper Company constructed a large copper smelting plant on the southwest border of New Mexico. The plant, at the time the largest of its kind in the world, was, from the beginning, a profitable operation for the company. Currently, it is a major installation producing more than 25 percent of U.S. Copper's lead and copper and 15 percent of its zinc.

The smelter is located on a narrow wedge of land opposite El Paso, Texas, and is the center of a community of 600 Mexican-Americans. Most of the working population of Coppertown is employed by the company. Shunned by the city fathers of El Paso, to which it nominally belongs geographically, the town has no paved streets, no garbage collection, no sewers, and no street lights. The typical house is a one-story adobe structure built up closely against the house next door and fronted by a ramshackle fence and a hot, dusty street.

Coppertown's residents have gone to U.S. Copper for help, and the company has responded by providing water for the community, and even by helping to rebuild the neighborhood church. According to Father Roberto Medina, the local priest, "The company has always shown more interest in our community than either the city or the state."

Pollution has long been a problem in Coppertown, and the company has made efforts over the years to combat it. In 1926, it installed its first particle-trapping baghouse, and as early as 1917, it had installed an electrostatic precipitator. Unfortunately, the problem was very difficult to overcome; as recently as 1970, the plant's stacks still emitted more than 500 tons of lead particles a year.

The company management believed that most of this pollutant was dispersed beyond Coppertown through the use of a giant 897-foot stack, but admitted that some local pollution might still be occurring because of ground-level leaks in the smelting process. The effectiveness of the stack was demonstrated, in 1979, by the fact that Mexico, just a few miles south of the smelter, had protested to the Department of State about across-the-border pollution.

Lead Poisoning in Coppertown

In March 1986, tragedy came to Coppertown, and U.S. Copper quickly became a villain to many residents. Some eighty children were found to have abnormally high levels of lead in their blood, and forty of them were hospitalized for observation and treatment.

The mayor of El Paso, envisioning an epidemic, requested that a federal health team be assigned to test the blood of more than five hundred children living outside Coppertown. "So far, the problem has been isolated in Coppertown, but if those tests show lead poisoning in white neighborhoods, you'll see a revolution in this city," says Homer Stringham, chairman of the city planning authority.

As far as children living in Coppertown itself, both the state of New Mexico and U.S. Copper ran independent blood tests and discovered a tragic truth: four children had more than 80 micrograms of lead per 100 grams of blood—a level that the U.S. Public Health Service defined as unequivocal lead poisoning and a medical emergency. Another sixty-six children showed blood levels about 40 micrograms, the acceptable upper limit of the normal range.

There is disagreement among doctors whether or not the children exhibited such typical lead poisoning traits as anemia. But even if the courtroom evidence supports the company's contention that none of the children suffered any damage, symptoms could appear later. Dr. John Fischer, a specialist in the pathology of lead poisoning at the Harvard Medical School, and a consultant on the case, states that "anything above 40 micrograms is cause for concern, because we aren't really sure of the minimum level at which damage to the brain begins."

Two years ago, the state sued U.S. Copper for violating air-quality standards near the plant, and the court ordered the company to install more ground-level controls. Although the company complied with the order, officials continued to press the suit. In collecting evidence they discovered, to their own amazement, the high lead content in the soil. "Our technicians were flabbergasted at the lead levels, and asked us to check if the decimal point was in the right place," exclaims Dr. Harry Lomax, director of the investigating team.

U.S. Copper was surprised, too. J. R. Walton, vice-president for smelting operations, says that the company concentrated on reducing stack emissions and never thought that lead deposits in the soil might be high enough to affect Coppertown. However, the wind-whipped lead particles have been building up in the soil for the past 92 years, and subsequent measurements by the company confirmed that the soil in Coppertown contains up to 1 percent lead—at least two hundred times greater than the national average. In addition, the state has found that the air near the town contains about 10 micrograms of lead per cubic meter. In comparison, lead concentration in most cities ranges from 2 to 5 micrograms.

Legal Actions

U.S. Copper is currently defending itself against two suits as a result of the recent findings. The state is suing for $4 million in damages, and eleven Coppertown families, charging that the company caused lead poisoning in their children, are suing for an additional $2.7 million. In addition, the authorities have made threats about forcing closure of the plant.

The residents of Coppertown are deeply divided. Some, especially those who work at the plant, maintain that the community is safe. Says one lady: "They said my grandchild has a high lead reading, but he looks as healthy as a horse to me." But Mr. Francisco Martinez, whose four-year-old boy was hospitalized for seventeen days, says bitterly: "I'm so angry at U.S. Copper that I can hardly get myself to face in the direction of the plant anymore." A number of families have already moved, and Dr. Lomax says flatly: "Coppertown is uninhabitable and should be condemned."

The company believes that the children were affected only because they played in contaminated dirt yards. They maintain that, although the smelters were one "contributing" factor to the lead buildup in the yards, other sources, especially automobiles, have contributed to lead pollution in Coppertown. And it is true that a state highway lies between the plant and the community.

Eventually, Coppertown may disappear altogether if it is finally determined that the place is simply too contaminated for human habitation. However, the real significance of the case, according to one official, "is that there are an awful lot of smelters in this country. If lead poisoning can happen here, it's possible we could be permitting the same bodily insults elsewhere."

A more quiet revolution will probably occur in government regulation of lead emissions. Until now, nearly all known cases of high lead levels have resulted from ingestion by traffic police officers of the lead fumes in auto exhaust. "This is the first time we've had an indication of widespread lead poisoning from an industrial source," says Morris Hainsworth, the federal official who recently headed the government examinations.

In the wake of the Coppertown discovery, the Environmental Protection Agency is preparing new emission standards for smelters. But EPA officials are not certain that emission standards will solve the kind of problem uncovered in Coppertown. Much of the local lead pollution no longer comes from the smelters themselves, but from lead particles deposited in the soil over the years and now circulated by the sandstorms that frequently hit the area. Whatever the EPA decides to do, the nation's lead and copper smelters almost certainly face tighter standards to go along with the already tough sulfur oxide regulations.

Excerpts from the Federal Air Quality Act of 1967

Findings and Purposes

Sec. 101. (a) The Congress finds:

(1) that the predominant part of the Nation's population is located in its rapidly expanding metropolitan and other urban areas, which generally cross the boundary lines of local jurisdictions and often extend into two or more states;

(2) that the growth in the amount and complexity of air pollution brought about by urbaniza-

tion, industrial development, and the increasing use of motor vehicles, has resulted in mounting dangers to the public health and welfare, including injury to agricultural crops and livestock, damage to and the deterioration of property, and hazards to air and ground transportation;

(3) that the prevention and control of air pollution at its source is the primary responsibility of states and local governments; and

(4) that federal financial assistance and leadership is essential for the development of cooperative federal, state, regional and local programs to prevent and control air pollution.

Cooperative Activities and Uniform Laws

Sec. 102. (a) The Secretary shall encourage cooperative activities by the states and local governments for the prevention and control of air pollution; encourage the enactment of improved, and, so far as practicable in the light of varying conditions and needs, uniform state and local laws relating to the prevention and control of air pollution; and encourage the making of agreements and compacts between states for the prevention and control of air pollution.

Research Investigations, Training, and Other Activities

Sec. 103. (a) The Secretary shall establish a national research and development program for the prevention and control of air pollution and as part of such program shall:

(1) conduct and promote the coordination and acceleration of, research, investigations, experiments, training, demonstrations, surveys, and studies relating to the causes, effects, extent, prevention, and control of air pollution;

(2) encourage, cooperate with, and render technical services and provide financial assistance to air pollution control agencies and other appropriate public or private agencies, institutions, and organizations, and individuals in the conduct of such activities....

Grants for Support of Air Pollution Planning and Control Programs

Sec. 105. (a) The Secretary is authorized to make grants to air pollution control agencies in an amount up to two-thirds of the cost of planning, developing, establishing, or improving, and grants to such agencies in an amount up to one-half of the cost of maintaining, programs for the prevention and control of air pollution and programs for the implementation of air quality standards authorized by this Act....

Air Quality Control Regions, Criteria, and Control Techniques

Sec. 107. (a)(1) The Secretary shall, as soon as practicable, but not later than one year after the date of enactment of the air quality Act of 1967, define for the purposes of the Act, atmospheric areas of the Nation on the basis of those conditions, including, but not limited to, climate, meteorology, and topography, which affect the interchange and diffusion of pollutants in the atmosphere....

Air-Quality Standards and Abatement of Air Pollution

Sec. 108. (a) The pollution of the air in any state or states which endangers the health of any persons, shall be subject to abatement as provided in this section.

(b) Consistent with the policy declaration of this title, municipal, state, and interstate action to abate air pollution shall be encouraged and shall not be displaced by Federal enforcement action except as otherwise provided by or pursuant to a court order under subsection (c), (b), or (k).

(c) If, after receiving any air quality criteria and recommended control techniques issued pursuant to Section 107, the Governor of a State, within ninety days of such receipt, files a letter of intent that such State will within one hundred and eighty days, and from time to time thereafter, adopt, after public hearings, ambient air quality standards applicable to any designated air quality control region or portions thereof within such State and within one hundred and eighty days thereafter, and from time to time as may be necessary, adopts a plan for the implementation, maintenance, and enforcement of such standards of air quality adopted, and as such standards and plans are established in accordance with the letter of intent and if the Secretary determines that such State standards are consistent with the air quality criteria and recommended control techniques issued pursuant to Section 107; that the plan is consistent with the purposes of the act insofar as it assures achieving such standards of air quality within a reasonable time; and that a means of enforcement by State action, including authority comparable to that in subsection (k) of this section, is provided, such State standards and plan shall be the air quality standard applicable to such State.

(2) If a state does not (A) file a letter of intent or (B) establish air quality standards in accordance with paragraph (1) of this subsection with respect to air quality control region or portion thereof and if the Secretary finds it necessary to achieve the purpose of this Act, or the Governor of any State affected by air quality standards established pursuant to this subsection petitions for a revision in such standards, the Secretary may after reasonable notice and a conference of representatives of appropriate Federal departments and agencies, interstate agencies, States, municipalities, and industries involved, prepare regulations setting forth standards of air quality consistent with the air quality criteria and recommended control techniques issued pursuant to Section 107 to be applicable to such air quality control region or portions thereof. If, within six months from the date the Secretary publishes such regulations, the State has not adopted air quality standards found by the Secretary to be consistent with the purposes of this Act, or a petition for public hearing has not been filed under paragraph (3) of this subsection, the Secretary shall promulgate such standards....

Standards to Achieve Higher Level of Air Quality

Sec. 109. Nothing in this title shall prevent a State, political subdivision, intermunicipal or interstate agency from adopting standards and plans to implement an air quality program which will achieve a higher level of ambient air quality than approved by the Secretary....

ASSIGNMENT QUESTIONS

1. What is the purpose of the federal Air Quality Act of 1967?
2. What mechanisms are provided in the act for the accomplishment of this purpose?
3. How much lead must be taken into the human system for lead poisoning to occur?
4. What are the effects of lead poisoning on the body?
5. How widespread is lead poisoning? Who would be most likely to become so afflicted?
6. What happened at Coppertown?
7. Who is at fault for the situation at Coppertown?
8. What should the company do?
9. What action would you recommend to the federal and state authorities?

10. What would be the consequences of your recommendations to the people now living in Coppertown?

NOTE

1. Exod. 15:10.

9
DISCRIMINATION IN EMPLOYMENT

Title VII of the 1964 Civil Rights Act

Title VII prohibits discrimination relative to any condition of employment. This includes hiring, firing, promotion, transfer, compensation, and assignment to training programs. Like many other laws, however, the 1964 Civil Rights Act does not define exactly what discrimination is. In fact, one clause in Title VII actually creates confusion by *permitting* employers to discriminate on the basis of sex, religion, or national origin if these characteristics are a "bona fide occupational qualification." Eventually, of course, the responsibility for defining exactly what discrimination in employment is became the obligation of the courts. The following are some of the key court decisions in this area.

GRIGGS v. *DUKE POWER CO.*

401 U.S. 424 (1971).

Facts of the Case

Prior to the passage of the Civil Rights Act of 1964, the Duke Power Company openly discriminated on the basis of race in the hiring and assigning of employees at its Dan River plant. The plant was organized into five operating departments: (1) labor, (2) coal handling, (3) operations, (4) maintenance, and (5) laboratory and testing. Blacks were employed only in the labor department, where the highest-paying jobs paid less than the lowest-paying jobs in the other four "operating" departments, in which only whites were employed. Promotions were normally made within each department on the basis of job seniority. Transferees into a department usually began in the lowest position.

In 1955 the company instituted a policy of requiring a high school education for initial assignment to any department except Labor, and for transfer from Coal Handling to any "inside" department (Operations, Maintenance, or Laboratory). When the company abandoned its policy of restricting blacks to the Labor Department in 1965, completion of high school was also made a prerequisite to transfer from Labor to any other department.

The company added a further requirement for new employees on July 2, 1965, the date on which Title VII became effective. To qualify for placement in any but the Labor Department, it became necessary to register satisfactory scores on two professionally prepared aptitude tests, as well as to have a high school education.

In September 1965 the company began to permit incumbent employees who lacked a high school education to qualify for transfer from Labor or Coal Handling to an "inside" job by passing two tests—the Wonderlic Personnel Test, which purports to measure general intelligence, and the Bennett Mechanical Comprehension Test. Neither was directed or intended to measure the ability to learn to perform a particular job or category of jobs. The requisite scores used for both initial hiring and transfer approximated the national median for high school graduates.

In Title VII of the Civil Rights Act of 1964, Congress provided for class actions in cases where the law was not being enforced. Under this provision, action was brought against the Duke Power Company by a group of black employees. All the petitioners were employed at the company's Dan River Steam Station, a power-generating facility located at Draper, North Carolina. At the time of the action, the company had 95 employees at the Dan River Station, 14 of whom were blacks and 13 of whom were involved in the suit.

Argument for the Company

There is no requirement in Title VII that employers abandon bona fide qualification tests, where, because of differences in background and education, members of some groups are able to perform better on these tests than members of other groups. An employer may set his qualifications as high as he likes, he may test to determine which applicants have these qualifications, and he may hire, assign, and promote on the basis of test performance.

During the debates on the Civil Rights Act of 1964, two of the legislation's supporters, Senators Clark and Case, explained to the Senate that tests which measure "applicable job qualifications" are permissible under Title VII. They assured the Senators that employers were not to be prohibited from using tests that determine *qualifications*. Certainly a reasonable interpretation of what the Senators meant was that nothing in the Act prevents employers from requiring that applicants be fit for the job.

Accepting this argument, it is clear that the Duke Power Company had established qualification tests that, in their best judgment, enabled it to screen out applicants of inferior quality. This it had every right to do under the law, and this it did.

Argument for the Employees

Regardless of the intention of the company, the requirements in question discriminate against blacks because they result in an unequal impact. On the record of the case, whites register far better on the company's requirements than do blacks. Basic intelligence must have the means of articulation to manifest itself fairly in a testing process. Because they are blacks, the petitioners have long received inferior educations in segregated schools. In North Carolina, the 1960 census statistics show that, while 34 percent of white males had completed high school, only 12 percent of black males had done so. Because of this inferior education received by blacks in North Carolina, the courts have barred the institution of a literacy test for voter registration on the ground that the test would abridge the right to vote indirectly on account of race.

Similarly, with respect to standardized tests, the EEOC in one case found that use of a battery of tests, including the Wonderlic and Bennett Tests used by the Company in the instant case, resulted in 58 percent of whites passing the tests, as compared with only 6 percent of the blacks. Admitting that test and requirements discriminate against blacks makes them, on their face, in violation of the Civil Rights Act unless it can be shown that they are specifically related to the jobs in question. Since the company does not claim any relationship between a high school graduation or intelligence tests and the work required in the Labor or Coal Handling Departments, and since the tests do discriminate on the basis of race, then they are illegal under the law.

DIAZ v. *PAN AMERICAN WORLD AIRWAYS*

442 F.2d. 385.

Finding by Tuttle, Circuit Judge

The facts in this case are not in dispute. Celio Diaz applied for a job as flight cabin attendant with Pan American Airlines in 1967. He was rejected because Pan Am had a policy of restricting its hiring for that position to females. He then filed charges with the Equal Employment Opportunity Commission (EEOC) alleging that Pan Am had unlawfully discriminated against him on the grounds of sex. The Commission found probable cause to believe his charge, but was unable to resolve the matter through conciliation with Pan Am. Diaz next filed a class action in the United States District Court for the Southern District of Florida on behalf of himself and others similarly situated, alleging that Pan Am had violated Section 703 of the 1964 Civil Rights Act by refusing to employ him on the basis of his sex; he sought an injunction and damages.

Pan Am admitted that it had a policy of restricting its hiring for the cabin attendant position to females. Thus, both parties stipulated that the primary issue for the District Court was whether, for the job of flight cabin attendant, being a female is a "bona fide occupational qualification (hereafter BFOQ) reasonably necessary to the normal operation" of Pan American's business.

The trial court found that being a female was a BFOQ (D.C., 311 F.Supp. 559). Before discussing its findings in detail, however, it is necessary to set forth the framework within which we view this case.

Section 703(a) of the 1964 Civil Rights Act provides, in part:

(a) It shall be an unlawful employment practice for an employer—(1) to fail or refuse to hire or to discharge any individual, or otherwise to discriminate against any individual with respect to his compensation, terms, conditions, or privileges of employment, because of such individual's race, color, religion, sex or national origin....

The scope of this section is qualified by Section 703(e) which states:

(e) Notwithstanding any other provision of this subchapter, (1) it shall not be an unlawful employment practice for an employer to hire and employ employees...on the basis of his religion, sex, or national origin in those certain instances where religion, sex, or national origin is a bona fide occupational qualification reasonably necessary to the normal operation of that particular business or enterprise....

Since it has been admitted that appellee has discriminated on the basis of sex, the result in this case, turns, in effect, on the construction given to this exception.

Argument for Mr. Diaz

We note, at the outset, that there is little legislative history to guide our interpretation. The amendment adding the word "sex" to "race, color, religion and national origin" was adopted one day before House passage of the Civil Rights Act. It was added on the floor and engendered little relevant debate. In attempting to read Congress' intent in these circumstances, however, it is reasonable to assume, from a reading of the statute itself, that one of Congress' main goals was to provide equal access to the job market for both men and women.

Attainment of this goal, however, is, as stated above, limited by the bona fide occupational qualification exception in Section 703(e). In construing this provision, we feel, that it would be totally anomalous to do so in a manner that would, in effect, permit the exception to swallow the rule. Thus, we adopt the EEOC guidelines which state "the Commission believes that the bona fide occupational qualification as to sex should be interpreted narrowly." Indeed, close scrutiny of the language of this exception compels this result. As one commentator has noted:

"The sentence contains several restrictive adjectives and phrases: it applies only *'in those certain instances'* where there are *'bona fide'* qualifications *'reasonably necessary'* to the operation of that *'particular'* enterprise. The care with which Congress has chosen the words to emphasize the function and to limit the scope of the exception indicates that it has no intention of opening the kind of enormous gap in the law which would exist if (for example) an employer could legitimately discriminate against a group solely because his employees, customers, or clients discriminated against that group. Absent much more explicit language, such a broad exception should not be assumed for it would largely emasculate the act" [emphasis added].

Argument for Pan American

Having reviewed the evidence submitted by Pan American regarding its own experience with both female and male cabin attendants it had hired over the years, the trial court found that Pan Am's current hiring policy was the result of a pragmatic process, "representing a judgment made upon adequate evidence acquired through Pan Am's considerable experience, and designed to yield under Pan Am's current operating conditions better *average* performance for its passengers than would a policy of mixed male and female hiring" [emphasis added]. The performance of female attendants was *better* in the sense that they were *superior* in such nonmechanical aspects of the job as "providing reassurance to anxious passengers, giving courteous personalized service and, in general, making flights as pleasurable as possible within the limitations imposed by aircraft operations."

The trial court also found that Pan Am's passengers overwhelmingly preferred to be served by female stewardesses. Moreover, on the basis of the expert testimony of a psychiatrist, the court found that an airplane cabin represents a unique environment in which an air carrier is required to take account of the special psychological needs of its passengers. These psychological needs are better attended to by females. This is not to say that there are no males who would not have the necessary qualities to perform these non-mechanical functions, but the trial court found that the actualities of the hiring process would make it more difficult to find these few males. Indeed, "the admission of men to the hiring process, in the present state of the art of employment selection, would have increased the number of unsatisfactory employees hired, and reduced the average levels of performance of Pan Am's complement of flight attendants."...In what appears to be a summation of the difficulties which the trial court found would follow from admitting males to this job the court said "that to eliminate the female sex qualification would simply eliminate the best available tool for screening out applicants *likely* to be unsatisfactory and thus reduce the *average* level of performance" [emphasis added].

SPURLOCK v. *UNITED AIRLINES*

475 F.2d. 215, 10th Cir., 1972.

Facts of the Case

The appellant Paul Spurlock, a black, brought this action alleging that United Airlines unlawfully discriminated against him because of his race in violation of Title VII of the Civil Rights Act of 1964.

The evidence established that on May 19, 1969, the appellant applied for the position of flight officer. At that time, appellant did not meet United's qualifications to be considered for flight officer. He was twenty-nine years of age, had two years of college, principally in music education, had logged 204 hours of flight time, and had obtained a commercial pilot's licence. United's minimum requirements for flight officer were 500 hours of flight time, twenty-one to twenty-nine years of age, a commercial pilot's license and instrument rating, and a college degree.

When appellant's application was received by mail in United's employment office, it was reviewed by a clerical employee. He circled in red the respects in which the appellant's qualifications were deficient. Appellant was then advised by letter that United had other applicants whose qualifications more nearly met United's requirements. No one at United saw or interviewed the appellant, and no one knew his race.

Argument for Spurlock

While it is important to examine the intent of a company charged with a Title VII violation, absence of discriminatory intent does not necessarily establish that the company's employment practices have no discriminatory *effect*. Title VII is aimed at the consequences of employment practices, not simply the motivation. Thus, when a plaintiff is claiming that the criteria used by a company in screening job applicants discriminate against a minority group, he need only establish that the use of such criteria has a discriminatory *result*. It is not necessary to prove a discriminatory intent but only that the discriminatory criteria were used deliberately, not accidentally.

In order to establish that United's flight officer qualifications resulted in discrimination against blacks, the appellant showed that out of the approximately 5,900 flight officers in United's employ at the time of the trial only 9 were blacks. Appellant contends that these statistics establish a prima facie case of racial discrimination. United claims that these bare statistics establish nothing unless accompanied by similar information as to the number of *qualified* black applicants for the flight officer position. The circuitousness of this bootstrap argument becomes obvious when one recalls that it is United's *qualifications* for flight officer that appellant claims are discriminatory against blacks. By showing the miniscule number of black flight officers in United's employ, the appellant established a prima facie case of racial discrimination in hiring practices. This is true even though it is clear from the record that United applied its employment criteria without regard to race or color.

Argument for United

Employment practices which are inherently discriminatory may nevertheless be valid if a business necessity can be shown. And pre-employment qualifications which result in discrimination may be valid if they are shown to

EXHIBIT 9-1 Failure Rate Relative to Flight Experience Among United Airlines Trainees (February 1965–April 1967)

Number of flight hours	*Number of trainees*	*Number of failures*	*Failure rate (%)*
200 or less	352	32	9
201–500	128	19	14
501–1,000	154	12	8
1,001–1,500	175	9	5
1,501–2,000	168	3	2
2,001–2,500	119	2	2
2,501–3,000	89	3	2
3,001–5,000	118	2	2
Total	1303	82	

be job-related. Thus, once the appellant had established a prima facie case of racial discrimination, the burden fell upon United to show that its qualifications for flight officer were job-related.

The two job qualifications that appellant challenges are the requirements of a college degree and a minimum of 500 flight hours. The evidence at trial showed that United does not train applicants to be pilots but instead requires that their applicants be pilots at the time of their application. It cannot seriously be contended that such a requirement is not job-related. United also showed through the use of statistics that applicants who have higher flight hours are more likely to succeed in the rigorous training program which United flight officers go through after they are hired (Exhibit 9-1).

The evidence also showed that because of the high cost of the training program, it is important to United that those who begin its training program eventually become flight officers.

With regard to the college degree requirement, United officials testified that it was a requirement which could be waived if the applicant's other qualifications were superior, especially if he had a lot of high quality flight time, that is, flight time in high speed jet aircraft. The evidence showed that United flight officers go through a rigorous training course upon being hired and then are required to attend intensive refresher courses at six-month intervals to ensure that all flight officers remain at peak performance ability. United officials testified that the possession of a college degree indicated that the applicant had the ability to understand and retain concepts and information given in the atmosphere of a classroom or training program. Thus, a person with a college degree, particularly one in the "hard" sciences, is more able to cope with the initial training program and the unending series of refresher courses than a person without a college degree.

When a job requires a small amount of skill and training and the consequences of hiring an unqualified applicant are insignificant, the courts should examine closely any pre-employment standard or criteria which discriminate against minorities. In such a case, the employer should have a heavy burden to demonstrate to the court's satisfaction that his employment criteria are job-related. On the other hand, when the job clearly requires a high degree of skill and the economic and human risks involved in hiring an unqualified applicant are great, the employer bears a correspondingly lighter burden to show that his employment criteria are job-related. The job of airline flight officer is clearly such a job. United's flight officers pilot aircraft worth as much as $20 million and transport as many as 500 passengers per flight. The risks involved in hiring an unqualified applicant are staggering. The public interest clearly lies in having the most highly qualified persons available to pilot airliners. The courts, therefore, should proceed with great caution before requiring an employer to lower his pre-employment standards for such a job.

SMITH v. *CITY OF EAST CLEVELAND*

520 F.2d. 492, 1975.

Elizabeth A. Smith, a 5-foot, 5-inch, 136-pound black woman, filed in district court a class action against the city of East Cleveland, charging that the city's use of minimum height and proportionate weight requirements in hiring its police officers unconstitutionally discriminated against her on the basis of sex.

The East Cleveland Administrative Code requires policy applicants to be at least 5 feet, 8 inches in height. City officials maintain that there is a relationship between the height of a police officer and physical strength, physical fitness, agility, ability to view crowds, ability to drive cars, arm reach, ability to absorb blows, and psychological advantage. Further, they claimed that forty-seven of forty-nine state highway patrols and police forces and twenty-nine of twenty-nine municipal police departments surveyed had height requirements ranging from 5 feet, 6 inches to 6 feet.

As a matter of policy, the city of East Cleveland has also followed certain weight guidelines or ranges to judge the fitness of an applicant. The 150-pound minimum weight requirement disqualified approximately 80 percent of the women, but only 26 percent of the men meeting the height requirement.

Plaintiffs contend that these requirements not only discriminate against women, but also discounted certain functions claimed to be related to height and weight because these functions actually took only a small portion of the average patrol officer's time, and because traffic-related matters accounted for more than three-fourths of the patrol officer's working time. In other words, they argued that the requirements were irrelevant to most of a police officer's actual job and thus not "bona fide occupational qualifications."

GREEN v. *MISSOURI PACIFIC RAILROAD*

523 F.2d 1290, 8th Cir., 1975.

Finding by Bright, Circuit Judge

The Missouri Pacific Railroad Company (MoPac) follows an absolute policy of refusing consideration for employment to any person convicted of a crime other than a minor traffic offense. Appellant Buck Green, who is black, raises the principal question of whether this policy violates Title VII of the Civil Rights Act of 1964, because this practice allegedly operates to disqualify blacks for employment at a substantially higher rate than whites and is not job related.

Green on his own behalf and as a class action filed this suit November 7, 1972, seeking declaratory and injunctive relief as well as back pay. The district court denied Green relief on his individual claim and that of the class. Green brings this timely appeal. We outline the undisputed facts.

On September 29, 1970, Green, then 29 years of age, applied for employment as a clerk at MoPac's personnel office in the corporate headquarters in St. Louis, Missouri. In response to a question on an application form, Green disclosed that he had been convicted in December 1967 for refusing military induction. He stated that he had served 21 months in prison until paroled on July 24, 1970. After reviewing the application form, MoPac's personnel officer informed Green that he was not qualified for employment at MoPac because of his conviction and prison record. Green, thereafter, sought relief under Title VII, and, when administrative conciliation failed, he brought this action.

Since 1948, MoPac has followed the policy of disqualifying for employment any applicant with a conviction for any crime other than a minor traffic offense.

Green makes the following contentions on this appeal: (1) MoPac's policy of not hiring any person convicted of a criminal offense has a racially discriminatory effect and violates Title VII; (2) this policy is not justified by any business necessity.

Although the employment practice in question is facially neutral, an employment test or practice which operates to exclude a disproportionate percentage of blacks violates Title VII unless the employer can establish that the practice is justified as a business necessity.

Initially, we note that the district court recognized statistical data offered into evidence by the plaintiff which indicate that blacks are convicted of crimes at a rate at least two to three times greater than the percentage of blacks in the populations of certain geographical areas. Dr. Ronald

Christensen, a qualified expert witness for the plaintiff, concluded that it is between 2.2 and 6.7 times as likely that a black person will have a criminal conviction record during his lifetime than that a white person will have such a record. He further concluded that in urban areas from 36.9 percent to 78.1 percent of all black persons would incur a conviction during their lifetimes, but that from only 11.6 percent to 16.8 percent of all white persons would acquire a conviction.

MoPac's records of employment applications at its corporate headquarters during the period from September 1, 1971, through November 7, 1973, disclose that 3,282 blacks and 5,206 whites applied for employment. Of these individuals, 174 blacks (5.3 percent of the black applicants) and 118 whites (2.23 percent of the white applicants) were rejected because of their conviction records. Thus, statistically, the policy operated automatically to exclude from employment 53 of every 1,000 black applicants but only 22 of every 1,000 white applicants. The rejection rate for blacks is two and one-half times that of whites under this policy.

Once a prima facie case of discrimination has been established, the defendants must show that the employment practice in question is justified by "business necessity."

MoPac proffers a number of reasons for claiming that its policy is a business necessity: (1) fear of cargo theft; (2) handling company funds; (3) bonding qualifications; (4) possible impeachment of an employee as a witness; (5) possible liability for hiring persons with known violent tendencies; and (6) alleged lack of normal character of persons with convictions.

STRAILEY v. *HAPPY TIMES NURSERY SCHOOL, INC.*

608 Federal Reporter, 2d Series, p. 327.

Strailey, a male, was fired by the Happy Times Nursery School after two years' service as a teacher. He alleged that he was fired because he wore a small gold ear-loop to school prior to the commencement of the school year. He then filed a suit on behalf of himself and all others similarly situated, seeking declaratory, injunctive, and monetary relief.

Argument for Mr. Strailey

Strailey contends that he was terminated by the Happy Times Nursery School because that school felt that it was inappropriate for a male teacher to wear an earring to school. He claims that the school's reliance on a stereotype—that a male should have a virile rather than an effeminate appearance—violates Title VII of the Civil Rights Act.

He also claims that in prohibiting certain employment discrimination on the basis of "sex," Congress meant to include discrimination on the basis of sexual orientation. He adds that discrimination against homosexuals disproportionately affects men and that this disproportionate impact and correlation between discrimination on the basis of sexual preference and discrimination on the basis of "sex" requires that sexual preference be considered a subcategory of the "sex" category of Title VII.

Argument for the Happy Times Nursery

On the other side it was argued that Congress had only the traditional notions of "sex" in mind when it enacted the Civil Rights Act. Later legislative activity makes this narrow definition even more evident. Several bills have been introduced to *amend* the Civil Rights Act to prohibit discrimination against "sexual preference." None have been enacted into law.

It was also noted that Congress has not shown any intent other than to restrict the term "sex" to its traditional meaning. Therefore,...the manifest purpose of Title VII's prohibition against sex discrimination in employment is to ensure that men and women are treated equally, absent a bona fide relationship between the qualifications for the job and the person's sex.

JOHNSON v. *TRANSPORTATION AGENCY, SANTA CLARA COUNTY, CALIFORNIA*

In 1978 the administrators of Santa Clara County, California, had it brought to their attention that the percentage of women on the county payroll was 14 percent lower than the area's labor market. In response they enacted a voluntary affirmative action program designed not only to correct this imbalance, but to move women into higher-level skill and salaried positions.

The plan was a voluntary action by the county even though there was no proven history of discrimination—they did it simply because there was evidence of a "manifest imbalance" in the number of women or minorities holding the positions in question. With regard to the skilled jobs, the county set a temporary goal of filling 36 percent of these jobs with women in an attempt to achieve a work force that mirrored the percentage of women in the area labor market.

Diane Joyce came to work for Santa Clara County in 1976. She worked for four years doing road work such as patching holes, shoveling asphalt, opening culverts, and so on, and in 1980 applied for a desk job as a dispatcher. Because women had not, previously to this time, applied for jobs directing the highway crews, all of the 238 workers employed there were men.

Paul Johnson, a white male with thirteen years of service in the agency, applied for a dispatcher's position at the same time as Diane Joyce. Johnson and Joyce were among seven applicants who scored above 70 on an oral exam. Joyce scored 73 and Johnson scored 75. The local supervisor picked Johnson based on his higher score, but the county's affirmative action coordinator recommended Joyce, and she was given the job. Johnson sued, claiming he was a victim of reverse discrimination.

Johnson's suit was based on Title VII of the Civil Rights Act, which makes it unlawful for an employer "to deprive any individual of employment opportunities or otherwise adversely affect his status as an employee because of such individual's race, color, religion, sex, or national origin."

Proponents of affirmative action contend that equality for all can be achieved only through temporary preferences given to blacks, women, and other groups that have historically suffered discrimination. Opponents argue that each individual has the right to be judged on merit. Setting special standards for blacks or women is demeaning and ultimately destructive, both to society and to those who are the intended beneficiaries.

ASSIGNMENT QUESTIONS

1. What are the threads or questions that tie these seven cases together?
2. Write down the following for each case:
   a. The basis for the alleged discrimination.
   b. The arguments for the potential or actual employee(s).
   c. The arguments for the company or municipality.
   d. A decision—as though you were the judge.
   e. The reasoning behind your decision.

3. Make a list of jobs in which employers should have the right (in your opinion) to discriminate on the basis of sex, religion, or national origin because the particular characteristic is a "bona fide occupational qualification."

10
KAISER ALUMINUM & CHEMICAL CORPORATION

443 U.S. 193.

The Facts of the Case

In 1974, the United Steelworkers of America and Kaiser Aluminum & Chemical Corporation entered into a master collective-bargaining agreement covering terms and conditions of employment at fifteen Kaiser plants. The agreement contained an affirmative action plan designed to eliminate conspicuous racial imbalances in Kaiser's then almost exclusively white craftwork forces. Black craft-hiring goals were set for each Kaiser plant equal to the percentage of blacks in the respective local labor forces. To enable plants to meet these goals, on-the-job training programs were established to teach unskilled production workers—black and white—the skills necessary to become craftworkers. The plan reserved for black employees 50 percent of the openings in these newly created in-plant training programs.

This case arose from the operation of the plan at Kaiser's plant in Gramercy, Louisiana. Until 1974, Kaiser hired as craftworkers for that plant only persons who had had prior craft experience. Because blacks had long been excluded from craft unions, few were able to present such credentials. As a consequence, prior to 1974 only 1.83 percent (5 out of 273) of the skilled craftworkers at the Gramercy plant were black, even though the work force in the Gramercy area was approximately 39 percent black.

Pursuant to the national agreement, Kaiser altered its craft-hiring practice in the Gramercy plant. Rather than hire already trained outsiders, Kaiser established a training program to train its production workers to fill craft openings. Selection of craft trainees was made on the basis of seniority, with the proviso that at least 50 percent of the new trainees were to be black until the percentage of black skilled craftworkers in the Gramercy plant approximated the percentage of blacks in the local labor force.

During 1974, the first year of the operation of the Kaiser-USWA affirmative action plan, thirteen craft trainees were selected from Gramercy's production work force. Of these, seven were black and six were white. The most senior black selected into the program had less seniority than did several white production workers whose bids for admission were rejected. Thereafter one of those white production workers, Brian F. Weber, instituted a class action suit in the United States District Court for the Eastern District of Louisiana.

Weber's complaint alleged that the filling of craft trainee positions at the Gramercy plant pursuant to the affirmative action program had resulted in junior black employees receiving training in preference to senior white employees, thus discriminating against Weber and other similarly situated white employees in violation of Sections 703(a) and (d) of Title VII of the Civil Rights Act of 1964.[1]

The District Court held that the plan violated Title VII, entered a judgment in favor of the plaintiff, and granted a permanent injunction prohibiting Kaiser and the USWA "from denying plaintiffs, Brian F. Weber and all other members of the class, access to on-the-job training programs on the basis of race." The decision was appealed, and a divided panel of the Court of Appeals for the Fifth Circuit affirmed, holding that all employment preferences based upon race, including those preferences incidental to bona fide affirmative action plans, violated Title VII's prohibition against racial discrimination in employment. The case was then appealed to the Supreme Court of the United States and was accepted for review.

Arguments for Kaiser and USWA

The only question before the court is the narrow statutory issue of whether Title VII forbids private employers and unions from voluntarily agreeing upon bona fide affirmative action plans that accord racial preferences in the manner and for the purpose provided in the Kaiser-USWA plan....

Respondent argues that Congress intended in Title VII to prohibit all race-conscious affirmative action plans. Respondent's argument rests upon a literal interpretation of Sections 703(a) and (d) of the Act. Those sections make it unlawful to "discriminate...because of...race" in hiring and in the selection of apprentices for training programs. Since, the argument runs, Title VII forbids discrimination against whites as well as blacks, and since the Kaiser-USWA affirmative action plan operates to discriminate against white employees solely because they are white, it follows that the Kaiser-USWA plan violates Title VII.

Respondent's argument is not without force. But it overlooks the significance of the fact that the Kaiser-USWA plan is an affirmative action plan voluntarily adopted by private parties to eliminate traditional patterns of racial segregation. In this context respondent's reliance upon a literal construction of Sections 703(a) and (d) is misplaced....It is a "familiar rule, that a thing may be within the letter of the statute and yet not within the statute, because not within its spirit, nor within the intention of its makers."...The prohibition against racial discrimination in Section 703 of Title VII must therefore be read against the background of the legislative history of Title VII and the historical context from which the Act arose....Examination of those sources makes clear that an interpretation of the sections that forbade all race-conscious affirmative action would: "bring about an end completely at variance with the purpose of the statute" and must be rejected...

Congress' primary concern in enacting the prohibition against racial discrimination in Title VII of the Civil Rights Act of 1964 was with "the plight of the Negro in our economy" 110 Cong. Rec. 6548 (1964) (remarks of Sen. Humphrey). Before 1964, blacks were largely relegated to unskilled and semi-skilled jobs....Because of automation the number of such jobs was rapidly decreasing....As a consequence, "the relative position of the Negro worker was steadily worsening. In 1947 the non-white unemployment rate was only 64 percent higher than the white rate; in 1962 it was 124 percent higher."...

Congress feared that the goals of the Civil Rights Act—the integration of blacks into the mainstream of American society—could not be achieved unless this trend were reversed. And Congress recognized that that would not be possible unless blacks were able to secure jobs "which have a future."...As Senator Humphrey explained to the Senate:

> What good does it do a Negro to be able to eat in a fine restaurant if he cannot afford to pay the bill? What good does it do him to be accepted in a hotel that is too expensive for his modest income? How can a Negro child be motivated to take full advantage of integrated education facilities if he has no hope of getting a job where he can use that education?

Accordingly, it was clear to Congress that "the crux of the problem [was] to open employment opportunities for Negroes in occupations which have been traditionally closed to them,"...and it was to this problem that Title VII's prohibition against racial discrimination was primarily addressed.

It plainly appears from the House Report accompanying the Civil Rights Act that Congress did not intend wholly to prohibit private and voluntary affirmative action efforts as one method of solving this problem. The Report provides:

> No bill can or should lay claim to eliminating all of the causes and consequences of racial and other types of discrimination against minorities. There is reason to believe, however, that national leadership provided by the enactment of Federal legislation dealing with the most troublesome problems *will create an atmosphere conducive to voluntary or local resolution of other forms of discrimination.*

Given this legislative history, we cannot agree with respondent that Congress intended to prohibit the private sector from taking effective steps to accomplish the goal that Congress designed Title VII to achieve. The very statutory words intended as a spur or catalyst to cause "employers and unions to self-examine and to self-evaluate their employment practices and to endeavor to eliminate, so far as possible, the last vestiges of an unfortunate and ignominious page in this country's history,"...cannot be interpreted as an absolute prohibition against all private, voluntary, race-conscious affirmative action efforts to hasten the elimination of such vestiges. It would be ironic indeed if a law triggered by a Nation's concern over centuries of racial injustice and intended to improve the lot of those who had been excluded from the American dream for so long,...constituted the first legislative prohibition of all voluntary, private, race-conscious efforts to abolish traditional patterns of racial segregation and hierarchy.

We need not today define in detail the line of demarcation between permissible and impermissible affirmative action plans. It suffices to hold that the challenged Kaiser-USWA affirmative action plan falls on the permissible side of the line. The purposes of the plan mirror those of the statute. Both were designed to break down old patterns of racial segregation and hierarchy. Both were structured to open employment opportunities for Negroes in occupations which have been traditionally closed to them.

At the same time, the plan does not unnecessarily trammel the interests of the white employees. The plan does not require the discharge of white workers and their replacement with new black hirees....Nor does the plan create an absolute bar to the advancement of white employees; half of those trained in the program will be white. Moreover, the plan is a temporary measure; it is not intended to maintain racial balance, but simply to eliminate a manifest racial imbalance. Preferential selection of craft trainees at the Gramercy plant will end as soon as the percentage of black skilled craftworkers in the Gramercy plant approximates the percentage of blacks in the local labor force.

We conclude, therefore, that the adoption of the Kaiser-USWA plan for the Gramercy plant falls within the area of discretion left by Title VII to the private sector voluntarily to adopt affirmative action plans designed to eliminate conspicuous racial imbalance in traditionally segregated job categories.

Arguments for Weber

In this case, the court is being asked to act contrary to the explicit language of the statute and arrive at this decision by means wholly incompatible with long-established principles of separation of powers. Under the guise of statutory "construction," the court is asked to rewrite Title VII to achieve what is described as a desirable result. It is asked to mend the statute to do precisely what both its sponsors and its opponents agreed the statute was *not* intended to do.

When Congress enacted Title VII after long study and searching debate, it produced a statute of extraordinary clarity, which speaks directly to the issue we consider in this case. In Section 703 (d) Congress provided:

> It shall be an unlawful employment practice for any employer, labor organization, or joint labor-management committee controlling apprenticeship or other training or retraining, including on-the-job training programs to discriminate against any individual because of his race, color, religion, sex, or national origin in admission to, or employment in, any program established to provide apprenticeship or other training.

Often we have difficulty interpreting statutes either because of imprecise drafting or because legislative compromises have produced genuine ambiguities. But, here, there is no lack of clarity, no ambiguity. The quota embodied in the collective-bargaining agreement between Kaiser and the steelworkers unquestionably discriminates on the basis of race against individual employees seeking admission to on-the-job training programs. And, under the plain language of Section 703(d), that is "an *unlawful* employment practice."

Oddly, our opposition seizes upon the very clarity of the statute almost as a justification for evading the unavoidable impact of its language. They blandly tell us that Congress could not really have meant what it said, for a "literal construction" would defeat the "purpose" of the statute—at least the congressional purpose as they divine it today. But how are judges supposed to ascertain the purpose of a statute except through the words Congress used and the legislative history of the statute's evolution?...Moreover...the legislative history makes equally clear that the supporters and opponents of Title VII reached an agreement about the statute's intended effect. That agreement, expressed so clearly in the language of the statute that no one should doubt its meaning, forecloses the reading which we are asked to give today.

Arguably, Congress may not have gone far enough in correcting the effects of past discrimination when it enacted Title VII. Gross discrimination against minorities—particularly against Negroes in the building trades and craft unions—is one of the dark chapters in the otherwise great history of the American labor movement. And I do not question the importance of encouraging voluntary compliance with the purposes and policies of Title VII. But that statute was conceived and enacted to make discrimination against *any* individual illegal, and I fail to see how "voluntary compliance" with the no-discrimination principle that is the heart and soul of Title VII as currently written will be achieved by permitting employers to discriminate against some individuals to give preferential treatment to others.

...If Congress had wanted to provide discriminatory preference for any group,...it could easily have drafted language allowing it. Far from doing so, Congress expressly *prohibited* the very discrimination against Brian Weber which the court is asked to approve. If "affirmative action" programs such as the one presented in this case are to be permitted, it is for Congress, not this court, to so direct.

Reading the language of Title VII against the background of its legislative history, and the historical context from which the Act arose, ...one is led inescapably to the conclusion that Congress fully understood what it was saying and meant precisely what it said. Opponents of the civil rights bill did not argue that employers would be permitted under Title VII voluntarily to grant preferential treatment to minorities to correct racial imbalance. The plain language of the statute too clearly prohibited such racial discrimination to admit of any doubt. They argued, tirelessly, that Title VII would be interpreted by federal agencies and their agents to require unwilling employers to racially balance their work forces by granting preferential treatment to minorities. Supporters of the Civil Rights Act responded, equally tirelessly, that the Act would not be so interpreted because not only does it not require preferential treatment of minorities, it also does not permit preferential treatment of any race for any reason. It cannot be doubted that the proponents of Title VII understood the meaning of their words, for seldom has similar legislation been debated with greater consciousness of the need for "legislative history" or with greater care in the making thereof, to guide the courts in interpreting and applying the law.

It is often observed that hard cases make bad

law. I suspect there is some truth to that adage, for the "hard" cases always tempt judges to exceed the limits of their authority, as the Court is asked to do today by totally rewriting a crucial part of Title VII to reach a "desirable" result. Cardozo no doubt had this type of case in mind when he wrote:

> The judge, even when he is free, is still not wholly free. He is not to innovate at pleasure. He is not a Knight-errant, roaming at will in pursuit of his own ideal of beauty or goodness. He is to draw his inspiration from consecrated principles. He is not to yield to spasmodic sentiment, to vague and unregulated benevolence. He is to exercise a discretion informed by tradition, methodized by analogy, disciplined by system, and subordinate to the "primordial necessity of order in the social life." Wide enough in all conscience is the field of discretion that remains. *The Nature of the Judicial Process*, 141 (1921)

What Cardozo tells us is beware the "good result," achieved by judicially unauthorized or intellectually dishonest means on the appealing notion that the desirable ends justify the improper judicial means. For there is always the danger that the seeds of precedent sown by good men for the best of motives will yield a rich harvest of unprincipled acts of others also aiming at "good ends."

ASSIGNMENT QUESTIONS

1. Summarize the facts in this case.
2. Outline the arguments for Mr. Weber.
3. What were the arguments for Kaiser Aluminum and USWA?
4. If you were on the Supreme Court, how would you vote in this case? Why?

NOTES

1. Section 703 (a), 78 Stat., as amended, 86 Stat. 109, 42 U.S.C. Section 2000-2 (a), provides:

   It shall be unlawful employment practice for an employer—

   (1) to fail or refuse to hire or to discharge any individual, or otherwise to discriminate against any individual with respect to his compensation, terms, conditions, or privileges of employment, because of such individual's race, color, religion, sex, or national origin; or

   (2) to limit, segregate, or classify his employees or applicants for employment in any way which would deprive or tend to deprive any individual of employment opportunities or otherwise adversely affect his status as an employee, because of such individual's race, color, religion, sex, or national origin.

   Section 703 (d), 78 Stat. 256, 42 U.S.C. Section 2000e-2 (d), provides:

   It shall be an unlawful employment practice for any employer, labor organization, or joint labor-management committee controlling apprenticeship or other training or retraining, including on-the-job training programs to discriminate against any individual because of his race, color, religion, sex, or national origin in admission to, or employment in, any program established to provide apprenticeship or other training.

11
THE KIDD COMPANY

Jennifer Andersen, after her graduation from UCLA, accepted a position as a management trainee with The Kidd Company, a Los Angeles–based firm involved in the design and manufacture of high-tech computer components. Organized in 1972, the company took great pride in its ultramodern manufacturing facilities and in a reputation for enlightened employment and personnel practices. The company operated a single-plant manufacturing facility and had approximately thirteen hundred employees.

Jennifer started out as an executive assistant in the Human Resources Department where she administered the company's affirmative action program. Company policy was that the makeup of the company work force should approximate the ethnic makeup of the community in which the plant was located and should have a proportion of male and female workers comparable to the percentages of both sexes in the general work force. Jennifer took pride in the fact that The Kidd Company was in the process of meeting its affirmative action goals. On the other hand, she was much disturbed over the fact that the enthusiasm that provided for ethnic and gender diversity in the manufacturing, technical, supervisory, and managerial staffs did not, in her opinion, extend to the compensation of individuals in those various groups.

Specifically, she felt that women working in what were traditionally female-dominated jobs within the company, such as secretaries and accounting clerks, were not being compensated fairly when compared with men working in traditionally male-dominated jobs, such as electronic technicians, computer operators, and draftsmen (called "drafters" by Jennifer). After some soul-searching, and a great deal of research, Jennifer concluded that the problem was of such importance that it was her responsibility to take some action to bring it to the attention of top management. Working mostly on her own time, she summarized her arguments for a formal comparable worth program in a memo she presented to her immediate superior, Henry J. Brown, along with a request that the material be forwarded up to the Executive Committee for consideration.

Memorandum

October 5, 1988

TO: Mr. Henry J. Brown
Manager, Human Resources Department

FROM: Jennifer Andersen
Executive Assistant

SUBJECT: Comparable Worth

The concept of "comparable worth" is now an important social, legal, and political issue facing many employers. Although the Supreme Court has not, as yet, issued a substantive ruling on the issue, advocates are pressing comparable worth class-action suits all over the country, and forward-thinking employers are developing programs that will solve this last area of blatant discrimination against their women employees.

Already, six states—Washington, Idaho, Minnesota, New Mexico, Iowa, and South Dakota—have adopted comparable worth laws. In addition, it is supported by feminist organizations, by politicians from both political parties, by labor unions attempting to include it in collective-bargaining agreements, and by enlightened businessmen attempting to anticipate future problems with their employees.

Some Definitions

"Comparable worth" is a system of resolving the problem of gender-based wage disparities based on the fundamental idea that every job has a determinable worth to the employer that can be measured and given a numerical value. This numerical value is based on things such as job skills required, physical effort needed, responsibility, and working conditions. Once jobs are assigned a numerical value, each job with the same value will receive equal pay—in other words, there will be equal pay for comparable worth.

In deciding what is comparable, other factors, such as market factors, will be deliberately disregarded. Thus, comparable worth is premised on the idea that workers should receive equal pay for *dissimilar* jobs where factors such as skill, effort, responsibility, and so on can be proven to be substantially equal or comparable. Therefore, the basic proposition underlying comparable worth is that it is possible to compare different jobs—even jobs that are totally dissimilar—and establish some kind of correct pay relationship between them. For example, in the suit against the state of Washington, the plaintiffs successfully paired clerk typists (usually women) with warehouse workers (usually men) and demonstrated that the two jobs were of comparable worth even though dissimilar and that there was no rational reason why they should have traditionally received significantly different levels of pay.

"Comparable worth" is not the same as "equal pay for equal work." Under the latter, an employer is required by law to pay equal wages to men and women who do the same or basically equivalent work. Thus, male secretaries should be paid the same as female secretaries, and female truck drivers should be paid the same as male truck drivers. The concept of comparable worth carries the idea of "equal pay for equal work" to its logical extension. It arises from the fact that some jobs are traditionally held by women—such as nurses, secretaries, retail clerks, and bank tellers—while other jobs—such as construction workers, truck drivers, and garbage collectors—are usually held by men. Further, women often receive lower pay in the traditional female jobs even though these jobs often require equal—or even greater—levels of skill, knowledge, responsibility, and so on than traditional men's jobs.

In summary, the comparable worth concept says that jobs which differ in work content may be comparable and should, therefore, be compensated for at the same rate. There should be equal pay for all employees—regardless of their gender—whose work is of equal value to this firm.

Arguments in Favor

It is a fact of life in the United States that women earn, on the average, less than two-thirds of what men earn. In addition, it is also true that very little progress has been made over the past twenty-five years in eliminating this disparity. Those who advocate comparable worth view it as the most efficient and effective method of dealing with this wage gap.

The first argument supporting comparable worth is the claim that there is a bias in wages and salaries paid to women. Not only do women fill a smaller percentage of managerial and administrative positions compared to men, but there also appears to be a pervasive and systematic undervaluation of work done by women that is not only accepted but really unquestioned. It exists in every industry, every occupation, and every profession—even in those dominated by female employees.

The second argument for comparable worth is that it really is possible to develop and apply methods by which the monetary value of various kinds of work can be measured and compared. In fact, techniques have been designed which allow for us to provide not only objective but dependable comparisons of the necessary requirements for different jobs.

The third argument has to do with the cost of implementation. Some businessmen claim that the cost of eliminating sex-based wage differentials will be prohibitively expensive to implement. These critics forget that only about 30 to 40 percent of the male-female earnings gap is due to discrimination. Nondiscrimination factors, such as female preference for part-time work, make up the balance. Also, no one has seriously suggested that we eliminate these pay inequities overnight. It will undoubtedly be a long and tedious process.

To sum up, I believe that comparable worth is an ideal that we should, as a company, adopt on its merits. It makes not just economic sense, but moral sense for the wages that we pay to be a reflection of the intrinsic value of the jobs performed. It can provide a standard that eliminates sex bias and compares wages on the basis of relevant, compensable factors.

Suggested Components of a System

Job Analysis. The fundamental core of any job evaluation system is the development of functional job descriptions. The person who knows most about a particular job is, of course, the person performing that job, so the most accurate job descriptions are obtained by interviewing employees. There are numerous guides for obtaining this kind of information through interviews by asking the following kinds of questions:

1. What do you actually do?
2. What are your most difficult duties?
3. What special skills are necessary?
4. What experience is required?
5. What special independent judgment is required to do your job?
6. What is the consequence if you make an error?
7. With whom do you interact?
8. What particular physical skills or effort is required?
9. What unusual working conditions exist?
10. Do you have supervisory responsibility?

Job Evaluation. Although it is not scientifically exact, job evaluation can be a valid method of establishing the relative value of

Job Classifications	Knowledge	Experience	Judgment	Independence	Accountability	Inter-relationships	Physical Skills	Environment	Physical Effort	Physical Risks	INDEX
Electronic Technician	30	16	15	12	14	8	6	8	8	6	123
Secretary	30	16	18	14	14	14	6	2	4	2	120
Computer Operator	24	24	15	16	14	12	6	2	4	2	119
Drafter	24	24	15	12	14	8	6	4	6	2	115
Maintenance Worker	18	24	12	8	11	6	6	8	12	8	113
Accounting Clerk	24	24	15	14	14	8	6	2	4	2	113

EXHIBIT 11-1 The Kidd Company: Job Evaluations

a wide variety of positions within an organization. For The Kidd Company I recommend the establishment of a Job Evaluation Committee composed of seven members representing the Production, Engineering, Marketing, Data Processing, Secretarial, Maintenance, and Accounting departments, with a chairperson chosen by the group. The ongoing function of the group will be to develop and maintain a system by which each of the job evaluation elements can be applied to the jobs in our company. For example, Exhibit 11-1 illustrates how this system could be applied to our own company.

EXHIBIT 11-2 The Kidd Company: Comparative Pay Rates

	Maximum Pay Rates	*Job Evaluation Index*	*Suggested Revised Rates*
Electronic technician	$8.87	123	$8.88*
Secretary	8.34	120	8.66
Computer operator	9.19	119	8.59
Drafter	8.34	115	8.30
Maintenance worker	8.11	113	8.16
Accounting clerk	7.91	113	8.16

$$^{*}\ \frac{\text{Sum of pay rates}}{\text{Sum of index nos.}} = \frac{\$50.76}{703} = \$.07219 \times 123 = \$8.88$$

With the job evaluation index in hand, we can then compare the maximum salaries that should be paid to the actual salary schedule currently operative within our company as shown in Exhibit 11-2.

The third column lists suggested maximum pay scales for each of the job positions illustrated. It is obvious from the data that female-dominated jobs, such as secretary and accounting clerk, are relatively underpaid and that male-dominated positions, such as computer operator and drafter, are relatively overpaid. Assuming that the company decides to implement comparable worth as an official policy, changes will have to be implemented slowly, since it will obviously be difficult to make radical pay rate changes overnight.

Many critics of comparable worth might suggest that the plan I have developed will have a serious impact on the profitability of our business. What they lose sight of is the fact that for the past half-century, wage and salary programs in companies of all sizes have had the same objectives as those who now propose the ideal of comparable worth. In spite of the prophets of doom, the principle of comparable worth can be absorbed within our current systems with only minor disruptions. I hope that you will take this proposal under serious consideration.

Memorandum

October 15, 1988

TO: Mr. Charles J. Ellerbee
President

FROM: Henry J. Brown
Manager,Human Resources
Department

SUBJECT: Comparable Worth Proposal

Enclosed you will find a copy of a memorandum recently submitted to me by Jennifer Andersen, an executive assistant/management trainee working in my department. She has asked that her memo be forwarded to you and to the Executive Committee, and I am doing so. Along with Jennifer's paper, I am also enclosing the following comments, which express my own opinion on the value of the comparable worth concept and how it would fit into our company.

The best place to start to examine the comparable worth issue is to consider the reasons for gender-based differences in pay. It is, of course, well accepted that women earn, on the average, about 60 percent as much as men. What should not be forgotten, however, is that there are legitimate reasons why this difference exists. Some of these reasons are

1. Women make up a larger portion of the part-time work force than do men, and this condition seems to be increasing. Since employers believe that the costs of part-time employment are higher than for full-time employment, and since there is a lower commitment on the part of the part-time employee, they usually have less job security and usually earn less than full-time workers.
2. Women tend to reject higher-paying jobs that have less desirable working conditions. As a group they prefer not to work surrounded by high temperatures, noise, or dirt or to accept positions where job requirements include heavy lifting, rotating shifts, or seven-day operation. For a variety of reasons, women tend to prefer weekday work, fixed shifts, light lifting, and pleasant work surroundings.
3. Women tend to reject some jobs out of hand, based on their perceptions of job requirements, even though there is no real reason why they could not perform well and even though the pay is better than jobs dominated by female workers.
4. Women, in general, have different external responsibilities than do men, spending more time with children and on home management, and because of this may be less flexible regarding working hours and other job demands.
5. Men and women often approach employment careers with different motivations. A man with little motivation, minimal attachment to his company, and with little interest in his job, may seek advancement because he needs the money to feed his family. On the other hand, a highly motivated woman with an excellent performance record and high aspirations may not accept a promotion because her husband is being transferred or her young children need her attention.
6. One of the crucial differences between employment patterns of men and women is continuity of employment. It is common for women to enter the work force for a few years and then withdraw for an extended period while their children are in their younger years. When they return to the work force, their real wages at reentry are usually lower than at withdrawal, and the reduction is greater the longer the interruption. The amount of the decline in wages has been calculated at 3.3 to 7.6 percent per year of absence from work.[1]
7. Women may earn less because of the occupations they choose. When they choose traditional "female jobs" such as teaching, nursing, and clerical and service work, they encourage the wage disparity to continue. If more women were to set their sights on higher-paying "nontraditional" jobs and acquire the skills needed to land them, this would help reduce the earnings difference.
8. Women may earn less than men because they have less education than men. Over 22 percent of all male workers have a college de-

gree, as compared to 17.5 percent of all female workers. This will change in the future, because among persons age 18 to 24, a larger proportion of women than men are enrolled in college.[2] For the present, though, the educational differential does remain an important contributing factor.

9. Women earn less than men because they are, on the average, less experienced and therefore less productive.
10. Women earn less than men because of an excess supply of women flooding the job market.
11. Finally, women earn less than men because men tend to belong to stronger and more aggressive labor organizations.

EXHIBIT 11-3 Job Worth Points as a Percentage of Points Assigned to Electricians

	WI	*IA*	*MN*	*WA*
Electrician	100	100	100	100
Licensed practical nurse (LPN)	150	124	79	108
Dental assistant	108	77	50	73
Telephone operator	91	64	49	60
Data entry operator	55	72	43	63

Source: Association of Washington Business, "Comparable Worth in the Private Sector: A Debate," *Pacific Northwest Executive*, July 1985, p. 22.

Difficulties in Implementation

Those who advocate comparable worth base its implementation on extensive use of job evaluation systems. The goal is to present objective comparisons of the skills, effort, and responsibilities required by vastly different jobs. The problem is that a totally objective plan for comparing and valuing dissimilar jobs—one which lacks bias and can be applied in the real world—just does not exist.

Any evaluation system necessarily involves subjective judgment in both its creation and application. There are no universally accepted standards of measurement, and experts differ among themselves about which factors should be measured and how many points should be assigned to each. This can be illustrated in Exhibit 11-3, which shows how various job evaluators rated five jobs differently in four different states—Wisconsin, Iowa, Minnesota, and Washington.

The chart shows that Minnesota rated LPNs lower than electricians while the other three states rated them higher—in the case of Wisconsin, considerably higher. Similar significant differences are seen in the case of dental assistants.

This chart points out the main illusion of comparable worth—that the different skills, working conditions, and responsibilities of jobs—can be expressed in formulas. They can't. The consequence is that it leads us to ask the wrong questions. The right question is not: Do we pay women's (or men's) jobs enough? But, rather, Do we pay enough for specific jobs to get qualified workers. If not, we need to determine what combination of higher salaries and qualifications is needed.

Comparable worth cannot be implemented fairly in the workplace because it is subjective and vague in concept with few objective guidelines, and because it is highly dependent upon the point of view of the job evaluator in comparing vastly dissimilar jobs.

Those who advocate comparable worth have a fundamental misunderstanding of how the labor markets function. Indexes developed from job evaluation systems do not tell us anything about the labor market, which can be capricious and highly localized. Even if two jobs were judged to be equal, one job might be difficult to fill and the other flooded with applicants. For example, in the Wisconsin state government, a legal secretary is paid $14,800 and a public defender investigator (level 3) $20,600. The experimental job evaluation system, however, rates the jobs as almost equal, even though 92 percent of the investigators are men and 100 percent of the secretaries are women. To eliminate "sex bias," the recommendation is to hike the legal secretaries salary 33 percent to $19,600.[3]

This sort of approach, which is similar to the one proposed for our company, assumes that it is as easy to hire secretaries as it is law school graduates—which is probably just not true. Again, the right question to ask is: What do we have to pay in order to get the quality of workers we need in each job position?

In conclusion, we would have chaos if comparable worth ever became an official policy of this company. Not only would it increase our labor costs, but both labor and management would be forced to abdicate their functions. Decisions we now make based on productivity, profitability, and the interaction of supply and demand would now be made by bureaucrats operating under an illusion of mathematical precision. Wage inequities between the sexes is not, in the final analysis, a problem that lends itself to solution by decree.

ASSIGNMENT QUESTIONS

1. Summarize the arguments of those who advocate comparable worth as a policy for the Kidd Company.
2. Outline how the system would work; the steps that would be taken.
3. Summarize the arguments of those who oppose comparable worth.
4. With which argument do you agree? Why?
5. If you disagree with comparable worth, what would you propose to do about the problem of sex-based discrimination in the workplace?

NOTES

1. Jacob Miner and Haim Ofek, "Interrupted Work Careers: Depreciation and Restoration of Human Capital," *Journal of Human Resources*, Vol. XVII, no. 1 (Winter 1982).
2. Sherri Miller, "The Incomparable Problems of Comparable Worth," *Consumers' Research*, October 1984, and Arthur Padilla, "The Economics and Politics of Comparable Worth," *North Carolina Review of Business and Economics* (Spring 1985) 9.
3. Robert J. Samuelson, "The Myths of Comparable Worth," *Newsweek*, April 22, 1985, p. 57.

12
THE PACIFIC CORPORATION

The Corporation

The Pacific Corporation is a large national conglomerate with factories and offices in many states of the union. Organized in 1927 as a construction company specializing in highway and parking lot work, the company expanded into a variety of areas following World War II, including electronics manufacturing, a chain of auto supply stores, and a large wholesale chicken processing plant. The geographical location of the company's various operations, although spread throughout the country, tend to be located in the American west.

The president and chief executive officer of the company is John T. Stevens, who has been with the Pacific Corporation for thirty-two years. Stevens ascended to the presidency on the retirement of Oscar R. Fredericks—who was elevated to chairman of the board. Stevens and Fredericks stay in close contact with each other and consult frequently on matters relating to the formulation of corporate policy. Their relationship can best be described as "amiable," and both have a strong interest in making sure that their company is viewed by their employees and by the public as socially responsible. In particular, they have made a concerted effort to manage Pacific so that it is a good place to work. The company had what amounted to an affirmative action program before federal legislation established that obligation, and management takes pride in the fact that women and minority group members have risen to positions of significant responsibility within the corporation.

The Petition

September 14, 1988

Mr. John Stevens, President
The Pacific Corporation
Oakland, California

Dear Mr. Stevens:

The following are employees of the National Chicken Processing Company, a division of your corporation.

It has come to our attention that one of our fellow employees, Frank Forbes, has been diagnosed as suffering with AIDS. In spite of his illness, he continues to come to work on a more or less regular basis to work in the accounting department of the company. We are aware of the fact that AIDS can be transmitted through a variety of ways and that, once it has been passed on, it is universally fatal.

We do not think it reasonable that we should have to work in a facility where the danger of a deadly and highly infectious disease is present. Accordingly, we are asking you by this petition that Mr. Forbes be separated from the company permanently so that none of us will be in danger from his presence.

We sincerely hope that it will not be necessary for us to take any kind of concerted action, such as work stoppage or some legal act, in order to solve this problem. We thank you for your assistance and hope that you can work out this difficulty to the satisfaction of all.

Signed by (following are 247 names)

____
____
____

The Letter

LAWYERS FOR THE AMERICAN WAY
Oakland, California

Mr. John T. Stevens
The Pacific Corporation
Oakland, California

Dear Mr. Stevens:

Mr. Frank Forbes, an employee of your National Chicken division, has asked us to represent him in the event that an action is necessary because of the discriminatory conduct of some of your employees.

As you no doubt know by now, Mr. Forbes is suffering from the initial stages of AIDS. Fortunately, he is able to work most of the time and is very anxious that he keep employed as long as he can while undergoing treatment.

I am sure that you know that it is not possible to contract AIDS through casual social contact and that your employees are under absolutely no danger from the continued employment of Mr. Forbes. He would appreciate it very much if official notice of your support for Mr. Forbes in his time of need, and of your unwillingness to bow to the uninformed opinions of bigots, could be stated officially under your letterhead and sent to him through our offices.

We would appreciate your prompt attention to this matter.

Sincerely,

G. W. Sawyer

The Memo

THE PACIFIC CORPORATION
Oakland, California

TO: Oscar R. Fredericks
President

FROM: John T. Stevens
Chairman

SUBJECT: Policy on AIDS

I have enclosed copies of two letters I recently received that present a problem that needs to be solved by the Board. I would strongly suggest that in addition to taking some kind of action with regard to Mr. Forbes, the Board should formulate a written policy to deal with future employees who might contract the AIDS virus.

Good luck on this....It's a tough one!

JTS

P.S. I had my executive assistant work up a package of materials on the subject of AIDS. It's enclosed. You might find it interesting and helpful.

jts/osb

The Package

THE PACIFIC CORPORATION
Oakland, California

TO: Mr. John T. Stevens
President

FROM: Iris R. Hansen
Executive Assistant

SUBJECT: Material on AIDS

Summary

In considering a policy on AIDS, it is best, I believe, to start out with the scientific facts. The following is based on the best information currently available:

1. AIDS is caused by a virus, usually called HIV.
2. The AIDS blood test is a test for antibodies to the virus and is a measure of whether a person is or is not infected. People who test positive are AIDS carriers. It is extremely unlikely that any person testing positive for the antibodies is not infected.
3. People who have the virus are infected for life. The virus integrates its genetic material into the genetic material of millions of human cells and remains. Someday there may be a medical treatment to control this infection, but there is little likelihood that there will ever be one to eliminate it.
4. The virus passes from human to human through (a) sexual intercourse, (b) the mixing of blood, or (c) from a mother to a child in the womb.
5. People can be infected for years with the virus with no symptoms. We are not sure the exact percentage of infected people that will eventually get sick from the virus, but it will likely vary from 50 to 100 percent.
6. No one knows when someone else who is infected is capable of infecting another person.

The enclosed "Scrapbook of AIDS Information" presents a summary of current information on the problem, including projections of the future course of the disease, and comments on the possibilities for an ultimate cure. Please let me know if I can provide any additional information.

AIDS Bulletin 1: Facts That Show It Affects You

INFECTION WITH THE HIV VIRUS IS A DEFINITE PREREQUISITE TO developing disease symptoms, although the incubation period for the development of either AIDS or ARC varies between 6 months to an indefinite number of years, probably 10–20.

DEATH AND/OR SUFFERING OCCURS BECAUSE OF OPPORTUNISTIC DISEASES which flourish in the absence of a healthy immune system.

HIV INFECTION IS PERMANENT, WITHIN INFECTED INDIVIDUALS, AND IN the population. No known, or foreseeable technique will remove the virus from the human body; therefore, this disease will never be eradicated. It is only possible to minimize the spread of infection. A cure seems as distant as a cancer cure.

HEALTH IMPLICATIONS OF BEING SEROPOSITIVE TO THE HIV VIRUS ARE increasingly alarming as statistics are accumulated. (Seropositive means that your blood contains antibodies to the AIDS virus because you have been exposed to this virus.) It is estimated that 57% of all seropositive people will develop AIDS, ARC, or another significant opportunistic disease within 15 years. The percentage rises with every new year's statistic. IT IS NOT KNOWN WHY SOME PEOPLE ARE MORE RESISTANT TO BECOMING SYMPTOMATIC; THEREFORE IT IS WISEST TO TAKE PRECAUTIONS AS IF INFECTION IS SYNONYMOUS WITH EVENTUAL DEVELOPMENT OF A LIFE-THREATENING DISEASE.

FACTORS STATISTICALLY CORRELATED WITH PROMOTING THE ONSET OF AIDS or ARC symptoms in seropositive people include incubation time, reexposure to HIV (therefore even two seropositive people need to practice safe sex), pregnancy, repeated stimulation of the immune system by any foreign antibodies, and possibly age.

INFECTION STATISTICS ARE STAGGERING. THE JANUARY 18, 1988, CDC AIDS publication reports that there are 50,000 AIDS CASES IN THE U.S., with 400 NEW AIDS CASES BEING REPORTED EACH WEEK. The World Health Organization estimates that 100,000 people IN THE WORLD will develop AIDS in 1988 and that 5–10 million people are seropositive. This figure seems exceedingly low since there are 70–100 seropositive people for every AIDS case. In the U.S. alone, the calculations are, therefore, 3.5–5 MILLION AMERICANS MAY BE ESTIMATED TO BE SEROPOSITIVE....The CDC article further states that the number of AIDS cases in the U.S. increased 58.5% over the increase in 1986.

Dr. Lynne Osman Elkin, professor of Biological Sciences, California State University, Hayward. Distributed by the CSUH AIDS Coordinating Committee.

A SCRAPBOOK OF AIDS INFORMATION

A Short History of Killer Illnesses

With the latest evidence suggesting that AIDS cases will be doubling every year, AIDS will soon take its place as one of the great plagues of history. The others have been truly terrible:

The Black Death. This plague killed from 25 to 50 million Europeans—from a quarter to a half of the population—in one three-year period ending in 1350. The Black Death, or bubonic plague, was spread to its victims through the air and through flea bites. The fleas picked up the germ from the millions of rats that lived among the filth in the city streets. Eventually, some of those who had become sick recovered and developed an immunity to the disease. As this segment of the population grew, fewer people became infected, and the plague eventually died down.

Smallpox. Smallpox racked Europe for centuries until a vaccine was found in 1796. After a vigorous inoculation campaign in Asia during the 1970s, the World Health Organization announced in 1979 that the disease had been wiped out.

Influenza. The flu epidemic of 1917–18 killed 500,000 Americans, and at the pace it was spreading, would have entirely wiped out civilization in a matter of weeks. Like the Black Death, people recovered from it and became immune.

Typhus. This epidemic originated in the crowded and dirty prison camps and refugee centers established in conjunction with World War I. Over 3 million people died before the conditions supporting its spread disappeared and the disease ran its course.

Polio. The polio epidemic killed some 22,000 Americans by paralysis and respiratory failure and infected some 400,000 others during its peak from 1943 to 1956. Children were forbidden by their parents from swimming in public pools, and attempts were made to quarantine entire communities. After the discovery of a vaccine in 1955 by Jonas Salk, polio all but vanished in the United States. It is still a problem in some Third World countries.

Syphilis. Like other sexually transmitted diseases, syphilis ravaged humankind for many centuries until the discovery and wide application of penicillin in the late 1940s. Even today, there is a wide variety of sexually transmitted diseases afflicting a substantial number of Americans—most of which respond to medical treatment. Syphilis itself continues to be a serious problem in the less developed parts of the world.

The uniqueness of AIDS becomes obvious when it is compared to these killer diseases of history. Unlike these diseases, AIDS is difficult to contract. Unlike the Black Death, it is not spread through the bite of an insect. Unlike smallpox, it is not spread through skin contact. Unlike influenza, it is not spread by airborne coughs and sneezes. Unlike typhus, it is not spread through contaminated food or water. Similar to syphilis in that it is transmitted through sexual contact, AIDS is unique in that it has the capacity to decimate whole populations. Since there is no evidence to suggest that AIDS will die out on its own, it is probable that if an AIDS vaccine is not developed within the next decade, the worldwide death toll could be in the tens of millions before the turn of the century.

Current Statistics

- AIDS has been reported in eighty-five countries, although it may have actually struck in over one hundred countries.[1]
- Some officials estimate that 10 million people around the world now carry the AIDS virus.[2]
- Blacks and Hispanics are twice as likely as whites to be ravaged by AIDS.[3]

- AIDS is a particularly difficult disease for minorities. Because they are poorer, they are less able to handle the heavy medical expenses attached to it, and as a consequence their health deteriorates more quickly. The average life expectancy of a Black or Hispanic with AIDS is as little as nineteen weeks after diagnosis, compared with two years for a white person.[4]
- In the future, AIDS is likely to become a pandemic—that is, a disease that by its sweep and scope has gone beyond an epidemic.[5]
- In the United States, about one in every thirty men between the ages of twenty and fifty, may already carry the virus.[6]
- More than 1 million Americans are thought to be infected with the virus, and more than 90 percent of them do not know it.[7]
- To date, most victims of AIDS have been drug users and homosexuals; however, there are indications that the disease has begun to spread among the heterosexual population. In 1982, only 12 percent of the women who contracted AIDS had received it through sexual activity—this had increased to 26 percent by 1986. The future course of the disease seems to be that it will increasingly be spread through heterosexual relations.[8]
- One frightening aspect of AIDS that is seldom mentioned is "AIDS dementia"—dementia meaning "a condition of deteriorating mentality, even madness or insanity." Recent studies of the brains of AIDS patients after death showed that 50 percent of them had sustained severe damage to the central nervous system that could be traced directly to AIDS-related viruses. Another estimate made by researchers at the Sloan-Kettering Cancer Center concludes that nearly 90 percent of AIDS patients will exhibit signs of dementia before they die.[9]
- Many experts believe that AIDS deaths are seriously underreported because of the social stigma attached to the disease. Instead of putting "AIDS" on the death certificate, the attending physician may put "viral encephalitis" to spare the family. The Center for Disease Control statisticians believe that this underreporting may come up to at least 10 percent of the total.[10]
- A recent study conducted by the San Francisco AIDS Foundation presented some discouraging conclusions. In spite of the fact that the city's homosexuals are well educated about AIDS, the 50 percent most at risk—those with an average of four to five sex partners a year—have not been convinced to alter their sexual habits. Two-thirds of them do not even feel threatened by AIDS.[11]
- A long-term study of the wives of hemophiliacs who became infected with AIDS through blood products suggests that the longer people carry the virus, the more contagious they become.[12]
- Statistics on the AIDS epidemic are kept by the Center for Disease Control, an agency of the federal government located in Atlanta. Exhibits 12-1 through 12-5 illustrate the type of public reporting done by the CDC and also support the conclusion that the AIDS problem is serious and growing.

Exhibit 12-1 AIDS Weekly Surveillance Report—U.S. AIDS Program—CDC, as of February 2, 1987 (U.S. cases reported to CDC)

A. TRANSMISSION CATEGORIES	*MALES CUMULATIVE*		*FEMALES CUMULATIVE*		*TOTAL CUMULATIVE*	
	NUMBER	*(%)*	*NUMBER*	*(%)*	*NUMBER*	*(%)*
Adults/Adolescents						
Homosexual/bisexual male	19,634	70%			19,634	66%
Intravenous (IV) drug user	4,048	15	1,051	51%	5,099	17
Homosexual male and IV drug user	2,318	8			2,318	8
Hemophilia/coagulation disorder	248	1	6	0	254	1
Heterosexual cases	574	2	563	27	1,137	4
Transmission, blood/components	363	1	201	10	564	2
Undetermined	721	3	232	11	953	3
Subtotal, % of all cases	27,906	93%	2,053	7%	29,959	100%
Children						
Hemophilia/coagulation disorder	22	9%	1	0%	23	5%
Parent with/at risk of AIDS	172	73	177	88	349	80
Transfusion, blood/components	34	14	18	9	52	12
Undetermined	8	3	5	2	13	3
Subtotal, % of all cases	236	54%	201	46%	437	100%
Total, % of all cases	26,142	93%	2,254	7%	30,396	100%

B. TRANSMISSION CATEGORIES BY RACIAL/ETHNIC GROUP	*WHITE NOT HISPANIC CUMULATIVE*		*BLACK NOT HISPANIC CUMULATIVE*		*HISPANIC CUMULATIVE*		*TOTAL CUMULATIVE*	
	NUMBER	*(%)*	*NUMBER*	*(%)*	*NUMBER*	*(%)*	*NUMBER*	*(%)*
Adults/Adolescents								
Homosexual/bisexual male	14,529	80%	2,854	39%	2,055	48%	19,634	66%
Intravenous (IV) drug abuser	943	5	2,595	35	1,528	36	5,099	17
Homosexual male and IV drug user	1,493	8	509	7	301	7	2,318	8
Hemophilia/coagulation disorder	218	1	14	0	17	0	254	1
Heterosexual cases	137	1	848	12	147	3	1,137	4
Transfusion, blood/components	433	2	88	1	32	1	564	2
Undetermined	334	2	408	6	190	4	953	3
Subtotal, % of all cases	18,087	60%	7,316	24%	4,270	14%	29,959	100%
Children								
Hemophilia/coagulation disorder	15	17%	5	2%	3	3%	23	5%
Parent with/at risk of AIDS	40	46	216	90	90	85	349	80
Transfusion, blood/components	29	33	13	5	10	9	52	12
Undetermined	3	3	7	3	3	3	13	3
Subtotal, % of all cases	87	20%	241	55%	106	24%	437	100%
Total, % of all cases	18,174	60%	7,557	25%	4,376	14%	30,396	100%

EXHIBIT 12-2 AIDS Weekly Disease Report—U.S. AIDS Program—CDC, 1981–1987 (2-2-87) (Cases of AIDS and case-fatality rates by half-year of diagnosis, United States)

		Number of Cases	*Number of Known Deaths*	*Case-Fatality Rate*
1981	Jan.–June	84	76	90%
	July–Dec.	177	159	90
1982	Jan.–June	360	312	87
	July–Dec.	634	547	86
1983	Jan.–June	1,201	1,023	85
	July–Dec.	1,570	1,302	83
1984	Jan.–June	2,390	1,878	79
	July–Dec.	3,139	2,392	76
1985	Jan.–June	4,260	2,926	69
	July–Dec.	5,271	3,002	57
1986	Jan.–June	6,049	2,490	41
	July–Dec.	5,092	1,159	23
1987	Jan.–Feb.	95	9	9
Total		30,396	17,338	57

AIDS Cases by Standard Metropolitan Statistical Area (SMSA) of Residence, 1987

SMSA of Residence	*Cumulative Total*
New York, NY	8,763
San Francisco, CA	3,086
Los Angeles, CA	2,586
Houston, TX	934
Miami, FL	901
Washington, DC	819
Newark, NJ	735
Chicago, IL	670
Philadelphia, PA	536
Dallas, TX	496
Atlanta, GA	468
Boston, MA	455
Nassau-Suffolk Cty, NY	376
Ft. Lauderdale, FL	340
Jersey City, NJ	339
Rest of United States	8,892
Total	30,396

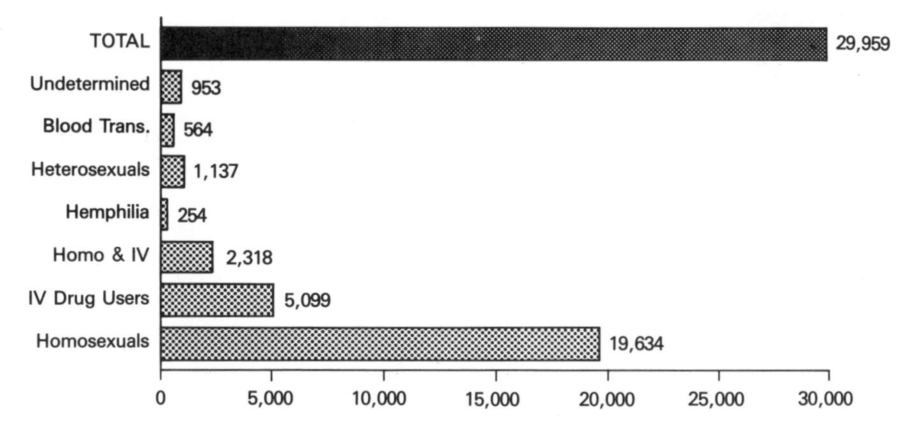

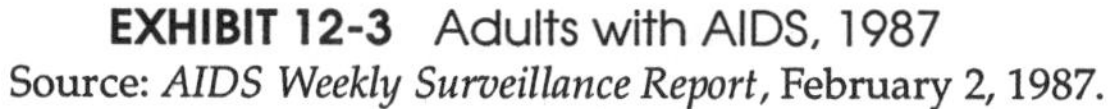
EXHIBIT 12-3 Adults with AIDS, 1987
Source: *AIDS Weekly Surveillance Report*, February 2, 1987.

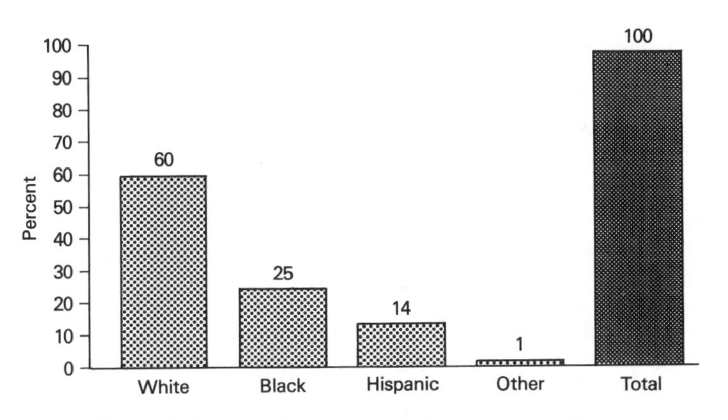

EXHIBIT 12-4 AIDS by Racial Groups, 1987
Source: *AIDS Weekly Surveillance Report*, February 2, 1987.

EXHIBIT 12-5 AIDS Case Fatality Rates, 1981–1987

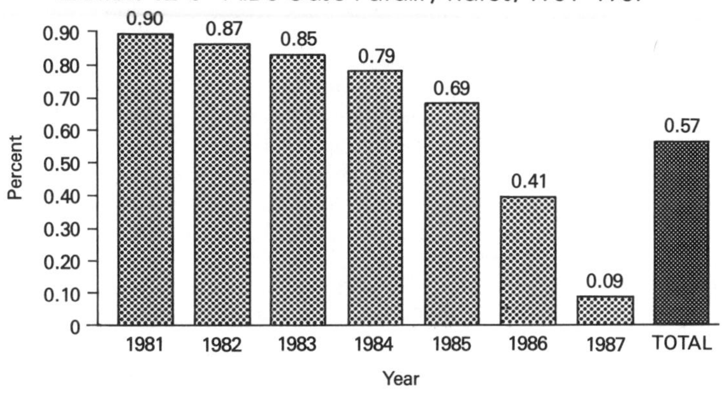

Source: *AIDS Weekly Surveillance Report*, February 2, 1987.

Future of AIDS

- AIDS is no longer just a disease afflicting homosexuals or drug users. There are at least 1.5 million carriers of the virus in the United States and each one puts his or her sex partners at risk. This fact has led many to express concern that the epidemic may soon be "breaking out" into the heterosexual community. By even the most conservative estimates, most experts agree that by 1991, AIDS will be one of the worst epidemics in U.S. history.[13]
- When AIDS first appeared, it was estimated that only about 10 percent of those who contracted the virus would eventually progress on to the disease. We now know that it has a dormant period of anywhere from four years to life and that up to 50 percent of those with the virus will die. Some researchers believe that unless a cure is developed, *all* of those exposed will eventually die.[14]
- According to some estimates, 100 million people could have the virus by the end of the century.[15]
- As AIDS spreads through our society, those who are afflicted will not be able to disguise the fact. The wasting away of the body, the lesions and spots on the skin, will quickly mark them as having the disease. If it is true that a significant percentage of our population will become incapacitated within 20 years, we could develop two societies—those who have it and those who don't.[16]
- U.S. Surgeon-General C. Everett Koop has compared AIDS with the Black Death, the bubonic plague that killed about 30 percent of the Western European population within a few years in the middle of the fourteenth century. To some, this comparison has seemed a bit hysterical; after all, there are only about 30,000 diagnosed AIDS victims in the United States today out of a total population of around 240,000,000. But bear the following in mind: between 1 and 2 million persons are carrying the virus that causes AIDS: once someone contracts the virus, it doesn't go away, and of those having the virus, 50 percent or more may eventually develop AIDS. If the present doubling rate keeps up (the number of AIDS victims doubles every eighteen months or so), millions will have the disease by the year 2000, and tens of millions will be carrying the lethal virus. So Dr. Koop is right on target when he makes his comparison with the Black Death. Unless things change drastically, a considerable fraction of the population of the United States will be killed off by AIDS in the next twenty-five years.[17]
- Health and Human Services Secretary Otis Bowen in a recent speech before the National Press Club stated that earlier epidemics such as typhus, smallpox, and even the Black Death will "look very pale by comparison" to AIDS.[18]
- The Center for Disease Control reported that three female health care workers had apparently become infected after a single exposure to AIDS-contaminated blood. The three cases described by the CDC were among the first involving exposure to blood *without* a needle prick; all three women, however, had breaks in their skin that could have allowed the virus to enter. In one instance, a health worker was infected with the AIDS virus when a vacuum-sealed test tube accidentally popped open and splashed blood into her face and mouth. CDC officials speculate that the AIDS virus may have passed through mucous membranes in her mouth. The second victim, an emergency room nurse, applied pressure for 20 minutes with her chapped and ungloved hands to a site where a catheter had been removed from an artery. The third woman, who was also not wearing gloves, was operating a blood separation machine that broke, splashing blood over her hands and forearms. She told investigators that she had an ear inflammation, which she may have touched before washing up.

WASHINGTON. Federal health officials now project that at least 450,000 Americans will have been diagnosed with AIDS by the end of 1993, and that as many as 100,000 new cases will be reported in that year.

The estimates represent the first major revisions in two years of the nation's projected AIDS caseload and are the first to extend the original Public Health Service figures beyond the 270,000 people expected to develop AIDS by 1991....said one official...with the present system these trends could mean the demise of the public hospitals in the United States....

In addition to predicting the future incidence of the disease, officials attempted to address many of the epidemic's most vexing problems. Scientists who presented the most recent data on vaccine research continued to call a vaccine a distant solution at best for the crisis.[19]

- Gradually, over the years, AIDS will begin to touch many aspects of our lives—our marriage rites, our sexual habits, our health care, and our insurance protection. Soon, most of us will know somebody who has died of AIDS. Our children will grow up in a different world, one where AIDS is an important part of everyone's life.

Costs to Society

- The estimated cost to take care of a single AIDS patient—between the time when he or she contracts the virus until death—varies depending upon who is doing the estimating, but the most recent studies suggest that it is somewhere in the vicinity of $150,000.
- By 1991 AIDS medical bills could total as much as $14 billion annually and that does not begin to address the losses in productivity from the deaths of people who die from AIDS in the prime of life.[20]

A Cure

- There is no cure for AIDS. The afflicted person is almost always dead within two years of diagnosis. The best estimate for a cure is that we should not expect much within the next ten years. Prospects for a vaccine are no better.
- Scientists report that AIDS is caused by two, or perhaps three, similar viruses, and that they have a previously unencountered tendency to mutate. This means that future forms of the disease might be transmitted with a greater or a lesser degree of difficulty—it could even become aerobic and as easy to catch as the common cold. These possibilities provide another strong reason for the rapid development of a vaccine or cure.[21]

ASSIGNMENT QUESTIONS

1. In your opinion, how much at risk from AIDS is the typical citizen?
2. How much a threat is AIDS to our society?
3. Should the government take any steps to protect society from those infected by the AIDS virus? What steps? Why or why not?
4. Who should pay for the treatment of AIDS victims?
5. With regard to the Pacific Corporation,
   a. How significant is the AIDS threat to the company's employees?
   b. How would you deal with the AIDS protest group?

c. Would you develop a policy statement to handle the problem? If so, what would the policy be?

6. What would *you* do if you found out that a fellow worker had AIDS?
7. In your opinion, what rights does an AIDS-afflicted person have with regard to employment, education, social activities, and so on?
8. How would you respond to the following statement: "AIDS is a self-inflicted disease. If people would behave themselves, the disease wouldn't spread. Because of this fact, I don't feel any obligation to grant special privileges or help to those who have contracted it."

NOTES

1. "You Haven't Heard Anything Yet," *Time*, February 16, 1987, p. 54.
2. Ibid., p. 54.
3. "The Uneven Odds," *U.S. News & World Report*, August 17, 1987, p. 31.
4. Ibid., p. 32.
5. "AIDS: At the Dawn of Fear," *U.S. News & World Report*, January 12, 1987, p. 60.
6. *Time*, June 15, 1987, p. 57.
7. "The Big Chill: Fear of AIDS," *Time*, February 16, 1987, p. 51.
8. Donald R. Ross, "Risk and Reality," *Vital Speeches of the Day*, July 14, 1987, p. 681.
9. "AIDS: Attacking the Brain," *U.S. News & World Report*, September 7, 1987, p. 48.
10. "AIDS," *U.S. News & World Report*, January 12, 1987, p. 63.
11. Ibid., p. 68.
12. "The Problem with Testing," *Newsweek*, June 15, 1987, p. 60.
13. Mortimer B. Zuckerman, "AIDS: A Crisis Ignored," *U.S. News & World Report*, January 12, 1987, p. 76.
14. Ross, *Risk.*, p. 682.
15. *Time*, June 15, 1987, p. 57.
16. "Myths," *U.S. News & World Report*, January 12, 1987, p. 67.
17. David R. Carlin, Jr., "Not by Condoms Alone," *Commonweal*, March 13, 1987, p. 32.
18. *Time*, February 16, 1987, p. 54.
19. "450,000 with AIDS by 1994," *Tri Valley Herald* (Dublin, California), June 6, 1988, p. 6.
20. *Time*, February 16, 1987, p. 54.
21. Ross, *Risk*, p. 682.

13
WELFARE FACTS

1. A person is poor if he or she falls into the category defined as such. The 1987 guidelines began at $5,500 a year for a single person and increased by $1,900 for each additional person in the family. Thus the poverty threshold for a family of four is $11,200.[1] The poverty index is based solely on money income and does not reflect the fact that many low-income persons receive noncash benefits such as food stamps, Medicaid, and public housing.

   According to the Census Bureau, 32.4 million Americans (or 13.6 percent of the population) lived in poverty in 1986, a statistically insignificant drop from the 33.1 million figure recorded in 1985 and about equal to the decline from the previous year.[2]

2. How much does the federal government spend each year to assist the poor and disadvantaged? The most visible program, Aid to Families with Dependent Children, reaches 11 million Americans and costs $17 billion in 1985. It also triggers automatic eligibility to receive Medicaid, which runs another $41 billion. When fifty-seven additional programs—including food stamps ($13 billion) and Supplemental Security Income ($12 billion)—are added, total welfare spending is more than $140 billion a year.[3]

3. The small drop in the poverty rate compared with a significant increase in median family income in 1986. The $29,460 figure was 4.2 percent higher than the 1985 median after adjusting for an inflation rate of 1.9 percent.[4]

4. Income distribution among American families in 1986 was as follows:[5]

Upper one-fifth of all families received 46.1 percent of total income.

Middle three-fifths of all families received 50.2 percent of total income.

Lowest one-fifth of all families received 3.8 percent of total income.

5. In 1986, 69 percent of those officially designated as poor were white, up from 66 percent in 1979. Whites accounted for 81 percent of the net increase in the poverty population between 1979 and 1985.[6]

6. Of the 10.1 million Americans who lost their jobs, owing to plant dislocations and a slack economy, between 1981 and 1986, nearly a third were still unemployed at the end of the

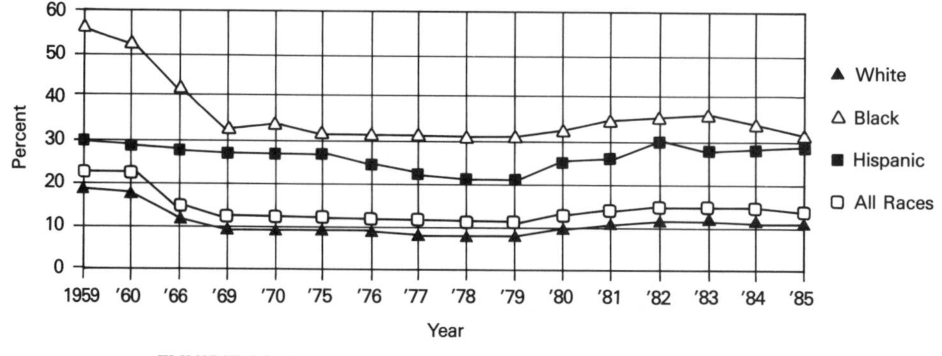

EXHIBIT 13-1 Persons Below Poverty Level, 1959–1985
Source: U.S. Bureau of The Census, *Current Population Reports*, Series P-60, no. 152-4.

period—and more than 30 percent were working at new jobs for 80 percent or less of their previous salaries. A tenth held part-time jobs only.[7]

7. Some 41.3 percent of all poor people over the age of 14 had a job in 1986. The "working poor" are the fastest-growing segment of the poverty population—8.9 million in 1986 compared with 6.5 million in 1979. The number of full-time, year-round workers who are poor has increased from 1.36 million in 1976 to 2.0 million in 1986.[8]
8. Children constitute 13.6 percent of all those in poverty. In 1986 20.5 percent of all American children, and almost a quarter of those under 6 years of age, lived below the poverty line.[9]
9. Funding for low-income programs over the Reagan years has decreased from $62.8 billion to $38.1 billion, a drop of 54 percent. This includes an 81 percent cut in subsidized housing, a 68 percent cut in training and employment services, and a 47 percent reduction in housing assistance for the elderly.[10]
10. According to a Census Bureau analysis, the number of Americans living in poverty may be as much as 11.5 million lower than previously reported. The bureau's study included the value of noncash federal assistance such as food stamps, and thereby reduced the number of officially poor people, in 1985, from 30.4 million to 21.5 million—reflecting a poverty rate of about 9.1 percent.[11]
11. What we have built is a Poverty Pentagon, the principal beneficiaries of which are not the poor but those who make their living from the poor. In New York City, the Community Service Society (a hundred-year-old social work agency) has examined how monies intended to meet the needs of that city's 1.4 million poor people (or one-fifth of its population) were actually spent. The study found that of the $14.5 billion spent on the poor in 1983 in the City of New York, 74 cents of every single dollar went to the service industry; only 26 cents was spent on the poor for rent, clothes, and other items of personal choice.[12]
12. One of the yardsticks by which the success of any society is measured is the manner in which it cares for its citizens who are least able to care for themselves. In this country, people of all political persuasions agree that government must assume some responsibility for improving the lives of our weakest members.
13. Exhibit 13-1 traces the levels of poverty in the total population and among various racial groups in the United States over the past quarter century.

ASSIGNMENT QUESTIONS

1. How much does the federal government spend, per capita, on helping the poor?

2. Does the government spend enough? What should it spend? For whom should it be expended?
3. Do business managers have any responsibility in aiding those below the poverty line? If yes, what should they do? If not, why not?
4. What do you think is your personal obligation to help those who are less fortunate?

NOTES

1. Wilbur J. Cohen, "Federal Poverty Guidelines Need Updating," *Los Angeles Times,* May 19, 1987, Sec. II, p. 5.
2. *The New York Times,* July 31, 1987, p. 8.
3. Ibid., p. 8.
4. Ibid., p. 8.
5. Ibid., p. 8.
6. *The New York Times,* November 19, 1987, p. 31 (L).
7. Ibid., p. 31.
8. Ibid., p. 31.
9. Ibid., p. 31.
10. *Washington Post,* February 1, 1988, p. A13.
11. *The Wall Street Journal,* October 3, 1986, p. 50.
12. Robert L. Woodson, "Saving the Poor from Their Saviors," *BYU Today,* February 1986.

14
MOTOROLA, INC.

The Motorola Corporation was founded in 1928, and for a period in the 1950s and 1960s was a major manufacturer of premier-quality television sets. Millions of Americans were happy owners of Motorola's big Quasar color consoles, and the company was contemplating competing successfully in the Far East and other foreign markets and had even built plants in Japan and Taiwan.

In 1974, as Japanese dumping in the United States and other markets cut into the business of all American television producers, Matsushita Electric (marketing under Panasonic, Technics, and other brand names) approached Motorola with an offer to purchase its Japanese TV manufacturing facilities. As a consequence, in March 1974, Matsushita bought Motorola's Japanese television manufacturing interests for $100 million, and Motorola agreed to retire from TV manufacturing, turning over its Japanese plant and closing its plants in Taiwan and the United States. Motorola received a sizable sum for a part of its business that had grown to be only marginally profitable and turned to other areas of electronics technology.

By 1982, Motorola, with sales of $6.7 billion, was fighting Texas Instruments to become the world's number one producer of semiconductors. Over the next five years, however, in something of a repeat of the company's experience as a television manufacturer, Japanese producers entered the semiconductor market and, competing both legally and illegally, began to eat into Motorola's market share. Between 1982 and 1987, while Motorola's sales of semiconductors rose from $1,219,000,000 to $2,450,000,000, its share of the worldwide market declined from 29 percent to 18 percent.[1]

Compounding its difficulties, Motorola's other electronic businesses—from modems to cellular phones—were under siege from foreign competitors. One highly profitable division in particular, the Pager Division, was under pressure from Japanese companies illegally dumping their products in the American market.

Other Causes of Motorola's Decline

In addition to fierce competition from abroad, the symptoms of Motorola's illness were twofold. The first was an uneven quality of products: although many products were well designed, many of these were poorly manufactured or assembled.

The second symptom was poor relations with its customers. Customers complained about delays in deliveries and about employees who were generally unresponsive to their needs. Customers claimed that they had difficulty in getting the simplest questions answered, and some compared dealing with Motorola with dealing with the federal government.

There were multiple causes for these symptoms, but the most important were the following:

1. *Poor-Quality Production Workers.* Many of Motorola's workers were deficient in reading and math abilities. At a time when assembly-line workers in Japan were often able to read computer manuals written in English, Motorola was facing the same problem other American companies faced—workers who were not only culturally illiterate but who couldn't perform basic mathematical functions and were unable to read above the most rudimentary level in their own language.
2. *Lack of Internal Communication.* Because marketing and production were frequently moving in different directions, products often had to be redesigned or new production had to be postponed until all the snafus could be cleared away.
3. *Inefficient Production Lines.* In addition to the marginal ability of the average production worker, the supervision and administration of production was wanting. The consequence of this was a high level of defects in finished products and the added expense of repairing and reassembling them.

ASSIGNMENT QUESTIONS

1. Suppose you have been chosen as the new chief executive officer of Motorola. What steps would you take to turn the company around? In particular, how would you improve the quality of the work force? Be specific.
2. How much is the American school system responsible for the problems American companies have in obtaining well-educated, highly motivated workers? What changes would you recommend in our educational system to prepare American youth more effectively for life in the computer age?
3. Assume that some of your classmates are cultural illiterates. What can *they* do to improve their knowledge of the world not only so that they might be able to earn a living, but so that their lives might be richer?

NOTE

1. *Business Week,* June 1, 1988, p. 80.

15
CONFIDENTIAL MEMORANDUM

TO: All Field Sales Personnel
FROM: C. R. Smith, General Sales Manager
The ElectroVac Vacuum Cleaner Company
SUBJECT: Improving Sales Performance

Declining sales for the past two quarters indicate that it is time we reviewed the basic sales techniques that have made this company the most successful in the field of direct house-to-house selling of vacuum cleaners. Remember that these techniques have enabled some of our salespeople to earn as much as $100,000 a year. We encourage you to follow them closely.

Hints to Improve Your Sales Techniques

1. *At the door.* Knock firmly if there is no bell. When the lady of the house comes to the door, take one step back. This will assure her that you are sincere and that you are not trying to "get your foot in the door." Explain that your primary purpose is not to sell cleaners, but to demonstrate it to "selected opinion leaders" in the neighborhood so that people can learn of its superior qualities.

   If she seems reluctant to invite you in, explain that you are new with the company and that you are required to demonstrate to a certain number of homes in order to keep your job. Although the success of this strategy will depend on your ability to convince her of your need "just to show it," many of our veteran salespeople have used this strategy successfully for years.
2. *The demonstration.* Once inside, with the equipment out and assembled, be sure and imply that the carpet "has apparently not been vacuumed yet today." Act surprised when told that it has been—comment that her old vacuum cleaner must not be working properly because (as she will see) the ElectroVac will release the dirt hidden within the carpet. Demonstration will always pull some dirt from even the cleanest carpet and should convince the housewife that the rug really isn't as clean as it should be.

If she is still not convinced, spread some of our special vacuum compound on the rug and demonstrate again. This compound is especially formulated to be picked up by a vacuum cleaner and will provide a dramatic demonstration.

3. *The regular close.* Ninety-nine out of a hundred housewives will admit after the demonstration that the ElectroVac does clean better than their old cleaner. With firm agreement on this point, make out the order form and ask "How much would you like to pay down?" At the same time, hand her the form and indicate the place where she must sign to confirm the order. Many prospects will sign at this point—once you have their signature, you can negotiate about the details.
4. *Alternative closes.* If the housewife resists signing with some comment about not being able to afford the machine, or not wanting to have any more monthly payments, use the following alternative closes in the order listed.
   a. *The health close*—Ask "Isn't the health of your family important?" When she responds affirmatively, say "Then you certainly will want to have a clean home, and the ElectroVac can help you do that more than anything else."
   b. *The small daily cost close*—Stress that payments are "only about 30 cents a day—I'm sure you spend more than that on things that don't improve the welfare of your family."
   c. *The "summer camp" close*—If she still resists, change your attitude from that of an interested friend to that of the poor salesman struggling to get along. Something on the order of the following might be appropriate: "Look, I'll level with you. The real reason I need this sale is that I have to get two more orders (or one, or three, or whatever seems to fit) to earn a trip to Florida for my wife and myself. My mother is living there, and in poor health and I want to see her one more time." This close can be varied to fit any circumstances that seem reasonable, but it should sound plausible.
5. *The trade-in.* Do not, repeat, do not talk about trade-ins until the prospect has signed on the dotted line. If she brings it up before that, make every effort to change the subject.

   When the subject is brought up *after* the sale is closed, ask her: "You wouldn't give me much for your old cleaner when it cleans as poorly as it does, would you?" If she agrees, offer her $5 just to take it off of her hands—you can usually make an extra $10 to $15 on the trade-in if this strategy works. If she insists on some kind of "fair" trade-in (she may have a relatively new machine), get out the blue book and show her the listed price. Since this price is low wholesale price, you will do well if she is willing to settle for it. In any case, the margin on the new sale will allow you considerable leeway in dickering on the old machine.

   One final point. Some salespeople are able to use the trade-in as a tool to close the sale of the new machine. Don't be afraid, as a last resort, to jack up the prices of both the new machine and the trade-in—if you think it might help to make the sale.

Remember that the achievement of a sale under unfavorable odds is the most exciting thing a salesperson can do, and I can guarantee you rewards both financially and in self-esteem if you will follow the outline suggested.

Good luck,

Charlie

ASSIGNMENT QUESTIONS

1. Do you object to the "confidential memorandum"? Why?
2. Defend the right of the sales manager to issue instructions such as those contained in the memo.
3. Should anything be done about this type of sales technique? What? By whom?

16
SEARS, ROEBUCK AND CO.

THE STIFFEL COMPANY, PLAINTIFF-APPELLANT
SEARS, ROEBUCK AND CO., DEFENDANT-APPELLEE

United States Court of Appeals, Seventh Circuit
January 23, 1963

376 U.S. 225 (1964).

The Appeal Court

Finding by Kiley, Circuit Judge

This is a patent infringement and unfair competition suit. Defendant answered that the patents in suit were invalid and that defendant was not guilty of unfair competition, and its counterclaim sought declaratory judgment accordingly. The District Court found the patents invalid, but found defendant guilty of unfair competition. From the judgment on these findings, each party has appealed.

The patents in suit are Stiffel Patent No. 2,793,286 and Stiffel Design Patent No. 180,251, both relating to floor to ceiling "pole lamps." The patents were issued to Theophile Stiffel in May 1957, and subsequently were assigned to plaintiff. The lamp was first shown to the public in 1956. Plaintiff learned from a Sears, Roebuck and Co. catalog in 1957 that pole lamps were being sold by Sears. It purchased a Sears lamp in Greensboro, North Carolina, and this suit followed.

The Stiffel pole lamp consists of a plurality of detachable tubular members of small diameter, joined together to form a single pole longer than the distance between floor and ceiling of a room. It carries three lamps, with swivel brackets, on the exterior of one of the sections. The lamps are served by wires "extending interiorly" down through and out the lower section of the pole. In use it is supported between floor and ceiling under compression of a spring contained in the uppermost section. The upper and lower ends are small round felt or rubber discs to protect ceiling and floor. The lower disc is at the end of an adjustable leg for making fine adjustments to the length of the pole.

The District Court found that the Stiffel pole lamp was anticipated in the prior act more than one year prior to the Stiffel patent application in January 1956, by Sears' public use and sale of the Deca pole lamp; and in printed publications. The question is whether the court erred in concluding, on these findings, that Stiffel Patent No. 2,793,286 is invalid.

The findings underlying the conclusion have substantial basis in the admitted use of the Deca poles by Sears in 1953 and 1954, and the evidence of their published illustrations, sketches and descriptions more than one year prior to the Stiffel patent application, and were sufficient to overcome the presumption of validity of the patent. We hold the conclusion of invalidity of Patent No. 2,793,286 is not clearly erroneous.

The Deca pole included all the essential elements of the Stiffel except the adjustable leg. Instead of the adjustable leg, the Deca pole employed an equivalent, i.e., sections of various lengths for adjusting height. The court was not required to find on the evidence that the adjustable leg was novel or was functionally different than the various sized sections of Deca pole which served the same purpose. This is also true of the Stiffel spring unit and the Deca pole sliding section and spring which have the same effect. And there is substantial evidence that Deca pole had the wire run "extended interiorly" within the pole.

The District Court's conclusion of invalidity of Design Patent No. 180,251 rests on findings that the Deca pole does not differ in ornamental design aspects from the Stiffel patented design, and that the Miller "lamp tree" was disclosed in several magazines in 1950 and 1954. Plaintiff challenges this conclusion.

The design patent claims only "the ornamental design for a lighting fixture as shown." The finding with respect to the Miller "lamp tree" anticipating the Stiffel design has sufficient support in the evidence of the disclosure of the lamp tree in printed publications. The finding is not clearly erroneous, and we need not therefore discuss the finding. We hold the conclusions of the invalidity of Design Patent No. 180,251 is not erroneous.

Because the District Court's conclusions with respect to the patents are not erroneous, it follows that the court did not err in its conclusion of noninfringement.

There is substantial basis in the evidence to support the findings underlying the conclusion that Sears was guilty of unfair competition. The evidence is: The lamp had a decided impact on the market in 1956 as something revolutionary in lighting fixtures. In four years (1956–1960) Stiffel shipped about $3,250,000 in pole lamps. They were widely advertised in national magazines. Sears "moved in" when they saw the Stiffel pole lamp was moving toward a mass market. Sears lamps are not labeled, and the Sears lamp retails at the wholesale price of the Stiffel lamp.

The Stiffel pole lamps and that of Sears made from a copy of a picture of the Stiffel lamp are before us as exhibits. A comparison of the two gives substantial support for the finding that the lamps have a remarkable sameness of appearance. And there is testimony of buyers for Marshall Field and Company and John M. Smyth Company of customer confusion. The finding that there is a likelihood of confusion and some actual confusion, as to the source of the lamps, is not clearly erroneous. The conclusion of unfair competition, based on the finding, is not erroneous.

SEARS, ROEBUCK AND CO. v. *STIFFEL COMPANY*

Certiorari to the United States Court of Appeals for the Seventh District
No. 108. Argued January 16, 1964—Decided March 9, 1964

The Supreme Court

Mr. Justice Black delivered the opinion of the Court:

The question in this case is whether a State's unfair competition law can, consistently with the federal patent laws, impose liability for or prohibit the copying of an article which is protected neither by a federal patent nor a copyright. The respondent, Stiffel Company, secured design and mechanical patents on a "pole lamp"—a vertical tube having lamp fixtures along the outside, the tube being made so that it will stand upright between the floor and a ceiling of a room. Pole lamps proved a decided commercial success, and soon after Stiffel brought them on the market Sears, Roebuck and Company put on the market a substantially identical lamp, which it sold more cheaply, Sears' retail price being about the same as Stiffel's wholesale price. Stiffel then brought this action against Sears in the United States District Court for the Northern District of Illinois, claiming in its first count that by copying its design Sears had infringed Stiffel's patents and in its second count that by selling copies of Stiffel's lamp Sears had caused confusion in the trade as to the source of the lamps and had thereby engaged in unfair competition under Illinois law. There was evidence that identifying tags were not attached to the Sears' lamps although labels appeared on the cartons in which they were delivered to customers, that customers had asked Stiffel whether its lamps differed from Sears', and that in two cases customers who had bought Stiffel lamps had complained to Stiffel on learning that Sears was selling substantially identical lamps at a much lower price.

The District Court, after holding the patents invalid for want of invention, went on to find as a fact that Sears' lamp was "a substantial exact copy" of Stiffel's and that the two lamps were so much alike, both in appearance and in functional details, "that confusion between them is likely, and some confusion has already occurred."

On these findings the court held Sears guilty of unfair competition, enjoined Sears "from unfairly competing with Stiffel by selling or attempting to sell pole lamps identical to or confusingly similar to" Stiffel's lamp, and ordered an accounting to fix profits and damages resulting from Sears' "unfair competition."

The Court of Appeals affirmed. That court held that, to make out a case of unfair competition under Illinois law, there was no need to show that Sears had been "palming off" its lamps as Stiffel lamps; Stiffel had only to prove that there was a "likelihood of confusion as to the source of the products"—that the two articles were sufficiently identical that customers could not tell who had made a particular one. Impressed by the "remarkable sameness of appearance" of the lamps, the Court of Appeals upheld the trial court's findings of likelihood of confusion and some actual confusion, findings which the appellate court construed to mean confusion "as to the source of the lamps." The Court of Appeals thought this enough under Illinois law to sustain the trial court's holding of unfair competition, and thus held Sears liable under Illinois law for copying and marketing an unpatented article.

ASSIGNMENT QUESTIONS

1. What were the issues under determination in this case?
2. Present a summary of the arguments put forth by the Stiffel Co.
3. What were the answering arguments on behalf of Sears?
4. How did the Court of Appeals decide? Why?
5. If you were a justice of the Supreme Court, how would you rule on this case? Why?

17
THE ALLEN COOKIE COMPANY

After working twenty-three years for the Amalgamated Baking Corporation, Truman Allen fulfilled the dream of many blue-collar workers by starting his own business. His available capital consisted of $7,800 he had put aside in U.S. Savings Bonds and $53,000 left to him by his mother's favorite uncle, Uncle Fred, who had been a successful dress shop owner.

After some searching, Mr. Allen located an ideal building for his purposes in a rundown section of town. The building was very large and very ugly—it had not been painted for years—and was surrounded by single-story houses populated largely by black and Spanish-speaking families. Since his capital was limited, Truman concentrated on essential machinery and office furnishings and did not make any exterior cosmetic improvements. He hired six production workers and a secretary and began to turn out cookies.

In truth, the Allen Cookie Company did not make high-quality cookies. Mr. Allen liked to describe his products as "good cookies for the money." He sold them not under his own name, but through large grocery and drug chains under a number of house brands. One of the company's best sellers was a sealed bag of mixed cookies sold widely throughout the area under titles such as "Family Pack" and "Jumbo Variety Pack."

As a series of successful years marked the solid position of his company in the cookie business, Truman gradually added lines of new products. He produced marshmallow-filled pink puff balls, chocolate-covered graham crackers, and mediocre-quality, semisweet animal crackers usually purchased by parents to keep their kids quiet in the supermarket. After eight years in the business, Mr. Allen had seventy-four employees, three new cars, and a 5,400-square-foot home in the exclusive High Point section of the city. That year, he took his wife on a six-week vacation to Europe.

In the spring of 1988, Mr. Allen's only son, Arlo, took a course entitled "Business Ethics and Social Responsibility" offered by the Political Science Department at Las Remos Community College. Greatly excited by his newfound knowledge, Arlo talked with his father about activities at the Allen Cookie Company. In particular, he was interested in "what the company was doing for society." "Dad," he said, "if you're going to be a good citizen as well as a businessman, you have to be socially responsible. What are you doing about your obligation to 'the people'?"

In quiet moments during the following weeks, Mr. Allen mulled over his son's concerns. After lengthy consideration, he had developed the following ideas:

Paint his building. This would improve the looks of the neighborhood and might encourage others to clean up and paint their places.

Hire some Spanish-speaking workers. At the moment, all his employees were either black or white. Mr. Allen was perfectly willing to hire the Spanish speaking, but had considered the language barrier to be insuperable.

Give money to poor people in the surrounding neighborhood. He didn't know how he would implement this idea, and had rejected it about as fast as he had thought of it.

Support a Little League team. Not only would this be relatively inexpensive, but the company name on the uniforms would provide a bit of advertising.

Only make high-quality cookies. Arlo had also been preaching a lot about the importance of quality products as well as social responsibility.

Truman discussed the problem one night with Charlie Rich, his shop foreman, and got this answer: "Why can't we just make cookies? Why do we have to worry about all this other stuff?"

Mr. Allen's problem was eventually solved by Mrs. Allen. She had recently (in particular, after their trip to Europe) developed a strong interest in classical music and was able to persuade her husband to make a sizable contribution to the Metropolitan Symphony. This contribution made Mr. and Mrs. Allen sponsors of the orchestra, and their names were listed on the concert programs together with a select number of other heavy contributors. He did have an argument with her about whether the contribution should be listed in their name or in the company name—he was thinking of more advertising—but her tearful, nearly hysterical reaction to his suggestion made him forget the notion.

As he accompanied his wife to the symphony week after week, Truman's initial lack of interest gradually changed to complete and total boredom. He tried to read a book during one concert, but his wife gave him a look that discouraged that kind of activity. Forced to listen to the music, Mr. Allen finally concluded that his boredom was caused by the kind of music they were playing. Now and then he would hear something familiar that he actually liked, but most of the time it was pretty bad. One "modern symphonic tone poem" sounded and looked like a bunch of lunatics running around hitting indiscriminately on xylophones.

He finally concluded that since he was giving a lot of money to the organization, he ought to have some say regarding the kind of music they would play. Accordingly, on one Monday morning, after a particularly unsatisfactory Saturday night concert, he dictated a letter to the chairman of the symphony board in which he stated that any future contributions from him would be dependent upon whether or not the orchestra played some music that he personally liked and approved of. He listed the following suggestions:

1. The orchestra should not play music composed by Communists. Given the nature of the Cold War, the playing of Communist music is not patriotic.
2. Part of the year's concert series should be given over to light programs such as those offered by the Boston Pops.
3. The orchestra should play some marches once in a while. "There is nothing like a rousing march by John Philip Sousa."
4. Celebrity guest conductors—like Johnny Cash or Merv Griffin—would make an evening with the symphony interesting and a lot of fun.

ASSIGNMENT QUESTIONS

1. Evaluate Mr. Allen's attempts to be socially responsible.
2. If you don't like what he did, what would you have him do?
3. What is the social responsibility of business?
4. To what groups are business managers responsible? (stockholders? employees? customers? neighbors? society? who?)
5. How does social responsibility fit in with obedience to the law, environmental concerns, product quality, minority rights, U.S. foreign policy, and so on?
6. Do you agree with the following: "The social responsibility of business is to maximize the wealth of the shareholders." Why or why not?

PART FOUR

THE PROBLEM OF ECONOMIC CONCENTRATION

When Theodore Roosevelt became president of the United States, he had yet to develop a personal philosophy regarding the huge corporations that had been formed over the prior quarter-century in most of our key industries. Having assumed the presidency in 1901, the same year as the world's first billion-dollar corporation, United States Steel, was formed by J. P. Morgan, he was very much aware of the tremendous public concern over the power and influence of the trusts. Eventually, Roosevelt concluded that large business organizations were necessary in a modern industrial society—he did not, however, believe that we had to put up with their excesses. In essence, he differentiated between good trusts and bad trusts. The cases in this section illustrate not only Roosevelt's attempts to apply the laws in the antitrust arena, but the activities of other presidents, the Congress, and the courts as well.

Case 18, *The Sherman Act,* outlines the basic law in dealing with economic concentration in the United States. The law, as stated, is not particularly complex as it is written, and the reader is encouraged to contemplate what it might mean in application. Case 19 covers the Supreme Court's first attempt to apply the Sherman Act—against the Sugar Trust—and illustrates how even the high court can make what is generally considered to be a wrong turn. This case also illustrates the influence of a well-written dissenting opinion.

Cases 20, *The Northern Securities Case;* 21, *The Rule of Reason;* 22, *The U.S. Steel Case;* and 23, *The Alcoa Case,* chart the course of the courts in attempting to determine the "real" meaning of "activities in restraint of trade" and "monopolization." The courts had to resolve such questions as: Is the possession of power to violate the law itself a violation of the law? What is reasonable and what is unreasonable restraint of trade? Is it possible for a monopolist to have monopoly forced upon it by customers demanding its products? How is business to operate under a government policy that requires it to compete, but which does not want it to win?

18
THE SHERMAN ACT (PUBLIC LAW 190)

An act to protect trade and commerce against unlawful restraints and monopolies.

Be it enacted by the Senate and House of Representatives of the United States of America in Congress assembled.

Sec. 1. Every contract, combination in the form of trust or otherwise, or conspiracy, in restraint of trade or commerce among the several States, or with foreign nations, is hereby declared to be illegal. Every person who shall make any such contract or engage in any such combination or conspiracy, shall be deemed guilty of a misdemeanor, and, on conviction thereof, shall be punished by fine not exceeding five thousand dollars, or by imprisonment not exceeding one year, or by both said punishments, in the discretion of the court.

Sec. 2. Every person who shall monopolize, or attempt to monopolize, or combine or conspire with any other person or persons, to monopolize any part of the trade or commerce among the several States, or with foreign nations, shall be deemed guilty of a misdemeanor, and, on conviction thereof, shall be punished by fine not exceeding five thousand dollars, or by imprisonment not exceeding one year, or by both said punishments, in the discretion of the court.

Sec. 3. Every contract, combination in form of trust or otherwise, or conspiracy, in restraint of trade or commerce in any Territory of the United States or of the District of Columbia, or in restraint of trade or commerce between any such Territory and another, or between any such Territory or Territories and any State or States or the District of Columbia, or with foreign nations, is hereby declared illegal. Every person who shall make any such contract or engage in any such combination or conspiracy, shall be deemed guilty of a misdemeanor, and, on conviction thereof, shall be punished by fine not exceeding five thousand dollars, or by imprisonment not exceeding one year, or by both said punishments, in the discretion of the court.

Sec. 4. The several circuit courts of the

United States are hereby invested with jurisdiction to prevent and restrain violations of this act; and it shall be the duty of the several district attorneys of the United States, in their respective districts, under the direction of the Attorney General, to institute proceedings in equity to prevent and restrain such violations. Such proceedings may be by way of petition setting forth the case and praying that such violation shall be enjoined or otherwise prohibited. When the parties complained of shall have been duly notified of such petition the court shall proceed, as soon as may be, to the hearing and determination of the case; and pending such petition and before final decree, the court may at any time make such temporary restraining order or prohibition as shall be deemed just in the premises.

Sec. 5. Whenever it shall appear to the court before which any proceeding under section four of this act may be pending, that the ends of justice require that other parties should be brought before the court, the court may cause them to be summoned, whether they reside in the district in which the court is held or not; and subpoenas to that end may be served in any district by the marshall thereof.

Sec. 6. Any property owned under any contract or by any combination, or pursuant to any conspiracy (and being the subject thereof) mentioned in section one of this act, and being in the course of transportation from one State to another, or to a foreign country, shall be forfeited to the United States, and may be seized and condemned by like proceedings as those provided by law for the forfeiture, seizure, and condemnation of property imported into the United States contrary to law.

Sec. 7. Any person who shall be injured in his business or property by any other person or corporation by reason of anything forbidden or declared to be unlawful by this act, may sue therefore in any circuit court of the United States in the district in which the defendant resides or is found, without respect to the amount in controversy, and shall recover threefold the damages by him sustained, and the costs of suit, including a reasonable attorney's fee.

Sec. 8. That the word "person," or "persons," wherever used in this act shall be deemed to include corporations and associations existing under or authorized by the laws of either the United States, the laws of any of the Territories, the laws of any State, or the laws of any foreign country.

Approved, July 2, 1890.

ASSIGNMENT QUESTIONS

1. What activities does the Sherman Act make illegal?
2. What agencies are to enforce the prohibitions contained in the act?
3. What penalties are provided for in the act?
4. In the act, what sort of redress is available to injured parties?
5. What do you think the authors of the act were trying to accomplish?

19
THE SUGAR CASE

United States v. *E. C. Knight Company*, 156 U.S. 1 (1895).

The American Sugar Refining Company was established to purchase, manufacture, and sell sugar in the American market. By 1890 it had grown to encompass 65 percent of the sugar produced and sold in the United States, with the remainder produced by four Pennsylvania companies—the E. C. Knight Company, Spreckels Sugar Refining Company, the Delaware Sugar House, and the Franklin Sugar Refining Company—and by the Revere Sugar Refinery in Boston. The national market share of the Pennsylvania companies was about 33 percent and that of the Boston company about 2 percent.

In March 1892, the American Sugar Refining Company obtained control over 98 percent of the sugar refining capacity in the United States by acquiring absolute control of the four Pennsylvania companies—exchanging its own stock for the stock of the concerns involved. According to the federal District Court, the purpose of the mergers was to obtain complete control over the refining and selling of sugar in the United States.

In consequence of the company's actions, the Justice Department brought suit against one of the parties to the combination—the E. C. Knight Company. Eventually, the case found its way to the Supreme Court.

The Opinion of the Court

The opinion of the Court was nearly unanimous in rejecting the government's case—only Justice Harlan dissented. Chief Justice Fuller delivered the opinion of the Court:

By purchase of the stock of the four Philadelphia refineries, with shares of its own stock, the American Sugar Refining Company acquired nearly complete control of the manufacturing of refined sugar within the United States. The bill charged that the contracts under which these purchases were made constituted combinations in restraint of trade, and that in entering into them the defendants combined and conspired to restrain the trade and commerce in refined sugar among the several States and with foreign nations, contrary to the act of Congress of July 2, 1890.

The relief sought was the cancellation of the agreements under which the stock was transferred; the redelivery of the stock to the parties respectively; and an injunction against the further performance of the agreements and further violations of the act.

The fundamental question is, whether conceding that the existence of a monopoly in manufacturing is established by the evidence, that monopoly can be directly suppressed under the act of Congress in the mode attempted by this bill.

The fact that an article is manufactured for export to another state does not of itself make it an article of interstate commerce, and the intent of the manufacturer does not determine the time when the article or product passes from control of the State and belongs to commerce.

No distinction is more popular to the common mind, or more clearly expressed in economic and political literature, than that between manufacture and commerce. Manufacture is transformation—the fashioning of raw materials into a change of form for use. The functions of commerce are different. The buying and selling and the transportation incidental thereto constitute commerce; and the regulation of commerce in the constitutional sense embraces the regulation at least of such transportation....If it be held that the term includes the regulation of all such manufacturers as are intended to be the subject of commercial transactions in the future, it is impossible to deny that it would also include all productive industries that contemplate the same thing. The result would be that Congress would be invested, to the exclusion of the States, with the power to regulate, not only manufacturers, but also agriculture, horticulture, stock raising, domestic fisheries, mining—in short, every branch of human industry. For is there one of them that does not contemplate, more or less clearly, an interstate or foreign market? Does not the wheat grower of the Northwest or the cotton planter of the South, plant, cultivate, and harvest his crop with an eye on the prices at Liverpool, New York and Chicago? The power being vested in Congress and denied to the States, it would follow as an inevitable result that the duty would devolve on Congress to regulate all of these delicate, multiform and vital interests—interests which in their nature are and must be local in all the details of their successful management.

Slight reflection will show that if the national power extends to all contracts and combinations in manufacture, agriculture, mining, and other production industries, whose ultimate result may affect external commerce, comparatively little of business operations and affairs would be left for state control.

It was in the light of well-settled principles that the act of July 2, 1890, was framed. Congress did not attempt thereby to assert the power to deal with monopoly directly as such; or to limit and restrict the rights of corporations created by the States or the citizens of the States in the acquisition, control, or disposition of property; or to regulate or prescribe the price or prices at which such property or the products thereof should be sold; or to make criminal the acts of persons in the acquisition and control of property which the States of their residence or creation sanctioned or permitted. Aside from the provisions applicable where Congress might exercise municipal power, what the law struck at was combinations, contracts, and conspiracies to monopolize trade and commerce among the several States or with foreign nations; but the contracts and acts of the defendants related exclusively to the acquisition of the Philadelphia refineries and the business of sugar refining in Pennsylvania, and bore no direct relation to commerce between the States or with foreign nations. The object was manifestly private gain in the manufacture of the commodity, but not alleged that the products of these refineries were sold and distributed among the several States, and that all the companies were engaged in trade or commerce with the several States and with foreign nations; but this was no more than to say that trade and commerce served manufacture to fulfill its function.

Sugar was refined for sale, and sales were probably made at Philadelphia for consumption, and undoubtedly for resale by the first purchasers throughout Pennsylvania and other States, and refined sugar was also forwarded by the companies to other States for sale. Nevertheless it does not follow that an attempt to monopolize, or the actual monopoly of, the manufacture was an attempt, whether executory or consummated, to monopolize commerce, even though, in order to dispose of the product, the instrumentality of commerce was necessarily invoked. There was nothing in the proofs to indicate any intention to put a restraint upon trade or commerce, and the fact, as we have seen, that trade or commerce might be indirectly affected was not enough to entitle complainants to a decree.

Justice Harlan's Dissenting Opinion

The Constitution which enumerates the powers committed to the nation for objects of interest to the people of all the States should not be subjected to an interpretation so rigid, technical and narrow, that those objects cannot be accomplished.

Congress is invested with power to regulate commerce with foreign nations and among the several States. The power to regulate is the power to prescribe the rule by which the subject regulated is to be governed. It is one that must be exercised whenever necessary throughout the territorial limits of the several States. The power to make these regulations is complete in itself, may be exercised to its utmost extent, and acknowledges no limitations, other than are prescribed in the Constitution.

What is commerce among the States? The decisions of this court fully answer the question. Commerce, undoubtedly, is traffic, but it is something more: it is intercourse. It does not embrace the completely interior traffic of the respective States—that which is carried on between man and man in a State, or between different parts of the same State and which does not extend to or affect other States—but it does embrace every species of commercial intercourse between the United States and foreign nations and among the States, and, therefore, it includes such traffic or trade, buying, selling, and interchange of commodities, as directly affects or necessarily involves the interests of the People of the United States. Commerce, as the word is used in the Constitution, is a unit, and cannot stop at the external boundary line of each State, but may be introduced into the interior. The genius and character of the whole government seem to be, that its action is to be applied to all the external concerns of the nation, *and to those internal concerns which affect the States generally*.

It is the settled doctrine of this court that interstate commerce embraces something more than the mere physical transportation of articles of property, and the vehicles or vessels by which such transportation is effected.

In my judgment, the citizens of the several States composing the Union are entitled, of right, to buy goods in the State where they are manufactured, or in any other State, without being confronted by an illegal combination whose business extends throughout the whole country, which by the law everywhere is an enemy to the public interests, and which prevents such buying, except at prices arbitrarily fixed by it. I insist that the free course of trade among the States cannot coexist with such combinations. When I speak of trade I mean the buying and selling of articles of every kind that are recognized articles of interstate commerce. Whatever improperly obstructs the free course of interstate intercourse and trade, as involved in the buying and selling of articles to be carried from one State to another, may be reached by Congress, under its authority to regulate commerce among the States. The exercise of that authority so as to make trade among the States, in all recognized articles of commerce, absolutely free from unreasonable or illegal restrictions imposed by combinations, is justified by an express grant of power to Congress and would redound to the welfare of the whole country.

While the opinion of the court in this case does not declare the act of 1890 to be unconstitutional, it defeats the main object for which it was passed. For it is, in effect, held that the statute should be unconstitutional if interpreted as embracing such unlawful restraints upon the purchasing of goods in one State to be carried to another State as necessarily arises from the *existence* of combinations formed for the purpose and with the effect, not only of monopolizing the ownership of all such goods in every part of the country, but of controlling the prices for them in all the States. This view of the scope of the act leaves the public, so far as national power is concerned, entirely at the mercy of combinations which arbitrarily control the prices of articles purchased to be transported from one State to another State. I cannot assent to that view. In my judgment, the general government is not placed by the Constitution in such a condition of helplessness that it must fold its arms and remain inactive while capital combines, under the name of a corporation, to destroy competition, not in one State only, but throughout the entire country, in the buying and selling of articles—especially the necessities of life—that go into commerce among the States.

To the general government has been committed the control of commercial intercourse among the

States, to the end that it may be free at all times from any restraints except such as Congress may impose or permit for the benefit of the whole country. The common government of all the people is the only one that can adequately deal with a matter which directly and injuriously affects the entire commerce of the country, which concerns equally all the people of the Union, and which it must be confessed, cannot be adequately controlled by any one State. Its authority should not be so weakened by construction that it cannot reach and eradicate evils that, beyond all question, tend to defeat an object which that government is entitled, by the Constitution, to accomplish. Powerful and ingenious minds, taking, as postulates, that the powers expressly granted to the government of the Union, are to be contracted by construction into the narrowest possible compass, and that the original powers of the States are retained if any possible construction will retain them, may, by a course of well digested, but refined and metaphysical reasoning, founded on these premises, explain away the Constitution of our country, and leave it, a magnificent structure, indeed, to look at, but totally unfit for use.

For the reasons stated I dissent from the opinion and judgment of the court.

ASSIGNMENT QUESTIONS

1. Summarize the important facts in the case.
2. Summarize the reasoning and conclusions of the majority opinion of the Court.
3. Justice Harlan made a strong dissent. What was his reasoning? What were his conclusions?
4. With which opinion do you agree? Why?
5. What principle of antitrust law is established in the *Sugar* case?

20
THE NORTHERN SECURITIES CASE

Northern Securities Co. v. *United States,* 193 U.S. 197 (1904).

In 1900, four great railroads connected the Midwest with the Pacific Ocean. The Southern Pacific connected San Francisco with Ogden, Utah, and also with the Port of New Orleans. The Union Pacific ran westward from Kansas City and Omaha to join up with the Southern Pacific. Much less famous, but equally impressive, were the Great Northern and Northern Pacific railways, connecting the Old Northwest with Oregon and Washington.

The Great Northern was the creature of that swashbuckling, one-eyed railway man, James J. Hill. Not only was he the only one to build a transcontinental railroad without heavy federal subsidy, but he is also generally acknowledged to have constructed the best of all the early railroads. While others were concerned principally with getting some kind of railroad over as much distance as possible in as short a time as possible, Hill was laying down solid roadbeds and building permanent bridges. The Great Northern reached the Pacific Coast in 1893.

Henry Villard, the promoter of the Northern Pacific, was much more a financier than a builder. In addition to federal help, Villard obtained vast sums by selling bonds to eastern and European investors. Since the western railroads were only earning about 2 percent when things were booming, it was evident that a business downturn would prevent the railroad from meeting the demands of its heavy load of fixed debt. In 1893, the Northern Pacific went into receivership; in 1896, it was reorganized by J. P. Morgan and Company.

James J. Hill and J. P. Morgan versus E. H. Harriman

At the turn of the century no single railroad had a system that connected the American Midwest with the Pacific Coast. The Union Pacific went as far east as Omaha and Kansas City and as far west as Ogden, Utah. The

Northern Pacific and Great Northern roads reached Seattle but had as their eastern endings St. Paul and Duluth. In spite of these shortcomings, it was, of course, possible for any of these roads to ship freight or passengers to any part of the nation, but this meant that they would have to work out cooperative arrangements with other railroads. But to men such as James J. Hill and J. Pierpont Morgan, the thought of depending on the cooperation of others to offer reasonable rates and through traffic was a persistent worry. To remedy this situation, Hill had, for some time before 1900, attempted to buy a railroad connecting St. Paul with Chicago—from which point he could ship to the eastern markets on railroads friendly to or dominated by Morgan interests.

In 1900, Hill's opportunity to do this came about through a number of fortuitous events. To begin with, when Morgan had reorganized the bankrupt Northern Pacific, he had turned to Hill as a man of proven ability to run a railroad and show profits. After some legal maneuvering, Hill and his associates purchased about $16,000,000 of Northern Pacific stock, about 10 percent of the total issued. This substantial minority holding, when combined with the shares under Morgan's control, gave them effective joint control of the railroad. The result was that, after 1896, although the Northern Pacific appeared to be in competition with Hill's Great Northern, and although it was a separate corporation, it was, in fact, under Hill's control.

The other circumstance favorable to Hill's scheme was that, in 1900, the directors of the Chicago, Burlington, and Quincy—the best road for his purpose—were willing to recommend to their shareholders that they accept a generous takeover bid. In exchange for bonds (secured, apparently, by the stock of the railroad they were buying) the Great Northern bought almost all of the 1,800,000 shares of capital stock of the Burlington Road.

Lurking in the wings, observing all this, was the president of the Union Pacific Railroad, E. H. Harriman. Although he had taken control of the Union Pacific a few months earlier, Harriman still did not have a convenient route into the Northeast. It was bad enough that Morgan and Hill could, if they chose, deny him service east of Omaha and Kansas City; it was even worse that they would now be in direct competition with him in Colorado and Nebraska.

In an attempt to improve his position, Harriman, in the early months of 1900, ordered his agents to buy stock in the Burlington Road. After spending $10,000,000 and acquiring about 10 percent of the total stock, Harriman went to Hill and Morgan and asked that the Union Pacific be permitted to join with them in the ownership and management of the Burlington. When he was refused, he left in a rage, saying, "Very well, it is a hostile act and you must take the consequences."[1]

Rebuffed in his attempt to cooperate with his opponents, Harriman chose a course of action both daring in scope and dangerous to accomplish. He resolved to buy control of the Northern Pacific, thereby to gain access to part control over the Burlington. Since the voting stock of the corporation was selling at about $100 per share, and since there were 1,550,000 shares outstanding—800,000 common and 750,000 voting preferred—he would have to spend a minimum of $77,500,000.

The campaign was launched at the beginning of April 1901. By May, Harriman had acquired a clear majority of the stock, over 780,000 shares, of which 410,000 were preferred and 370,000 common. The task was made easier by the fact that J. P. Morgan was in Europe for a rest and Hill was wandering around the western end of his empire, in Seattle.

As Harriman continued to purchase huge numbers of Northern Pacific shares, the price of the stock began to inch upward. In Seattle, Hill became aware that something was going on somewhere. Typical of him, he ordered a special train, had the tracks cleared, and broke the intercontinental speed record in getting to New York City. Once there, he confronted Harriman's broker, Jacob Schiff, with the charge that Schiff was representing Harriman in attempting to gain control of Northern Pacific. Schiff readily admitted that he and Harriman had, indeed, been working to gain control of the Burlington by such a back-door method and further stated that it was done in response to a failure to cooperate on the part of Hill and Morgan. Greatly excited, Hill rushed to J. P. Morgan and Company, where Robert Bacon, a Morgan partner, cabled Morgan in Europe. He asked for permission to get into the market to buy Northern Pacific common stock.

Morgan's agents moved quickly because the chance of success was small and depended upon a quirk in Northern Pacific's capital structure. By the time Hill discovered the plot, Harriman had acquired over 50 percent of the total common and voting preferred stock. *But* the Board of Directors, still under the domination of Morgan and Hill, had the right, if they chose, to retire the voting preferred—after which, control would depend upon the ownership of the common stock. By Friday, May 3, 1901, neither party owned a clear majority of the 800,000 outstanding shares of common. Morgan was considerably short, and Harriman needed about 30,000 shares.

The dramatic events that followed this near impasse can be summarized as follows:

Friday, May 3

- Schiff claimed that the Harriman interests had obtained an overwhelming majority of the stock desired.
- Harriman was stricken ill and confined to his home.

Saturday, May 4

- Harriman, worried because the common stock issue is still not settled, and concerned that Morgan might get the voting preferred retired, telephoned Kuhn, Loeb & Company (Schiff's firm) and instructed them to purchase 40,000 shares of Northern Pacific common for his account.
- Schiff attended services at his synagogue and could not be reached for many hours by Harriman's order.
- Schiff was finally located, but advised against further buying—in effect, Harriman's order was ignored.

Sunday night, May 5

- A cable from Morgan arrived authorizing his lieutenants in New York to buy Northern Pacific stock.

Monday, May 6

- The Morgan forces took the floor at the Stock Exchange, bidding for Northern Pacific common and buying all they could at any price.
- The price of Northern Pacific common rose from 110 to 131.
- From his sick bed, Harriman—now aware that things were not going well—railed at Kuhn, Loeb & Company.

Tuesday morning, May 7

- The Morgan forces continued to buy.
- The price of Northern Pacific common rose to 149.
- From France, Morgan ordered that the stock be bought at any price.

Tuesday afternoon, May 7

- The Morgan forces had gained control of 150,000 shares of common stock and claimed victory.
- The Harriman forces claimed victory based on their control of more than 50 percent of all the voting stock—including the voting preferred.

Wednesday, May 8

- Unaware of the contest between Morgan-Hill and Harriman, speculators began to sell Northern Pacific stock short—expecting to buy it back later at lower prices. But since every share of stock purchased by the contending parties was taken out of the market, no stock was available for repurchase.

Thursday, May 9

- Rumors of the "corner" spread through the market.
- Speculators made frantic efforts to obtain Northern Pacific shares at any price.
- The price of Northern Pacific common rose to $1,000 a share.
- All other securities in the market suffered price declines of from 15 to 40 percent.
- Money became very scarce, with loans being made at 40 to 60 percent interest.
- Speculators dumped everything they had to get funds to buy Northern Pacific stock.

Friday, May 10

- The stock market crash was felt in all the world's financial centers.
- J. P. Morgan rushed to his European headquarters in Paris.
- Morgan called reporters "idiots" and "rascals" and threatened one of them with murder.
- Morgan cabled emergency orders to New York: money was loaned to needy brokerage houses, demands for delivery of stock were delayed, and the delivery price was set at $150 per share.
- The Morgan forces claimed victory.
- Harriman claimed that Morgan could not legally retire the voting preferred.
- In response to an inflamed public opinion and heavy criticism in the press, both parties signed peace terms. In the formation of the new Northern Pacific Board, Morgan remained dominant, but Harriman had representation.

The Formation of the Northern Securities Company

In the aftermath of their titanic battle with Harriman, Morgan and Hill decided that they had to do two things to bring permanent peace to the western railroads. The first was to establish a holding company to control both the Northern Pacific and the Great Northern; the second was to bring Harriman into the enterprise so as to ensure his cooperation. Accordingly, the Northern Securities Corporation was organized as a holding company in the state of New Jersey on November 13, 1901. In four months, the company had gained control of 96 percent of the common stock of Northern Pacific and 76 percent of the stock of the Great Northern. Through ownership in these two corporations, the holding company also owned the Burlington Road.

The makeup of the board of directors of Northern Securities was living proof of the new era of cooperation—six directors represented Northern Pacific; four, the Great Northern; three, Harriman; and two, no specific railroad.

Theodore Roosevelt versus J. P. Morgan

Two months before the formation of the Northern Securities Company, Theodore Roosevelt had become president of the United States. As vice-president, Roosevelt had developed his personal opinion on the trusts and was now prepared to put it into action. He believed that large business units were necessary in a modern society but did not believe that we had to put up with their excesses. Sometimes called the "good trust–bad trust" philosophy, his program was designed to reap the benefits of modern industry while controlling those who engaged in unacceptable promotional or monopoly practices.

The announcement by Philander Knox, the attorney general of the United States, that the government was bringing action against Northern Securities under the antitrust law was a severe shock to Morgan, Hill, and Harriman. Not only were they in the middle of a court battle against the state of Minnesota, but prior to this action had sincerely believed that Roosevelt was favorable to their views. After all, he *was* a Republican, and he was from New York State! Morgan went to visit the president. In that famous meeting, he complained about the way he had been treated and suggested: "If we have done anything wrong, send your man to my man and they can fix it up."[2] Refusing to accept the notion that he and Morgan ran the country between the two of them, the president made clear his intention to push forward with the action against Northern Securities.

Arguments Before the Supreme Court

After being tried before the lower federal courts, the *Northern Securities* case, as expected, eventually ended up before the Supreme Court. The argument for the defendants was made by a number of attorneys. George B. Young presented the following case.

1. For some years prior to 1901 the two railway companies had been engaged in an enterprise of building up a great interstate and Oriental commerce.
2. In April, 1901, they purchased nearly all the Burlington shares at a cost of over $200,000,000. They made the purchase not with any view of placing the two companies, their shares or their commerce, under a single control.
3. Immediately after this purchase, persons interested in the Union Pacific attempted to obtain the stock control of the Northern Pacific, their object being to prevent the carrying out of the enterprise of the defendant railway companies, and especially to prevent the use of the Burlington road in carrying out that enterprise.
4. This "raid" (as it is called) on the Northern Pacific stock failed, the failure being largely due to an error of the raiders in buying preferred instead of common stock. But there was imminent danger that another like attempt might be made and be successful.
5. Such a raid, if successful, would destroy the commerce the railway companies were building up, and in aid of which they had bought the Burlington shares....
6. In forming the Northern Securities Co., it was the intention of its promoters that it should acquire, if it could, a majority of Northern Pacific Stock, thereby protecting such stock from future raids, and protecting the commerce of the railways from the ruin that would result from a successful raid....

The defendants contend as to the Sherman-Antitrust Act and its meaning:

1. The act is wholly a criminal law, directed to the punishment and prevention of crime. The remedy by injunction, etc., given by the fourth section is not to protect property interests, but solely to prevent "violations of this Act" (i.e., crimes, for every violation of the act is a crime, and, without this section, would not be within the competence of a court of equity to restrain by injunction).
2. Being a criminal statute, the act is not to be enlarged by construction. The first section cannot be stretched so as to make criminal...every agreement, combination or conspiracy that merely tends to restrain commerce among the States, or that confers on the parties to it or any one else the power to restrain trade.
3. The act makes unlawful and criminal every contract, combination or conspiracy in direct restraint of interstate trade or commerce.

   The gist of the crime is the contract, combination or conspiracy, and the offense is complete on the making of such contract, be done to carry it out, and though trade be not in fact restrained.

   But to constitute a combination or conspiracy in restraint of interstate trade or commerce, the parties must combine or conspire to do acts, which if performed, will of themselves restrain such trade or commerce, and will directly restrain it—that is, acts which operate directly on such commerce.

Francis Lynde Stetson and David Willcox, for defendants Morgan, Bacon, and Lamont, submitted the following brief:

The transactions alleged are entirely lawful in their character. They consisted merely in the organization of a lawful corporation of New Jersey, and in the sale to, and purchase by it, of property lawfully salable. All the acts were expressly authorized by law. The legal effect of the transaction has been that the owner of stock in one of the railway companies has sold the same to the Securities Company, and has received there for stock of the Securities Company, which company owns the stock not merely of one of the railway companies, but the stock of both....These transactions being lawful are not affected by allegations as to the motive which actuated them. As the means employed were lawful, the only question must be whether the result accomplished was unlawful.

An intent to violate the Anti-Trust Act, and therefore to commit a crime, could not in any case be inferred, but must be actually proved.

No indirect or remote effect of these lawful transactions upon competition between the railway companies could bring them within the Federal Anti-Trust Act.

The mere fact that a contract has the effect of restraining trade or suppressing competition in some degree does not render it injurious to the public welfare and thus bring it within the police power.

The Sherman Act is a criminal statute pure and simple and its meaning and effect as now determined must also be its meaning and effect when made the basis of a criminal proceeding.... Criminal intent is essential to constitute a crime, and the testimony bearing thereon is always a question for the jury.

Regardless of all other considerations presented on this argument, the judgment under review must be reversed unless it is to be established as a matter of law that the mere possession of the power to control all the means of two competing interstate commerce carriers operates as the effectual exercise of such power and directly affects interstate commerce, notwithstanding the fact that such power has never been exercised by its possessors, and the further fact that it is perfectly practicable for them to exercise it in a perfectly proper way.

Attorney General Knox argued for the United States:

It has been the ever present aim of those dominating the policy of the Great Northern and the Northern Pacific, during the past few years, to bring about a community of interest or some closer form of union to the end that the motive from which competition springs might be extinguished. On at least three prior occasions Mr. Hill and Mr. Morgan and their associates acted in concert in transactions affecting both roads: the attempted transfer of half the stock of the Northern Pacific to the Great Northern in exchange for a guarantee of the bonds of the Northern Pacific which was held to be violative of the laws of Minnesota, the joint purchase of the Burlington in 1901, and in the events leading up to the panic of May, 1901. After the refusal to admit the Union Pacific to an interest in the Burlington purchase, those in control of the Union Pacific attempted to acquire control of the Northern Pacific and as soon as Mr. Hill and Mr. Morgan heard of this attempt they reached an understanding to oppose it in concert, and this resulted in the threat to retire the preferred stock of the Northern Pacific, and the subsequent conference at which the plan announced in the statement of June 1, in the Wall Street Summary, was arranged. The testimony of defendants shows that the incorporation of the Securities Company, and its acquisition of a large majority of the stock of both railway companies were the designed results of a plan or understanding between the defendants Hill and Morgan and their associates, which was carried out to the letter by the parties thereto. The facts, as the Government asserts them, are recapitulated in the opinion of the Circuit Court.

On the facts as proved the Government maintains that a combination has been accomplished by means of the Securities Company which is in violation of Section 1 of the act of July 2, 1890; the defendants have monopolized or attempted to monopolize a part of the interstate or foreign commerce of the United States.

The primary aim of Congress in passing the act was not to create new offenses but to pronounce and declare a rule of public policy to cover a field wherein the Federal government has supreme and exclusive jurisdiction. As the United States has no common law, contracts in restraint of trade would not be repugnant to any law or rule of policy of the United States in the absence of a statute, and the controlling purpose of the act was to declare that the public policy of the nation forbade contracts, combinations, conspiracies, and monopolies in restraint of interstate and international trade and commerce, and the jurisdiction conferred upon courts of equity to restrain violations of the act was intended as a means to uphold and enforce the principle of public policy therein asserted, not as a means to prevent the commission of crimes.

The Anti-Trust Act was purposely framed in broad and general language in order to defeat subterfuges designed to evade it. It is framed in sweeping and comprehensive language which includes every combination, regardless of its form or structure, in restraint of trade or commerce, and every person, natural or artificial, monopolizing, attempting to monopolize, or combining with any other person to monopolize any part of such trade or commerce.

The form or framework is immaterial. Congress, no doubt, anticipated that attempts would be made to defeat its will through the "contrivances of powerful and ingenious minds," and to meet these it used the broad and all-embracing language found in the act; and it is in this light that that language is to be construed. And the device of a holding corporation for the purpose of circumventing the law can be no more effectual than any other means.

In exercising its power over commerce Congress may to some extent limit the right of private contract, the right to buy and sell property, without violating the Fifth Amendment. It may declare that no contract, combination, or monopoly which restrains trade or commerce by shutting out the operation of the general law of competition shall be legal.

The Government does not claim that ordinary corporations and partnerships formed in good faith in ordinary course of business come within the prohibitions of the act because incidentally they may to some extent restrict competition, but those where the corporation or partnership is formed for the purpose of combining competing businesses. The act embraces not only monopolies but attempts to monopolize. The term monopoly as used by modern legislators and judges signifies the combining or bringing together in the hands of one person or set of persons the control, or the power of control, over a particular business or employment, so that competition therein may be suppressed.

A combination or monopoly exists within the meaning of the act even if the immediate effect of the acts complained of is not to suppress competition or to create a complete monopoly. It is sufficient to show that they tend to bring about those results.

It is not essential to show that the person or persons charged with monopolizing or combining have actually raised prices or suppressed competition, or restrained or monopolized trade or commerce in order to bring them within the condemnation of the act. It is enough that the necessary effect of the combination or monopoly is to give them the power to do those things. The decisive question is whether the power exists, not whether it has been exercised.

ASSIGNMENT QUESTIONS

1. Summarize the story of the formation of the Northern Securities Company.
2. What was Theodore Roosevelt's antitrust policy?
3. Why do you think Hill and Morgan reacted as they did to the news that the Roosevelt administration was bringing suit against them?
4. What was the argument for the defendants? Has it merit?
5. Summarize the argument for the government.
6. If you had been serving as a member of the Court, how would you have voted in this case? Justify your decision.

NOTES

1. George Kennan, *E. H. Harriman,* Vol. I (New York: Houghton Mifflin, 1922), p. 290.
2. Frederick Lewis Allen, *The Great Pierpont Morgan* (New York: Harper & Brothers, 1949).

21
THE RULE OF REASON

Throughout the nineteenth century, a tradition had grown in the government of the United States that the chief justice of the Supreme Court would be chosen from outside the Court. In 1910, President Taft broke with this tradition by appointing Justice Edward White as the new chief justice. The reasons behind this action by the president have never been clear to historians, although it is suggested by some that he acted in response to a unanimous demand on the part of the other justices.

In some ways the appointment of White was a good one. He was respected and honest and was an excellent administrator. In at least one sense, however, it was not a good choice. More than offsetting White's personal characteristics was the fact that he could not, apparently, express his opinions in clear English. "Indeed, it has been said that his opinions were 'models of what judicial opinions ought not to be,' his favorite mode of thought and expression was so intricate and elusive that his arguments have wrongly, though understandably, been called sophistical."[1]

This flaw in White's otherwise impressive makeup is particularly distressing since he wrote the opinion for what is generally considered to be the most important case in the first half-century of the Sherman Act, the *Standard Oil* case of 1911.[2] The scholar, investigating the opinion of the Court, is continually confronted with single sentences such as the following:

> And it is worthy of observation, as we have previously remarked concerning the common law, that although the statute by the comprehensiveness of the enumerations embodied in both the first and second sections makes it certain that its purpose was to prevent undue restraints of every kind or nature, nevertheless by the omission of any direct prohibition against monopoly in the concrete it indicates a consciousness that the freedom of the individual right to contract when not unduly or improperly exercised was the most efficient means for the prevention of monopoly, since the operation of the centrifugal and centripetal

forces resulting from the right to freely contract was the means by which monopoly would be inevitably prevented if no extraneous or sovereign power imposed it and no right to make unlawful contracts having a monopolistic tendency were permitted.

Such defects of style badly mar the usefulness of the *Standard Oil* case as a source document and often force the researcher to turn not to the original opinion, but to other people's explanations of what the opinion says. The following is based only partially on some of the more understandable of White's statements.

Background

The Standard Oil Co., being both one of the oldest and largest of the trusts, was generally considered by critics of American business to be the arch devil of the monopoly movement. Not only did Standard Oil have nearly complete control over the national supply of kerosene—"the poor man's source of light"—but it had received much bad publicity as a result of some of its actions in rising to dominance over the oil industry. A litany of unfair and unscrupulous practices was repeated in newspapers and in the popular magazines of the era. Of particular importance was the sensational exposé produced by Ida Tarbell in her serialized *History of the Standard Oil Company*.

Given the general climate of hostility toward Standard Oil, it is no surprise that suit was initiated against the trust during Theodore Roosevelt's second term in office. Having vanquished Morgan in the *Northern Securities* case, he was now intent on taking on that other Goliath, John D. Rockefeller. The case is important not only because it marks the beginning of modern antitrust actions, the judges being presented with a record twenty-three volumes of printed matter, aggregating about twelve thousand pages, and running to nearly five million words. The government's case was prepared with meticulous detail and so impressed the circuit judges that they behaved according to the fondest hopes of the Justice Department, delivering an opinion that closely followed the reasoning of the *Northern Securities* case. Eventually, of course, the case found its way to the Supreme Court.

The Opinion of Mr. Chief Justice White

White's opinion, for the majority of the Court, can be broken down into two main parts. The first part is a recital of the facts in the case; the second, the reasoning and conclusions making up the decision.

The Facts

After noting the amount of material to be digested by the Court in making this decision, White lists the firms involved, the charge against them, and presents a short history of the Standard Oil Company.

The bill and exhibits, covering one hundred and seventy pages of the printed record, was filed on November 15, 1906. Corporations known as Standard Oil Company of New Jersey, Standard Oil Company of California, Standard Oil Company of Indiana, Standard Oil Company of Iowa, Standard Oil Company of Nebraska, Standard Oil Company of New York, Standard Oil Company of Ohio and sixty-two other corporations and partnerships, as also seven individuals were named as defendants. The bill was divided into thirty numbered sections, and sought relief upon the theory that the various defendants were engaged in conspiring "to restrain the trade and commerce in petroleum, commonly called 'crude oil,' in refined oil, and in the other products of petroleum."

After noting that the conspiracy was alleged to have been formed in about 1870 by John D. Rockefeller, William Rockefeller, and Henry M. Flagler, White summarized the history of the company.

In 1870, John D. and William Rockefeller and several other named individuals, who, prior to 1870 had been separate partnerships, engaged in the oil refining business, organized a corporation known as the Standard Oil Company. Other individual defendants soon afterwards became participants in the "illegal combination" so that by 1872, the combination had acquired all but 3 or 4 of the 35 or 45 oil refineries in Cleveland.

By reason of this power, the combination was able to obtain "preferential rates and rebates in many and devious ways" over their competitors from railway companies. Through this advantage, nearly all the company's competitors were either forced out of business or joined the combination. As a result of this strong position, the Standard Oil Company of Ohio was able to (a) acquire refineries in other states; (b) obtain control of the pipe lines used for transporting oil from the oil fields to refineries in Cleveland, Pittsburgh, Titusville, Philadelphia, New York, and New Jersey, and (c) eventually obtain a complete mastery over the oil industry, controlling 90 per cent of production, shipping, refining, and selling petroleum and its products, and thus was able to fix the price of crude and refined petroleum and to restrain and monopolize all interstate commerce in those products.

The Sins of Standard Oil

After sketching the rise and growth of the company, White listed the unacceptable activities of Standard Oil (or, as he called them, "averments") as follows:

1. Rebates, preferences, and other discriminatory practices in favor of the combination by railroad companies;
2. Restraint and monopolization by control of pipe lines, and unfair practices against competing lines;
3. Contracts with competitors in restraint of trade;
4. Unfair methods of competition, such as local price cutting at the points where necessary to suppress competition;
5. Espionage of the business of competitors, the operation of bogus independent companies, and payment of rebates on oil, with the like intent;
6. The division of the United States into districts and the limiting of the operations of the various subsidiary corporations as to such districts so that competition in the sale of petroleum products between such corporations had been entirely eliminated and destroyed;
7. Enormous and unreasonable profits earned by the Standard Oil Trust as a result of the monopoly.

The Opinion

White's principal thesis was that, when the Sherman Act prohibits "every contract in restraint of trade," the words must be understood to mean every contract that *unreasonably* restrains trade. This opinion virtually created a new antitrust law, ignoring both the written text of the Sherman Act and the many court opinions already on the books. In emphasizing the intent and methods of the combination instead of its results, White believed that he was building on the common law, which, in his opinion prohibited:

> Contracts or acts which were unreasonably restrictive of competitive conditions, whether from the nature or character of the contract or act, or where the surrounding circumstances were such as to justify the conclusion that they had not been entered into or performed with the legitimate purpose of unreasonably forwarding personal interest and developing trade, but, on the contrary, were of such character as to give rise to the inference or presumption that they had been entered into or done with the intent to do wrong to the general public and to limit the right of individuals, thus restraining the free flow of commerce and tending to bring about the evils, such as enhancement of prices, which were considered to be against public policy.

Applying the Rule of Reason to the facts of the *Standard Oil* case, White found the defendants guilty, and orders were subsequently issued calling for the breaking up of the Standard Oil Trust.

ASSIGNMENT QUESTIONS

1. For what specific reasons was Standard Oil judged to be in violation of the Sherman Act?
2. Compare the decision in the *Standard Oil* case with that in the *Northern Securities* case. Was the law changed?
3. Liberals denounced Chief Justice White's decision as taking the teeth out of the Sherman Act. How could this be true since the Oil Trust was found guilty?
4. In 1913, in the *United Shoe Machinery* case, the Court found nothing to condemn in the case of a company possessing a virtual monopoly (95 percent) of the shoe machinery business in the United States. Justify this decision based on the Rule of Reason.
5. Do you agree with the Rule of Reason as an interpretation of the Sherman Act? Why or why not?

NOTES

1. William Letwin, *Law and Economic Policy in America* (New York: Random House, 1965), p. 256.
2. *United States* v. *Standard Oil,* 173 Fed. 177.

22
THE U.S. STEEL CASE

United States v. *United States Steel Corporation,* 251 U.S. 417 (1920).

Formation of United States Steel Corporation

The organization of United States Steel in 1901 marked the culmination of a chain of events within the steel industry which began in 1889. During that 12-year period, the structure of the industry changed from hundreds of competing firms, to one of oligopoly, with the United States Steel Corporation the leader in pricing and policies.

Consolidation began in 1889 with the formation of the Illinois Steel Corporation. A combining of three previously independent companies, this firm had an annual pig iron capacity of 750,000 tons and an authorized stock of $18,000,000. Three years later, Andrew Carnegie formed his Carnegie Steel Corporation with a capital stock of $25,000,000. The largest company in the steel industry at that time, Carnegie Steel had an annual capacity of 1,200,000 tons of pig iron. Other large firms were organized from smaller, previously competing firms in the early 1890s—among them were Jones and Laughlin, the Pennsylvania Steel Company, and Colorado Fuel and Iron.

Unlike later consolidations, these firms tended to lack integration, since ownership within the industry was usually concentrated in single functional areas. For example, the mining of iron ore was almost always a business by itself, and few firms had extensive holdings of ore lands. In addition, the actual production of raw steel was controlled by a limited number of companies, and most concerns producing finished articles purchased their supply of semifinished steel instead of making it themselves. The transportation of materials was also accomplished through independent companies. However, even at this early stage movements toward integration were already taking shape. Carnegie allied himself with the H. C. Frick Coke Company to lock up supplies of coking coal, and other firms—especially those with production facilities near coal or iron beds—made similar moves.

Admitting that there was some movement toward consolidation, the keynote of the steel industry in the early 1890s was still that of competition. Under intense pressure from declining prices during these years, however, competing companies began engaging in a number of cooperative activities. The most common of these was the pool—a mutual agreement between competing companies to fix prices and divide up markets so as to ensure each participant a "fair share" of the business. There were pools in most segments of the industry, but few of them were rarely successful for long.

The main problem with pools was that, since they were illegal under the common law, they were not enforceable in the courts. In addition, there was continual disagreement over specific provisions by parties to them. When times turned bad, they tended to be universally ignored, and even in good times there is little evidence that they were faithfully abided by. It is doubtful if a single pool agreement, and there were many of them, was ever honestly kept by all parties. It was common for those participating in the pool to seek to gain an advantage over their competitors while the pool was in the formation stage. In at least one instance a corporate representative was stationed outside a building where a pool conference was being held. When the agreement had been reached, the company's man in the conference casually signaled through a window and the outside man ran to contact customers with offers undercutting the agreed-upon price schedule.

Although the pools failed, they did demonstrate to sharp minds, such as Andrew Carnegie's, the advantages to be gained through combination and integration. He moved quickly to capture ore lands and transportation facilities in the Great Lakes region, and at once stirred integration activities on the part of other large firms. In the late 1890s about a dozen very large steel combines were formed to control, between them, over half the steelmaking capacity of the nation. Three of these concerns, Federal Steel, Carnegie Steel, and National Steel, together had about 45 percent of the steel ingot production. A near monopoly was had by the American Steel and Wire Company, which controlled over 90 percent of the nail and wire business. Further, near-monopolies were secured in sheet steel, tin plate, bridge fabrication, and welded tubing.

As large as these consolidations were, they left the industry divided into two parts. There were the "primary producers," those firms making ingots and semifinished products, and the "secondary producers," consisting of companies making tubing, finished sheet, wire, and other products. The significance of this was that the three largest primary producers—Carnegie, Federal and National—in spite of their size and power, were ultimately dependent upon secondary manufacturers to buy their products.

For some period after this latest round of consolidations, the situation remained reasonably stable. The large firms restricted their activity to making crude steel products, and the secondary producers concentrated on finished items. This period of peace was broken when the makers of lighter steel forms began to lay plans to produce the crude steel products previously purchased from primary producers. This happened at a time when the larger firms had just finished making substantial investments in expanding their production facilities. Faced with the loss of their best customers, the primary producers were forced to plan expansion in the direction of finished products, and the industry was disturbed by the possibility of fierce competition.

Andrew Carnegie, probably the most dynamic of the big industrialists, typified the activities of the primary producers during this critical period. He set in motion a series of operations which, if completed, would have forced his competitors out of business and made him the absolute dictator of the steel industry. It was "war to the knife and the knife to the hilt." Never before had a multimillionaire run amok with such force and fury. He announced his intention to have only one profit from the ore to the finished product.

To fight Rockefeller, he ordered seven new ore carriers. To fight the Pennsylvania

Railroad, he set surveying teams at work planning a railroad from Pittsburgh to the sea. To fight the National Tube Company he announced the purchase of land for a vast new tubing mill. To fight the American Steel and Wire Company, a new rod mill was to be erected near Pittsburgh. And to fight all the other steel companies, he proclaimed that $10 million was to be spent on technical improvements that would put his mills beyond the reach of competition.

At this critical moment in American industrial history, the leaders of a number of the larger firms—under the guidance of J. P. Morgan—resolved to create a final consolidation of the consolidations. Since it was believed by Morgan that the steel industry would never settle down as long as Carnegie had a position of influence, the Carnegie interests were purchased and combined with those of other steel firms to form the United States Steel Corporation.

With the formation of U.S. Steel, the process of consolidation begun in 1889 was completed. From an industry composed of hundreds of highly competitive firms, the steel industry was transformed so that a single giant firm owned three-fifths of the productive capacity and the rest was spread among eight or nine other firms. The extent of the consolidations is demonstrated in Exhibit 22-1. U.S. Steel was formed from 12 firms that had previously been 226 independent and competing firms made up of 146 separate works and 1,216 plants. The total capitalization of the new trust was $1,400,000,000, making it the world's first billion-dollar corporation.

A Peaceful Industry

Morgan's man in charge of U.S. Steel was the upright and honest judge Elbert Gary of Illinois. Gary realized that the company was

EXHIBIT 22-1 Report on the Steel Industry

Number of Original Companies	*Consolidated into*	*Final Consolidation*
20	Carnegie Company	United States Steel Corporation
18	Federal Steel Co.	
13	National Steel Co.	
32	American Steel and Wire	
16	National Tube Co.	
13	Shelby Steel Tube Co.	
38	American Tin Plate	
30	American Sheet Steel	
14	American Steel Hoop	
29	American Bridge Co.	
2	Lake Superior Iron	
1	Bessemer Steamship Co.	
226		

146 works consisting of		
	Bessemer converters	33
	Furnaces	423
	Rolling mills	421
	Wire mills	61
	Pipe and tube works	55
	Galvanizing and tinning	38
	Other mills and plants	156
	Miscellaneous	29
		1,216 plants

Source: U.S. Bureau of Corporations, *Report on the Steel Industry* (Washington, D.C.: Government Printing Office, 1911), p. 106.

in mortal danger because of adverse public reaction to the sheer size of the venture, and because of increasing government interest in the effects such a business would have on competition. To counter these attitudes, Gary resolved to create for the new company the reputation the "Good Trust." By using the corporation's power sparingly, by establishing a reputation for honesty and fair dealing with the public, by being friendly and cooperative with government officials, he hoped to guarantee the continued existence of the company.

Within a very short period, the steel industry was characterized by stable prices and the sort of industrial peace that could have been prescribed by J. P. Morgan himself. Details of prices and other industry data for the years after the formation of U.S. Steel are shown in Exhibits 22-2 through 22-4.

EXHIBIT 22-3 Operating Profits of Major Steel Companies as a Percentage of Gross Fixed Assets, 1901–1915

	1901–1905	*1906–1910*	*1911–1915*
Armco	4.4%	24.9%	8.5%
Bethlehem	8.9	10.1	14.0
Crucible	6.9	7.0	9.8
Republic	9.0	10.3	8.2
United States Steel	14.4	14.0	8.8
Youngstown	13.5	22.3	11.3

Source: Gertrude G. Schroeder, *The Growth of Major Steel Companies, 1900–1950* (Baltimore, Md.: The Johns Hopkins University Press, 1953), p. 175.

EXHIBIT 22-2 Relative Prices and Purchasing Power of Iron and Steel, United States

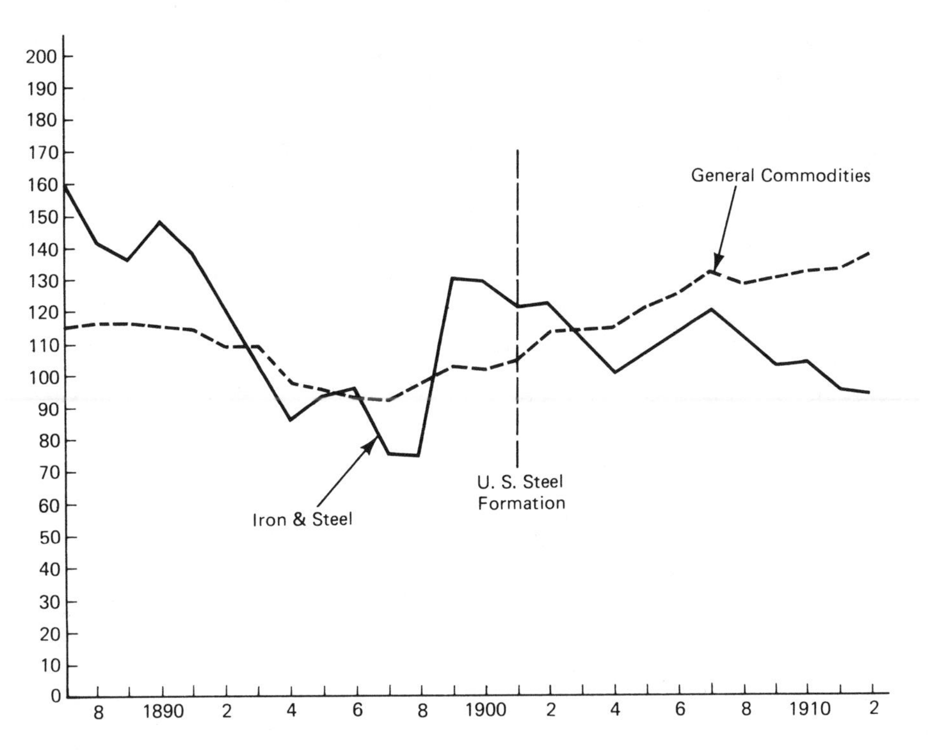

Source: Arundel Cotter, *The Authentic History of the United States Steel Corporation* (New York: The Moody Magazine and Book Company, 1916), p. 183.

EXHIBIT 22-4 U.S. Steel Corporation Subsidiaries and Other Steel-Producing Companies, 1901–1920

	Production (thousands of gross tons)			
Year	*U.S. Steel*	*Other Companies*	*U.S. Total*	*U.S. Steel as % of U.S. Total*
1901	8,855	4,618	13,473	65.7
1902	9,750	5,197	14,947	65.2
1903	9,174	5,361	14,535	63.1
1904	8,413	5,447	13,860	60.7
1905	12,006	8,018	20,024	60.0
1906	13,529	9,869	23,398	57.8
1907	13,100	10,263	23,363	56.1
1908	7,839	6,184	14,023	55.9
1909	13,355	10,600	23,955	55.8
1910	14,179	11,916	26,095	54.3
1911	12,753	10,923	23,676	53.9
1912	16,901	14,350	31,251	54.1
1913	16,656	14,645	31,301	53.2
1914	11,826	11,687	23,513	50.3
1915	16,376	15,775	32,151	50.9
1916	20,911	21,863	42,774	48.9
1917	20,285	24,776	45,061	45.0
1918	19,583	24,879	44,462	44.0
1919	17,200	17,471	34,671	49.6
1920	19,278	22,855	42,133	45.8

Source: United States Steel Corporation, *T.N.E.C. Papers, Comprising the Pamphlets and Charts Submitted...to the Temporary National Economic Committee*, Vol. II, p. 142.

United States v. *U.S. Steel Corp.*

Ten years after the formation of the United States Steel Corporation, in 1911, the U.S. government brought suit against the company under the Sherman Act. It took six years for the case to make its way to the Supreme Court, where it was argued on March 9, 1917. The case was reargued late in 1919, and on March 1, 1920, the Court rendered its decision.

Argument for the Government

The Steel Corporation is a combination in restraint of trade because it is not the result of natural trade growth but is a mere instrumentality for combining competing corporations which together occupy an overwhelming preponderant position in trade and commerce in iron and steel products generally. The group of independent plants and businesses combined under one control through the corporation included the largest and most powerful competitors in practically every branch of the iron and steel industry....

The preponderant position and the dominance of this combination is manifested by its capital as compared with that of competitors; its proportion of the total production; its proportion of ore reserves; its control over transportation of ore; its effect upon prices; concerted maintenance of prices under its leadership; and opinion as to its power....

The contention that the case must fail because the combinations have not increased prices, or limited production, or degraded the quality of product, or decreased wages, or decreased the price of raw materials, or oppressed competitors, loses sight of the broader policy of the act, which was, not to wait until the evils enumerated are already upon us, but to prevent their occurrence by striking at their underlying cause—undue concentration of commercial power through the process of combination.

The test of the legality of a combination, therefore, is not its present effect upon prices, wages, etc., nor its present conduct toward the remaining competitors, but its effect upon competition. If its effect is unduly to restrict competition, then it is immaterial that for the time being the combination may exercise its power benevolently. This defense of good conduct has been interposed in many cases of this character, and as many times rejected. Nor is forbearance by a combination from the exercise of its power to drive the remaining competitors from the field, or to prevent new ones from entering, on any different footing from good conduct of any other sort. The cases make no such distinction. Obviously, where a combination takes in so large a proportion of the competitors or competitive units that effective competition no longer exists, it can be no defense to say that the combination is doing nothing to prevent the restoration of competitive conditions.

Argument for the Steel Corporation

The Government insists that, as a matter of law, the suppression of competition is undue whenever the combination controls units which together occupy a preponderant position in a given industry, and this without regard to the intentions of those who form it or the after conduct of the combination. We submit that no such test is warranted either by the language of the Anti-Trust Act or by the decisions of this court. Whether restraint is unreasonable, and therefore, undue, depends on three things: (1) the extent of such control; (2) the method by which such control was brought about; and (3) the manner in which such control has been exercised.

We submit that *a priori* reasoning as to the direct or necessary effect of the organization of the Steel Corporation or as to the result produced by its preponderant position in the industry, if it has such a position, is uncalled for in the present case. When the evidence in the case was closed, thirteen years of the active life of the Corporation had passed. If restraint of trade or monopoly necessarily resulted from its formation or from its so-called preponderant position in the industry, evidence of such restraint or monopoly would appear somewhere in its history; and if such evidence does not appear, it is reasonable to conclude that no such result inhered in its organization or position.

Nor is an intent to monopolize or restrain trade evinced by the conduct of the Corporation after its formation. Throughout its whole career the Corporation has pursued the objects declared by its founders at the time of its formation, decreasing the cost of production, increasing wages, decreasing prices, and greatly extending trade in steel products both at home and abroad. Its treatment of both competitors and consumers has been fair and just; it has neither attempted to oppress the one nor to coerce the other. The few plants which it has purchased since its formation were offered to it, and they were purchased only because they were needed in the development of the Corporation's business.

Instead of monopolizing the manufacture of steel, the Corporation's percentage of the country's production has steadily decreased; instead of monopolizing the supply of ore, the Corporation has confined its purchases to two or three localities, and in the locality where its holdings are the largest it has relatively less than many of its competitors and less than its own experts and the experts of its competitors testify that it ought to have.

We insist that the acquisition of a preponderant position in a trade or manufacture without unlawful intent and without excluding practices, does not constitute restraint of trade or monopoly either at common law or under the Federal Anti-Trust Act when no actual monopoly or actual restraint of trade results therefrom. How could it? Size in itself is nothing as we have already shown. And power to do wrong cannot be confounded with wrongdoing itself without leading to hopeless confusion. We are dealing with a criminal statute. If the acquisition of power to violate a statute is the equivalent of its violation, then all men are guilty, for all have acquired the power to violate not one but many statutes.

In the *Standard Oil* case the combination was condemned because the court thought the conclusion of wrongful purposes and illegal combination was overwhelmingly established by the circumstances surrounding the organization and the after-conduct of the company, showing an ever present intent to drive competitors out of the field. Nothing, we submit, could be more unreasonable than to condemn every corporation, without regard to its purposes or practices, which happens to exceed in size or trade power any other competitor in the field. A rule which would lead to that result, instead of protecting commerce—which was the object of the Anti-Trust Act—would tend to throttle and destroy it by driving or keeping out of the competitive field all but the incompetents and inefficients.

Opinion of the Court

Mr. Justice McKenna delivered the opinion of the Court:

Our consideration should be of not what the Corporation had power to do or did, but what it has now power to do and is doing. What can be urged against the Corporation? It is greater in size and productive power than any of its competitors, equal or nearly equal to them all, but its power over prices was not and is not commensurate with its power to produce.

It is true there is some testimony tending to show that the Corporation had such power, but there was also testimony tending strongly to the contrary. The company's officers and, as well, its competitors and customers, testified that its competition was genuine, direct and vigorous, and was reflected in prices and production. No practical witness was produced by the government in opposition. Its contention is based on the size and asserted dominance of the Corporation—alleged power for evil, not the exertion of the power in evil. Or as counsel put it, "a combination may be illegal because of its purpose; it may be illegal because it acquires a dominating power, not as a result of normal growth and development, but as a result of a combination of competitors." Such composition and its resulting power constitute, in the view of the government the offense against the law, and yet it is admitted "no competitor came forward and said he had to accept the Steel Corporation's prices."

The situation is indeed singular, and we may wonder at it, wonder that the despotism of the Corporation, so baneful to the world in the representation of the Government, did not produce protesting victims.

The Government, therefore, is reduced to the assertion that the size of the Corporation, the power it may have, not the exertion of the power, is an abhorrence to the law, or as the Government says, "the combination embodied in the Corporation unduly restrains competition by its *necessary effect*, and therefore is unlawful regardless of purpose."

It is the inevitable logic of the Government's argument that competition must not only be free, but that it must not be pressed to the ascendancy of a competitor, for in ascendancy there is the menace of monopoly. The fallacy of this is, to us, obvious.

The Corporation was formed in 1901, no act of aggression upon its competitors is charged against it, it confederated with them at times in offense against the law, but abandoned that before this suit was brought, and since 1911 no act in violation of law can be established against it except its existence—if that be in violation of the law. This is urged by the Government, as we have seen.

It is difficult to see how there can be restraint of trade when there is no restraint of competitors in the trade nor complaints by customers. The Corporation is undoubtedly of impressive size and it takes an effort of resolution not to be affected by it or to exaggerate its influence. But we must adhere to the law and the law does not make mere size an offense or the existence of unexerted power an offense. It, we repeat, requires overt acts and trusts to its prohibition of them and its power to repress or punish them. It does not compel competition nor require all that is possible.

ASSIGNMENT QUESTIONS

1. Summarize the historical facts behind and the reasons for the formation of the United States Steel Corporation.
2. What happened to U.S. Steel during the years between its formation and the decision of the Supreme Court in 1920?
3. What was the argument for the defense?
4. Summarize the argument for the defense.
5. In brief, what was the opinion of the Court? What effect would this opinion have on the Rule of Reason?
6. Do you agree with the opinion of the Court? Why or why not?

23
THE ALCOA CASE

United States v. *Aluminum Company of America*, 148 Fed.2d. 416, 1945.

Aluminum (or aluminium) is our most modern metal, having become commercially available only in the twentieth century. Its name comes from the Latin "alumen," the name of a natural-appearing aluminous sulfate. Although aluminum is never in a free state naturally, it is still the third most abundant element, making up 8 percent of the earth's crust. Compounds of aluminum are present in almost all animals, vegetables, and minerals.

Production of Aluminum

The industrial production and use of aluminum was delayed because it is one metal that cannot be produced by direct melting—such as iron, copper, lead, and so on. The combination of a great affinity for oxygen and a high melting point result in the loss of most of the aluminum created as vapor during the melting process. The metal that remains is too impure for use.

The development of a process to efficiently produce pure aluminum took many hundreds of years and the contributions of a number of scientists—each building on the success of his predecessors.

500 B. C. Aluminous sulfate was used as an astringent and to fix dyes in cloth.

1200s. Crystaline alum was first made from alumen salts.

1600s. Alum was successfully produced from clay. At this date it was still not known that it had a metallic base.

1809. Sir Humphry Davy proved that aluminum was a metal. He produced it by electrolysis and gave the new metal its name.

1825. Hans Christen Oersted attempted to solve the production problems of aluminum by the use of chemicals. He had some limited success.

1845. Frederich Wohler, using chemicals, finally produced enough aluminum to measure its physical qualities. He managed to make particles as large as pinheads.

1854. Robert Wilhelm Bunsen (of Bunsen burner fame) invented the process of producing aluminum by the electrolysis of molten anhydrous sodium chloride. At this stage, however, aluminum was only a curiosity, since the electrical power needed was obtained from storage batteries, which made the cost prohibitive.

1886. Charles Hall (United States) and Paul Héroult (France) almost simultaneously developed the modern electrolysis method of producing aluminum. Finally, a practical method existed.

Alcoa

The Aluminum Company of America was organized under the laws of Pennsylvania on September 18, 1888. Since its organization, Alcoa has always engaged in the production and sale of ingot aluminum, and after 1895, was also engaged in the fabrication of aluminum into many finished and semifinished products. In 1889, Alcoa made arrangements with Charles Hall, the inventor of the electrolytic process, to have Hall's patent assigned to the company. Thus, Alcoa had a legal monopoly of the manufacture of pure aluminum for the next seventeen years, or until 1906, when the patent expired.

Meanwhile, a man named Bradley had invented a process by which the smelting process could be carried on without the use of external heat, as had previously been necessary, and for this improvement he obtained a patent in 1892. Bradley's invention resulted in tremendous savings in the cost of manufacturing aluminum, so that, although after the expiration of the Hall patent in 1906, anyone could manufacture aluminum by the electrolytic process; for practical purposes no one could compete with the holder of Bradley's patent until it expired in 1909.

In 1903, Alcoa obtained exclusive right to use the Bradley patent. Thus, until 1909, Alcoa had either a monopoly of the manufacture of virgin aluminum ingot or the monopoly of a process that eliminated all competition.

The Consent Decree of June 7, 1912

The extraction of aluminum from alumina requires large amounts of electrical energy, which is nearly always obtained from water power. Beginning as early as 1895, Alcoa obtained power from several companies by contracts, containing in at least three instances, agreements binding the power companies not to sell or deliver power to anyone else for the production of aluminum. In addition, Alcoa also entered into cartel arrangements with foreign manufacturers of aluminum by which arrangements were made to divide up the world market and, in some cases, to fix prices.

These cartels and restrictive covenants and certain other practices resulted in a suit filed by the United States against Alcoa. The result was a decree entered by consent on June 7, 1912, declaring several of these covenants unlawful and also declaring invalid other restrictive covenants obtained before 1903 relating to the sale of aluminum.

The Government Suit Against Alcoa

During the three decades following the expiration of the Hall and Bradley patents, Alcoa continued to dominate the aluminum market in the United States. As aluminum became an increasingly important metal for industrial and military purposes, this position drew an increasing amount of criticism from within and without the government. Finally, in April 1937, the government filed a complaint against the company, charging that it was monopolizing interstate and foreign commerce in the manufacture and sale of virgin aluminum. The government asked that Alcoa be dissolved.

The action came to trial on June 1, 1938 and proceeded without much interruption until August 14, 1940, when the case was closed after more than 40,000 pages of testimony had been taken. The judge took time to consider the evidence, and delivered an oral opinion that occupied him from September 30 to October 9, 1941. He took time to prepare findings of fact and conclusions of law which he filed on July 14, 1942, and he entered final judgment dismissing the complaint on July 23 of that year. The petition for an appeal, and assignments of error, were filed on September 14, 1942. On June 12, 1944, the Supreme Court, declaring that a quorum of six justices qualified to hear the case was lacking, referred the appeal to the Second Circuit Court of Appeals for adjudication.

Judge Learned Hand

The chief judge of the Second Circuit Court of Appeals was Judge Learned Hand. Judge Hand was a remarkable jurist, considered by many to be among the finest to ever serve in this country. Circumstances (mostly political) prevented him from ever attaining the United States Supreme Court, but his position in the Second Circuit Court of Appeals, in New York City, gave special importance to his decisions. As chief judge, he wrote more than two thousand decisions touching virtually all legal fields. The son and grandson of judges, Hand received his M.A. and LL.B. from Harvard, where he studied under Santayana and William James. In 1959, in his eighty-seventh year, Judge Hand celebrated a record fifty years of service in the U.S. judiciary. The occasion was marked by a special session of his court in which Chief Justice Earl Warren paid him tribute on behalf of the American bench and bar.

The *Alcoa* Decision

The *Alcoa* decision is considered to be one of Judge Hand's most important decisions. Certainly, it is recognized as a landmark in the development of antitrust law.

The following excerpts from this decision present Judge Hand's basic arguments and conclusions.

The most important question in this case is whether the monopoly of Alcoa's production of virgin ingot, secured by the two patents until 1909, and in part perpetuated between 1909 and 1912 by the unlawful practices, forbidden by the decree of 1912, continued for the ensuing twenty-eight years; and whether, if it did, it was unlawful under Sec. 2 of the Sherman Act. It is undisputed that throughout this period Alcoa continued to be the single producer of virgin ingot in the United States; and the government argues that this without more was enough to make it an unlawful monopoly. It also takes an alternative position: that in any event during this period Alcoa consistently pursued unlawful exclusionary practices, which made its dominant position certainly unlawful, even though it would not have been, had it been retained only by "natural growth." Finally, it asserts that many of these practices were of themselves unlawful, as contracts in restraint of trade under Section 1 of the Act.

Alcoa's position is that the fact that it alone continued to make virgin ingot in this country did not, and does not, give it a monopoly of the market; that it was always subject to the competition of imported virgin ingot, and of what is called "secondary" ingot; and that even if it had not been, its monopoly would not have been retained by unlawful means, but would have been the result of a growth which the Act does not forbid, even when it results in monopoly. We shall first consider the amount and character of this competition; next, how far it established a monopoly; and finally, if it did, whether that monopoly was unlawful under Section 2 of the Sherman Act.

Character of Competition

From 1902 onward until 1928 Alcoa was making ingot in Canada through a wholly owned subsidiary; so much of this as it imported into the United States it is proper to include with what it produced here. In the year 1912 the sum of these two items represented nearly 91 percent of the total amount of virgin ingot available for sale in this country. This percentage varied year by year up to and including 1938; in 1913 it was about 72 percent; in 1921 about 68 percent; in 1922 about 72 percent; with these exceptions it was always over 80 percent of the total and for the last five years 1934–38 inclusive it averaged over 90 percent.

The effect of such a proportion of the production upon the market we reserve for the time being, for it will be necessary first to consider the nature and uses of secondary ingot, the name by which the industry knows ingot made from aluminum scrap. This is of two sorts, though for our purposes it is not important to distinguish between them.

One of these is the clippings and trimmings of sheet aluminum, when patterns are cut out of it, as a suit is cut from a bolt of cloth. The chemical composition of these is obviously the same as that of the sheet from which they come and, although they are likely to accumulate dust or other dirt in the factory, this may be removed by well known processes. If a record of the original composition of the sheet has been preserved, this scrap may be remelted into new ingot, and used again for the same purpose. Nevertheless, there is an appreciable sales resistance even to this kind of scrap, and for some uses (airplanes and cables among them) fabricators absolutely insist upon virgin: just why is not altogether clear.

The other source of scrap is aluminum which has once been fabricated and the article, after being used, is discarded and sent to the junk heap...as for example, cooking utensils, like kettles and pans, and the pistons or crank cases of motorcars. These are made with a substantial alloy and to restore the metal to its original purity costs more than it is worth. However, if the alloy is known both in quality and amount, scrap, when remelted, can be used again for the same purpose as before. In spite of this, as in the case of clippings and trimmings, the industry will ordinarily not accept ingot so salvaged upon the same terms as virgin.

Alcoa's Control of the Market

There are various ways of computing Alcoa's control of the aluminum market. The judge figured its share—during the years 1929–1938, inclusive—as only about 33 percent; to do so he included secondary and excluded that part of Alcoa's own production which it fabricated and did not therefore sell as ingot. If, on the other hand, Alcoa's total production, fabricated and sold, be included, and balanced against the sum of imported virgin and secondary, its share of the market was in the neighborhood of 64 percent for that period.

The percentage we have already mentioned—over 90—results only if we both include all Alcoa's production and exclude secondary. That percentage is enough to constitute a monopoly; it is doubtful whether 60 or 64 percent would be enough; and certainly 33 percent is not. Hence it is necessary to settle what we shall treat as competing in the ingot market. That part of its production which Alcoa itself fabricates, does not of course ever reach the market as ingot; and we recognize that it is only when a restriction of production either inevitably affects prices, or is intended to do so, that it violates Section 1 of the Sherman Act.

However, even though we were to assume that a monopoly is unlawful under Section 2 only in case it controls prices, the ingot fabricated by Alcoa, necessarily had a direct effect upon the ingot market. All ingot—with trifling exceptions—is used to fabricate intermediate, or end, products; and therefore, all intermediate, or end, products which Alcoa fabricates and sells, reduce the demand for ingot itself. We cannot therefore agree that the computation of the percentage of Alcoa's control over the ingot market should not include the whole of its ingot production.

We conclude therefore that Alcoa's control over the ingot market must be reckoned at over 90 percent.

Reasons to Oppose Monopoly

It is settled, at least as to Section 1 of the Sherman Act, that there are some contracts restricting competition which are unlawful, no matter how beneficent they may be; no industrial emergency will justify them; they are absolutely forbidden. Chief Justice Taft said as much of contracts dividing a territory among producers; the Supreme Court unconditionally condemned all contracts fixing prices; and the same notion originally extended to all contracts—reasonable or unreasonable—which restrict competition. The decision in the *Standard Oil* case, in 1912, certainly did change this, and since then it has been accepted law that not all contracts which in fact put an end to existing competition are unlawful. Starting, however, with the authoritative premise that all contracts fixing prices are unconditionally prohibited, the only possible difference between them and a monopoly is that while a monopoly necessarily involves an equal, or even greater, power to fix prices, its mere existence might be thought not to constitute an exercise of that power. That distinction is nevertheless purely formal; it would be valid only so long as the monopoly remained wholly inert; it would disappear as soon as the monopoly began to operate; for when it did—that is, as soon as it began to sell at all—it must sell at some price, and the only price at which it could sell is a price which it itself fixed. Thereafter the power and its exercise must needs coalesce. Indeed it would be absurd to condemn such contracts unconditionally, and not to extend the condemnation to monopolies; for the contracts are only steps toward that entire control which monopoly confers; they are really partial monopolies.

But we are not left to deductive reasoning. Although in many settings it may be proper to weigh the extent and effect of restrictions in a contract against its industrial or commercial advantages, this is never to be done when the contract is made with intent to set up a monopoly. A monopoly is always an unreasonable restraint of trade.

Perhaps, it has been idle to labor the point at length; there can be no doubt that the vice of restrictive contracts and of monopoly is really one, it is the denial to commerce of the supposed protection of competition. To repeat, if the earlier stages are proscribed, when they are parts of a plan, the mere projecting of which condemns them unconditionally, the realization of the plan itself must also be proscribed.

We have been speaking only of the economic reasons which forbid monopoly; but, as we have already implied, there are others, based upon the belief that great industrial consolidations are inherently undesirable, regardless of their economic results. In the debates in Congress, Senator Sherman himself in the passage quoted below stated that among the purposes of Congress in 1890 was a desire to put an end to great aggregations of capital because of the helplessness of the individual before them.

> If the concerted powers of this combination are intrusted to a single man, it is a kingly prerogative, inconsistent with our form of government, and should be subject to the strong resistance of the State and national authorities.
>
> The popular mind is agitated with problems that may disturb social order, and among them all none is more threatening than the inequality of condition, of wealth, and opportunity that has grown within a single generation out of the concentration of capital into vast combinations to control production and trade and to break down competition. These combinations already defy or control powerful transportation corporations and reach State authorities. They reach out their arms to every part of our country. They are imported from abroad. Congress alone can deal with them, and if we are unwilling or unable there will soon be a trust for every production and a master to fix the price for every necessity of life.

Throughout the history of the statutes it has been constantly assumed that one of their purposes was to perpetuate and preserve, for its own sake and in spite of possible cost, an organization of industry in small units which can effectively compete with each other. We hold that Alcoa's monopoly of ingot was of the kind covered by Section 2.

Alcoa and Monopoly

It does not follow because Alcoa had such a monopoly, that it "monopolized" the ingot market; it may not have achieved monopoly; monopoly may have been thrust upon it. If it had been a combination of existing smelters which united the whole industry and controlled the production of all aluminum ingot, it would certainly have "monopolized" the market. In several decisions the Supreme Court has decreed the dissolution of such combinations, although they had engaged in no unlawful trade practices.

Nevertheless, it is unquestionably true that from the very outset the courts have at least kept in reserve the possibility that the origin of a monopoly may be critical in determining its legality; and for this they had warrant in some of the congressional debates which accompanied the passage of the act. This notion is usually expressed by saying that size does not determine guilt; that there must be some "exclusion" of competitors; that the growth must be something else than "natural" or "normal"; that there must be a "wrongful intent," or some other specific intent; or that some "unduly" coercive means must be used. At times there has been emphasis upon the use of the active verb, "monopolize," as the judge noted in the case at bar.

What engendered these compunctions is reasonably plain; persons may unwittingly find themselves in possession of a monopoly, automatically so to say; that is, without having intended either to put an end to existing competition, or to prevent competition from arising when none had existed; they may become monopolists by force of accident. Since the Act makes "monopolizing" a crime, as well as a civil wrong, it would be not only unfair, but presumably contrary to the intent of Congress, to include such instances. A market may, for example, be so limited that it is impossible to produce at all and meet the cost of production except by a plant large enough to supply the whole demand. Or there may be changes in taste or in cost which drive out all but one purveyor.

A single producer may be the survivor out of a group of active competitors, merely by virtue of his superior skill, foresight and industry. In such cases a strong argument can be made that, although, the result may expose the public to the evils of monopoly, the Act does not mean to condemn the resultant of those very forces which it is its prime object to foster. The successful competitor, having been urged to compete, must not be turned upon when he wins. The most extreme expression of this view is in *United States v. United States Steel Corporation*. Justice McKenna for the majority said:

> The corporation is undoubtedly of impressive size, and it takes an effort of resolution not to be affected by it or to exaggerate its influence. But we must adhere to the law, and the law does not make mere size an offense, or the existence of unexerted power an offense. It, we repeat, requires overt acts and trusts to its prohibition of them and its power to repress or punish them. It does not compel competition, nor require all that is possible.
>
> The Act offers no objection to the mere size of a corporation, nor to the continued exertion of its lawful power, when that size and power have been developed by natural growth and obtained by lawful means, although its resources, capital and strength may give to such corporation a dominating place in the business and industry with which it is concerned. It is entitled to maintain its size and the power that legitimately goes with it, provided no law has been transgressed in obtaining it.

Whatever authority the *U.S. Steel* opinion had was diminished by the Supreme Court in the case against Swift & Company. In that case, Justice Cardozo said:

> Mere size is not an offense against the Sherman Act unless magnified to the point at which it amounts to a monopoly...but size carries with it an opportunity for abuse that is not to be ignored when the opportunity is proved to have been utilized in the past.

Alcoa's size was "magnified" to make it a monopoly; indeed, it has never been anything else; and its size, not only offered it an "opportunity for abuse," but it utilized its size for abuse, as can be easily seen.

It would completely misconstrue Alcoa's position in 1940 to hold that it was the passive beneficiary of a monopoly, following upon an involuntary elimination of competitors by automatically operative economic forces. Already in 1909, when its last lawful monopoly position ended, it sought to strengthen its position by unlawful practices, and these concededly continued until 1912. In that year it had two plants in New York, at which it produced less than 42 million pounds of ingot; in 1934 it had 5 plants and its production had risen to about 327 million pounds, an increase of almost eight-fold. Meanwhile not a pound of ingot had been produced by anyone else in the United States. This increase and this continued and undisturbed control did not fall undesigned into Alcoa's lap; obviously it could not have done so. It could only have resulted from a persistent determination to maintain the control, with which it found itself vested in 1912. There were at least one or two abortive attempts to enter the industry, but Alcoa effectively stalled all competition, and succeeded in holding the field alone. True, it stimulated demand and opened new uses for the metal, but not without making sure that it could supply what it had evoked. There is no dispute as to this; Alcoa avows it as evidence of the skill, energy and initiative with which it has always conducted its business; as a reason why, having won its way by fair means, it should be commended, and not dismembered. We need charge it with no moral derelictions after 1912; we may assume that all it claims for itself are true.

The only question is whether it falls within the exception established in favor of those who do not seek, but cannot avoid, the control of a market. It seems to us that that question scarcely survives its statement. It was not inevitable that it should always anticipate increases in the demand for ingot and be prepared to supply them. Nothing compelled it to keep doubling and redoubling its capacity before others entered the field. It insists that it never excluded competitors; but we can think of no more effective exclusion than progressively to embrace each new opportunity as it opened, and to face every newcomer with new capacity already geared into a great organization, having the advantage of experience, trade connections and the elite of personnel.

Alcoa answers that it positively assisted competitors, instead of discouraging them. That may be true as to fabricators of ingots; but what of it? They were its market for ingot, and it is charged only with a monopoly of ingot. We can find no instance of its helping prospective ingot manufacturers.

In order to fall within Section 2 of the Sherman Act, the monopolist must have both the power to monopolize, and the intent to monopolize. To read the passage as demanding any "specific" intent, makes nonsense of it, for no monopolist monopolizes unconscious of what he is doing. So here, Alcoa meant to keep, and did keep, that complete and exclusive hold upon the ingot market with which it started. That was to "monopolize" that market, however innocently it otherwise proceeded. So far as the judgment held that it was not within Section 2, it must be reversed.

ASSIGNMENT QUESTIONS

1. How did Alcoa obtain a dominant position in the aluminum market?
2. What is the significance of the consent decree of 1912?
3. What is the principal question considered in the case?
4. What was the government's main argument? What was Alcoa's?
5. What portion of the aluminum market was held by Alcoa? Did this constitute a monopoly? What percentage of a market is needed, according to Judge Hand, to constitute a monopoly?
6. What reasons are given for opposition to monopoly?
7. Summarize the *Alcoa* decision and indicate its significance in relation to the Rule of Reason.

PART FIVE

GOVERNMENT'S ROLE IN MAINTAINING COMPETITION

In addition to attempting to maintain competition by law, the intent of the Congress has also been to somehow make the competition fair. In this section, particular applications of laws designed to halt specific anticompetitive practices or to prevent monopoly in its incipiency are illustrated. Case 24, *The American Tobacco Company,* applies the decisions developed in earlier cases under conditions in which the evidence presented by the government was wholly circumstantial. This was the first case where minutes of secret meetings and details of sub rosa agreements were replaced by reams of statistical evidence suggesting, in the words of the U.S. attorney, "a conscious parallelism of action."

Cases 25 and 26 are concerned with the necessity to define markets in order to determine the market impact in a monopoly or oligopoly situation. In addition, the second case marks an attempt to apply antitrust law in a situation where a part owner is also a supplier to a major corporation. Cases 27 and 28 are concerned with price discrimination under the Robinson-Patman Act. In the *Utah Pie Case,* the courts accepted the definition that predatory pricing was pricing below cost and then attempted to develop a methodology for determining the relevant cost of a particular product or line of products. The *Morton Salt Company* (Case 28), also charged with price discrimination, presented a defense based on the fact that the maximum price discount in question was open and available to *any* purchaser of 50,000 cases of salt. It was further suggested that not allowing such discounts might foster a kind of "soft" competition and ultimately be harmful to consumers.

24
THE AMERICAN TOBACCO COMPANY

328 U.S. 781 (1946).

Mr. Justice Burton delivered the opinion of the Court:

The petitioners are the American Tobacco Company, Liggett & Myers Tobacco Company, R. J. Reynolds Tobacco Company,...and certain officials of the respective companies who were convicted by a jury, in the District Court of the United States for the Eastern District of Kentucky, of violating Sections 1 and 2 of the Sherman Anti-Trust Act.

Each petitioner was convicted on four counts: (1) conspiracy in restraint of trade; (2) monopolization; (3) attempt to monopolize; and (4) conspiracy to monopolize....No sentence was imposed under the third count as the Court held that that count was merged in the second. Each petitioner was fined $5,000 on each of the other counts, making $15,000 for each petitioner and a total of $225,000. Seven other defendants were found not guilty.

The Circuit Court of Appeals for the Sixth Circuit, on December 8, 1944, affirmed each conviction....All the grounds urged for review of these judgments were considered here on petitions....On March 26, 1945, this Court granted the petitions but each was limited to the question whether actual exclusion of competitors is necessary to the crime of monopolization under Section 2 of the Sherman Act....

While the question before us, as briefly stated in the Court's order, makes no express reference to the inclusion, in the crime of "monopolization," of the element of "a combination or conspiracy to acquire and maintain the power to exclude competitors to a substantial extent," yet the trial court, in its...instructions to the jury, described such a combination or conspiracy as an "essential element" and an "indispensable ingredient" of that crime in the present cases. We therefore include that element in determining whether the foregoing instructions correctly stated the law as applied to these cases. In discussing the legal issue we shall assume that such a combination or conspiracy to monopolize has been established. Because of the presence of that element, we do not have here the hypothetical case of parties who themselves have not "achieved" monopoly but have had monopoly "thrust upon" them....

The present opinion is an application of the law to the facts as they were found by the jury and which the Circuit Court of Appeals held should not be set aside. The trial court's instruction did not call for proof of an "actual exclusion" of competitors on the part of the petitioners. For the purposes of this opinion, we shall assume, therefore, that an actual exclusion of competitors by the petitioners was not claimed or established by the prosecution. Simply stated the issue is: Do the facts called for by the trial court's definition of monopolization amount to a violation of Section 2 of the Sherman Act?

The Facts of the Conspiracy

Although there is no issue of fact or question as to the sufficiency of the evidence to be discussed here, nevertheless, it is necessary to summarize the principal facts of that conspiracy to monopolize certain trade, which was charged in the fourth count. These facts demonstrate also the vigor and nature of the intent of the petitioners to exclude competitors in order to maintain that monopoly if need or occasion should offer itself to attempt such an exclusion. To support the verdicts it was not necessary to show power and intent to exclude all competitors, or to show a conspiracy to exclude all competitors. The requirement stated to the jury and contained in the statute was only that the offenders shall "monopolize any part of the trade or commerce among the several states, or with foreign nations." This particular conspiracy may well have derived special vitality, in the eyes of the jury, from the fact that its existence was established, not through the presentation of a formal written agreement, but through the evidence of widespread and effective conduct on the part of petitioners in relation to their existing or potential competitors....

The fact, however, that the purchases of leaf tobacco and the sales of so many products of the tobacco industry have remained largely within the same general group of business organizations for over a generation, inevitably has contributed to the ease with which control over competition within the industry and the mobilization of power to resist new competition can be exercised. A friendly relationship within such a long established industry, is in itself not only natural but commendable and beneficial, as long as it does not breed illegal activities. Such a community of interest, however, provides a natural foundation for working policies and understandings favorable to the insiders and unfavorable to outsiders. The verdicts indicate that practices of an informal and flexible nature were adopted and that the results were so uniformly beneficial to the petitioners in protecting their common interests as against those of competitors that, entirely from circumstantial evidence, the jury found that a combination or conspiracy existed among the petitioners from 1937 to 1940, with power and intent to exclude competitors to such a substantial extent as to violate the Sherman Act as interpreted by the trial court.

The position of the petitioners in the cigarette industry from 1931 to 1939 is clear....Although American, Liggett and Reynolds gradually dropped in their percentage of the national domestic cigarette production from 90.7 percent in 1931 to 73.3 percent, 71 percent and 68 percent respectively in 1937, 1938 and 1939, they have accounted at all times for more than 68 percent, and usually for more than 75 percent, of the national production. The balance of the cigarette production has come from six other companies....

The further dominance of American, Liggett and Reynolds within their special field of burley blend cigarettes, as compared with the so-called "10 cent cigarettes," is also apparent. In 1939, the 10 cent cigarettes constituted about 14 ½ percent of the total domestic production. Accordingly, the 68 percent of the total cigarette production enjoyed by American, Liggett and Reynolds amounted to 80 percent of that production within their special field of cigarettes....

The foregoing demonstrates the basis of the claim of American, Liggett and Reynolds to the title of the "Big Three."...Without adverse criticism of it, comparative size on this great scale inevitably increased the power of these three to dominate all phases of their industry....

The Findings of the Lower Court

The verdicts show that the jury found that the petitioners conspired to fix prices and to exclude undesired competition against them in the purchase of the domestic type of flue-cured tobacco and of burley tobacco....

The Government introduced evidence showing that, although there was no written or express agreement discovered among American, Liggett and Reynolds, their practices included a clear course of dealing. This evidently convinced the jury of the existence of a combination or conspiracy to fix and control prices and practices as to domestic leaf tobacco, both in restraint of trade as such, and to establish a substantially impregnable defense against any attempted intrusion by potential competitors into these markets.

It appeared that petitioners refused to purchase tobacco on these markets unless the other petitioners were also represented thereon. There were attempts made by others to open new tobacco markets but none of the petitioners would participate in them unless the other petitioners were present. Consequently, such markets were failures due to the absence of buyers....

The Government presented evidence to support its claim that, before the markets opened, the petitioners placed limitations and restrictions on the prices which their buyers were permitted to pay for tobacco....

Competition also was eliminated between petitioners by the purchase of grades of tobacco in which but one of them was interested. To accomplish this, each company formulated the grades which it alone wished to purchase. The other companies recognized the grades so formulated as distinctive grades and did not compete for them. While the differences between the grades so formulated were distinguishable by the highly trained special buyers, they were in reality so minute as to be inconsequential....

Each company determined in advance what portion of the entire crop it would purchase before the market for that season opened. The petitioners then separately informed their buyers of the percentage of the crop which they wished to purchase and gave instructions that only such a percentage should be purchased on each market. The purchases were spread evenly over the different markets throughout the season. No matter what the size of the crop might be, the petitioners were able to purchase their predetermined percentages thereof within the price limits determined upon by them, thus indicating a stabilized market....

At a time when the manufacturers of lower priced cigarettes were beginning to manufacture them in quantity, the petitioners commenced to make large purchases of the cheaper tobacco leaves used for the manufacture of such lower priced cigarettes. No explanation was offered as to how or where this tobacco was used by petitioners. The compositions of their respective brands of cigarettes calling for the use of more expensive tobaccos remained unchanged during this period of controversy and up to the end of the trial. The Government claimed that such purchases of cheaper tobacco evidenced a combination and a purpose among the petitioners to deprive the manufacturers of cheaper cigarettes of the tobacco necessary for their manufacture, as well as to raise the price of such tobacco to such a point that cigarettes made therefrom could not be sold at a sufficiently low price to compete with the petitioner's more highly advertised brands.

The verdicts show also that the petitioners conspired to fix prices and to exclude undesired competition in the distribution and sale of their principal products....The list prices charged and the discounts allowed by petitioners have been practically identical since 1923 and absolutely identical since 1928. Since the latter date, only seven changes have been made by the three companies and those have been identical in amount.

Circumstantial Evidence

The following record of price changes is circumstantial evidence of the existence of a conspiracy and of a power and intent to exclude competition coming from cheaper grade cigarettes....On June 23, 1931, Reynolds, without previous notification or warning to the trade or public, raised the list price of Camel cigarettes, constituting its leading cigarette brand, from $6.40 to $6.85 a thousand. The same day American increased the list price for Lucky Strike cigarettes, its leading brand, and Liggett the price for Chesterfield cigarettes, its leading brand, to the identical price of $6.85 a thousand. No economic justification for this raise was demonstrated.

Before 1931, certain smaller companies had manufactured cigarettes retailing at 10 cents a package, which was several cents lower than the retail price for the leading brands of the petitioners. Up to that time, the sales of the 10 cent cigarettes were negligible. However, after the above described increase in list prices of the petitioners in 1931, the 10 cent brands made serious inroads upon the sales of the petitioners. These cheaper brands of cigarettes were sold at a list price of $4.75 a thousand and from 1931 to 1932 the sales of these cigarettes multiplied 30 times, rising from 0.28 percent of the total cigarette sales of the country in June, 1931, to 22.78 percent in November, 1932. In response to this threat of competition from the manufacturers of the 10 cent brands, the petitioners, in January, 1933, cut the list price of their three leading brands from $6.85 to $6 a thousand. In February, they cut again to $5.50 a thousand. The evidence tends to show that this cut was directed at the competition of the 10 cent cigarettes....Following the first price cut by petitioners, the sales of the 10 cent brands fell off considerably. After the second cut they fell off to a much greater extent. When the sale of the 10 cent brands had dropped from 22.78 percent of the total cigarette sales in November, 1932, to 6.43 percent in May, 1933, the petitioners, in January, 1934, raised the list price of their leading brands from $5.50 back up to $6.10 a thousand....The petitioners, in 1937, again increased the list prices of their above named brands to $6.25 a thousand and in July, 1940, to $6.53 a thousand.

There was evidence that when dealers received an announcement of the price increase from one of the petitioners and attempted to purchase some of the leading brands of cigarettes from the other petitioners at their unchanged prices before announcement of a similar change, the latter refused to fill such orders until their prices were also raised, thus bringing about the same result as if the changes had been precisely simultaneous....

Conclusions

It is not the form of the combination or the particular means used but the result to be achieved that the statute condemns. It is not of importance whether the means used to accomplish the unlawful objective are in themselves lawful or unlawful. Acts done to give effect to the conspiracy may be in themselves wholly innocent acts. Yet, if they are part of the sum of the acts which are relied upon to effectuate the conspiracy which the statute forbids, they come within its prohibition. No formal agreement is necessary to constitute an unlawful conspiracy....The essential combination or conspiracy in violation of the Sherman Act may be found in a course of dealing or other circumstances as well as in an exchange of words....Where the circumstances are such as to warrant a jury in finding that the conspirators had a unity of purpose or a common design and understanding, or a meeting of minds in an unlawful arrangement, the conclusion that a conspiracy is established is justified. Neither proof of exertion of the power to exclude nor proof of actual exclusion of existing or potential competitors is essential to sustain a charge of monopolization under the Sherman Act....

The material consideration in determining whether a monopoly exists is not that prices are raised and that competition actually is excluded but that power exists to raise prices or to exclude competition when it is desired to do so....

In the present cases, the petitioners have been found to have conspired to establish a monopoly and also have the power and intent to establish and maintain the monopoly. To hold that they do not come within the prohibition of the Sherman Act would destroy the force of that Act. Accordingly, the instructions of the trial court under Section 2 of the Act are approved and the judgment of the Circuit Court of Appeals is *Affirmed*.

ASSIGNMENT QUESTIONS

1. For what specific actions was the American Tobacco Company found to be in violation of the antitrust laws?
2. The government was never able to show with direct evidence that the Big Three had any plan for joint action. In light of this, how was it able to establish its case?
3. What principles of law were established in this case?
4. Compare the Court's opinion with the *Alcoa* decision.

25
THE CELLOPHANE CASE

UNITED STATES v. *E. I. DU PONT DE NEMOURS & CO.*

Appeal from the United States District Court
for the District of Delaware
No. 5. Argued October 11, 1955—Decided June 11, 1956

351 U.S. 377 (1956).

Mr. Justice Reed delivered the opinion of the Court:

The United States brought this civil action against E. I. du Pont de Nemours and Company. The complaint, filed December 13, 1947, in the United States District Court for the District of Columbia, charged du Pont with monopolizing, attempting to monopolize and conspiracy to monopolize interstate commerce in cellophane and cellulosic caps and bands in violation of Section 2 of the Sherman Act. After a lengthy trial, judgment was entered for du Pont on all issues.

The government's direct appeal attacks only the ruling that du Pont has not monopolized trade in cellophane. At issue for determination is only this alleged violation by du Pont of Section 2 of the Sherman Act.

During the period that is relevant to this action, du Pont produced almost 75 percent of the cellophane sold in the United States, and cellophane constituted less than 20 percent of all flexible packaging materials sales. This was the designation accepted at the trial for the materials listed in Finding 280 (see Exhibit 25-1).

EXHIBIT 25-1 Total U.S. Sales of Flexible Packaging Materials versus du Pont Cellophane Sales (1949)

	Thousands of square yards	
Glassine, greaseproof, and vegetable parchment papers	3,125,826	
Waxing papers	4,614,685	
Sulfite bag and wrapping papers	1,788,615	
Aluminum foil	1,317,807	
Cellophane	3,366,068	
Cellulose acetate	133,982	
Pliofilm, polyethylene, Saran, and Cry-O-Rap	373,871	
Total	14,720,854	100.0%
Total du Pont cellophane production	2,629,747	17.9%

The Finding of the Lower Court

The Government contends that, by so dominating cellophane production, du Pont monopolized a "part of the trade or commerce" in violation of Section 2. Du Pont agrees that cellophane is a product which constitutes a part of commerce within the meaning of Section 2, but it contends that the prohibition of Section 2 against monopolization is not violated because it does not have the power to control the price of cellophane or to exclude competitors from the market in which cellophane is sold. The court below found that the "relevant market for determining the extent of du Pont's market control is the market for flexible packaging materials," and that competition from those other materials prevented du Pont from possessing monopoly powers in its sale of cellophane.

The Government asserts that cellophane and other wrapping materials are neither substantially fungible nor like priced. For these reasons, it argues that the market for other wrappings is distinct from the market for cellophane and that the competition afforded cellophane by other wrappings is not strong enough to be considered in determining whether du Pont has monopoly powers. Market determination is necessary under du Pont's theory to determine whether an alleged monopolist violates Section 2. The ultimate consideration in such a determination is whether the defendants control the price and competition in the market for such part of trade or commerce as they are charged with monopolizing. Every manufacturer is the sole producer of the particular commodity it makes but its control in the above sense of the relevant market depends upon the availability of alternative commodities for buyers: i.e., whether there is a cross-elasticity of demand between cellophane and the other wrappings. This interchangeability is largely gauged by the purchase of competing products for similar uses considering the price, characteristics and adaptability of the competing commodities. The court below found that the flexible wrappings afforded such alternatives. This court must determine whether the trial court erred in its estimate of the competition afforded cellophane by other materials.

The Development of Cellophane

I. Factual Background

For consideration of the issue as to monopolization, a general summary of the development of cellophane is useful.

In the early 1900s, Jacques Brandenberger, a Swiss chemist, attempted to make tablecloths impervious to dirt by spraying them with liquid viscous (a cellulose solution available in quantity from wood pulp) and by coagulating this coating. His idea failed, but he noted that the coating peeled off in a transparent film. This first "cellophane" was thick, hard, and not perfectly transparent film, but Brandenberger apparently foresaw commercial possibilities in his discovery. By 1906 he developed the first machine for the manufacture of transparent sheets of regenerated cellulose. The 1908 product was not satisfactory, but by 1912, Brandenberger was making a salable thin flexible film used in gas masks. He obtained patents to cover the machinery and the essential ideas of his process.

It seems to be agreed, however, that the disclosures of the early patents were not sufficient to make possible the manufacture of commercial cellophane. The inadequacy of the patents is partially attributed to the fact that the essential machine (the Hopper) was improved after it was patented. But more significant was the failure of these patents to disclose the actual technique of the process. This technique included the operational data acquired by experimentation.

In 1917 Brandenberger assigned his patents to La Cellophane Société Anonyme and joined the organization.

An important factor in the growth of cellophane production and sales was the perfection of moistureproof cellophane, a superior product of du Pont research and patented by that company through a 1927 application. Plain cellophane has little resistance to the passage of moisture vapor. Moistureproof cellophane has a composition added which keeps moisture in and out of the packed commodity. This patented type of cellophane has had a demand with much more rapid growth than the plain.

Between 1928 and 1950, du Pont's sales of plain cellophane increased from $3,131,608 to $9,330,776. Moistureproof sales increased from $603,222 to $89,850,416, although prices were continuously reduced. It could not be said that this immense increase in use was solely or even largely attributable to the superior quality of cellophane or to the technique or business acumen of du Pont, though doubtless those factors were important. The growth was a part of the expansion of the commodity-packaging habits of business, a by-product of general efficient competitive merchandising to meet modern demands. The profits, which were large, apparently arose from this trend in marketing, the development of industrial use of chemical research and production of synthetics, rather than from elimination of other producers from the relevant market.

Applicable Antitrust Law

II. The Sherman Act and the Courts

The Sherman Act has received long and careful application by this court to achieve for the nation the freedom of enterprise from monopoly or restraint envisaged by the Congress that passed the Act in 1890. Because the Act is couched in broad terms, it is adaptable to the changing types of commercial production and distribution that have evolved since its passage. Chief Justice Hughes wrote for the Court that "As a charter of freedom, the Act has a generality and adaptability comparable to that found to be desirable in constitutional provisions."

It was said in *Standard Oil Co.* v. *United States,* that fear of the power of rapid accumulations of individuals and corporate wealth from the trade and industry of a developing national economy caused its passage. Units of traders and producers snowballed by combining into so-called "trusts." Competition was threatened, control of prices was feared. Individual initiative was dampened. While the economic picture has changed, large aggregations of private capital, with power attributes, continue. Mergers have continued. Industries such as steel, automobiles, tires, chemicals, have only a few production organizations. A considerable size is often essential for efficient operation in research, manufacture and distribution.

Judicial construction of antitrust legislation has generally been left unchanged by Congress. This is true of the Rule of Reason. While it is fair to say that the Rule of Reason is imprecise, its application in Sherman Act litigation, as directed against enhancement of price or throttling of competition, has given a workable content to antitrust legislation. It was judicially declared a proper interpretation of the Sherman Act in 1911, with a strong, clear-cut dissent challenging its soundness on the ground that the specific words of the Act covered every contract that tended to restrain or monopolize. This court has not receded from its position on the Rule. There is not, we think, any inconsistency between it and the development of the judicial theory that agreements as to maintenance of prices or division of territories are in themselves a violation of the Sherman Act. It is logical that some agreements and practices are invalid *per se,* while others are illegal only as applied to particular situations.

III. The Sherman Act, Section 2—Monopolization

The only statutory language of Section 2 pertinent on this review is: "Every person who shall monopolize...shall be deemed guilty...." Our cases determine that a party has monopoly power if it has, over "any part of the trade or commerce among the several states," a power of controlling prices or unreasonably restricting competition.

If cellophane is the "market" that du Pont is found to dominate, it may be assumed it does have monopoly power over that "market." Monopoly power is the power to control prices or exclude competition. It seems apparent that du Pont's power to set the price of cellophane has been limited only by the competition afforded by other flexible packaging materials. Moreover, it may be practically impossible for anyone to commence manufacturing cellophane without full access to du Pont's technique. However, du Pont has no power to prevent competition from other wrapping materials. The trial court consequently had to determine whether competition from the other wrappings prevented du Pont from possessing monopoly power in violation of Section 2. Price and competition are so intimately entwined that any discussion of theory must treat them as one. It is conceivable that price could be controlled without power over competition or vice versa. This approach to the determination of monopoly power is strengthened by this Court's conclusion in prior cases that, when an alleged monopolist has power over price and competition, an intention to monopolize in a proper case may be assumed.

If a large number of buyers and sellers deal freely in a standardized product, such as salt or wheat, we have complete or pure competition. Patents, on the other hand, furnish the most familiar type of classic monopoly. As the producers of a standardized product bring about significant differentiations of quality, design, or packaging in the product that permit differences of use, competition becomes to a greater or less degree incomplete and the producer's power over price and competition greater over his article and its use, according to the differentiation he is able to create and maintain. A retail seller may have in one sense a monopoly on certain trade because no one else makes a product of just the quality or attractiveness of his product, as for example in cigarettes. Thus one can theorize that we have monopolistic competition in every nonstandard commodity with each manufacturer having power over the price and production of his own product. However, this power that, let us say, automobile or soft-drink manufacturers have over their trademarked products is not the power that makes an illegal monopoly. Illegal power must be appraised in terms of the competitive market for the product.

Determination of the competitive market for commodities depends on how different from one another are the offered commodities in character of use, how far buyers will go to substitute one commodity for another. For example, one can think of building materials as in commodity competition but one could hardly say that brick competed with steel or wood or cement or stone in the meaning of the Sherman Act litigation; the products are too different. This is the inter-industry competition emphasized by economists. On the other hand, there are certain differences in the formulae for soft drinks but one can hardly say that each one is an illegal monopoly. Whatever the market may be, we hold that control of price or competition establishes the existence of monopoly power under Section 2. Section 2 requires the application of a reasonable approach in determining the existence of monopoly power just as surely as did Section 1. This of course does not mean that there can be a reasonable monopoly. Our next step is to determine whether du Pont has monopoly power over cellophane; that is, power over its price in relation to or in competition with other commodities. The charge was monopolization of cellophane. The defense, that cellophane was merely a part of the relevant market for flexible packaging materials.

IV. The Relevant Market

When a product is controlled by one interest, without substitutes available in the market, there is monopoly power. Because most products have possible substitutes, we cannot give infinite range to the definition of substitutes. Nor is it a proper interpretation of the Sherman Act to require that products be fungible to be considered in the relevant market.

The Government argues:

> We do not here urge that in no circumstances may competition of substitutes negative possession of monopolistic power over trade in a product. The decisions make it clear at the least that the courts will not consider substitutes other than those which are substantially fungible with the monopolized product and sell at substantially the same price.

But where there are market alternatives that buyers may readily use for their purposes, illegal monopoly does not exist merely because the product said to be monopolized differs from others. If it were not so, only physically identical products would be a part of the market. To accept the Government's argument, we would have to conclude that the manufacturers of plain as well as moistureproof cellophane were monopolists, and so with films such as Pliofilm, foil, glassine, polyethylene, and Saran, for each of these wrapping materials is distinguishable. These were all exhibits in the case. New wrappings appear, generally similar to cellophane: is each a monopoly? What is called for is an appraisal of the "cross-elasticity" of demand in the trade.

The Opinion of the Supreme Court

The varying circumstances of each case determine the result. In considering what is the relevant market for determining the control of price and competition, no more definite rule can be declared than that commodities reasonably interchangeable by consumers for the same purposes make up that "part of the trade or commerce," monopolization of which may be illegal. As respects flexible packaging materials, the market geographically is nation-wide.

Industrial activities cannot be confined to trim categories. Illegal monopolies under Section 2 may well exist over limited products in narrow fields where competition is eliminated. That does not settle the issue here. In determining the market under the Sherman Act, it is the use or uses to which the commodity is put that control. The selling price between commodities with similar uses and different characteristics may vary, so that the cheaper product can drive out the more expensive. Or, the superior quality of higher priced articles may make dominant the more desirable. Cellophane costs more than many competing products and less than a few. But whatever the price, there are various flexible wrapping materials that are bought by manufacturers for packaging their goods in their own plants or are sold to converters who shape and print them for use in the packaging of the commodities to be wrapped.

Cellophane differs from other flexible packaging materials. From some it differs more than from others. It may be admitted that cellophane combines the desirable elements of transparency, strength and cheapness more definitely than any of the others. Comparative characteristics have been noted thus:

> Moistureproof cellophane is highly transparent, tears readily but has high bursting strength, is highly impervious to moisture and gases, and is resistant to grease and oils. Heat sealable, printable, and adapted to use on wrapping machines, it makes an excellent packaging material for display and protection of commodities.
>
> Other flexible wrapping materials fall into four major categories: (1) opaque nonmoistureproof wrapping paper designed primarily for convenience and protection in handling packages; (2) moistureproof films of varying degrees of transparency designed primarily either to protect, or to display and protect, the products they encompass; (3) nonmoistureproof transparent films designed primarily to display and to some extent protect, but which obviously do a poor protecting job where exclusion or retention of moisture is important; and (4) moistureproof materials other than films of varying degrees of transparency (foils and paper products) designed to protect and display.

But, despite cellophane's advantages, it has to meet competition from other materials in every one of its uses. Food products are the chief outlet, with cigarettes next. The Government makes no challenge to the findings that cellophane furnishes less than 7 percent of wrappings for bakery products, 25 percent for candy, 32 percent for snacks, 35 percent for meat and poultry, 27 percent for crackers and biscuits, 47 percent for fresh produce, and 34 percent for frozen foods. Seventy-five to eighty percent of cigarettes are wrapped in cellophane. Thus, cellophane shares the packaging market with others. The over-all result is that cellophane accounts for 17.9 percent of flexible wrapping materials, measured by the wrapping surface.

Moreover a very considerable degree of functional interchangeability exists between these products. Except as to permeability to gases, cellophane has no qualities that are not possessed by a number of other materials. Meat will do as an example of interchangeability. Although du Pont's sales to the meat industry have reached

19,000,000 pounds annually, nearly 35 percent, this volume is attributed "to the rise of self-service retailing of fresh meat." In fact, since the popularity of self-service meats, du Pont has lost a considerable portion of this packaging business to Pliofilm. Pliofilm is more expensive than cellophane, but its superior physical characteristics apparently offset cellophane's price advantage. While retailers shift continually between the two, the trial court found that Pliofilm is increasing its share of the business. One further example is worth noting. Before World War II, du Pont cellophane wrapped between 5 and 10 percent of baked and smoked meats. The peak year was 1933. Thereafter du Pont was unable to meet the competition of Sylvania and of greaseproof paper. Its sales declined and the 1933 volume was not reached again until 1947. It will be noted that greaseproof paper, glassine, waxed paper, foil and Pliofilm are used as well as cellophane.

An element for consideration as to cross-elasticity of demand between products is the responsiveness of the sales of one product to price changes of the other. If a slight decrease in the price of cellophane causes a considerable number of customers of other flexible wrappings to switch to cellophane, it would be an indication that a high cross-elasticity of demand exists between them; that the products compete in the same market. The court below held that the "great sensitivity of customers in the flexible packaging markets to price or quality changes prevented du Pont from possessing monopoly control over price." The record sustains these findings.

Conclusions

We conclude that cellophane's interchangeability with the other materials mentioned suffices to make it a part of this flexible packaging material market. There is no cellophane market distinct and separate from the market for flexible packaging materials; the market for flexible packaging materials is the relevant market for determining the nature and extent of du Pont's market control; and du Pont has at all times competed with other cellophane manufacturers of other flexible packaging materials in all aspects of its cellophane business.

The "market" which one must study to determine when a producer has monopoly power will vary with the part of commerce under consideration. The tests are constant. That market is composed of products that have reasonable interchangeability for the purposes for which they are produced—price, use and qualities considered. While the application of the tests remain uncertain, it seems to us that du Pont should not be found to monopolize cellophane when that product has the competition and interchangeability with other wrappings that this record shows.

On the findings of the District Court, its judgment is *Affirmed*.

ASSIGNMENT QUESTIONS

1. Outline the main issues in this case.
2. Summarize the opinion of the Court, and state a general principle to be gained from the decision.
3. Develop a strong dissenting opinion in opposition to the opinion of the majority of the Court.

26

DU PONT AND ITS 23 PERCENT STOCK INTEREST IN GENERAL MOTORS

United States v. *E. I. du Pont de Nemours & Company*, 353 U.S. 586 (1957).

In 1949, the Justice Department brought an action against the du Pont Company, charging that a purchase by du Pont, in 1917–1919, of a 23 percent stock interest in General Motors resulted in a violation of Section 7 of the Clayton Act. The essence of the charge was that by means of the close relationship between the two companies, du Pont had obtained an illegal preference over competitors in the sale of automobile finishes and fabrics to GM—thus "tending to create a monopoly in a line of commerce."

The case was tried in the United States District Court for the Northern District of Illinois. After a lengthy trial, the court concluded that the Government had failed to prove its case, and dismissed the complaint. An appeal was made to the Supreme Court, and arguments were presented on November 14–15, 1956.

Argument for the Government

The primary issue is whether du Pont's dominant position as GM's supplier of finishes and fabrics was achieved on competitive merit alone, or because its ownership of General Motors' common stock gave it sufficient influence to keep competition out. If the latter case is true, then there has been the creation of monopoly in a line of commerce.

The first paragraph of Section 7, pertinent here, provides:

> That no corporation engaged in commerce shall acquire, directly or indirectly, the whole or any part of the stock or other share capital of another corporation engaged also in commerce, where the effect of such acquisition may be to substantially lessen competition between the corporation whose stock is so acquired and the corporation making the acquisition, or to restrain such commerce in any section or community, or tend to create a monopoly of any line of commerce.

Section 7 is designed to stop in its incipiency not only a substantial lessening of competition between corporations, when one firm buys the stock of a competing firm, but also to stop monopoly in a relevant market as a result of the acquisition. Acquisitions solely for investment purposes are excepted.

The Application of Section 7 to Vertical Acquisitions

We are met at the threshold with the argument that Section 7, before its amendment in 1950, applied only to an acquisition of the stock of a competing corporation, and not to an acquisition by a supplier corporation—in other words, that the statute applied only to horizontal and not to vertical acquisitions. This is the first case presenting the question in this court.

It must be admitted that during the 35 years before this action was brought, the Government did not invoke Section 7 against vertical acquisitions. The Federal Trade Commission has said that the section does not apply to vertical acquisitions. However, the courts have the duty to reconcile administrative interpretations with the broad antitrust policies laid down by Congress. The failure of the Commission to act is not a binding administrative interpretation that Congress did not intend vertical acquisitions to come within the purview of the Act.

Section 7 is framed to reach not only the corporate acquisition of stock of a competing corporation, where the effect may be to substantially lessen competition between them, but also the corporate acquisition of stock of any corporation, competitor or not, where the effect may be either (1) to restrain commerce in any section or community, or (2) tend to create a monopoly of any line of commerce. The amended complaint does not allege that the effect of du Pont's acquisition may be to restrain commerce in any section or community but alleges that the effect was to tend to create a monopoly in a particular line of commerce.

Examination of the events in the Congress during the passage of the Clayton Act lends support to our interpretation of the meaning of the bill. Senator Chilton, one of the Senate managers of the act, explained that the House conferees insisted that to prohibit just acquisitions where the effect was "substantially" to lessen competition would not accomplish the designed aim of the statute, because "a corporation might acquire the stock of another corporation, and there would be no lessening of competition, but the tendency might be to create a monopoly or to restrain trade or commerce." "Therefore," said Senator Chilton, "there was added...the following: 'Or to restrain such commerce in any section or community or tend to create a monopoly of any line of commerce.' " This construction of the section, as embracing three separate and distinct effects of a stock acquisition, has also been recognized by a number of federal courts.

We hold that any acquisition by one corporation of all or any part of the stock of another corporation, competitor or not, is within the reach of the section whenever the reasonable likelihood appears that the acquisition will result in a restraint of commerce or in the creation of a monopoly of any line of commerce. Thus, although du Pont and General Motors are not competitors, there was at the time of the suit a reasonable likelihood of monopoly of any line of commerce. Judge Maris correctly stated in *Transamerica Corp.* v. *Board of Governors,*

> A monopoly involves the power to...exclude competition when the monopolist desires to do so. Obviously, under section 7 it was not necessary...to find that...the defendant had actually achieved monopoly power but merely that the stock acquisitions under attack had brought it measurably closer to that end. For it is the purpose of the Clayton Act to nip monopoly in the bud. Since by definition monopoly involves the power to eliminate competition, a lessening of competition is clearly relevant in the determination of the existence of a tendency to monopolize. Accordingly, in order to determine the existence of a tendency to monopoly in any line of business the area or areas of existing effective competition in which monopoly power might be exercised must first be determined.

The Relevant Market

Our opponents argue that there exists no basis for finding of a probable restraint or monopoly within the meaning of Section 7 because the total General Motors market for finishes and fabrics constituted only a negligible percentage of the total market for these materials for all uses, including automobile uses. It is stated in the General Motors brief that in 1947 du Pont's finish sales to

General Motors constituted 3.5 percent of all sales of finishes to industrial users, and that its fabric sales to General Motors comprised 1.6 percent of the total market for the type of fabric used by the automobile industry.

Determination of the relevant market is a necessary predicate to a finding of a violation of the Clayton Act because the threatened monopoly must be one which will substantially lessen competition "within the area of effective competition." Substantiality can be determined only in terms of the market affected. The record shows that automobile finishes and fabrics have sufficient peculiar characteristics and uses to constitute them products sufficiently distinct from all other finishes and fabrics to make them a "line of commerce," within the meaning of the Clayton Act.

General Motors is the colossus of the giant automobile industry. It accounts annually for upwards of two-fifths of the total sales of automobile vehicles in the Nation. In 1955 General Motors ranked first in sales and second in assets among all United States industrial corporations and became the first corporation to earn over a billion dollars in annual net income. In 1947 General Motors' total purchases of all products from du Pont were $26,628,274, of which $18,938,229 (71 percent) represented purchases from du Pont's Finishes Division. Of the latter amount purchases of "Duco" totaled $12,224,798 (65 percent). Purchases by General Motors of du Pont fabrics in 1948 amounted to $3,700,000, making it the largest account of du Pont's Fabrics Division. Expressed in percentages, du Pont supplied 67 percent of General Motors' requirements for finishes in 1946 and 68 percent in 1947. In fabrics du Pont supplied 52.3 percent of requirements in 1946, and 38.5 percent in 1947. Because General Motors accounts for almost one-half of the automobile industry's annual sales, its requirements for automobile finishes must represent approximately one-half of the relevant market for these materials. Because the record shows that quantitatively and percentagewise du Pont supplies the largest part of General Motors' requirements, we must conclude that du Pont has a substantial share of the relevant market.

The Applicable Time

The appellees argue that the Government could not maintain this action in 1949 because Section 7 is applicable only to the acquisition of stock and not to the holding or subsequent use of the stock. This argument misconceives the objective toward which Section 7 is directed. The Clayton Act was intended to supplement the Sherman Act. Its aim was primarily to arrest apprehended consequences of intercorporate relationships before those relationships could work their evil, which may be at or any time after the acquisition, depending upon the circumstances of the particular case.

To accomplish the Congressional aim, the Government may proceed at any time that an acquisition may be said with reasonable probability to contain a threat that it may lead to a restraint of commerce or tend to create a monopoly of a line of commerce. Even when the purchase is solely for investment, the plain language of Section 7 contemplates an action at any time the stock is used to bring about, or in attempting to bring about, the substantial lessening of competition.

The History of du Pont–GM Relations

The du Pont Company's commanding position as a General Motors supplier was not achieved until shortly after its purchase of a sizeable block of General Motors stock in 1917. At that time its production for the automobile industry and its sales to General Motors were relatively insignificant. General Motors then produced only about 11 percent of the total automobile production.

Before the first block of General Motors stock was acquired, du Pont was seeking markets for its nitrocellulose, artificial leather, celluloid, rubber-coated goods, and points and varnishes in demand by automobile companies. In that connection, the trial court expressly found that "reports and other documents written at or near the time of the investment show that du Pont's representatives were well aware that General Motors was a large consumer of products of the kind offered by du Pont," and that John J. Raskob, du Pont's Treasurer and the principal promoter of the investment, "for one, thought that du Pont would ultimately get all that business."

The company's interest in buying into General Motors was stimulated by Raskob and Pierre S. du Pont, then du Pont's president, who acquired personal holdings of General Motors stock in 1914....On December 19, 1917, Raskob submitted a Treasurer's Report to the du Pont Finance Committee recommending a purchase of General Motors stock in the amount of $25,000,000. That report makes clear that more than just a profitable investment was contemplated. A major consideration was that an expanding General Motors would provide a substantial market needed by the burgeoning du Pont organization. Raskob's summary of reasons in support of the purchase includes this statement: "Our interests in the General Motors Company will undoubtedly secure for us the entire Fabrikoid Pyralin (celluloid), paint and varnish business of those companies, which is a substantial factor."

This background of the acquisition, particularly the plain implications of the contemporaneous documents, destroys any basis for a conclusion that the purchase was made "solely for investment." However, immediately after the acquisition, du Pont's influence growing out of it was brought to bear within General Motors to achieve primacy for du Pont as General Motors' supplier of automobile fabrics and finishes.

Two years were to pass before du Pont's total purchases of General Motors stock brought its percentage to 23 percent of the outstanding stock and its aggregate outlay to $49,000,000. During that period, Pierre du Pont and GM President, W. C. Durant worked under an arrangement giving du Pont primary responsibility for GM finances and Durant the responsibility for operations. J. A. Haskell, du Pont's former sales manager and vice-president, became the General Motors vice-president in charge of the operations committee. The trial judge said that Haskell "...was willing to take the responsibility of keeping du Pont informed of General Motors affairs during Durant's regime."

Haskell frankly and openly set about gaining the maximum share of the General Motors market for du Pont. In a contemporaneous 1918 document, he reveals his intention to "pave the way for perhaps a more general adoption of our material," and he was thinking "how best to get cooperation [from the several General Motors Divisions] whereby makers of such of the low priced cars as it would seem possible and wise to get transferred will be put in the frame of mind necessary for its adoption [du Pont's artificial leather]."

Haskell set up lines of communication within General Motors to be in a position to know at all times what du Pont products and what products of du Pont competitors were being used. It is not pure imagination to suppose that such surveillance from that source made an impressive impact upon purchasing officials. It would be understandably difficult for them not to interpret it as meaning that a preference was to be given to du Pont products. Haskell also actively pushed the program to substitute Fabrikoid artificial leathers for genuine leather and sponsored use of du Pont's pyralin sheeting through a liaison arrangement set up between himself and the du Pont sales organization.

Thus sprung from the barrier, du Pont quickly swept into a commanding lead over its competitors, who were never afterwards in serious contention. In less than four years, by August 1921, Lammont du Pont, then a du Pont vice-president and later Chairman of the Board of General Motors, in response to a query from Pierre S. du Pont, then Chairman of the Board of both du Pont and General Motors, "whether General Motors was taking its entire requirements of du Pont products from du Pont," was able to reply that four of General Motors' eight operating divisions bought from du Pont their entire requirements of Fabrikoid, four their entire requirements of rubber cloth, and seven their entire requirements of Pyralin and celluloid. Lammont du Pont quoted du Pont's sales department as feeling that "the condition is improving and that eventually satisfactory conditions will be established in every branch, but they wouldn't mind seeing things going a little faster."

The fact that sticks out in this voluminous record is that the bulk of du Pont's production has always supplied the largest part of the requirements of the one customer in the automobile industry connected to du Pont by a stock interest. The inference is overwhelming that du Pont's commanding position was promoted by its stock interest and was not gained solely on competitive merit.

This is not to say that considerations of price, quality and service were overlooked by either du Pont or General Motors. Pride in its products and its high financial stake in General Motors' success would naturally lead du Pont to try to supply the best. But the wisdom of this business judgment cannot obscure the fact, plainly revealed by the record, that du Pont purposely employed its stock to pry open the General Motors market to entrench itself as the primary supplier of General Motors' requirements for automobile finishes and fabrics.

It is hoped that the judgment of the District

Court will be reversed and that equitable relief will be obtained appropriate to the public interest.

Argument for du Pont

To begin, it should be noted that in the District Court, the trial of these issues took nearly seven months. The Court heard 52 witnesses, including most of the principal actors, and received over 2,000 exhibits. The evidence contained in the 8,283 page transcript of record covers in minute detail the facts bearing on the Government's charge that du Pont, by coercion, agreement, control or influence, had interfered unlawfully with General Motors' purchasing and manufacturing policies. On the basis of this evidence, the District Court found that the Government had failed to prove its case.

The Government now proposed that the Supreme Court disregard the carefully documented findings of fact of the District Court. The court's decision will be far reaching. Although Section 7 of the Clayton Act was enacted in 1914—over 40 years ago—this is the first case in which the United States or the Federal Trade Commission has sought to apply it to a vertical integration. Likewise, this appears to be the first case in which it ever has been argued that Section 7 is applicable to a stock acquisition which took place many years before. The Court, if it accepts both of these contentions, must disregard the language and purpose of the statute, 40 years of administrative practice, and all the precedents except one District Court decision.

Summary

We believe that the Government is in error in (1) attempting to apply Section 7 to a vertical acquisition; (2) proposing that the time chosen by the Government in bringing the action is controlling rather than the time of the acquisition, and (3) concluding that, even if we accept these theories of illegality, that the findings of the trial court should be disregarded.

Section 7 of the Clayton Act does not make unlawful all intercorporate acquisitions and mergers. It does not apply to acquisitions of physical assets. It applies only to certain acquisitions of stock, and even then with important exceptions. The first paragraph of Section 7, which is the statutory provision primarily involved in this case, provides:

> That no corporation engaged in commerce shall acquire, directly or indirectly, the whole or any part of the stock or other share capital of another corporation engaged also in commerce, where the effect of such acquisition may be to substantially lessen competition between the corporation making the acquisition, or to restrain such commerce in any section or community, or tend to create a monopoly of any line of commerce.

This paragraph makes unlawful only those intercorporate stock acquisitions which may result in any of three effects: (1) substantially lessen competition between the acquiring and the acquired corporations; (2) restrain commerce in any section or community; or (3) tend to create a monopoly of any line of commerce. The Government concedes that since General Motors and du Pont have never been in competition with each other, number (1) does not apply. The questions before us are whether the other unlawful effects, namely, restraint of commerce in any section or community and tendency to create a monopoly of any line of commerce, are applicable to this case, and, if so, whether the 1917–1919 acquisition of General Motors stock by du Pont resulted or may result in either of those unlawful effects.

Section 7 has never been authoritatively interpreted as prohibiting the acquisition of stock in a corporation that is not engaged in the same line of business as the acquiring corporation. Although the language of the Act is ambiguous, the relevant legislative history, administrative practice, and judicial interpretation support the conclusion that Section 7 does not apply to vertical acquisitions.

Legislative History

The report of the House Committee on the Judiciary presented by Representative Clayton, stated emphatically that the provisions relating to stock acquisitions by corporations, which originally appeared as Section 8 of the bill, were intended to eliminate the evils of *holding companies*. Although a "holding company" was defined as a "company that holds the stock of another company or companies," the one "evil" referred to was that a holding company "is a means of holding under one control the *competing* companies whose stocks it has thus acquired."

The extensive debates on the bill in each House of the Congress contain many detailed discussions of the provisions relating to intercorporate stock acquisitions. These discussions are devoid of any suggestion that the provisions were to apply to vertical acquisitions. On the contrary, these provisions of the bill were repeatedly described as prohibiting the acquisition of stock of competing companies. The one specific reference to a vertical acquisition during the entire debate on these provisions ended with a flat statement by Senator Reed to the effect that the bill as then written would *not* prevent a steel manufacturer from acquiring stock in an ore producing corporation, a classic type of vertical integration.

A reading of the legislative history of the bill leaves the distinct impression that intercorporate relationships between buyers and sellers which resulted in noncompetitive preferences were intended to be dealt with exclusively by the provision forbidding interlocking directorates, if not covered by the specific prohibitions of certain price discriminations, and of certain exclusive selling or leasing contracts.

Forty years of administrative practice provides additional support for this view. Neither the Department of Justice nor the Federal Trade Commission, the two principal enforcing agencies, has brought any action under old Section 7 (other than this case) that has not involved a stock acquisition in allegedly competing corporations. The Federal Trade Commission repeatedly has declared its understanding that Section 7, prior to its amendment in 1950, applied only to competing corporations.

The Applicable Time

In this case, the Government is challenging, in 1949, a stock acquisition that took place in 1917–1919. Without advance reasons to support its conclusions, it holds that in deciding whether the effect of the stock acquisition is such as to violate Section 7, the time chosen by the Government in bringing its suit is controlling rather than the time of the acquisition of the stock. This seems to us to ignore the language and structure of Section 7, the purpose of the Clayton Act, and all existing administrative and judicial precedents.

The Clayton Act was not intended to replace the Sherman Act in remedying actual restraints and monopolies. Its purpose was to supplement the Sherman Act by checking anticompetitive tendencies in their incipiency, before they reached the point at which the Sherman Act comes into play. This purpose was well stated in the Senate Report on the bill:

> Broadly stated, the bill, in its treatment of unlawful restraints and monopolies, seeks to prohibit and make unlawful certain trade practices which, as a rule, singly and in themselves, are not covered by the Sherman Act, or other existing antitrust acts, and thus, by making these practices illegal, to arrest the creation of trusts, conspiracies, and monopolies in their incipiency and before consummation.

This purpose places emphasis on the probable anticompetitive effects of transactions or occurrences viewed as of the date of their occurrence. If, at the time of the stock acquisition, a potential threat to competition is apparent, the acquisition is unlawful under Section 7. If, on the other hand, a potential threat to competition is not then apparent, an antitrust violation is not involved unless subsequent use of the stock constitutes a restraint of trade prohibited by the Sherman Act.

The Government ignores the all-important lawfulness or unlawfulness of the stock acquisition at or about the time it occurred, and limits its attention to the probable anticompetitive effects of the continued holding of the stock at the time of suit, some 30 years later. The result is to subject a good-faith stock acquisition, lawful when made, to the hazards that the continued holding of the stock may make the acquisition illegal through unforeseen developments. Such a view is not supported by the statute and violates elementary principles of fairness. The Government may set aside a transaction which was entirely lawful when made, merely by showing that it would have been unlawful had it occurred at the time of suit, many years later. The growth of the acquired corporation, a fortuitous decline in the number of competitors, or the achievement of control by an accidental diffusion of other stock may result, under this test, in rendering the original lawful acquisition unlawful.

The Government's holding is unfair to the individuals who entered into transactions on the assumption, justified by the language of Section 7, that their actions would be judged by the facts available to them at the time they made their decision.

Du Pont as a Supplier to General Motors

The remaining issues are factual: (1) whether the record establishes the existence of a reasonable probability that du Pont's competitors will be foreclosed from securing General Motors' trade, and (2) whether the record establishes that such foreclosure, if probable, involves a substantial and significant share of the relevant market and significantly limits the competitive opportunities of others trading in that market. In discussing these factual issues, we meet the Government on its own ground, that is, we assume that the old Section 7 applies to vertical acquisitions, and that the potential threat at the time of suit is controlling. Even on that basis the record does not support the Government's conclusion that Section 7 was violated by this 1917–19 stock acquisition.

This is not a case where a supplier corporation has merged with its customer corporation with the result that the supplier's competitors are automatically and completely foreclosed from the customer's trade. In this case, the only connection between du Pont, the supplier, and General Motors, the customer, is du Pont's 23 percent stock interest in General Motors. A conclusion that such a stock interest automatically forecloses du Pont's competitors from selling to General Motors would be without justification. Whether a foreclosure has occurred in the past or is probable in the future is a question of fact turning on the evidence in the record.

According to the Government, the basic facts are said to be that du Pont had no standing as a General Motors' supplier before the stock purchases of 1917–1919, that it gained a "commanding position" after the stock purchases, and that certain items of evidence tend to indicate that du Pont hoped to get and actually did get a preference in General Motors' trade. From these alleged facts the Government draws the conclusion that du Pont has misused its 23 percent stock interest in General Motors "to entrench itself as the primary supplier of General Motors' requirements for automobile finishes and fabrics." With these words, the Government disregards the District Court's unequivocal findings to the effect that du Pont was a principal supplier to General Motors prior to the 1917–1919 stock purchases, that du Pont maintained this position in the years following the stock purchases, and that for the entire 30-year period preceding the suit, General Motors purchases of du Pont's products were solely based on the competitive merits of these products. The evidence supporting these findings of the District Court may be summarized as follows:

Du Pont is primarily a manufacturer of chemicals and chemical products. Thousands of its products could be used by General Motors in manufacturing automobiles, appliances and machinery. Despite du Pont's sales efforts over a period of 40 years, General Motors buys many of the commodities produced by du Pont from du Pont's competitors. The Government is ignoring the many products which General Motors declines to buy from du Pont or which it buys only in small quantities, and is concentrating on the few products which du Pont has sold in large volume to General Motors for many years—paints and fabrics. Before examining the history of these large volume purchases, it is essential to understand where and by whom purchasing decisions within General Motors have been made.

For many years, General Motors has been organized into some 30 operating divisions, each of which has final authority to make, and does make, its own purchasing decisions. This decentralized management system places full responsibility for purchasing decisions on the officers of the respective divisions. To speak of "selling to General Motors" is, therefore, misleading. A prospective supplier, instead of selling to General Motors, sells to Chevrolet, or Frigidaire, or Delco Light, as divisions. Moreover, when there are several plants within a division, each plant frequently has its own purchasing agent and presents a separate selling job.

The record discloses that each division buys independently, that the pattern of buying varies greatly from one division to another, and that within each division purchases from du Pont have fluctuated greatly in response to price, quality, service and other competitive considerations. For example, Oldsmobile is the only division which buys antifreeze from du Pont and one of the two car divisions which does not finish its cars with Duco. Buick alone buys du Pont motor enamel, and Cadillac alone uses du Pont's copper electroplating exclusively. Thus the alleged nefarious influence arising from du Pont's stock interest apparently affects the Oldsmobile antifreeze buyer, but not the Oldsmobile paint buyer; the paint buyers at Chevrolet, Buick and Pontiac, but not the antifreeze or electroplating buyers; and the electroplating buyer at Cadillac, but not the Cadillac paint buyer.

The Relevant Market

Finally, even assuming the correctness of the Government's conclusion that du Pont's competitors have been or will be foreclosed from General Motors' paint and fabric trade, it is still necessary to resolve one more issue in favor of the Government in order to reverse the District Court. It is necessary to hold that the Government proved that this foreclosure involves a substantial share of the relevant market and that it significantly limits the competitive opportunities of others trading in that market.

The Government holds that the relevant market in this case is the automobile market for finishes and fabrics, and not the total industrial market for these products. The Government reaches that conclusion because in its view "automotive finishes and fabrics are sufficiently distinct from all others finishes and fabrics." We are not told what these "peculiar characteristics" are. Nothing is said about finishes other than that Duco represents an important contribution to the process of manufacturing an automobile. Arbitrary conclusions are not an adequate substitute for analysis of the pertinent facts contained in the record.

The record does not show that the fabrics and finishes used in the manufacture of automobiles have peculiar characteristics differentiating them from the finishes and fabrics used in other industries. Duco was first marketed not to General Motors, but to the auto refinishing trade and to manufacturers of furniture, brush handles, and pencils. In 1927, 44 percent of du Pont's sales of colored Duco, and 51.5 percent of its total sales, were to purchasers other than auto manufacturers. Although the record does not show exact figures for all years, it does show that a substantial portion of du Pont's sales of Duco have continued to be for non-automotive uses.

In 1947, when du Pont's sales of paints to General Motors totaled about $15,400,000, the total national market for paints and finishes was $1,248,000,000, of which $552,000,000 was for varnishes, lacquers, enamels, thinners, and dopes, the kinds of finishes sold primarily to industrial users. There is no evidence of record that these industrial finishes are not competitive with Duco. There is considerable evidence that many of them are. It is probable that du Pont's total sales of finishes to General Motors in 1947 constituted less than 3.5 percent of all sales of industrial finishes.

The burden was on the Government to prove that a substantial share of the relevant market would, in all probability, be affected by du Pont's 23 percent stock interest in General Motors. The Government proved only that du Pont's sales of finishes and fabrics to General Motors were large in volume, and that General Motors was the leading manufacturer of automobiles during the later years covered by the record. The Government did not show that the identical products were not used on a large scale for many other purposes in many other industries. Nor did the Government show that the automobile industry in general, or General Motors in particular, comprised a large or substantial share of the total market. What evidence there is in the record affirmatively indicates that the products involved do have wide use in many industries, and that an insubstantial portion of this total market would be affected even if an unlawful preference existed or were probable.

For the reasons stated, we conclude that Section 7 of the Clayton Act, prior to its amendment in 1950, did not apply to vertical acquisitions; that the Government failed to prove that there was a reasonable probability at the time of the stock acquisition (1917–1919) of a restraint of commerce or a tendency toward monopoly.

ASSIGNMENT QUESTIONS

1. What is the central issue under consideration in this case?
2. Summarize the government's argument.
3. What was du Pont's counterargument?

4. For what reason did both sides refer to the legislative history of the Clayton Act in their arguments?
5. Is it proper for a court to overturn forty years of prior administrative practice and court decisions?
6. Do you agree with the following statement: "Law is not the path to social reform. We must resist the alluring prospect that our world can be changed in the courts rather than by legislators."
7. What would be your decision in this case? Why?
8. If the Supreme Court decides in favor of the government, what sort of remedy could be applied to the situation? Would du Pont have to sell its 23 percent stock interest? (At the time of the case, it had an estimated market value of $3.5 billion.) What problems can you see in this?

27
THE UTAH PIE COMPANY

Utah Pie Co. v. *Continental Baking Co.*, 386 U.S. 685 (1967).

The Utah Pie Company (UPC) is a Utah corporation which, since 1927, has been baking pies in its plant in Salt Lake City and selling them in Utah and surrounding states. The company was founded by the Rigby family and since its inception has continued to be owned and operated by members of that family. Of the firm's eighteen employees in 1957, nine were family members.

In 1957 Utah Pie entered the frozen pie business, offering frozen apple, cherry, boysenberry, peach, pumpkin, and mince pies to the consuming public. This initial venture did so well that in 1958 the company constructed a new plant in Salt Lake City specifically to produce frozen pies.

UPC sold its pies under the "Utah" brand. It also sold pies of like grade and quality under the house brand "Frost 'N' Flame" to Associated Grocers, and in 1961 it began selling to American Food Stores under the "Mayfresh" label. It also sold pumpkin and mince frozen pies on a seasonal basis to Safeway under Safeway's own "Bel-air" label. From its beginning in 1957, Utah Pie's frozen pie business was very successful and became a major part of the firm's total product line. A summary of UPC's operations is shown in Exhibit 27-1.

EXHIBIT 27-1 The Utah Pie Company: Operating Data, 1957–1961

	1957	*1958*	*1959*	*1960*	*1961*
Net worth	$ 31,651				$ 68,802
Sales	238,000	$353,000	$430,000	$504,000	589,000
Net income	–6,461	7,090	11,897	7,636	6,216

The Utah Frozen Pie Market

The major competitive weapon in the Utah frozen pie market was price. The location of UPC's plant gave it natural advantages in the Salt Lake City marketing area, and it entered the market at a price below the going prices for competitors' comparable pies. For most of the period under consideration here—from 1958 through 1961—its prices were the lowest in the Salt Lake City market. It was, however, challenged by each of its major competitors at one time or another and for varying periods, and there was evidence to show that the frozen pie price structure deteriorated during the same period.

Utah Pie Company's principal competitors in the frozen pie business were Pet Milk Company, Carnation Company, and Continental Baking. UPC, which entered the market at a price of $4.15 per dozen at the beginning of the relevant period, was selling "Utah" and "Frost 'N' Flame" pies for $2.75 per dozen some forty-four months later. Pet, which was offering pies at $4.92 per dozen in February 1958, was offering "Pet-Ritz" and "Bel-air" pies at $3.56 and $3.46 per dozen, respectively, in March and April 1961. Carnation's price in early 1958 was $4.82 per dozen, but it was selling at $3.46 per dozen at the conclusion of the period, meanwhile having been down as low as $3.30 per dozen. The price range recorded by Continental ran from a 1958 high of over $5.00 per dozen to a 1961 low of $2.85 per dozen.

The Salt Lake City sales volumes and market shares of the main competitors in the frozen pie business are shown in Exhibit 27-2.

EXHIBIT 27-2 Salt Lake City Frozen Pie Market, 1958–1961

Company	*Unit Volume (in doz.)*	*Percentage of Market*
	1958	
Carnation	5,863	10.3%
Continental	754	1.3
Utah Pie	37,970	66.5
Pet	9,336	16.4
Others	3,137	5.5
Total	57,060	100.0%
	1959	
Carnation	9,625	8.6
Continental	3,182	2.9
Utah Pie	38,372	34.3
Pet	39,639	35.5
Others	20,911	18.7
Total	111,729	100.0%
	1960	
Carnation	22,372	12.1
Continental	3,350	1.8
Utah Pie	83,894	45.5
Pet	51,480	27.9
Others	23,473	12.7
Total	184,565	100.0%
	1961	
Carnation	20,067	8.8
Continental	18,067	8.3
Utah Pie	102,690	45.3
Pet	66,786	29.4
Others	18,565	8.2
Total	226,908	100.0%

Pet Milk

Pet Milk entered the frozen pie business in 1955, acquired plants in Pennsylvania and California to augment the production of its existing plant in Michigan, and undertook a large advertising campaign to market its "Pet-Ritz" brand of frozen pies. Pet's initial emphasis in the Utah market was on quality, but in the face of competition from regional and local companies and in an expanding market where price proved to be a crucial factor, Pet was forced to take steps to reduce the price of its pies to the ultimate consumer.

First, Pet successfully concluded an arrangement with Safeway, which is one of the three largest customers for frozen pies in the Salt Lake market, whereby it would sell frozen pies to Safeway under the latter's own "Bel-air" label at a price significantly lower than it was selling its comparable "Pet-Ritz" brand in the same Salt Lake market and elsewhere. The initial price on "Bel-air" pies was slightly lower than Utah's price for its "Utah" brand of pies at the time, and near the end of the period, the "Bel-air" price was comparable to the "Utah" price but higher than Utah's price for its "Frost 'N' Flame" brand.

Second, it introduced a 20-ounce economy pie under the "Swiss Miss" label and began selling the new pie in the Salt Lake market in August 1960 at prices ranging from $3.25 to $3.30 for the remainder of the period. This pie was at times sold at a lower price in the Salt Lake City market than it was sold in other markets.

Third, Pet became more competitive with respect to the prices for its "Pet-Ritz" proprietary label. For eighteen of the relevant forty-four months beginning in 1958, its offering price for Pet-Ritz pies was $4.00 per dozen or lower and $3.70 or lower for six of these months. In seven of the forty-four months, Pet's prices in Salt Lake were lower than prices charged in the California markets. This was true, although selling in Salt Lake involved a 30 to 35-cent freight cost.

The Carnation Company

The Carnation Company, which operated a single plant in California, entered the frozen dessert pie business in 1955, the same year as Pet Milk, through the acquisition of "Mrs. Lee's Pies," which was then engaged in manufacturing and selling frozen pies in Utah and elsewhere under the "Simple Simon" label. Carnation also quickly found the market extremely sensitive to price. Carnation decided, however, not to enter an economy product in the market and offered only its quality "Simple Simon" brand. Its primary method of meeting competition in its markets was to offer a variety of discounts and other reductions, and the technique was successful. In 1958, for example, Carnation enjoyed 10.3 percent of the Salt Lake City market, and although its volume of pies sold in that market increased substantially in the next year, its percentage of the market temporarily slipped to 8.6 percent. The year 1960 was a turnaround one for Carnation in the Salt Lake City market; it more than doubled its volume of sales over the preceding year and captured 12.1 percent of the market. While the price structure in the market deteriorated rapidly in 1961, Carnation remained an important competitor.

After Carnation's temporary setback in 1959, it instituted a new pricing policy to regain business in the Salt Lake City market. This involved a slash in price of 60 cents per dozen pies, which brought Carnation's price to a level well below its costs, and well below the other prices prevailing in the market. The impact of this move was felt immediately, and the other major sellers in the market reduced their prices. Carnation's best year during this period was 1960 and involved eight months during which the prices in Salt Lake City were lower than prices charged in other markets. This situation continued into 1961. During this period, the prices charged by Carnation in Salt Lake City were well below the prices it charged in other markets, and in all but August 1961, the Salt Lake City delivered price was 20 to 50 cents lower than the prices charged in distant San Francisco.

Continental Baking

Continental Baking was a large national corporation with plants in Virginia, Iowa, and California. At first, Continental was only a minor player in the Salt Lake City frozen pie business. Its sales of frozen 22-ounce dessert pies, sold under the "Morton" brand, amounted to only 1.3 percent of the market in 1958, 2.9 percent in 1959, and 1.8 percent in 1960. Its problems were primarily that of cost and in turn that of price, the controlling factor in the market. In late 1960 it worked out a co-packing arrangement in California by which fruit would be processed directly from the trees into the finished pie without large intermediate packing, storing, and shipping expenses. Having improved its position, it attempted to increase it share of the Salt Lake City market by utilizing a local broker and offering short-term price concessions in varying amounts.

Carnation's efforts were not particularly successful at first. Then in June 1961, it offered its 22-ounce frozen apple pies in the Utah area at $2.85 per dozen. It was then selling the same pies at substantially higher prices in other markets. The Salt Lake City price was less than its direct cost plus an allocation for overhead. Utah's going price at the time for its 24-ounce "Frost 'N' Flame" apple pie sold to Associated Grocers was $3.10 per dozen and for its "Utah" brand $3.40 per dozen. At its new prices, Continental sold pies to American Grocers in Pocatello, Idaho, and to American Food Stores in Ogden, Utah. Safeway also purchased 6,250 dozen, its major requirements for about five weeks. Another purchaser ordered 1,000 dozen. Utah Pie's response was immediate. It reduced its price on all its apple pies to $2.75 per dozen. Continental refused Safeway's request to match UPC's price, but renewed it offer at the same prices effective July 31 for another two-week period.

The Suit

As the competition in the Salt Lake City market continued to heat up in 1961, it became obvious to the management of UPC that Pet, Carnation, and Continental were selling pies in Utah at prices lower than they were selling pies of like grade and quality in other markets considerably closer to their plants. Accordingly, on September 8, 1961, Utah Pie filed suit claiming treble damages against the three companies, claiming that they had injured UPC's competitive position by selling frozen fruit pies at discriminatory prices in the Salt Lake City market, thereby violating Section 2(a) of the Clayton Act.

The Decisions of the Courts

Jury Trial. The jury rejected the allegation by UPC that the Big Three had acted in concert against it in some kind of conspiracy, but found that they had individually violated Section 2(a) of the Clayton Act and were therefore guilty of price discrimination.

Court of Appeals. The Appeals Court overturned the verdict of the jury trial. In its view the central issue was whether the evidence against the allegedly price-discriminating competitors was sufficient to support a finding of probably injury to competition. The court held that there was little evidence of an adverse effect on competition.

The Supreme Court. The Supreme Court reversed the decision of the Court of Appeals. It reasoned that the lower court's finding of no probable adverse effect on competition was overcome by the decline in the share of the market held by the Utah Pie Company. Furthermore, the Court found evidence that the Robinson-Patman Act was violated in the working of the competitive process itself, since the price level in Utah was eroded as a result. The core of the Supreme Court holding is contained in the following sentences of the opinion:

> The major competitive weapon in the Utah market was price. The location of petitioner's plant gave it natural advantages in the Salt Lake City marketing area and it entered the market at a price below the then going prices for the respondent's comparable pies. For most of the period involved here [1958–1961], its prices were the lowest in the Salt Lake City market. It was, however, challenged by each of the respondents at one time or another and for varying periods. There was ample evidence to show that each of the respondents contributed to what proved to be a deteriorating price structure over the period covered by this suit, and each of the respondents in the course of the ongoing price competition sold frozen pies in the Salt Lake market at prices lower than it sold pies of like grade and quality in other markets considerably closer to their plants.
>
> Section 2(a) does not forbid price competition which will probably injure or lessen competition by eliminating competitors, discouraging entry into the market, or enhancing the market shares of the dominant sellers. But Congress has established some ground rules for the game. Sellers may not

sell like goods to different purchasers at different prices if the result may be to injure competition.

The frozen pie market in Salt Lake City was highly competitive. At times Utah Pie was a leader in moving the general level or prices down, and at other times each of the respondents also bore responsibility for the downward pressure on the price structure. We believe that the Act reaches price discrimination that erodes competition as much as it does price discrimination that is intended to have immediate destructive impact. In this case, the evidence shows a drastically declining price structure which the jury could rationally attribute to continued or sporadic price discrimination. The jury was entitled to conclude that "the effect of such discrimination may be substantially to lessen competition...or to injure, destroy, or prevent competition with any person who either grants or knowingly receives the benefit of such discrimination,...Proper application of that standard here requires reversal of the judgment of the Court of Appeals.

Dissenting Opinion

Mr. Justice Stewart, with whom Mr. Justice Harlan joins, dissenting.

I would affirm the judgment, agreeing substantially with the reasoning of the Court of Appeals....There is only one issue in this case in its present posture: Whether the respondents engaged in price discrimination "where the effect of such discrimination may be substantially to lessen competition or tend to create a monopoly in any line of commerce, or to injure, destroy, or prevent competition with any person who either grants or knowingly receives the benefit of such discrimination."...Phrased more simply, did the respondents' actions have the anticompetitive effect required by the statute as an element of a cause of action?

The Court's own description of the Salt Lake City frozen pie market from 1958 through 1961 shows that the answer to that question must be no. In 1958 Utah Pie had a quasi-monopolistic 66.5% of the market. In 1961—after the alleged predations of the respondents—Utah Pie still had a commanding 45.3%, Pet had 29.4%, and the remainder of the market was divided almost equally between Continental, Carnation, and other, small local bakers. Unless we disregard the lessons so laboriously learned in scores of Sherman and Clayton Act cases, the 1961 situation has to be considered more competitive than that of 1958. Thus, if we assume that the price discrimination proven against the respondents had any effect on competition, that effect must have been beneficent.

That the Court has fallen into the error of reading the Robinson-Patman Act as protecting competitors, instead of competition, can be seen from its unsuccessful attempt to distinguish cases relied upon by the respondents. These cases are said to be inapposite because they involved "no general decline in price structure" and no "lasting impact upon prices." But lower prices are the hallmark of intensified competition.

The Court of Appeals squarely identified the fallacy which the Court today embraces:

> ...a contention that Utah Pie was entitled to hold the extraordinary market share percentage of 66.5, attained in 1958, falls of its own dead weight. To approve such a contention would be to hold that Utah Pie was entitled to maintain a position which approached, if it did not in fact amount to a monopoly, and could not exist in the face of proper and healthy competition.

I cannot hold that Utah pie's monopolistic position was protected by the federal antitrust laws from effective price competition, and I therefore respectfully dissent.

ASSIGNMENT QUESTIONS

1. Summarize the important facts in the *Utah Pie* case.
2. Assume that you were the vice-president for marketing of a large national baking company in 1958. What strategy would you use to successfully enter and compete in the Salt Lake City frozen pie market?

3. Identify the arguments in the majority opinion of the Supreme Court.
4. What are the arguments for the dissenting opinion?
5. If you were a member of the Supreme Court, with which opinion would you agree? Give reasons for your answer.

28
THE MORTON SALT CASE

328 U.S. 781 (1946).

History of the Clayton Act

By 1912, the year that Woodrow Wilson was elected president, many in Congress felt that the Sherman Act, passed in 1890, had proved to be ineffective in halting the growth of trusts and monopolies. Large consolidations and mergers continued to be organized, and the "trusts" continued to flourish.

The Rule of Reason, enumerated by the Supreme Court in 1911 in the *Standard Oil* case, was regarded by many persons as having fatally weakened the Sherman Act. The result was a concerted effort to develop more effective means of preserving the free enterprise system.

Political agitation for curbing the power of the trusts grew to the point where all major parties in the national campaign of 1912 denounced the monopolistic trends and carried planks on their platforms calling for remedial legislation.

The leadership in the effort to strengthen the antitrust laws was assumed by President Wilson, who, in a series of messages to Congress, urged further legislative action. The Congress acted in 1914 by passing the Clayton Act. Its essential purpose was preventative—to check anti-competitive acts in their incipiency before they reached the dimensions of Sherman Act violations. In short, Congress intended to establish a standard much less rigorous than that which had become required under the Sherman Act. As stated in the Senate Report on the bill:

> Broadly stated, the bill, in its treatment of unlawful restraints and monopolies, seeks to prohibit and make unlawful certain trade practices which, as a rule, singly and in themselves, are not covered by the Sherman Act, or other existing anti-trust acts, and thus, by making these practices illegal to arrest the creation of trusts, conspiracies, and monopolies in their incipiency and before consummation.[1]

Section 2 of the Clayton Act

Sec. 2. It shall be unlawful for any person engaged in commerce to discriminate in price between different purchasers of commodities...where the effect of such discrimination may be to substantially lessen competition or tend to create a monopoly in any line of commerce: provided, that nothing herein contained shall prevent discrimination in price between purchasers of commodities on account of differences in the grade, quality, or quantity of the commodity sold, or that makes only due allowance for differences in the cost of selling or transportation, or discrimination in price in the same or different communities made in good faith to meet competition....

The Robinson-Patman Act

The Robinson-Patman Act of 1936 amended and amplified Section 2 of the Clayton Act. Section 2 did not forbid price discrimination where the consequence was a tendency to create monopoly among buyers. Specifically, it did not protect independents from the effects of the use of bargaining power by mass distributors, since it failed to limit quantity discounts to manufacturers' actual cost savings and did not prevent special discounts and allowances.

With the active assistance of the U.S. Wholesale Grocers Association (an anti-chain-store group), the Congress produced what is really a revision of Section 2 of the Clayton Act.

Section 2 of the Robinson-Patman Act

Sec. 2. (a) It shall be unlawful for any person engaged in commerce...to discriminate in price between different purchasers of commodities of like grade and quality...where the effect of such discrimination may be substantially to lessen competition or tend to create a monopoly in any line of commerce....*Provided,* that nothing herein contained shall prevent differentials which make only due allowance for differences in the cost of manufacture, sale, or delivery resulting from the differing methods or quantities in which such commodities are to such purchasers sold or delivered; *Provided,* however, that the Federal Trade Commission may, after due investigation and hearing to all interested parties, fix and establish quantity limits, and revise the same as it finds necessary, as to particular commodities or classes of commodities where it finds that available purchasers in greater quantities are so few as to render differentials on account thereof unjustly discriminatory or promotive of monopoly in any line of commerce; and the foregoing shall then not be construed to permit differentials based on differences in quantities greater than those so fixed and established....

Federal Trade Commission v. Morton Salt Co.

Mr. Justice Black delivered the opinion of the Court:

The Federal Trade Commission, after a hearing, found that the Morton Salt Company, which manufactures and sells table salt in interstate commerce, had discriminated in price between different purchasers of like grades and qualities, and concluded that such discriminations were in violation of Section 2 of the Clayton Act...as amended by the Robinson-Patman Act....It accordingly issued a cease and desist order....Upon petition of the company the Circuit Court of Appeals, with one judge dissenting, set aside the Commission's findings and order....

The company manufactures several different brands of table salt and sells them directly to (1) wholesalers or jobbers, who in turn resell to the retail trade, and (2) large retailers, including chain store retailers. The company sells its finest brand of table salt, known as Blue Label, on what it terms a standard quantity discount system available to all customers. Under this system the purchasers of this brand differ according to the quantities bought. These prices are as follows, after making allowances for rebates and discounts:

	Per case
Less-than-carload purchases	$1.60
Carload purchases	1.50
5,000-case purchases in any consecutive 12 months	1.40
50,000-case purchases in any consecutive 12 months	1.35

Only five companies have ever bought sufficient quantities of salt to obtain the $1.35 per case price. These companies could buy in such quantities because they operate large chains of retail stores in various parts of the country. As a result of this low price these five companies have been able to sell Blue Label salt at retail cheaper than wholesale purchasers from Morton could reasonably sell the same brand of salt to independently operated retail stores, many of whom competed with the local outlets of the five chain stores.

First. Morton Salt's basic contention, which it argues this case hinges upon, is that its "standard quantity discounts, available to all on equal terms, as contrasted, for example, to hidden or special rebates, allowances, prices or discounts, are not discriminatory within the meaning of the Robinson-Patman Act." Theoretically, these discounts are equally available to all, but functionally they are not. For as the record indicates, no single independent retail grocery store, and probably no single wholesaler, bought as many as 50,000 cases or as much as $50,000 worth of table salt in one year. Furthermore, the record shows that, while certain purchasers were enjoying one or more of Morton's standard quantity discounts, some of their competitors made purchases in such small quantities that they could not qualify for any of the company's discounts, even those based on carload shipments. The legislative history of the Robinson-Patman Act makes it abundantly clear that Congress considered it to be an evil that a large buyer could secure a competitive advantage over a small buyer solely because of the large buyer's quantity purchasing ability. The Robinson-Patman Act was passed to deprive a large buyer of such advantages except to the extent that a lower price could be justified by reason of a seller's diminished costs due to quantity manufacture, delivery or sale, or by reason of the seller's good faith effort to meet a competitor's equally low price.

Section 2 of the original Clayton Act had included a proviso that nothing contained in it should prevent "discrimination in price...on account of differences in the grade, quality, or quantity of the commodity sold, or that makes only due allowance for difference in the cost of selling or transportation."...That section has been construed as permitting quantity discounts, such as these here, without regard to the amount of the seller's actual savings in cost attributable to quantity sales or quantity deliveries. The House Committee Report on the Robinson-Patman Act considered that the Clayton Act's proviso allowing quantity discounts so weakened Section 2 "as to render it inadequate, if not almost a nullity." The Committee considered the present Robinson-Patman amendment to Section 2 "of great importance." Its purpose was to limit "the use of quality price differentials to the sphere of actual cost differences."...And it was, in furtherance of this avowed purpose—to protect competition from all price differentials except those based in full on cost savings—that Section 2(a) of the amendment provided "that nothing herein contained shall prevent differentials which make only due allowance for differentials in the cost of manufacture, sale, or delivery resulting from the differing methods or quantities in which such commodities are to such purchasers sold or delivered."

Second. The Government interprets the opinion of the Circuit Court of Appeals as having held that in order to establish "discrimination in price" under the Act the burden rested on the Commission to prove that Morton's quantity discount differentials were not justified by its cost savings. The company does not so understand the Court of Appeals decision, and furthermore admits that no such burden rests on the Commission. We agree that it does not. First, the general rule of statutory construction that the burden of proving justification or exemption under a special exemption to the prohibitions of a statute generally rests on the one who claims its benefits, requires that Morton undertake this proof under the proviso of Section 2(a). Secondly, Section 2(b) of the Act specifically imposes the burden of showing justification upon one who is shown to have discriminated in prices.

Third. It is argued that the findings fail to show that the company's discriminatory discounts had in fact caused injury to competition. There are specific findings that such injuries had resulted from Morton's discounts, although the statute does not require the Commission to find that injury has actually resulted. The statute requires no more than that the effect of the prohibited price discriminations "may be substantially to lessen competition...or to injure, destroy, or prevent competition." After a careful consideration of this provision of the Robinson-Patman Act, we have said that "the statute does not require that the discrimination must in fact have harmed competition, but only that there is a reasonable possibility that they 'may' have such an effect."

Fourth. It is argued that the evidence is inadequate to support the Commission's findings of injury to competition. As we have pointed out, however, the Commission is authorized by the Act to bar discriminatory prices upon the "reasonable possibility" that different prices for like goods to competing purchasers may have the defined effect on competition. That Morton's quantity discounts did result in price differentials between competing purchasers sufficient in amount to influence their resale prices of salt was shown by evidence. This showing, in itself, is adequate to support the Commission's appropriate findings that the effect of such price discriminations may be substantially to lessen competition...and to injure, destroy, and prevent competition.

It is also argued that Morton's less-than-carload sales are very small in comparison with the total volume of its business and for that reason we should reject the Commission's finding that the effect of the carload discrimination may substantially lessen competition and may injure competition between purchasers who are granted and those who are denied this discriminatory discount. To support this argument, reference is made to the fact that salt is a small item in most wholesale and retail businesses and in consumers' budgets. For several reasons we cannot accept this contention.

There are many articles in a grocery store that, considered separately, are comparatively small parts of a merchant's stock. Congress intended to protect a merchant from competitive injury attributable to discriminatory prices on any or all goods sold in interstate commerce, whether the particular goods constituted a major or minor portion of his stock. Since a grocery store consists of many comparatively small articles, there is no possible way effectively to protect a grocer from discriminatory prices except by applying the prohibitions of the Act to each individual article in the store.

The judgment in this case is for the Government.

ASSIGNMENT QUESTIONS

1. For what reasons did Congress pass the Clayton Act?
2. Summarize Section 2 of the Clayton Act.
3. Is *any* price discrimination allowed under the Clayton Act?
4. What defect in the Clayton Act brought on the Robinson-Patman Act?
5. What does Section 2(a) of the Robinson-Patman Act add to the Clayton Act?
6. Summarize the facts in the *Morton Salt* case.
7. What was Morton Salt Company's basic defense?
8. What was the opinion of the Court?
9. As a consumer, do you approve or disapprove of the Court's decision in this case? Why?

NOTE

1. S. Report No. 698, 63rd Congress, 2nd Session 1 (1914), p. 68.

PART SIX
TRUTH IN ADVERTISING

Section 5 of the Federal Trade Commission Act states that "Unfair methods of competition in commerce, and unfair or deceptive acts or practices in commerce, are declared unlawful." Since the passage of that act in 1914, the federal government has prosecuted more than thirty-three hundred cases of deception in advertising and other business practices. The law, as it has developed, does not protect the public from tasteless or boring or repetitious advertisements; it does, however, attempt to protect us from actions on the part of advertisers that are deceptive or unfair.

In Case 29, *The Colgate-Palmolive Company,* a television commercial purported to show that Colgate's Rapid Shave shaving cream was potent enough to shave sandpaper with an ordinary razor blade. But it was a hoax. What appeared to be sandpaper was actually grains of sand sprinkled on Plexiglas. In its defense, Colgate claimed that sandpaper really could be shaved if it were soaked for over an hour and that the mock-up was necessary because the very fine sandpaper used looked like plain paper on television.

In Case 30, *Mattell, Inc.,* the Federal Trade Commission (FTC) charged the company with deceptive advertising even though the ads were completely truthful. The commercials showed toy racers speeding over their tracks and seeming to move like bullets. This was merely a "special effect" which was achieved by filming the racers at close range from clever angles. The commission charged that even though the representation was technically accurate, it was nevertheless misleading.

Case 31, *The Continental Baking Company*, concerns action brought against the company for television commercials claiming that Continental products, such as Wonder Bread and Hostess snack cakes, actually contained higher levels of vitamins and nutrients than competing products. The government maintained that the company should be able to, but could not, prove such a contention, while the company, in its defense, characterized its ads as containing only innocent puffery—which had little impact on the actual purchasing decisions made by consumers.

29
THE COLGATE-PALMOLIVE COMPANY

380 U.S. 374 (1964).

Ted Bates & Company, a New York advertising agency, prepared for the Colgate-Palmolive Company three one-minute commercials designed to show that Rapid Shave shaving cream could soften even the toughness of sandpaper. Each of the commercials contained the same "sandpaper test." The announcer informed the audience that "To prove Rapid Shave's super-moisturizing power, we put it right from the can onto this tough, dry sandpaper. It was apply...soak...and off in a stroke." While the announcer was speaking, Rapid Shave was applied to a substance that appeared to be sandpaper, and immediately thereafter a razor was shown shaving the substance clean.

In actual fact, sandpaper of the type depicted in the commercials could not be shaved immediately following the application of Rapid Shave, but required a substantial soaking period of approximately 80 minutes. Furthermore, even when sandpaper was soaked in Rapid Shave for the necessary time, the inadequacies of television transmission made it appear to viewers as nothing more than plain, colored paper. Because of this, the substance resembling sandpaper was in fact a simulated prop, or "mock-up," made of Plexiglas to which sand had been applied.

The FTC issued a complaint against Colgate and Bates charging that the commercials were false and deceptive, but a hearing examiner dismissed the complaint because, in his opinion, neither misrepresentation—concerning the actual moistening time or the identity of the shaved substance—was a material one that would mislead the public.

The Commission reversed the hearing examiner. It found that since Rapid Shave could not shave sandpaper within the time depicted in the commercials, Bates and Colgate had misrepresented the product's moisturizing power. Moreover, the Commission found that the undisclosed use of a Plexiglas substitute for sandpaper was an additional material misrepresentation. Even if the sandpaper could be shaved just as depicted in the commercials, the Commission found that viewers had been misled into believing that they had seen it done with their own eyes. As a result of these findings the Commission entered a cease-and-desist order. Colgate and Bates appealed to the Court of Appeals, and the case eventually worked its way up to the Supreme Court.

Opinion of the Court

In reviewing the issues in the case, it is well to remember the respective roles of the Commission and the courts in the administration of the Federal Trade Commission Act. When the Commission was created by Congress in 1914, it was directed by Section 5 to prevent "unfair methods of competition in commerce." Congress amended the Act in 1938 to extend the Commission's jurisdiction to include "unfair or deceptive acts or practices in commerce"—a significant amendment showing Congress' concern for consumers as well as for competitors.

This statutory scheme necessarily gives the Commission an influential role in interpreting Section 5 and in applying it to the facts of particular cases arising out of unprecedented situations....This court has frequently stated that the Commission's judgment is to be given great weight by reviewing courts. This admonition is especially true with respect to allegedly deceptive advertising since the finding of a Section 5 violation rests so heavily on inference and pragmatic judgment.

We accept the Commission's determination that the commercials involved in this case contained three representations to the public: (1) that sandpaper could be shaved by Rapid Shave; (2) that an experiment had been conducted which verified this claim; and (3) that the viewer was seeing this experiment for himself. Colgate admits that the first two representations were made, but deny that the third was. The Commission, however, found to the contrary, and, since this is a matter of fact resting on an inference that could reasonably be drawn from the commercials themselves, the Commission's finding should be sustained.

We agree with the Commission that the undisclosed use of plexiglass [sic] in the commercials was a material deceptive practice, independent and separate from the other misrepresentation found. We find unpersuasive Colgate's claim that it will be impractical to inform the viewing public that it is not seeing an actual test, experiment or demonstration. Further, we think it inconceivable that the ingenious advertising world will be unable, if it so desires, to conform to the Commission's insistence that the public not be misinformed....If it becomes impossible or impractical to show simulated demonstrations on television in a truthful manner, this indicates that television is not a medium that lends itself to this type of commercial, not that the commercial must survive at all costs.

The Dissenting Opinion

Mr. Justice Harlan, whom Mr. Justice Stewart joins, dissenting in part.

In this case, the Court must assume that the advertiser can perform the experiment in question and that the demonstration is as simple as it appears on television. The only question here is what techniques the advertiser may use to convey essential truth to the television viewer. If the claim is true and valid, then the technique for projecting that claim, within broad boundaries, falls purely within the advertiser's art. The warrant to the FTC is to police the verity of the claim itself.

I do not agree that the use of "mock-ups" by the television advertiser is of itself a deceptive trade practice. Further, while there was an independent deceptive element in this commercial, I do not think this record justifies the broad remedial order issued by the Commission. I would remand the case to the Commission for further proceedings.

"Mock-ups" as Such

The faulty prop in the Court's reasoning is that it focuses entirely on what is taking place in the studio rather than on what the viewer is seeing on his screen. That which the viewer sees with his own eyes is not, however, what is taking place in the studio, but an electronic image. If the image he sees on the screen is an accurate reproduction of what he would see with the naked eyes were the experiment performed before him with sandpaper in his home or in the studio, there can hardly be a misrepresentation in any legally significant sense.

In this case, assuming that Rapid Shave could soften sandpaper as quickly as it does sand-covered plexiglass [sic], a viewer who wants to entertain his friends by duplicating the actual experiment could do so by buying a can of Rapid Shave and some sandpaper. If he wished to shave himself, and his beard were really as tough as sandpaper, he could perform this part of his morning ablutions with Rapid Shave in the same way as was the plexiglass [sic], shaved on television.

I do not see how such a commercial can be said to be "deceptive" in any legally acceptable use of that term.... Nor can I readily understand how the accurate portrayal of an experiment by means of a mock-up can be considered more deceptive than, for example, the use of mashed potatoes to convey the glamorous qualities of a particular ice cream.

It is commonly known that television presents certain distortions in transmission for which the broadcasting industry must compensate. Thus, [on black and white television] a white towel will look a dingy gray, but a blue towel will look a sparkling white. On the Court's analysis, an advertiser must achieve accuracy in the studio even though it results in an inaccurate image being projected on the home screen.... All that has happened here is that a demonstration has been altered in the studio to compensate for the distortions of the television medium, but in this instance in order to present an accurate picture to the television viewer.

In short, it seems to me that the proper legal test in cases of this kind concerns not what goes on in the broadcasting studio, but whether what is shown on the television screen is an accurate representation of the advertised product and of the claims made for it.

ASSIGNMENT QUESTIONS

1. Summarize the important facts in this case.
2. What was the reasoning and the opinion of the Supreme Court majority?
3. Summarize the dissenting opinion.
4. If you were a justice on the Court, how would you have voted in this case? Why?
5. Formulate a policy statement that will serve to guide an advertising firm in its use of mock-ups in television commercials.

30
MATTEL, INC.

79 F.T.C. 653.

Complaint

Paragraph 1. Respondent Mattel, Inc., is a corporation organized, existing and doing business under and by virtue of the laws of the State of Delaware, with its principal office locate in Hawthorne, California.

Par. 2. Mattel, Inc., is now and has been engaged in the manufacture, packaging, advertising, offering for sale, sale and distribution of toys and related products, including toys designated Hot Wheels, and the Dancerina Doll, to the public and to distributors and retailers for resale to the public.

Par. 3. In the course and conduct of its business, Mattel, Inc., has caused and continues to cause its toys and related products to be packaged, sold, shipped and distributed from its place of business in the State of California or from the state of manufacture to purchasers thereof located in various states of the United States.

Par. 5. In the course and conduct of their aforesaid businesses and for the purpose of inducing the purchase of the Hot Wheels and Dancerina Doll toys, respondents have made statements and pictorial representations in:

1. advertising appearing on product packages; and
2. advertising which respondents have prepared, utilized and caused to be broadcast on television stations located in various States of the United States.

Par. 6. By and through the use of the aforesaid advertisements, respondents have represented, directly and by implication, that:

1. The Dancerina Doll walks or dances by itself without assistance.
2. A Hot Wheels set as packaged and sold con-

tains all parts or accessories shown or depicted in such advertisements.

Par. 7. In truth and fact:

1. The Dancerina Doll does not walk or dance by itself or without assistance, but requires the assistance of an operator to perform such movements.
2. A Hot Wheels set as packaged and sold does not contain all parts or accessories shown or depicted in such advertisements. Certain of such parts or accessories are obtainable only by way of separate purchase.

Therefore, the advertisements referred to in Paragraphs five and six were and are deceptive.

Par. 8. The aforesaid advertisements purport to accurately and truthfully depict or describe the appearance or performance of the Hot Wheels toy. However, by and through the use of a manner of presentation including, but not limited to, special camera, filming, or sound techniques, said advertisements exaggerate or falsely represent said appearance or performance.

Therefore, said advertisements were and are unfair or deceptive.

Par. 9. By and through the use of a manner of presentation including, but not limited to, special camera, filming or sound techniques, the aforesaid advertisements convey a sense of involvement or participation in the use of the Hot Wheels toy which falsely represents the actual use of the toy.

Therefore, said advertisements were and are unfair or deceptive.

Par. 10. Respondents' aforesaid advertising was and is addressed primarily to children. In that advertising, respondents have utilized statements of endorsement as to the worth, value or desirability of the Hot Wheels toy by persons well known to the public as racing car drivers. Said statements were offered on the basis of and in connection with the experience and renown of said persons as racing car drivers. The nature of that experience and renown, however, extends to actual auto racing. It has not provided said persons with a special competence or expertise on which to base a judgment of the worth, value or desirability to children of the Hot Wheels toy, or with special competence or expertise in the formation of judgments on which children should be induced to rely.

Therefore, the use of such advertisements was and is unfair or deceptive.

Par. 11. Mattel, Inc., has caused to be printed on the Hot Wheels package the statement "Drag chutes slow them down after their 200 mph sprint down the drag strip." This statement describing velocity misrepresents the speed attainable by the car under ordinary or normal conditions of use.

Par. 12. Mattel, Inc., sells and distributes several varieties of toy racing car and track sets under the brand name Hot Wheels. Said sets are not identical in their dimensions and methods of operation, and in certain cases contain parts which are incompatible in their function and use with parts of other of said sets. Respondents in their advertising fail to disclose such incompatibility. The aforesaid advertisements have the tendency and capacity to mislead prospective purchasers or consumers who may reasonably expect parts of said Hot Wheels sets to be compatible.

Therefore, said practices were and are unfair or deceptive.

Par. 13. Mattel, Inc.'s toys including the Hot Wheels and Dancerina Doll toys, are designed primarily for children, and are bought either by or for the benefit of children. Respondent's deceptive and unfair advertising thus unfairly exploits a consumer group unqualified by age or experience to anticipate or appreciate the possibility the representations may be exaggerated or untrue. Further, the respondent unfairly plays upon the affection of adults, especially parents and other close relatives, for children, by inducing the purchase of toys and related products through deceptive or unfair claims of their performance, which claims appeal both to adults and to children who bring the toys to the attention of the adults. As a consequence of Mattel's exaggerated and untrue representations, toys are purchased in the expectation that they will have characteristics to perform acts not substantiated by the facts. Consumers are thus misled to their disappointment and competing advertisers who do not engage in deceptive or unfair advertising are unfairly prejudiced.

Par. 15. The aforesaid acts and practices of Mattel, as herein alleged, were and are all to the prejudice and injury of the public and of respondent's competitors and constituted and now constitute, unfair methods of competition in commerce and unfair and deceptive acts and practices in commerce in violation of the Federal Trade Commission Act.

Order

It is ordered, That Mattel, Inc., a corporation and its officers, agents, representatives and employees,...do forthwith cease and desist from:

1. Portraying or describing in an advertisement addressed to children the performance, operation or use of such products by or through the use of:
   a. Any film or camera techniques which result in any visual perspective of such product which purports to be but is not one which a child can experience in the ordinary use of such product, when the effect of such visual perspective in the context of the advertisement as a whole is to misrepresent the product's performance, operation or use to the age group or age groups of children to whom the advertisement is addressed.
   b. Any sequence of different visual perspectives which purports to depict perspectives which a child can experience but which changes faster than a child can change his visual perspectives in the ordinary use of such product, when the effect of such sequence in the context of the advertisement as a whole is to misrepresent the product's performance, operation or use to the age group or age groups of children to whom the advertisement is addressed, taking into consideration the level of knowledge, sophistication, maturity, and experience of such age group or age groups....
   c. Camera over-cranking or under-cranking to depict a performance characteristic of such product which does not exist or cannot be perceived under ordinary conditions of the product's use,...if the effect...is to misrepresent the product's performance...
2. Using in broadcast, print or package advertising of such products, addressed to children, any endorsements or other similar statements as to the worth, value or desirability to children of any such product, by any living person...when such endorsements are offered on the basis of or in connection with any experience, special competence or expertise which the public may reasonably be expected to associate with such person, unless the person making the statement has acquired a degree or type of experience, special competence, or expertise which qualified him to form the judgements expressed.
3. Portraying or describing in any advertisement two or more of such products which are sold or distributed under the brand name Hot Wheels, if such products must be purchased separately, unless such advertisement establishes which of the products advertised therein must be purchased separately.
4. Commencing the...exhibition...within any twelve month period following the date of this order...advertisements for toys advertised under the brand name Hot Wheels...if the toys advertised...would reasonably be expected by purchasers to be, but are not, compatible in use and function with one another under ordinary conditions of use....
5. Representing that any toy car or other toy vehicle travels at any specific velocity other than that velocity determined by measuring the distance actually elapsed when both distance and time are calculated during the normal or ordinary conditions of use of such car or other toy vehicle.
6. Failing to disclose on their packages that the Dancerina doll or other similar motorized ballerina, dancing or walking doll requires human assistance to walk or dance if such is the fact....

It is further ordered, That the respondent corporation shall, within sixty days after service upon it of this order, file with the Commission a report in writing setting forth in detail the manner and form in which it has complied with the provisions of this order....

ASSIGNMENT QUESTIONS

1. List the allegedly deceptive claims broadcast on television by Mattel—according to the Federal Trade Commission.
2. Develop an argument defending the right of Mattel to air the kind of television commercials that brought on action by the FTC.
3. What was the basis of the criticism of the Mattel commercials by the Commission?
4. What are your personal feelings on the issue? How much creative license should be given to advertisers? How much protection do you need as a consumer?
5. What is the significance of the Consent Decree or "order" published by the FTC? Why would Mattel agree to abide by such an order?

31
CONTINENTAL BAKING COMPANY

83 F.T.C. 865.

For many years, one of the most prominent American food-producing companies has been Continental Baking, a Delaware corporation with offices and main place of business located in Rye, New York. A national concern, it has produced and sold bakery products under familiar brand names such as Wonder Bread and Hostess snack cakes.

In the process of persuading consumers to buy its products, Continental Baking, through its advertising agency, Ted Bates & Company, of New York City, has disseminated advertisements through magazines, newspapers, radio broadcasts, and television commercials. In the period from 1964 through 1970 the corporation spent at least $57,595,000 for this purpose. Typical statements and representations made in its advertisements follow.

Advertisements and Commercials for Wonder Bread

Four television commercials asked children how big they wanted to be and then through time sequence photography depicted a child dramatically growing taller and larger. These commercials opened showing a young child with "HOW BIG DO YOU WANT TO BE?" overprinted. The announcer said "Wonder asks, How big do you want to be?" Various children answered as they are photographed, "Big enough so that the barber won't have to cut my hair in a baby's chair," "Big enough to be a cheerleader," "Big enough to sink a basket," "Big enough to dance with my girlfriend," "Big enough to go surfing," "Big enough to wear my daddy's shoes," "Big enough to see the parade," "Big enough to ride a two-wheeler," "About ten times bigger than my sister," "Big enough to reach things without a chair," and "Bigger than George, he's my dog." After the children told how big they wanted to be, the announcer stated, "He'll never need Wonder Bread more than right now, because the time to grow bigger and stronger is during the Wonder Years—ages one through twelve—the years when your child grows to ninety percent of his adult height." During this audio message the child was pictured growing rapidly, apparently from a very young child to a twelve-year-old in physical stature. Then the audio portion continued: "How can you help? By serving nutritious Wonder enriched bread. Wonder helps build strong bodies twelve ways. Each delicious slice of Wonder Bread supplies protein for muscle, minerals for strong bones and teeth, carbohydrates for energy, vitamins for nerves. All vital elements for growing minds and bodies." During this message a second segment of the child's growth sequence was shown. The commercial ended with parents serving their child Wonder Bread and the audio stating "During the Wonder Years—the growth years—help your child grow bigger and stronger. Serve Wonder Bread. Wonder helps build strong bodies twelve ways."

Four 30-second versions of the television commercials just described showed only one growth sequence. Two of these commercials had the following audio: "Wonder asks, How big do you want to be? Big enough to sink a basket. Bigger than George, he's my dog. And the time to grow bigger and stronger is during the Wonder Years—ages one through twelve—when your child grows to ninety percent of his adult height. How can you help? By serving nutritious Wonder Bread. Each delicious slice supplies protein, minerals, carbohydrates, and vitamins, so during the Wonder Years help your child grow bigger and stronger. Serve Wonder Bread. Wonder helps build strong bodies twelve ways."

Three 30-second television commercials opened with scenes of children playing as the announcer stated, "These are the Wonder Years—ages one through twelve—when your child actually grows to ninety percent of his adult height." As the announcer explained that "each slice of Wonder Bread supplies protein for muscle, minerals for strong bones and teeth, carbohydrates for energy, vitamins for nerves, all vital elements for growing minds and bodies," a child was shown eating Wonder Bread with an insert overprinted showing a child in four different stages of growth. Underneath were the printed words "protein," "minerals," "carbohydrates," and "vitamins," respectively. The commercials ended with the announcer imploring "To help make the most of these Wonder Years, serve Wonder Bread. Wonder helps build strong bodies twelve ways."

A number of Wonder Bread television commercials were broadcast on the program "Bozo Circus" on Channel 9 in Chicago. Representative of these commercials was the following audio portion:

UNCLE NED: Say, how many of you would like to grow up to be as big as an elephant? That's pretty big isn't it? And, of course, no one really wants to be quite that big. But you are going to do a lot of growing in the next few years, and it is fun thinking about how big you'll be. You know, one thing that's so important to your growing is the kind of food you eat. You need to eat the right kinds of food. Yes, foods that are good for you, like Wonder enriched bread. Because Wonder is baked with vitamins and other good things that help you grow up big and strong and have energy for worktime and playtime fun. And you know what fun Wonder is to eat. Yes, just look at this delicious Wonder Bread sandwich, so tender and light, just the way you like it. You can enjoy Wonder so many times during the day: for your sandwiches at lunch, after-school snacks, perhaps with your evening meal, too. So Mom, when your kids tell you how big they want to be—remember, they'll never need Wonder more than right now. Wonder helps build strong bodies 12 ways!"

Numerous Wonder Bread television commercials were broadcast on the network television program "Captain Kangaroo." Representative of these was the following audio portion:

CAPTAIN KANGAROO: Mr. Moose, I have an interesting question for you. If you could be as big as you wanted to be...how big would you want to be?

MR. MOOSE: Gee...as big...as big as big...I know! As big as a tree! Then I could see everything around me for miles and miles.

CAPTAIN KANGAROO: Wouldn't that be fun, Mr. Moose!

MR. MOOSE: Yes! Do you think eating Wonder Bread would get me that big?

CAPTAIN KANGAROO: Well...not quite as big as a tree...but Wonder does help boys and girls grow up big and strong, and give them energy for work and play. Each slice of Wonder is baked with vitamins and other good things that help you grow.

MR. MOOSE: And Wonder tastes so good, too.

CAPTAIN KANGAROO: It does indeed—it's so light and tender and white, baked soft just the way you like it best. Great for lunchtime sandwiches...and anytime snacks. You'll want to enjoy Wonder enriched bread soon. Mothers, please look for the red, yellow, and blue balloons printed on every wrapper. Remember, Wonder helps build strong trees—uh, bodies! 12 ways!

In addition to broadcasts on television, numerous commercials were broadcast on radio containing similar scripts, and advertisements appeared in national magazines, and in newspapers, picturing children at play with copy such as the following overprinted: "Make the most of their 'Wonder Years.' You can do the most for your children's growth during their 'Wonder Years'—ages one through twelve. These are the years when your children actually grow to ninety percent of their adult height. Each slice of Wonder Bread during the 'Wonder Years' give children protein for muscles, minerals for strong bones, carbohydrates for energy, vitamins for nerves...all vital elements for growing minds and bodies. Helps build strong bodies twelve ways!"

The Complaint Regarding Wonder Bread

In 1970, the Federal Trade Commission charged that Continental Baking represented directly and by implication that:

1. Wonder Bread is an outstanding source of nutrients, distinct from other enriched breads.
2. Consuming Wonder Bread in the customary manner that bread is used in the diet will provide a child age one to twelve with all the nutrients in recommended quantities that are essential to healthy growth and development.
3. The optimum contribution a parent can make to his or her child's nutrition during the formative years of growth is to assure that the child consumes Wonder Bread regularly.
4. The protein supplied by Wonder Bread is complete protein of high nutritional quality necessary to assure maximum growth and development.

The Commission charged that the following were the actual facts with regard to Wonder Bread:

1. Wonder Bread is not an outstanding source of nutrients, distinct from other enriched breads. Wonder Bread is a standardized enriched bread, and all enriched breads are required by law to contain minimum levels of certain nutrients. The amount and kind of nutrients contained in Wonder Bread are the same as those contained in most other enriched breads. Wonder Bread does not contain the maximum amounts of nutrients permitted by law, as promulgated in Stan-

dards of Food Identity of the Food and Drug Administration. Wonder Bread contains only 38 percent of the maximum calcium permitted, 57 percent of the maximum riboflavin permitted, 72 percent of the maximum niacin permitted, 76 percent of the maximum iron permitted, and 83 percent of the maximum thiamin permitted.

2. Consuming Wonder Bread in the customary manner that bread is used in the diet will not provide a child age one to twelve with all the nutrients, in recommended quantities, that are essential to healthy growth and development. Wonder Bread provides only eight of the seventeen nutrients recognized as essential for which Recommended Dietary Allowances, designed for the maintenance of good nutrition, have been established for children and adults. One slice of Wonder Bread does not contain significant amounts of vitamin A, vitamin D, vitamin C, folacin, vitamin E, vitamin B_6, vitamin B_{12}, iodine, and magnesium, all of which are nutrients recognized as essential for the maintenance of good nutrition.

   The following amounts of Wonder Bread depending upon age and sex must be consumed daily by children, age one through twelve, in order to obtain the Recommended Dietary Allowance of the nutrients which Wonder Bread does provide:

a. Calcium	40 to 68 slices
b. Phosphorous	24 to 40 slices
c. Iron	18 to 33 slices
d. Niacin	13 to 27 slices
e. Protein	12 to 23 slices
f. Riboflavin	12 to 25 slices
g. Thiamin	7 to 15 slices

3. Parents cannot rely on Wonder Bread to provide their children with all nutrients that are essential to healthy growth and development.
4. Assuring that the child consumes Wonder Bread regularly is not the optimum contribution that a parent can make to his or her child's nutrition during the formative years of growth.
5. The protein supplied by Wonder Bread is not complete protein of high nutritional quality necessary to assure maximum growth and development.

Based on these statements, the FTC concluded that the advertisements referred to above were misleading in material respects and constituted "false advertisements." Further, the Commission claimed, these practices were particularly reprehensible because they were directed primarily to children, who aspire for healthy and rapid growth and development, and parents, who have strong emotional concerns for the healthy physical and mental growth of their children.

Representations Regarding Hostess Snack Cakes

Typical of the advertisements regarding Hostess snack cakes were the following:

1. An advertisement appearing in national magazines pictured a child eating a Hostess snack cake and used the following copy:

"A major nutritional advance from Hostess. Snack Cakes with body-building vitamins and iron. Look for the big 'V' on every new package of Hostess Cup Cakes, Twinkies and Fruit Pies! It's the nutritional advance that takes the guesswork out of which Snack Cakes to buy! These famous Hostess Snack Cakes now give your children more than good taste...they give them important nutrition, too. So why settle for just cake—give them Hostess Snack Cakes fortified with body building vitamins and iron to grow on. Thank Hostess...for the good taste kids love and good nutrition they need."

2. A television commercial depicted a mother in a grocery store looking at different snacks. The audio portion stated: "Snacks, snacks, everywhere snacks. Welcome to the snack cake jungle. Everywhere you look, snack cakes for the kids." The mother asks, "Are there any that have more than good taste?" As the visual portion depicts a Hostess display the audio portion continues: "Yes! Hostess announces Snack Cakes now fortified with vitamin and iron. You can thank Hostess bakers for new vitamin-fortified snack cakes with the good taste kids love and good nutrition they need." The mother carries away an armload of Hostess Snack Cakes, and the vi-

sual portion switches to children eating the cakes. The audio continues: "Like new Hostess Cup Cakes! That chocolaty devil's food cake with creamy filling and fudge icing now gives your children more than good taste. It gives them important nutrition, too. Because now Hostess Cup Cakes are fortified with body-building vitamins and iron to grow on. Yes there are snack cakes with more than good taste. New vitamin-fortified Hostess Snack Cakes. Look for the 'V' on packages of Hostess Cup Cakes. Thank Hostess for the good taste kids love, and the good nutrition they need." Other television commercials used the same copy except for substituting the products Hostess Twinkies or Hostess Fruit Pies instead of Hostess Cup Cakes.

The Complaint Regarding Hostess Snack Cakes

The Federal Trade Commission charged that Continental Baking, through the use of advertisements such as the foregoing, represented directly and by implication that:

1. The fortification of Hostess Snack Cakes with vitamins and iron constituted a major nutritional advance that has just been developed for providing children with good nutrition.
2. The fortification of Hostess Snack Cakes with vitamins and iron constituted a major nutritional advance that was unavailable in other baked goods used for snacks by children.
3. Hostess Snack Cakes provided all the vitamins recognized as essential to the healthy growth and development of children.

In truth and fact, the Commission charged that:

1. The fortification of Hostess Snack Cakes with vitamins and iron did not constitute a major nutritional advance that had just been developed for providing children with good nutrition. The fortification of Hostess Snack Cakes is the nutritional equivalent of using enriched flour to make the cakes, a process which adds certain amounts of vitamins B_1 and B_2, niacin, and iron. Such enrichment of baked goods has been developed and used for more than thirty years.
2. The fortification of Hostess Snack Cakes with vitamins and iron did not constitute a major nutritional advance that was unavailable in other baked goods used for snacks by children.
3. Hostess Snack Cakes do not provide in significant quantities all the vitamins recognized as essential to the healthy growth and development of children. In fact, they provide in significant quantities only three of the ten vitamins that have been recognized as essential by the Food and Nutrition Board of the National Academy of Sciences.
4. The representation that Hostess Snack Cakes provide children with good nutrition fails to disclose the material fact that the cakes are composed primarily of sugar.

Therefore, the Commission concluded, the advertisements referred to were and are misleading in material respects and constituted "false advertisements" as that term is defined in the Federal Trade Commission Act.

Continental's Responses to the Charges

The Continental Baking Company made a very lengthy and carefully reasoned response to the FTC's charges. Among the arguments and statements it presented were the following:

1. The company presented the testimony of Dr. Steuart Henderson Britt, a psychologist with extensive experience in marketing, advertising, consumer behavior, and consumer understanding of advertising. Dr. Britt had studied the films of the Wonder Bread commercials, examined print advertising for Wonder Bread, and had further examined roughly one thousand verbatim responses from consumers. It was his opinion that this advertising did not represent, and would not be understood by consumers to suggest, that Wonder Bread is an outstanding source of nutrients distinct from other enriched breads

or that Wonder Bread is a uniquely nutritious bread. It was, further, Dr. Britt's opinion that the advertisements involved in the case did not make any of the representations asserted by the Commission.

2. In response to the charges that Wonder Bread's advertising represented the product to have *all* nutrients essential to healthy growth and development, the corporation pointed out that no commercial placed in evidence expressly made this claim.
3. Although a child of three or four might understand that Wonder Bread by itself could cause a child's growth, the word "help" that is used there is very clear to an adult.
4. There is no evidence that the reference to protein in Wonder Bread represents to consumers that it is complete protein of high nutritional quality necessary to assure maximum growth and development. In any event, Continental maintained that the protein in Wonder Bread was, in fact, of a nutritional quality sufficient to assure maximum growth and development when Wonder Bread was consumed in the customary manner that bread is used in a diet.
5. A study sponsored by Continental showed that in July 1971, 72.3 percent of the respondents surveyed regarded all brands of white bread the same in terms of nutrition and that only 5 percent of the respondents surveyed thought that Wonder Bread stood out on nutrition from other breads.

   The study also demonstrated that consumer perceptions of the nutritional superiority of a bread may develop in the absence of nutritional advertising. Arnold and Pepperidge Farms brands, which together have about one-half the market share of Wonder Bread and have never been advertised on a nutritional basis, are mentioned as being nutritionally superior by virtually the same number of persons as the number that mentioned Wonder Bread.

   From these data, Continental's consultant, Dr. Rossi, concluded that, in spite of great differences in advertising expenditures, both Arnold and Pepperidge Farm brands were regarded by consumers as being more nutritious than Wonder Bread.
6. Questions concerning the impact of television commercials on children have been the subject of only a very limited amount of empirical research. The principal body of research that does exist consists of studies by Scott Ward under grants received from the National Institute of Mental Health which deal with the effects of television advertising on children from the ages of five to twelve.

   In general, Ward's research reflects that there is a potential for either literal belief of and/or confusion concerning television commercials among a small proportion of very young children. Even by the age of five to seven there are substantial numbers of children who are skeptical about television commercials. The potential for literal belief or confusion that does occur in some young children decreases with age, to a point around age eight where children generally exhibit a clear, consistent, and widespread reaction that television commercials cannot be taken as literally true. Even young children who are exposed to fantasy in television commercials may disbelieve it because it does not conform to their own experience with reality....

   Over the age of six, children increasingly recognize that the fantasy present in Wonder Bread television commercials constitutes a "television trick" and are increasingly skeptical about it....

   All witnesses agreed that the impact on children of television advertising is far outweighed by other factors, particularly the nature of the child's relationships with other human beings, and especially his parents.

7. Continental summarized its arguments as follows:
   a. Wonder Bread advertisements had no impact on consumers that was specific to the attribution of nutrition or was a function of the claims made.
   b. The commercials in question generated a "halo effect" which was not shown to be the result of the nutritional content of the commercials.
   c. Exposure to Wonder Bread television advertising that promotes nutrition does not cause consumers to perceive Wonder Bread as more nutritious than other breads.
   d. None of the challenged advertising for Wonder Bread contained, either directly or by implication any of the representations alleged in the complaint.

ASSIGNMENT QUESTIONS

1. Make a summary of the facts both pro and con in this case. Further, make a summary of those statements on either side that are more opinions than facts.
2. How do you feel as a consumer about the FTC's charges against Continental Baking? Do the advertisements in question, in your opinion, lead other people to view Wonder Bread and Hostess Snack Cakes as more nutritious than they otherwise would? Does this lead them to buy products that they would not otherwise buy?
3. Make up a strong argument supporting the Commission's case.
4. Develop a summary of the arguments in defense of Continental Baking.
5. If you were a member of the Federal Trade Commission, how would you vote in this case—for Continental Baking or against. What sort of remedy would you suggest?

PART SEVEN
INTERNATIONAL BUSINESS

In Part VII the cases have a number of objectives. One is to consider the actions that should be taken by an American company operating in South Africa, an allegedly racist country; a second is to investigate the validity of arguments for and against the imposition of protective tariffs on goods imported into the United States; and a third is to consider the charges laid by many Americans against Japanese industry—specifically that that country's competitive success against us is based on unfair and conspiratorial methods rather than on fair methods and free trade.

Case 32, *The Dow Chemical Company,* attempts to present, from the testimony of those directly involved in the controversy, both criticism and defense of the Republic of South Africa and of the three hundred American firms doing business there. Proper action toward that country is difficult to determine given the facts of apartheid on the one hand and the crucial position that South Africa holds because of its strategic location and critical resources on the other.

Case 33, *The Boston Banana Company,* relates the story of a banana company located in Worcester, Massachusetts, that has managed to grow bananas using surplus combat stoves and vast sheets of Saran Wrap. At a retail price of $1 per banana, the company is having some difficulty in competing with foreign bananas and applies to the U.S. Tariff Commission for a tariff that "will be competitive in that it will only equalize the costs of production at home and abroad—along with a reasonable profit." Arguments for and against protective tariffs are presented, such as to protect infant industries, to avoid domestic unemployment, for national defense ("If our domestic industry were allowed to wither under the pressure of foreign competition, we would be forced to rely, in time of war, on foreign sources of supply.").

Case 34, *The Japanese Conspiracy*, contains testimony from a number of sources relating to the motivations and methodologies behind those Japanese industrialists who have brought about the "Japanese Miracle." Although it is fairly easy to conclude that the Japanese have been playing the "American game" in a distinct and possibly uniquely Japanese manner, solutions to the problems they have created are neither obvious nor without their risks and costs.

32
THE DOW CHEMICAL COMPANY

Dow Chemical is a worldwide American-based corporation with 26,000 employees in the United States and an equal number in other countries. In 1959 Dow opened a small sales office in Johannesburg, South Africa. At the current time, Dow employs a work force of about two hundred in that country—a third of them black—and operates one plant and three sales offices. Its total investment in South Africa is about $20 million. Dow's South African sales run about $60 million a year, or about half of 1 percent of the company's 1986 total. Profits for 1986 were about the same percentage.

Among the products Dow sells in South Africa is Rifadin, the drug usually recommended for treating tuberculosis, which strikes about 100,000 people each year in South Africa, most of whom are black. Rifadin is the only product Dow sells directly to the government of South Africa.

Historical Background

Foreign settlement of the geographical area now known as South Africa came during the seventeenth and eighteenth centuries, when immigrants began to come from The Netherlands and Britain. The conflicts between the conservative, religious Dutch (known as Boers) and the more liberal English ultimately led to two wars, the second of which, The Boer War, in 1899, led to British control of the country.

In spite of British control as a consequence of their military victory, the Boers worked to develop political support among the whites of South Africa, and in 1948, their Nationalist Party won the general elections and took control of the government. One of the consequences of their control was that British plans for a society of equal racial communities were replaced by a Boer system of apartheid, based on the separation of the races.

Today, South Africa's population totals about 33 million people. About two-thirds of the people are black, one-tenth are colored (mixed races), and 3 percent are Asian (meaning Indian). The remaining 15 percent—five million citizens—are white. Slightly less than half of the whites are descendants of the Boers. The consequence is that the 15 percent of the population that is white, in effect, rules over the rest.

In time the rest of the world became increasingly aware that the underlying philosophy of the South African government was segregation and racism. Opposition and contempt for South Africa as a society grew among most other nations in the Western World. In 1961 South Africa was forced out of the British Commonwealth, and since 1974 the country has been excluded from plenary sessions of the United Nations.

Over the past fifteen years, U.S. companies have been increasingly part of the apartheid debate. In the beginning, they were expected only publicly to express opposition to apartheid, but in the late 1970s they were pressured to abide by the Sullivan Principles, named after the Rev. Leon Sullivan, a Philadelphia minister and civil rights activist.

The original Sullivan Principles called for the following:

1. Nonsegregation of the races in all eating, comfort, and work facilities.
2. Equal and fair employment practices for all employees.
3. Equal pay for all employees doing equal or comparable work for the same period of time.
4. Initiation and development of training programs that will prepare, in substantial numbers, blacks and other nonwhites for supervisory, administrative, clerical, and technical jobs.
5. Increasing the number of blacks and other nonwhites in management and supervisory positions.
6. Improving the quality of employees' lives outside the work environment in such areas as housing, transportation, schooling, recreation, and health.

Later, other provisions were added, including one in 1984 committing American companies operating in South Africa to support the repeal of all apartheid laws.

The consequence of efforts by "Sullivan Companies" in South Africa led to significant changes—at least by South African standards. Workplaces have been desegregated; common medical, pension, and insurance plans have been set up for all employees; blacks have received more frequent and larger pay raises than whites; and the number of blacks in supervisory and management positions has increased steadily. In addition, American companies have invested hundreds of millions of dollars in a variety of social programs in South Africa.

Over the past decade, antiapartheid sentiment has grown stronger in the United States and other countries. At first, universities, pension funds, and other investment groups were urged to sell stock in any company that refused to abide by the Sullivan Principles. This gradually changed to calls for *divestiture,* under which stock was to be sold if a company had any investment in South Africa. Divestiture then became *disinvestment,* requiring companies with assets in South Africa to leave the country altogether unless the government changed its position on apartheid. The idea behind disinvestment was to send a message to the South African government that it would have to reconsider its racial policies or pay a heavy economic and political price.

In 1986, the U.S. Congress passed tough economic sanctions against South Africa and then overrode President Reagan's veto of the bill. Prohibitions include new investments in South Africa, new bank loans to the South African government, and imports of coal, iron, steel, uranium, textiles, Krugerrands, and agricultural products from South Africa. Also outlawed are nuclear cooperation between the two countries and sale of computer technology to the South African police or military.

Dow's Reaction to Apartheid

The first public statement from the corporation came in March 1983 in the company magazine. This issue included the following quote: "Dow firmly opposes apartheid. Indeed, we know of no U.S.-based corporation in South Africa that does not oppose it. But the question at bottom is how do you best oppose a national policy that you find abhorrent?"[1]

In July 1984, Paul Oreffice, Dow's chief executive officer, issued an updated statement of Dow's position, and in May 1966, Ned Brandt, a senior public affairs executive, wrote: "We have made no secret of our repugnance for the apartheid system. We have supported and participated actively in all sorts of protests against these evils....We do not see how our pulling out of South Africa would help them [black South Africans] at all—it would, indeed, cause them grievous injury through loss of jobs, educational assistance, health aids and other contributions we have made and continue to make."[2]

Ted Doan, former president of Dow and board member, made the following comments after a recent trip to South Africa: "The South African government is not particularly appealing. Bureaucratic, over-regulating, stuck with a lousy idea called Apartheid, and perhaps trapped in a philosophy that mixes too closely church, state and love of land...". About those advocating unconditional withdrawal from South Africa, he wrote, "...I'm struck by the complete vagueness of thought when it comes to solutions. The Crusaders have their heart in the Right place, their goal of liberation seems fine, at least in theory, but their understanding of economics, business development and job creation is not only poor, it is abysmal."[3]

Dow's Contributions

Although Dow's South African operation is relatively small—its two hundred employees contrast with Coca-Cola's four thousand, General Motors and Mobil Oil's more than three thousand, and other firms that have more than two thousand—it has been active in helping to improve the social situation. Specifically,

Blacks in South Africa are the only Dow employees in the world whose housing loans are guaranteed by the company.

Dow provides six scholarships per year for black students at the University of Zululand.

Dow has adopted a black school in Soweto, the Phenfeni Senior Secondary School, and spends $10,000 to $20,000 per year to upgrade facilities and buy books and equipment. The company also packed and shipped a 26,000-volume contribution to the school's library.

Dow gave a medical library worth $750,000 to MEDUNSA, the Medical University of Southern Africa. The company also provides scholarships to train black doctors at the university.

Leave or Stay?

To those who have studied the problem, Dow's presence in South Africa likely seems more complicated than expected. On the one hand, those advocating immediate withdrawal cite the growing political pressure in the United States; the threat of shareholder resolutions among those owning Dow stock; deteriorating social, economic, and political conditions in South Africa; and the possibility of future, highly public, problems for Dow if some action is not taken in the near future.

Those wanting Dow to stay will argue the wrongness of giving in to seemingly uninformed pressure groups. They'll also cite Dow's responsibility to employees there, especially the blacks. Some will say that pulling out won't make any significant difference in any case.

While the Dow management ponders its alternatives, several of the largest American companies announce plans to leave. When General Motors, Coca-Cola, and IBM all announce their intentions, pressure builds on Dow to follow their example.

STATEMENT OF JOHN PAYTON

National Bar Association Before the House Committee on Foreign Affairs Subcommittee on Africa, May 22, 1980.

Good morning Mr. Chairman. My name is John Payton and with me is my colleague James Hackney. We are here today to testify on behalf of the National Bar Association, founded over 50 years ago to represent the interests of black lawyers in this country. Historically, the National Bar Association has been concerned with numerous domestic and international civil rights issues. In recent years the National Bar Association has been actively involved in the dialogue concerning the crisis in Southern Africa. We welcome this opportunity to discuss United States corporate involvement in South Africa. At your request, we will comment on the Sullivan Principles, a code of conduct voluntarily adopted by some United States corporations doing business in South Africa. Before discussing the Sullivan Principles, we will review the political and economic context in which they exist. With a full appreciation of the magnitude of the political, economic and social oppression of black people in South Africa, the inadequacy and hollow symbolism of the Sullivan Principles are clearly revealed.

I The Reality of Apartheid

Black South Africans have no rights.

They have no right to citizenship. Under South African law, blacks must be citizens of the so-called "homelands." These homelands were established to accommodate the 72 percent of the country that is black, yet they constitute only 13 percent of the total land area of South Africa. Blacks are forcibly relocated to these generally barren, worthless areas. Over 2,115,000 blacks have been relocated and such mass relocations are planned to continue until substantially all Africans have been removed from the "white areas."

Blacks have no right to own land outside the homelands. Only a limited number of blacks may lease land. The natural desire of people to own their own property is rendered meaningless by laws of South Africa.

Blacks have no right to vote.

Blacks have no freedom of movement. Absolute physical segregation of the races is ensured by influx control laws by which all blacks must carry with them special identification and must observe rigid curfews.

Blacks have no right to free association or free expression. For even a murmur of dissent or an effort at political organization, they are subject to indefinite detention without charges, beating, banning, torture or death.

Blacks have no right to maintain the integrity of their families. Families are uprooted by the forced relocation of people to the homelands areas. Husbands often must live in all male hostels near their employment while their families live in the homelands.

South Africa's public relations managers would lead us to believe that, in recent years, the government has undertaken measures designed to improve the living conditions of black South Africans and to reform the apartheid system. The truth is that the quality of life for black South Africans has not improved in the last several years—it has significantly deteriorated.

During this time, the denial of political and civil rights has become more systematic, if more refined in its public presentation. Last week, Prime Minister Botha's government dramatically announced its plan for a new constitution. However, in the words of the *Washington Post*, blacks are intended to play only a "walk-on part." The black majority will have no meaningful role in the creation of the new constitution. Affirming the policy of separate development in the new constitution, Botha stated: "I do not believe in a unitary state or in a unitary society." As *The New York Times* stated in an editorial,

> The sad truth is that the new "reform" further confirms Prime Minister P. W. Botha's retreat from his early promises to bring South Africa's blacks to a position of greater economic and political influence. Without such an evolution, no peaceful development seems conceivable.

The response of the South African system to black protest has also grown more repressive. In 1976, when thousands of blacks demonstrated in the streets of Soweto, the South African regime responded by killing at least 700 demonstrators and arresting hundreds more. Police killed at least 26 of those arrested while they were in detention centers. In late 1977, Steve Biko, a prominent black leader was killed while in police custody. His death and the failure of the South African government adequately to explain the circumstances of his death, shocked the conscience of the world.

In 1979, a labor strike erupted in Port Elizabeth over the treatment of the black employees. The government's response to the nonviolent strike was to arrest and detain or ban the labor leadership. In recent weeks, thousands of colored students have been arrested and detained for their protests against the inferior educational system for nonwhites.

In fact, just last week, the government announced proposed legislation relating to arrest and detention. The new proposal provides that no person shall disclose to any person the fact that any particular person has been arrested or is being detained...or anything purporting to be such information.

The logic of apartheid dictates that racial oppression, and indeed, oppression of all people critical of the system, will intensify rather than become ameliorated. This is because the South African Government is unwilling to make the only concession that will satisfy the legitimate demands of the blacks: political equality and full civil rights.

II United States Corporate Involvement in South Africa

As racial oppression in South Africa has intensified, United States corporate involvement in South Africa has increased. This involvement has strengthened the South African economy and government by providing key assistance in the most strategic sectors of the economy and contributing to the efforts of the South African regime to become self-sufficient. Since 1966 direct investment by United States corporations increased from $490 million to $1.8 billion, and presently accounts for 17 percent of the foreign investment in South Africa. Over 75 percent of the total United States investment in South Africa is attributable to a dozen corporations, and the operations of those corporations are concentrated in the most crucial areas of the economy. United States businesses account for 33 percent of the motor vehicle market; 44 percent of the petroleum products market; and 70 percent of the computer market.

Automobiles, oil, and computers are essential components of the South African economy, and the United States corporations dominating these sectors have demonstrated a willingness to cooperate with and to do business with the South African Government.

Both Ford and General Motors sell vehicles to the South African military avoiding United States Commerce Department regulations prohibiting such sales by manufacturing the vehicles in South Africa without using any parts made in the United States. GM has developed a contingency plan, to be activated in the case of civil unrest or national emergency, to cooperate fully with the South African Ministry of Defense, including actual surrender of the company's facilities to the military, manufacturing vehicles directly for the military, and even encouraging its white employees to form and join local defense units.

South Africa has no domestic oil production. Because of its racist policies, every member of OPEC has refused to sell oil to South Africa. There is strong evidence that United States oil companies assist South Africa in obtaining its oil needs despite these boycotts. More disturbing is the fact that South Africa is relying on the Fluor Corporation, a California based engineering and construction company, to become energy self-sufficient. Fluor has signed a $4.2 billion contract to design and supervise the expansion of the South African Coal, Oil and Gas Corporation's coal to oil conversion plant (SASOL II). This is the largest economic undertaking in South African history and is projected to provide 30–50 percent of South Africa's energy needs.

Of the United States computer companies in South Africa, IBM, Control Data, Hewlett-Packard, NCR, Sperry Rand, Burroughs, and Honeywell each include the South African government among their major clients. Computers supplied by these companies are used by the South African Government to implement the pass laws, control the law of migratory labor, and to create an information bank that keeps the government informed on the entire adult black population. Furthermore, all of South Africa's key industries rely on United States computers....

III The Sullivan Principles

Faced with a rising tide of sentiment against doing business with a country whose existence is based on a political system totally repugnant to the world community, United States corporations have sought to justify their continued presence in South Africa and to protect billions of dollars in investment by embracing the Sullivan Principles. The Sullivan Principles were quickly adopted not only by a significant portion of United States corporations doing business in South Africa, but by the South African Government which reviewed, revised and approved the Principles.

The Sullivan Principles have failed to promote peaceful change in South Africa. Moreover, the Principles have failed to achieve their more limited purpose, to "contribute greatly to the general economic welfare of all the people of the Republic of South Africa." We will examine the effect or non-effect of each principle on the lot of black workers—three years after the promulgation of the code....

Principle 3. Equal pay for all employees doing equal or comparable work for the same period of time.

This principle has no effect for the great majority of black workers; 71 percent of black workers employed in United States corporations work in job categories that employ no whites. Ninety-nine percent of the workers employed in the top job categories are white; 1 percent is black.

Principle 1. Nonsegregation of the races in all eating, comfort and work facilities.

While some United States corporations no longer post signs that segregate their facilities according to race, the majority of the facilities are *still* segregated through the use of more subtle but equally effective means of discrimination. Initially, some companies substituted color-keyed signs for explicitly racial signs. Currently, the discriminatory effect is maintained by assigning separate plant facilities to hourly workers and salaried workers, when the overwhelming majority of wage workers are black and the overwhelming majority of salaried workers are white.

Principle 2. Equal and fair employment practices for all employees.

This principle has been amplified to contain an ambiguous statement encouraging companies to "support" the elimination of discrimination against black trade unions and to "acknowledge generally" the right of blacks to join or form their own trade unions. There is no requirement that the companies recognize or negotiate with unions. In fact, an overwhelming majority of signatories do not negotiate with *any* union—white or black. Only two companies recognize a black trade union, and only one has actually signed a contract....

Principle 4. Initiation and development of training programs that will prepare, in substantial numbers, blacks and other nonwhites for supervisory, administrative, clerical and technical jobs.

South African law cripples this principle by reserving skilled positions for whites. For example, black artisan-trainees are ineligible for certificates of competency, without which they cannot be employed. Closed shop agreements between white unions and their employers reserve skilled positions for members of white trade unions.

Principle 5. Increasing the number of blacks and other nonwhites in management and supervisory positions.

Approximately half the United States companies responded to the most recent Sullivan questionnaire employed no blacks in managerial or supervisory positions. Even the successful completion by all blacks presently enrolled in training programs of responding companies would result in the employment of blacks in only 3 percent of the managerial and 6 percent of the professional positions.

Principle 6. Improving the quality of employees' lives outside the work environment in such areas as housing, transportation, schooling, recreation and health.

Unlike the first five principles which purport to improve the work environment of blacks, the sixth principle holds out the nebulous promise of improving the quality of black employees' lives. As we have demonstrated earlier in this testimony, apartheid controls the quality of black South African lives. Token philanthropy is a palliative that does not address the pervasive tyranny of apartheid.

IV National Bar Association Position and Recommendations

The National Bar Association has thus far attempted to set forth the grim reality of the South African experience in order to point out the negligible consequences which the "Sullivan Principles"—even if mandatory—would have on the prospects for ameliorating the condition of South African blacks.

The National Bar Association takes the position that the President and the Congress must take decisive and uncompromised action by prohibiting United States companies from directly or indirectly doing business in South Africa. This would require disinvestment of all current commercial interests of United States companies in South Africa, a ban on all new investments, and the immediate termination of all exportation to and importation from South Africa....

The National Bar Association does not cry wolf. Ours is the calm judgment that the situation in South Africa is deteriorating and, absent fundamental changes, will ultimately explode into racial warfare. Such a circumstance could not but help to tear at the seams of our own multiracial society if we remain ambivalent or noncommittal....

Arguments will be heard that continued economic intercourse with South Africa benefits blacks thereby providing them with jobs and income. Slavery in the United States was rationalized in a similar way.

The American black community is unanimous in calling for comprehensive economic sanctions against South Africa....Recently, more than one thousand black leaders and elected officials, representing over three hundred organizations, and millions of constituents across the country, met to adopt a national political, social, economic and international agenda for the decade of the eighties. That agenda, to which the National Bar Association subscribed, called for the immediate cessation of all economic, diplomatic, political and cultural relations with South Africa....

TALK BY MR. ROBERT KEELEY

Deputy Assistant Secretary of State for African Affairs. "U.S. Policy and South Africa" Workshop, Detroit, December 13, 1979.

...South Africa is a unique country because the dominant feature of its internal arrangement is a system known as apartheid which is a policy of keeping the races apart and in fact very unequal. The whites there have monopolized political and economic power and they keep for themselves a disproportionate share of the wealth produced by all South Africans.

Within its region South Africa can be called a superpower. It can close transportation links which are vital to its neighbors, maintains a powerful defense force, manufactures an array of weapons, influences significantly all the economies of all other countries in that region of southern Africa, and also exercises de facto power over Namibia and at times threatens to project its power into Zimbabwe-Rhodesia.

South Africa's mineral wealth is also one of a kind in the world. Although diamonds and gold are the most renowned of the minerals found there, the platinum group metals, uranium and chrome might be the most strategically vital for the United States and our allies in Europe and Japan. Quite frankly the United States role in South Africa is peripheral rather than central in the process of change taking place there. We assume that the pressures on the South African Government to make the distribution of opportunities and benefits equal and to accept majority rule will prevail in the end. Most of these pressures for change must be generated from within South Africa by the needs of its economy for more highly skilled workers, by the desire of the South African Government to give everyone some stake in that society so that they are loyal to it but most of all by the insistent demands of the unenfranchised majority, that is the black population, for a political system that depends on their informed consent rather than on that of a particular minority group within the nation.

The United States presence in South Africa is quite limited. We have approximately 16 percent of foreign investment there, the American firms operating in South Africa employ approximately 1 percent of the labor force. We have a large deficit in our trade with South Africa, in our bilateral trade. But we do feel that we have a unique role to play there and that is to deny the validity of the apartheid system and its successors, to distance ourselves from it and to encourage other forces working for peaceful change. We play this role in several different roles which I would like to review for you briefly:

Since 1963 we have maintained an arms embargo against South Africa. In 1977 the United Nations Security Council made the embargo mandatory for all countries. We severely restrict travel of South African military personnel to the United States and of ours to South Africa. This year the military personnel in the United States Embassy in Pretoria and of the South African Embassy in Washington were sharply reduced. Despite our trade deficit we follow restrictive commercial policies with regard to South Africa. There are no active commercial promotions, we withdrew our commercial attachés. No export/import bank activities are permitted except for guarantees on private loans to firms with good labor practices as permitted by the Evans amendment adopted last year. There is no transfer of United States origin goods or technology to or for the use of South African military or police. We formally urge United States firms in South Africa to subscribe to and implement the Sullivan Principles.

Let me also note that the United States Government takes this particular position only with regard to South Africa. I stress again its unique case. We regret that not all the United States firms have followed the lead of Ford and Kellogg's in recognizing black unions....We make strenuous efforts to direct our public diplomacy toward all of South Africa's people. We sponsor several dozen South African students studying here at the post-graduate level. We fund training programs for black trade unionists. We have a large exchange program to bring blacks and whites here to explore the process of change in our own society. Clearly there is a great deal more to be done in this area....

We fund United Nations operations to maintain and educate South African refugees and to provide humanitarian assistance to dissidents and their families within South Africa. We limit official contacts with the South African Government and we restrict official travel. Clearly business does not go on as usual with South Africa. We have provided political asylum to South Africans in the United States, we criticize specific human rights violations there, we are just now in the process of completing a very candid report on the human rights situation in South Africa which will be submitted to the Congress by January of next year.

"A WORLD IN MICROCOSM"

Backgrounder Issued by the Information Counselor, South African Embassy, Washington, D.C.—July 1980.

> The Republic of South Africa is very much the world in microcosm. Approximately 24 million people with various origins and languages live there side by side. They include almost 5 million whites, 2 million colored, 800,000 Asians, 5 million Zulu, 2 million Xhosa, 3 million North and South Sotho, 2 million Tswana, and 2.5 million representing smaller nationalities. Not one of these groups is culturally homogeneous, each comprises several distinctive subcultural units. The human mosaic stretches from the primitive Bushman to the sophisticated city dwellers of Johannesburg and Soweto, where faces, clothes and costumes reflect cultures from all over the globe.
>
> The human history of South Africa is an engrossing record of material, social and political achievement, decisively influenced by the confluence of diverse ethnic groups.

South Africa's Human Mosaic

The Bushmen and Hottentots, nomadic food gatherers who ranged between the far interior and the southern shores of the subcontinent, were the first indigenous peoples of South Africa, preceding black and white alike. More amenable to social contact than the Bushman, the pastoral Hottentot nomads in and around the Cape of Good Hope, were more readily drawn under the influence of mid-17th century Dutch and British immigrants. Deculturization and the ravages of three smallpox epidemics led to the disintegration of the main Hottentot tribes and their subsequent progressive assimilation with Negroid and East Indian slaves and white sailors, soldiers and officials. Eventually, through intermingling, there crystallized a new ethnic group—the Cape Coloreds.

The arrival of whites and blacks, too, was the result of major migratory movements. For the Dutch, wanting to consolidate and expand their lucrative trade with the Orient, the Cape was a logical place to set up a ship refueling and replenishment station halfway between Western Europe and the East. But what had in 1652 been envisaged as only a limited commercial enterprise, gradually evolved for the white settlers as a base for the development of a vigorous new nation. Meanwhile, several ethnic black tribes from the regions of the great lakes of Central East Africa were migrating southwards along the east coast of the continent. This population movement was a series of successive waves as the peoples involved reacted to the push and pull of inter-tribal wars and the search for better crop and hunting land.

Approximately a century after the establishment of the Cape settlement, the south-westerly migration of black tribes and the north-easterly expansion of white pioneers finally led to a confrontation between blacks and whites, primarily in the south-central portion of Africa.

Then, the beginning of the 20th century also brought in an Asian population, the fourth main population group, to South Africa. Starting with mostly Asian laborers brought in to work the Natal sugar-cane fields in 1860, these laborers were followed in increasing numbers by relatives, individual traders and Asian workers for other tasks besides agriculture.

The Whites

The socio-economic structure of the South African whites today shows a diversity of cultural, economic, social and religious backgrounds. According to the 1970 census, 56 percent of the whites in South Africa are Afrikaans and 38 percent English-speaking, while more than 1 percent use both Afrikaans and English as their home languages. More than 5 percent of the white population have a home language other than Afrikaans and English, including German,...Portuguese, and Dutch.

Historically and biogenetically the white population of South Africa has ties with a great variety of European peoples. The Netherlands and Britain made the largest contribution....

The Afrikaner genesis dates back to the arrival of the first pioneers at the Cape more than 300 years ago. The vast exodus of Boer pioneers from the British-administered Cape Colony in the 1830s (colloquially known as the Great Trek) was a further milestone in the evolution of the Afrikaner people.

This breakaway from English domination was accelerated and consolidated by two wars of independence waged against the British Empire. Few people realize that these two wars were the first major struggles in Africa for emancipation from colonial rule. In fact, Afrikaner nationalism was the first coherent nationalist movement on the Continent of Africa. By the late 1800s the Afrikaners had long outgrown their original settler status. Their ties with Europe had become progressively more tenuous, and at the start of the 20th century Afrikaners were, to all intents and purposes, a fully established nation with their own distinctive language and way of life....The Afrikaners are the descendants of the only white emigrant group from the Old World to evolve a language of their own in South Africa. In 1925 Afrikaans became the second official language of the country, alongside English.

Approximately 38 percent of South Africa's white population is English-speaking. Ethnically not as coherent and demographically not as indigenous as the Afrikaners, this group of approximately 1.5 million people embraces, apart from smaller enclaves of non-Anglo-Saxon origin, mainly persons of British descent. Early British emigration to South Africa was a steady influx of individual officials and traders, interspersed with larger population groups such as the 1820 settlers and those drawn by events such as the diamond and gold discoveries in the late 19th century, South Africa's second war of independence and the two world wars.

Measured by the accepted criteria of nationhood, the whites of South Africa constitute a full-fledged, independent nation. Despite their diverse European origins they have evolved a nationhood and a distinctive identity of their own. They are not a mere temporary projection of Western Europe anymore than white Americans are in the United States. They are white Africans.

The Black Peoples of South Africa

The blacks of South Africa do not constitute a single homogeneous people or ethnic entity. They are subdivided into four main cultural–linguistic groups, namely the Nguni, Sotho-Tswana, Venda and Shangaan-Tsonga. These subdivisions are based principally on historical, linguistic and cultural differences and can in turn be subdivided into nine separate ethnic groups, each with its own language, legal system, life-style, values and socio-political identity.

In life-style and language the Zulu nation, for example, differs as much from the Tswana nation as the French differ from the Italians.

The Sotho-Tswana

The Sotho-Tswana group is a patriarchal society and its members are traditionally agriculturalists and pastoralists. Among the first blacks to come south across the Zambezi river, this group embraces three distinctive peoples—the Tswana, South Sotho and North Sotho.... The three Sotho nations have many cultural characteristics in common, but there are also important differences separating them, especially in language and in political and tribal organization.

The Venda

The Venda people are a unique division of the South African blacks. Many of their customs are not found among any other black people in South Africa. The Venda are related to blacks living across the Limpopo river in Zimbabwe, and their language, Chivenda, is related to languages in Zimbabwe. The Venda people consist of 27 tribes.

The Venda nation became independent on September 13, 1979. Venda has considerable mining potential. Large deposits of copper, vermiculite, graphite, phosphates and high grade coal are available. Venda is about the same size as the State of Delaware.

The Shangaan-Tsonga

The Shangaan-Tsonga people, of mixed origin, are settled mainly in the Limpopo River Valley in Mozambique. Those living in South Africa have their own black state called Gazankulu, a small country in the north, near Venda and Mozambique. The name Shangana originated when the Tsonga people were dominated by the Zulu Chief Soshangane after he had fled from another Zulu Chief, Chaka, and established his Gaza empire in Mozambique in 1835. Many Tsonga migrated when this happened and the descendants of these early immigrants still prefer the name Tsonga. They were followed by others who were true subjects of Soshangane—hence the name Shangana. Their settlement in South Africa is of fairly recent origin, the latest settlers having arrived in 1895 after the defeat of their chief, Ngungunyane, by the Portuguese. Gazankulu advanced to self-government status in 1973.

The Nguni

The Nguni tribes are concentrated mainly in the eastern and south-eastern areas of South Africa. This major cultural–linguistic division comprises the Xhosa, Swazi and Zulu nations.

The Asian Community

The Asian community owes its presence in South Africa primarily to farmers in the early British colony of Natal, who recruited Asian laborers for their sugar plantations.

The Asians in South Africa are not culturally homogeneous. There are marked differences between linguistic groups.... The Asians of South Africa are a prosperous community. Many are excellent and successful shopkeepers and businessmen.

The Colored People

The origin of the colored people, a community of mixed ethnic descent, dates back to 1652. The colored people include two subcultural groups, viz. the Griquas and Cape Malays. Many coloreds have distinguished themselves in the fields of ballet, fine arts and literature.

WHY SOUTH AFRICA SHRUGS AT SANCTIONS

Peter Brimelow, "Why South Africa Shrugs at Sanctions," *Forbes,* March 9, 1987, p. 101.

"Comment is free, but facts are sacred." This was the creed of the great *Manchester Guardian* Editor C. P. Scott, a liberal journalist renowned for his courageous appeals for reason at a time when jingoist emotions ran high in Britain during the Anglo–Boer War (1899–1902). Throughout the Free World today emotions again run powerfully against the Boers' descendants, who run a racist regime in South Africa. With Congress's enactment of the Comprehensive Antiapartheid Act of 1986, the United States is firmly committed to waging economic war against Afrikaner rule in South Africa. How effective is this economic warfare? Wishful thinking aside, what are the facts—the sacred facts? In this report from South Africa, *Forbes* cuts through the comment and rhetoric and gets at the facts.

To the casual American observer, South Africa today looks unnervingly normal. The main cities are modern, clean and multiracially bustling; the grosser forms of segregation apparently vanished as part of State President P. W. Botha's much derided reforms. By American standards, in fact, relations between the races seem oddly gentle. The sun shines, prices are gratifyingly low in dollar terms—South Africa is one of the remaining tourist bargains—and the dinner talk is of the May 6 election, in which Botha's National Party is expected to run not against the fierce challenges mounted by his political opponents on the left and—especially—on the right, but against American interference. It seems likely to be an easy victory for Botha, one of the first tangible results of the U.S. economic sanctions.

These, of course, are superficial impressions. But the black townships are quiet, patrolled by the army, and the school boycott has ended. Two years after the African Congress' Oliver Tambo made his New Year's message a call to "render South Africa ungovernable," it isn't. And no one thinks it will be anytime soon.

Such a sense of relief is spreading among South Africa's 4.6 million whites that the antigovernment *Johannesburg Star* has felt obliged to headline a cautionary story BEWARE SANCTIONS "EUPHORIA." But the managers of many foreign-owned South African companies have a very good reason to feel euphoric: Sanctions have made them rich. This has happened because foreign corporations couldn't simply pick up their factories and go home, as advocates of divestment seemed to think they would. They have had to sell them, frequently to the incumbent managers in the form of leveraged buyouts, often for a fraction of market value, because everyone knew they were desperate. Some companies that have recently decided to pull out: IBM, Coca-Cola, Procter & Gamble. Some deals have been so attractive that American managers have chosen to join in, as in the case of the South African subsidiary of General Motors.

Alternatively, foreign firms have been selling out to other interests. Some are exotic: Craig Williamson, who worked undercover inside the African National Congress for several years, recently became head of a unit empowered to purchase foreign assets on behalf of GMR, an Italian group....More typical: In November Anglo-American Corp., one of the five capital pools that dominate the South African economy, acquired South Africa's biggest bank, Barclays National, from its British parent, Barclays Bank Plc., long a target for antiapartheid protesters. Significantly, Anglo paid $8.06 for stock trading at $10.30. Barclays will get only about half that because of the machinations of South Africa's ingenious two-tier foreign exchange system. And South Africa will save some 30 million rand ($14 million) in foreign dividend payments annually.

Over the years, disinvestment has been a tremendous boon to a vital component of the South African government-industrial complex: the $650 million Allied Electronics Corp. Ltd (Altron), with operations in the electronics, telecommunications and electrical power fields. Altron's chairman is William Venter, 52, one of many Afrikaners now prominent in what had once been the exclusively English-speaking preserve of business. Venter has said that his "big break" came in 1976, when he was able to persuade ITT to begin selling its South African subsidiary to him. This became the nucleus of the first major South African–controlled electronics company. "If I had to thank anybody," says Venter, "I think I would thank the American church groups who had played such a major role in making people like ITT feel uncomfortable."

Subsequently Altron acquired a string of other foreign subsidiaries from the U.S., Britain, France and Holland, including Motorola and, most recently, Asia.

Today the integrated equal-pay work force at Altron's headquarters at Boksburg, near Johannesburg, pores over its circuit boards placidly enough. But their employer is widely regarded as one of Pretoria's chosen instruments, a preferred supplier in telecommunications and in defense electronics.

The ability to bid on government contracts is one of the advantages local managements gain when freed from foreign ownerships. They can also cut out the costly social-responsibility programs often implemented to conform with the "Sullivan Principles," the code of corporate conduct for U.S. subsidiaries developed by Leon Sullivan, the Philadelphia clergyman and GM director. Sullivan recently added the further principle that U.S. corporations should actually engage in efforts to challenge South African law, and has said that he will call for complete withdrawal if "apartheid" is not ended by May 31. (Many Americans use "apartheid" to mean "white rule" in general. But to South Africans it has a specific meaning: "petty apartheid," or segregation, and "grand apartheid," or ultimate territorial partition, policies developed by former National Party leader Hendrik Verwoerd and now publicly disavowed by Botha.)

Now, one South African merchant bank is using the list of Sullivan signatories as a marketing tool to locate potential buyouts. From this point of view, disinvestment has been a cheap form of corporate restructuring, quite possibly enhancing the efficiency of the South African economy.

Which is not to say that economic sanctions will have no effect on South Africa—in the long run. With fewer foreign firms and no capital imports, the South African economy will grow more slowly than otherwise. The best guess is it will average up to 3% a year, instead of the 5% to 6% of the 1960s. But it will grow. And it will be that much less vulnerable.

Much of what sanctions are doing to South Africa, in fact, is just the mirror image of what many countries have done to themselves: insistent on Soviet-style self-sufficiency, protectionism, restrictions on foreign ownership. Thus are foreign proponents of disinvestment achieving for South Africa almost precisely what Canadian nationalists have advocated with only partial success against U.S. ownership north of the border.

The difference is that the South African economy, with its sophisticated industrial base and its resources, is better fitted than most for autarky, even if externally imposed. A remarkable 60% of its export earnings are from low-volume, high-value, difficult-to-sanction items like precious metals, diamonds, and strategic minerals. According to most estimates, it can generate almost all of its annual capital needs internally; it actually sustained a net outflow of long-term capital after 1976 until the South African authorities imposed a debt moratorium in mid-1985.

To the extent that sanctions are effective, the South African economy will reorient itself away from exports and toward import substitution, much of which would previously have been uneconomic. At a price, the South Africans have the technical capacity to build practically anything. They have already demonstrated this by responding to the oil and arms embargoes in the 1960s and 1970s with stepped-up production at the Sasol oil from coal plants, which now supply 70% of their liquid fuel needs, and at the government-backed Armaments Corp. of

South Africa Ltd. (Armscor). The firm now exports arms to 23 countries. Armscor's G-5 self-propelled howitzer, which has a tactical nuclear capability and is supposedly the finest of its type in the world, has been seen recently in action in Iraq.

However, South African businessmen are surprisingly confident about their ability to export even easily sanctionable goods. Sanctions-busting has already been developed to a high art. Revealing its secrets is a serious crime in South Africa, although this has not prevented the English-language press from exposing false labeling of canned fruit and alleged schemes to launder goods through a free port in Britain's Isle of Man. But South Africa has already had considerable success evading formal trade bans—over half the country's exports are already categorized as "all other," which is viewed as a partial euphemism. And it can draw on Rhodesian experience: The coordinator of the Department of Finance's antisanctions effort was governor of the Rhodesia Reserve Bank, Desmond Krogh.

Far Eastern markets are expected to remain accessible—and adaptable. South African coal exports in 1986 and 1987 are likely to remain at the 40-million-ton mark, despite the loss of 10 million tons to the French and Danish embargoes, because fierce price-cutting by the South Africans in the Far East is displacing the Australian coal exporters. And an official at the Committee on Pipe and Tube Imports alleges that Thailand, not previously a pipe-maker, has undermined U.S. steel sanctions by producing pipes using South African steel. Where there is a will to make a dollar, or a mark or a franc or a lira, there is usually a way.

Or a ruble, for that matter. South African businessmen are confident they will be able to deal through the Soviet bloc. It's tempting to dismiss such claims as bravado. But the Soviets did become one of Rhodesia's major illicit trade partners during its unilateral independence, notably in re-exporting Rhodesian chrome to the U.S., and South Africans have long had intimate, secret relations with them through their participation in the De Beers–managed diamond cartel. Some evidence of the South Africans' sincerity: the real pain in their eyes when discussing the commissions Marxist middlemen charge. Soviet duplicity is dependable, but it is expensive.

"Commissions" work in black Africa, too. "We can sell anything we want to Africa," says one Afrikaner businessman.

"But they can't pay," points out his colleague.

"The Americans will give them alms."

No doubt the Americans will give increased economic aid to black African countries whose trade with South Africa is being reduced by sanctions; Senator Edward Kennedy has proposed $700 million over five years. And undoubtedly a good part of U.S. aid will find its way to South Africa through purchases of South African goods and services.

Still, sanctions will have some immediate impact. Some exporters, like South Africa's fruit growers, are highly alarmed. Marketing officials say North American and Scandinavian sanctions may cost 12.5% to 15% of fresh fruit sales, and they see little possibility of evasion. The industry employs 220,000 nonwhites.

Here, amid the carefully tended apple orchards of the western Cape, the cutting edge of sanctions is visible at last. Every year farm manager Bernard Napier buses over 200 Xhosas from the autonomous Transkei "National State" to augment the "Colored" (mixed-race) work force on the Graymead farm. As always in Africa, their earnings support several people at home. When the new workers arrive from their homeland, they are so undernourished Napier has to feed them up to strength before they can work. If alternative markets cannot be found, the apple trees on which Napier has depended for more than 40 years of his life could be plowed under. Back in the Transkei, the blacks will starve.

This, in a nutshell, is the real trouble with sanctions as a political weapon: They hurt the blacks more than the whites. South Africa is not a nation but a small empire of 23 million people, a sociologists' paradise of different ethnic groups interdependent in fantastically complicated ways. In its peculiar political economy, the dominant cast of 2.7 million Afrikaners are by far the best insulated. Some 40% of them are the employees of the South African state and its dependents: in the civil service, defense force, police. The 1.8 million English-speaking whites, who tend to be on the liberal side of white politics but are outvoted, are in business and therefore more exposed, although much less so than the best-placed nonwhites, the 800,000 Indians and 2.8 million Coloreds, who have just been given the right to vote for their own assemblies. The 15.2 million blacks, unskilled labor with no vote in a country without any social security net, are intensely vulnerable. And the situation of the estimated 1.9 million blacks from the neighboring "Front Line" states to the north, where they support probably 10 million people, is the most desperate of all.

In theory, the whites could pass most of the costs of sanctions through to the blacks in general and to the front line states in particular. In practice, they have been less ruthless—up to now. Despite emitting threatening noises, Pretoria, unlike Nigeria, has not yet expelled its foreign workers. Nor has it acted decisively to end inflation, currently 18% a year, apparently because, like Washington in the 1970s, it is under the delusion that it can and must put jobs first by maintaining high levels of demand. Interacting with South Africa's steeply progressive tax code, this has resulted in unlegislated tax increases so severe that many believe them to be the most important cause of white emigration. Inflation, not insurrection, may be the real threat to white rule in South Africa.

During Oliver Tambo's recent visit to Washington, he told Georgetown University students that white wealth must be redistributed to "raise the impoverished standard of living for millions of our people." This is because he obviously views the South African economy as a static pile of wealth, unfairly monopolized by whites. But the fact is that, despite its highly visible modern sector, South Africa is actually a poor country. Its total gross national product is only $51 billion, one-third of Australia's and 1% of the U.S.,' a mere $2,232 per capita. That's not enough to go around. The whites, 19.3% of the population and possessors of all the vital technical skills, already contribute 93% of income tax revenue and pay European levels of tax. South Africa is a microcosm of the world—except that its First World is taxed to subsidize its Third World.

Most of Africa has always lived in primeval poverty. Even in South Africa, 1 million blacks are still subsistence farmers. But in South Africa economic activity organized by whites has gradually drawn the blacks out of their tribal lands, into the cash economy and into the cities—to the great consternation of the architects of apartheid. Driving the whites out or depriving them of incentives would reverse this dynamic process and eventually cause economic collapse.

The South African economy may be small by world standards, but it nevertheless composes over one-third of sub-Saharan Africa's total gross domestic product. It is the locomotive that has been pulling the subcontinent out of subsistence farming and out of looming Malthusian tragedy. The last 20 years have been an economic disaster for black Africa, with per capita GNPs falling 16% in the first half of the 1980s alone. Remittances from foreign workers in South Africa provide badly needed foreign exchange for other African countries; it is their natural trading partner and also the most reliable transport route for their exports.

South Africa's economy may prove more adaptable than anyone expects. For example, if Afrikaners can eschew their deep respect for legal forms, the country could exploit the advantages of being outlawed by ignoring international patents and copyrights, as Taiwan has done—one reason legislating against license agreements, as some sanctioneers urge, could prove self-defeating. A favorite plan: to duplicate the Canadian Maple Leaf gold coin, since the South African authorities obligingly hosted the Canadians when they were planning their own coin, only to find Canada's leader in the sanctions campaign.

South Africa could also find a source of growth in deregulation. At least 3 million blacks work in the "shadow economy," in contravention of laws many of which were part of apartheid's very substantial apparatus of economic control. Even opening a store, for example, required multiple permissions. Legalizing these activities could have profound economic and social consequences.

A very visible case study: the proliferation of black-owned minibuses, called "combis," on South Africa's roads. Partly as a result of the murderous riots in Soweto and the accompanying boycott of the state-subsidized bus company Putco, the police have largely ceded the transport of blacks to these usually illegal private operators and no longer attempt to maintain Putco's monopoly or enforce safety standards. There are now an estimated 40,000 such black cabs in South Africa—an industry that is booming regardless of sanctions.

South Africans call these fairly labor-intensive, low-technology activities "inward industrialization." They hope to do the same thing with black housing. They think it may enable the economy to keep growing and providing work when import-substitution opportunities are exhausted.

A further unspoken advantage of outlaw status: It could allow South Africa to reverse its drift, impelled by its newly legal, highly politicized black labor unions and by well-intentioned international opinion, toward becoming a high-wage economy for the employed few. In a textbook demonstration of the unintended consequences of minimum wage law, this drift has resulted in mechanization, the substitution of capital for labor, and no wages at all for the unlucky black majority.

Many South African white liberals blame U.S. sanctions for undercutting Botha's reforms....they are part of Afrikaner history, which, contrary to myth, did not consist of landing at the Cape in 1652 and blasting everyone flat but, instead, involved a complex process of coercion, cooperation and diplomacy.

Sanctions were important as a threat; as a reality, they are like pushing on a string. Having imposed them, the U.S. no longer has much influence in South Africa. Unless, of course, we want to send in the Marines.

WHY THE WEST NEEDS SOUTH AFRICA[4]

Carl F. Noffke, Institute for American studies at the Rands Afrikaans University (RAU).

Soviet Chairman Andrei Gromyko was once quoted as saying: "America's greatest weakness is its inability to understand the Soviet Union's final goal."

We are now well into the eighties—A decade of confrontation and conflict. Africa has become a key area in the political battle ground between the Soviet Union and the United States of America. What happens in Africa in the next few years will be of the utmost concern to the Western powers.

Southern Africa is an area of immense chaos, of instability, conflict and confrontation.

Of all the black countries in Africa, the only three reasonably stable ones are Kenya, Botswana and Swaziland. In Southern Africa the only secure stable and economically well developed country is the Republic of South Africa. It has the resources, the proven skills, achievements and manpower to assist and help neighboring states to move as close as possible, in African terms, to a lifestyle and political base resembling that of the West. Yet, South Africa is being deliberately sabotaged and undermined by its erstwhile Western allies.

Few countries in Africa can claim to have democratic constitutions. The most frequently quoted example of a black democracy is Botswana. Democracy succeeds in Botswana on account of three facts: its homogeneous population, its natural resources and the economic and security benefits which flows from having stable, protective South Africa as a neighbor. South Africa itself is a democracy as far as the whites, the Asians and the coloureds are concerned. Increasingly the base of democracy is being broadened in South Africa and it will shortly include blacks up to the highest levels of government. To judge South Africa properly in the political sense of the word, it is necessary to note that Africa, including the adjacent island states, consists of 51 countries which are internationally recognized. At the time of writing three of these countries, Botswana, Mauritius and Gambia (all with small populations), could be described in relative terms as functioning democracies, ruled by the will of the majority on the basis of universal adult franchise, with a legally constituted and freely operating opposition. Of the remaining 48 countries only two, namely the Republic of South Africa and Namibia, have the base of democracy being widened to any significant extent. These two countries are, in fact, moving towards the much cherished democratic ideals. In the rest of Africa the form of government includes dictatorships, rule by military juntas and rule by a single party or party rule which excludes major population groups.

The reasons why democracies do not flower in Africa is simple to explain. However, few political commentators come to grips with the realities of Africa. As Prof. George N. Barrie so succinctly explained recently: "Constitutionalism, with its corollary of political rights and civil liberties (fundamental freedom), is the product of centuries of Western political thought and history, starting with the Greeks and manifesting itself in the Magna Carta, the Declaration of Independence and the Bill of Rights of the United States Constitution (and in the constitutions of such countries as West Germany and France)."[5]

It is difficult for forms of democracy and human rights to evolve in Africa. As Prof. Barrie views this dilemma: "The seeds are simply not there." It is therefore incumbent upon the United States and other Western countries to seek out those governments which are committed to the expansion of the Western concept of democracy and the expansion of the free enterprise system. Those few countries should be actively assisted in their evolutionary endeavors. This handful of countries includes South Africa.

The West Ignores South Africa's Achievements

The opposite is happening. Positive developments in South Africa are being ignored and Western governments have embarked upon a vast agenda of sanctions which, to quote President Reagan, "would feed violence and invite Marxist tyranny."[6]

South Africa is, warts and all, politically the most stable country in Africa. This is most unusual given the vast campaign of terrorism, and economic and psychological warfare waged by the Soviet Union and the intense sanctions campaign coming from the West.

South Africa's resilience in the face of an immense international campaign is most remarkable. Its position on the continent of Africa is also unique. It has the only First World economic structure on the continent of Africa and it is increasingly becoming a sophisticated industrial power. It ranks among the first 20 trading countries. It is an industrial and commercial giant on the African continent and it offers immense opportunities of economic and technical assistance to its neighbours. It is one of the few countries in Africa with more than one political party. Democracy is expanding in South Africa while it is withering in much of the rest of Africa, where 30 states have one-party (or no party) systems and eleven countries are military dictatorships.[7]

South Africa is in many ways a remarkable country. It has moved within the short period of six decades from a poverty stricken underdeveloped country to a regional military and economic power to be reckoned with.

With only 5 percent of the African continent's population and 4 percent of its land area, South Africa has more than 20 percent of Africa's total output of goods and services. It produced 37 percent of Africa's steel in 1982, generated 54 percent of Africa's electricity and employed 39 percent of the agricultural tractors available on the continent.

But apart from the fact that South Africa has more automobiles, trucks, telephones, permanent dwellings, highways, skyscrapers, industries and more paved roads than any country in Africa, in addition to the best equipped military force, it is considered to be the Persian Gulf of Metals and Minerals in the world. The country has a vast reserve of minerals and metals which are essential to the economies of the industrialized world. A number of these metals and minerals could be described as strategic....

West's Dependence on South Africa's Minerals

...One of the shrewdest, most informed judges of the global competition for strategic mineral supplies is Dr. W. C. J. van Rensburg, Director of the Texas Mining and Mineral Resources Research Institute at the University of Texas, Austin. He analyzed the U.S.A.'s dependence on imported sources of strategic minerals in 1981. In noting that the USSR had sharply reduced exports while entering the market as an importer of a number of key metals, Dr. van Rensburg concluded that these developments foreshadow growing competition for world supplies of strategic minerals.[8]

Dr. van Rensburg has warned that unfortunately it appears that the lessons of two world wars, in which the availability of adequate supplies of strategic minerals played an important role in the eventual outcome, have been forgotten. Present indications are that the USA and its allies are vulnerable to disruptions in the supply of a number of key strategic minerals.

The key metals supplied by South Africa to the Western industrial countries are used in almost everything from soap dishes and automobile bumpers to the turbine blades in jet engines, automobile catalytic converters, the production of high-quality glass, fiber-optics manufacturing equipment, as a chemical and petroleum catalyst, an ingredient for cancer drugs, film, plates, X-rays, electronics, drill bits for machines, tools and oil wells, to produce special steels and to manufacture aerosol propellants. In the case of titanium it accounts for up to 40 percent of the total weight of specialized military aircraft.

Analysts agree that chrome would be the hardest to eliminate from the US material diet.[9] According to a Shearson Lehman Brothers publication: "The world industrial economy would be hard pushed to operate at normal levels without stainless steel. There are alternative alloy steels, but they tend not to have the same qualities as stainless steels in such areas as corrosion resistance."

Smashing ties with South Africa would cost the West half a million jobs. The economic and military system of the United States and Europe would be dislocated and billions of dollars in business threatened. The study was made by the Institute for European Economic Studies in London, in conjunction with the Ecole Superieure de Commerce in Reims and the Fachhochschule Reutlingern in West Germany.[10]

The study said a boycott would cost the West 500,000 jobs, including 250,000 in the United Kingdom, 130,000 in West Germany and 122,000 in the USA.

South Africa was seen by the group as one of the most valuable trading partners in the world because of its mineral exports. It was added that for some strategic metals there are no substitutes at any price. "Industrialized countries must have them or write off a good part of their technological advance," the group concluded.

Without these metals one cannot build a jet engine or automobile, run a train, build a power plant, process food, run a clean restaurant or hospital operating room, build a computer or clean up air or water.

SA Plays Important Role in Southern Africa

Putting considerations related to the West aside, South Africa plays an immense role in the subcontinent of Africa. In many respects South Africa is the economic anchor and main supplier in the area.

Southern Africa is roughly the size of Western Europe with a population of approximately 80 million. South Africa provides enormous work opportunities for the citizens of the neighbouring black states. It is estimated that some 1,500,000 foreign blacks do in fact work in South Africa. If one assumes that each of these workers supports six people back home, which is a fair average in Africa, then it means that approximately nine million black women and children in the neighbouring states depend for their daily bread on wages earned in South Africa.

South Africa and most of the economically viable countries in Southern Africa form a close economic unit. In fact, the relations are such that the closeness could be compared to the European Economic Community. At least 45 percent of the combined total imports and exports of Malawi, Zimbabwe, Zambia and Zaire are carried to and from South African ports by the South African Transportation Services. Virtually all imports and exports of Botswana, Lesotho and Swaziland are routed through South Africa....

But perhaps the strategic importance of South Africa astride the Indian and the Atlantic Oceans is even more important than its mineral wealth and its status as Africa's premier industrial power. South Africa is today strategically even more important than in 1969 when the American National Security Council concluded in a secret memorandum, that the strategic importance of Southern Africa increased with the closing of the Suez Canal following the 1967 Middle East war and increased Soviet naval activities in the Indian Ocean.

Significant Increase in Soviet Activity in Region

Since 1969 the Soviet Union has increased its military and economic influence in Africa, especially in Southern Africa. Angola and Mozambique are now dominated by the Soviet Union, while Zimbabwe, Zambia and Tanzania are leaning toward the Soviet Union. South Africa is the only stumbling block preventing the Soviet Union from assuming total control of Southern Africa, to take over its immense resources and then to control the most important naval choke point in the world, the Cape Sea Route. But the Republic of South Africa has proved in every sense a tough nut to crack.

The American policy of Constructive Engagement aimed at enhancing America's interests in Southern Africa has proved to be a failure. It has failed not on account of the policy and the basic concepts guiding the Reagan administration's policies in the area but because it is now being used to undermine the only dependable ally of the US in the area. South Africa is indisputably the economic, industrial, military and mining giant of Africa, with a total work force of 10 million (in 1980). During the past few years, mainly as a result of the political pressure which escalated on Capital Hill and growing resentment within the US Department of State's ranks over Pres. Reagan's approach toward South Africa, the policy has been turned around. The United States has become an adversary of South Africa and is employing sanctions to undermine the country. The consequences for the West, if the present tendencies and pressure continue, will be disastrous....

Significant Changes Underway

South Africa is moving rapidly toward the accommodation of all its citizens in all levels of government. All citizens will share all levels of political power. It seems as if nothing which is proposed by South Africa is acceptable to Western pressure groups. It is perhaps necessary to look again at what that outstanding American international expert, Hon. George W. Ball, had to say when he criticized the Carter policy toward South Africa in 1977: "Diplomacy, like politics, is the art of the possible, and if we use our leverage toward an unachievable end, we will 'create a mess.' "[11] Add Gann and Duignan: "A peaceful but imperfect solution for South Africa is preferable to a perfect solution achieved by violent means."

EXHIBIT 32-1 Mineral Dependence of the United States

The Republic of South Africa is not dependent on the United States for any mineral, strategic or otherwise. South Africa contains all essential minerals except bauxite and petroleum. South Africa has methodically reduced its dependence on the latter through the construction of three coal-to-oil plants over the past 30 years.

The United States, however, relies on South Africa for a variety of strategic minerals:

Mineral	*U.S. Import Dependence (%)*	*Supplied by South Africa (%)*	*S.A. Share of World Reserves (%)*
Chromium	100	56	84
Ferrochromium	98	44	50
Diamonds	100	67	29
Gold	21	13	63
Fluorspar	83	29	46
Manganese	99	33	93
Ferromanganese	75	43	15
Platinum	84	67	83
Vanadium	52	54	61
Uranium	30	24	17
Cobalt	95	61	11

Source: Office of Africa, ITA, U.S. Department of Commerce, 1985, 1986.

MINERAL RESERVES
Combined South Africa and USSR

Mineral	*S.A. (%)*	*USSR (%)*	*Combined (%)*
Platinum	79	20	99
Manganese	71	21	92
Chromium	78	12	90
Vanadium	20	60	80
Gold	59	16	75
Fluorspar	46	4	50
Cobalt	46	4	50
Uranium	17	13	30

Source: U.S. Bureau of Mines; U.S. Department of Commerce, 1985, 1986; *1985 South Africa Yearbook.*

EXHIBIT 32-2 U.S. Mineral Import Dependence

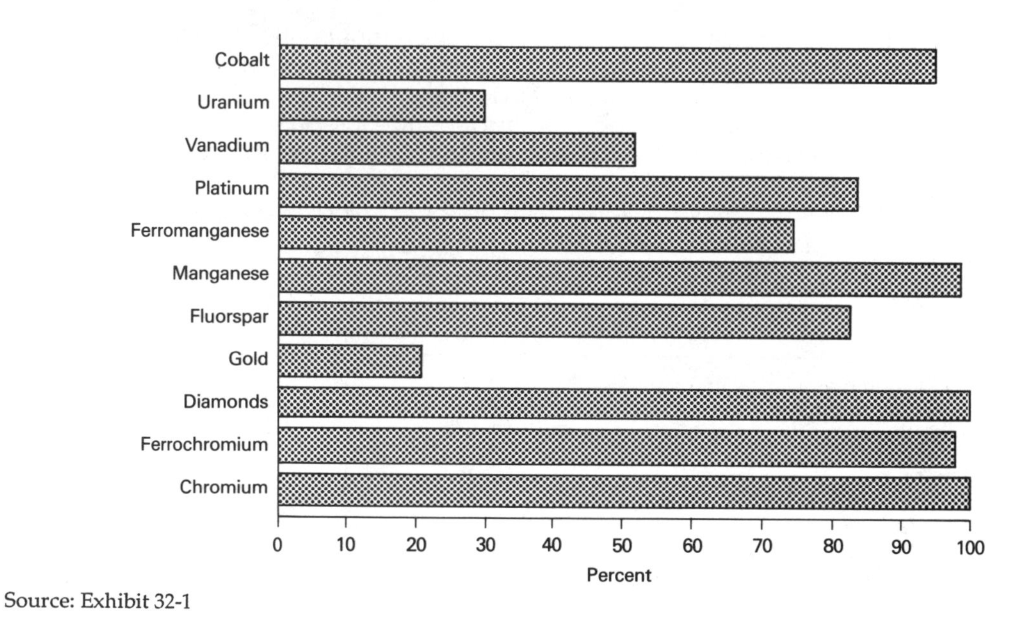

Source: Exhibit 32-1

EXHIBIT 32-3 South Africa's Share of World Minerals

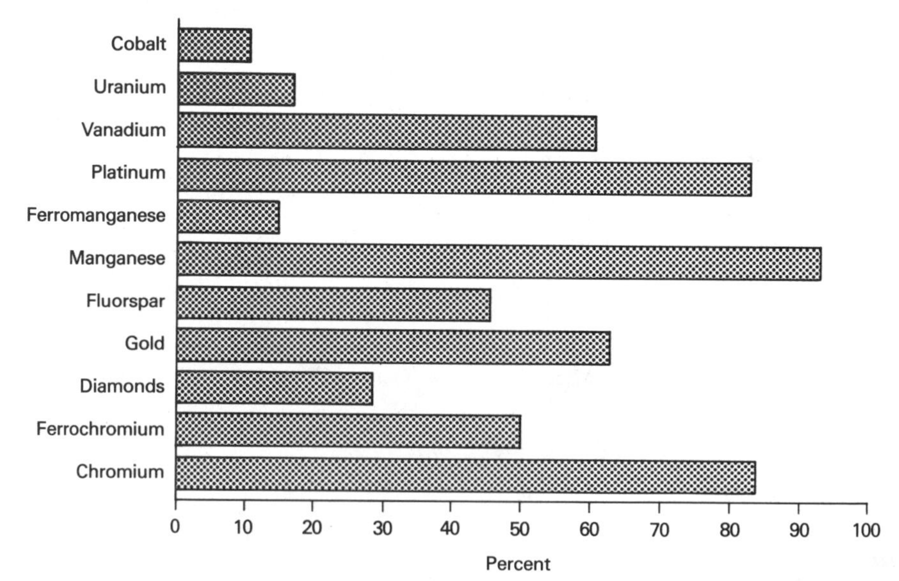

Source: Exhibit 32-1

SOUTH AFRICA TO MAXIMIZE SEGREGATION[12]

Bill Would Evict Blacks from White Neighborhoods

David Crary, Associated Press.

JOHANNESBURG, South Africa—The government on Friday proposed tough measures to enforce residential segregation, and critics said it could mean mass eviction of blacks from white areas.

"The new amendment has a clear political message—apartheid is alive and well," said Mahamed Dangor, spokesman for a group which has fought to block evictions of blacks living illegally in whites-only areas.

Government opponents condemned the proposal to tighten enforcement of the Group Areas Act, which segregates residential areas by race.

The government has not strictly enforced the 35-year-old act in recent years, angering conservative whites opposed to integrated neighborhoods. The proposed amendment is viewed as an accommodation to right-wing whites before nationwide municipal elections....

"The government indicates once again its absolute obsession with skin color as a norm on which to base South Africa's political, social and economic life," said the anti-apartheid Independent Party.

Tian van der Merwe, a Parliament member for the anti-apartheid Progressive Federal Party, called the new measures "so harsh and so brutal" that up to 200,000 blacks could be evicted on short notice.

The Group Areas Amendment bill calls for hiring inspectors to check for violations of the law. It would make it easier for authorities to confiscate property and to evict and prosecute people living in areas not designated for their race group.

The maximum fine for a property owner who allows a person to live outside his race group area would be increased from the current $175 to $4,300. The maximum prison sentence would be increased from two years to five years.

The bill also would negate a court ruling that violators cannot be evicted until alternative housing is found.

A second bill proposed Friday, the Free Settlement Areas Bill, would allow the creation of the first legal multiracial residential areas, subject to approval by President P. W. Botha and other officials. No neighborhood could be integrated against the wishes of its residents.

Botha's National Party favors gradual race reform but is committed to preserving white "group rights" such as segregated neighborhoods and schools.

The National Party has held power for 40 years but has been losing ground to the far-right Conservative Party which opposes all concessions to South Africa's 26-million black majority.

The Labor Party, which controls the mixed-race chamber of Parliament, said the Group Areas Act "cannot be amended and must be repealed."

"We once again call on the Nationalist government to repeal this immoral, ungodly, and iniquitous act that has been, and still is, the cause of so much hurt, pain and suffering," the party said.

South Africa has a housing surplus in white areas and a severe shortage of black townships. Many whites have been moving from inner cities to suburban areas, leaving urban landlords little choice but to rent to non-whites in "white" neighborhoods such as Hillbrow in Johannesburg and Woodstock in Cape Town.

ASSIGNMENT QUESTIONS

1. What is the approximate racial mix in South Africa?
2. Summarize the charges made by those who are critical of the South African government and society.
3. What do the critics want the U.S. government to do about South Africa? What do they want U.S. corporations to do?
4. Outline the response of the South African government and others to charges made by the critics of South Africa.
5. What course of action would you recommend to Dow Chemical Company?

NOTES

1. Richard K. Long, "Dow and South Africa," *Vital Speeches of the Day,* April 11, 1987.
2. Ibid., p. 522.
3. Ibid., p. 522.
4. Carl F. Noffke, "Why the West Needs South Africa," *International Conservative Insight,* January–February 1987, p. 20.
5. George N. Barrie, "The US and Human Rights for Africa: A Cryptic 1986 Assessment, *American Review* (RAU), Winter 1986.
6. *The Citizen* (Johannesburg), September 29, 1986, p. 8.
7. *Farica Insight,* published by the Africa Institute Pretoria, Vol. 15, no. 3, 1985.
8. *I.P.C. Business Press,* USA, January 1981.
9. "Four Vital Metals," *The Star* (Johannesburg), April 2, 1986.
10. "West Cannot Live Without SA Minerals," *The Star* (Johannesburg), September 7, 1984.
11. George Ball, "Asking for Trouble in South Africa," *Atlantic Monthly,* October 1977.
12. *The Valley Times* (Dublin, Calif.), July 2, 1988, p. 2B.

33
THE BOSTON BANANA COMPANY

In August 1988, the Fair Tariff Committee of the National Banana Council (the FTC of NBC) petitioned the U.S. Tariff Commission, under the "escape clause" of the Trade Expansion Act of 1962, for the imposition of higher tariffs or lower quotas on imported bananas.

In response to this petition, the commission held hearings as part of an investigation of the request. All interested parties were invited to appear and present arguments. Because the New England banana industry was relatively new, the Tariff Commission lacked significant information in its files and was anticipating making its decision basically on the information obtained through the hearings.

The New England Banana Industry

The banana is one of the world's most important fruits, being consumed extensively throughout the tropics and in many parts of the temperate zones. In the United States, bananas have been a staple household fruit since the midnineteenth century. Traditionally, bananas have been grown in Central American countries such as Costa Rica, Honduras, Guatemala, Mexico, and Panama.

In 1977, a refugee Jamaican national and former right-wing revolutionary, named Manuelo Portfolio, escaped from Martinique and came to live in Worcester, Massachusetts. Portfolio never lost his interest in growing bananas even though he was now living in an area where bananas rarely grow naturally. In 1979, he organized the Boston Banana Company (BBC) and developed a method for the mass cultivation of bananas using vast sheets of Saran Wrap and surplus combat stoves from the Indo-Chinese War. His bananas were sold under the brand name Ye Olde Boston Bananas (YOBBs).

The main competitive difficulty faced by the BBC was in relation to the pricing structure of the industry. Bananas imported from Central America sold for 19 cents per pound.

BBC, because of its much higher costs, was forced to sell its bananas at 89 cents per pound at the wholesale level. With the normal retail markup, this set the retail price of YOBBs at between $1.10 and $1.25 per pound.

For the first three years of its existence, BBC was able to increase its annual sales by 15 percent per year through a number of successful promotional programs. In the beginning, customers had purchased the bananas more or less out of curiosity to taste genuine Massachusetts bananas—or to be able to show their friends bananas costing more than $1.00 a pound. To maintain this initial burst of sales, Portfolio next conducted a sub rosa campaign through Boston underground newspapers that was built on the premise that Ye Olde Boston Banana peels could be dried and smoked with much the same effects as marijuana. When this fad died down, he further stimulated sales by a dual campaign: to the younger people he advertised YOBBs as an aphrodisiac, and to the older people he played on the snob appeal of brand-name $1.00 bananas combined with a heavy emphasis on the importance of buying American products—this promotion was based on the catchy slogan, "Don't Let Any Foreign Fruits in Your House."

Formation of the FTC of the NBC

By early 1988, it had become obvious to observers of the American banana industry that BBC was fighting a losing battle in attempting to maintain its 0.0001 market share. Sales had declined steadily for over a year, and Mr. Portfolio anticipated that if something was not done, he would have to lay off his two production workers.

After some careful analysis of the situation, he decided that his best course would be to apply to the U.S. Tariff Commission for relief from foreign competition. Prior to making official application, he organized his production staff and bookkeeper (Mrs. Portfolio) into the National Banana Council. To press his demands, Mr. Portfolio and the bookkeeper formed a subcommittee called the Fair Tariff Committee.

Testimony Before the Tariff Commission

In his appearance before the commission, Mr. Portfolio made the following statement:

My name is Manuelo Portfolio. I am president of the Boston Banana Company, a member of the board of directors of the National Banana Council, and chairman of that organization's Fair Trade Committee. I am accompanied today by my chief accountant and by two members of my production staff.

I appreciate the opportunity to speak before this subcommittee, and hope that I might be able to present our position to you in a clear and concise manner. Banana growing is a relatively new industry in the United States, but I believe that it has the potential for becoming a most important sector of our economy. I believe that our request for relief should be granted for the following reasons:

1. It is a tradition in the United States that the Congress will use tariffs to protect infant industries from unfair competition from abroad. The American steel industry never could have survived competition from European steel mills during its early years had it not been for the protection of tariffs. In the same manner, we are only asking that protection be extended to our industry in the expectation that increasing economies of scale will eventually enable North American bananas to compete with Central American products.

   Our philosophy is that of a "competitive tariff." This concept is based on the idea that in all protective legislation the true principle of protection is best maintained by the imposition of such duties as will equal the difference between the cost of production at home and abroad, together with a reasonable profit to American business. The notion underlying this equalization of costs of production is that of enabling the domestic producer to compete on even terms with the foreign producer. Thus, it can be seen that we seek no unfair advantage over foreign producers. All we ask for is the right to compete on an equal basis through the establishment of competitive tariff.

2. We seek protection from cheap foreign labor. It is well known that workers in many foreign countries are paid slave labor rates, that American workers are simply unable to accept such low wages, and that they consequently must be protected by their elected representatives in Congress from the importation of certain foreign goods. In our business, we pay our production workers an average of $4.85 per hour—U.S. government statistics indicate that workers in Central American banana plantations earn between 65 and 90 cents per hour. If cheap foreign labor is allowed to produce and export to this country items that can be produced here, no American workingman's job will be safe.
3. We seek to avoid domestic unemployment. Unless something is done within the next few months, I fully anticipate that 100 percent of our BBC's production staff will be out of work. These workers, and their families, will probably have to resort to unemployment compensation, and may possibly end up on welfare. Because of the specialized nature of their training, they will not only be unemployed, but in many cases, unemployable.
4. The final enumerated reason is probably the most important of all. At a time when the very foundations of Western civilization are being threatened by atheistic Communism, we must always consider the national defense implications of decisions such as that now under consideration.

   The armed forces of the United States of America consume over 20 million pounds of bananas in a single year. If our domestic industry was allowed to wither under the pressure of foreign competition, we would be forced to rely, in time of war, on foreign sources of supply. It is not likely that the American public would be willing to see our boys in the trenches go without these foods that are part of the American way of life.

In summary, let me say this. The rapid increase of imports in the banana industry is a threat that can cause the bankruptcy of the domestic industry. Bananas are a highly specialized product, and facilities used for growing bananas cannot be easily converted to other agricultural uses. Already there is pressure on employment levels in this industry. No matter how much we mechanize, we will not be able to compete with lower-cost foreign companies. We hope that the commission will look with favor on our petition.

ASSIGNMENT QUESTIONS

1. Summarize the history and the difficulties of the Boston Banana Company.
2. What were the reasons underlying Portfolio's request for relief? Deal with each of them in turn. Do they have validity?
3. If you were a member of the commission, how would you decide in this case? Why?

34
THE JAPANESE CONSPIRACY

CONGRESSIONAL RECORD

Congressional Record, Vol. 134, no. 22, March 1, 1988. Excerpted by permission of Marvin J. Wolf from *The Japanese Conspiracy* (New York: Empire Books). Copyright 1983, Marvin J. Wolf.

The SPEAKER pro tempore. Under a previous order of the House, the gentlewoman from Maryland [Mrs. BENTLEY] is recognized for 60 minutes.

MRS. BENTLEY. Mr. Speaker, a conference committee of the Congress is in the process of working out a trade bill on which we voted last fall. We are all concerned about what is happening to the industrial base of the United States, which is a very important part of our national security.

In connection with my research on the subject of trade and the industrial base, I have come across a book that I believe explains a great deal about what has happened to that industrial base and how it was forced to move overseas. This book is entitled *The Japanese Conspiracy,* written by Marvin J. Wolf, an author who lives in Los Angeles. Between his military assignment and civilian life, Mr. Wolf has lived or spent more than a decade in Japan....

Mr. Wolf points out that Japanese business has come to be universally regarded with a near-mythic mixture of fear and admiration, even envy. Demigods of trade, the Japanese are seen as mysteriously energetic, tirelessly shrewd, part of an irresistible tide. In America, in Europe, Latin America, the Middle East, Southeast Asia, throughout the developed and undeveloped world, the West watches passively as the Japanese seize one market after another.

In scarcely a dozen years Japan has increased its annual exports of high-technology products more than seven-fold, to more than $40 billion....

Many estimates, including those by the American Productivity Center and by the Japan Economic Council, predict that Japan will surpass the United States as the world's leading economic power by the year 2000. The JEC, an advisory group to the Prime Minister's office, has already outlined Japan's conquest in simple terms. By the turn of the century...the per capita income of the Japanese will be $21,200, compared with only $17,000 in the United States and less in Western Europe.

The trade statistics in Japan's favor are startling and growing in awesome proportions each year. In 1970, Japan's balance of payments surplus with the United States was only $1 billion, a meaningless sum to a nation the size of America, then exporting some $150 billion a year to the world. By 1980, the $1 billion had magically mushroomed to $10 billion, a large, significant trade imbalance, but still not one that threatened the economic sanctity of America, or of the West.

But within two years, the force of the Japanese export onslaught would be fully felt throughout the world. In 1982, America's trade deficit would rise to $30 billion, most of which—$21 billion—would be with one nation, Japan. Staggered by that red ink, Americans were soon to learn that 1983 would be considerably worse and each year after, even worse. As Japanese computers, television sets, radios, pharmaceuticals, cameras, cars, video recorders, stereos, bicycles, subway cars, tractors, and motorcycles flooded the American markets, estimates of the 1983 Japanese trade balance with the United States—initially $30 billion—rose to $35 billion and more.

And last year it is predicted that the final figures will show it is about $60 billion.

Along with these deficits have come increased unemployment in America and Western Europe, as more and more workers move from assembly to unemployment lines. The Japanese trade surplus accounts for the direct loss of over 1 million American jobs, and as many or more in Western Europe. Ultimately the toll is much greater as the industrial infrastructure of the western world is weakened.

"No industry is immune from trade deficits," Alfred E. Eckes, chairman of the U.S. International Trade Commission, warned in August 1983. Each $1 billion in trade deficits, he reveals, is equal to about 25,000 U.S. jobs lost. "Problems that have hit footwear, apparel, steel, and autos may soon impact the chemical industry, pharmaceuticals, and other high-technology sectors," Eckes says. France, Sweden, West Germany, and other European nations are suffering these same deficits with Japan as that nation assaults their domestic markets.

Surprisingly, many Americans and Europeans believe that the Japanese deserve their success. Almost four out of five polled by the *Los Angeles Times* in May 1983, felt that the prime reason for the success of Japanese products is "cheaper labor costs," followed by superior management. "Our management is old-fashioned," is the common complaint. If the Japanese are beating the Western nations, this argument states, it is our own fault. We've been unwilling to work as hard; we demand wages that are too high. After all, our Calvinist consciences mutter, the Japanese demonstrate unrivaled energy and skill; it is no wonder their productivity is the envy of the world. They are shrewd bargainers, but outmaneuvering your opponent has always been the essence of good business. We must learn to do better; we must emulate the Japanese, say many. We need to adopt quality circles and other storied Japanese management techniques.

There is obviously much to be learned from the Japanese. But their skill and productivity, though impressive, is not the major reason for their stunning international success. Behind their massive penetration of foreign markets is a system of business activity which can best be described as economic totalitarianism, a government-directed enterprise in which all the energies of Japan have been mobilized to overwhelm the world competition. It is a national conspiracy directed from a central command post, a squat 11-story building in central Tokyo, the headquarters of MITI, the Ministry of International Trade and Industry. The elements that comprise the conspiracy come from every facet of Japanese life: unelected bureaucrats; industrialists; *shinko-zaibatsu*, the reconstituted cartels; labor union officials; politicians; and submissive workers. Even co-opted Americans and Europeans contribute to the new power of Japan.

The Japanese themselves have termed their centrally run operation the "Bureaucratic-Industrial Complex," one that is becoming as potentially dangerous to world stability as the military-political threat of the Soviet Union. But while Russian dissimulation seems to persuade only the naive, the Japanese have brilliantly disguised their conspiracy on a convincing cloak of free enterprise. They thus confound and confuse those in the West who have become unwitting partners in Japan's economic aggression.

Although Japan now boasts a democratic political system not unlike America's and Western Europe's, its business methods bear little resemblance to free market capitalism, or even the semisocialist-style capitalism of France, Great Britain, and Italy, which still follow the conventions and ethics of international trade.

Business the Japanese way is unique and often difficult to understand for those not familiar with its nuances. From the Western viewpoint, it regularly flouts the rules of ethical behavior, yielding to the obsessive need to win at any cost. Joseph J. Sullivan, a former employee of Sony, has repeated a telling conversation with Japanese industrialist Akio Morita, president of Sony. "Sullivan San," Morita said, "militarily we could never defeat the United States, but economically we can overcome the United States and become number one in the world."

Individual Japanese industries are efficient, but not to the degree the world has been led to believe. Much of their advantage is based on unsavory practices. Japan has borrowed or copied foreign technology, or acquired it through joint venture agreements which it has later disavowed. When this has failed they have resorted to bribery, industrial espionage and outright theft. Its industries often act in concert, as did the prewar Japanese cartels, the *zaibatsu*, targeting their competitors in other nations and dumping their products at a temporary loss in order to win larger and larger shares of the world's markets and eventually achieve monopoly positions. The Japanese educate their scientists and engineers in American and European universities; they then return home to use their new skills in a trade war against those who educated them. Japan, it is now becoming clear, is winning the trade war because it refuses to play by the rules.

...the desire to become *itchiban*—No. 1—has created a tense, uneven, and unfair relationship between Japan and its trading neighbors. Not only does Japan insist on imposing Byzantine import barriers to shield its domestic market from outside competition, but its export trade policies include predatory pricing, secret government subsidies, the targeting of advanced technology industries in America and elsewhere, and restrictions on direct foreign investments....

In addition,...intervention by MITI forces Japanese firms to "Buy Japan," to purchase exclusively from domestic suppliers despite price and quality disadvantages, and to pursue an overaggressive export policy with the world. On one occasion, a group of Japanese television manufacturers found cheating the United States Government claimed that MITI had "compelled" them to do it. These, and still other methods, are at the core of a privately owned but state directed form of capitalism modeled after a military campaign.

1430

Japan has been portrayed as a worker's paradise in which employees are perpetually grateful to a benevolent management. In fact,...Japanese corporations exploit many of their workers, particularly women and millions of temporary and part-time workers who are denied the much-heralded Japanese corporate benefits. Early retirement at age 55 forces skilled, mature workers with inadequate pensions back on the job market, usually starting all over at the bottom. Instead of true labor unions, the Japanese employ company unions, which are used less for collective bargaining than to enforce discipline and boost productivity.

Some in the West—including government leaders who could act to confront this worldwide industrial conspiracy—are reluctant to see our Japanese allies in a negative light. But contemporary history demonstrates that whenever it has been convenient for them, the Japanese have bent, distorted, and abused existing American, European, and Japanese legislation and contractual arrangements in order to gain corporate and national advantage. Where avoidance, obfuscation, and shrewdness have failed, they have lied to achieve the defeat of their industrial partners and to further their quest for what they believe is their national manifest destiny—economic supremacy.

The Japanese industrial conspiracy has numerous layers of complexity, which, as we shall see, involve every aspect of the Japanese and world economy. One is a hypocritical, but effective, policy which insists on free trade for Japan throughout the world, while Japan uses every possible device, from tariffs to truculence, to close its domestic markets. America and the European Economic Community (EEC) have complained, often bitterly, that Japan does not practice what it preaches. Japan's response, for more than 20 years, has been to deny that there are any restrictions, and then to promise to "liberalize" the particular ones that trading partners point out. And we in the United States have certainly experienced that, on item after item.

"Trying to move the Japanese on trade is like peeling an onion," [stated] William Piez, who directed the U.S. Embassy's Tokyo trade office in early 1983. "You start taking the layers off, but you're never sure if there will be anything inside at the end. The whole thing is a rather zen experience." Piez was referring to the fact that behind the formal trade barriers that Japan had officially lifted, there is a maze of informal ones, including standards and inspection procedures that crudely, but effectively, block imports.

In 1982, Foreign Minister Yoshio Sakurauchi claimed that "Japan is one of the most open markets in the world." A few weeks after that comment was made, the Japanese ambassador to the United States, Nobuhiko Ushiba, told reporters: "There is no example in recent history of a nation liberalizing trade policy as fast as Japan." What a farce.

The reality, of course, is just the opposite....European Economic Community spokesman Giules Anouilh places it in perspective: "Japan, with a population of 117 million, imports no more manufactured goods than Switzerland with a population of 6.4 million"—6.4 million versus 117 million. The Japanese answer, sounding ridiculous by contrast, comes from Norishige Hasegawa, chairman of a committee to promote trade with America. "We're already importing what we need, Parker pens, Cross pencils, and French neckties," he says with no trace of irony.

Japan's protectionist policy, which insures the basic strength of its domestic industries against fair competition while it assaults foreign markets with its exports, is not an ad hoc program. It has been carefully orchestrated by MITI, which by persuasion and arm twisting, manipulates Japan's import and export strategy, down to the behavior of customs officials. "We enable the Japanese to bring in everything they want when they don't even give us the right of entry," commented Charles L. Nicolosi, an analyst in the New York offices of Dean Witter Reynolds.

As the world's leading manufacturer of automobiles, for example, Japan sells millions of its cars in the United States and Europe, but imports few. Before a car is shipped to the United States, each Japanese manufacturer certifies that it meets United States product and safety standards; America accepts the certifications and freely admits the Japanese imports. But the Japanese view every import into their market as currency lost in the war of trade balances.

If a foreign product does finally penetrate the protectionist barriers, the Japanese respond with elaborate tactical maneuvers. The cigarette war is an excellent illustration of their ingenuity in blocking imports. Achieving even a minuscule 1.5 percent share of the Japanese cigarette market required American manufacturers to absorb a prohibitive 35 percent tariff. But the official tobacco monopoly was still worried that some Japanese might prefer a foreign cigarette to a cheaper, if inferior, homegrown product.

In a guerrilla war of harassment, certifications by foreign manufacturers are disregarded by Japanese customs. Every car, every baseball bat, every foreign product attempting entry to Japan is subject to elaborate testing, and those not meeting standards must be reworked to meet them before entry is allowed. The handful of United States cars imported in Japan, and in 1986 that figure was 2,500, compared with the 3 million or more that they sent in here, are sometimes virtually rebuilt in Yokohama harbor before leaving the Japanese customs area, and that cost, of course, is borne by the importer, and that raises the cost of the car four- or fivefold.

A six-page battle plan was issued by the Japanese cigarette industry to thousands of distributors and retailers, detailing such tactics as placing limits on the stocking of foreign brands, actually removing them from small vending machines, and eliminating point-of-purchase displays for foreign cigarettes in prominent locations. Compliance by retailers is assured: the Japan Tobacco and Salt Corporation [JTSC] has absolute control over the licensing and supply of all tobacco products in Japan.

In early 1983, in response to American diplomatic pressures, Japan made a great show of lowering cigarette import duties to 20 percent. But Japan's trade defenses are mobile. Almost immediately after this seeming concession, the price of all cigarettes was uniformly raised by 9 cents, wiping out much of the tariff cut's effect on imported cigarettes....

Despite facetious comments about "Parker pens," Japan has enormous need for at least one American commodity—food. It would not only help correct the United States trade imbalance, but would be a boon for Japanese consumers, who are victimized by Japan's inefficient agricultural industry. A Tokyo housewife must expect to pay $35 a pound for the best sirloin steak while Japanese ranchers, whose average herd consists of 2.5 cattle, get only 7 percent of that price, or about $2 a pound. The rest of the money is eaten up by an archaic distribution system of as many as two dozen middlemen, most of whom have never seen a live cow, a beef carcass, or even a raw steak. If a foreign supplier of beef—American, Australian, Argentine, or otherwise—should attempt to maneuver past these legions of middlemen, Japan has a final revetment; import quotas on foreign beef are kept so low that Japanese farmers sell virtually all their production at exorbitant retail prices, and it is, of course, the Japanese consumer who pays.

The Japanese face no such restraints in their trade with the West, who openly welcome most Japanese imports because of their price and quality, unaware of the permanent disruption it creates in their economies.

...Japan starts out with an enormous advantage in reaching its goal of industrial conquest. Unlike America, Germany, France, the Soviet Union, or Israel, Japan does not pay for most of its own defense. Former U.S. Senator Paul J. Fannin of Arizona calls it a

$70 billion a year subsidy from the United States, the sum they would spend if we did not protect them from potential aggressors. "With this tremendous advantage," says Fannin, "the Japanese now dominate one after another of our markets. Radio, TV, recorders, small calculators, motorcycles, bicycles, sporting goods, and now the manufacture of automobiles, farm machinery, road equipment and electrical generators, is suffering from this subsidized competition."

World reaction to the Japanese capture of world markets has varied from numbness to shock to impotent outrage, and even despair. Responding to a poll by Opinion Research Corp. of Princeton, N.J., three-fourths of 500 American opinion leaders from business, labor, Congress, academia, and the media stated that Japanese trading policies systematically violate internationally accepted business and trade practices.

More than two-thirds of Americans surveyed by the *Los Angeles Times* poll said U.S. policy should restrict imports to protect American industry and American jobs. American politicians from the President down have tried to persuade Japan to impose restrictions on its exports and to open their own markets to American goods. But it has been to little avail. The Japanese response has been a cascade of cosmetic changes and a public relations blitz incorporating blithe denials of wrong-doing along with righteous indignation. Japanese trade policy, they maintain, is strictly a matter for the Japanese to decide.

Many Japanese, exultant at their new world prominence, are immune to criticism about their business methods, but some do express anguish over Japan's reputation. "Our mercantile image has once again been tarnished," says Kinji Yajama, a retired Tokyo Institute of Technology professor. "We Japanese are now being regarded as a scheming bunch of villains around the United States. It will take years for us to improve our image to what it had been before."

...Japanese political commentator Akira Sono has warned his fellow Japanese of the friction that their economic war is beginning to generate worldwide. Trade relations between the United States and Japan, he says, have deteriorated to the point where "the Japanese people are reminded of the pre–World War II ABCD [American-British-Chinese-Dutch] encirclement of Japan, and European Community nations are taking an equally high-handed posture."

1445

This has happened, Sono explained, because "Japan has been treating foreign products like unwanted stepchildren. Japanese politicians and bureaucrats seem incapable of demonstrating a spirit of fair play. Consumers seldom criticize the economic structure that causes them hardship through high commodity prices. The people cannot appreciate economic democracy because they have not assimilated the political democracy that was forced on them as a result of defeat in war."

Sono adds: "Perhaps the Japanese will reach maturity for the first time when foreign countries shut out Japan's exports. Recent Japan–United States relations resemble those of the spring of 1941. The free nations of the world might come to look upon Japan as an outcast. The results might be more disastrous than the defeat in World War II."

The Declining Position of American Industry

Exhibits 34-1 and 34-2 illustrate how American companies are losing their domestic market to foreign competition. In electronics, shoes, machine tools, automobiles, and computers, foreign producers have improved their positions in the U.S. market since 1981. With regard to television manufacturers, there were seventeen American companies in the industry in 1970. By 1988 only Zenith was still in domestic production.

EXHIBIT 34-1 Share of U.S. Market Held by Foreign Goods

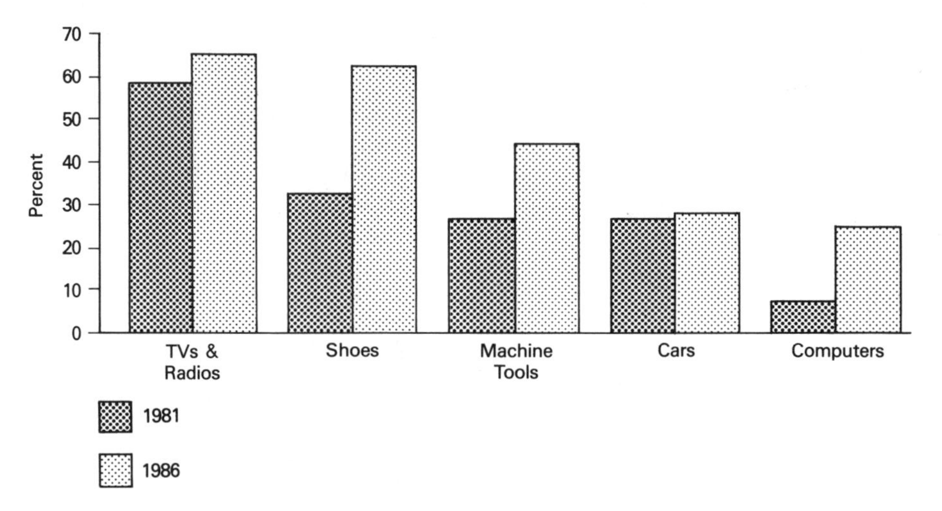

Source: *U.S. News & World Report*, February 2, 1987, p. 19.

EXHIBIT 34-2 Number of Major TV Producers by Country, 1970–1988

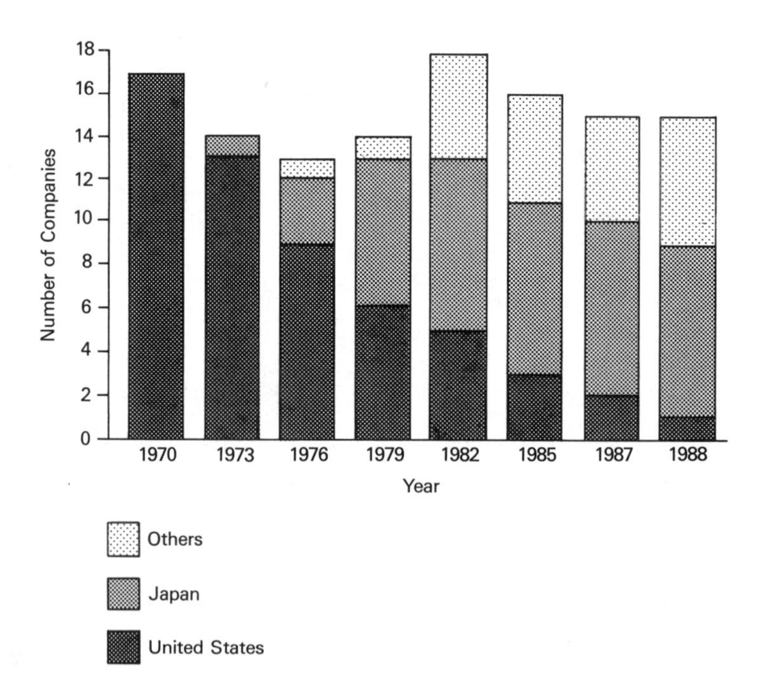

Source: *Newsweek*, August 3, 1987, p. 36.

JAPAN'S CLOUT IN THE U.S.: IT'S TRANSLATING ECONOMIC MIGHT INTO INFLUENCE

Business Week, July 11, 1988, p. 64.

A new wave of Japanese wealth is washing over America, and it has little to do with government bonds or corporate securities. The new currency is influence. As Japan increases its investment in the U.S., it is also becoming a full-fledged member of the American political, cultural, and intellectual debate in a way that no other nation has achieved.

Japanese companies are spending heavily to shape the way Americans view them. They are pouring tens of millions of dollars into U.S. education, from Ivy League colleges to elementary schools in Kentucky. Museums, universities, public television stations, and think tanks are competing for—and getting—Japanese money. The Japanese are also wielding political power from the grass roots to the top echelons of Washington. The same words that describe Japan's economic strategy apply to what the Japanese call their "soft-side" activities: Systematic. Coordinated. Long-term.

There is nothing improper about it. America and most larger nations attempt to spread their ideas around the world. For Japan, though, the motive is primarily economic. As Japan's investments overflow from financial assets into real property such as plants and skyscrapers, the Japanese want more than just an open U.S. market for their exports—they want to protect their broad stake here. That means becoming more sophisticated in pulling America's political strings. "They've learned how to play us like a violin," says Lester C. Thurow, dean of the Sloan School of Management at Massachusetts Institute of Technology. "Japan's say in the U.S. decision-making will rise as their investments go from passive to active."

Japan's newfound clout came of age this year when Toshiba Corp. defeated efforts to impose harsh sanctions on it in retaliation for a subsidiary's selling of restricted propeller technology to the Soviet Union. Japan's lobbyists also played a key role in stalling major trade bills in Washington and prevailed on other issues as well, including registration of foreign investments. At the state level, they obtained generous incentives to build plants while beating back legislation such as unitary taxes in 12 states.

Status Quo

But their effort goes beyond specific political objectives. Japan wants to help shape the American agenda and to reinforce a notion that America's economic problems are mainly homegrown. Most of all, Japan wants to maintain a political and economic status quo to prevent surprises from threatening its economic stake. "They're interested in creating an environment in which they can make money," says Bernard Karsh, director of the Center for East Asian Studies at the University of Illinois and a Japan-watcher for 30 years. "I see this as a major effort to come in and stay, to legitimate their presence."

Although the U.S. and Japan share important economic and security goals, they are also competitors. What is unique about Japan's position is that never before in modern history has an economic adversary wielded so much influence on a rival's home ground.... Japan's government, foundations, and companies will spend at least $310 million this year on soft-side activities, not including advertising. That's still small compared with Japan's direct investment of at least $35 billion and exports of $85 billion a year. But it allows for an astonishing range of activities....

For lawyers, public relations advisers, academics, economists, journalists, and political consultants, Japan's spending is a growth industry, far outstripping OPEC's influence-buying. For the American Enterprise Institute, the Brookings Institution, and other influential think tanks, Japanese money is becoming important. And universities from Massachusetts to California are providing a steady stream of research and information to Japan. "They're investing in the cutting edge of ideas," says Peter G. Peterson, chairman of the Blackstone Group, a Wall Street firm with major Japanese clients, who is also chairman of the Council on Foreign Relations and the Institute for International Economics....

Many top-echelon Americans who have no financial links with Japan are members of what critics call the "Cherry Blossom Crowd"—people who befriend Japan because of special relationships and favors and for reasons of principle....All this leads Chalmers Johnson, a Japan expert at the University of California at San Diego, to conclude that "Japan has undue influence in the U.S."

Compromised Judgment

Some observers even argue that America's long-cherished exchange of ideas is endangered. Argues Pat Choate, Washington vice-president for policy analysis at TRW Inc.: "In the marketplace of ideas, the Japanese seek people who will amplify their views and then they pour in money. They dominate the adviser corps." Most professionals who take grants from the Japanese say there are no strings attached. But a few disagree. "Everyone who gets money from Japan has to worry about not offending Japan," says Ronald A. Morse, formerly head of the Asia program at the Woodrow Wilson International Center for Scholars in Washington and now development officer at the Library of Congress....

Japanese companies spend an estimated $45 million a year on public relations—much of it for image-building. There are some 400,000 Japanese on assignment in the U.S., many of whom see it as their job to promote Japan's case....The Japanese also have well-established U.S. listening posts, including consuls in 15 cities—who monitor American attitudes for Tokyo....

Japan's Ministry of International Trade and Industry (MITI) is also becoming a much more active player inside the U.S. In part, the ministry operates through the Japan External Trade Organization (JETRO), which once concentrated exclusively on promoting Japanese exports. Now a major JETRO focus is collecting information in Washington, wooing prominent journalists, and hosting elegant receptions at top-flight hotels. JETRO maintains offices in seven American cities.

Beneath these two governmental bodies is a bewildering array of private and quasi-private organizations, some of which enjoy a combination of Japanese and U.S. financing. There are Japan-America Societies in at least 20 cities and Japanese Chambers of Commerce in dozens more....

The lesson is that Japan's economic prowess, both in imports and investment, does not exist in a vacuum. As it makes itself felt in U.S. social and political agendas, it can have a subtle but important impact on the big policy questions facing the U.S. What is well-founded criticism and what is simply anti-Japanese? What constitutes protectionism? What is dumping? What are the effects of Japanese investment? On issues such as these, the Japanese are learning to shape the debate. And that will test the character and integrity of America's institutions far more than any wave of imports ever did.

Japanese-Endowed Chairs at MIT

Daichi Kangyo Bank
  Finance
Fujitsu
  Electrical Engineering
Fukutake Publishing
  Media Laboratory
Kokusai Denshin Denwa
  Media Laboratory
Kyocera
  Material Sciences
Matsushita
  Electrical Engineering
Mitsubishi
  Finance
Mitsui
  International Management
  Contemporary Technology (2)
NEC
  Computers/Communications
  Software
Nippon Steel
  Civil Engineering/Policy
Nomura Securities
  Finance
TDK
  Materials
Toyota
  Materials

THE U.S. AND JAPAN—SOME FACTS

Fact. The United States ranks fifth among the world's five leading industrial nations in increasing manufacturing output per hour over the past decade. Exhibit 34-3 illustrates our relative decline.

EXHIBIT 34-3 Increase in Manufacturing Output per Hour, 1979–1985

Japan	5.7%
Britain	4.2
France	3.8
West Germany	3.2
United States	3.1

Source: U.S. Department of Labor.

Fact. In spite of the fact that they are less productive, American factory workers continue to be the highest paid in the world. As shown in Exhibit 34-4, factory workers in the United States earn twice as much as Japanese workers and nine times as much as Korean workers.

EXHIBIT 34-4 Average Hourly Compensation for Factory Workers, 1975–1985

	1975	*1980*	*1985*
United States	6.35	9.75	12.82
West Germany	6.35	12.15	9.60
Japan	2.90	5.80	6.45
Britain	3.50	7.15	6.14
South Korea	.55	1.10	1.44

Source: U.S. Department of Labor.

Fact. Imports now account for 13.6 percent of the goods and services purchased in the U.S., up from 10.8 percent five years ago.

Fact. As recently as 1981, the U.S. shipped nearly 43 percent of the world's computers. By 1985, the share had slipped to just over 34 percent.

Fact. Over 70 percent of the value of components in an IBM personal computer is made in Japan and Singapore.

Fact. Japan's takeover of semiconductor chips, now 47 percent of world sales, raises the possibility that someday the Pentagon won't be able to buy the chips it needs from American companies.

Fact. In the mid-1950s, the Ampex Corporation of Redwood City, California, developed a videotape recorder for use by television stations. Today, Ampex still produces the commercial machines, but not a single U.S. company manufactures home videocassette recorders, one of today's hottest consumer electronics items.

In 1987 a number of Japanese companies were found guilty of dumping computer chips in the U.S. market by the International Trade Commission. One of the companies found guilty was Hitachi, which was shown to have sent the following instructions to its American distributors:

Quote 10 percent below competition
If they requote...
Bid 10 percent under again
The bidding stops when Hitachi wins...
Win with the 10 percent rule...
Find AMD and Intel sockets...
Quote 10 percent below their price...
If they requote...
Go 10 percent *again*
Don't quit until you *win*...
25 percent profit margin
Guaranteed.

Such practices are totally illegal. But even if they are caught and punished—which they rarely are—the damage to our manufacturers and our markets has already been done.[1]

Motorola...makes an excellent car-phone telephone system. For several months it has been trying to get the Japanese government's permission to sell this system throughout Japan in competition with the Japanese firm NTT. The Japanese government hemmed and hawed. Finally it said it would divide the car-phone market into two sectors and "allow" Motorola access to one of them. But the sector Motorola has been offered doesn't include Tokyo, which alone accounts for more than half of the Japanese car-phone market.[2]

Japanese banking assets in the United States, barely measurable a decade ago, now exceed $200 billion, and Japanese banks now hold nearly 9 percent of U.S. commercial and industrial loans....The list of the world's largest banks was once dominated by U.S. names—even as late as 1979, there was only one Japanese bank among the largest ten. But now, there are six Japanese names and only one American among the ten largest banks ranked by total assets, and eight Japanese banks are on the list of the top ten in market capitalization. And this is not a situation involving just a few large banks—sixteen of the world's twenty largest banks are based in Japan, as are twenty-two of the top thirty.[3]

Kao Corporation, Japan's leading packaged-goods company, recently purchased Andrew Jergens Company, a division of American Brands, Inc., and the well-known producer of Jergen's Lotion, for $350 million, outbidding other buyers by more than $100 million. Kao intends to use Jergens to sell its Japanese brands in the United States.[4]

ASSIGNMENT QUESTIONS

1. Outline the strategic elements of "The Japanese Conspiracy." Do you agree with these allegations? Why or why not?
2. What happened to the American television industry? Who is at fault here? American companies such as Sears, Roebuck? American consumers? The U.S. government? Does it really matter that the United States no longer has a consumer electronics industry?
3. Should we be concerned over rising Japanese power and influence in our country? How great is that influence, and in what ways is it manifested? If the trend continues, what might we anticipate in the future in U.S.-Japanese relations?
4. Summarize the state of national defense expenditures and obligations of the United States as compared with Japan. Is this a satisfactory situation? Why or why not? What specific changes would you recommend?
5. Should the U.S. government take some kind of action to reduce the enormous trade deficit we have with the Japanese? What are the implications for the economic well being of our country if the situation continues or gets worse? Formulate a set of policy recommendations for consideration by the president and the Congress that might resolve the situation.

NOTES

1. Richard A. Voell, "Unbinding Gulliver," *Vital Speeches of the Day*, April 9, 1987, p. 662.
2. Ibid., p. 661.
3. Serge Bellanger, "The Japanese Invasion," *The Bankers Magazine*, July–August 1987, p. 50.
4. *Business Week*, October 3, 1988, p. 38.

PART EIGHT

REGULATION IN THE PUBLIC INTEREST

In addition to acting as a policeman to keep competition alive and somehow fair, government in this country has moved to serve as a promoter of certain kinds of activities in business. In addition, it has moved to protect the public against other kinds of business activities. In this part, we examine some of these rather narrow areas of interest where government has established rules, regulations, and laws specifically tailored to accomplish limited objectives. Case 35, *Fanny's Famous Foods,* for example, is concerned with the Securities and Exchange Commission. A small investor has put his life's savings into a fly-by-night franchise operation and has lost all of it. It is apparent, as well, that the financial statements prepared by a national accounting firm "in conformance with generally accepted accounting principles" simply have not presented a full and fair picture of the operations of Fanny's Famous Foods. Issues raised are relative to the responsibility of the SEC in an instance like this, any possible liability that the accounting firm might have, and alternatives (if any) open to the poor investor.

Case 36, *Tobacco in America,* sketches the history of tobacco use in the United States over the past two hundred years, emphasizes the profits made by those corporations involved in providing tobacco products to the American public, and measures the cost to the country from tobacco use in both human lives and treasure.

Students are asked to consider appropriate actions to be taken by government against a substance that causes more deaths of Americans per year than were killed in all the wars in this century.

The Bell Telephone Company, Case 37, is concerned with publicly regulated telephone companies offering services which allow seedy entrepreneurs the opportunity to sell "Dial-A-Porn" messages to the public. Should society tolerate this kind of business? Does the First Amendment to the Constitution, providing that "Congress shall make no law...abridging the freedom of speech," preclude any kind of regulatory action by government? Is there a relationship between pornography of this sort and serious sexual crimes?

In Case 38, *Regulation of Network Radio Broadcasting,* the activities of the Federal Communications Commission are central to the material presented. The central issue under consideration is the proper function of the FCC, and the court had to decide whether the Commission served simply a police function in regulating traffic on the airways or acted as a kind of manager concerned with the business arrangements and the program content of the network broadcasters.

35
FANNY'S FAMOUS FOODS

Marvin Smith

Marvin Smith was a man in his mid-sixties who retired in 1966 after thirty-five years with the Harrison Iron Works in Skokie, Illinois. During his working years, Mr. Smith was at various times a common laborer, an apprentice ironworker, and for the last twenty-two years with the iron works a specialist in making steel and aluminum railings. In his retirement he lived upon social security benefits and a pension paid him from the Ironworker's retirement fund. In addition, he had savings of approximately $54,000.

Although Mr. Smith's income was sufficient to pay for a reasonably comfortable living for him and his wife, he frequently wished that he had additional money to provide for some travel and to pay for the expenses of his hobby of collecting and polishing rocks. Not wanting to spend his accumulated $54,000, and finding savings bank interest insufficient for his needs, he spent some time during the month of January 1967 filling out coupons and reading up on potential investment opportunities. Although he wanted, if possible, substantial income or capital appreciation, he was also fearful of losing that which he had. His money had been accumulated over so many years by doing without frills so that $100 per month could be regularly put into savings.

Investment Opportunity

In February, Mr. Smith received some general information on franchise retailing, and a prospectus from Fanny's Famous Foods. Fanny's Famous Foods, or FFF as it was known, was a fast-food franchise system headquartered in Chattanooga, Tennessee. It dealt in "genuine fried chicken" and was named after the famous star of the Country and Western Hour, Fanny Diamond. Exhibit 35-1 is a copy of the information he received on franchising.

EXHIBIT 35-1

NEWSLETTER

Investment Counseling Service

FRANCHISING—THE WAVE OF THE FUTURE

The day of the Mom and Pop grocery is ending along with the dominance of the wholly owned branches of many national firms. In their place has risen an entirely new concept in retailing. This is the franchise system. It combines the best of two worlds: the expertise, financial power, and organizing abilities of the large business firm is combined with the independent small business. The result has been an incredible spread of franchised outlets across the country. The basic reason for this expansion is that, in our opinion, franchised outlets have approximately 12 times the chance of being successful as do other new businesses.

The result of this success is shown below, in which it is shown that nearly one-third of all retail sales are now being made through franchised outlets.

Franchise Industry Summary
1965 Estimates

Annual sales	$100 billion
Percent of total retail sales	30
Percent of GNP	12
Firms engaged in franchising	1,200
Franchised outlets	500,000
Annual growth rate	45,000

Investment Opportunities

This great movement provides increasingly attractive opportunities for people wanting to invest their money in relatively secure but rapidly growing firms. In fact, it is generally recognized that the financial community is more interested in the franchising sector than in any other part of the economy at the present time. Nationally, publicly owned companies have seen the advantages to be gained from franchising, and are rapidly expanding in that area. RCA has acquired the Hertz Corporation, ITT has purchased Avis, Pillsbury has bought Burger King Corporation, United Fruit has acquired A & W Rootbeer, Beneficial Finance has purchased Western Auto Supply, and General Foods now owns Burger Chief Restaurants.

In addition to movements into franchising by nationally known firms, there is a vigorous movement on the part of franchising firms to themselves become public corporations. Climbing on the bandwagon, famous entertainers and sports stars have lent their names to a host of franchising endeavors. We have Dizzy Dean's Beef and Burger, Mickey Mantle's Country Cooking Restaurants, Al Hirt's Sandwich Saloons, Tennessee Ernie Ford's Steak'n Biscuit, and Johnny's American Inns (Johnny Carson).

All of these firms are hoping to emulate the example of Kentucky Fried Chicken and McDonald's. These companies have made millionaires of those who were fortunate enough to get in early, and are now, because of their phenomenal growth and high profitability, commanding from 30 to 40 times earnings in the stock market.

What does this mean to you, the investor? We think that it means that you should seriously consider putting some of your funds into this most exciting and most rewarding area of American business. Of course, nothing is a sure thing, but if there ever was one, it is in this NEW WAVE that is sweeping the country!

A Final Note: As investment counselors, we are very impressed with the opportunities now open to invest in a relatively new franchise system, Fanny's Famous Foods. This is a Chattanooga, Tennessee, firm operated by Jeb (Stonewall) Stewart, a man who was almost governor of the state, and a man who has a record of success in many fields. For your information we have included copies of the company's latest financial statements (see Exhibits 35-2 and 35-3).

Mr. Smith took the information of FFF—in particular the financial statements—to a close friend of his, a Mr. Homer Osborne. Mr. Osborne had once worked in a brokerage firm in St. Louis, and Mr. Smith considered him to be the neighborhood expert on these matters. The statements (shown in Exhibits 35-2 and 35-3, together with the accompanying information on the background and prospects for FFF, convinced Mr. Osborne that the investment was a sound one, and he recommended that Marvin invest some of his savings in the venture. Accordingly, on February 27, 1967, Mr. Smith arranged the purchase of $20,000 in FFF common stock. At that time, it was selling at 15 times earnings, or $32.50 per share.

During the remainder of 1967, Mr. Smith spent part of each day admiring the rise of FFF stock in *The Wall Street Journal* and in discussing his growing wealth with Mr. Osborne. His enthusiasm for the stock led him to invest an additional $10,000 late in the year.

In March 1968, the annual report of Fanny's Famous Foods was received by Mr. Smith. The financial statements included in the report are shown in Exhibits 35-4 and 35-5. By this time, the market price of the firm's stock had risen to over 30 times earnings, or $72 per share, and Mr. Smith calculated (with the assistance of Mr. Osborne) that if he invested the remainder of his savings, and if the current trend continued, by 1970 he would have a net worth of about $300,000. At that point he could decide whether to keep the investment as it was, to put it into securities bringing immediate interest and dividends, or to put it all in the bank and live off savings bank interest for the rest of his days. In May 1968, he invested an additional $24,000—the balance of his savings—and now had a total investment of $54,000 in FFF stock. The market value of his stock was about $80,000.

Down the Other Side of the Mountain

During the next few months, Mr. Smith had the satisfaction of watching his investment continue to go up in price. In October 1968,

EXHIBIT 35-2 Fanny's Famous Foods Statement of Profit and Loss Year Ending December 31, 1966

Sales and other income	
Sales of franchises	$3,175,000
Royalties on retail sales	243,000
	3,418,000
Deduct:	
Selling expenses	308,200
Administrative and general expenses	875,500
Interest expense	59,000
	1,243,200
Profit before taxes	$2,174,800

EXHIBIT 35-3 Fanny's Famous Foods Balance Sheet as of December 31, 1966

Assets	
Current assets	
Cash	$ 76,000
Government securities at cost	350,000
Royalties receivable	24,300
Notes receivable (current portion)	508,000
	958,700
Long-term assets	
Notes receivable (noncurrent portion)	2,832,000
Securities	63,900
	2,895,900
Fixed assets	
Land	205,000
Building	360,000
Equipment and fixtures	72,000
	637,000
Less accumulated depreciation	28,000
	609,000
Total assets	$4,463,600
Liabilities and Stockholders' Equity	
Current liabilities	
Accounts payable	$ 104,000
Bank loans	650,000
Income taxes payable	163,000
Interest payable	3,700
	923,300
Fixed liabilities	
Real estate mortgage	320,000
Capital	
Common stock	500,000
Preferred stock	200,000
Earned surplus	2,520,300
	3,220,300
Total liabilities and net worth	$4,463,600

EXHIBIT 35-4 Fanny's Famous Foods
Statement of Profit and Loss Year Ending December 31, 1967

Sales and other income	
Sales of franchises	$7,450,000
Royalties on retail sales	320,000
	7,770,000
Deduct:	
Selling expenses	542,000
Administrative and general expenses	1,250,000
Interest expense	73,000
	1,865,000
Profit before taxes	$5,905,000

FFF was selling at 36 times earnings, or $82 per share. Mr. Smith's personal fortune was now calculated at $96,000 and growing.

From that high of $82, FFF shares began to slip downward early in December 1968. Mr. Smith watched with anxiety the steady decline until FFF was selling at $52 per share in mid-1969. In August 1969, an "investment analyst" in one of the large New York papers wrote a report highly critical of Fanny's Fast Foods' products, leadership, and prospects. As a result, the stock almost immediately dropped $16, to $36 per share. This drop was never recovered, and the price of the stock was pushed even lower by unfavorable financial reports issued during the fall of the year.

In May 1970, Mr. Smith received the company's annual report for 1969. Unlike previous reports, it was unimpressive in both content and presentation, and contained a set of depressing financial statements (see Exhibits 35-6 and 35-7). Mr. Smith was stunned to note that sales had declined from $7,770,000 in 1967 to $6,450,000 in 1968 to only $2,050,000 in 1969.

The market's reaction to the very unfavorable 1969 report was a precipitous decline in the stock price until it was selling at under $10 per share. Mr. Smith watched with numb disbelief each day in the paper as his savings were slowly wiped out. Quarterly reports issued by the company in June indicated a further deterioration in the firm's position, and by the time the second quarterly report was issued in late August, the stock was selling at $4.20 and was nearly inactive. In late September, Fanny's Famous Foods filed for bankruptcy. Assets were given as $137,000 and liabilities as $3,600,000. It was estimated that holders of common stock would not be able to recover any of their investment in the bankruptcy proceedings.

Mr. Smith Strikes Back

Since he no longer was speaking to his ex-friend and ex-advisor, Mr. Osborne, Marvin Smith went to his local legal aid society to see

EXHIBIT 35-5 Fanny's Famous Foods
Balance Sheet as of December 31, 1967

Assets	
Current assets	
Cash	$ 94,600
Government securities at cost	285,000
Royalties receivable	32,500
Notes receivable (current portion)	1,450,000
	1,862,100
Long-term assets	
Notes receivable (noncurrent portion)	7,600,000
Securities	75,000
	7,675,000
Fixed assets	
Land	105,000
Building	360,000
Equipment and fixtures	82,000
	547,000
Less accumulated depreciation	53,000
	494,000
Total assets	$10,031,100
Liabilities and Stockholders' Equity	
Current liabilities	
Accounts payable	$ 154,000
Bank loans	1,250,000
Income tax payable	315,000
Interest payable	11,400
	1,730,400
Fixed liabilities	
Real estate mortgage	310,000
	310,000
Capital	
Common stock	900,000
Preferred stock	400,000
Earned surplus	6,690,700
	7,990,700
Total liabilities and net worth	$10,031,100

EXHIBIT 35-6 Fanny's Famous Foods Statement of Profit and Loss Year Ending December 31, 1969

Sales and other income	
Sales of franchises	$1,470,000
Royalties on retail sales	580,000
	2,050,000
Deduct:	
Selling expenses	274,000
Administrative and general expenses	1,075,000
Interest expense	137,000
	1,486,000
Profit before taxes	$ 564,000

EXHIBIT 35-7 Fanny's Famous Foods Balance Sheet as of December 31, 1969

Assets	
Current assets	
Cash	$ (2,100)
Royalties receivable	49,600
Notes receivable (current portion)	1,237,500
	1,285,000
Long-term assets	
Notes receivable (noncurrent portion)	13,280,000
	13,280,000
Fixed assets	
Land	205,000
Building	360,000
Equipment and fixtures	85,000
	650,000
Less accumulated depreciation	57,000
	593,000
Total assets	$15,158,000
Liabilities and Stockholders' Equity	
Current liabilities	
Accounts payable	$ 472,000
Bank loans	2,140,000
Income tax payable	417,000
Interest payable	23,000
	3,052,000
Fixed liabilities	
Real estate mortgage	320,000
	320,000
Capital	
Common stock	1,300,000
Preferred stock	600,000
Earned surplus	9,886,000
	11,786,000
Total liabilities and net worth	$15,158,000

if there was any kind of action he could take to recover at least part of his loss. The man at the legal aid society was a senior at Central Illinois School of Law and admitted that his experience in this area was limited. However, he suggested to Mr. Smith that he begin by writing to the Securities and Exchange Commission about his problem. Mr. Smith did this, and his letter is shown in Exhibit 35-8.

In addition to advising Mr. Smith to write a letter to the SEC, the novice lawyer introduced him to an accountant friend of his, a Mr. Morris Adams, who spent some time looking carefully into the literature and re-

EXHIBIT 35-8 Letter from Marvin Smith to the SEC

24 Oskiola Street
Skokie, Illinois

October 23, 1970

Securities and Exchange Commission
Washington, D.C.

Gentlemen:

In February 1967, I began to invest in the stock of Fanny's Famous Foods. In September of this year, the company went bankrupt, and I lost my entire life's savings of $54,000. I feel that I have been cheated out of my money and want to know what you are going to do about it.

I thought that the purpose of the SEC was to protect people from losing their money in the stock market. If that is true, please let me know how you can help me. If it is not true, then I don't know what your purpose is.

I hope that you are investigating Fanny's Famous Foods. I will wait for your letter indicating how you can help me.

Sincerely,

Marvin Smith

ports that had induced Mr. Smith to make his investment. The financial statements had been prepared by a branch of the national accounting firm of Wilkinson, Clark and McCleary and had written across the bottom, "prepared in accordance with generally accepted principles of accounting."

Adams reached the conclusion that the financial statements were very misleading in the things they did not state and recommended that Mr. Smith consider a suit against the accounting firm on the grounds that the statements they prepared did not fairly present the condition of FFF, and that investors, as a result, could be, and in this case had been, led to invest funds where they otherwise would not have done so. The suit as filed asked damages in the sum of $350,000.

ASSIGNMENT QUESTIONS

1. Why did Fanny's Famous Foods go out of business?
2. What misled Mr. Smith (and Mr. Osborne) into thinking that the company had a chance of long-term success?
3. What do you imagine the response of the SEC will be to Mr. Smith's letter?
4. Is the accounting firm in any way at fault? What is the firm's obligation in preparing financial statements of publicly held firms?
5. Can you propose some legislation to protect small investors from losing their savings such as happened in this case?

36
TOBACCO IN AMERICA

1493. Christopher Columbus becomes the first European to smoke, learning it from the Indians of San Salvador.

1604. King James I blasts smoking as "a custom loathsome to the eye, hateful to the nose, harmful to the brain, and dangerous to the lungs."

1850. Reformers preach that smoking undermines morals and leads to heavy rum drinking.

1866. Tobacco becomes the salvation of a south ravaged by the Civil War.

1900. Lung cancer is such a rare medical phenomenon that only 134 cases can be found in the entire medical literature.

1911. R. J. Reynolds Industries produces the first blended cigarette.

1920. Cigarette smoking becomes chic and modern.

1925. Nine states prohibit cigarette smoking.

1945. Ronald Reagan sends cartons of cigarettes to wounded veterans in hospitals.

1963. U.S. consumption of cigarettes peaks at 4,345 per person.

1964. The U.S. Surgeon General declares that smoking causes lung cancer, heart disease, and other respiratory illnesses.

1965. Labels warning of health dangers are required on cigarette packages.

1967. Forty-two percent of adults smoke in America.

1971. Faced with antismoking messages aired under the FCC "fairness doctrine," cigarette makers withdraw advertisements from TV and radio.

1972. The Surgeon General issues the first report suggesting that secondhand smoke is a danger to nonsmokers.

1975. Minnesota passes the first state law requiring businesses, restaurants, and other institutions to establish no-smoking areas.

1981. A Japanese study of 91,000 women found that women married to men who smoked more than one pack of cigarettes per day were almost twice as likely to die from lung cancer as were women married to nonsmokers. Similar findings resulted from studies in Greece and one by the Louisiana State University Medical Center in New Orleans.

1983. The federal government doubles the excise tax on cigarettes to 16 cents per package.

1983. The rise in lung cancer deaths in women—about 6 percent annually between 1973 and 1983—reflects the fact that women took up smoking in large numbers about 20 years later than men.

1983. San Francisco becomes the first major city to limit smoking in the workplace.

1984. Treatment of diseases caused by smoking, coupled with lost earnings from tobacco-related illness and premature death, costs the country almost $60 billion a year.

1985. Some 30.4 percent of adults smoke.

1985. James L. Repace, an indoor air specialist at the EPA, writes a highly publicized report concluding that up to five thousand people die annually of lung cancer induced by secondhand smoke.

1985. Pacific Northwest Bell Telephone notifies its 15,000 employees that smoking will no longer be allowed at work—anywhere, anytime.

1986. Surgeon General Koop and the National Research Council publish results of studies linking secondhand smoke to lung cancer and respiratory disease in nonsmokers. The government curtails smoking in federal buildings, and the Defense Department orders the military services to cut down as well.

1986. Cigarette smoking results in an annual production of 150,000 new cases of lung cancer and 130,000 deaths from lung cancer.

1986. Cigarettes sales average 3,274 per person and only 32 percent of adults say they smoke.

1986. Operating profits for Philip Morris's U.S. Tobacco division reach $2.4 billion on sales of $7.1 billion, a 34 percent gross return. No. 2, R. J. Reynolds's domestic operations earn more than $1.4 billion on sales of $4.7 billion before taxes. The two companies hold about 70 percent of the American cigarette market.

1986. The Washington State Appeals Court rules that Helen McCarthy, an eleven-year employee of the state Human Services Department, can sue for damages. She claims that her allergy to smoke was so exacerbated by workplace fumes that she developed chronic pulmonary disease—and that her employer was liable.

1988. Turner Broadcasting System, Inc., establishes a policy of not hiring those who smoke.

1988. The Tobacco Institute contends that the government's studies on secondhand smoke are based on surveys, not actual measurements of exposure to smoke. RJR Nabisco claims that it takes a nonsmoker 24 hours in a tiny, smoke-filled bar to inhale the nicotine equivalent of one cigarette.

1988. Ninety percent of those who contract lung cancer die within five years. 80 to 85 percent of all lung cancers are directly linked to prolonged tobacco use.

1988. Tobacco is the largest nonfood cash crop grown on the face of the earth. Six major American companies produce 600 billion cigarettes every year for sale. Their industry is essentially unregulated by any scientific or agricultural watchdog agency of the federal or any state government.

1988. Cigarettes remain the most heavily promoted product in the United States, with the six major tobacco companies spending more than $2 billion on advertising and sales promotion.

1988. Approximately 350,000 to 500,000 Americans will die of smoking-related causes this year.

1988. More Americans die in one year from tobacco-related diseases than were killed in the Spanish-American War, World War I, World War II, the Korean conflict, and the war in Vietnam—combined.

ASSIGNMENT QUESTIONS

1. What actions would you like the U.S. government to take in relation to tobacco smoking in this country? Specifically, what would you recommend with regard to:

a. Tobacco advertising.
b. Sales of cigarettes.
c. Smoking in public places.
d. Education regarding the hazards of smoking.
e. Federal support payments to tobacco farmers.

2. In congressional testimony in 1986, the American Civil Liberties Union opposed proposals to prohibit tobacco advertising. The ACLU's central argument was:

   It is not enough to assert that health would improve if persons stopped using tobacco. The Congress would need to build a credible case that banning the advertisements would improve public health. This premise of the tobacco ad-ban advocates is in substantial doubt. The evidence to date that tobacco advertising in fact is a substantial reason why persons begin to smoke, or continue to smoke once they start, is largely unpersuasive.

3. Would you approve of a federal law outlawing the production, distribution, promotion, and sale of tobacco products in the United States? Why or why not.

37

THE BELL TELEPHONE COMPANY: "REACH OUT AND TOUCH SOMEONE"[1]

In the 1920s, the Bell Telephone Company began providing recorded messages which gave the time of day and weather to its customers. The technology developed for such message services enabled Bell to provide these services at reduced costs because an operator did not have to handle the calls and give the information. Such recorded messages were called "Dial-it" services.

By the 1970s, this service had expanded and included recordings such as dial-a-joke and sports score lines. The telephone company was solely responsible for the content, distribution, and advertising of the recorded messages.

In the early 1980s, the Federal Communications Commission ruled that providing information by recorded messages was a service beyond the permissible scope of the telephone companies' authority. As a result of this ruling, the entire telephone Dial-it service network was transformed.

Today, the delivery of all recorded message services involves two entities: the information provider, which is responsible for the content, distribution, and advertising of the message, and, the telephone company, which is responsible for transmitting the calls and billing the caller.

The recorded messages referred to as "Dial-A-Porn" began in 1982 after deregulation of the Dial-it service. With the advent of telephone deregulation, some telephone companies began holding lotteries to select providers of recorded messages or Dial-it services. One provider of Dial-A-Porn service was a winner in the lottery conducted in New York State and by February of 1983 was offering Dial-A-Porn services over three telephone lines. It had acquired the lines either through the lottery process or by leasing them from other lottery winners. This company has become one of the leading Dial-A-Porn providers in the market.

There are two types of Dial-A-Porn calls. The first, involves the customer dialing a number and carrying on a live conversation with a paid performer on the other end of the line. The performer who answers the call will talk to the caller in terms as sexually explicit as the caller desires and may encourage him or her to perform sexual acts during the course of the phone conversation. The call may last up to 45 minutes and the caller is billed on his or her credit card for an amount usually between $15 and $30.

The second type of Dial-A-Porn call involves the receipt of a prerecorded message when the caller dials the designated number. These calls are a part of the Mass Announcement Network Service (MANS) and all begin with the prefix 976. MANS recorded messages provide other information such as prayers, racetrack results, weather forecasts, sports scores, time of day, and children's stories. The caller is charged for each call to this service on his or her monthly telephone bill.

The Dial-A-Porn recorded messages often consist of verbal illustrations of sex acts. These acts are frequently described by the performer as though they were actually occurring during the call with the caller and the performer actually participates in the acts. The acts described may include lesbian sexual activity, sodomy, rape, incest, excretory functions, bestiality, sadomasochistic abuse, and sex acts with children. One Dial-A-Porn number in California offers the caller a choice of five "pleasures" including descriptions of sadomasochistic abuse, urination, and anal intercourse. To make it easier for callers, the telephone companies have issued such numbers as 976-FOXX, 976-4LUV, 976-SLUT, 976-LUST upon the request of one Dial-A-Porn provider. These numbers indicate the nature of the 976 service.

Distribution

Dial-A-Porn recordings are now available locally in New York, Los Angeles, San Francisco, Philadelphia, Denver, Pittsburgh, Baltimore, Washington, D.C., and other major cities across the country. These services generate large numbers of calls.

Many Dial-A-Porn providers can communicate 57-second messages to a maximum of 50,000 callers per hour without any caller receiving a busy signal. During one day in May 1983, 800,000 calls were placed to one sexually explicit recorded message service. In the year ending February 29, 1984, 180 million calls were made to the same numbers.

In 1984, Dial-A-Porn recordings represented 44 percent of the 27 million messages on the "976" exchanges offered by Pacific Bell. This figure dropped to 27 percent in 1985, but was due to an increase in the volume of other "976" offerings.

Dial-A-Porn providers and the telephone companies realize significant revenues from the Dial-A-Porn services. When a caller is charged on his or her monthly telephone bill for prerecorded Dial-A-Porn messages, the provider of the message and the telephone company divide the revenues according to local tariffs. The telephone company generally earns from 2 to 19 cents for a 1-minute call with the remainder going to the Dial-A-Porn provider.

In New York, one Dial-A-Porn provider earns 2 cents per call and the telephone company earns 9.4 cents. In California, Dial-A-Porn providers earn $1.26 per call while the telephone company earns 74 cents. In some other areas, Dial-A-Porn providers earn $1.45 per call while the telephone companies receive 50 cents. At 2 cents per call in New York City, one major Dial-A-Porn provider earned $16,000 a day and a total of $3.6 million for the year ending February 29, 1984. The telephone company for the state of New York has earned as much as $35,000 a day from Dial-A-Porn calls. Pacific Bell estimates that their company earned $12 million from Dial-A-Porn calls between October 1984 and October 1985.

Not all Dial-A-Porn calls are local calls. Eighty percent of the calls made to Dial-A-Porn recordings provided by one major service in New York are local calls and 20 percent are long distance. A direct long-distance call from Michigan to a Dial-A-Porn number in New York costs the caller 58 cents per message after five o'clock in the evening and 23 cents per message after eleven o'clock at night.

Telephone companies face a dilemma as a result of the rapid rise of Dial-A-Porn. The telephone companies support the MANS concept as a means of providing information to the public and earning revenues to help keep basic telephone rates down. However, they have been subjected to mounting public criticism for helping to provide sexually explicit messages to anyone who can dial the assigned number.

In response, some companies have taken legal action against Dial-A-Porn providers. For example, one telephone company has refused to offer Dial-A-Porn services at an estimated revenue loss of $500,000 per year.

One telephone company recommended to the Commission several steps to alleviate the growing Dial-A-Porn problems. It proposed that all advertising clearly and plainly disclose the cost of the telephone call. If an individual is unaware of the charge or if a child makes an unauthorized call, the company should offer a one-time adjustment of the telephone bill to delete the charges. They also suggested that a telephone subscriber could have "976" access "blocked" from his or her lines.

The advertising of Dial-A-Porn numbers has become pervasive. In the San Francisco area, Dial-A-Porn numbers are listed in the White Pages of the telephone directory under "Dial-it" and in the Yellow Pages under "Recorded Announcement." Listings under the San Francisco Yellow Pages heading include "Adult Fantasy," "Gay Phone," and "High Society."

In addition to telephone directories, the numbers are also openly advertised in sexually explicit magazines and tabloids. For example, the June 1985 issue of one leading sexually explicit magazine contained ten pages of Dial-A-Porn advertisements. Many of these publications are sold on the public streets with the Dial-A-Porn numbers openly displayed.

Dial-A-Porn numbers have also been advertised in a major California newspaper, although many newspapers have now discontinued the advertisements. In addition, Dial-A-Porn numbers are found in magazines in convenience stores and newsstands and are passed around among children and even written on walls.

Moreover, some Dial-A-Porn advertising is deceptive. Advertisements often refer to "free phone sex" or "free love" when in fact callers are charged on their telephone bill if they make the call. This misapprehension is especially common among younger callers and minors.

The effect of Dial-A-Porn calling on these younger callers can be particularly traumatic. In 1985 Dr. Victor Cline conducted research involving fourteen children (eleven boys and three girls) and their parents on the effects of Dial-A-Porn on children. He found that each of the children displayed an addictive behavior toward the Dial-A-Porn recordings. Cline reported that none of the children stopped placing the calls until they were admonished by their parents upon discovery of the practice. The research also concluded that the children retained very vivid and recurring memories of the Dial-A-Porn recordings. Cline observed that the children exhibited characteristics of embarrassment, guilt, and shame about their involvement with Dial-A-Porn. He also suggested that the long-term effects of the Dial-A-Porn experience may be the most alarming.

Parents have also become frustrated with the availability of Dial-A-Porn when they discover that their children have become secret and habitual callers, sometimes running up large phone bills in the process. On a day in June 1986, twelve-year-old Brian Thompson, living in Hayward, California, spent more than two hours listening to Dial-A-Porn messages. Two weeks later he sexually assaulted a four-year-old girl. In consequence, the parents of both children brought a joint suit against Pacific Telephone for $10 million, charging that Dial-A-Porn was responsible. The core of their argument was that Pacific Bell and pornographers had taken away from them their rights as parents to train their children with regard to what is right and wrong. Since it is impossible for parents to police kids 24 hours a day, Bell Telephone has an obligation not to provide temptations such as Dial-A-Porn.

In December 1987 a judicial ruling declined to shut down the services pending a trial, but did order Pacific Bell to block "976" calls from individual phones when requested to do so by customers. In the twelve months after the Brian Thompson incident, Pacific Bell made an estimated $13.5 million in profits from Dial-A-Porn. Some prosecutors charge that the majority of customers continue to be children.[2]

ASSIGNMENT QUESTIONS

1. How profitable is Dial-A-Porn to the telephone companies and to the providers of this kind of service?
2. Should society tolerate this kind of business? What would you recommend that government should do?
3. The First Amendment to the Constitution of the United States provides that "Congress shall make no law...abridging the freedom of speech, or of the press." According to some legal experts, the regulation of pornography constitutes an abridgment of the freedom of speech, or an abridgment of freedom of the press, and is therefore unconstitutional. Do you agree? Why or why not?
4. What power do you think that government at any level should have to regulate any of the following:
   a. Adult book stores
   b. X-rated videotapes and movies
   c. Broadcasting of X-rated materials on public or cable TV systems
   d. Child pornography
   e. The selling of mainstream sexually explicit magazines—such as *Playboy, Penthouse, Hustler,* and *Forum*—in supermarkets and "stop and shop" convenience stores
   f. Sexually explicit computer subscription services such as SEXTEX (an "uncensored erotic" service), GENDERNET (an "information source for the transvestite and transsexual), ODYSSEY II (designed for nudists and swingers), and SYSLAVE (the "kinkiest in L.A.")
5. Alaska and Nevada residents buy five times as many pornography magazines per capita as do residents of North Dakota and have a rape rate that is six times as high. An FBI study of thirty-seven murderers confessing multiple killings found that twenty-nine used hard- and soft-core pornography to fuel their anticipatory fantasies. Should facts such as these lead to strict government regulation of the sale of this kind of material?

NOTES

1. U.S. Attorney General's Commission on Pornography, *Final Report of the Attorney General's Commission on Pornography* (Washington D.C.: U.S. Department of Justice, 1986), p. 365.
2. *Time*, December 21, 1987, p. 58.

38
REGULATION OF NETWORK RADIO BROADCASTING

Radio communication, as it developed around the beginning of the twentieth century, took two separate forms. Wireless telegraphy was developed to send and receive information in the form of Morse code messages, and then radiotelephony was devised so that voice messages could be sent over electromagnetic waves.

The Development of Wireless Telegraphy

By 1898, scientists throughout the world were conducting experiments with radio waves. Well-known researchers such as Popov in Russia, Braun in Germany, Muirhead in Britain, and Nikola Tesla in the United States were among them. Despite this competition, the first commercial radio service was installed by a relatively unknown Italian named Guglielmo Marconi.

In 1894, Marconi had read about the discovery of electromagnetic waves by Heinrich Hertz, and had set out to construct a transmitter and receiver at the University of Bologna. By the close of 1895, he had signaled 1.2 miles across the family estate, and had developed a fanatical faith in possibilities of radio for worldwide communications. Initially, he decided to promote his wireless telegraph as a means of communicating with ships at sea rather than as a competitor to the established cable and wire telegraph services.

By 1898, he had extended his transmissions to 30 miles, obtained a British patent, and formed a company to utilize his inventions. During the next two years he performed a number of feats that excited the imagination of the public. During Ireland's Kingstown Regatta, he put a transmitter in a tugboat and reported to shore on the positions of the yachts when they were beyond the sight of land. He gained further fame by providing communications for Queen Victoria from her summer residence to the royal yacht a few miles away where Prince Edward was convalescing. In March 1899, he made his first wireless transmission across the English Channel.

After successfully signaling 150 miles in 1900, Marconi set out to demonstrate conclusively the abilities of the wireless by attempting to send a message across the Atlantic. A powerful transmitter was built at Poldhu, England, and Marconi sailed for St. John's, Newfoundland, taking along two assistants, receiving equipment, wire, and several kites and balloons. On December 12, 1901, using an antenna made of 400 feet of wire tied to a kite, Marconi heard the first radio message sent across the Atlantic Ocean. News of the feat created worldwide interest and excitement.

During the next decade, Marconi attempted to expand his business by persuading shipowners that shipboard wireless was a necessity for safety reasons. Most of them continued to believe that it was an expensive luxury. This attitude was altered completely under the dramatic circumstances of collision at sea.

On the night of January 23, 1909, the White Star liner *Republic*, with 550 people on board, was rammed by the Italian ship *Florida*, carrying 1,500 persons. Both ships were badly damaged, with the *Republic* rapidly sinking and the *Florida* in a much crippled condition and in grave danger of sinking. The accident occurred in the fog 26 miles off the Massachusetts coast, and the *Republic*'s wireless operator was able to send a distress call to a nearby coastal station. Within minutes other ships were on their way to the scene. Assistance was so speedy in arriving that only six lives were lost in transferring all passengers from both ships to the rescue ship *Baltic*.

One result of this demonstration of the value of shipboard wireless was the passage, by the Congress, of the Wireless Ship Act of 1910. This act, which marks the first federal attempt to in any way regulate radio communication, forbade any steamer carrying or licensed to carry 50 or more persons to leave any American port unless equipped with an efficient wireless device in charge of a skilled operator. The enforcement of this legislation was given to the Secretary of Commerce and Labor, who was in charge of the administration of marine navigation laws.

The Development of Radiotelephony

American contributions to the rapidly developing field of radio began with the work of Reginald Fessenden of the University of Pittsburgh and the U.S. Weather Bureau. Under the auspices of a company formed by two Pittsburgh financiers to support his work, Fessenden performed highly original and technically successful work. In December 1900 he transmitted speech for over a mile, and although the sound quality was poor, inaugurated radiotelephony.

Six years later, on Christmas Eve, 1906, Fessenden made what is generally regarded as the world's first radio broadcast. Good-quality voice and music were heard by numerous surprised ship-to-shore wireless operators within 15 miles of his transmitter at Brant Rock off the Massachusetts coast.

Lee De Forest entered the radio field with a Ph.D. from Yale and a great desire for fame and fortune. Most of the technical advancements he claimed made little contribution to the progress of radio communications, but he gained much publicity for radio by performing numerous feats demonstrating radio's capabilities. For example, in 1908 he broadcast from the top of the Eiffel Tower in Paris, and in 1910 broadcast the voice of Caruso from the Metropolitan Opera House in New York. His extravagant claims for his achievements and his boundless confidence in the growth of radio captured the public imagination and made it very receptive to later developments. By 1912, when the United States ratified the first international radio treaty, the need for general regulation of radio communication had become urgent. To fulfill our obligation under the treaty, Congress enacted the Radio Act of 1912. This law forbade the operation of radio equipment without a license from the Secretary of Commerce and Labor, allocated certain frequencies to government use, and imposed certain restrictions upon the character of wave emissions, the transmission of distress signals, and the like.

Growth of Commercial Broadcasting in the United States

The enforcement of the Radio Act of 1912 presented no serious problems prior to World War I. Questions of interference arose only rarely because there were many more frequencies available than there were stations in existence. During the war, this situation continued to exist, although the techniques and art of broadcasting were considerably advanced.

Radio broadcasting to homes began in earnest in the early 1920s. Frank Conrad, an engineer with Westinghouse in Pittsburgh, began making a series of broadcasts from his garage that attracted the attention of hobbyists. Henry P. Davis, Westinghouse vice-president, received notice of Conrad's activity and developed the idea that the company could profitably build radio receivers. In addition, he persuaded Westinghouse to sponsor a transmitting station with a regular broadcasting schedule in Pittsburgh. Over the next few years, events such as the broadcasting of election returns, the blow-by-blow reporting of the Dempsey-Carpentier fight, and performance of the Chicago Civic Opera brought wide fame to radio and greatly stimulated the sale of receivers. The National Broadcasting Company was organized and expanded under the brilliant leadership of David Sarnoff, and the Columbia Broadcasting System was established with William S. Paley as president.

Sarnoff predicted, to much general amusement, that RCA would be able to sell a million "radio music boxes" within three years. Actually, he proved to be a bit conservative. RCA sold somewhat over a million during that period, and other firms found it difficult to keep up with demand. By the end of 1924 there were an estimated three million receiving sets in use, and 538 stations were on the air to provide entertainment and information.

These early years of broadcasting were marked by chaos. Since the Act of 1912 had not set aside any particular frequencies for the use of private broadcast stations, the secretary of commerce simply selected two frequencies, 750 and 833 kilocycles, and licensed all stations to operate upon one or another of these channels. No attempt was made to regulate station power or broadcast hours. When two or more stations were in one locality, they had to work out an agreement among themselves. In some areas stations divided the time fairly—in others they tried to drown out their rivals with greater power or circumvent them by using a slightly different frequency.

The number of stations increased so rapidly, however, and the situation became so chaotic, that the secretary, upon the recommendation of the National Radio Conference which met in Washington in 1923 and 1924, established a policy of assigning specified frequencies to particular stations. The entire radio spectrum was divided into numerous bands, each allocated to a particular kind of service. The frequencies, ranging from 550 to 1,500 kilocycles (ninety-six channels in all, since the channels were separated from each other by 10 kilocycles), were assigned to the standard broadcast stations. But the problems created by the enormously rapid development of radio were far from solved. The increase in the number of channels was not enough to take care of the constantly growing number of stations. Since there were more stations than available frequencies, the secretary of commerce attempted to find room for everybody by limiting the power and hours of operation in stations in order that several stations might use the same channel. The number of stations multiplied so rapidly, however, that by November 1925, there were almost 600 stations in the country, and there were 175 applications for new stations. Every channel in the standard broadcast band was, by that time, already occupied by at least one station, and many by several. The new stations could be accommodated only by extending the standard broadcast band, at the expense of the other types of services, or by imposing still greater limitations upon time and power. The National Radio Congress which met in November 1925 opposed both of these methods and called upon Congress to remedy the situation through legislation.

The Secretary of Commerce was powerless to deal with the situation. For reasons convincing only to the courts, it had been ruled that he could not deny a license to an otherwise legally qualified applicant on the ground that the proposed station would interfere with existing private or governmental stations. In addition, on April 26, 1926, an Illinois district court held that the secretary had no power to even impose restrictions as to power and hours of operation. This same court ruled that a station's use of a frequency not assigned to it was not a violation of the Radio Act of 1912. The last straw was an opinion by the attorney general of the United States on July 8 that the secretary of commerce had no power under the Radio Act of 1912 to regulate the power, frequency, or hours of operation of stations. In response, the next day the secretary issued a statement abandoning all efforts to regulate radio and urging the stations to cooperate in self-regulation.

But the plea of the secretary went unheeded. From July 1926 to February 1927 almost two hundred new stations went on the air. These new stations used any frequency they desired, regardless of the interference thereby caused to others. Existing stations changed to other frequencies and increased their power and hours of operation at will. The result was chaos and confusion. With everybody on the air, nobody could be heard. The situation became so intolerable that the president, in his message of December 7, 1926, appealed to Congress to enact a comprehensive radio law.

The Radio Act of 1927 and the Communications Act of 1934

The plight into which radio fell in the mid-1920s was attributable to certain fundamental characteristics of radio as a means of communication—its facilities are limited, they are not available to all who may wish to use them, and the radio spectrum is simply not large enough to accommodate everybody. Because of this fixed natural limitation upon the number of stations that can be operated without interfering with others, regulation was believed necessary to ensure full development. The Radio Act of 1927 was the first comprehensive scheme of control over radio communication. The act created the Federal Radio Commission, composed of five members, and endowed the Commission with wide licensing and regulatory powers.

The provisions of the Radio Act of 1927 were included in broader legislation passed by Congress seven years later—in the Communications Act of 1934. Section 1 of the Communications Act states its purpose of "regulating interstate and foreign commerce in communication by wire and radio so as to make available, so far as possible, to all the people of the United States a rapid, efficient, nation-wide, and world-wide radio communication service with adequate facilities at reasonable charge."

Section 301 particularizes this general purpose with respect to radio: "It is the purpose of this Act, among other things, to maintain the control of the United States over all the channels of interstate and foreign radio transmission; and to provide for the use of such channels, but not the ownership thereof, by persons for limited periods of time, under license granted by Federal authority, and no such license shall be construed to create any right, beyond the terms, conditions, and periods of the license." To that end a commission composed of seven members was created, with broad licensing and regulatory powers.

Section 303 provides: "Except as otherwise provided in this Act, the Commission from time to time, as public convenience, interest, or necessity requires, shall—

(a) Classify radio stations;
(b) Prescribe the nature of the service to be rendered by each class of licensed stations and each station within any class;
(f) Make such regulations not inconsistent with law as it may deem necessary to prevent interference between stations and to carry out the provisions of this Act...;
(g) Study new uses for radio, provide for experimental uses of frequencies, and generally encourage the larger and more effective uses of radio in the public interest;
(i) Have authority to make special regulations applicable to radio stations engaged in chain broadcasting;
(r) Make such rules and regulations and prescribe such restrictions and conditions, not inconsistent with law, as may be necessary to carry out the provisions of this Act....

Investigation of the Networks

During the first four years of the commission's existence, the growth of the national radio networks continued at an accelerated pace. One result of this was a rising wave of criticism directed at monopoly in radio broadcasting and the commission's apparent inaction. In response, on March 18, 1938, the FCC undertook a comprehensive investigation to determine whether special regulations pertaining to radio stations engaged in chain broadcasting were required in the "public interest, convenience, or necessity."

On April 6, 1938, a committee of three commissioners was designated to hold hearings and make recommendations to the full commission. This committee held public hearings for seventy-three days over a period of six months, from November 14, 1938 to May 19, 1939. Order No. 37, announcing the investigation and specifying the particular matters which would be explored at the hearings, was published in the *Federal Register,* and copies were sent to every station licensee and network organization. Notices of the hearings were also sent to these parties. Station licensees, national and regional networks, and transcription and recording companies were invited to appear and give evidence. Other persons who sought to appear were afforded an opportunity to testify. Ninety-six witnesses were heard by the committee, forty-five of whom were called by the national networks. The evidence covers twenty-seven volumes, including over eight thousand pages of transcript and more than seven hundred exhibits. The testimony of the witnesses called by the national networks fills more than six thousand pages, the equivalent of forty-six hearing days.

The committee found that at the end of 1938 there were 660 commercial stations in the United States and that 341 of these were affiliated with national networks. These figures, the committee noted, did not accurately reflect the relative prominence of the three national network companies, since stations affiliated with the national networks utilized more than 97 percent of the total nighttime broadcasting power of all the stations in the country. NBC and CBS together controlled more than 85 percent of the total nighttime wattage, and the broadcast business of the three national network companies amounted to almost half of the total business of all stations in the United States.

The committee submitted a report to the commission on June 12, 1940, stating its findings and recommendations. Thereafter, briefs on behalf of the networks and other interested parties were filed before the full commission, and on November 28, 1940, the commission issued proposed regulations which the parties were requested to consider in the oral arguments held on December 2 and 3, 1940.

Chain Broadcasting Regulations

The regulations, which the commission characterized as "the expression of 'the general policy we will follow in exercising our licensing power' " are addressed in terms to station licensees and applicants for station licenses. They provide, in general, that no licenses shall be granted to stations or applicants having specified relationships with networks. Each regulation is directed at a particular practice found by the commission to be detrimental to the public interest.

The Commission found that a number of network abuses were amenable to correction within the powers granted it by Congress:

1. Exclusive affiliation of station. The Commission found that the network affiliation agreements of NBC and CBS customarily contained a provision that prevented the station from broadcasting the programs of any other network. The Commission believed that the effect of this provision was to hinder the growth of new networks, to deprive the listening public in many areas of service to which they were entitled, and to prevent station licensees from exercising their statutory duty of determining which programs would best serve the needs of their community. The Commission observed that in areas where all the stations were under contract exclusively to either NBC or CBS, the public was deprived of the opportunity to hear programs presented by Mutual.

   To take a case cited in the report; In the fall of 1939 Mutual obtained the exclusive right to broadcast the World Series baseball games. It offered this program of outstanding national interest to stations throughout the country, including NBC and CBS affiliates in communities having no other stations. CBS and NBC immediately invoked the "exclusive affiliation" clauses of their agreements with these stations, and as a result thousands of persons in many sections of the country were unable to hear the broadcasts of the games.

2. Territorial exclusivity. The Commission found another type of "exclusivity" provision in network affiliation agreements whereby the network bound itself not to sell programs to any other station in the same area. The effect of this provision, designed to protect the affiliate from competition of other stations serving the same territory, was to deprive the listening public of many programs that might otherwise be available. If an affiliated station rejected a network program, the "territorial exclusivity" clause of its affiliation agreement prevented the network from offering the program to other stations in the area.

   The Commission concluded, "It is not in the public interest for the listening audience in an area to be deprived of network programs not carried by one station where other stations in that area are ready and willing to broadcast the programs."

3. Term of affiliation. The standard NBC and CBS affiliation contracts bound the station for a period of five years, with the networks having the exclusive right to terminate the contracts upon one year's notice. The Commission, relying upon Section 307 of the Communications Act of 1934, under which no license to operate a station can be granted for a longer term than three years, found the five-year affiliation term to be contrary to the policy of the Act. Accordingly, the Commission adopted Regulation 3.103: "No license shall be granted to a standard broadcast station having any contract, arrangement, or understanding, express or implied, with a network organization which provides, by original term, provisions for renewal, or otherwise for the affiliation of the station with the network organization for a period longer than two years."

4. Option time. The Commission found that network affiliation contracts usually contained so-called network optional time clauses. Under these provisions the network could upon twenty-eight days' notice call upon its affiliates to carry a commercial program during any of the hours specified in the agreement as "network optional time." For CBS affiliates "network optional time" meant the entire broadcast day. For twenty-nine outlets of NBC on the Pacific Coast, it also covered the entire broadcast day; for substantially all of the other NBC affiliates it included 8 1/2 hours on weekdays and 8 hours on Sunday.

   In the Commission's judgment these optional time provisions, in addition to imposing serious obstacles in the path of new networks, hindered stations in developing a local program service.

   The Commission undertook to preserve the advantages of option time as a device for stabilizing the industry, without unduly impairing the ability of local stations to develop local program service. The text of the proposed regulation read: "No license shall be granted to a standard broadcast station which options for network programs any time subject to call on less than fifty-six days' notice, or more time than a total of three hours within each of four segments of the broadcast day, as herein described. The broadcast day is divided into four segments, as follows: 8:00 A.M. to 1:00 P.M.; 1:00 P.M. to 6:00 P.M.; 6:00 P.M. to 11:00 P.M.; and 11:00 P.M. to 8:00 A.M.

5. The right to reject programs. The Commission found that most network affiliation contracts contained a clause defining the right of the station to reject network commercial programs. While seeming in the abstract to be fair, these provisions, according to the Commission's finding, did not sufficiently protect the "public interest." As a practical matter, the licensee could not determine in advance whether the broadcasting of any particular network program would or would not be in the public interest. "It is obvious that from such skeletal information [as the networks submitted to the stations prior to the broadcasts] the station cannot determine in advance whether the program is in the public interest, nor can it ascertain whether or not parts of the program are in one way or another offensive. In practice, if not in theory, stations affiliated with networks have delegated to the networks a large part of their programming functions. In many instances, moreover, the network delegates the actual production of programs to advertising agencies. These agencies are far more than mere brokers or intermediaries between the network and the advertiser. To an ever-increasing extent, these agencies actually exercise the function of program production. Thus it is frequently neither the station nor the network, but rather the advertising agency, which determines what broadcast programs shall contain. Under such circumstances, it is especially important that individual stations, if they are to operate in the public interest, should have the practical opportunity as well as the contractual right to reject network programs.

Reactions to the Proposed Regulations

Upon request of the networks, the commission postponed the effective date of the regulations while additional petitions were submitted and hearings granted. Finally, on October 11, 1941, the effective date was established as November 11. In response, NBC and CBS brought suit on October 30 to prevent enforcement of the proposed regulations. The networks contended that the commission went beyond the regulatory powers conferred upon it by the Communications Act of 1934 in interfering in the business affairs of the networks; that the regulatory powers of the FCC are limited to the engineering and technical aspects of radio communication and cannot be extended to embrace business arrangements. The lower courts ruled in favor of the FCC, and upon appeal, the cases eventually went to the U.S. Supreme Court. The Court affirmed the decisions rendered against the networks and ordered that the regulations be enforced.

ASSIGNMENT QUESTIONS

1. Is government regulation of radio and TV really necessary? If so, how can those who operate the stations maintain the freedom to comment on and criticize government actions?
2. Do radio and TV networks perform a necessary function? Summarize the values and dangers of network radio and TV.
3. Outline the method by which the chain broadcasting regulations were developed. How can industry representatives make their feelings known to the commission members?

4. Summarize the regulations as presented in the case. What was the intent of the commission in developing the regulations?
5. What was the argument used by those who opposed the chain broadcasting regulations? Do you agree?
6. Is there any general principle to be gained from the government's efforts to control communication? Why isn't it just as logical for government to control newspapers, magazines, and motion pictures? What particular characteristics have industries such as radio and TV that cause them to require regulation?

PART NINE
BUSINESS RELATIONS WITH OTHER GROUPS

Traditionally, business management has been described as being responsible to the owners of a corporation. In recent years, however, other groups have come forth claiming that business managers also have a duty to account to them. These interest groups include workers, customers, neighbors, and even a group described as "society." In this section we consider business relations with some of these other groups. In Case 39, *The Lomax Baby Furniture Company,* and Case 40, *The Case of the OSHA Cowboy,* environmental and product safety are the focal points of our interest. The business manager has an unusual challenge in this area because he or she has to develop safety policies given the inefficiency and ineptness of the federal agency involved. In the latter case, the reader is presented with the challenge of developing a perfectly safe cowboy and horse through the addition of safety equipment and rules.

The *Natural, Organic, and Health Foods* case (Case 41) relates some of the arguments for and against health foods but really leaves conclusions in this area to the reader. The important question is not whether "natural, organic, or health" foods are better for us. The important question has to do with what role we want government to take in those cases where consumers are not actually being harmed—only being cheated by being sold supermarket food at health food prices. What should be the role of the Food and Drug Administration?

39

THE LOMAX BABY FURNITURE COMPANY

TO: David H. Lomax, President

FROM: Roxanne P. Dickson, Safety Director

SUBJECT: Safety Policies

As the company's newly appointed safety director, I have been asked to recommend policies in the areas of product and occupational safety. Since these are two completely separate areas, I will make separate recommendations for each of them.

At the outset, distinction should be made among the three types of safety concerns—environmental, occupational, and consumer. The differences between them can be illustrated by a simple example. Suppose that in manufacturing a certain item, a dangerous chemical is produced. This chemical may present a threat to workers in the plant (occupational safety), it may present a hazard to the public at large if released into the atmosphere (environmental safety), or it may be carried by the items produced until it is purchased by a customer (consumer safety).

In these recommendations, I will not be suggesting policies in environmental safety because this is an area of little concern for the company. As a manufacturing facility, we are fortunate in that we neither create nor distribute through the environment significant air, water, or noise pollution. Since we do have some real problems in the areas of occupational and product or consumer safety, I will concentrate on those areas.

Some Background and History on Safety Legislation

1450. During the Middle Ages, workers in Europe routinely died of industry-related illnesses. Some died from lead poisoning ("lead colic"), some expired due to dust inhalation ("grinders' consumption"), and mercury poisoning regularly killed those who used it to cure beaver hats.

1700. The first paper on occupational diseases was written by Ramazzini in Italy.

1880. In the United States there was some awareness of health and safety problems in some occupations—such as rats and an occasional worker in the sausage, and wide publicity given to the horrors of work in slaughterhouses and coal mines. The emphasis at this time was on health problems stemming from the consumption or use of the products produced, with less attention paid to health problems relating to the workplace. In fact, prior to 1900, workers were usually considered responsible for accidents or job-related illnesses. If the injured or sick worker sought remedy from his employers, he or she was forced to turn to the courts, where the employers usually won.

1908. The first worker's compensation law was passed in the United States covering federal workers.

1911. On March 25, 1911, 150 employees, mostly young women, died in a fire at the Triangle Shirtwaist Company. Subsequent investigation showed that, because emergency exits had been locked to keep employees from stealing, workers had died heaped against exits or had jumped from the top floors of the building to the cement sidewalks below. In response to the resulting public indignation, the New York Legislature established a commission to investigate industrial working conditions. The result was the enactment of safety legislation in New York State. In most other states, safety regulations were still largely left up to employers.

1925. The *Monthly Labor Review* reported that one-third to one-half of all electric linemen were accidentally killed while on the job.[1]

1931. The Food and Drug Administration was established to administer laws concerning purity, safety, and labeling accuracy of certain foods and drugs.

1936. The Walsh-Healey Public Contract Act provided that all work performed on federal contracts in excess of $10,000 had to be done in safe workplaces.

1937. The Agricultural Marketing Service was established to set grades and standards for most farm commodities, to inspect egg production, and to administer product and process safety acts, licenses, and bonded warehouses.

1950. During this decade, many corporations established the position of Safety Director, and began serious programs aimed at preventing accidents and educating employees on safety matters. Safety posters and regular safety reports became a normal and accepted part of business life.

1960. In the 1960s, industrial accident frequency rates actually began to rise, and business critics, such as Ralph Nader, pointed out serious flaws and problems in safety practices. New and possibly dangerous substances were introduced into industrial processes.

1970. As part of President Johnson's Great Society legislation, the Congress enacted the Occupational Safety and Health Act of 1970. The law provided for the following:

1. Employers must maintain a safe working environment.
2. The Occupational Safety and Health Administration (OSHA) was to conduct regular safety investigations.
3. Penalties were set for employers who allow unsafe conditions to exist.
4. Established the Occupational Safety and Health Administration to administer safety regulations.
5. An assistant secretary of labor was to head up the agency.
6. OSHA will have the power to set standards for safety and health which will have the force of law.

Also in 1970, the National Highway Traffic Safety Administration was established to set safety standards for trucks and autos and to certify compliance.

1972. The law establishing the Consumer Product Safety Commission gave it the power to establish mandatory product safety standards, and to ban the sale of products that fail to comply.

This sketchy history does not, of course, attempt to include all the laws passed on the state and federal level to promote occupational and product safety. I could have included legislation such as the Longshoremen's and Harbor Worker's Compensation Act of 1927, or the Safe Drinking Water Act of 1974. Without attempting to list *all* pertinent legislation, it is evident that any particular company or plant now faces a multiplicity of governmental regulations and procedures in the safety area. Further, each agency has not only different procedures but may also have differing aims in its investigations. For example, "Both OSHA and the FDA regard the presence of rats in a food processing plant as an unacceptable hazard, the former because of danger to consumers. If an inspector from the Food and Drug Administration finds rats on the premises, the processor can only be fined if the inspector can convince the local United States Attorney to prosecute and the case is won. If an OSHA inspector finds the plant out of compliance with OSHA regulations on vermin control, the manufacturer can be cited and fined virtually on the spot. Because of overlapping regulations by FDA and OSHA, the same violation can lead to very different outcomes depending upon which agency smells the rat."[2]

Policy Recommendation —Product Safety

The main agency for dealing with product safety is the Consumer Products Safety Commission. Fortunately, or unfortunately, depending on your viewpoint, the commission has not compiled a particularly impressive record since its formation. Its main problem stems from the fact that, in establishing priorities, the CPSC relies heavily on a very arbitrary hazards index. A kind of running score is kept on each product according to the severity of accidents associated with it and these calculations are added up periodically to produce a score for each product. By comparing these scores, the CPSC can decide which products are in need of regulation.

The specific problems with this method are, first, that it assumes that all products are used with the same frequency. Thus, a product with a high score of total accidents but a low per unit accident rate is more likely to be investigated and regulated than a product with a high per unit accident rate but a low total score because there are so few units at large. Second, the index takes no account of the age of the products involved. Presumably, a very old model of a certain consumer good might be less safe simply because it has outlived its useful life. Finally, the most arbitrary part of the hazard index calculation is the establishment of weights designed to reflect the seriousness of each accident. Thus, a death is worth 2,516 points while a sprained ankle is worth 10 points. There is no evidence that this kind of arbitrary ranking is the result of any scientific or even well-reasoned study.

A less important but still major problem is that the CPSC is very slow in its proceedings. In 1975, the commission received forty-two petitions under the Consumer Product Safety Act. Only four of these had been resolved by the end of 1976, and these had taken an average of 265 days. Ten other cases had taken an average of 326 days and were still pending.[3]

Based on these facts about CPSC, it might seem a profitable policy to simply ignore product safety and assume that our chances of being investigated or in any way regulated in this area are very slim. However, there is more at stake here. Possibly a short review of this company's most significant experience with a product safety problem might be in order.

Prior to 1968 the spacing between the slats of the baby cribs we produced was approximately 4 inches. This was about the same as the rest of the industry and seemed to be safe enough to prevent babies from being hurt. However, in 1968, a presidential commission, with great fanfare and subsequent bad publicity for us, announced that the spacing of currently produced crib slats was sufficiently wide so that the body of a baby could slip through the slats until stopped by its skull. The baby could then strangle itself as it hung outside the crib. As you will remember, under intense pressure from the media, our trade association, without making a systematic analysis, voluntarily adopted a standard of 3.25 inches between slats. We got more bad press when the Bureau of Product Safety of the FDA—a forerunner of the CPSC—determined that a safe spacing was

2.375 inches, nearly an inch smaller than the industry standards. In April 1973, a mandatory spacing standard of 2.375 inches was adopted.

I believe that we can learn a number of valuable lessons from our experience with the federal agencies and crib slat spacing:

1. The nature of our products is such that any hint of safety problems will have disastrous effects on our sales. As you may remember, we lost millions on our crib lines between 1968 and 1973.
2. Government agencies will make sure that any investigation of our industry will receive the widest possible publicity.
3. It will be good business to formalize company efforts at ensuring product safety and in making such formalization part of our promotional and advertising campaigns.

In addition to these economic factors, it is also my opinion that a company such as ours, in a responsible position in American industry, will want to have a basic presupposition of ethical conduct and social responsibility underlying its operating policies. Because of this, and because of the arguments noted earlier, I suggest that a company policy in the area of product safety might be stated as follows:

POLICY: WE WILL BE UNCOMPROMISING IN OUR EFFORTS TO PRODUCE PRODUCTS THAT WILL BE USEFUL AND ALSO COMPLETELY SAFE FOR INFANTS.

Policy Recommendation —Occupational Safety

Although nobody wants to criticize the general concept of worker safety, OSHA has turned out to be among the most unpopular agencies involved in the regulation of business. The main reason why this is so turns on the method that the agency has developed to ensure safety in those businesses it investigates. The agency has specified "engineering controls"—machine enclosures and the like—as the only acceptable way to meet safety standards. It has done this even in those cases where business managers and industrial engineers may believe that such changes may not only be economically prohibitive, but significantly less effective than personal protection—such as earmuffs in high-noise situations.

Further criticism of OSHA is premised on its apparent congressional mandate to, in effect, seek absolute safety for everyone instead of trying to just minimize the inevitable risks of an industrial society. Put another way, OSHA assumes that every worker is an idiot and wants the work site organized with a level of protection that would prevent him from hurting himself in spite of his lack of common sense. In addition, the agency was also encouraged to impose its judgment on employers instead of leaving them any choice between different approaches to safety precautions—they have prescribed details rather than performance standards.

One of the consequences of all this has been the promulgation of standards that are not only, at times, unrealistic, but that for sheer volume are almost unmanageable for OSHA and the industry alike. For example, the steel industry is staggering under a load of fifty-six hundred regulations from twenty-seven different agencies—and OSHA accounts for four thousand of these rules.[4]

In the consideration of factors suggesting an appropriate policy for our company, we should keep in mind that, in spite of its large budget for compliance, OSHA has a nearly impossible task to accomplish. Its major problem is that its mandate covers more than four million companies. The consequence is that inspections are quite infrequent—which certainly blunts the effectiveness of enforcement as an incentive to comply. As can be seen in Exhibit 39-1, the total number of OSHA inspections during 1972 and 1973 was approximately eighty-two thousand. Assuming that the agency is making about forty thousand inspections a year—still quite a number—the chances of any one of the four million businesses being inspected is only 1 percent per year.

EXHIBIT 39-1 OSHA Initial Inspections from July 1972 to May 1974 by Size of Establishment

Number of employees	*Inspections*	
	Number	*% of Total*
0–15	32,184	39%
16–25	9,138	11
Over 25	40,660	50
Total	81,982	100%

Source: Department of Health, Education and Welfare and Certain Independent Agencies Appropriation for Fiscal Year 1976. Hearings, Subcommittee of the Senate Committee on Appropriations, 94th Congress, 1st Session, 1975, pt 2, p. 976.

Equally important as the infrequency of inspections are the minimal consequences for being found out of compliance. As can be seen in Exhibit 39-2, the average fine for violations was $25.

In the twelve months of 1977, OSHA levied a total of $12,400,000 in fines—an almost laughably small amount—but to meet, for example, OSHA's 90-decibel factory noise standard, American industry would have to pay $13 billion.[5] Aside from noting that this kind of expenditure is nonproductive, it suggests to me that, after consideration of the infrequency of inspection and the relatively small fines involved for noncompliance, the cost of complying with OSHA standards far outweighs the costs of violating them.

EXHIBIT 39-2 OSHA Citations, July 1972 to March 1974

Category	*Number of citations*	*Average fine*
Nonserious	360,102	$ 16
Serious	4,330	648
Willful, repeat, or imminent danger	523	1,104
Total	364,955	$ 25

Source: Department of Health, Education and Welfare and Certain Independent Agencies Appropriation for Fiscal Year 1976. Hearings, Subcommittee of the Senate Committee on Appropriations, 94th Congress, 1st Session, 1975, pt 2, p. 967.

This is the key point and the basis for a new company policy on occupational safety. One additional fact that should be emphasized is that our production facilities, although not in technical compliance with OSHA standards, are perfectly safe, and that our employees are fitted with the most modern personal safety equipment. The effectiveness of our program is proven by our excellent safety record over the past few years in spite of the lack of a formal safety department until this year. With education, our record should be outstanding. To bring us in full compliance with OSHA standards, we would have to do the following kinds of things:

1. Change all our fire extinguishers to a different (but not particularly more effective) type and raise them by 2 inches from where currently hanging.
2. All our railings would have to be lowered—to a uniform height that we believe is less safe than they are now.
3. All exit signs would have to be replaced—they are all visible and lighted but are slightly off from the OSHA standard.
4. Some of our machinery is completely unprotected, but is located where only an idiot would go. In one case, a worker would have to proceed without authorization onto a narrow catwalk to even get near it—yet OSHA standards would require that it be covered.
5. We would likely have to replace our giant multiple press. Although it makes a noise in excess of OSHA requirements—94 decibels—all those who work on or near it are required to wear heavy ear protection. In actual use it has never been a problem, except for a couple of workers who had to be transferred to other departments or fired for not wearing the required equipment.

The cost of making these changes, in the estimation of our engineering department, would be about $1,400,000 if we do not replace the big press, and about $2,200,000 if such replacement is required.

Based on (1) the high costs of compliance,

(2) the fact that we are a safe organization even though not in compliance with OSHA standards, (3) the infrequency of OSHA inspections, and (4) the minimal consequences of being found out of compliance, I would recommend the following policy:

POLICY: WE WILL MAINTAIN HIGH STANDARDS OF OCCUPATIONAL SAFETY FOR OUR WORKERS, WILL COOPERATE WITH GOVERNMENT INSPECTORS, AND DO OUR BEST TO COMPLY WITH THEIR RECOMMENDATIONS TO US.

In effect, what this policy means is that we will do the best job as we see it to make this a safe place to work, but that we will make no attempt to comply with OSHA standards until we are forced to do so as the result of an inspection.

I will appreciate your comments on these recommendations.

ASSIGNMENT QUESTIONS

1. Distinguish among occupational, product, and environmental safety.
2. For what are the following agencies responsible: FDA, OSHA, CPSC?
3. Summarize criticisms of the CPSC.
4. Rephrase the suggested policy on product safety and summarize the rationale underlying it.
5. Why is OSHA among the most unpopular agencies involved in the regulation of business?
6. What is the policy recommendation for the company on occupational safety? What is the justification given for this policy? Is it a good policy?
7. The policy recommendation regarding occupational safety appears to be at variance with notions of corporate social responsibility. Explain.

NOTES

1. *Monthly Labor Review*, 1925, p. 172.
2. Martin C. Schnitzer, *Contemporary Government and Business Relations* (Chicago: Rand McNally, 1978), p. 183.
3. Nina Cornell, Robert Noll, and Barry Weingast, "Safety Regulations," in Henry Owen and Charles L. Schultz, editors, *Setting National Priorities: The Coming Decade* (Washington D.C.: The Brookings Institution, 1976), p. 8.
4. *Business Week*, April 4, 1977, p. 79.
5. Ibid., p. 74.

40
THE CASE OF THE OSHA COWBOY

TO: Randell J. "Tex" Doty
Lazy D Ranch
Cowley, Wyoming

FROM: I. M. Murchison
Washington, D.C.

SUBJECT: OSHA Violations

As a result of my inspection tour through your area this past month, I am required under the Occupational Safety and Health Act (July 1972) to inform you of certain violations found in your ranching operation. Specifically, I found that those individuals designated as "cowboys" are grossly in violation of the law with regard to the installation and use of both safety and environmental equipment. This is to serve as official notification that the following conditions must be cleared up within 90 days or we will have to take legal action.

Violations

1. The "cowboy hat," although colorful and traditional, does not provide real protection in the event of a fall from the horse.
2. There is no protection whatsoever for the worker's ears in the event of cold weather or the shock of a gun being fired.
3. Provision for head restraint and a padded back on the saddle to support the back itself are missing.
4. Backup lights are missing.
5. There are no directional signals to warn closely following horses of sudden turns.
6. There is no shoulder harness to keep the worker securely on the horse.
7. There is no automatic air-filled chest protector similar to the air bags used in cars.
8. There is no provision for repelling bug spray to keep flies off both horse and rider.
9. No seat belt (a shocking omission!).

10. In place of the traditional chaps, our research office recommends quilted pants and knee pads.
11. There is no system for taking care of "emissions" from the horse itself. This is absolutely required under environmental laws.
12. The currently used steel horseshoes work fairly well on soft surfaces, but are prone to cause dangerous sparks on cement surfaces.
13. No provision is made for stopping the horse if the worker should fall asleep at night while on patrol.
14. The worker is completely lacking in eye protection against dust in the air or against harsh desert sunlight.
15. The worker has no way to see to the rear without turning his or her head around.
16. No headlights to see ahead at night.
17. No provision to ensure that the horse itself has good vision.
18. Current-style stirrups provide little protection to the toes.
19. No safety net to catch the worker in case he should fall off the horse.
20. No provision to protect the horse and rider in case the horse itself slips and starts to fall.

One of our inspectors will be in your area in October to discuss the changes and improvements you have made.

ASSIGNMENT QUESTION

1. Make a list of the equipment and changes you would recommend to Tex so that his cowboys will be in compliance with the law.

41

NATURAL, ORGANIC, AND HEALTH FOODS

THE HEALTH FOOD MOVEMENT

J. Garnwell DuBairre

Although it is not possible to pick out a date when the current concern over what we eat began, a good place to begin might be in 1962. Of course, before that time there were many people who were interested in "health foods," but the publication of Rachel Carson's book *Silent Spring* forced many previously unconcerned Americans to consider seriously for the first time problems brought on by the use of chemical fertilizers, pesticides, and additives in food production. Stories began to come to light about mercury in our fish, of *Salmonella* in our powdered milk, and of beef full of cancer-causing DES growth hormones. Led by the Sierra Club, the Environmental Defense Fund, and the Izaak Walton League, environmentalists began to question the purity and nutritional value of everything from eggs to water.

In addition to doubts stemming from the use of chemicals in farming and food production, many people came to believe that these systems also robbed food of much of its nourishment. Criticism was leveled at white bread (as nutritional as cotton), breakfast cereals (the boxes they came in were more nutritious), mass-produced chickens (full of chemicals and hormones), canned vegetables (boiled so that most of their value was taken from them), and even the all-American hot dog (full of water, fillers, and fat).

In response to these concerns regarding food purchased in regular supermarkets, many people have turned to so-called "health food stores," which have spread throughout most cities. Together with the growth in health food outlets has grown the problem facing consumers of determining what is and what is not "health food." There are no official or even traditional definitions of words such as "organic," "natural," or "health" food. The technical definition of "organic" is that it means any compound containing carbon—which includes any kind of plant or animal life. But informal usage has used "organic" to mean the absence of chemical insecticides, fertilizers, and preservatives in food production. It is likely that most people concerned about modern nutrition would accept the following definitions:

Natural foods: those marketed without preservatives or other artificial ingredients.

Organic foods: those foods produced as natural foods, but also excluding the use of chemical pesticides and fertilizers.

Health foods: a very broad term which includes not only natural and organic foods, but also dietetic, vegetarian, and some products containing artificial chemicals.

The Main Conclusions

Those of us who have embraced the truths of the health food movement usually agree on the following:

1. *Many of our commercially produced foods contain harmful chemicals and pesticides that have been added during production.* The use of additives has been increasing dramatically. In many cases it has not been established that these additives are necessary; in other cases, although it has been established that an additive may have some value, it often has not been adequately tested.
2. *Organic fertilizers produce foods that are superior nutritionally to foods grown with chemical fertilizers.* In addition to poisoning our foods, the heavy use of chemical fertilizers has aggravated our ecological problems—for example, the heaviest damage to Lake Erie has been done not by industry, but by chemical fertilizers applied to nearby farmlands and carried by streams and rivers into the lake.
3. *Certain foods have such high nutritional value that they almost act as miracle foods.* Foods such as whole grains, wheat germ, and blackstrap molasses do more than just provide high-quality nutrition. They actually have special health-giving, even curative powers.
4. *Because modern foods are nutritionally deficient, we need to regularly take vitamins.* These should not be vitamins based on chemicals, but natural vitamins—for example, it is better to obtain vitamin C through rose hips than through ascorbic acid pills.
5. *High levels of natural vitamins taken into the body will actually cure a variety of physical problems.* It is well established, for example, that massive, regular doses of vitamin C will both prevent colds and help to cure them if contracted.

Special Health Foods

As I noted in point 3, certain foods have come to be generally recognized by nutritionists as having especially high nutritional or curative powers. Some of the foods recognized by the national health food magazines, lecturers, and authors of health food books are as follows:

1. *Raw foods.* One of the strongest notions held by those of us who have studied and worked in this area is the recognition that raw foods are much more nutritious than are cooked foods. The fact underlying this truth is, of course, that almost all vitamins and minerals are lost in the cooking process. Many people now substitute pure apple juice as a breakfast drink in place of orange or tomato juice, since the former can be obtained without sugar or preservatives added, while the latter is usually processed and full of chemicals.
2. *Wheat bread.* The typical loaf of white bread sold in the supermarket is not only as tasteless as cotton, but it is so full of chemicals and has lost so much of its nutritive value in the manufacturing process that it is nearly useless as a food. We are lucky that it is possible to buy alternative bread made with whole-wheat grains, containing a natural supply of protein, calcium, the B vitamins, and many other nutrients. To make whole-wheat bread even better for us, we can add honey, brown sugar, sea salt, and spring water.
3. *Honey.* One so-called food that no thinking person should ever eat is refined sugar. Not only does it lack nutritional value, it contains

a heavy dose of calories not often needed by those who consume it. On the other hand, honey is not only sweeter than sugar, but it also contains the vitamins removed from processed sugar, and iron, calcium, and many other minerals.

4. *Blackstrap molasses.* Blackstrap molasses, a by-product of sugar refining, is a concentrated food especially high in iron. Many people find its thick texture and pleasant taste a welcome addition to their diet. Health food experts have shown that it cures insomnia, alleviates nervous conditions, restores hair color, and even extends life itself.
5. *Goat's milk.* First of all, goat's milk is inherently a better food than milk from cows. It has more calcium and vitamins, and also has smaller fat globules—which makes it easier to digest. Further, all commercially available cow's milk has been pasteurized and generally homogenized. In the process of doing these things, much of the food value is destroyed. In particular, there is a loss of vitamin C and thiamin.
6. *Granola cereals.* These crunchy, good-to-eat cereals usually have things like wheat germ, oats, sesame seeds, coconut, and brown sugar in them. At least two dozen brands are on the market.
7. *Seeds.* Sesame seeds, pumpkin seeds, and sunflower seeds are very good for you. They are not only very rich in protein, calcium, and the B vitamins, but have strong sexual stimulation powers.
8. *Wheat germ.* I recommend adding wheat germ to lower-quality cereals and as a general additive in cooking and baking. It is a good source of natural vitamin E and contains many amino acids.
9. *Lecithin.* Lecithin is a substance that occurs naturally in the body, and that acts to break up cholesterol in the blood so that it doesn't build up on artery walls and cause high blood pressure. By adding lecithin to the diet, the natural substance within the body can be augmented and assisted. Lecithin is available in an oil form combined with fish oil, or in tablet form.
10. *Sprouts.* Sprouts are a kind of "superfood," as they contain very high amounts of vitamins and protein. They can be easily and cheaply grown at home in simple containers.
11. *Organic meats.* Most of the commercially grown meat available in the supermarkets contains hormones and antibiotics. I recommend "organic" chickens and meat, even though the prices are usually much higher.

As a consequence of the continued acceptance of the truths developed within the health food movement, it is now possible to purchase organic and natural foods in department stores and in special sections of supermarkets—as well as in specialty stores. Health food sales are up dramatically over the past few years, and many new converts appear each year to the cause of healthy food, healthy bodies, and richer, more useful lives.

ABOUT PESTICIDES

United Fresh Fruit and Vegetable Association, "About Pesticides," *Nutrition Notes,* Number 61 (Washington, D.C.: March 1974).

Unless people learn to do without eating, they must contest their right to live with bugs, bacteria, fungi, hematodes, molluscs, weeds, rodents, viruses and other organisms that are pests under some circumstances. Some of them reduce both the quantity and quality of available food, while at the same time human population increases and requires more food. Today, even with extensive pest control programs, U.S. agriculture loses about a third of its potential crop production to pests. Without modern pest control, losses would at least double, according to expert estimates.[1]

Some people advocate banning all agricultural chemicals. Secretary of Agriculture Earl L. Butz said that if agricultural chemicals were banned, he would not like to be the one to decide which 50 million of our people should starve. Probably his 50 million estimate is low.

The fact is it is practically impossible to grow profitable commercial crops of fruits and vegetables, especially those of high quality, without application of pesticides. One reason is that these crops are much more vulnerable to pests than they were 100 years ago. This increased vulnerability is built in to the way fruits and vegetables must be grown now. To satisfy our nation's needs, they must be grown on relatively large tracts of a single crop for mechanized operations and in specialized areas. This concentration of a kind of food a particular pest requires means that the pest can multiply enormously in a short time if unchecked. Not only are the tracts large and devoted to one type of plant, but the plants are closer together than in former years. This intensive planting is to provide large yields per acre by use of more fertilizer and water. This kind of agriculture also makes things delightfully easy for the bugs and other assorted pests. Beyond that, the same genetic varieties are used year after year because of their proven value, and also favor pests.[2,3]

People not only need enough fruits and vegetables and other crops but they also demand and are entitled to good quality. They are not satisfied with scrubby, misshapen, poorly colored, insect- and disease-damaged produce. It takes pesticides not only to grow fruits and vegetables but to grow them with the sort of quality that makes them welcome to the tables of our people.

Some of those who constantly attack use of pesticides insist it is possible to meet pest attacks by means of biological controls, such as sex attractants, insect or viral predators and the like. It is true that such controls are desirable and should be used wherever practical. However, biological controls that are effective enough to ensure commercial crops are rare. Pesticides must be used now and in the foreseeable future, under strict governmental regulations.

FOOD PRODUCTION AND ACCEPTANCE: CONSUMER ATTITUDES AND PROBLEMS[4]

Thomas A. Jukes, "Food Production and Acceptance: Consumer Attitudes and Problems," *Feedstuffs* (Minneapolis, Minn.: Miller Publishing Company, December 23, 1974), p. 18.

In 1972 and 1973, the Food and Drug Administration introduced a number of new regulations—which are not enforced yet, but were put on the books for subsequent enforcement—about nutrition labeling. About the Recommended Daily Allowances (RDA) and about the limits that would be permitted in over-the-counter products on vitamin content, particularly with regard to vitamins A and D. The health food industry felt threatened by this and immediately started to take measures against it. For example, there was a rally at the Cow Palace in San Francisco last winter and various performers on the stage were health food addicts, whipping up enthusiasm leading cheers against the FDA, shouting and saying that "the FDA is going to take the vitamins away from you." A great misrepresentation went on.

Then there was introduction of the Hosmer Bill in the House which specifically stripped the FDA of its authority to regulate the levels of vitamins that were sold over-the-counter in food supplements. There was bipartisan support for this in the House. Letter writing was started and great pressure was brought on congressmen.

Then a corresponding bill, S2801, was introduced in the Senate by Senator William Proxmire. Write-in campaigns were conducted by the National Health Federation and the Rodale Press. There was a form letter in *Prevention* magazine last May for readers to sign and send to their senator, urging passage of the Proxmire bill. (*Prevention* magazine has a circulation of 1,375,000. It should be read by all nutritionists. Currently, it is much more important to read *Prevention* magazine than to read the *Journal of Nutrition*.)

On September 23, the Senate passed the Proxmire bill by a vote of 78 to 10, in spite of an appeal by Senator Edward Kennedy from the floor to defeat it and in spite of impressive statements on behalf of science during the Senate hearings. A joint committee was set up between the House and Senate to reconcile the two bills so that the entire measure could be made into law....

Support for the Proxmire bill is based on misrepresentation. Its only effect on vitamin sales is to limit the size of the dose per pill. Vitamin enthusiasts can continue to pop vitamin pills all day long even if the bill is defeated as it should be.

Against the bill were not only the Nutrition Consortium group, but also the American Medical Association, Consumers Union, the American Association of Retired Persons, the American Pharmaceutical Manufacturers Association, and Ralph Nader's group. But nevertheless, it passed in the initial votes. This is where nutrition stands in the halls of Congress today.

Attitudes Toward Nutrition

To understand why such legislation is accepted we have to realize that there has been a great change in current attitudes toward nutrition....I list 15 points I think are all contributing toward the public rejection of scientific nutrition.

1. Rejection of establishment: "Back to Nature"
2. *Silent Spring*
3. Sensitive analytical methods
4. Delaney Clause
5. Cyclamates, aminotriazole, DES, DDT, dieldrin
6. Mass media stories on "poisons in your food"
7. Names of additives on labels
8. Environmentalism
9. Misinformation by scientists and charlatans
10. Growth of anti-intellectualism and "anti-science"
11. Propaganda by "organic" and "health" food industries
12. Urbanization of population and alienation from agriculture
13. Mistrust of private enterprise and "agribusiness"
14. Lack of understanding of toxicology
15. Replacement of scientific debate by advocacy proceedings

Organic Food Movement

Most of us haven't paid much attention to the promoters of the organic food movement. But we're going to have to pay a lot more attention to them, to their ideas and their prejudices because they are having an increased impact on legislation.

First, they are very well off for money. As Exhibit 41-1 shows, the cost of organic foods is high. These figures are based on a survey carried out by the U.S. Department of Agriculture in Washington, D.C., in 1972. USDA priced standard foods in the regular department and the organic department of a supermarket, in a health food store, and a natural food store.

What is fascinating about this is that the supermarket had its own organic department charging about twice as much as the regular price for the food. It seemed to be quite ingenious in its pricing: notice that the pricing of organic food in the supermarket was intermediate between the health food store and the natural food store, so it wasn't rocking the boat. What would an alert supermarket manager do if he ran out of organic chickens? I leave that to your imagination. I think that he would be perfectly justified in going over and taking some of the regular chickens and carrying them across the store. Because, confidentially, there is no difference between an organic chicken and a regular chicken.

EXHIBIT 41-1 Cost of Organic Food, USDA Survey

	Price			
	Supermarket			
Food	*Regular department*	*Organic department*	*Health food store*	*Natural food store*
Canned apple juice, ($/qt)	0.29	0.65	0.75	0.51
Dried peaches ($/lb)	0.73	1.32	1.63	1.55
Corn meal ($/lb)	0.14	0.30	0.44	0.21
Honey ($/lb)	0.55	0.79	1.05	0.50
Fryer chickens ($/lb)	0.33	0.59	0.75	—
Home apples ($/lb)	0.20	0.30	—	0.20
Cucumbers ($/lb)	0.19	0.79	0.69	0.57
Total of 5 items listed by all 4 outlets ($)	1.90	3.85	4.61	3.34
Rip-off of regular price		103%	143%	76%
Market basket of 29 standard foods ($)	11.00	20.30	21.90	17.80
Rip-off		85%	99%	62%

Exhibit 41-2 extends this topic to a survey that was made by the New York State Department of Agriculture. This was reported at the public hearings in the matter of Organic Foods on December 1, 1972, before Louis J. Lefkowitz, attorney general of the state of New York. The representatives of the New York Department of Agriculture presented their findings and they also responded to examination by the Attorney General. For example, he asked one of these inspectors:

"Did you come upon a store that was selling fish?"

"Yes."

"What was the price of that fish, compared to ordinary fish?"

"The organic flounder ranged in price from $1.88 to $1.99 a pound [these are 1972 figures]; in contrast, the regular supermarket was $1.25 to $1.78."

"Did the man selling the fish tell you why it was organic?"

"Yes. He claimed that it was caught in the pollution-free, mineral-rich Atlantic Ocean."

"Did he have a sign to that effect?"

EXHIBIT 41-2 New York Survey of Organic Foods

Organic food	*Label*	*Laboratory findings*	*Higher cost of organic food (%)*
Carrots	Organic carrots	0.02 ppm DDE	60
Tea	100% natural orange flavor tea	2.98 ppm DDT, 2.02 ppm lindane, 0.17 ppm dieldrin	167
Raisins	Organic raisins	0.16 ppm ethylene	121
Dried prunes	Organic prunes	0.5 ppm ketones, 0.04 ppm DDT, 0.02 ppm methoxychlor	43
Chow chow (relish)	Organic chow	0.02 ppm TDE	256
Sesame candy	An organic chew	0.03 ppm DDT, 0.01 ppm DDE	76
Beets	Organic beets	0.03 ppm DDT, 0.01 ppm DDE	56
Fruit cereal	Natural organic	0.21 ppm malathion	

"Yes, he had a sign. I took a picture of that sign after interviewing that gentleman in the store."

The report stated that 30 percent of the organic foods contained pesticide residues, and about 25 percent of the supermarket foods contained pesticide residues. The supermarket foods were not advertised as not containing pesticides. The supermarket foods were complying with the law. They contained pesticide residues that were within the limits of tolerance.

The organic foods were advertised as being raised in pesticide-free soils, etc. The only one that was a little bit high was the 100 percent natural orange flavor tea that was pretty high in chlorinated hydrocarbons, but still within tolerance levels. The other pesticide residues were present in insignificant quantities. The cost of the organic foods ranged from 43 percent to 266 percent more than the regular food. One product that was interesting was pickled beets. They were advertised as not containing any acid.

What is an "organic" food? We are always trying to get an exact definition of this. One was elicited during these hearings from Mr. Robert Rodale who heads *Prevention* magazine. Mr. Rodale defined organic foods as follows:

Organically grown food is food grown without pesticides; grown without artificial fertilizers; grown in soil whose humus content is increased by the additions of organic matter; grown in soil whose mineral content is increased with applications of natural mineral fertilizers; has not been treated with preservatives, hormones, antibiotics, etc.

Asked what his qualifications were in nutrition, he said that he was a nutrition journalist and that he had majored in journalism. He was then asked why he was challenging the trained people in nutrition, and he said: "They have had millions of dollars fed into their laboratories by food companies with a vested interest in this kind of food."

...The *Prevention* system for better health is described by the Rodale Press, and reflects the psychology of Mr. J. J. Rodale, who invented the word "organic" as referred to in organic gardening or organic farming. Here are some of the ideas that he has set forth in the summary of the *Prevention* system for better health:

1. *Impossible* to get all the vitamins and minerals from food.
2. *Bone meal* stopped tooth decay overnight, also gets rid of canker sores within 48 hours.
3. *Vitamin C* protects against bacterial and virus infections, detoxifies cadmium and nitrite, etc.
4. *Vitamin E* in high-dosage overruns physiological dam and "helps" in arteriosclerosis, ulcers, etc.
5. *Zinc* in pumpkin seeds protects male prostate gland against enlargement and incompetence.
6. *Bioflavonoids* may play a powerful role in preventing clots and embolisms.
7. *Sunflower seeds* beneficial to eyesight, complexion, etc.
8. *Garlic* should be eaten every day. Prevents polio, cures intestinal infections, including amebic dysentery.
9. *Herb teas* vs. asthma, nervous headache, arthritis, etc.

You will see the reflection of these prejudices quite wide-spread throughout many publications today....

No one objects to "health food" fans eating dried seaweed and drinking cider vinegar. But when this movement seeks to place restrictive legislation on the regulation of quackery, it is time to write your congressmen.

The "health" food and "organic" food industries encourage their customers to medicate themselves with various nutritional remedies rather than to seek competent medical advice for degenerative diseases. Officials of the National Health Federation strongly oppose any legislation limiting the advertising of health food supplements. They were afraid that wild claims for "health foods" will be restricted.

WHEN IT COMES TO FOOD, THE PUBLIC IS MYTH-TAKEN

"When It Comes to Food, the Public Is Myth-Taken," *University of Utah Review* (Salt Lake City), April 7, 1978.

If spinach were invented today, the United States government would have to ban it.

The same goes for potatoes, lima beans, shrimp, oysters, almonds and rhubarb, says a University medicinal chemist.

"Because of the levels of cyanide, solanine, oxalic acid and other toxins in these foods, they'd never receive Food and Drug Administration approval if they were synthetic," says Dr. David Roll, professor and associate dean for academic affairs in the College of Pharmacy.

"There is a dangerous myth widely believed in America today that natural is good and synthetic is bad," Roll says. "I feel safer about what is in processed food than what is in many so-called 'natural' foods because food additives have been subject to much more thorough testing and analysis."

Roll is an adviser to the American Council on Science and Health, a consortium of American scientists. The council was formed recently to promote a rational and balanced approach to the evaluation and regulation of chemicals in our food and environment.

Roll says the widespread paranoia about chemicals in the environment during the past decade has led to irrational myths about food.

"People began to notice that chemicals were being added to food and forgot that food is made of chemicals. A potato contains 150 different chemicals. We are plagued by irrational and meaningless words such as 'natural,' 'organic' and 'health foods.'

" 'Natural' has become a big promotional word. 'Natural' doesn't mean much in terms of quality or safety. Botulism toxin is natural but it is one of the most toxic substances known. Food additives (nitrates, nitrites) are necessary in some foods to prevent botulism. It is a myth that only substances added to foods are poisonous," Roll says.

"Health food" is another meaningless term, he says. "Why is a cucumber or spinach health food and a burrito or a hamburger not? Anyone who ate an exclusive diet of one or the other would probably end up with serious nutritional deficiencies."

Roll says a peculiar form of ignorance is that of people who say they "won't eat anything I can't pronounce." Such people would probably avoid food with this label:

> Contents: Water, triglycerides of stearic, palmitic, oleic and linoleic acids; myosin and actin; glycogen, collagen, lecithin, cholesterol, dipotassium phosphate, myoglobin and urea. Warning: May contain steroid hormones of natural origin.

That, he says, is beef steak.

Milk is made of water, twelve fats, six proteins, lactose, nine salts, seven acids, three pigments, seven enzymes, eighteen vitamins, six miscellaneous compounds and three gasses that would take a page to list by their chemical names.

Another myth is that manure is better fertilizer and produces plants and vegetables richer in nutrients than synthetic chemical fertilizers. "A plant's roots don't absorb the nitrogen in manure," he notes. "Only when it has been broken down by bacteria in the soil into nitrite can it be taken up by the roots, and it is then indistinguishable from the nitrate in synthetic fertilizers.

"It is a myth that plants grown on poor or worn-out soil have fewer nutrients. With the exception of certain trace minerals, the nutrient content of plants is genetically determined. It is the same in any soil. The quality of the soil affects only the yield per acre, or whether the plant will grow at all."

Roll notes that some scientists believe the advent of processed foods with antioxidant preservatives has actually been responsible for the decline in the nation's stomach cancer rate. One theory is that these antioxidant additives protect the stomach from the natural cancer-causing agents in food.

Roll also says there is no reason to completely avoid "refined" sugar and flour products. "There is no evidence that eating brown bread is more healthful than eating white bread. Some of the nutrients that are lost in the refining process are not even necessary, and others can easily be made up by other foods we eat.

"In fact, there are some substances in whole grains that actually prevent the absorption of some nutrients. Phytic acid, for example, interferes with the absorption of calcium, iron and other trace minerals.

"Contrary to popular belief, honey is no more nutritious than sugar," Roll says. "But I am not going to stop eating honey even though it may contain small quantities of a cancer-causing agent derived from pollen.

"A variety of food is probably the best way to insure that you get all the nutrients we know about and any we don't know of. By that I don't mean 42 varieties of crackers and pastries.

"We have the best, most nutritious food supply of any country in the world, but people have to use common sense to benefit from it," Roll adds.

ASSIGNMENT QUESTIONS

1. Define "organic," "natural," and "health" foods.
2. Summarize the arguments of those who advocate "organic" or "natural" foods.
3. Outline arguments by the scientific establishment critical of the health food industry.
4. Which side has the better argument? Why? Be specific.
5. What should be done about health or natural food stores that cheat the public? Who should do it? FDA? FTC? State agencies?
6. Should people be allowed to take as many vitamins as they want without government interference? What are the two sides of the argument?

NOTES

1. "Pesticides—The Issues," *The Alternatives* (Berkeley: University of California, February 1972).
2. *A National Plant Disease Detection and Information Program,* American Phytopathological Society, 1973.
3. *Agricultural Chemicals, What They Are/How They Are Used,* Manufacturing Chemists Association.
4. The accompanying comments on organic food and environmentalism in agriculture are adopted from a speech given by Thomas H. Jukes at the 1974 Texas Nutrition Conference. Dr. Jukes holds a B.S. in agriculture and a Ph.D. in medical biochemistry. His early work was involved with riboflavin, nicotine, vitamin B_6, pan-

tothenic acid, and chlorine; from 1942 until the early 1960s he was with Lederle Laboratories, where he worked on antibiotics, vitamins, cancer chemotherapy, and nutrition. In 1963 he moved to the Space Sciences Laboratory, University of California, Berkeley, as a professor in residence, medical physics.

AFRICAN DESIGNS
FROM TRADITIONAL SOURCES

AFRICAN DESIGNS
FROM TRADITIONAL SOURCES

by Geoffrey Williams

Dover Publications, Inc., New York

Published in Canada by General Publishing Company, Ltd., 30 Lesmill Road, Don Mills, Toronto, Ontario.
Published in the United Kingdom by Constable and Company, Ltd.

African Designs from Traditional Sources is a new work, first published by Dover Publications, Inc., in 1971.

DOVER *Pictorial Archive* SERIES

International Standard Book Number: 0-486-22752-9
Library of Congress Catalog Card Number: 76-162027

Manufactured in the United States of America
Dover Publications, Inc.
31 East 2nd Street
Mineola, N.Y. 11501

Preface

The aim of this book is to present a sampling of the best in African art and design on the level at which it is finally judged—its own vigor and life. Such a work can never fully document all that the Dark Continent has produced, but it is hoped that a glimpse will be had, and a record will be maintained, of an art that can be both frighteningly barbaric and eloquently beautiful.

After suffering the successive rape by slave traders and empire builders, traditional African culture and the art it produced is fast disappearing through the force of economic necessity. It is hoped, therefore, that this book will produce an awareness, and stimulate a reaction, that will give rise to a new African art based on its own precedent.

The original plates for this book have in the main been produced by linocut prints, this being the most obvious technique for reproducing what is largely a carved art form. For myself, to retrace the exact lines of the original artist working in wood or stone has provided a new dimension of understanding. Pen and ink drawings have been used for the remainder of the plates. The reader seeking the three-dimensional view of African art is referred to the all too few books on the subject, many of which are contained in my own list of references.

I am indebted to all those people who have given encouragement and comment on the work, in particular to Wopko Jensma, who was so involved in the original idea, and to my wife for her unwavering help and inspiration.

GEOFFREY WILLIAMS

April 1971

A map of Africa showing the tribes and sites mentioned in this book will be found following the plates.

List of Illustrations

SYMBOLIC AND
SIMPLE GEOMETRIC MOTIFS

REPETITIVE DESIGNS AND TEXTURAL PATTERNS

ANIMALS
AND MYTHICAL FIGURES

HUMAN BEINGS

MASKS

ARTIFACTS AND OBJECTS
WITH FIGURAL COMPONENTS

ABSTRACT AND
COMPLEX GEOMETRIC MOTIFS

Source References

MUSEUMS
AND COLLECTIONS

1. Africana Museum, Johannesburg (Republic of South Africa).
2. Mr. and Mrs. Allen Alperton, New York.
3. American Museum of Natural History, New York.
4. Mr. and Mrs. Ernst Anspach, New York.
5. Emil J. Arnold, New York.
6. Art Institute of Chicago.
7. Mr. and Mrs. William R. Bascom, Berkeley, California.
8. British Museum, London.
9. Brooklyn Museum.
10. Buffalo Museum of Science.
11. Louis Carré Gallery, Paris.
12. W. Claes, Antwerp.
13. Mr. and Mrs. A. Cohen, New York.
14. Commercial Museum, Philadelphia.
15. Coray Collection, Agnuzzo, Lugano (Switzerland).
16. Former G. Dehondt Collection, Brussels.
17. Eliot Elisofon, New York.
18. Field Museum of Natural History, Chicago.
19. Capt. A. W. Fuller.
20. Mrs. Edith Gregor Halpert, New York.
21. Hamburgisches Museum für Völkerkunde und Vorgeschichte, Hamburg.

22. Mr. and Mrs. Gaston de Havenon, New York.
23. André Held, Ecublen (Switzerland).
24. Ipswich Museum.
25. Jucker Collection, Milan.
26. Henri Kamer, Milan.
27. Pierre Langlois, Paris.
28. Former H. Lavachery Collection, Brussels.
29. H. V. Leemputen, Antwerp.
30. Manchester University Museum.
31. Former Henri Matisse Collection, Nice.
32. Mrs. Katherine W. Merkel, Gates Mills, Ohio.
33. William Moore, Los Angeles.
34. Dr. and Mrs. Muensterberger, New York.
35. Mr. Joseph Muller.
36. Musée des Arts Africains et Océaniens, Paris.
37. Musée de l'Homme, Paris.
38. Musée Royal de l'Afrique Centrale, Tervuren (Belgium).
39. Muséum d'Histoire Naturelle, La Rochelle.
40. Museum für Völkerkunde, Berlin.
41. Museum für Völkerkunde, Frankfurt.
42. Museum für Völkerkunde, Leipzig.
43. Museum of African Art, Washington.
44. Museum of Primitive Art, New York.
45. Natal Museum, Pietermaritzburg (Republic of South Africa).
46. National Museum, Gaberones (Botswana).
47. Newbury Museum (England).
48. Maurice Nicard, Paris.
49. Nigerian Museum, Lagos (Nigeria).
50. Peabody Museum, Harvard University, Cambridge, Mass.
51. Peace Memorial Museum, Zanzibar (Tanzania).
52. Pitt Rivers Museum, Oxford.
53. Margaret Webster Plass, Philadelphia.
54. Prempeh II Jubilee Museum, Kumasi (Ghana).

55. Mr. and Mrs. Paul Rabut, Westport, Conn.
56. Charles Ratton, Paris.
57. Rijksmuseum voor Volkenkunde, Leiden (Netherlands).
58. Mr. and Mrs. Harold Rome, New York.
59. Royal Ontario Museum of Archaeology, Toronto.
60. Sammlung für Völkerkunde der Universität Zürich, Zurich (Switzerland).
61. Schomberg Collection, New York.
62. Mr. and Mrs. Clark Stillman, New York.
63. James Johnson Sweeney, New York.
64. Mrs. Edgar D. Taylor, Los Angeles.
65. Paul Tishman, New York.
66. Margaret Trowell, London.
67. Former Tristan Tzara Collection, Paris.
68. Uganda Museum, Kampala.
69. Université de Gand, Ghent (Belgium).
70. University Museum of Archaeology and Ethnology, Cambridge (England).
71. University of Pennsylvania Museum, Philadelphia.
72. G. Van de Kerken, Brussels.
73. Alex Van Opstall, St. Genèse, Rhodes.
74. Rene Van der Straete, Brussels.
75. Pierre Vérité, Paris.

PUBLICATIONS

76. Breuil, Abbé Henri, *The Tsibab Ravine,* The Trianon Press, London, for the Calouste Gulbenkian Foundation, 1959.
77. Duerden, Denis, *African Art,* in the series *The Colour Library of Art,* Paul Hamlyn, London, 1968 (in U.S.: International Publications Service, N.Y.).
78. Goodall, Elizabeth; G. K. Cooke & Desmond Clarke, *Prehistoric Rock Art of the Federation of Rhodesia and Nyasaland,* National Publications Trust of Rhodesia and Nyasaland, Rhodesia, 1959 (in U.S.: Humanities Press, N.Y.).
79. Junod, Henri P.; Walter W. Battiss, G. H. Franz & J. W. Grossert, *The Art of Africa,* Shuter & Shooter, Pietermaritzburg, 1958.
80. Kyerematen, A. A. Y., *Panoply of Ghana,* Longmans Green & Co., London, 1964.

81. Leiris, Michel, & Jacqueline Delange, *African Art,* in the series *The Arts of Mankind,* Thames and Hudson, London, 1967.

82. Leuzinger, Elsy, *Africa: the Art of the Negro Peoples,* Methuen, 1960 (in U.S.: *Art of Africa,* in the series *Art of the World,* Crown, N.Y.).

83. Olbrechts, Frans M., *Les arts plastiques du Congo Belge,* Editions Erasme, Brussels, 1959.

84. Olderogge, Dmitry, & Werner Forman, *Art of Africa: Negro Art,* Paul Hamlyn, London, 1969 (in U.S.: International Publications Service, N.Y.).

85. Paulme, Denise, *African Sculpture,* Elek Books, London, 1962.

86. Rachewiltz, Boris de, *Introduction to African Art,* John Murray, London, 1966 (in U.S.: New American Library, N.Y.).

87. Segy, Ladislas, *African Sculpture,* Dover, N.Y., 1958.

88. Slack, Lina M., *Rock Engravings from Driekops Eiland,* Centaur Press, Fontwell (Sussex), 1962 (in U.S.: Albert Saifer, West Orange, N.J.).

89. Trowell, Margaret, *African Design,* Faber and Faber, London, 1960 (in U.S.: revised ed., Praeger, N.Y., 1965).

90. Trowell, Margaret, & K. P. Wachsmann, *Tribal Crafts of Uganda,* Oxford University Press, London, 1953.

91. Tyrrell, Barbara, *Tribal Peoples of Southern Africa,* Tri-Ocean, San Francisco, 1968.

The following books are valuable items of reference:

Elisofon, Eliot, *The Sculpture of Africa,* Thames and Hudson, London, 1958.

Fagg, William, *Tribes and Forms in African Art,* Methuen, London, 1965 (in U.S.: Tudor, N.Y.).

Meauzé, Pierre, *African Art: Sculpture,* Weidenfeld and Nicolson, London, 1968 (in U.S.: World, N.Y.).

Plass, Margaret Webster, *African Miniatures: the Goldweights of the Ashanti,* Lund Humphries, London, 1967 (in U.S.: Praeger, N.Y.).

Robbins, Warren, *African Art in American Collections,* Praeger, N.Y., 1966.

Sweeney, James Johnson, *African Negro Art,* W. W. Norton & Co., N.Y., for The Museum of Modern Art, 1935 (reprinted by Arno, N.Y.).

Wingert, Paul S., *The Sculpture of Negro Africa,* Columbia University Press, N.Y., 1950.

Symbolic and Simple Geometric Motifs

The numbers in parentheses throughout the plate section refer to the list of Source References on pages xix–xxii. The designs on the plates have been rendered either from objects or illustrations of objects in the corresponding museums and collections (sources 1–75) or from illustrations in the corresponding publications (sources 76–91).

Top: Carved motif on Pende wooden sculpture, Congo-Kinshasa. (43)

Bottom: Two Bushman rock engravings from Driekops Eiland, Republic of South Africa. (88)

1

Three Bushman rock engravings from lower Riet River, Cape Province, Republic of South Africa. (79)

Three Bushman rock engravings from lower Riet River, Cape Province, Republic of South Africa. (79)

3

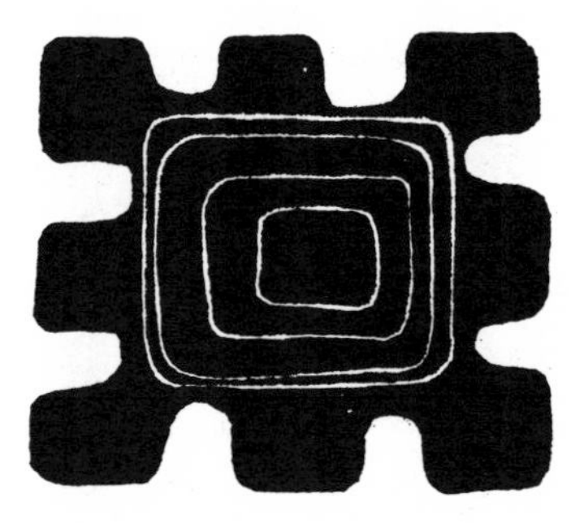

Top: Ashanti bronze gold weight, Ghana. (53)
Middle: Mud wall relief at Bida, Nigeria. (89)
Bottom: Carved wood motif on Tswana spoon handle, Botswana. (46)

Three mud wall reliefs at Bida, Nigeria. (89)

Top: Sundi woven mat design from the lower Congo area. (38)
Bottom: Two woven cloth motifs from the upper Senegal area. (8)

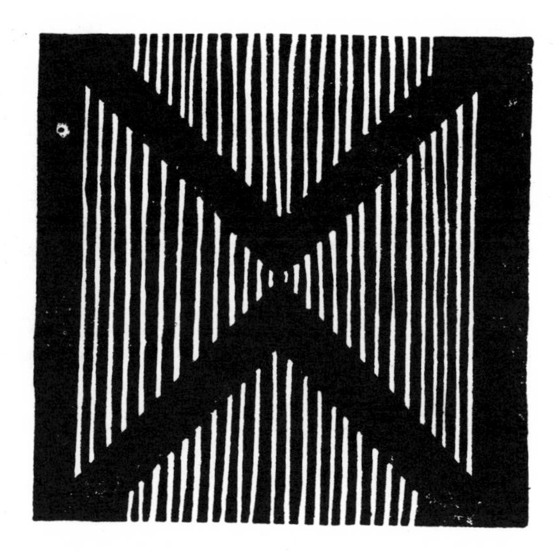

Top: Carved wood motif on Yaka comb, Congo-Kinshasa. (29)
Middle: Bangba painted wall motif, Congo-Kinshasa. (89)
Bottom: Tswana beadwork belt motif, Botswana. (46)

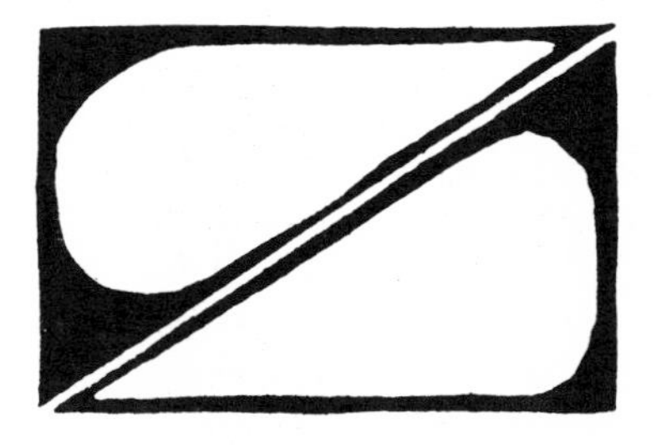

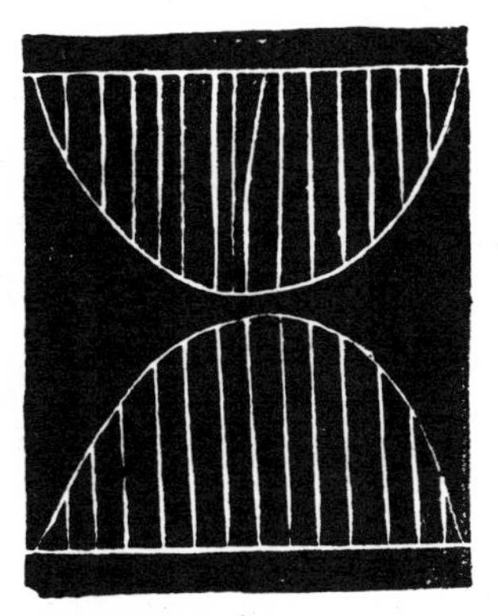

Top left: Ibo painted wall motif, Nigeria. (89)
Top right: Carved wood motif on Yaka comb, Congo-Kinshasa. (83)
Bottom: Carved wood motif on Kuba comb, Congo-Kinshasa. (83)

Top: Carved wood motif on Kuba urn base, Congo-Kinshasa. (72)
Middle and bottom: Mud wall relief designs at Kano, northern Nigeria. (89)

Top: Carved wood motif on Djokwe comb, Congo-Kinshasa. (59)
Middle: Ashanti bronze gold weight, Ghana. (53)
Bottom: Carved wood motif on Lunda comb, Congo-Kinshasa. (28)

Top: Carved design on Basa wooden figure, Liberia. (50)
Bottom left: Mbun woven raffia design, Congo-Kinshasa. (8)
Bottom right: Carved motif on Bembe wooden mask from the lower Congo area. (81)

Top: Mbun woven raffia design, Congo-Kinshasa. (8)
Middle: Segment of Yoruba carved calabash bowl, Nigeria. (8)
Bottom: Yombe torso cicatrization, Congo-Kinshasa. (81)

Left: Design on coiled basket from Barotseland, Zambia. (8)
Right: Mud wall relief at Bida, Nigeria. (89)

Top: Mud wall relief at Kano, northern Nigeria. (89)
Bottom: Bushongo raffia velour design, Congo-Kinshasa. (65)

Top: Zulu woven mat, Republic of South Africa. (79)
Bottom: Design from plaited prayer mat from Zanzibar, Tanzania. (51)

Top: Woven cloth design from the upper Senegal area. (8)
Bottom: Design from plaited prayer mat from Zanzibar, Tanzania. (51)

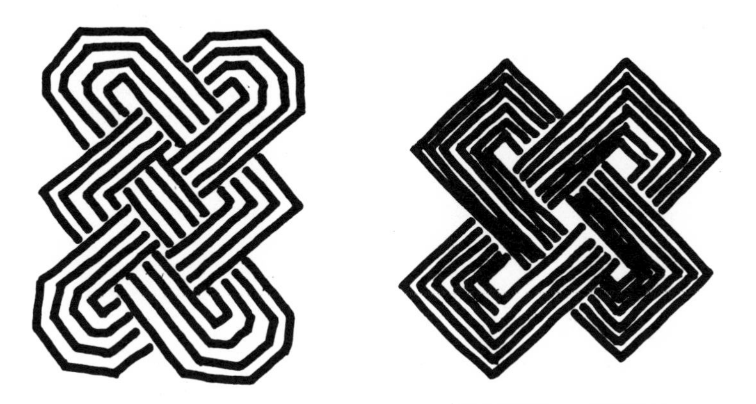

Top: Ivory carving on Yoruba sword handle, Nigeria. (8)
Bottom left: Bushongo embroidered raffia motif, Congo-Kinshasa. (8)
Bottom right: Carved motif on Yoruba wooden door, Nigeria. (37)

Three symbolic mud wall reliefs from Uganda, the upper two representing the disposition of opposing armies in war. (90)

Top: Carved relief on side of Venda wooden drum, Republic of South Africa/ Rhodesia. (1)

Middle and bottom: Carved motifs on Bemba wooden sculpture, Congo-Kinshasa. (42)

Top left: Benin chased bronze plaque motif, Nigeria. (8)
Top right: Mud wall relief at Kano, northern Nigeria. (89)
Bottom left and right: Hausa stucco relief designs, Nigeria/Niger. (81)

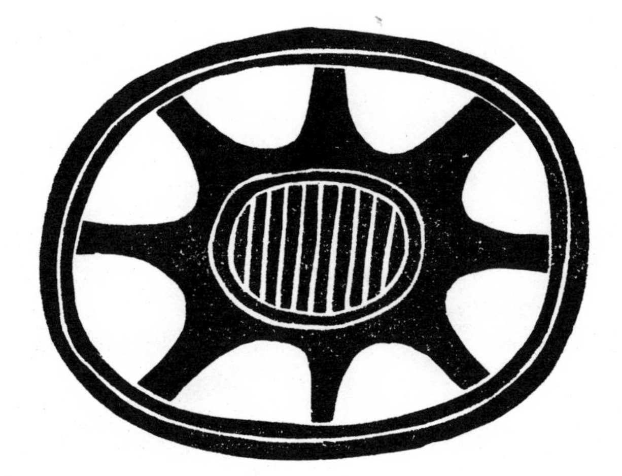

Top: Carved motif on Kuba wooden sculpture, Congo-Kinshasa. (73)
Middle: Senufo earth-dyed cloth, Ivory Coast/Mali/Upper Volta. (37)
Bottom: Carved motif from Bushongo wooden vessel, Congo-Kinshasa. (38)

Two Ashanti cast bronze gold weights, Ghana. (45)

Three Ashanti cast bronze gold weights, Ghana. (top and bottom, 54; middle, 8)

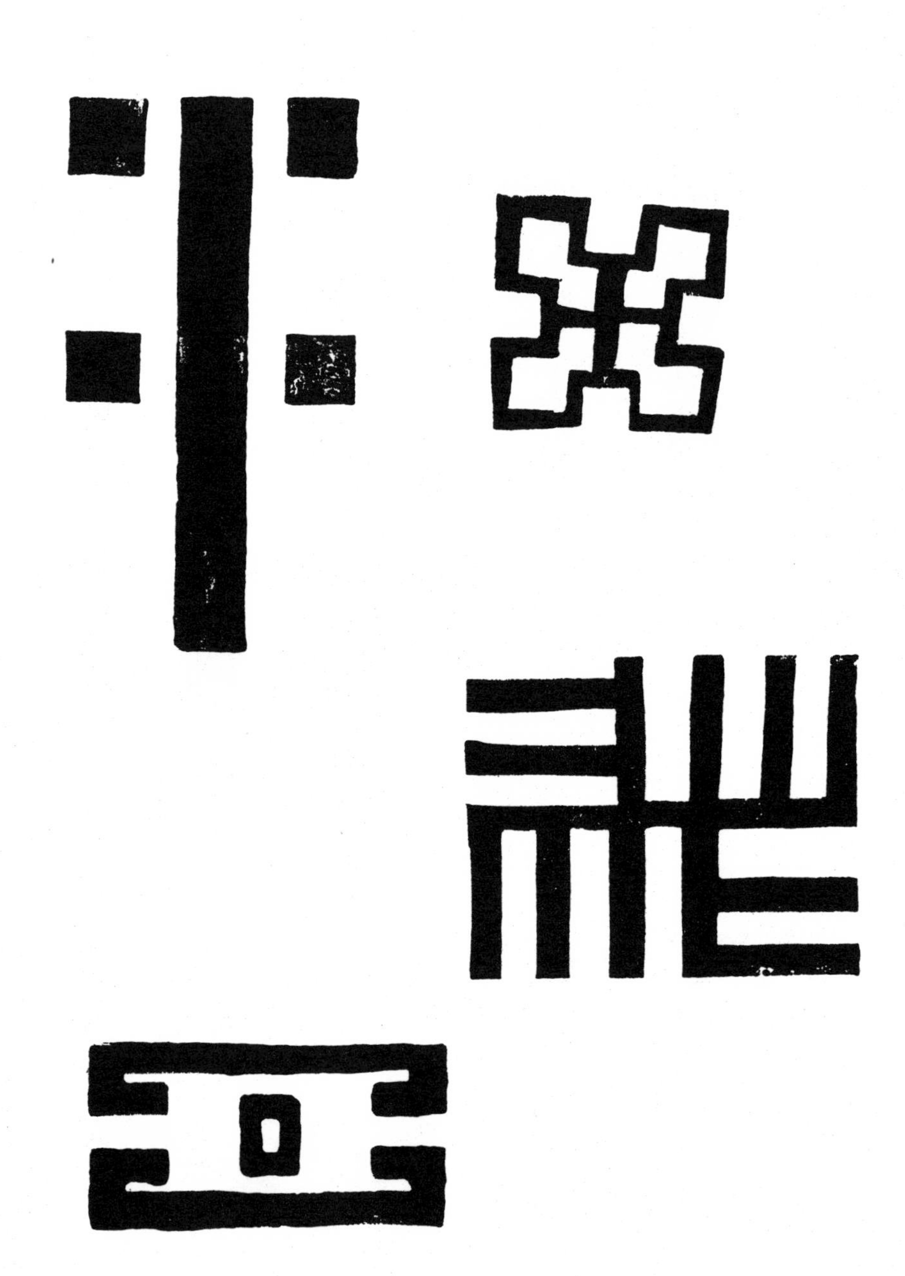

Top left: Motif on Tsonga bead headdress, Republic of South Africa/Mozambique/Swaziland. (1)

Top right: Ashanti "Adinkira" printing stamp, Ghana. (8)

Middle: Ashanti cast bronze gold weight, Ghana. (80)

Bottom: Motif on Ndebele bead bracelet, Republic of South Africa. (91)

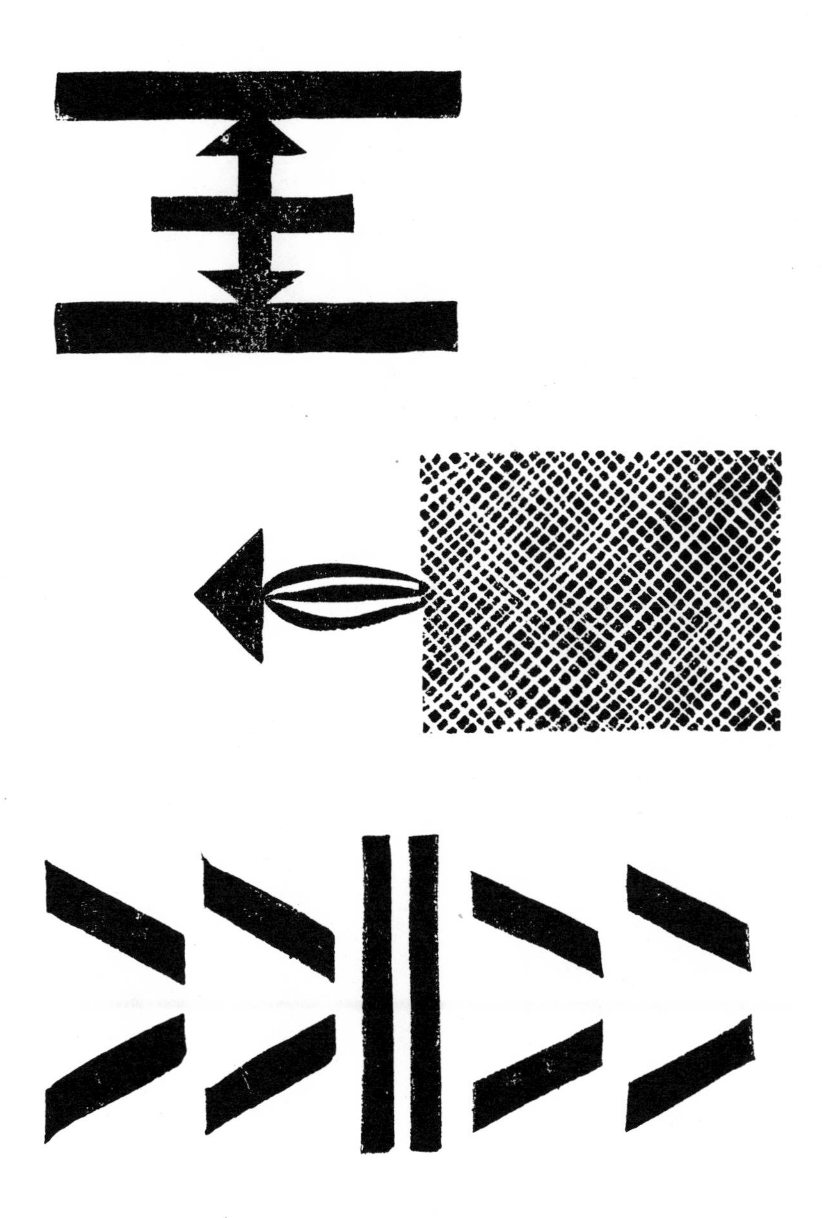

Top: Woven cloth motif (from southern Nigeria?). (8)
Middle: Carved wood motif on Yoruba door, Nigeria. (37)
Bottom: Zulu bead bracelet design, Republic of South Africa. (1)

Top: Two Ashanti "Adinkira" printing stamps, Ghana. (8)
Bottom left: Motif on Benin cast bronze plaque, Nigeria. (40)
Bottom right: Motif on Benin hide appliqué fan, Nigeria. (8)

Top left: Segment of carved calabash bowl, southern Nigeria. (30)

Top right: Carved motif on Senufo wooden door, Ivory Coast/Mali/Upper Volta. (71)

Bottom: Fan in hide appliqué, southern Nigeria. (8)

Top: Ashanti cast bronze gold weight, Ghana. (56)
Middle and bottom: Two painted cloth designs from Ghana. (8)

Repetitive Designs and Textural Patterns

Two Ashanti "Adinkira" printing stamps, Ghana. (top, 8; bottom, 54)

Two Ashanti "Adinkira" printing stamp patterns, Ghana. (8)

Two Ashanti "Adinkira" printing stamp patterns, Ghana. (8)

Top: Scraped calabash design on bowl, Dahomey. (37)

Middle: Repetitive design on sewn grass mat of the Hima (the Hamitic pastoral people), Uganda. (68)

Bottom: Painted design on cow dung pot, Kordofan area, Sudan. (8)

Top left: Incised pattern on wooden milk pot from French Somaliland. (37)
Top right: Repetitive design on inside face of Tswana woven basket, Botswana. (46)
Bottom: Carved pattern on Bushongo wooden vessel, Congo-Kinshasa. (38)

Top: Carved pattern on base of Kuba wooden cup, Congo-Kinshasa. (81)
Middle: Pattern on Bushongo sewn mat, Congo-Kinshasa. (38)
Bottom: Carved pattern on Djokwe wooden "bush piano," Congo-Kinshasa. (41)

Top: Benin carved wood pattern, Nigeria. (71)
Bottom: Ibo painted wall pattern, Nigeria. (89)

Top: Bambara dyed cloth pattern, Mali. (38)
Bottom: Pattern on Djokwe carved wooden panel, Congo-Kinshasa. (59)

Top: Carved pattern on Kongo wooden sculpture, Congo-Kinshasa/Congo-Brazzaville/Angola. (15)

Middle: Carved pattern on Yoruba ivory jug, Nigeria. (8)

Bottom: Carved pattern on Bushongo wooden drum, Congo-Kinshasa. (8)

Top: Common Zulu wood-carving motif, Republic of South Africa. (45)

Middle: Common Tsonga pottery motif, Republic of South Africa/Mozambique/Swaziland. (79)

Bottom: Bushongo raffia pile cloth pattern, Congo-Kinshasa. (71)

Top: Carved pattern on Luba wooden sculpture, Congo-Kinshasa. (12)
Middle: Carved pattern on Dogon wooden sculpture, Mali. (56)
Bottom: Bushongo embroidered cloth pattern, Congo-Kinshasa. (8)

Top and middle: Two Bushongo embroidered cloth patterns, Congo-Kinshasa. (8)
Bottom: Woven basketry pattern from the lower Congo area. (37)

Top: Carved design on Yoruba wooden divination vessel, Nigeria. (7)
Left: Plaited mat pattern from Zanzibar, Tanzania. (66)
Right: Carved design on wooden milk pot from French Somaliland. (37)

Top: Bambara printed cloth pattern, Mali. (37)
Middle: Bushongo woven wall matting design, Congo-Kinshasa. (89)
Bottom: Bushongo embroidered cloth, Congo-Kinshasa. (8)

Top and middle: Bushongo embroidered cloth patterns, Congo-Kinshasa. (8)
Bottom: Kuba raffia velour pattern, Congo-Kinshasa. (65)

Top: Carved design on Kuba wooden cup, Congo-Kinshasa. (8)
Middle and bottom: Bushongo embroidered cloth design, Congo-Kinshasa. (8)

Top: Pattern on woven cloth rug from the upper Senegal area. (8)
Middle: Mbun woven basketry relief, Congo-Kinshasa. (8)
Bottom: Kuba pattern in raffia velour, Congo-Kinshasa. (65)

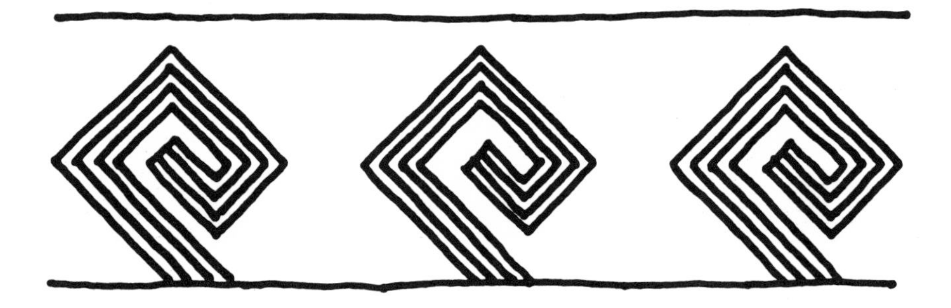

Top: Woven mat pattern from the lower Congo area. (38)
Bottom: Carved motif on Bushongo wooden box, Congo-Kinshasa. (10)

Top: Carved design on Bushongo wooden box, Congo-Kinshasa. (10)
Middle: Pattern on woven casing for casket from the lower Congo area. (8)
Bottom: Carved design on Kuba wooden cup, Congo-Kinshasa. (87)

Top: Pattern on Hausa embroidered cloth, Nigeria/Niger. (52)
Middle: Ashanti cast bronze pattern on box, Ghana. (53)
Bottom: Kiga design scorched into calabash jug, Uganda. (68)

Top: Scraped calabash motif on drinking vessel, Dahomey. (37)
Middle: Sotho wall mosaic pattern, South Africa. (81)
Bottom: Blackened wood relief on basket, Congo-Kinshasa. (38)

Top: Bushongo carved wood pattern, Congo-Kinshasa. (86)
Middle: Carved pattern on Kuba wooden sculpture, Congo-Kinshasa. (8)
Bottom: Nupe decorated calabash pattern, Nigeria. (8)

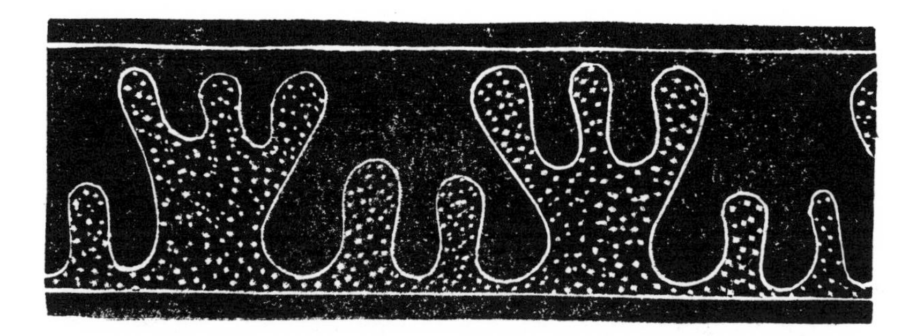

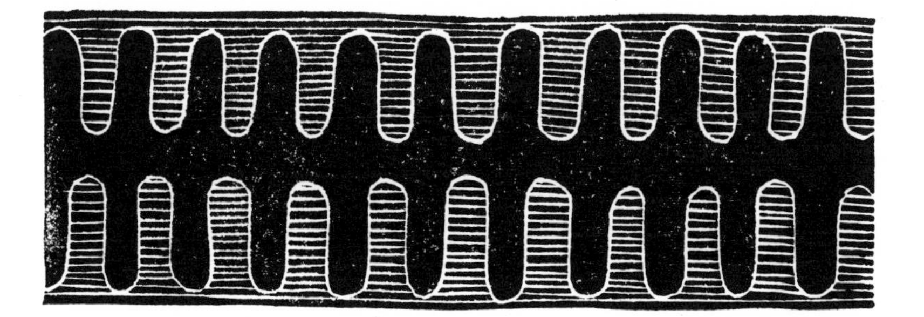

Top and middle: Beaten brass design on Ashanti vases, Ghana. (top, 86; middle, 37)
Bottom: Blackened wood relief on basket, Congo-Kinshasa. (38)

Left: Mbala incised earthenware decoration, Congo-Kinshasa. (61)
Right: Beaten decoration on Ashanti bronze vase, Ghana. (33)

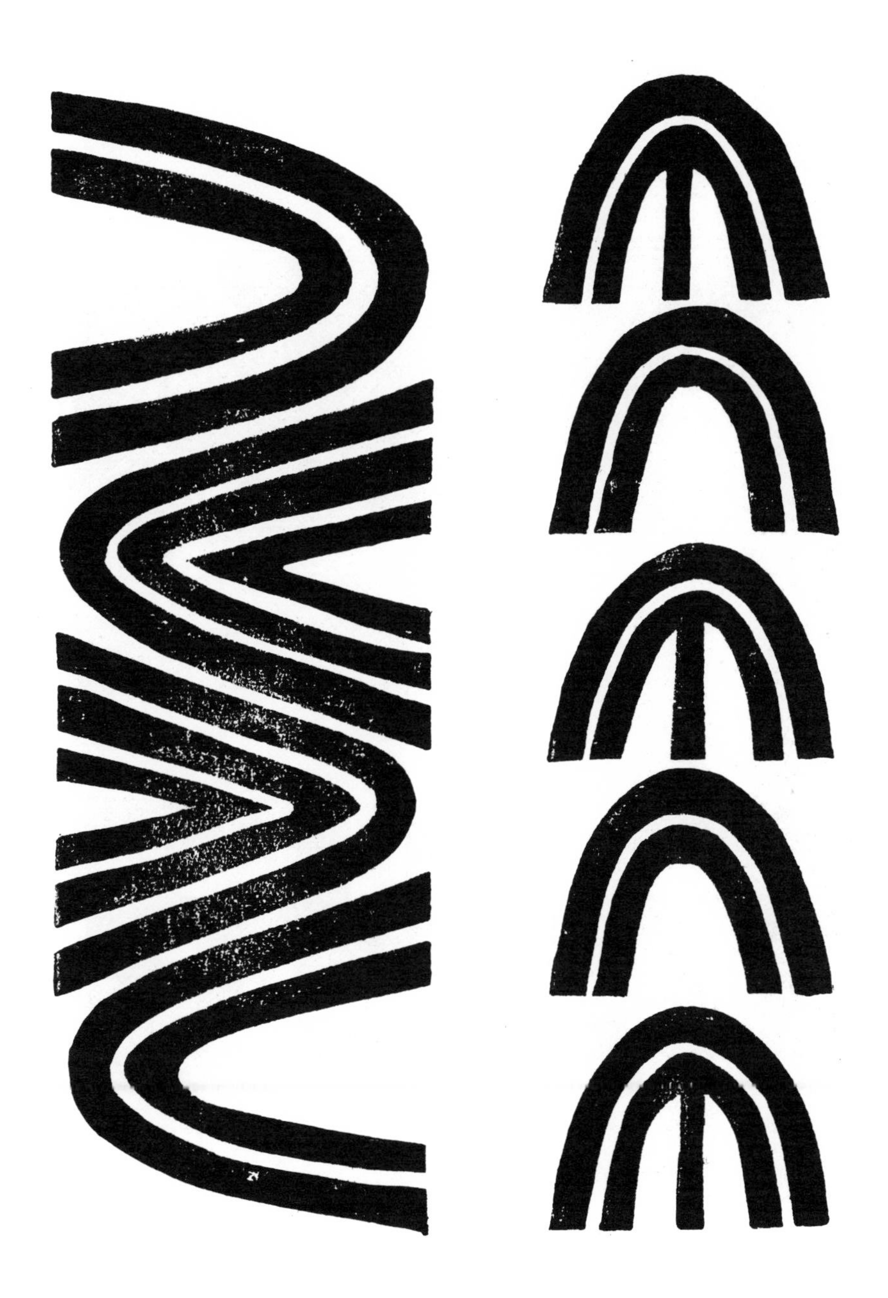

Two carved patterns on Kuyu wooden sculpture, Congo-Brazzaville. (75)

Top: Mbala discharge-printed cloth pattern, Congo-Kinshasa. (37)
Bottom: Bushongo embroidered cloth pattern, Congo-Kinshasa. (8)

Continuous design applied on Benin bronze sculpture, Nigeria. (86)

Top: Wood carving on side of Bushongo drum, Congo-Kinshasa. (59)
Bottom: Moulded design on Ibo clay pot, Nigeria. (8)

Top: Carved relief on Bushongo wooden drinking vessel, Congo-Kinshasa. (38)
Bottom: Beaten pattern on brass sculpture, Dahomey. (3)

Top: Ashanti "Adinkira" stamp printed cloth pattern, Ghana. (8)
Bottom: Beaten pattern on Ashanti bronze urn, Ghana. (33)

Top: Beadwork design on Bali calabash cover, Cameroon. (8)
Bottom: Benin carved wood pattern, Nigeria. (24)

Top: Bushongo carved wood pattern, Congo-Kinshasa. (9)
Bottom: Carving on wooden keg from the lower Congo area. (38)

Top: Beadwork design on Okavango apron, Botswana. (46)
Bottom: Basketweave pattern on Nyoro pot stand, Uganda. (68)

Top: Coiled basketwork design from Barotseland, Zambia. (8)
Bottom: Basketweave design on casket casing from the lower Congo area. (38)

Two Bushongo raffia pile cloth patterns, Congo-Kinshasa. (top, 71; bottom, 8)

Top: Tufted cloth pattern, Congo. (31)
Bottom: Bushongo sewn raffia mat pattern, Congo-Kinshasa. (38)

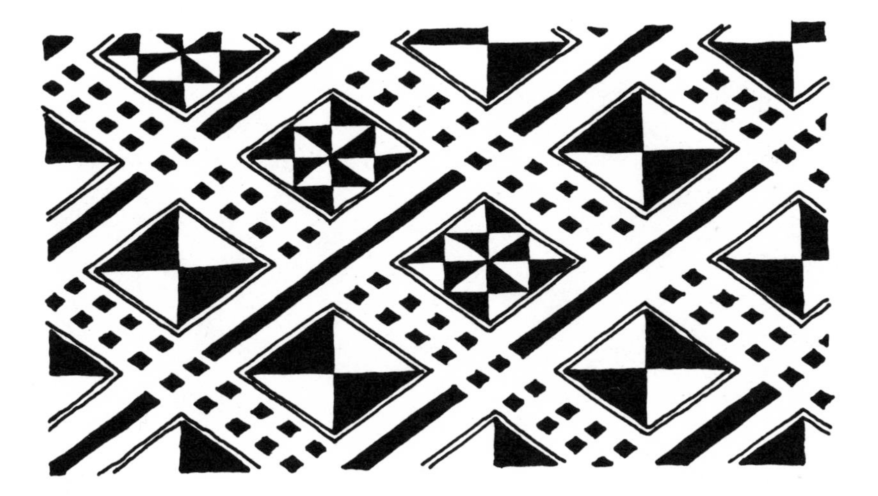

Top: Kuba raffia velour pattern, Congo-Kinshasa. (65)
Bottom: Huana raffia pile cloth pattern, Congo-Kinshasa. (60)

Top: Beadwork pattern on seat of stool from Cameroon. (84)
Bottom: Kuba raffia velour pattern, Congo-Kinshasa. (65)

Animals and Mythical Figures

Two scraped calabash bird designs on drinking vessel, Dahomey. (37)

Top left: Carved bird design on Dogon wooden door, Mali. (48)
Top right and bottom: Ashanti gold weights in form of birds, Ghana. (top, 71; bottom, 8)

Top: Woven mat bird design from the lower Congo area. (38)
Bottom: Brass repoussé bird design on Ashanti urn, Ghana. (8)

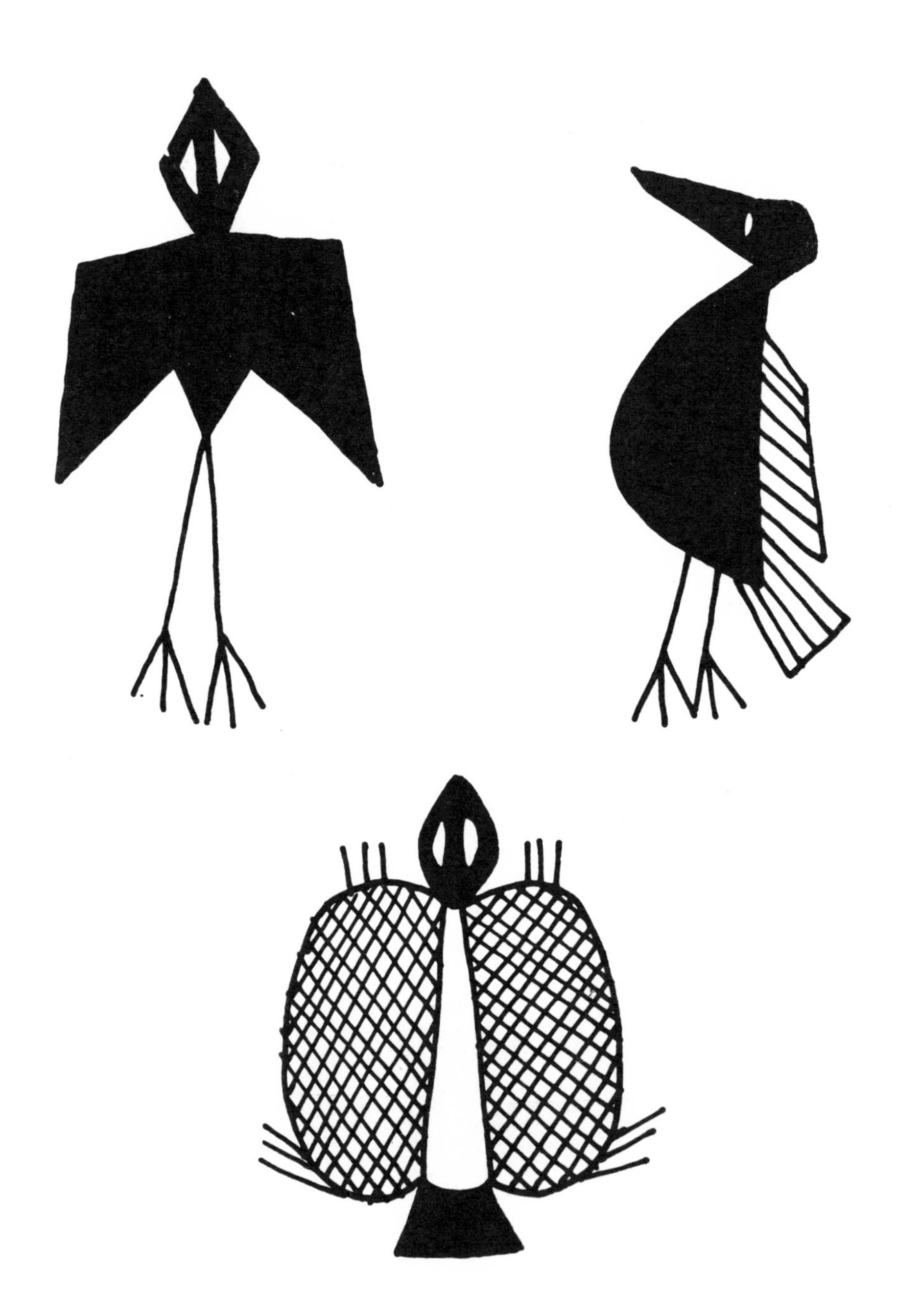

Three bird designs on Senufo earth-dyed cloth, Ivory Coast/Mali/Upper Volta. (37)

Top: Carved bird design on Yoruba wooden door, Nigeria. (37)
Bottom: Ashanti gold weight in form of bird, Ghana. (53)

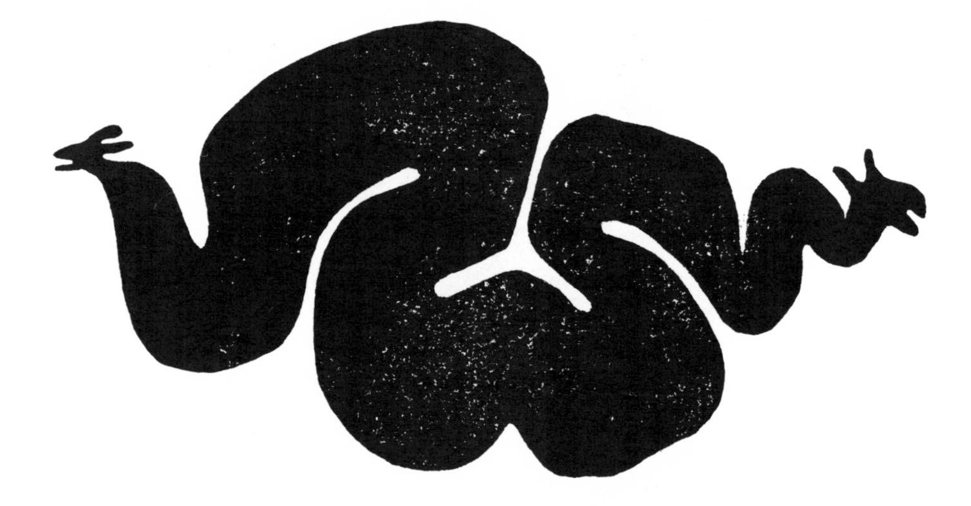

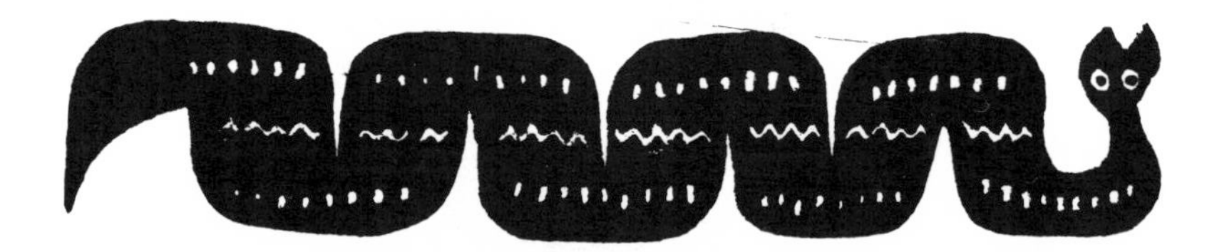

Top: Bushman rock painting of double-headed snake, South Africa. (78)
Bottom: Scraped calabash snake design, Dahomey. (37)

Top: Ashanti scraped calabash snake and lizard design, Ghana. (45)
Bottom: Scraped calabash lizard design, Dahomey. (37)

Top: Carved turtle design on Senufo wooden door, Ivory Coast/Mali/Upper Volta. (71)
Bottom: Carved lizard design on Senufo wooden door, Ivory Coast/Mali/Upper Volta. (17)

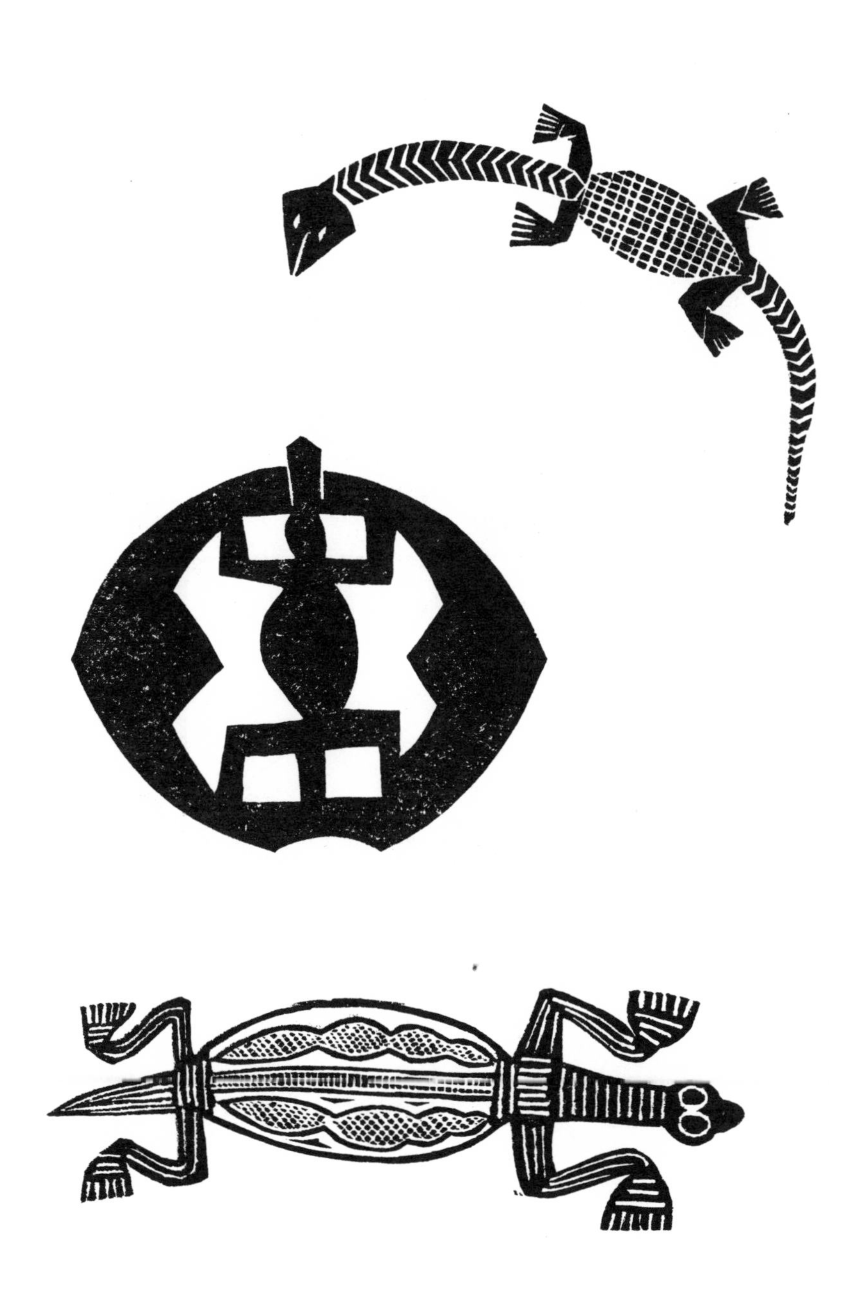

Top: Carved wooden lizard on Yoruba door, Nigeria. (37)

Middle: Carved wooden headcrest on Senufo sculpture, Ivory Coast/Mali/Upper Volta. (44)

Bottom: Scraped lizard design on calabash lid, Dahomey. (37)

Top: Carved lizard on Dogon wooden door, Mali. (48)

Middle: Ashanti "Adinkira" stamp in form of double crocodile with common stomach, Ghana. (54)

Bottom: Lizard carved on Dan wooden effigy, Liberia. (20)

Top: Stylized scorpion design on scraped calabash, Dahomey. (37)
Bottom left: Ashanti gold weight in form of scorpion, Ghana. (75)
Bottom right: Ashanti gold weight in form of stylized lizard, Ghana. (75)

Top: Frog relief carved onto Bushongo wooden goblet, Congo-Kinshasa. (38)
Left: Scraped calabash frog design, Dahomey. (37)
Right: Stylized frog design carved onto Bagam wooden sheath, Cameroon. (70)

Top: Scraped calabash goat design, Dahomey. (37)
Bottom: Bariba (Barba) scraped calabash antelope design, Dahomey. (37)

Top: Woven mat antelope design from the lower Congo area. (38)
Bottom: Nupe decorated horse profile, Nigeria. (8)

Top: Carved soapstone zebra from Zimbabwe, Rhodesia. (8)
Middle: Small mammalian design carved on Fang bone counter, Gabon. (85)
Bottom: Fanti scraped calabash dog design, Ghana. (47)

Top: Scraped calabash lion design, Dahomey. (37)
Bottom: Carved soapstone monkey design from Zimbabwe, Rhodesia. (37)

Two scraped calabash cattle designs, Dahomey. (37)

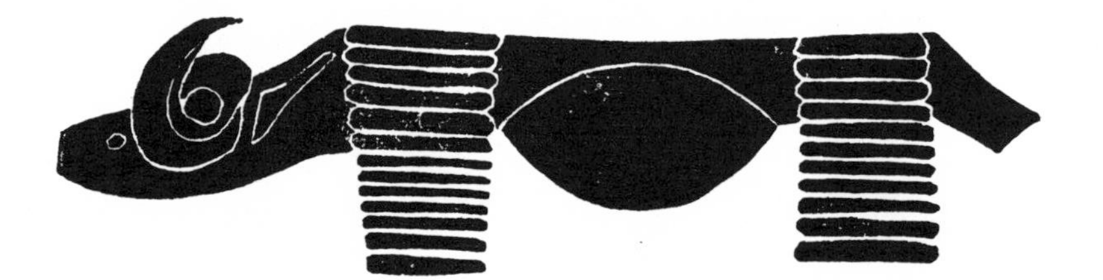

Top: Rock graffito rhinoceros from the Fezzan, Libya. (86)
Bottom: Profile of Rotse wood headrest in form of water buffalo, Zambia. (50)

Top: Benin elephant design on hide fan, Nigeria. (19)

Bottom: Elephant carved onto Senufo wooden door, Ivory Coast/Mali/Upper Volta. (23)

Benin stylized design of feeding elephant in carved ivory, Nigeria. (8)

Top: Ashanti gold weight in form of chameleon, Ghana. (8)
Bottom: Rock painting of mythical elephant, Mashonaland, Rhodesia. (78)

Top: Benin catfish design in carved ivory, Nigeria. (8)
Bottom: Ashanti gold weight in form of fish, Ghana. (75)

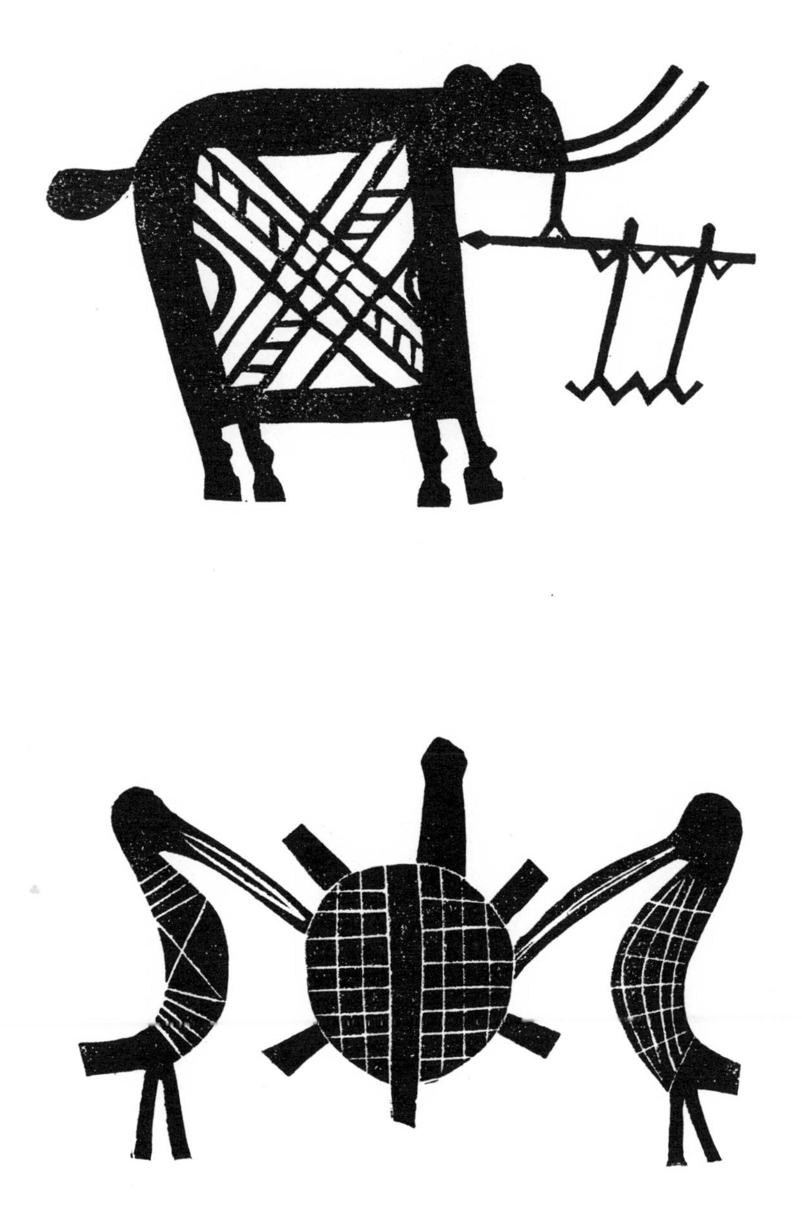

Top: Incised gourd hunting scene, Sudan area. (50)

Bottom: Pelican and turtle design carved on Senufo wooden door, Ivory Coast/Mali/Upper Volta. (17)

Bushman rock painting from the Tsibab ravine depicting two mythical creatures, South-West Africa. (76)

Bushman rock painting of mythical creature from Mashonaland, Rhodesia. (78)

Human Beings

Top: Carved bone design on Yaunde counter, Cameroon. (82)
Bottom: Bushman rock painting from the Tsibab ravine, South-West Africa. (76)

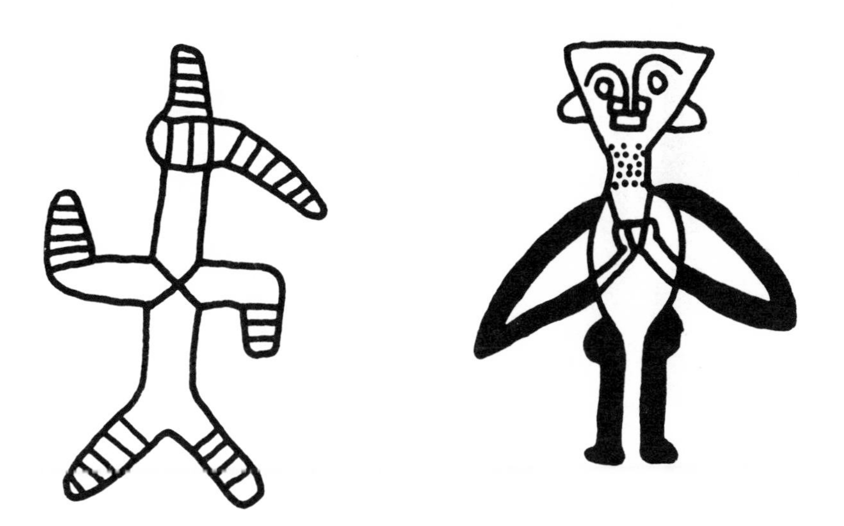

Top: Mangbetu incised and burnt wood design, Congo-Kinshasa. (3)
Left: Dogon painted figure on stone, Mali. (34)
Right: Raffia tapestry design, Cameroon. (50)

Two Bushman rock paintings, Republic of South Africa. (79)

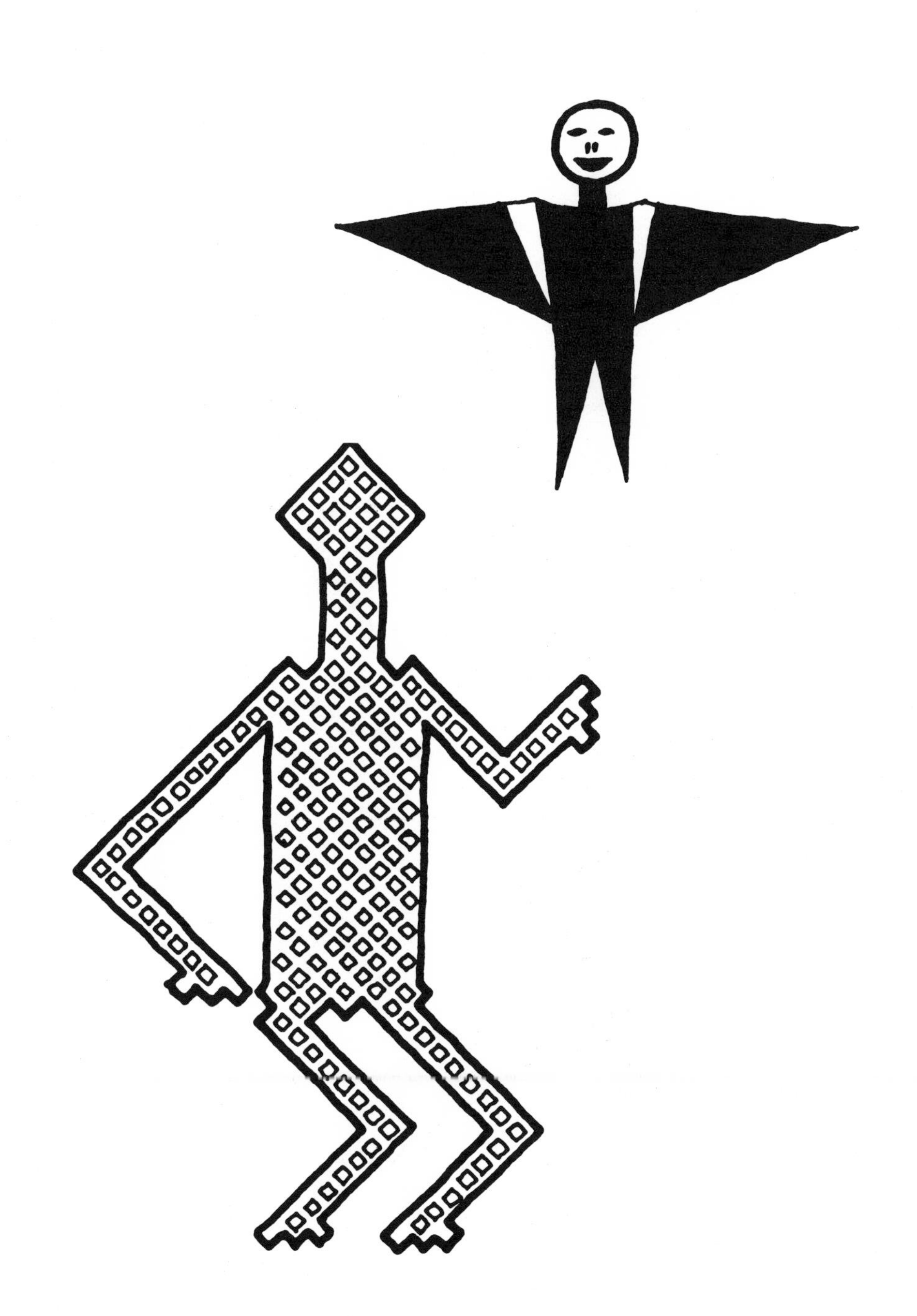

Top: Kamba engraved calabash figure, Kenya. (8)
Bottom: Woven mat figure, from the lower Congo area. (38)

Top: Bushman rock painting from the Tsibab ravine, South-West Africa. (76)
Bottom: Bushman rock painting from Ladybrand, Republic of South Africa. (79)

Bushman rock painting from the Tsibab ravine, South-West Africa. (76)

Two carved groups on Yoruba wooden door, Nigeria. (37)

Left: Senufo carved wooden figure, Ivory Coast/Mali/Upper Volta. (23)
Right: Zulu carved wooden figure, Republic of South Africa. (8)

Profile of Dogon wooden sculpture, Mali. (71)

Carved wooden figure from the northern Congo. (16)

Kongo soapstone stele relief, Angola. (57)

Carved wooden fetish figure from the Congo. (71)

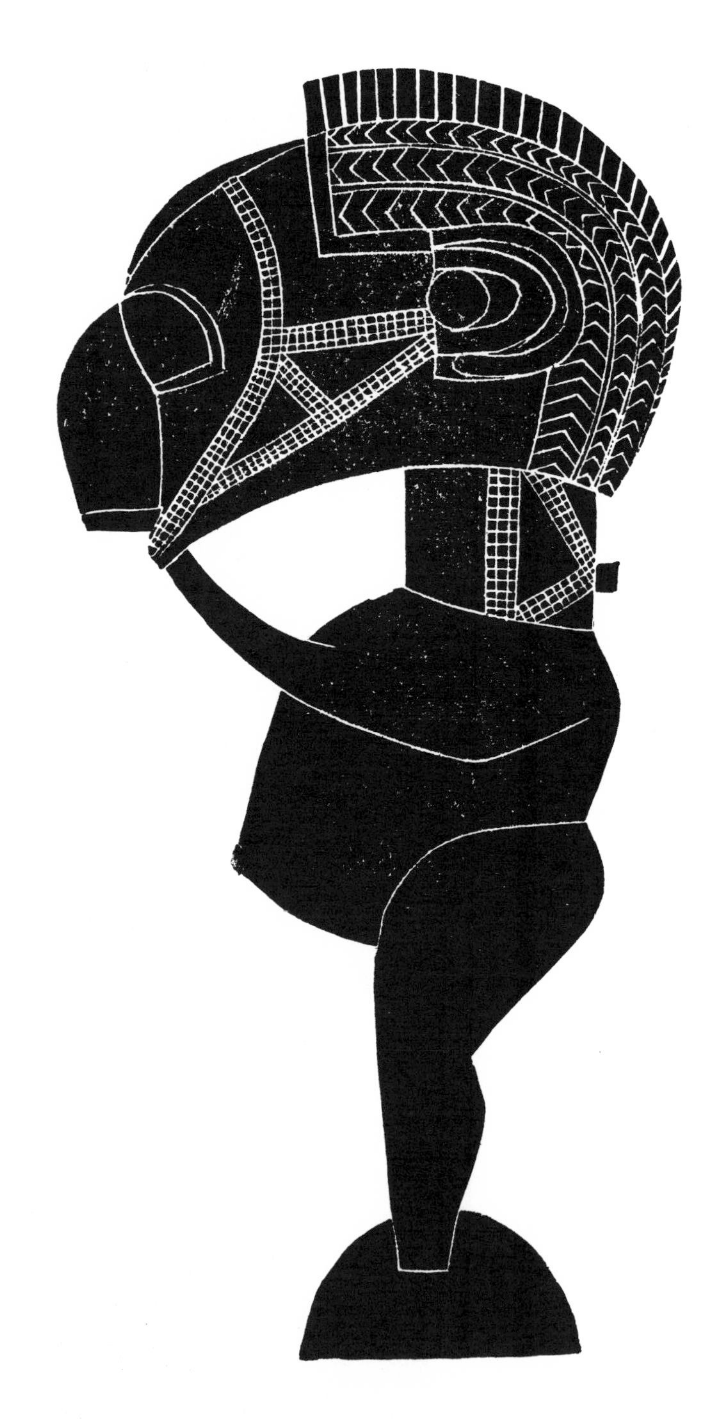

Baga carved wooden guardian figure, Guinea. (55)

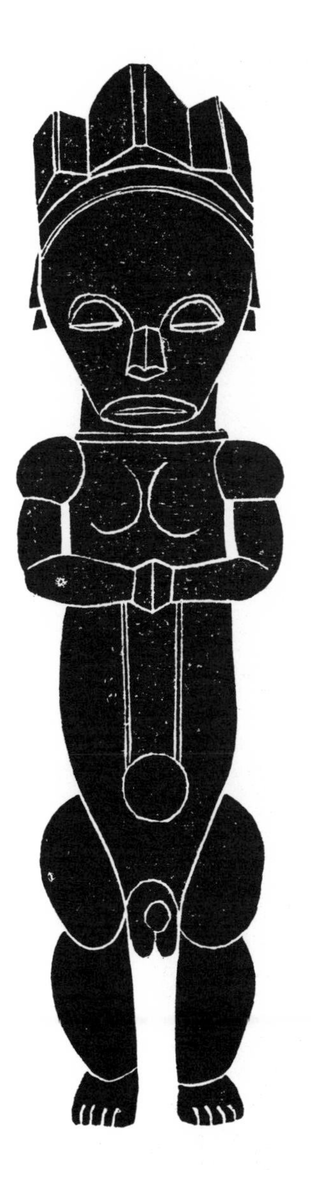

Left: Fang wooden guardian figure, Gabon. (9)
Right: Huana carved bone amulet, Congo-Kinshasa. (62)

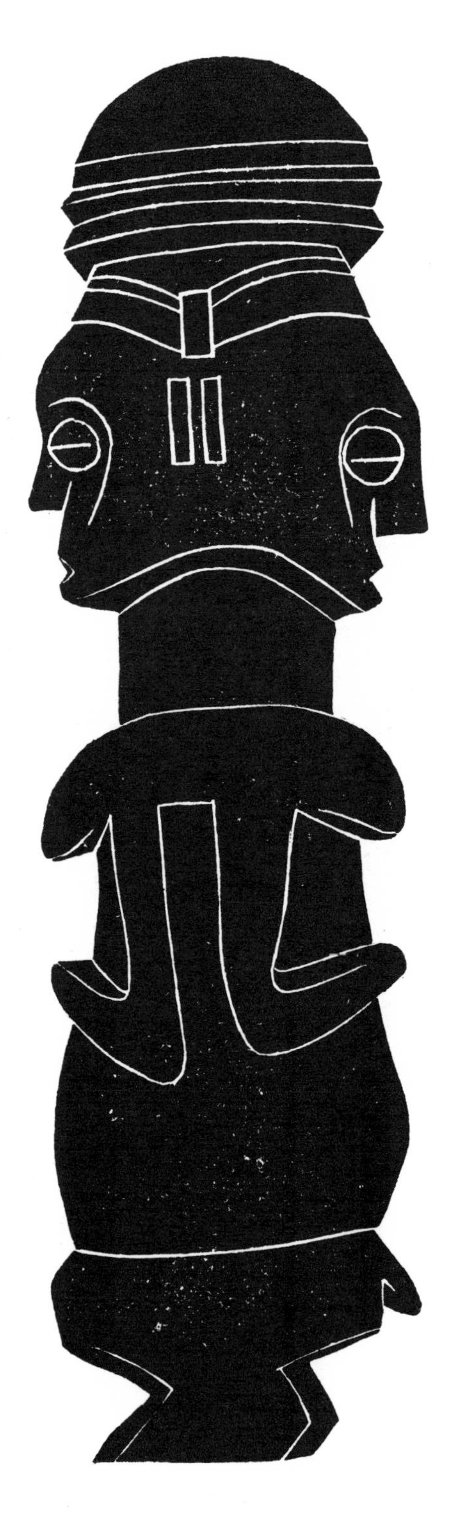

Suku double figure in wood, Congo-Kinshasa. (2)

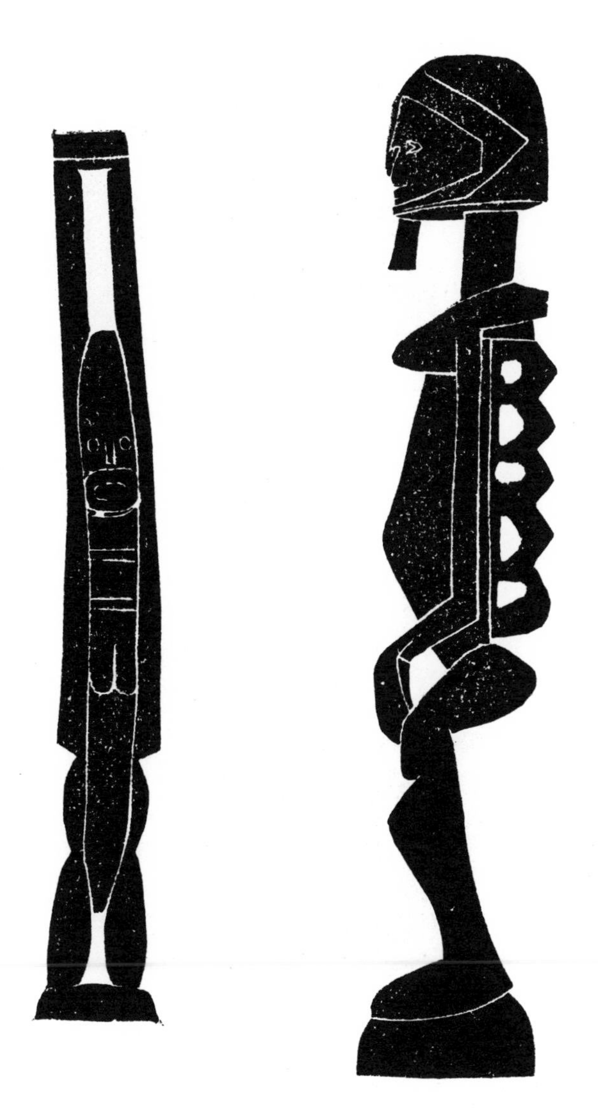

Left: Dogon wooden "Nommo" figure, Mali. (81)
Right: Dogon wooden cult figure, Mali. (63)

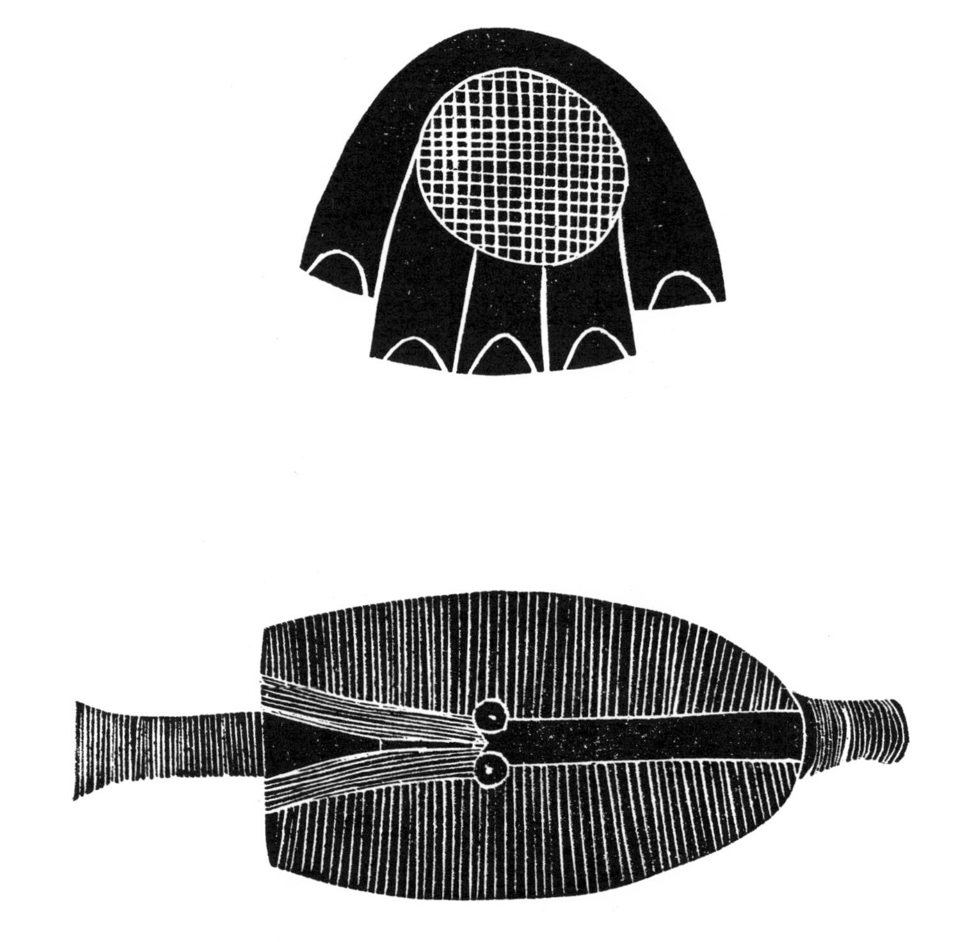

Top: Hand design on Songo-Meno wooden bell, Congo-Kinshasa. (62)
Bottom: Kota wood and brass reliquary figure, Gabon. (37)

Huana carved ivory pendant, Congo-Kinshasa. (87)

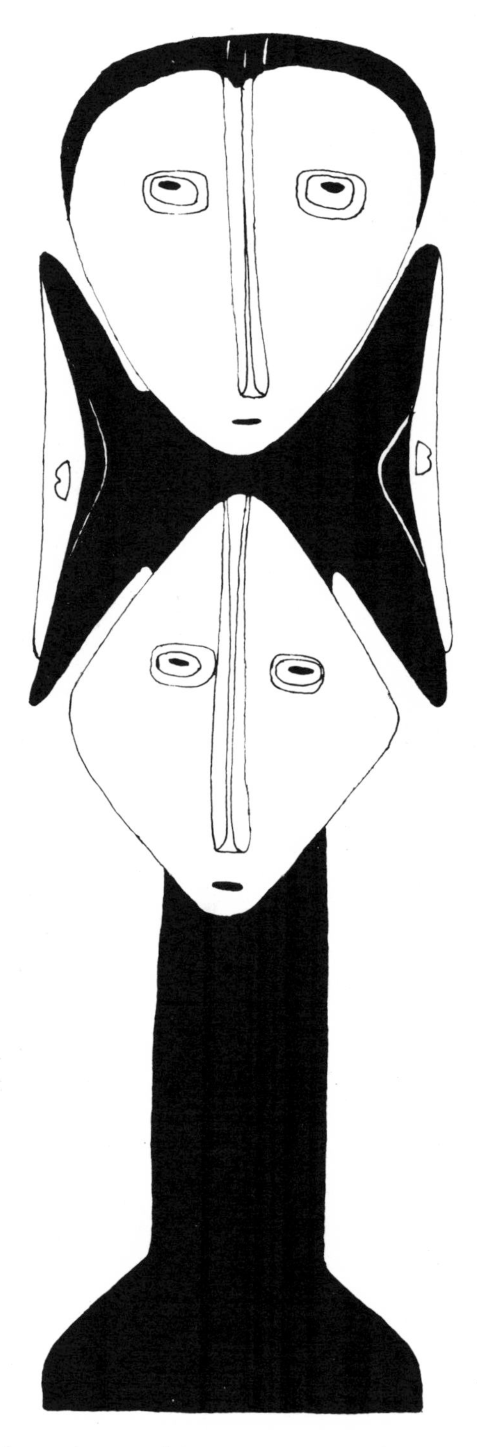

Lega six-faced pigmented wooden ritual figure, Congo-Kinshasa. (4)

Left: Fanti wooden fertility doll, Ghana. (2)
Right: Ashanti wooden fertility figure, Ghana. (59)

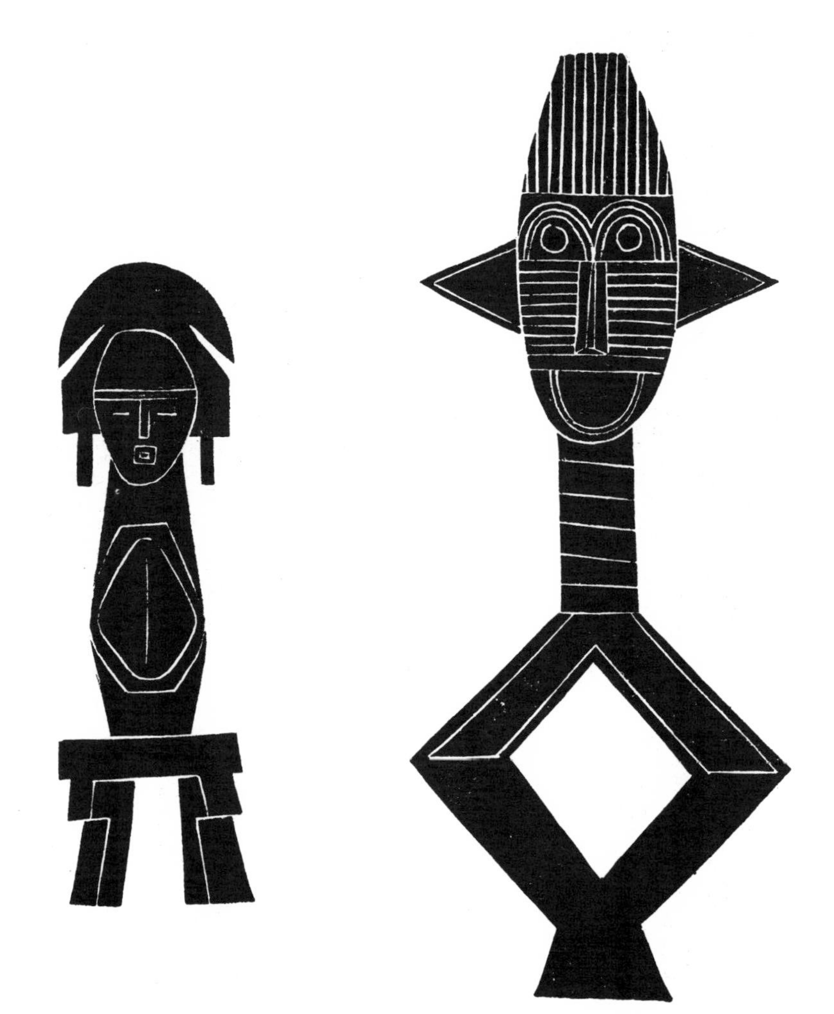

Left: Kota wooden figure on stool, Gabon. (71)
Right: Kota wood, brass and copper reliquary, Gabon. (5)

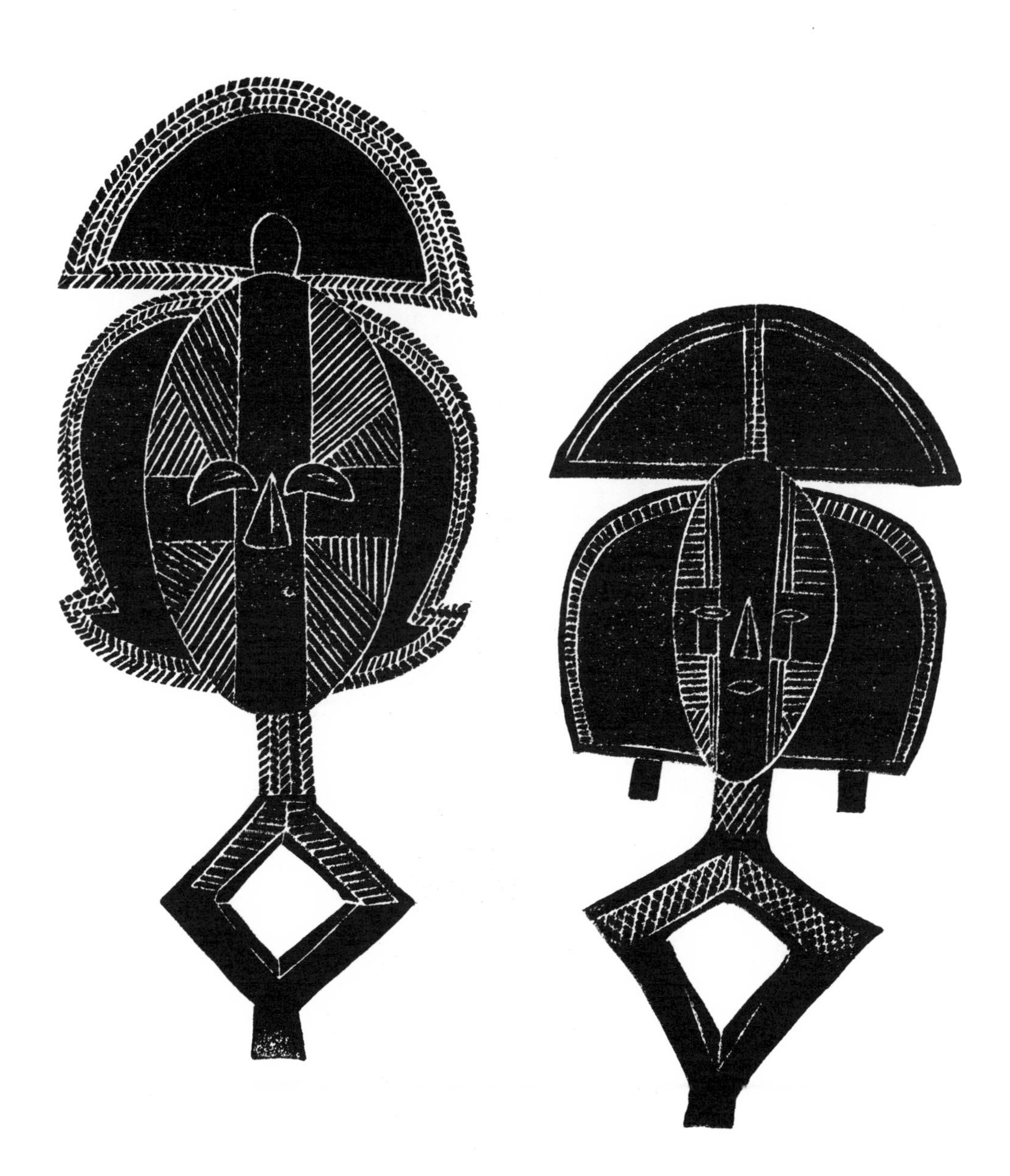

Two Kota hammered bronze and wood funerary figures, Gabon. (left, 25; right, 59)

Kota wood, brass and copper reliquary figure, Gabon. (53)

Masks

Left: Lega painted wooden mask, Congo-Kinshasa. (38)
Right: Shilluk dung-covered calabash mask, Sudan. (40)

Kwele wooden mask, Congo-Brazzaville. (39)

Landuman wooden helmet mask, Guinea. (32)

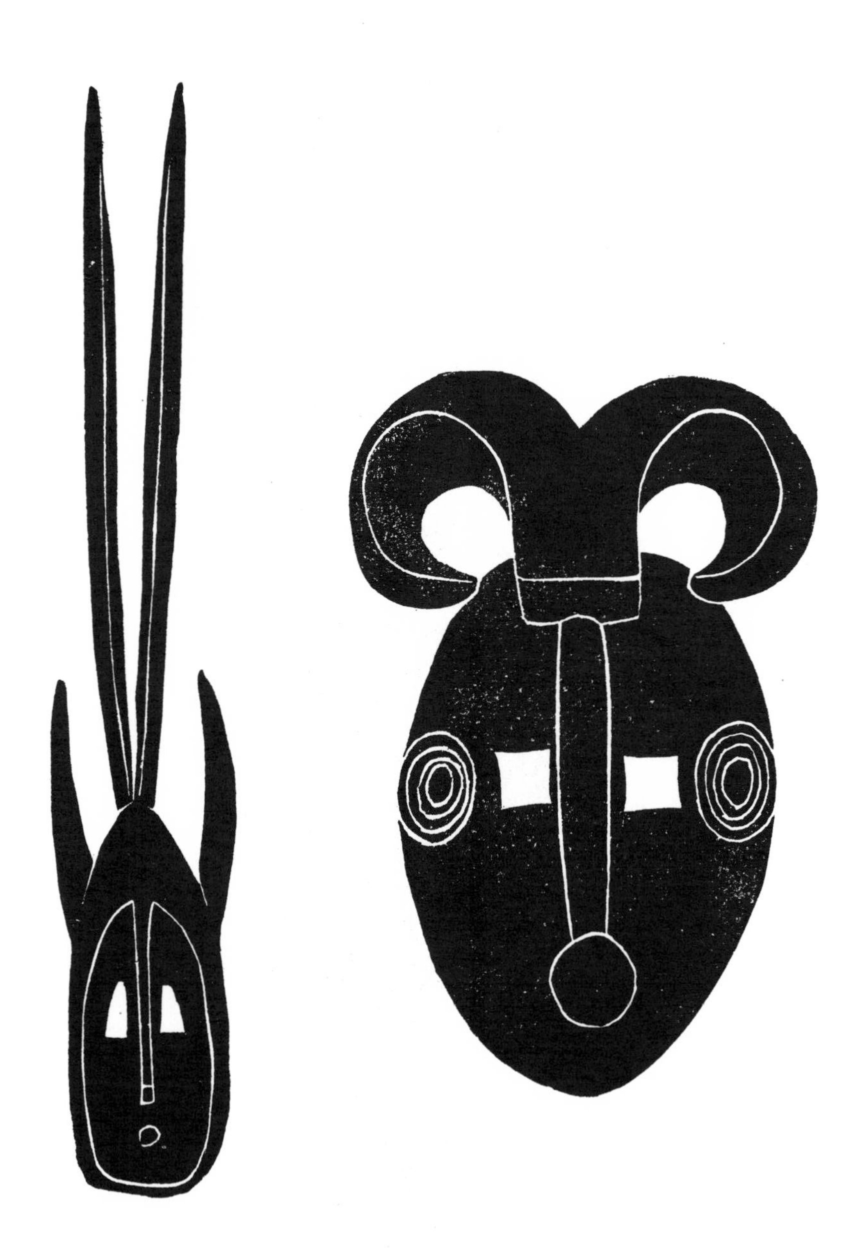

Left: Dogon wooden mask, Mali. (37)
Right: Ogoni society wooden mask of the Yoruba, Nigeria. (49)

Wooden mask from Mali. (36)

Left: Baule wooden mask, Ivory Coast. (73)
Right: Eastern Pende painted wood mask, Congo-Kinshasa. (3)

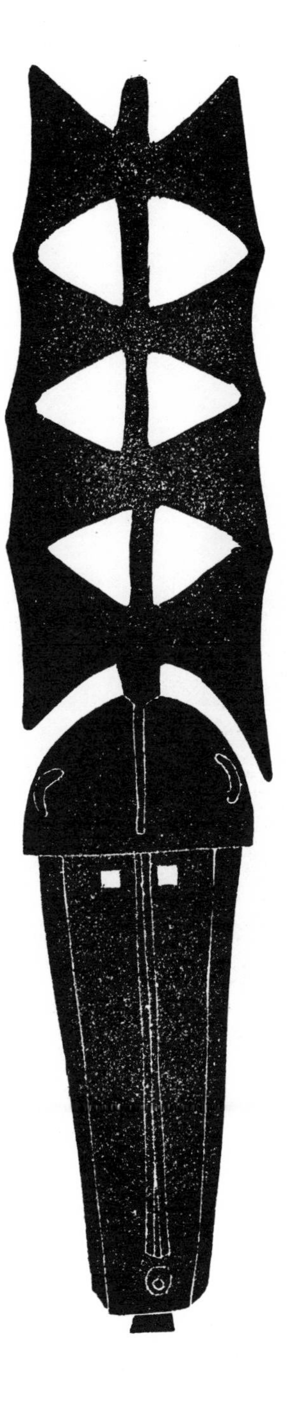

Bobo wooden dance mask, Upper Volta. (64)

Senufo wooden mask, Ivory Coast/Mali/Upper Volta. (87)

Senufo wooden mask, Ivory Coast/Mali/Upper Volta. (9)

Boa wooden mask, Congo-Kinshasa. (6)

Kwele painted wooden dance mask, Congo-Brazzaville. (44)

Bena-Kanioka wooden mask, Congo-Kinshasa. (21)

Polychrome wooden mask from the Congo. (67)

Tetela painted wooden mask, Congo-Kinshasa. (8)

Luba painted wooden and china-clay mask, Congo-Kinshasa. (38)

Polychrome wooden mask from the Congo. (86)

Bembe wooden mask from the lower Congo area. (32)

Senufo light bronze double-faced mask, Ivory Coast/Mali/Upper Volta. (26)

Ijo wooden mask, southern Nigeria. (8)

Nupe wooden mask, Nigeria. (8)

Baule ivory bracelet, Ivory Coast. (65)

Dogon wooden mask, Mali. (81)

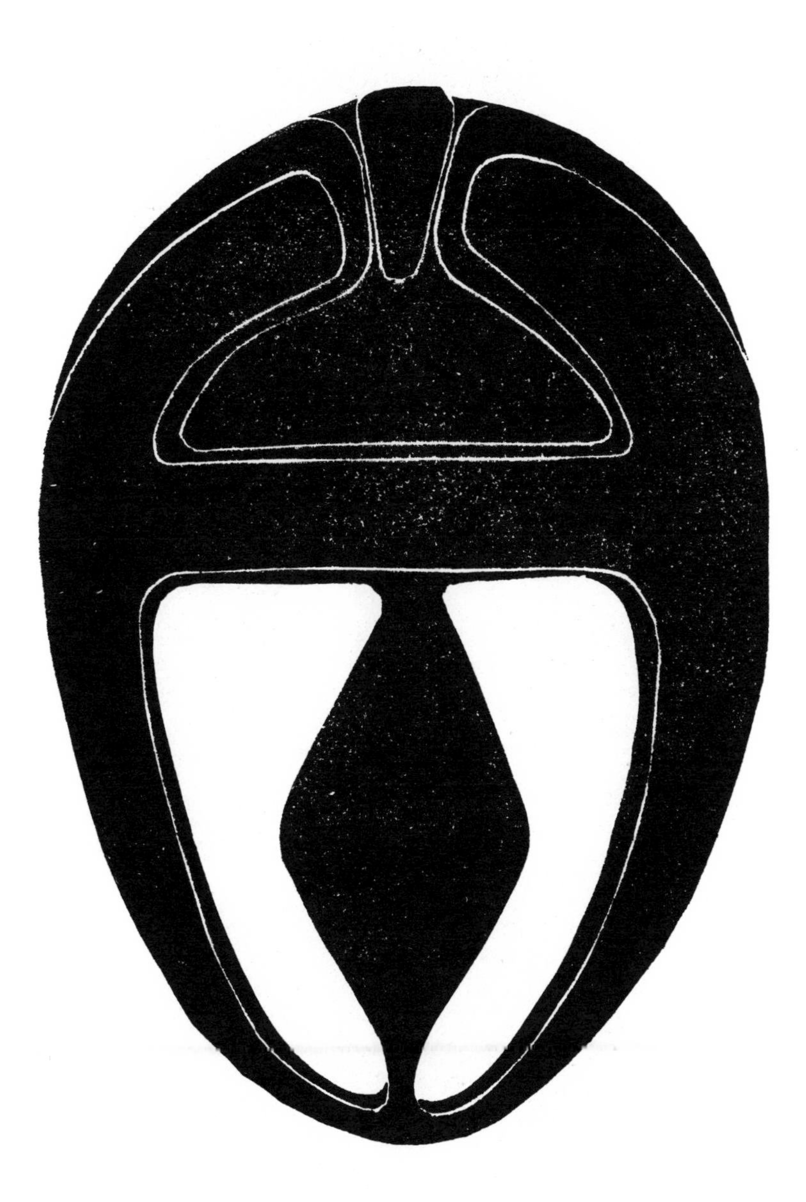

Toma wooden mask, Liberia/Guinea. (65)

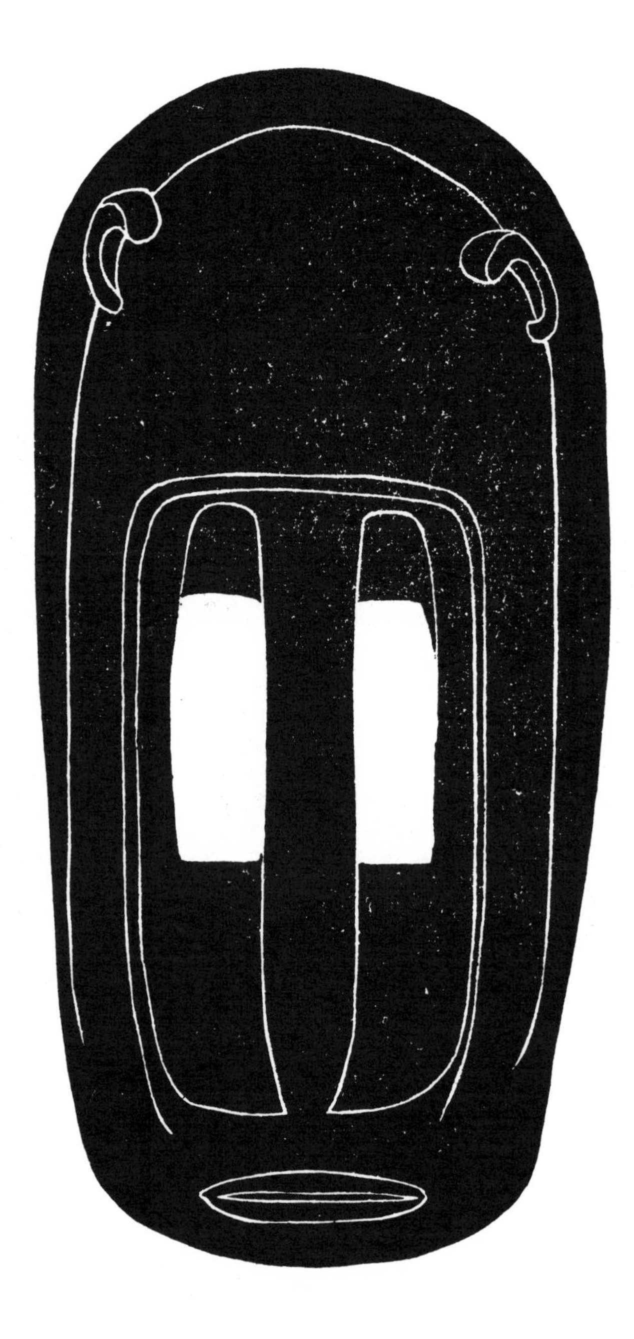

Dogon wooden "mask of the black monkey," Mali. (37)

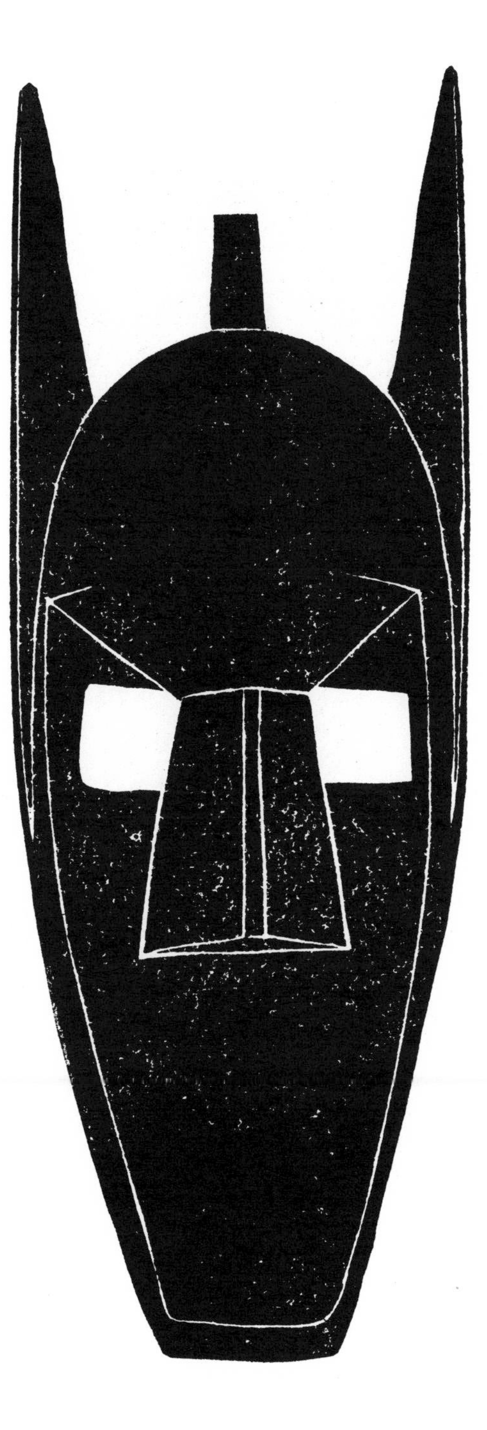

Wooden mask from Ivory Coast. (11)

Ibo wooden mask of the water spirit, Nigeria. (8)

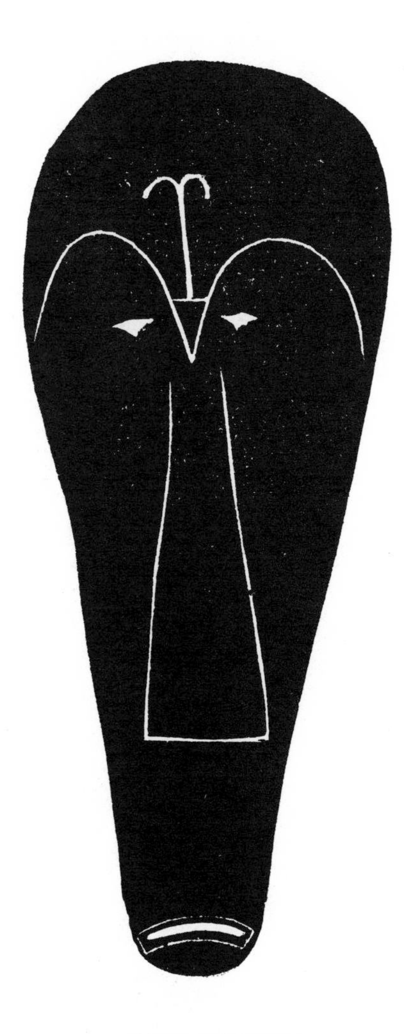

Fang wood and china-clay mask, Gabon. (40)

Bafo painted wooden mask, Cameroon. (40)

Djokwe wooden mask, Congo-Kinshasa. (38)

Fang wooden sculpture, Gabon. (44)

Artifacts and Objects with Figural Components

Ganda terracotta water jug, Uganda. (8)

Djokwe decorated wooden comb, Congo-Kinshasa. (87)

Top: Profile of Duala wooden stool, Cameroon. (77)
Bottom: Shona wooden headrest in form of buffalo, Rhodesia/Mozambique. (58)

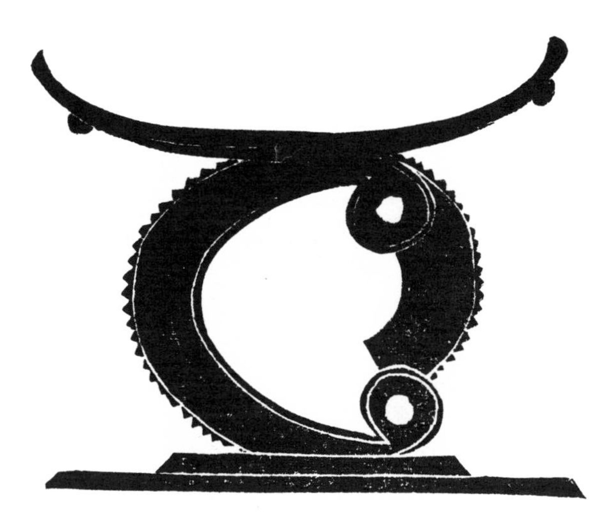

Top: Ashanti wooden stool, Ghana. (37)
Bottom: Carved wooden headrest from East Africa. (50)

Top: Makalanga carved wooden headrest, Mashonaland, Rhodesia. (87)
Bottom: Carved wooden headrest from Mashonaland, Rhodesia. (8)

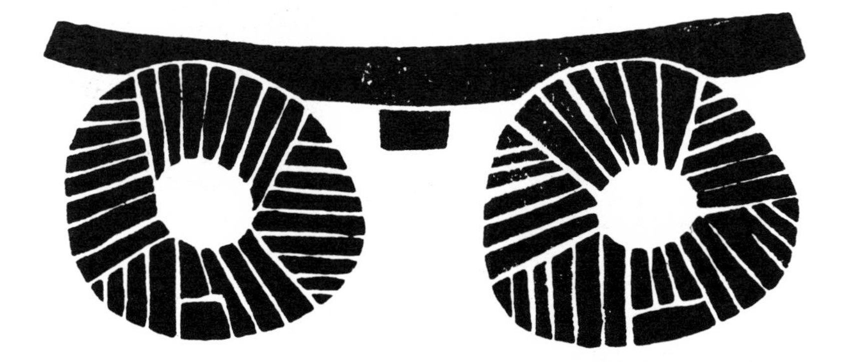

Two Tsonga wooden headrests, Republic of South Africa/Mozambique/Swaziland. (1)

Left: Ashanti ceremonial ivory spoon, Ghana. (8)
Right: Rotse ceremonial wooden spoon, Zambia. (65)

Top: Profile of quartz ritual stool from Ife. (8)
Bottom: Plan view of ceremonial wooden stool from Senegal. (14)

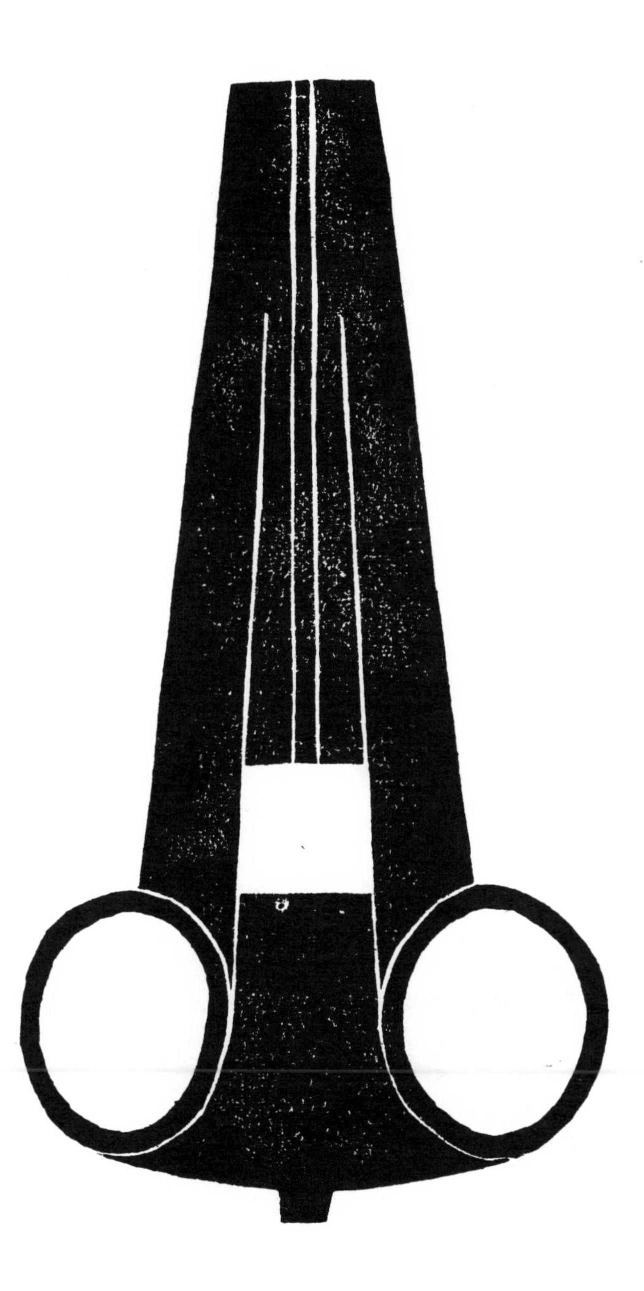

Profile of Ovambo wooden bellows, Angola/South-West Africa. (1)

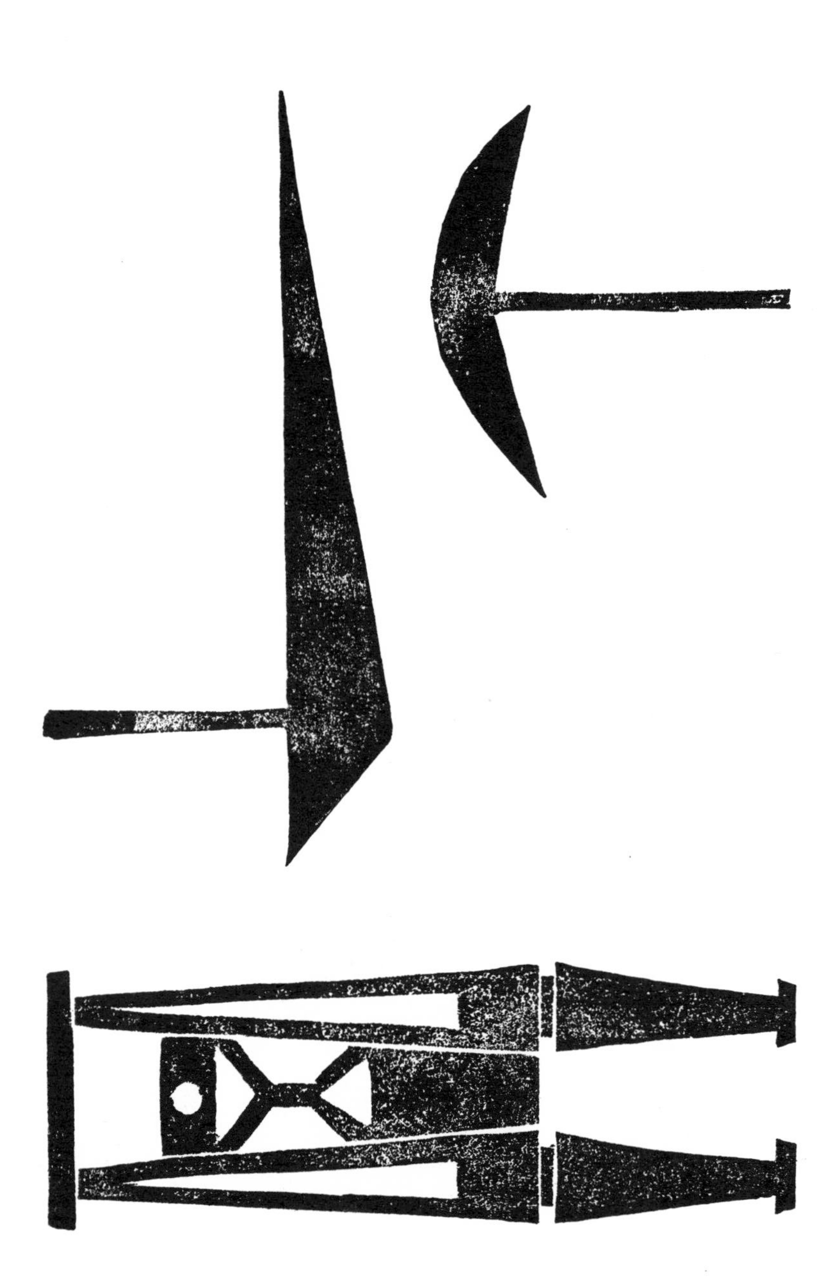

Top: Two Tswana axe heads, Botswana. (46)

Bottom: Double hunting knife and wooden sheath from Ngamiland, Botswana. (46)

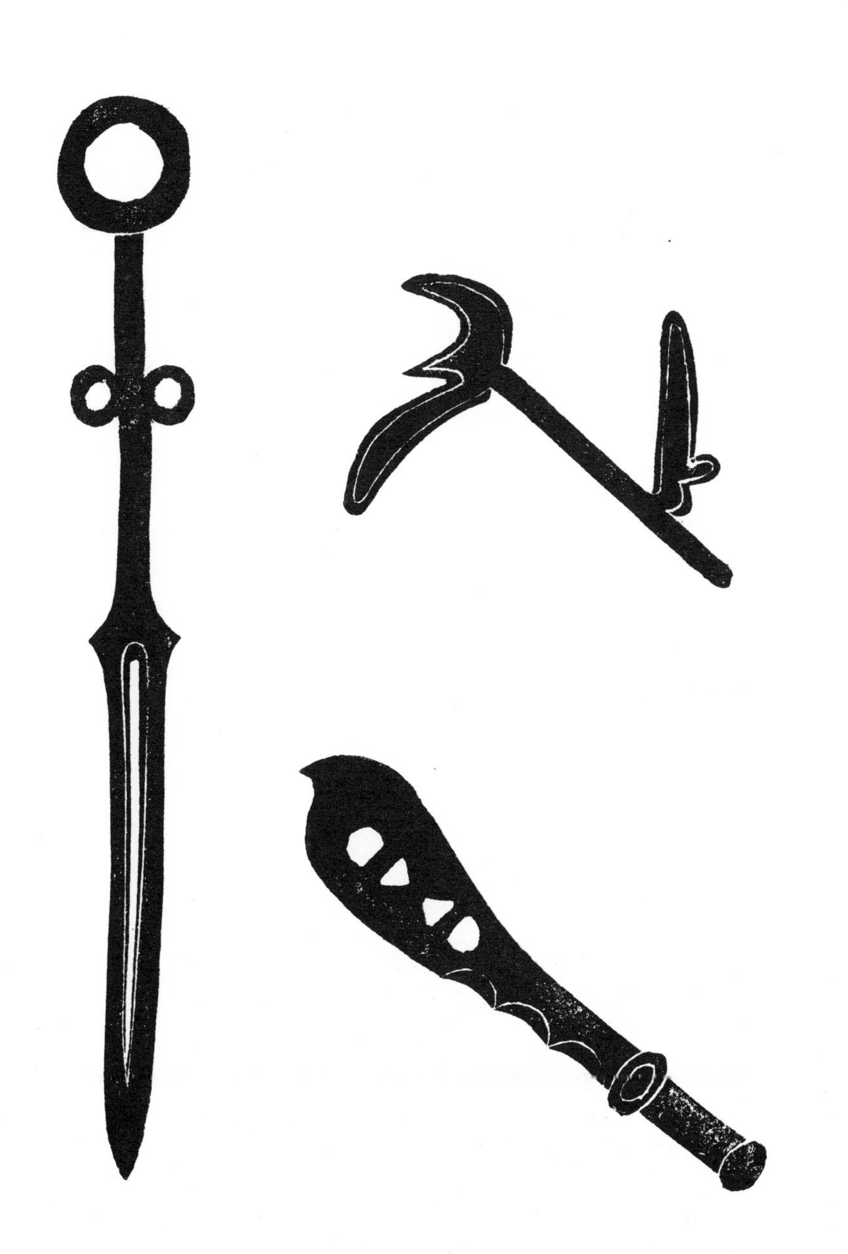

Left: Mangbetu ivory hairpin, Congo-Kinshasa. (81)
Top right: Zande throwing knife, Congo-Kinshasa/Central African Republic. (38)
Bottom right: Sword from hammered copper sculpture, Dahomey. (56)

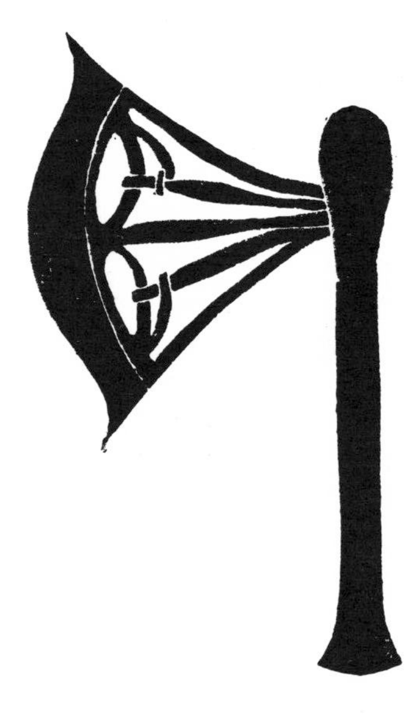

Left: Songe cast iron axe, Congo-Kinshasa. (69)
Right: Jekri wooden paddle profile, Nigeria. (52)

Two Bambara wooden headdresses in form of antelope, Mali. (left, 71; right, 82)

Ashanti wooden heddle pulley, Ghana. (58)

Left: Profile of Banda wooden comb, Central African Republic. (41)
Right: Profile of Djokwe wooden comb head, Congo-Kinshasa. (59)

Dogon wooden ritual axe shaft head, Mali. (81)

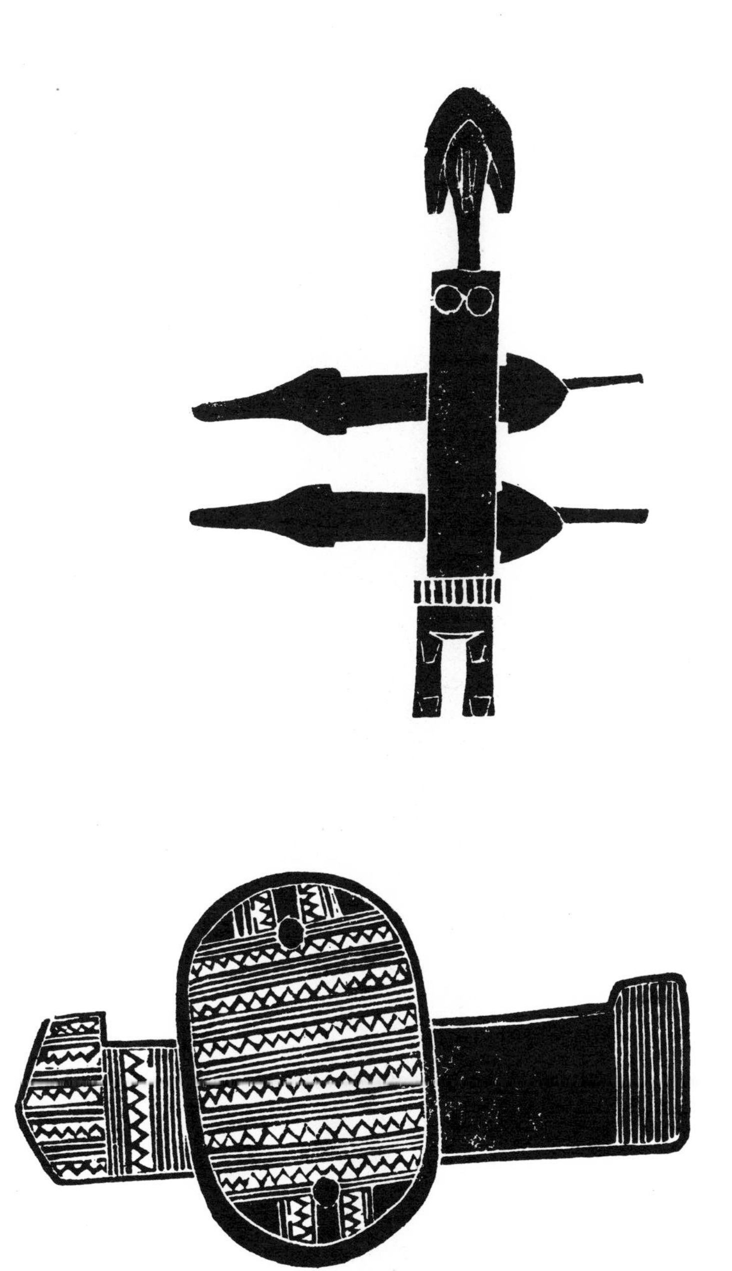

Top: Profile of Bambara wooden effigy door latch, Mali. (13)
Bottom: Profile of Dogon wooden door latch, Mali. (22)

Symbolic wooden crest to human figure grave post from southern Madagascar (Malagasy Republic). (71)

Baule carved wooden door panel, Ivory Coast. (35)

Left: Ceremonial staff from Dahomey. (82)
Right: Ivory ritual axe head from Abomey, Dahomey. (37)

Two raffia allegorical tapestry designs, Cameroon. (50)

Bariba engraved calabash design, Dahomey. (37)

Ashanti carved wooden door panel, Ghana. (36)

Ibo carved funerary stone, Nigeria. (49)

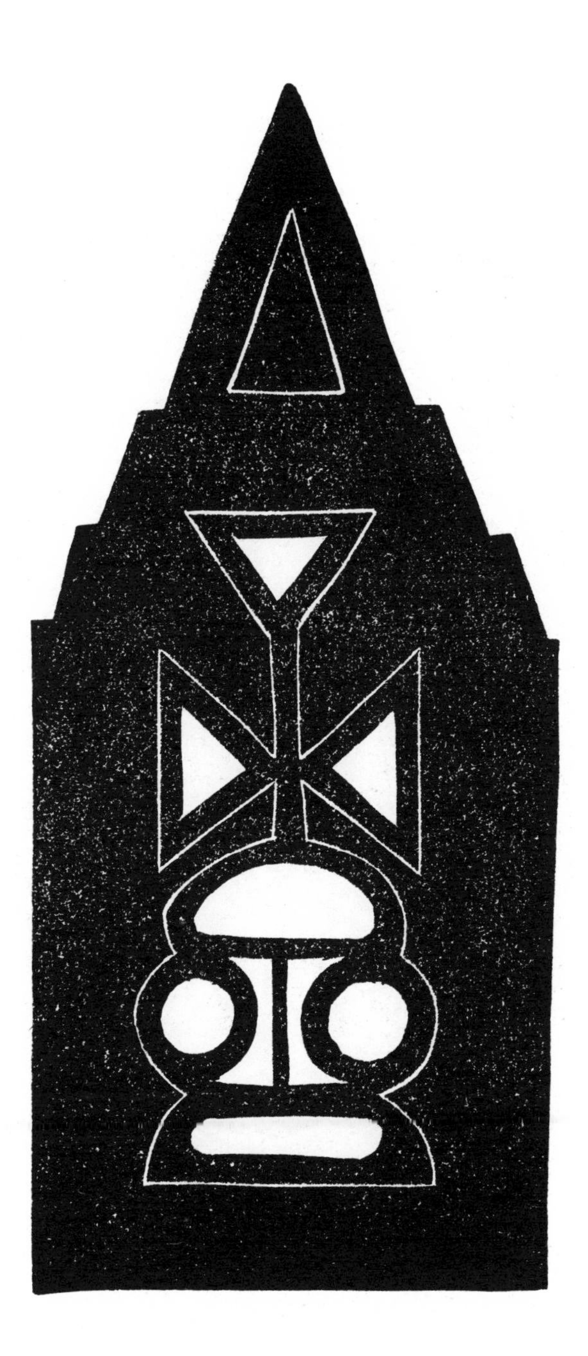

Fon carved altar slab, Dahomey. (81)

Design on Kuba carved wooden cosmetic box, Congo-Kinshasa. (81)

Top: Suku painted wooden spandrel panel over doorway, Congo-Kinshasa. (81)
Bottom: Bagam carved design on wooden sheath, Cameroon. (70)

Carved wooden panel on Djokwe "bush piano," Congo-Kinshasa. (41)

Abstract and Complex Geometric Motifs

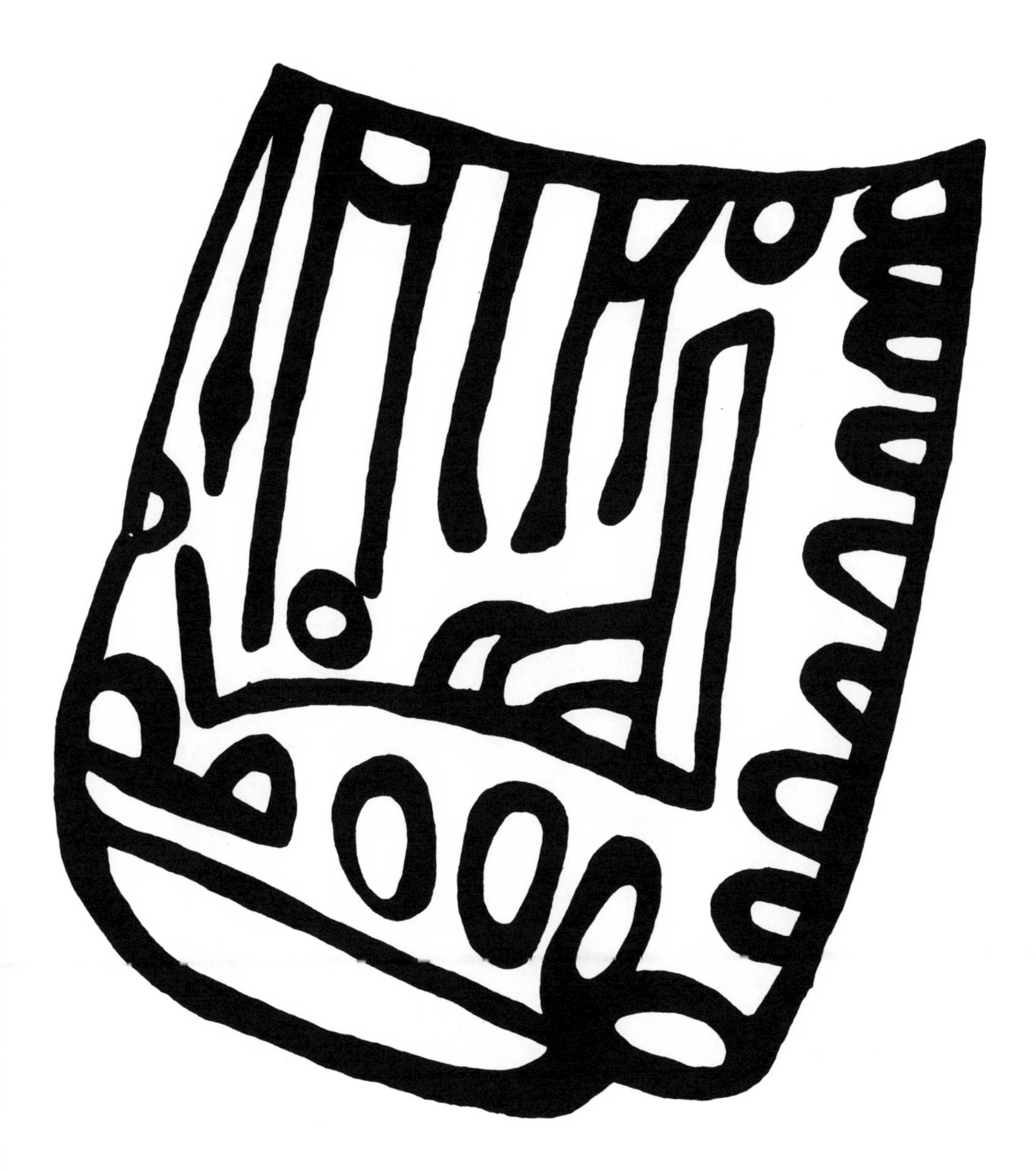

Schematic Bushman wall painting at Nachikufu, Rhodesia. (78)

Luo abstract wall painting, Kenya. (89)

Bangba symbolic wall painting, Congo-Kinshasa. (89)

Ndebele beadwork design on apron, Republic of South Africa. (46)

Top: Ndebele painted wall design, Republic of South Africa. (79)
Middle: Ndebele beadwork design on loin apron, Republic of South Africa. (46)
Bottom: Tusi sewn matting screen, Rwanda, etc. (66)

Top: Carved design on Kuba wooden spoon, Congo-Kinshasa. (81)
Bottom: Ndebele painted wall design, Republic of South Africa. (81)

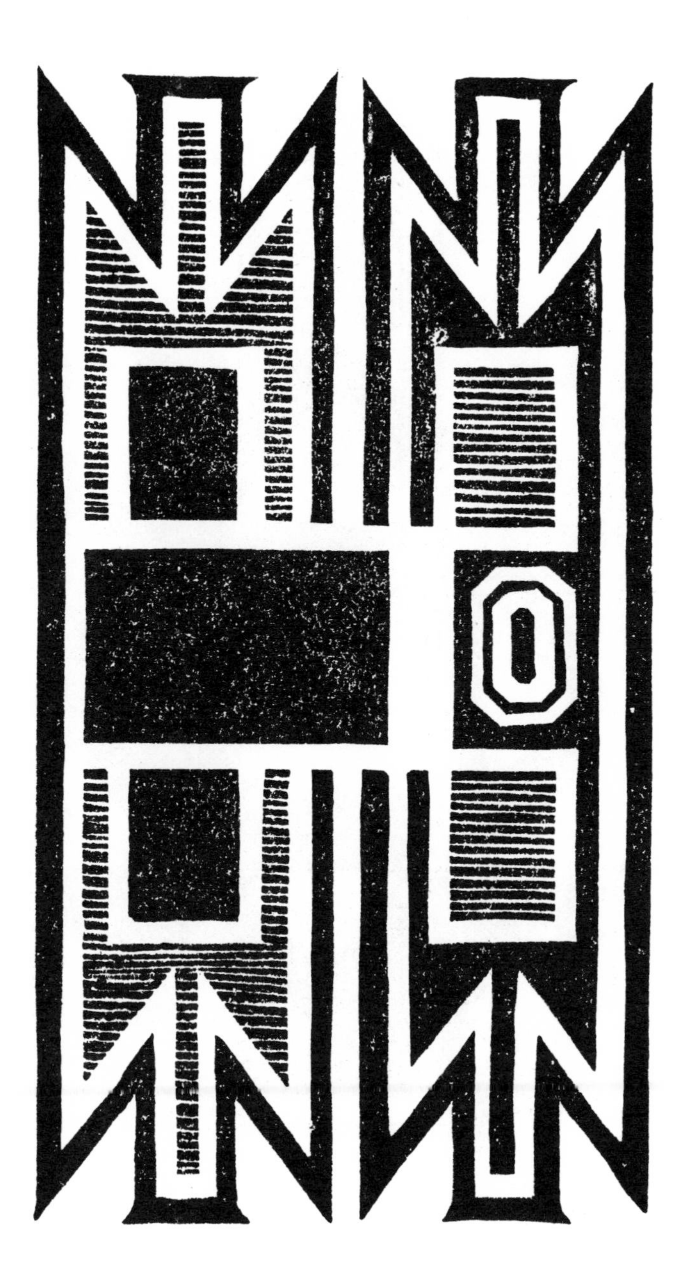

Ndebele painted wall façade, Republic of South Africa. (79)

Ashanti cast bronze gold weight, Ghana. (56)

Tusi sewn matting screen, Rwanda, etc. (66)

Kikuyu engraved wood dancing board, Kenya. (8)

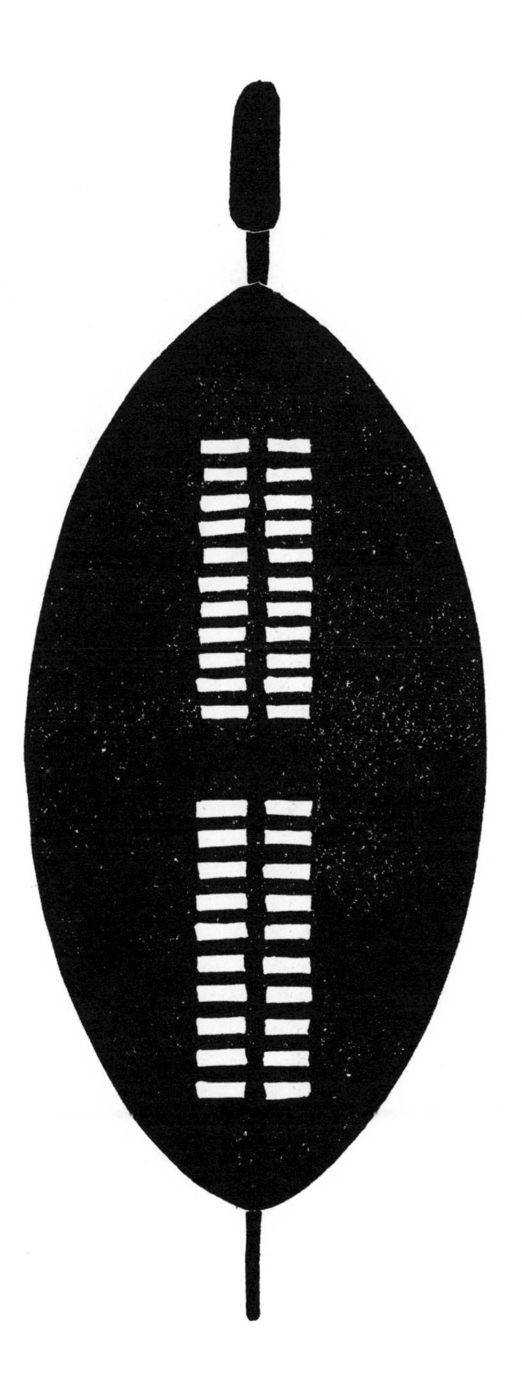

Common Zulu hide shield design, Republic of South Africa. (91)

Top: Kikuyu painted wooden shield, Kenya. (8)
Bottom: Masai painted hide shield, Kenya. (89)

Songye grooved and painted wooden shield, Congo-Kinshasa. (81)

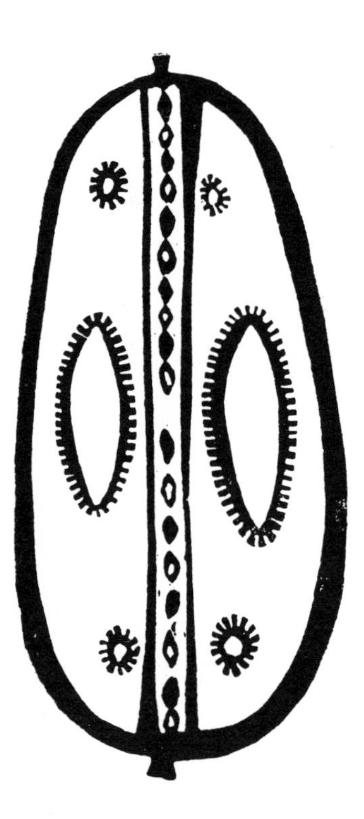

Two Masai painted hide shields, Kenya. (left, 89; right, 30)

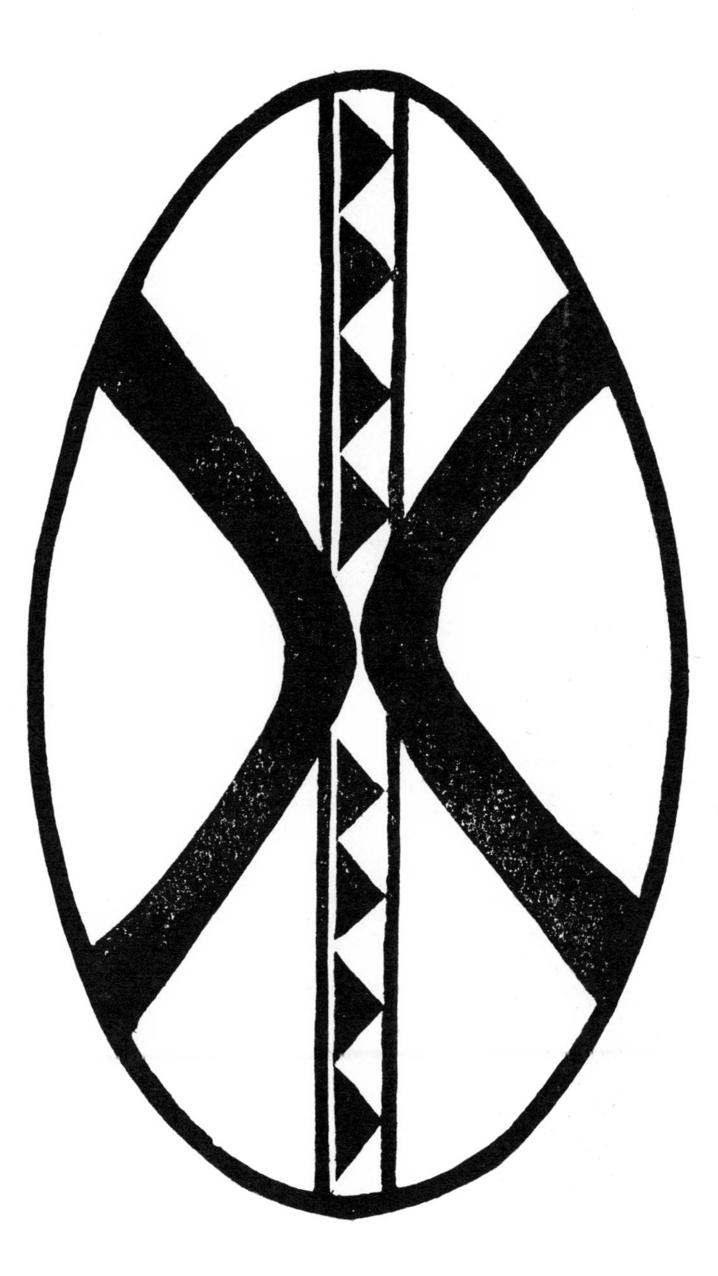

Masai painted hide shield, Kenya. (30)

Tswana bead apron design, Botswana. (46)

Kgalagadi bead apron design, Botswana. (46)

Carved design on Dogon wooden door latch, Mali. (27)

Bushongo design of palm cloth strips applied onto plain palm cloth backing, Congo-Kinshasa. (38)

Mangbetu raffia pile cloth design, Congo-Kinshasa. (38)

Left: Part of mud relief façade of house at Kano, northern Nigeria. (89)
Right: Ashanti cast bronze lid of gold dust box, Ghana. (8)

Profile of ceremonial wooden chair back from Ghana. (80)

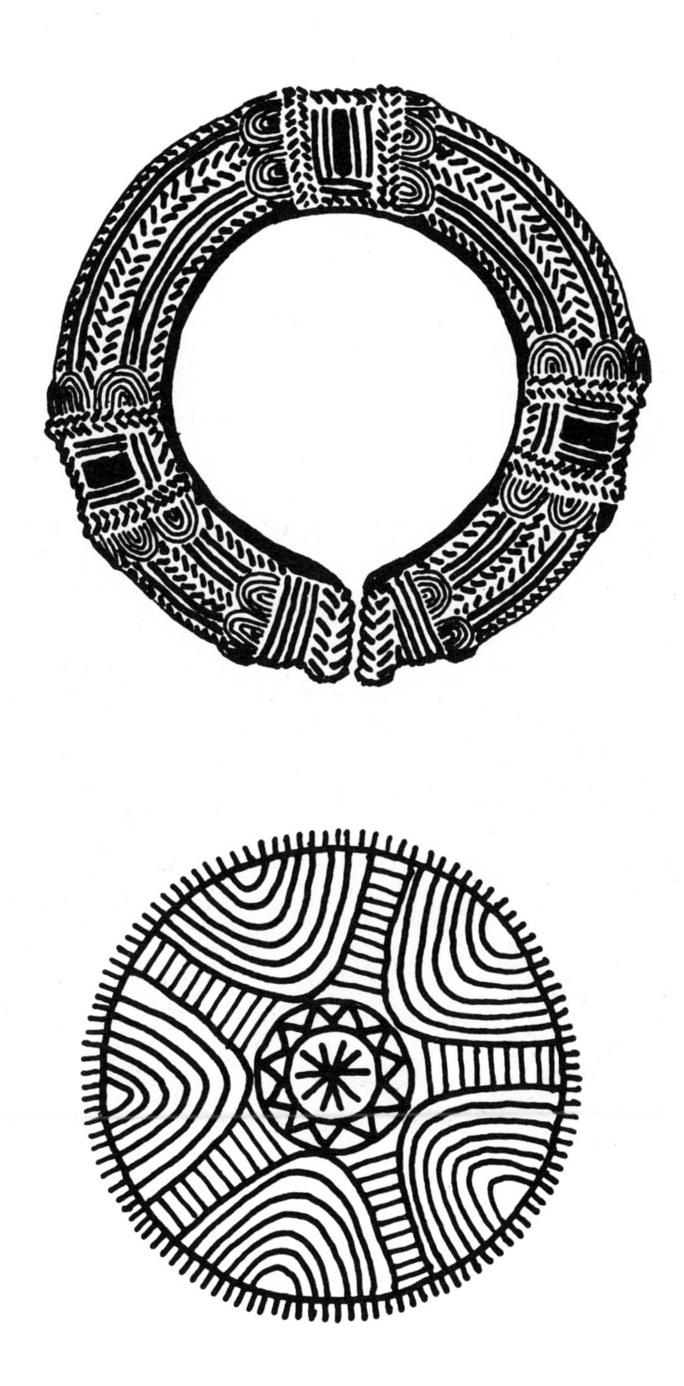

Top: Bronze bracelet, possibly from the time of the Ghana Empire, Mali. (37)
Bottom: Ashanti brass lid to gold dust box, Ghana. (53)

Kamba wooden stool with hammered wire decoration, Kenya. (8)

Mud relief on wall of house at Kano, northern Nigeria. (89)

Kamba wooden stool with hammered wire decoration, Kenya. (8)

Bambara design printed on cloth by the discharge method, Mali. (37)

Benin decorated hide fan, Nigeria. (18)

Map of Africa

TUNISIA
MOROCCO
IFNI
ALGERIA
LIBYA
EGYPT
(U.A.R.)
FEZZAN
SPANISH
SAHARA
MAURITANIA
MALI
NIGER
SUDAN
Senegal River
CHAD
KORDOFAN
SENEGAL
GAMBIA
Dogon
Hausa
Bambara
UPPER VOLTA
Kano
GUINEA
Bobo
Bariba
DAHOMEY
NIGERIA
PORTUGUESE
GUINEA
Landuman
Senufo
GHANA
TOGO
Nupe
Bida
Baga
IVORY
COAST
Ashanti
CENTRAL
AFRICAN REPUBLIC
ETHIOPIA
Yoruba
Ife
[BENIN]
Shilluk
SIERRA
LEONE
Toma
Ibo
Kumasi
LIBERIA
Baule
Fanti
Bali
CAMEROON
Banda
Fon
Jekri
Ijo
Bagam
Zande
Dan
Abomey
Lagos
Yaunde
Bangba

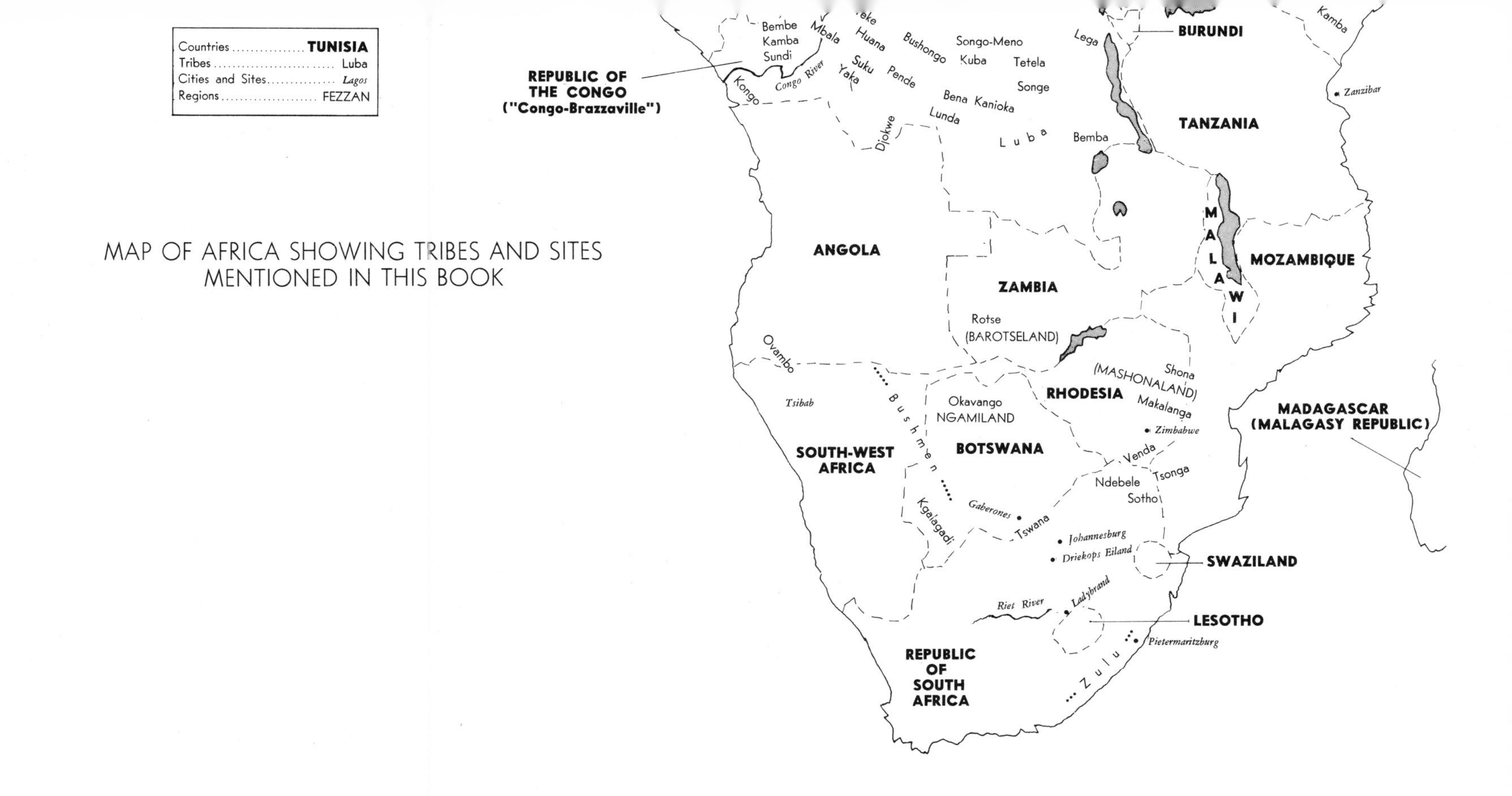
Countries .... TUNISIA
Tribes .... Luba
Cities and Sites............... Lagos
Regions .... FEZZAN
MAP OF AFRICA SHOWING TRIBES AND SITES MENTIONED IN THIS BOOK
REPUBLIC OF THE CONGO ("Congo-Brazzaville")
Bembe
Kamba
Sundi
Mbala
Huana
Bushongo
Songo-Meno
Kuba
Tetela
Songe
Suku
Yaka
Pende
Bena Kanioka
Lunda
Luba
Djokwe
Kongo
Congo River
Lega
BURUNDI
Bemba
TANZANIA
Kamba
Zanzibar
ANGOLA
ZAMBIA
MALAWI
MOZAMBIQUE
Rotse
(BAROTSELAND)
Ovambo
Shona
(MASHONALAND)
RHODESIA
Makalanga
Zimbabwe
Okavango
NGAMILAND
Bushmen
Tsibab
SOUTH-WEST AFRICA
BOTSWANA
MADAGASCAR (MALAGASY REPUBLIC)
Venda
Ndebele
Tsonga
Sotho
Gaberones
Kgalagadi
Tswana
Johannesburg
Driekops Eiland
SWAZILAND
Riet River
Ladybrand
LESOTHO
Pietermaritzburg
Zulu
REPUBLIC OF SOUTH AFRICA

A CATALOG OF SELECTED
DOVER BOOKS
IN ALL FIELDS OF INTEREST

A CATALOG OF SELECTED DOVER BOOKS IN ALL FIELDS OF INTEREST

THE BOOK OF BEASTS: Being a Translation from a Latin Bestiary of the Twelfth Century, T. H. White. Wonderful catalog real and fanciful beasts: manticore, griffin, phoenix, amphivius, jaculus, many more. White's witty erudite commentary on scientific, historical aspects. Fascinating glimpse of medieval mind. Illustrated. 296pp. 5⅜ × 8¼. (Available in U.S. only) 24609-4 Pa. $5.95

FRANK LLOYD WRIGHT: ARCHITECTURE AND NATURE With 160 Illustrations, Donald Hoffmann. Profusely illustrated study of influence of nature—especially prairie—on Wright's designs for Fallingwater, Robie House, Guggenheim Museum, other masterpieces. 96pp. 9¼ × 10¾. 25098-9 Pa. $7.95

FRANK LLOYD WRIGHT'S FALLINGWATER, Donald Hoffmann. Wright's famous waterfall house: planning and construction of organic idea. History of site, owners, Wright's personal involvement. Photographs of various stages of building. Preface by Edgar Kaufmann, Jr. 100 illustrations. 112pp. 9¼ × 10.
23671-4 Pa. $7.95

YEARS WITH FRANK LLOYD WRIGHT: Apprentice to Genius, Edgar Tafel. Insightful memoir by a former apprentice presents a revealing portrait of Wright the man, the inspired teacher, the greatest American architect. 372 black-and-white illustrations. Preface. Index. vi + 228pp. 8¼ × 11. 24801-1 Pa. $9.95

THE STORY OF KING ARTHUR AND HIS KNIGHTS, Howard Pyle. Enchanting version of King Arthur fable has delighted generations with imaginative narratives of exciting adventures and unforgettable illustrations by the author. 41 illustrations. xviii + 313pp. 6⅛ × 9¼. 21445-1 Pa. $5.95

THE GODS OF THE EGYPTIANS, E. A. Wallis Budge. Thorough coverage of numerous gods of ancient Egypt by foremost Egyptologist. Information on evolution of cults, rites and gods; the cult of Osiris; the Book of the Dead and its rites; the sacred animals and birds; Heaven and Hell; and more. 956pp. 6⅛ × 9¼.
22055-9, 22056-7 Pa., Two-vol. set $21.90

A THEOLOGICO-POLITICAL TREATISE, Benedict Spinoza. Also contains unfinished *Political Treatise*. Great classic on religious liberty, theory of government on common consent. R. Elwes translation. Total of 421pp. 5⅜ × 8½.
20249-6 Pa. $6.95

INCIDENTS OF TRAVEL IN CENTRAL AMERICA, CHIAPAS, AND YUCATAN, John L. Stephens. Almost single-handed discovery of Maya culture; exploration of ruined cities, monuments, temples; customs of Indians. 115 drawings. 892pp. 5⅜ × 8½. 22404-X, 22405-8 Pa., Two-vol. set $15.90

LOS CAPRICHOS, Francisco Goya. 80 plates of wild, grotesque monsters and caricatures. Prado manuscript included. 183pp. 6⅝ × 9⅝. 22384-1 Pa. $4.95

AUTOBIOGRAPHY: The Story of My Experiments with Truth, Mohandas K. Gandhi. Not hagiography, but Gandhi in his own words. Boyhood, legal studies, purification, the growth of the Satyagraha (nonviolent protest) movement. Critical, inspiring work of the man who freed India. 480pp. 5⅜ × 8½. (Available in U.S. only)
24593-4 Pa. $6.95

ILLUSTRATED DICTIONARY OF HISTORIC ARCHITECTURE, edited by Cyril M. Harris. Extraordinary compendium of clear, concise definitions for over 5,000 important architectural terms complemented by over 2,000 line drawings. Covers full spectrum of architecture from ancient ruins to 20th-century Modernism. Preface. 592pp. 7½ × 9⅜. 24444-X Pa. $14.95

THE NIGHT BEFORE CHRISTMAS, Clement Moore. Full text, and woodcuts from original 1848 book. Also critical, historical material. 19 illustrations. 40pp. 4⅝ × 6. 22797-9 Pa. $2.50

THE LESSON OF JAPANESE ARCHITECTURE: 165 Photographs, Jiro Harada. Memorable gallery of 165 photographs taken in the 1930's of exquisite Japanese homes of the well-to-do and historic buildings. 13 line diagrams. 192pp. 8⅜ × 11¼. 24778-3 Pa. $8.95

THE AUTOBIOGRAPHY OF CHARLES DARWIN AND SELECTED LETTERS, edited by Francis Darwin. The fascinating life of eccentric genius composed of an intimate memoir by Darwin (intended for his children); commentary by his son, Francis; hundreds of fragments from notebooks, journals, papers; and letters to and from Lyell, Hooker, Huxley, Wallace and Henslow. xi + 365pp. 5⅜ × 8. 20479-0 Pa. $5.95

WONDERS OF THE SKY: Observing Rainbows, Comets, Eclipses, the Stars and Other Phenomena, Fred Schaaf. Charming, easy-to-read poetic guide to all manner of celestial events visible to the naked eye. Mock suns, glories, Belt of Venus, more. Illustrated. 299pp. 5¼ × 8¼. 24402-4 Pa. $7.95

BURNHAM'S CELESTIAL HANDBOOK, Robert Burnham, Jr. Thorough guide to the stars beyond our solar system. Exhaustive treatment. Alphabetical by constellation: Andromeda to Cetus in Vol. 1; Chamaeleon to Orion in Vol. 2; and Pavo to Vulpecula in Vol. 3. Hundreds of illustrations. Index in Vol. 3. 2,000pp. 6⅛ × 9¼. 23567-X, 23568-8, 23673-0 Pa., Three-vol. set $37.85

STAR NAMES: Their Lore and Meaning, Richard Hinckley Allen. Fascinating history of names various cultures have given to constellations and literary and folkloristic uses that have been made of stars. Indexes to subjects. Arabic and Greek names. Biblical references. Bibliography. 563pp. 5⅜ × 8½. 21079-0 Pa. $7.95

THIRTY YEARS THAT SHOOK PHYSICS: The Story of Quantum Theory, George Gamow. Lucid, accessible introduction to influential theory of energy and matter. Careful explanations of Dirac's anti-particles, Bohr's model of the atom, much more. 12 plates. Numerous drawings. 240pp. 5⅜ × 8½. 24895-X Pa. $4.95

CHINESE DOMESTIC FURNITURE IN PHOTOGRAPHS AND MEASURED DRAWINGS, Gustav Ecke. A rare volume, now affordably priced for antique collectors, furniture buffs and art historians. Detailed review of styles ranging from early Shang to late Ming. Unabridged republication. 161 black-and-white drawings, photos. Total of 224pp. 8⅜ × 11¼. (Available in U.S. only) 25171-3 Pa. $12.95

VINCENT VAN GOGH: A Biography, Julius Meier-Graefe. Dynamic, penetrating study of artist's life, relationship with brother, Theo, painting techniques, travels, more. Readable, engrossing. 160pp. 5⅜ × 8½. (Available in U.S. only) 25253-1 Pa. $3.95

HOW TO WRITE, Gertrude Stein. Gertrude Stein claimed anyone could understand her unconventional writing—here are clues to help. Fascinating improvisations, language experiments, explanations illuminate Stein's craft and the art of writing. Total of 414pp. 4⅝ × 6⅜. 23144-5 Pa. $5.95

ADVENTURES AT SEA IN THE GREAT AGE OF SAIL: Five Firsthand Narratives, edited by Elliot Snow. Rare true accounts of exploration, whaling, shipwreck, fierce natives, trade, shipboard life, more. 33 illustrations. Introduction. 353pp. 5⅜ × 8½. 25177-2 Pa. $7.95

THE HERBAL OR GENERAL HISTORY OF PLANTS, John Gerard. Classic descriptions of about 2,850 plants—with over 2,700 illustrations—includes Latin and English names, physical descriptions, varieties, time and place of growth, more. 2,706 illustrations. xlv + 1,678pp. 8½ × 12¼. 23147-X Cloth. $75.00

DOROTHY AND THE WIZARD IN OZ, L. Frank Baum. Dorothy and the Wizard visit the center of the Earth, where people are vegetables, glass houses grow and Oz characters reappear. Classic sequel to *Wizard of Oz*. 256pp. 5⅜ × 8. 24714-7 Pa. $4.95

SONGS OF EXPERIENCE: Facsimile Reproduction with 26 Plates in Full Color, William Blake. This facsimile of Blake's original "Illuminated Book" reproduces 26 full-color plates from a rare 1826 edition. Includes "The Tyger," "London," "Holy Thursday," and other immortal poems. 26 color plates. Printed text of poems. 48pp. 5¼ × 7. 24636-1 Pa. $3.50

SONGS OF INNOCENCE, William Blake. The first and most popular of Blake's famous "Illuminated Books," in a facsimile edition reproducing all 31 brightly colored plates. Additional printed text of each poem. 64pp. 5¼ × 7. 22764-2 Pa. $3.50

PRECIOUS STONES, Max Bauer. Classic, thorough study of diamonds, rubies, emeralds, garnets, etc.: physical character, occurrence, properties, use, similar topics. 20 plates, 8 in color. 94 figures. 659pp. 6⅛ × 9¼. 21910-0, 21911-9 Pa., Two-vol. set $15.90

ENCYCLOPEDIA OF VICTORIAN NEEDLEWORK, S. F. A. Caulfeild and Blanche Saward. Full, precise descriptions of stitches, techniques for dozens of needlecrafts—most exhaustive reference of its kind. Over 800 figures. Total of 679pp. 8⅛ × 11. Two volumes. Vol. 1 22800-2 Pa. $11.95 Vol. 2 22801-0 Pa. $11.95

THE MARVELOUS LAND OF OZ, L. Frank Baum. Second Oz book, the Scarecrow and Tin Woodman are back with hero named Tip, Oz magic. 136 illustrations. 287pp. 5⅜ × 8½. 20692-0 Pa. $5.95

WILD FOWL DECOYS, Joel Barber. Basic book on the subject, by foremost authority and collector. Reveals history of decoy making and rigging, place in American culture, different kinds of decoys, how to make them, and how to use them. 140 plates. 156pp. 7⅞ × 10¾. 20011-6 Pa. $8.95

HISTORY OF LACE, Mrs. Bury Palliser. Definitive, profusely illustrated chronicle of lace from earliest times to late 19th century. Laces of Italy, Greece, England, France, Belgium, etc. Landmark of needlework scholarship. 266 illustrations. 672pp. 6⅛ × 9¼. 24742-2 Pa. $14.95

A CONCISE HISTORY OF PHOTOGRAPHY: Third Revised Edition, Helmut Gernsheim. Best one-volume history—camera obscura, photochemistry, daguerreotypes, evolution of cameras, film, more. Also artistic aspects—landscape, portraits, fine art, etc. 281 black-and-white photographs. 26 in color. 176pp. 8⅜ × 11¼. 25128-4 Pa. $12.95

THE DORÉ BIBLE ILLUSTRATIONS, Gustave Doré. 241 detailed plates from the Bible: the Creation scenes, Adam and Eve, Flood, Babylon, battle sequences, life of Jesus, etc. Each plate is accompanied by the verses from the King James version of the Bible. 241pp. 9 × 12. 23004-X Pa. $8.95

HUGGER-MUGGER IN THE LOUVRE, Elliot Paul. Second Homer Evans mystery-comedy. Theft at the Louvre involves sleuth in hilarious, madcap caper. "A knockout."—Books. 336pp. 5⅜ × 8½. 25185-3 Pa. $5.95

FLATLAND, E. A. Abbott. Intriguing and enormously popular science-fiction classic explores the complexities of trying to survive as a two-dimensional being in a three-dimensional world. Amusingly illustrated by the author. 16 illustrations. 103pp. 5⅜ × 8½. 20001-9 Pa. $2.25

THE HISTORY OF THE LEWIS AND CLARK EXPEDITION, Meriwether Lewis and William Clark, edited by Elliott Coues. Classic edition of Lewis and Clark's day-by-day journals that later became the basis for U.S. claims to Oregon and the West. Accurate and invaluable geographical, botanical, biological, meteorological and anthropological material. Total of 1,508pp. 5⅜ × 8½.
21268-8, 21269-6, 21270-X Pa. Three-vol. set $25.50

LANGUAGE, TRUTH AND LOGIC, Alfred J. Ayer. Famous, clear introduction to Vienna, Cambridge schools of Logical Positivism. Role of philosophy, elimination of metaphysics, nature of analysis, etc. 160pp. 5⅜ × 8½. (Available in U.S. and Canada only) 20010-8 Pa. $2.95

MATHEMATICS FOR THE NONMATHEMATICIAN, Morris Kline. Detailed, college-level treatment of mathematics in cultural and historical context, with numerous exercises. For liberal arts students. Preface. Recommended Reading Lists. Tables. Index. Numerous black-and-white figures. xvi + 641pp. 5⅜ × 8½.
24823-2 Pa. $11.95

28 SCIENCE FICTION STORIES, H. G. Wells. Novels, *Star Begotten* and *Men Like Gods,* plus 26 short stories: "Empire of the Ants," "A Story of the Stone Age," "The Stolen Bacillus," "In the Abyss," etc. 915pp. 5⅜ × 8½. (Available in U.S. only)
20265-8 Cloth. $10.95

HANDBOOK OF PICTORIAL SYMBOLS, Rudolph Modley. 3,250 signs and symbols, many systems in full; official or heavy commercial use. Arranged by subject. Most in Pictorial Archive series. 143pp. 8⅛ × 11. 23357-X Pa. $5.95

INCIDENTS OF TRAVEL IN YUCATAN, John L. Stephens. Classic (1843) exploration of jungles of Yucatan, looking for evidences of Maya civilization. Travel adventures, Mexican and Indian culture, etc. Total of 669pp. 5⅜ × 8½.
20926-1, 20927-X Pa., Two-vol. set $9.90

THE BLUE FAIRY BOOK, Andrew Lang. The first, most famous collection, with many familiar tales: Little Red Riding Hood, Aladdin and the Wonderful Lamp, Puss in Boots, Sleeping Beauty, Hansel and Gretel, Rumpelstiltskin; 37 in all. 138 illustrations. 390pp. 5⅜ × 8½. 21437-0 Pa. $5.95

THE STORY OF THE CHAMPIONS OF THE ROUND TABLE, Howard Pyle. Sir Launcelot, Sir Tristram and Sir Percival in spirited adventures of love and triumph retold in Pyle's inimitable style. 50 drawings, 31 full-page. xviii + 329pp. 6½ × 9¼. 21883-X Pa. $6.95

AUDUBON AND HIS JOURNALS, Maria Audubon. Unmatched two-volume portrait of the great artist, naturalist and author contains his journals, an excellent biography by his granddaughter, expert annotations by the noted ornithologist, Dr. Elliott Coues, and 37 superb illustrations. Total of 1,200pp. 5⅜ × 8.
Vol. I 25143-8 Pa. $8.95
Vol. II 25144-6 Pa. $8.95

GREAT DINOSAUR HUNTERS AND THEIR DISCOVERIES, Edwin H. Colbert. Fascinating, lavishly illustrated chronicle of dinosaur research, 1820's to 1960. Achievements of Cope, Marsh, Brown, Buckland, Mantell, Huxley, many others. 384pp. 5¼ × 8¼. 24701-5 Pa. $6.95

THE TASTEMAKERS, Russell Lynes. Informal, illustrated social history of American taste 1850's–1950's. First popularized categories Highbrow, Lowbrow, Middlebrow. 129 illustrations. New (1979) afterword. 384pp. 6 × 9.
23993-4 Pa. $6.95

DOUBLE CROSS PURPOSES, Ronald A. Knox. A treasure hunt in the Scottish Highlands, an old map, unidentified corpse, surprise discoveries keep reader guessing in this cleverly intricate tale of financial skullduggery. 2 black-and-white maps. 320pp. 5⅜ × 8½. (Available in U.S. only) 25032-6 Pa. $5.95

AUTHENTIC VICTORIAN DECORATION AND ORNAMENTATION IN FULL COLOR: 46 Plates from "Studies in Design," Christopher Dresser. Superb full-color lithographs reproduced from rare original portfolio of a major Victorian designer. 48pp. 9¼ × 12¼. 25083-0 Pa. $7.95

PRIMITIVE ART, Franz Boas. Remains the best text ever prepared on subject, thoroughly discussing Indian, African, Asian, Australian, and, especially, Northern American primitive art. Over 950 illustrations show ceramics, masks, totem poles, weapons, textiles, paintings, much more. 376pp. 5⅜ × 8. 20025-6 Pa. $6.95

SIDELIGHTS ON RELATIVITY, Albert Einstein. Unabridged republication of two lectures delivered by the great physicist in 1920–21. *Ether and Relativity* and *Geometry and Experience*. Elegant ideas in non-mathematical form, accessible to intelligent layman. vi + 56pp. 5⅜ × 8½. 24511-X Pa. $2.95

THE WIT AND HUMOR OF OSCAR WILDE, edited by Alvin Redman. More than 1,000 ripostes, paradoxes, wisecracks: Work is the curse of the drinking classes, I can resist everything except temptation, etc. 258pp. 5⅜ × 8½. 20602-5 Pa. $4.50

ADVENTURES WITH A MICROSCOPE, Richard Headstrom. 59 adventures with clothing fibers, protozoa, ferns and lichens, roots and leaves, much more. 142 illustrations. 232pp. 5⅜ × 8½. 23471-1 Pa. $3.95

PLANTS OF THE BIBLE, Harold N. Moldenke and Alma L. Moldenke. Standard reference to all 230 plants mentioned in Scriptures. Latin name, biblical reference, uses, modern identity, much more. Unsurpassed encyclopedic resource for scholars, botanists, nature lovers, students of Bible. Bibliography. Indexes. 123 black-and-white illustrations. 384pp. 6 × 9. 25069-5 Pa. $8.95

FAMOUS AMERICAN WOMEN: A Biographical Dictionary from Colonial Times to the Present, Robert McHenry, ed. From Pocahontas to Rosa Parks, 1,035 distinguished American women documented in separate biographical entries. Accurate, up-to-date data, numerous categories, spans 400 years. Indices. 493pp. 6½ × 9¼. 24523-3 Pa. $9.95

THE FABULOUS INTERIORS OF THE GREAT OCEAN LINERS IN HISTORIC PHOTOGRAPHS, William H. Miller, Jr. Some 200 superb photographs capture exquisite interiors of world's great "floating palaces"—1890's to 1980's: *Titanic, Ile de France, Queen Elizabeth, United States, Europa,* more. Approx. 200 black-and-white photographs. Captions. Text. Introduction. 160pp. 8⅜ × 11¾. 24756-2 Pa. $9.95

THE GREAT LUXURY LINERS, 1927–1954: A Photographic Record, William H. Miller, Jr. Nostalgic tribute to heyday of ocean liners. 186 photos of Ile de France, Normandie, Leviathan, Queen Elizabeth, United States, many others. Interior and exterior views. Introduction. Captions. 160pp. 9 × 12. 24056-8 Pa. $9.95

A NATURAL HISTORY OF THE DUCKS, John Charles Phillips. Great landmark of ornithology offers complete detailed coverage of nearly 200 species and subspecies of ducks: gadwall, sheldrake, merganser, pintail, many more. 74 full-color plates, 102 black-and-white. Bibliography. Total of 1,920pp. 8⅜ × 11¼. 25141-1, 25142-X Cloth. Two-vol. set $100.00

THE SEAWEED HANDBOOK: An Illustrated Guide to Seaweeds from North Carolina to Canada, Thomas F. Lee. Concise reference covers 78 species. Scientific and common names, habitat, distribution, more. Finding keys for easy identification. 224pp. 5⅜ × 8½. 25215-9 Pa. $5.95

THE TEN BOOKS OF ARCHITECTURE: The 1755 Leoni Edition, Leon Battista Alberti. Rare classic helped introduce the glories of ancient architecture to the Renaissance. 68 black-and-white plates. 336pp. 8⅜ × 11¼. 25239-6 Pa. $14.95

MISS MACKENZIE, Anthony Trollope. Minor masterpieces by Victorian master unmasks many truths about life in 19th-century England. First inexpensive edition in years. 392pp. 5⅜ × 8½. 25201-9 Pa. $7.95

THE RIME OF THE ANCIENT MARINER, Gustave Doré, Samuel Taylor Coleridge. Dramatic engravings considered by many to be his greatest work. The terrifying space of the open sea, the storms and whirlpools of an unknown ocean, the ice of Antarctica, more—all rendered in a powerful, chilling manner. Full text. 38 plates. 77pp. 9¼ × 12. 22305-1 Pa. $4.95

THE EXPEDITIONS OF ZEBULON MONTGOMERY PIKE, Zebulon Montgomery Pike. Fascinating first-hand accounts (1805–6) of exploration of Mississippi River, Indian wars, capture by Spanish dragoons, much more. 1,088pp. 5⅜ × 8½. 25254-X, 25255-8 Pa. Two-vol. set $23.90

DEGAS: An Intimate Portrait, Ambroise Vollard. Charming, anecdotal memoir by famous art dealer of one of the greatest 19th-century French painters. 14 black-and-white illustrations. Introduction by Harold L. Van Doren. 96pp. 5⅜ × 8½.
25131-4 Pa. $3.95

PERSONAL NARRATIVE OF A PILGRIMAGE TO ALMANDINAH AND MECCAH, Richard Burton. Great travel classic by remarkably colorful personality. Burton, disguised as a Moroccan, visited sacred shrines of Islam, narrowly escaping death. 47 illustrations. 959pp. 5⅜ × 8½. 21217-3, 21218-1 Pa., Two-vol. set $17.90

PHRASE AND WORD ORIGINS, A. H. Holt. Entertaining, reliable, modern study of more than 1,200 colorful words, phrases, origins and histories. Much unexpected information. 254pp. 5⅜ × 8½. 20758-7 Pa. $5.95

THE RED THUMB MARK, R. Austin Freeman. In this first Dr. Thorndyke case, the great scientific detective draws fascinating conclusions from the nature of a single fingerprint. Exciting story, authentic science. 320pp. 5⅜ × 8½. (Available in U.S. only) 25210-8 Pa. $5.95

AN EGYPTIAN HIEROGLYPHIC DICTIONARY, E. A. Wallis Budge. Monumental work containing about 25,000 words or terms that occur in texts ranging from 3000 B.C. to 600 A.D. Each entry consists of a transliteration of the word, the word in hieroglyphs, and the meaning in English. 1,314pp. 6⅞ × 10.
23615-3, 23616-1 Pa., Two-vol. set $27.90

THE COMPLEAT STRATEGYST: Being a Primer on the Theory of Games of Strategy, J. D. Williams. Highly entertaining classic describes, with many illustrated examples, how to select best strategies in conflict situations. Prefaces. Appendices. xvi + 268pp. 5⅜ × 8½. 25101-2 Pa. $5.95

THE ROAD TO OZ, L. Frank Baum. Dorothy meets the Shaggy Man, little Button-Bright and the Rainbow's beautiful daughter in this delightful trip to the magical Land of Oz. 272pp. 5⅜ × 8. 25208-6 Pa. $4.95

POINT AND LINE TO PLANE, Wassily Kandinsky. Seminal exposition of role of point, line, other elements in non-objective painting. Essential to understanding 20th-century art. 127 illustrations. 192pp. 6½ × 9¼. 23808-3 Pa. $4.50

LADY ANNA, Anthony Trollope. Moving chronicle of Countess Lovel's bitter struggle to win for herself and daughter Anna their rightful rank and fortune—perhaps at cost of sanity itself. 384pp. 5⅜ × 8½. 24669-8 Pa. $6.95

EGYPTIAN MAGIC, E. A. Wallis Budge. Sums up all that is known about magic in Ancient Egypt: the role of magic in controlling the gods, powerful amulets that warded off evil spirits, scarabs of immortality, use of wax images, formulas and spells, the secret name, much more. 253pp. 5⅜ × 8½. 22681-6 Pa. $4.50

THE DANCE OF SIVA, Ananda Coomaraswamy. Preeminent authority unfolds the vast metaphysic of India: the revelation of her art, conception of the universe, social organization, etc. 27 reproductions of art masterpieces. 192pp. 5⅜ × 8½.
24817-8 Pa. $5.95

ILLUSTRATED GUIDE TO SHAKER FURNITURE, Robert Meader. All furniture and appurtenances, with much on unknown local styles. 235 photos. 146pp. 9 × 12. 22819-3 Pa. $7.95

WHALE SHIPS AND WHALING: A Pictorial Survey, George Francis Dow. Over 200 vintage engravings, drawings, photographs of barks, brigs, cutters, other vessels. Also harpoons, lances, whaling guns, many other artifacts. Comprehensive text by foremost authority. 207 black-and-white illustrations. 288pp. 6 × 9. 24808-9 Pa. $8.95

THE BERTRAMS, Anthony Trollope. Powerful portrayal of blind self-will and thwarted ambition includes one of Trollope's most heartrending love stories. 497pp. 5⅜ × 8½. 25119-5 Pa. $8.95

ADVENTURES WITH A HAND LENS, Richard Headstrom. Clearly written guide to observing and studying flowers and grasses, fish scales, moth and insect wings, egg cases, buds, feathers, seeds, leaf scars, moss, molds, ferns, common crystals, etc.—all with an ordinary, inexpensive magnifying glass. 209 exact line drawings aid in your discoveries. 220pp. 5⅜ × 8½. 23330-8 Pa. $4.50

RODIN ON ART AND ARTISTS, Auguste Rodin. Great sculptor's candid, wide-ranging comments on meaning of art; great artists; relation of sculpture to poetry, painting, music; philosophy of life, more. 76 superb black-and-white illustrations of Rodin's sculpture, drawings and prints. 119pp. 8⅜ × 11¼. 24487-3 Pa. $6.95

FIFTY CLASSIC FRENCH FILMS, 1912–1982: A Pictorial Record, Anthony Slide. Memorable stills from Grand Illusion, Beauty and the Beast, Hiroshima, Mon Amour, many more. Credits, plot synopses, reviews, etc. 160pp. 8¼ × 11. 25256-6 Pa. $11.95

THE PRINCIPLES OF PSYCHOLOGY, William James. Famous long course complete, unabridged. Stream of thought, time perception, memory, experimental methods; great work decades ahead of its time. 94 figures. 1,391pp. 5⅜ × 8½. 20381-6, 20382-4 Pa., Two-vol. set $19.90

BODIES IN A BOOKSHOP, R. T. Campbell. Challenging mystery of blackmail and murder with ingenious plot and superbly drawn characters. In the best tradition of British suspense fiction. 192pp. 5⅜ × 8½. 24720-1 Pa. $3.95

CALLAS: PORTRAIT OF A PRIMA DONNA, George Jellinek. Renowned commentator on the musical scene chronicles incredible career and life of the most controversial, fascinating, influential operatic personality of our time. 64 black-and-white photographs. 416pp. 5⅜ × 8¼. 25047-4 Pa. $7.95

GEOMETRY, RELATIVITY AND THE FOURTH DIMENSION, Rudolph Rucker. Exposition of fourth dimension, concepts of relativity as Flatland characters continue adventures. Popular, easily followed yet accurate, profound. 141 illustrations. 133pp. 5⅜ × 8½. 23400-2 Pa. $3.50

HOUSEHOLD STORIES BY THE BROTHERS GRIMM, with pictures by Walter Crane. 53 classic stories—Rumpelstiltskin, Rapunzel, Hansel and Gretel, the Fisherman and his Wife, Snow White, Tom Thumb, Sleeping Beauty, Cinderella, and so much more—lavishly illustrated with original 19th century drawings. 114 illustrations. x + 269pp. 5⅜ × 8½. 21080-4 Pa. $4.50

CATALOG OF DOVER BOOKS

AMERICAN CLIPPER SHIPS: 1833–1858, Octavius T. Howe & Frederick C. Matthews. Fully-illustrated, encyclopedic review of 352 clipper ships from the period of America's greatest maritime supremacy. Introduction. 109 halftones. 5 black-and-white line illustrations. Index. Total of 928pp. 5⅜ × 8½.
25115-2, 25116-0 Pa., Two-vol. set $17.90

TOWARDS A NEW ARCHITECTURE, Le Corbusier. Pioneering manifesto by great architect, near legendary founder of "International School." Technical and aesthetic theories, views on industry, economics, relation of form to function, "mass-production spirit," much more. Profusely illustrated. Unabridged translation of 13th French edition. Introduction by Frederick Etchells. 320pp. 6⅛ × 9¼. (Available in U.S. only) 25023-7 Pa. $8.95

THE BOOK OF KELLS, edited by Blanche Cirker. Inexpensive collection of 32 full-color, full-page plates from the greatest illuminated manuscript of the Middle Ages, painstakingly reproduced from rare facsimile edition. Publisher's Note. Captions. 32pp. 9⅜ × 12¼. 24345-1 Pa. $4.95

BEST SCIENCE FICTION STORIES OF H. G. WELLS, H. G. Wells. Full novel *The Invisible Man,* plus 17 short stories: "The Crystal Egg," "Aepyornis Island," "The Strange Orchid," etc. 303pp. 5⅜ × 8½. (Available in U.S. only)
21531-8 Pa. $4.95

AMERICAN SAILING SHIPS: Their Plans and History, Charles G. Davis. Photos, construction details of schooners, frigates, clippers, other sailcraft of 18th to early 20th centuries—plus entertaining discourse on design, rigging, nautical lore, much more. 137 black-and-white illustrations. 240pp. 6⅛ × 9¼.
24658-2 Pa. $5.95

ENTERTAINING MATHEMATICAL PUZZLES, Martin Gardner. Selection of author's favorite conundrums involving arithmetic, money, speed, etc., with lively commentary. Complete solutions. 112pp. 5⅜ × 8½. 25211-6 Pa. $2.95

THE WILL TO BELIEVE, HUMAN IMMORTALITY, William James. Two books bound together. Effect of irrational on logical, and arguments for human immortality. 402pp. 5⅜ × 8½. 20291-7 Pa. $7.50

THE HAUNTED MONASTERY and THE CHINESE MAZE MURDERS, Robert Van Gulik. 2 full novels by Van Gulik continue adventures of Judge Dee and his companions. An evil Taoist monastery, seemingly supernatural events; overgrown topiary maze that hides strange crimes. Set in 7th-century China. 27 illustrations. 328pp. 5⅜ × 8½. 23502-5 Pa. $5.95

CELEBRATED CASES OF JUDGE DEE (DEE GOONG AN), translated by Robert Van Gulik. Authentic 18th-century Chinese detective novel; Dee and associates solve three interlocked cases. Led to Van Gulik's own stories with same characters. Extensive introduction. 9 illustrations. 237pp. 5⅜ × 8½.
23337-5 Pa. $4.95

Prices subject to change without notice.

Available at your book dealer or write for free catalog to Dept. GI, Dover Publications, Inc., 31 East 2nd St., Mineola, N.Y. 11501. Dover publishes more than 175 books each year on science, elementary and advanced mathematics, biology, music, art, literary history, social sciences and other areas.